A New Star-Rating System & Other Exciting News from Frommer's!

In our continuing effort to publish the savviest, most up-to-date, and most appealing travel guides available, we've added some great new features.

Frommer's guides now include a new **star-rating system.** Every hotel, restaurant, and attraction is rated from 0 to 3 stars to help you set priorities and organize your time.

We've also added **seven brand-new features** that point you to the great deals, in-the-know advice, and unique experiences that separate travelers from tourists. Throughout the guide, look for:

Finds	Special finds—those places only insiders know about
Fun Fact	Fun facts—details that make travelers more informed and their trips more fun
Kids	Best bets for kids—advice for the whole family
Moments	Special moments—those experiences that memories are made of
Overrated	Places or experiences not worth your time or money
Tips	Insider tips—some great ways to save time and money
Value	Great values—where to get the best deals

We've also added a **"What's New"** section in every guide—a timely crash course in what's hot and what's not in every destination we cover.

Here's what the critics say about Frommer's:

Other Great Guides for Your Trip:

Frommer's Adventure Guides: South America
Frommer's South America
Frommer's Peru

Frommer's®

Argentina & Chile

2nd Edition

by Shane Christensen, Haas Mroue
& Kristina Schreck

Wiley Publishing, Inc.

Published by:

Wiley Publishing, Inc.

909 Third Ave.
New York, NY 10022

ISBN 0-7645-2538-7
ISSN 1532-9968

Editor: Christine Ryan
Production Editor: Suzanna R. Thompson
Cartographer: Elizabeth Puhl
Photo Editor: Richard Fox
Production by Wiley Indianapolis Composition Services

Front cover photo: Llamas in the Andean Altiplano region, Chile
Back cover photo: Torres del Paine National Park, Chile

For information on our other products and services or to obtain technical support, please contact our Customer Care Department within the U.S. at 800-762-2974, outside the U.S. at 317-572-3993 or fax 317-572-4002.

Wiley also publishes its books in a variety of electronic formats. Some content that appears in print may not be available in electronic formats.

Manufactured in the United States of America

5   4   3   2   1

Contents

List of Maps

About the Authors

To do Argentina right, **Shane Christensen** (chapters 1, 2, 3, 4, 5, 6, 7, 9, and the appendix) moved in with a Porteño family, committed himself to a rigorous steak-only diet, searched Buenos Aires for the perfect tango partner, and added a rich Argentine accent to his Mexican-learned Spanish. With his nascent Argentine credentials, he roamed the country's far corners, finding that no place in South America offers such geographic diversity and cultural distinction. A California native, Shane has written extensively in South America, Western Europe, and the United States for the Berkeley Guides, Fodor's, and *The Wall Street Journal.*

Haas Mroue (chapters 1, 8, 14, 15, 16, and 17) has not stopped traveling since he was a child accompanying his single mother (who worked for the U.N.) on trips around the world. Haas traveled extensively in Argentina and Chile doing research to update this guidebook (crossing the Andes twice by bus). A freelance travel writer based in the United States, he covers a diverse number of destinations, from Bangkok to Monte Carlo to Santorini, for various publications. His short stories, poems, and travel pieces have appeared in a variety of publications—including *Interiors Magazine,* the *Michigan Quarterly Review,* the *Literary Review,* National Geographic guides, and Britannica.com, among many others—and his work has been broadcast on the BBC World Service and Starz! cable channel. He's the author of *Frommer's Memorable Walks In Paris* and *Frommer's Paris from $80 a Day,* and is a contributor to *Frommer's Gay & Lesbian Europe* and *Frommer's Europe from $70 a Day.* When not on the road, he lives on the Olympic Peninsula in Washington.

Kristina Schreck (chapters 1, 10, 11, 12, 13, and the appendix) has traveled extensively throughout Latin America and has lived and worked in Argentina and Chile for 8 years. She is the former managing editor of *Adventure Journal* magazine, and is co-author of the first edition of *Frommer's Argentina & Chile.* Kristina currently resides in Santiago and the Andes, where she works year-round for Ski Portillo (and although she thinks it is the greatest ski resort in the world, to be fair, she asked an independent, impartial source to edit Chile skiing coverage in this guide).

An Invitation to the Reader

In researching this book, we discovered many wonderful places—hotels, restaurants, shops, and more. We're sure you'll find others. Please tell us about them, so we can share the information with your fellow travelers in upcoming editions. If you were disappointed with a recommendation, we'd love to know that, too. Please write to:

Frommer's Argentina & Chile, 2nd Edition
Wiley Publishing, Inc. • 909 Third Ave. • New York, NY 10022

An Additional Note

Please be advised that travel information is subject to change at any time—and this is especially true of prices. We therefore suggest that you write or call ahead for confirmation when making your travel plans. The authors, editors, and publisher cannot be held responsible for the experiences of readers while traveling. Your safety is important to us, however, so we encourage you to stay alert and be aware of your surroundings. Keep a close eye on cameras, purses, and wallets, all favorite targets of thieves and pickpockets.

New! Frommer's Star Ratings & Icons

Every hotel, restaurant, and attraction listing in this guide has been ranked for quality, value, service, amenities, and special features using a star-rating scale. In country, state, and regional guides, we also rate towns and regions to help you narrow down your choices and budget your time accordingly. Hotels and restaurants in the Very Expensive and Expensive categories are rated on a scale of one (highly recommended) to three stars (exceptional). Those in the Moderate and Inexpensive categories rate from zero (recommended) to two stars (very highly recommended). Attractions, towns, and regions are rated according to the following scale: zero stars (recommended), one star (highly recommended), two stars (very highly recommended), and three stars (must-see).

In addition to the rating system, we also use seven icons to highlight insider information, useful tips, special bargains, hidden gems, memorable experiences, kid-friendly venues, places to avoid, and other useful information:

| *Finds* | *Fun Fact* | *Kids* | *Moments* | *Overrated* | *Tips* | *Value* |

The following abbreviations are used for credit cards:

| AE | American Express | DISC | Discover | V | Visa |
| DC | Diners Club | MC | MasterCard | | |

FROMMERS.COM

Now that you have the guidebook to a great trip, visit our website at **www.frommers.com** for travel information on nearly 2,500 destinations. With features updated regularly, we give you instant access to the most current trip-planning information available. At Frommers.com, you'll also find the best prices on airfares, accommodations, and car rentals—and you can even book travel online through our travel booking partners. At Frommers.com, you'll also find the following:

- Online updates to our most popular guidebooks
- Vacation sweepstakes and contest giveaways
- Newsletter highlighting the hottest travel trends
- Online travel message boards with featured travel discussions

What's New in Argentina & Chile

The second edition of *Frommer's Argentina & Chile* expands its coverage of Argentina, adding the up-and-coming tourist regions of **Córdoba** and **Mendoza**—a must for those keen to visit Argentina's marvelous wine region and surrounding mountains—and including the summer beach resort of **Mar del Plata.**

ARGENTINA

Many readers will wonder how Argentina's economic crisis has affected the tourism industry and the rest of the country. First, prices have been slashed across the board, from hotels and restaurants to tourist attractions and shopping. Argentina has become a bargain for foreign travelers. You should be aware, however, that many hotels and other establishments have introduced different prices for foreigners than for Argentines. Confirm prices before agreeing to the service. Prices quoted in this book are quoted in dollars only, but realize that high inflation and volatile exchange rates will limit their accuracy.

Of course, the country is no bargain for Argentines, who have stopped jet-setting to places like Miami and Punta del Este (a popular beach resort in Uruguay) and are instead staying at home or traveling domestically. This economic crisis is popularly viewed as the worst in Argentina's history, and everyone feels it. Poverty has skyrocketed, young people can't find jobs, and some children face malnutrition as families struggle to get bread on the table. One result is an increase in crime, particularly in the big cities, and travelers must now take extra precautions when visiting Argentina.

In general, the tourism industry is one of the few sectors that has benefited from the devalued currency. Hotel occupancies have risen as foreign tourists rush to take advantage of cheap goods and services. Travelers pump life into hotels, restaurants, taxis, and shops with their dollars. And there is growing recognition that tourism provides oxygen for the struggling economy, or, as some signs now read EL TURISMO ES TRABAJO (tourism is work). The result: Travelers to Argentina are catered to in a way they never were in the past.

BUENOS AIRES Travelers will find Buenos Aires far cheaper than at any time in recent memory, and quality hotels, restaurants, shops, and tourist attractions are all open for business. Due to the economic crisis, however, travelers should avoid walking alone and should not take taxis off the streets. Call a radio-taxi or *remise* (private, unmetered taxi) instead.

Accommodations In Recoleta, the the **Four Seasons Hotel** (© 11/4321-1200; www.fourseasons.com/buenos aires) has moved into the luxurious Park Tower and French-rococo La Mansión, where Madonna stayed during the filming of *Evita*. The Four Seasons offers among the best service you will find in Buenos Aires.

Closer to Plaza San Martín, the classy new **Sofitel** (© 11/4909-1454; www.sofitel.com) blends Parisian decor with traditional Art Deco styles. Staff members come to work dressed in designer French uniforms, reaffirming the impression that this city is more European than South American.

Two newly opened **Loi Suites** (© 11/5777-8950; www.loisuites. com.ar), with locations in Recoleta and downtown, provide good-value accommodations with service and style. Those looking for more inexpensive accommodations should consider the intimate **Bel Air Hotel** (© 11/4021-4000; www.hotelbelair.com.ar), as close as Buenos Aires comes to offering a simple boutique hotel.

Dining The city's most fashionable neighborhood for eating out is now Las Cañitas in Old Palermo, also called "Palermo Hollywood." Las Cañitas takes its inspiration from New York's SoHo, its crowded sidewalks leading past trendy ethnic, international, and Argentine restaurants.

It is said that you have not seen Buenos Aires until you stop for a coffee or whisky at **La Biela** (© 11/4804-0449), and indeed this thoroughbred Argentine bar has become one of the city's cultural landmarks. Today, artists, politicians, and neighborhood executives (as well as a fair number of tourists) all frequent La Biela, which serves breakfast, informal lunch plates, ice creams, and crepes.

Exploring Buenos Aires The stunning new **Museo de Arte Latinoamericano de Buenos Aires** (or **Malba;** © 11/4808-6500), which vaguely resembles New York's Museum of Modern Art, houses the private art collection of Eduardo Constantini. One of the most impressive collections of Latin American art anywhere, temporary and permanent exhibitions showcase names like Antonio Berni, Pedro Figari, Frida Kahlo, Cândido Portinari, Diego Rivera, and Antonio Siguí.

MAR DEL PLATA The ailing economy has limited the number of flights whisking Porteños off to Miami and Punta del Este, Uruguay, and a greater number of Argentines are spending their summers in Argentina's most popular beach resort. Mar del Plata's long, winding coastline offers crowded, tan-bodied beaches and excellent nightlife from December to March, along with beautiful landscapes further inland. The **Sheraton** (© 22/3499-9000; www.sheraton. com), built on a golf course and facing the ocean, is by far the best place to stay if you visit.

THE CARRETERA AUSTRAL A convenient, scenic, and very comfortable way to travel from Puerto Montt to Chaitén has just begun: catamarans that make the trip in 4 hours. **Catamaranes del Sur** (© 02/482308; www.catamaranesdelsur.cl) operates three times a week and costs $40 one-way, $72 round-trip.

PATAGONIA & TIERRA DEL FUEGO El Calafate The newest hot spot in El Calafate is a sleek wine bar that opened in the fall of 2002. **Casimiro,** Av. del Libertador 963 (© 029/492590), feels more like a big city bistro than a small town restaurant with its chic decor and exquisite wine collection—not to mention the excellent Patagonian specialties.

Ushuaia Although nobody's going to arrive in Ushuaia from Antarctica, many are taking the opportunity to go the other way. Flights to remote Seymour Island began in early 2003 and represent the only air link to Antarctica. The twice-weekly flights are aboard a converted Air Force cargo jet. The 1-day round-trip excursion, organized by **Aerored** (© 11/4328-1923 in Buenos Aires), includes a 3-hour tour of Antarctica.

CHILE

The Chilean tourism industry has lost a lot of business to neighboring Argentina, now that prices there have hit rock bottom. However, worldwide interest in Chile continues to grow wildly in popularity, mostly because Chile offers wonderful landscapes and adventure-travel opportunities that are incomparable to its Andean neighbor. As a result of this growing interest in Chile, the country's tourism infrastructure continues to improve with new hotels, a brand-new major highway, refined service, and easier trip planning.

The bad news is that the entry fee for first-time visitors from the United States has risen sharply to $100, regardless of age, but it's good for the life of the visitor's passport. This fee is intended as a reciprocity fee for the U.S. government's recent decision to charge Chileans $100 for a visa application.

It's comical how fast telephone numbers in Chile change, and how these telephone numbers are immediately reassigned to a residence. All numbers in this book have been meticulously updated; however, do not be surprised if, occasionally, a Juan Doe answers without any idea of what you're talking about. Have your hotel help you find any updated numbers.

GETTING THERE By Plane United Airlines, in the face of its recent bankruptcy, has pulled out of Chile completely. This is bad news for residents in California, as United Airlines offered the only nonstop flight to Santiago. However, the Costa Rican airline **Lacsa** (of the Taca group) now offers low-cost flights with just one stop if you're flying from San Francisco or Los Angeles. Also, **Delta** has entered the scene, sometimes offering fares as low as $450 during the off season if you fly out of Atlanta. Sign up for the Delta newsletter to be advised of special fares. **AeroContinental** and **Avant,** two airlines that once flew domestic routes within Chile, have both folded, and now visitors flying domestically have one option: **Lan-Chile.**

Australians and New Zealanders have faster and more convenient access to Chile now that **Qantas** has begun offering more direct flights than ever before to Santiago, without a stopover in Papeete.

GETTING AROUND The total overhaul of the portion of the PanAmerican Highway that runs from Puerto Montt to the north of Chile is finished at last, drastically improving what used to be a rather frightening drive into an efficient, modern artery. Of course, modernity comes with a price, meaning hundreds of tollbooths that dot its length or sit at highway exits and entrances. Some are as cheap as 30¢, but others are as high as $5, so always have pesos on hand.

SANTIAGO   Accommodations The drop in the value of the peso and increased competition mean that hotel prices have either lowered considerably or at least have maintained their rates from even 3 or 4 years ago, especially in Santiago. When searching for a hotel room, don't be afraid to investigate rates for hotels that might seem well beyond your budget as these hotels often advertise incredible bargains, especially for multiple-day stays.

New on the scene in Santiago is South America's first **Ritz-Carlton** hotel, El Alcalde 15 (© **800/241-3333** from the U.S., or 23/629619), which was scheduled to open in May 2003 (after this book went to press). Though touted as Santiago's current top five-star hotel, many detractors say it won't surpass the quality and service of the **Hyatt Regency Santiago.**

Dining   Dining out in Santiago has never been so enjoyable. The capital city's culinary revolution seemingly sees no end, with the dozens of new hip, innovative eateries and improvements in food quality and atmosphere in classic restaurants. Diners now find wonderful updates on Chilean cuisine and international options from Czech to sushi to Mexican. Now if only the rest of the country would follow suit.

VIÑA DEL MAR   The garden city's newest lodging option is the **Hotel del Mar,** a five-star (though a little closer to 4-star) hotel that abuts the grand, classic casino. Its beautiful seaside views and a sumptuous indoor pool and gym are draws, but this hotel needs to work out a few bugs in its service, which is truly lackluster. Great location nonetheless.

THE CENTRAL VALLEY   Chile's wine industry has seen unbelievable growth and an unprecedented improvement in quality over the past few years. The days of the cheap bottle of Chilean wine are slowly coming to an end, as wineries shift toward growing premium wines and quietly jacking up worldwide prices. This has all led to a major improvement in the wine-tasting circuit, and the new **Hotel Santa Cruz Plaza,** Plaza de Armas 286, Santa Cruz (✆ **72/821 010**), in the heart of the Colchagua Valley, serves as an excellent jumping-off point to sample the wonderful varieties Chile has to offer. The Hotel Santa Cruz will organize day tours with the **Ruta del Vino,** or you can just rent a car and explore at your own pace.

THE CHILEAN LAKE DISTRICT
Pucón   Pucón's new airport (no phone), minutes from the center of town, is now operational, saving you from the tedious 1½-hour drive from Temuco. **LanChile** (✆ **600/ 600-4000**) jets arrive from Santiago

on Friday and Sunday, in high season only.

A brand-new hotel just opened on Pucón's shady main plaza, steps from all the shops and restaurants. **Hotel Huincahue,** Miguel Ansorena 23 (✆/fax **45/443540**), has a lovely outdoor pool hidden in the lush back garden with a breathtaking view of the volcano.

Pucón's newest eatery originated in Punta del Este, Uruguay, and is the sole Uruguayan steakhouse in the region. **La Maga,** Fresia 125 (✆ **45/ 444277**), serves the best steaks in town in a cozy setting just steps from the main plaza.

Villarrica   Southern Chile's top new hotel opened in November 2002 and is the height of luxury. The **Villarrica Park Lake Hotel,** Camino Villarrica Pucón Km 13 (✆ **45/450000**), has 69 elegant rooms, all with incredible lake views, and a full service spa and fitness center.

Valdivia   The Aires Buenos International Hostel, General Lagos 1036 (✆/fax **63/206304**), opened in 2002 in one of the town's most beautiful historical mansions. In addition to private rooms with ensuite bathrooms, there are bunk beds for $8.50 for those traveling on a tight budget.

Puerto Octay   The region's newest hideaway is the **Hotel & Cabañas Centinela,** Península de Centinela (✆/fax **64/391326**), which recently opened at the tip of the peninsula overlooking the Osorno Volcano. In addition to the rustic lodge that used to house a bordello, there are rows of *cabañas* for rent directly on the hotel's private beach.

Puerto Varas   There are two notable additions to the vibrant restaurant scene in Puerto Varas, and both are excellent. **Kika's,** Walker Martínez 584 (✆ **65/234703**), serves distinctive cuisine blending old German favorites with local ingredients such as grilled Patagonian venison with sauerkraut. Its wine list is made up entirely of award-winning Chilean vintages. **Mediterráneo,** Santa Rosa 068, on the corner of Portales (© **65/237 268**), serves up imaginative Chilean-Mediterranean fusion dishes in a great location with a view of the water.

Puerto Montt   Finally, a deluxe hotel has opened in Puerto Montt. The sleek seven-story **Gran Pacífico,** Urmeneta 719 (© **65/482100**), towers over the city's harbor and offers breathtaking views from its Art Deco rooms that come with large-screen TVs and small marble bathrooms.

1

The Best of Argentina & Chile

Argentina and Chile—separated by the serrated peaks of the Andes Mountains—combine to blanket the southern half of South America; the distance from Chile's northern tip to the southern tail of Argentina's Tierra del Fuego spans almost 4,830km (3,000 miles). And the scope of experience to be found here is no less grand: from the cosmopolitan bustle of Buenos Aires to the desolate moonscape of Chile's Atacama Desert; from the tropical jungles and thunderous falls of Iguazú to the tundra and glaciers of Torres del Paine National Park. Whether you've come to meander the quiet towns of Chile's Lake District or dance the night away in a smoky, low-lit tango bar, your trip to the Southern Hemisphere won't disappoint. In this chapter, we've selected the best that Argentina and Chile have to offer—museums, outdoor adventures, hotels, and more. So read on and start planning!

1 The Most Unforgettable Travel Experiences

- **Learning to Dance Tango in Buenos Aires:** *Salones de baile,* as tango salons are called, blanket the city; the most famous are in San Telmo. In these salons, you can watch traditional Argentine tango danced by all generations, and most offer lessons before the floor opens up to dancers. You won't find many novices on the dance floor after midnight, however. See chapter 3.
- **Visiting the Recoleta Cemetery:** This beautiful cemetery in Buenos Aires houses enormous, expensive mausoleums competing for grandeur—a place where people can remain rich, even after death. Among the only non-aristocrats buried here is Eva Perón, or "Evita." See chapter 3.
- **Wandering Caminito Street in La Boca:** Capture the flavor of early Buenos Aires on this short historic street, which is also considered an outdoor museum. The Caminito is famous for the

brightly colored sheet-metal houses that border it and for the sculptures, paintings, and wall murals you'll find along the street. Performers and dancers are here every day. See chapter 3.
- **Visiting Iguazú Falls:** One of the world's most spectacular sights, Iguazú boasts over 275 waterfalls fed by the Iguazú River. In addition to the falls, Iguazú encompasses a marvelous subtropical jungle with extensive flora and fauna. See chapter 4.
- **Riding the "Train to the Clouds":** The *Tren a las Nubes* is one of the world's great railroad experiences. The journey through Argentina's Northwest takes you 434km (269 miles) through tunnels, turns, and bridges, culminating in the breathtaking La Polvorilla viaduct. You will cross magnificent landscapes, making your way from the multicolored Lerma valley through the deep canyons and rugged peaks of the

Argentina & Chile

Quebrada del Toro and on to the desolate desert plateau of La Puña. See chapter 5.

- **Traveling the Wine Roads of Mendoza:** Less commercialized than their European and American counterparts, Mendoza's wineries are free to visit and easily accessible along roads known locally as *los Caminos del Vino*. There are about 80 wineries that formally offer tours and tastings. See chapter 7.

- **Sailing Through the Andes Between Chile & Argentina:** Why fly or drive when you can sail through the Andes? Two companies work together to provide boat journeys between Ensenada, Chile, and Bariloche, Argentina. It's a dazzling, though low-key, cruise that's worth the journey only on a clear day. The cruise takes visitors through the emerald waters of Lago Todos los Santos and the rugged peaks and rainforest of Vicente Pérez Rosales National Park in Chile, and in Argentina across Lake Nahuel Huapi to Puerto Blest. The trip can be done in 1 or 2 days. See "Essentials" under "San Carlos de Bariloche," in chapter 8, and "Parque Nacional Vicente Pérez Rosales & The Lake Crossing To Argentina" under "Lake Llanquihue, Frutillar & Puerto Varas," in chapter 14.

- **Bronzing in Punta del Este in Summer:** As Porteños (residents of Buenos Aires) will tell you, anyone who has a peso left to travel on heads to Punta del Este for summer vacation. The glitzy Atlantic coast resort in Uruguay is packed with South America's jet set from December to February and offers inviting beaches and outstanding nightlife. See chapter 9.

- **Waking Up in Santiago After a Rainstorm:** Santiago is a magnificent city, but it's usually hidden under a blanket of smog that would make even Paris look like Detroit. If you're lucky enough to catch Santiago after a rainstorm has cleared the skies, try to make it to the top of Cerro San Cristóbal for a breathtaking view of the city spread below the towering, snow-capped Andes. Few cityscapes in the world compare. See "Barrio Bellavista & Parque Metropolitano" under "Seeing the Sights," in chapter 11.

- **Exploring the Madcap Streets of Valparaíso:** The ramshackle, colorful, and sinuous streets of Valparaíso offer a walking tour unlike any other. Apart from the picturesque Victorian mansions and tin houses that seem cut into every shape possible, terraced walkways wind around the various hills that shoot up from downtown, and there are plenty of antique funiculars to lift you to the top. Great restaurants and cafes can be found at every turn to rest aching feet. Valparaíso is like a diamond in the rough, and part of the fascination is touring the faded remains of this once-thriving port town. See chapter 12.

- **Catching a Full Moon in the Valle de la Luna:** Nothing could be more appropriate, or dreamier, than an evening under the glow of a full moon in the Valley of the Moon. This region of the Atacama Desert was named for its otherworldly land formations and salt-encrusted canyons that supposedly resemble the surface of the moon, a comparison that is hard to dispute, especially when these formations are cast under an eerie, nighttime glow. The full moon "experience" is popular enough that nearly all tour companies in San Pedro plan excursions. See chapter 13.

- **Sailing the Fjords of Southern Chile:** Quietly sailing through the lush beauty of Chile's southern fjords is an experience that all can afford. There are two breathtaking trajectories: a 3-day ride between Puerto Natales and Puerto Montt, and a 1- to 6-day ride to the spectacular Laguna San Rafael Glacier. Backpackers on a shoestring as well as those who need spiffier accommodations all have options. These pristine, remote fjords are often said to be more dramatic than those in Norway, but the scenery isn't the only pleasure here—often, the camaraderie that grows between passengers is what in the end makes for such a fulfilling trip. See chapter 14.

- **Soaking in Hot Springs:** The volatile Andes not only builds volcanoes, but it also produces steaming mineralized water that is used to fill hot springs complexes from the desert north to the Aisén region. Chileans often take to these waters to relieve arthritis and rheumatism problems, but most take a soothing soak to relax. These hot springs seem to have

been magically paired by nature with outdoor adventure spots, making for a thankful way to end a day of activity. The Lake District is a noted "hot spot," especially around Pucón. See chapter 14.

- **Driving the Carretera Austral:** It's a tough, crunchy drive along 1,000km (620 miles) of gravel road, but that is precisely why Chile's "Southern Highway" has kept the crowds at bay. This natural wonderland, saturated in green and hemmed in by jagged, snow-capped peaks, offers a journey for those seeking to travel through some of Chile's most remote and stunning territory. It can be done in a variety of directions and segments, but you'll need a rental car. There are plenty of great stops along the way, including rainforest walks, the idyllic mountain valley of Futaleufú, the wet primeval forest of Parque Quelat, Puyuhuapi and its luxury thermal spas, and the city of Coyhaique. See chapter 16.

2 The Most Charming Small Towns

- **Salta, Argentina:** Salta sits in the Lerma valley of Argentina's Northwest with an eternal springlike climate, and boasts Argentina's best-preserved colonial architecture. It's surrounded by the fertile valley of the provincial capital, the polychrome canyons of Cafayate, and the desolate plateau of La Puña. See chapter 5.

- **Villa Carlos Paz, Argentina:** A quick getaway from Córdoba, Villa Carlos Paz surrounds the picturesque Ebalse San Roque. Although it's actually a reservoir, vacationers treat San Roque like a lake, swimming, sailing, and windsurfing in its gentle waters. Year-round, people come to Carlos Paz to enjoy outdoor activities

by day and party by night. See chapter 6.

- **La Falda, Argentina:** An excellent base from which to explore the Punilla, La Falda lies between the Valle Hermoso (Beautiful Valley) and the Sierras Chicas. Argentines come here for rest and relaxation, not wild entertainment. Crisp, clean air, wonderful hikes, and quiet hotels are the draw. See chapter 6.

- **San Martín de los Andes, Argentina:** City planners in San Martín had the sense to do what Bariloche never thought of: to limit building height to two stories and to mandate continuity in the town's alpine architecture. The result? Bariloche is crass whereas

San Martín is class, and the town is a year-round playground to boot. Relax, swim, bike, ski, raft, hunt, or fish—this small town has it all. See chapter 8.

- **Villa La Angostura, Argentina:** Villa La Angostura has everything its neighbor Bariloche has and more. This is where you go to escape the crowds and savor the sense of exclusivity. Great restaurants go hand in hand with cozy lodging. The town is spread along one street and along the shore of Nahuel Huapi Lake, with plenty of hiking, biking, and boating nearby; there's a great little ski resort, too. The wood-heavy construction is eye-catching, and the location is sumptuous. See chapter 8.

- **Colonia del Sacramento, Uruguay:** Just a short ferry trip from Buenos Aires, Colonia is Uruguay's best example of colonial life. The Old Neighborhood contains brilliant examples of colonial wealth and many of Uruguay's oldest structures. Dating from the 17th century, this beautifully preserved Portuguese settlement makes a perfect day trip. See chapter 9.

- **San Pedro de Atacama, Chile:** Quaint, unhurried, and built of adobe brick, San Pedro de Atacama has drawn Santiaguinos (residents of Santiago) and expatriates the world over who have come to experience the mellow charm and New Age spirituality that wafts through the dusty roads of this town. Its location in the driest desert in the world makes for starry skies and breathtaking views of the weird and wonderful land formations that are just a stone's throw away. See chapter 13.

- **Pucón, Chile:** Not only was Pucón bestowed with a stunning location at the skirt of a smoking volcano and the shore of a glittering lake, it's also Chile's self-proclaimed adventure capital, offering so many outdoor activities you could keep busy for a week. But Pucón also has plenty of low-key activities if your idea of a vacation is plopping yourself down on a beach. You'll find everything you want and need without forfeiting small-town charm (that is, if you don't come with the Jan and Feb crowds). Wood-hewn restaurants, pubs, and crafts stores fill downtown, blending harmoniously with the forested surroundings. See chapter 14.

- **Frutillar & Puerto Varas, Chile:** Built by German immigrants who settled here in the early 1900s, these neighboring towns bear the clear stamp of Prussian order and workmanship, from the crisp lines of trees to the picturesque, shingled homes and tidy plazas ringed with roses. If you're lucky, you can still catch a few old-timers chatting in German over coffee and *kuchen* (a dense cake). Both towns feature a glorious view of Volcán Osorno and a lakefront address, a picture-postcard location that makes for an excellent boardwalk stroll. If that isn't enough, both towns also offer above-par lodging and a few of the best restaurants in the country. See chapter 14.

- **Futaleufú, Chile:** Nestled in a green valley surrounded by an amphitheater of craggy, snow-encrusted peaks, Futaleufú is made of colorful, clapboard homes and unpaved streets, and is without a doubt one of the prettiest villages in Chile. The population of 1,200 swells during the summer when the hordes descend for rafting adventures on the nearby Class V river, but it hasn't changed the town's fabric too dramatically, and locals rarely saunter past a visitor without a tip of the hat and a *"Buenas tardes."* See chapter 16.

3 The Best Outdoor Adventures

- **Discovering Iguazú Falls by Raft:** A number of tour companies operate rafts that speed toward the falls, soaking their awestruck passengers along the way. This is the best way to experience the sound and fury of Iguazú's magnificent *cataratas.* See chapter 4.
- **Traveling Beyond the Falls into the Iguazú Jungle:** This is a place where birds like the great dusky swift and brilliant morpho butterflies spread color through the thick forest canopy. You can easily arrange an outing into the forest once you arrive in Iguazú. See chapter 4.
- **Raging Down the Mendoza River:** Mendoza offers the best white-water rafting in Argentina, and during the summer months, when the snow melts in the Andes and fills the Mendoza River, rafters enjoy up to Class IV and V rapids. Rafting is possible year-round, but the river is colder and calmer in winter months. See chapter 7.
- **Skiing Las Leñas:** One of South America's top ski destinations, Las Leñas boasts more slopes than any single resort in the Americas, with 40 miles of runs, excellent snow, and typically small crowds. Las Leñas also offers an active nightlife in winter. See chapter 7.
- **Climbing Aconcagua:** At 6,960m (22,829 ft.), Cerro Aconcagua is the highest peak in the entire Western Hemisphere. Those hoping to reach the top must buy a 20-day permit, which costs $200 (including emergency medical insurance). The climb is not technically difficult, but it demands strength and endurance. See chapter 7.
- **Rafting or Horseback Riding in the Cajón de Maipo:** Okay, it's not even close to rafting the Futaleufú, but the Maipo River whips up enough exciting rapids for a thrill and, best of all, it's just a 45-minute drive from Santiago. The Maipo River winds through the Cajón del Maipo, a hemmed-in, alpine valley that is so fragrant and pleasant it seems worlds away from the smoggy metropolis. To get deep into the Andes, saddle up for a full- or half-day horseback ride. Beginners and kids are welcome, too. Contact **Cascada Expediciones** in Santiago at ℂ **22/342274.** See chapter 12.
- **Skiing or Snowboarding Portillo:** It's been around for 54 years, and the steep chutes of **Portillo** still raise fear in the hearts of those about to make the descent on a pair of skis or snowboard. This is where the speed-skiing record was broken, where Fidel Castro spent the night, and where a Who's Who of northern ski lovers come in search of the endless winter. The grand yet rustic hotel is a single, all-inclusive destination, much like a cruise ship in the sky: no lift lines, a stunning location, great nightlife, a warm social ambience, and lots for kids to do, too. Call ℂ **800/829-5325** in the United States, or 22/630606 in Santiago. See chapter 12.
- **Summiting a Volcano:** There's something more thrilling about summiting a volcano than any old mountain, especially when the volcano threatens to blow at any

given time. Chile is home to a large share of the world's volcanoes, some of which are perfectly conical and entirely feasible to climb, such as Volcán Villarrica in Pucón and Volcán Osorno near Puerto Varas. Active Villarrica is a relatively moderate climb to the gaseous crater, followed by a fun slide on your rear down a human toboggan chute. Osorno offers a more technical climb, roping up for a crampon-aided walk past glacier crevasses and caves. Electrifying views are included with the package, from the ocean and into Argentina. For Volcán Villarrica, contact **Aguaventura** (© 45/444246) or **Sol y Nieve** (© 45/441070); for Volcán Osorno, contact **Tranco Expediciones** (© 65/311311). See chapter 14.

- **Rafting or Kayaking the Futaleufú River:** With churning river sections that are frightening enough to be dubbed "Hell" and "The Terminator," the Class V Futaleufú River, or the "Fu," as it's known, is solemnly revered by rafting and kayaking enthusiasts around the world as one of the most difficult to descend. A little too much excitement for your nerves? Rafting companies offer short-section rafting trips on the Futaleufú and down the tamer, crystalline waters of the neighboring Espolón River—kayak schools use this stretch, too. The scenery here redefines mountain beauty.

Contact **Bío Bío Expeditions** (© 800/246-7238, or 530/582-6865 in the U.S.). See chapter 16.

- **Face to Face with the Perito Moreno Glacier:** Few natural wonders in South America are as magnificent or as easily accessed as the Perito Moreno Glacier. You can drive right up to it, park, and descend a series of walkways that take you directly to the 48m-plus (160-ft.-plus) wall of turquoise ice—an unforgettable experience. To get really close, strap on a pair of crampons and take a walk across the glacier's surface to admire the sculpted walls and caves and changing tonal variety of blues. Nearly all travel agencies in Calafate book this excursion. See chapter 17.

- **Trekking in Torres del Paine:** This backpacking mecca just keeps growing in popularity, and it's no wonder. Torres del Paine is one of the most spectacular national parks in the world, with hundreds of kilometers of trails through ever-changing landscapes of jagged peaks and one-of-a-kind granite spires, undulating meadows, milky, turquoise lakes and rivers, and mammoth glaciers. The park has a well-organized system of *refugios* and campgrounds, but there are also several hotels, and visitors can access the park's major highlights on a day hike. See chapter 17.

4 The Best Hotels

- **Alvear Palace Hotel,** Buenos Aires (© 11/4808-2100): The most exclusive hotel in Buenos Aires and one of the top hotels in the world, the Alvear reflects the Belle Epoque era in which it was designed. Luxurious bedrooms and suites have private butler service, and the hotel's guest list reflects the top names in Argentina and visitors from abroad. See p. 47.

- **Four Seasons Hotel,** Buenos Aires (© 11/4321-1200): In 2002, the Four Seasons took over what was already one of the city's most luxurious properties. There are two parts to this landmark hotel—the 12-story Park Tower housing the majority of the guest rooms, and the turn-of-the-20th-century French-rococo La Mansión with seven elegant suites and a handful of private event rooms. See p. 50.

- **Marriott Plaza Hotel,** Buenos Aires (© **11/4318-3000**): This historic hotel was the grande dame of Buenos Aires for much of the 20th century, a gathering place of Argentine politicians, foreign dignitaries, and international celebrities. It remains one of the city's most impressive hotels. See p. 52.

- **Sheraton International Iguazú,** Puerto Iguazú (© **0800/888-9180,** local toll-free, or 37/5749-1800): If you visit Iguazú Falls, the Sheraton International Iguazú enjoys the best location by far. It's the only hotel on the Argentine side situated within the national park; half the rooms overlook the falls, and guests are within easy walking distance of the waterfall circuits. See p. 88.

- **Park Hyatt Mendoza,** Mendoza (© **26/1441-1234**): Peering majestically over the Plaza de la Independencia, the new Park Hyatt is the top hotel from which to explore the region's wineries. Sweeping columns of granite and stone showcase the lobby, and an impressive collection of Mendocino art pays tribute to local culture. See p. 125.

- **Llao Llao Hotel & Resort,** near Bariloche (© **02944/448530;** fax 02944/445789): If you're looking for a memorable evening and your pocketbook can afford it, this is your place. The world-renowned Llao Llao Hotel & Resort's style was influenced by Canadian-style mountain lodges, and the hotel's

magnificent alpine setting is one of the best in the world. Antler chandeliers, pine-log walls, and Oriental rugs set the mood, and the "winter garden" cafe overlooking Lake Nahuel Huapi is divine. The hotel boasts every amenity imaginable, including its own golf course, and service is impeccable. See p. 144.

- **Belmont House,** Montevideo (© **02/600-0430**): A boutique hotel in Montevideo's peaceful Carrasco neighborhood, Belmont House offers its privileged guests intimacy and luxury close to the city and the beach. Small elegant spaces with carefully chosen antiques and wood furnishings give this the feeling of a wealthy private home. See p. 173.

- **Radisson Montevideo Victoria Plaza Hotel,** Montevideo (© **02/902-0111**): Montevideo's center-piece hotel is situated next to Plaza Independencia in the heart of downtown. Spacious guest rooms boast French-style furnishings and upgraded amenities, and the hotel's restaurant, Arcadia, is outstanding. See p. 173.

- **Conrad Resort & Casino,** Punta del Este (© **042/491-111**): This resort dominates social life in Punta del Este. Luxurious rooms have terraces overlooking the beach, and there's a wealth of outdoor activities from tennis and golf to horseback riding and watersports. Nightlife centers on the Conrad's 24-hour casino, nightclub, and theater performances. See p. 179.

- **Hotel Carrera,** Santiago (© **26/982011;** fax 26/721083): This, the grande dame of Santiago hotels, has been a classic since it opened its revolving brass doors in 1940. The hotel's front rooms and glitzy rooftop pool overlook the historic Plaza Constitución. The hotel was for decades the social center of Santiago's elite. The English-style rooms are elegant, and the amenities and services are first rate. Newer five-star hotels such as the Hyatt, the Ritz Carlton, and the Sheraton have given the Carrera a run for its money, but these North American chains can't match the Carrera's old-world glamour and history. See p. 208.

- **Hotel Orly,** Santiago (℃ 22/318947; fax 22/520051): The Hotel Orly is an ideal little inn for those who look for personal service and intimate accommodations to compensate for the overwhelming hustle and bustle of Santiago. The hotel is inside a converted, French-style mansion, and there's a compact interior garden patio and bar. It's located smack-dab in the middle of everything in Providencia. See p. 214.
- **Hacienda Los Lingues,** near San Fernando (℃ 22/355446 in Santiago; fax 22/357604): Step back in time to the 17th century with a visit to one of Chile's oldest hotels, located in the rural heartland of the central valley south of Santiago. Los Lingues has been in the same family hands for more than 400 years, and each venerable room has been lovingly and individually decorated with personal touches such as family antiques, photos, and other collectibles. Like all haciendas, Los Lingues wraps around a plant-filled patio and fountain, but you'll also find a small chapel, a stately main building, and one of the country's finest horse breeding farms. The hotel offers day visits that include lunch in the hacienda's grand wine cellar. See p. 272.
- **Hotel Explora** in San Pedro de Atacama and **Hotel Explora Salto**

Chico in Torres del Paine (℃ 22/066060 in Santiago; fax 22/284655): Few hotels have generated as much press in Latin America as the two all-inclusive Explora lodges in San Pedro de Atacama and Torres del Paine. A dynamite location has helped, of course, but great service, cozy rooms with out-of-this-world views, interiors that are equally elegant and comfortable, and guided outdoor trekking, horseback riding, and biking excursions are what really put these hotels above par. The lodges were designed by several of Chile's top architects, built of native materials, and decorated with local art. See p. 284 and p. 416.

- **Lodge Terrantai,** San Pedro de Atacama (℃ 55/851140; fax 55/851037): This minimalist-style, small inn is virtually unrecognizable from the other adobe buildings that flank it, but once inside, you know that great care went into the renovation of this 100-year-old building. The hotel's design effortlessly blends clean, contemporary lines and simple river-rock walls with the building's original antique adobe structure and thatched roof. Quiet, understated, and cheaper than Hotel Explora, Terrantai also offers packages that include excursions around the area. See p. 285.
- **Hotel Antumalal,** Pucón (℃ 45/441011; fax 45/441013): This low-slung, Bauhaus-influenced country inn is one of the most special places to lodge in Chile. Located high above the shore of Lake Villarrica and a sloping, terraced garden, the hotel literally sinks into its surroundings, offering a cozy ambience and number-one view of the evening sunset. A warm welcome and a room with

no lock are all part of making you feel at home. Outstanding cuisine, too. See p. 302.

- **Termas de Puyuhuapi Spa & Hotel,** near Puyuhuapi (©/fax **22/256489** in Santiago): This is arguably the best hotel/thermal spa facility in Chile. Spread across a remote cove on the Ventisquero Sound, this one-of-a-kind resort is nestled in pristine rainforest and is reachable only by boat. The hotel itself has become the region's top attraction, drawing day visitors who come for a soak in one of the handful of indoor or outdoor pools or treatments in the state-of-the-art spa. The accommodations are wonderfully comfortable and the food is outstanding. Many overnighters include the hotel's package trips with an additional trip to the Laguna San Rafael Glacier. See p. 374.

- **Los Notros,** Perito Moreno Glacier, near Calafate (© **11/4814-3934** in Buenos Aires; fax 11/4815-7645): Location is everything at the Los Notros hotel, which boasts a breathtaking view spanning one of Argentina's great wonders, the Perito Moreno Glacier. The hotel blends contemporary folk art with a range of colorful hues, and this, along with impeccable rooms that come with a dramatic view of the electric-blue tongue of the glacier, make this lodge one of the most upscale, unique lodging options in Argentina. The hotel arranges excursions around the area and occasional informative talks, and there are plenty of easy chairs and lounges for sitting and contemplating the glorious nature surrounding you. See p. 429.

- **Hotel José Nogueira,** Punta Arenas (© **61/248840;** fax 61/248832): Originally the home of one of Punta Arenas's wealthiest families, the Nogueira offers the chance to spend the night in a historic landmark, the principal rooms of which have been preserved as a museum to give visitors a look at the outlandish luxury that must have seemed dramatically out of place in the Patagonia of the early 1900s. The upper floors have been converted into handsome, classically designed rooms that come with marvelously high ceilings. The mansion's glass-enclosed patio now houses the hotel's excellent restaurant, La Pérgola, and the cellar is now an evening pub. See p. 399.

5 The Best Dining Experiences

- **Cabaña las Lilas,** Buenos Aires (© **11/4313-1336**): Widely considered the best *parrilla* (grill) in Buenos Aires, Cabaña las Lilas is always packed. The beef comes exclusively from the restaurant's private *estancia* (ranch). The steaks are outstanding. See p. 56.

- **Catalinas,** Buenos Aires (© **11/4313-0182**): This is without doubt the most recognized international restaurant in Buenos Aires, its kitchen a model of culinary diversity and innovation. In addition to Chef Pardo's enormous Patagonian toothfish steaks, his grilled lamb chops—sprinkled with rosemary and fresh savory—are famous throughout Argentina. See p. 60.

- **De Olivas i Lustres,** Buenos Aires (© **11/4867-3388**): This magical restaurant in Old Palermo serves Mediterranean cuisine in a small, rustic dining room where antiques, olive jars, and wine bottles are on display. Each candlelit table is individually decorated. See p. 59.

- **Katrine,** Buenos Aires (© 11/ 4315-6222): One of the top dining choices in Buenos Aires, Katrine (named after the Norwegian chef-owner, who can be found almost every day in the kitchen) serves exquisite cuisine in a loud and festive dining room. See p. 56.
- **1884,** Mendoza (© 11/4313- 1336): Inside Bodega Escorihuela, Francis Mallman has created Mendoza's top restaurant, his cuisine blending his Patagonian roots with his French culinary training. Dishes are prepared with matching wine selections, with Malbec and Syrah topping the list. You can easily combine a tour of the bodega in the same visit. See p. 126.
- **Arcadia,** Montevideo (© 02/ 902-0111): Arcadia, an elegant restaurant atop the Plaza Victoria, is a quiet paradise in Montevideo. Tables are nestled in semiprivate nooks with floor-to-ceiling bay windows in a dining room decorated with Italian curtains and crystal chandeliers. See p. 175.
- **La Bourgogne,** Buenos Aires and Punta del Este (© 11/4805-3857 in Buenos Aires, and 042/482- 007 in Punta del Este): Jean-Paul Bondoux is the top French chef in South America, splitting his time between La Bourgogne in Punta del Este and its sister restaurant tucked inside the Alvear Palace Hotel, Buenos Aires. A member of Relais & Châteaux, La Bourgogne serves exquisite cuisine inspired by Bondoux's Burgundy heritage. See p. 57 and p. 180.
- **Agua,** Santiago (© 22/630008). Perhaps Santiago's most hip and innovative restaurant, Agua is *the* chic place to see and be seen. The minimalist design of concrete and glass is as fashionable and tasteful

as the fusion cuisine. The young chef at Agua has catapulted to culinary fame in Santiago for his delicious creations, especially his extensive use of seafood dishes. You'll even find mahimahi imported from Easter Island on the menu, and there are outstanding meat and vegetarian dishes as well. Excellent wine list, too. See p. 225.
- **Astrid y Gastón,** Santiago (© 26/509125). Named for the Peruvian and German couple who own and run this wonderful restaurant with such care, Astrid y Gastón is one of the newest and most remarkable restaurants in Santiago—the reason you'll often need to make reservations days in advance. The chef uses the finest ingredients, combined so that each plate bursts with flavor and personality; here, you'll find French, Spanish, Peruvian, and Japanese influences, as well as impeccable service, an on-site sommelier, and a lengthy wine list. If you can afford it, don't miss dining here. See p. 223.
- **Europeo,** Santiago (© 22/ 083603). Europeo is named for its cuisine: central European–based cuisine expertly prepared by the restaurant's Swiss-born and -trained chef. In a word, the food is heavenly, and the offer of a more upscale main dining area and a more economical adjoining cafe makes the Europeo suitable for any budget. Not only are the entrees mouthwatering (try the leg of lamb in a merlot sauce and served over polenta), but also the Austrian-style desserts are heavenly. See p. 225.
- **Bar Liguria,** Santiago (© 22/ 357914): This lively yet cozy restaurant is a Providencia hot spot, often filling before 10pm

and spilling out onto tables on the sidewalk. The mix of actors, artists, businessmen, and locals ensures a vibrant crowd, and you can check out all the action from the Liguria's 19th-century-style wood bar, where sharply dressed waiters rush to and fro, serving pisco sours and good bistro dishes. See p. 225.

- **Enoteca/Camino Real,** Santiago (© 22/321758): If you've been graced with clear skies, you'll spend more time staring out the window of the Camino Real than concentrating on the food before you (you're paying more for the view than the food anyway). This restaurant sits high atop the Cerro San Cristóbal and affords a breathtaking eyeful of the sprawl of Santiago and the Andes that rise majestically behind it. If there's no time to dine, order a drink and admire the sunset as the city lights twinkle on. See p. 224.

- **Aquí Está Coco,** Santiago (© 22/358649): This place is wildly popular with foreign visitors, with good reason: The kitsch atmosphere is as fun as the food is mouthwatering. The restaurant is spread over two levels of a 140-year-old home and festooned with oddball and nautically themed gadgets and curios. Arrive a little early and enjoy an aperitif in the cavelike, brick cellar lounge. Seafood is the specialty here. See p. 223.

- **Merlin,** Puerto Varas (© 65/233105): This little restaurant has the good sense to celebrate the bounty of fresh regional products available in the Lake District by offering creative, flavorful food that arrives at your table *prepared,* not just "cooked." Fresh fish and shellfish, meats, and vegetarian dishes are seasoned with flair, using fresh herbs and spices. The restaurant occupies the first floor of an old home, with cozy, candlelit tables. See p. 333.

- **Latitude 42** at the Yan Kee Way Lodge, Ensenada (© 65/212030). Worth the drive from Puerto Varas, this gorgeous restaurant boasts superb views of the Osorno Volcano and delectable cuisine served in a beautiful dining room. The talented chef uses locally grown produce to create imaginative dishes that come as close to nouvelle cuisine as you're ever going to get in southern Chile. Service is impeccable and there's a cigar bar and a cellar for wine tasting, as well. See p. 337.

- **La Calesa,** Valdivia (© 63/225437): Don't overlook a Peruvian restaurant in Chile, especially La Calesa. The spicy, delectable cuisine brought to Valdivia by an immigrant family from Peru is as enjoyable as the architecture of the 19th-century home in which the restaurant is housed. Soaring ceilings, antique furniture, great pisco sours at an old wooden bar, the river slowly meandering by . . . need we say more? See p. 321.

- **Remezón,** Punta Arenas (© 61/241029): You'll have to come to the end of Chile for some of the country's best cuisine. This unassuming little restaurant consistently garners rave reviews by diners. Sumptuous dishes prepared with local king crab, lamb, and goose are the highlight here, as are the incredible desserts. If that weren't enough, the warm welcome and personal contact with the chef leave you feeling happy and well fed. See p. 402.

- **Kapué Restaurant,** Ushuaia (© 02901/422704): King crab features predominantly on the menu at the Kapué, in puff pastries, soufflés, and fresh-on-the-plate, but nearly every dish here is as refined and delectable. The gracious, family-run service is as pleasant as the view of the Beagle Channel, and the restaurant's new wine bar really sets it apart from other eateries in town. See p. 442.

6 The Best Museums

- **Caminito,** Buenos Aires: At the center of La Boca lies the Caminito, a short pedestrian walkway that is both an outdoor museum and marketplace. Each day, tango performers dance alongside musicians, street vendors, and artists. Surrounding the street are shabby metal houses painted in dynamic shades of red, yellow, blue, and green. See p. 66.
- **Museo Nacional de Bellas Artes,** Buenos Aires: This museum contains the world's largest collection of Argentine sculptures and paintings from the 19th and 20th centuries. It also houses European art dating from the pre-Renaissance period to the present day. The collections include notable pieces by Manet, Goya, El Greco, and Gaugin. See p. 71.
- **Malba-Colección Constantini,** Buenos Aires: This stunning new private museum houses one of the most impressive collections of Latin American art anywhere. Temporary and permanent exhibitions showcase names like Antonio Berni, Pedro Figari, Frida Kahlo, Cândido Portinari, Diego Rivera, and Antonio Siguí. Many of the works confront social issues and explore questions of national identity. See p. 70.
- **Museo Arqueológico Provincial,** Jujuy: The Provincial Archaeological Museum displays archaeological finds representing more than 2,500 years of life in the Jujuy region, including a 2,600-year-old ceramic goddess, a lithic collection of arrowheads, the bones of a child from 1,000 years ago, and two mummified adults. See p. 103.
- **Manzana Jesuítica,** Córdoba: The Jesuit Block, which includes the Society of Jesus's Church, the Domestic Chapel, the National University of Córdoba, and the National School of Monserrat, has been the intellectual center of Argentina since the early 17th century. Today, the entire complex is a historic museum, although the churches still hold Mass, the cloisters still house priests, and the schools still enroll students. See p. 110.
- **Museo Fundacional,** Mendoza: The Foundational Museum displays what remains of the old city, ravaged by the 1861 earthquake. Chronicling the early history of Mendoza, the museum begins by looking at the culture of the indigenous *huarpes* and continues with an examination of the city's development through Spanish colonization to independence. An underground chamber holds the ruins of the aqueduct and fountain that once provided Mendoza's water supply. See p. 120.
- **Iglesia, Convento y Museo de San Francisco,** Santiago: One step into this museum and you'll feel like you've been instantly beamed out of downtown Santiago. This is the oldest standing building in Santiago and home to a serene garden patio where the only sounds are a trickling fountain and the cooing of pigeons. The museum boasts 54 paintings depicting the life and death of San Francisco, one of the largest and best-conserved displays of 17th-century art in South America. On the altar of the church, you'll see

the famous *Vírgen del Socorro,* the first Virgin Mary icon in Chile. See p. 231.

- **Museo Chileno de Arte Precolombino,** Santiago: More than 1,500 objects related to indigenous life and culture throughout the Americas make the Precolumbian Museum one of the best in Santiago. Artifacts include textiles, metals, paintings, figurines, and ceramics from Mexico to Chile. All objects are handsomely lit and mounted throughout seven exhibition rooms that are divided into the Mesoamérica, Intermedia, Andina, and Surandina regions of Latin America. The museum is housed in the old Royal Customs House built in 1807. If you need a break, there's a patio with a small cafe and a good bookstore to browse. See p. 229.

- **Palacio de la Real Audiencia/ Museo Histórico Nacional,** Santiago: The National History Museum holds a superb collection of more than 70,000 colonial-era pieces, from furniture to suits of armor to home appliances. This fascinating grab bag of artifacts is laid out in 16 display rooms within the lemon-colored, neoclassical Palacio de la Real, built in 1807 and the historic site of the first Chilean congressional session. The museum will give you insight into the history of the lives of Chileans, and it's conveniently located on the Plaza de las Armas. See p. 228.

- **Casa Pablo Neruda,** Isla Negra: This was Nobel prize–winning poet Pablo Neruda's favorite home, and although his other residences in Valparaíso and Santiago are as eccentric and absorbing, this is the best preserved of the three. The home is stuffed with books by his favorite authors and the whimsical curios, trinkets, and toys he

collected during his travels around the world, including African masks, ships in bottles, butterflies, and more. The museum can be found in Isla Negra, south of Valparaíso, and you need to plan a half-day trip to get there. See p. 259.

- **Museo Arqueológico Padre le Paige,** San Pedro de Atacama: This little museum will come as an unexpected surprise for its wealth of indigenous artifacts, such as "Miss Chile," a leathered mummy whose skin, teeth, and hair are mostly intact, as well as a display of skulls that show the creepy ancient custom of cranial deformation practiced by the elite as a status symbol. The Atacama Desert is the driest in the world, and this climate has produced some of the best-preserved artifacts in Latin America, on view here. See p. 282.

- **Museo de Colchagua,** Santa Cruz: Here, you'll find a stunning collection of everything from pre-Hispanic objects throughout the Americas, to local Indian artifacts, to Spanish conquest–era helmets and artillery, to immigrant household items and farm machinery, and more. This museum is a not-to-be-missed stop while visiting the wine country. Unbelievably, the museum is really the private collection of a local man who earned his fortune in bomb manufacturing and arms dealing, and because he cannot leave the country (and risk arrest by the FBI), he has reinvested in projects such as this in his hometown. See p. 270.

- **Museo Marítimo y Presidio de Ushuaia,** Ushuaia: The United States used to send its worst criminals to Alcatraz, but Argentina took isolation to a whole new level and shipped its criminals to the end of the world. Ushuaia was built from the forced labor of these prisoners, whose former penitentiary you can now tour. While walking the echoing halls of the prison, try imagining what it must have been like to know that any escape plan was futile: After all, where would you go? And where would you change out of your comical, black-and-white striped wool uniform (also on display)? See p. 437.

- **Museo Regional Braun Menéndez,** Punta Arenas: The Braun Menéndez Regional Museum is the former home of one of Patagonia's wealthiest families. Tapestries, furniture from France, Italian marble fireplaces, hand-painted wallpaper—this veritable palace is a testament to the Braun family's insatiable need to match European elite society. Several small salons are devoted to ranching and maritime history, but the grandeur of this museum is really the reason for a visit. See p. 395.

- **Museo Salesiano Maggiorino Borgatello,** Punta Arenas: There's so much on display here that you could spend more than an hour wandering and marveling at the hodgepodge collection of archaeological artifacts, photo exhibits, petroleum production interpretative exhibitions, ranch furniture, industrial gadgets, and, best of all, the macabre collection of stuffed and mounted regional wildlife gathered by a Salesian priest. See p. 395.

2

Planning Your Trip to Argentina

A little advance planning can make the difference between a good trip and a great trip. What do you need to know before you go? When should you go? What's the best way to get there? How much should you plan on spending? What safety or health precautions are advised? All the basics are outlined in this chapter—the when, why, and how of traveling to and around Argentina.

1 The Regions in Brief

Argentina is the world's eighth-largest country. To the north, it is bordered by Bolivia, Paraguay, Brazil, and Uruguay, the latter situated directly northeast of Buenos Aires. The Andes cascade along Argentina's western border with Chile, where the continent's highest peaks stand. The polychromatic hills and desert plateau of the nation's Northwest are as far removed from the bustling activity of Buenos Aires as are the flat grasslands of Las Pampas from the dazzling waterfalls and subtropical jungle of Iguazú. The land's geographic diversity is reflected in the people, too: Witness the contrast between the capital's largely immigrant population and the indigenous people of the Northwest. For me, Argentina's cultural distinction and geographic diversity make this South America's most fascinating travel destination.

Many people who spend at least a week in Argentina choose between traveling to Iguazú Falls and the Northwest. To see the spectacular falls of Iguazú from both the Argentine and Brazil sides, you need at least 2 full days. A visit to the geographically stunning Northwest, where Argentina's history began and traces of Incan influence still appear, requires 3 or more days. If you choose to head south to the Lake District and Patagonia, you can do it in a week, but you'd spend a good chunk of that time just getting down there. Better to allot 2 weeks and allow time to savor the distinctive landscape.

BUENOS AIRES & THE PAMPAS
Buenos Aires, a rich combination of South American energy and European sophistication, requires at least several days (a week would be better) to explore. In addition to seeing the city's impressive museums and architectural sites, take time to wander its grand plazas and boulevards, to stroll along its fashionable waterfront, and to engage in its dynamic culture and nightlife. A thick Argentine steak in a local *parrilla* (grill), a visit to a San Telmo antiques shop, a dance in a traditional tango salon—these are the small experiences that will connect you to the city's soul.

The heartland of the country is the Pampas, an enormous fertile plain where the legendary gaucho (Pampas cowboy) roams. It includes the provinces of Buenos Aires, southern Santa Fe, southeastern Córdoba, and eastern La Pampa. The pampas today contain many of the major cities, including the capital. One-third of Argentines live in greater Buenos Aires. For more, see chapter 3.

MISIONES   This small province of Mesopotamia enjoys a subtropical climate responsible for the region's flowing rivers and lush vegetation. The spectacular Iguazú Falls are created by the merger of the Iguazú and Parana rivers at the border of Argentina, Brazil, and Paraguay. For more, see chapter 4.

NORTHWEST   The Andes dominate the Northwest, with ranges between 4,877m and 7,010m (16,000 ft.–23,000 ft.). It is here that South America's tallest mountain, Aconcagua, stands at 6,959m (22,831 ft.) above sea level. The two parallel mountain ranges are the Salto-Jujeña, cut by magnificent multicolored canyons called *quebradas*. This region is often compared with the Basin and Range region of the southwestern United States, and can be visited from the historic towns of Salta and Jujuy. For more, see chapter 5.

THE LAKE DISTRICT   Argentina's Lake District extends from Junín de los Andes south to Esquel—an Alpine-like region of snowy mountains, waterfalls, lush forest, and, of course, glacier-fed lakes. San Martín de los Andes, Bariloche, and Villa La Angostura are the chief destinations here, but this isn't an area where you stay in one place for long. Driving tours, boating, skiing—you'll be on the move from the moment you set foot in the region. For more, see chapter 8.

Considering the enormous, flat pampa that separates Buenos Aires from the Lake District, and the region's proximity to the international border with Chile, many visitors opt to include a trip to Chile's Lake District while here. (For more information, see chapter 14.) To avoid the crowds, I highly recommend that you plan a trip during the spring or fall (see "When to Go," below).

PATAGONIA   Also known as **Magallanes** or the **Deep South,** this dry, arid region at the southern end of the continent has soared in popularity over the past 5 years. We've grouped both Argentina and Chile in one Patagonia chapter because the majority of travelers visit destinations in both countries while here. Patagonia is characterized by vast, open pampa; the colossal Northern and Southern Ice Fields and hundreds of glaciers; the jagged peaks of the Andes as they reach their terminus; beautiful emerald fjords; and wind, wind, wind. Getting here is an adventure—it usually takes 24 hours if coming directly from the United States or Europe. But the long journey pays off in the beauty and singularity of the region. El Calafate is a tourist-oriented village adjacent to the Perito Moreno Glacier, which beckons visitors from around the world to stand face-to-face with its tremendous wall of ice. El Chaltén is a tiny village of 200 whose numbers swell each summer with those who come to marvel the stunning towers of mounts Fitz Roy, Cerro Torre, and Puntiagudo. This is the second most-visited region of Argentina's Los Glaciares National Park and quite possibly its most exquisite, for the singular nature of the granite spires here that shoot up, torpedolike, above massive tongues of ice that descend from the Southern Ice Field. For more, see chapter 17.

TIERRA DEL FUEGO   Even more south than the Deep South, this archipelago at the southern extremity of South America is, like Patagonia, shared by both Chile and Argentina. The main island, separated from the mainland by the Strait of Magellan, is a triangle with its base on the Beagle Channel. Tierra del Fuego's main town is Ushuaia, the southernmost

Argentina

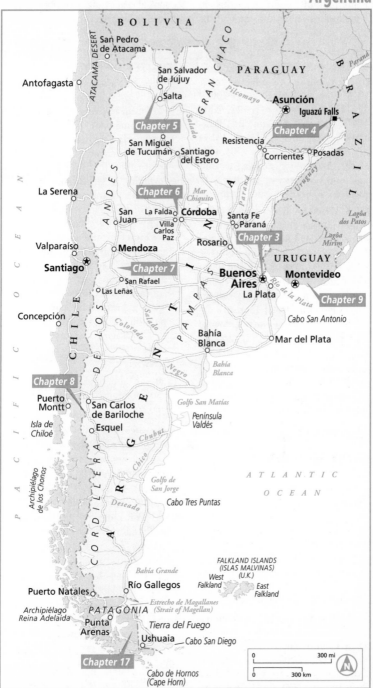

BOLIVIA

San Pedro
de Atacama

ATACAMA DESERT

Antofagasta

San Salvador
de Jujuy

Salta

GRAN CHACO

PARAGUAY

Pilcomayo

Asunción

Iguazú Falls

Chapter 5

San Miguel
de Tucumán

Santiago
del Estero

Salado

Chapter 4

Resistencia

Corrientes

Posadas

Paraná

BRAZIL

La Serena

ANDES

Chapter 6

Mar
Chiquito

San
Juan

La Falda

Córdoba

Villa
Carlos
Paz

Santa Fe

Paraná

Chapter 3

Lagôa
dos Patos

Valparaíso

Mendoza

Rosario

Uruguay

Lagôa
Mirim

Santiago

Chapter 7

URUGUAY

Buenos
Aires

Montevideo

San Rafael

Las Leñas

La Plata

Río de la Plata

Chapter 9

Concepción

Salado

Colorado

PAMPAS

Cabo San Antonio

Bahía
Blanca

Mar del Plata

ARGENTINA

Negro

Bahía
Blanca

CHILE

Chapter 8

Puerto
Montt

San Carlos
de Bariloche

Esquel

Golfo San Matias

Península
Valdés

Isla de
Chiloé

CORDILLERA DE LOS ANDES

Chubut

Chico

Golfo de
San Jorge

A T L A N T I C

O C E A N

Archipiélago
de los Chonos

Deseado

Cabo Tres Puntas

PACIFICO OCEAN

Bahía Grande

FALKLAND ISLANDS
(ISLAS MALVINAS)
(U.K.)

West
Falkland

East
Falkland

Puerto Natales

Río Gallegos

Archipiélago
Reina Adelaida

PATAGONIA

Punta
Arenas

Estrecho de Magallanes
(Strait of Magellan)

Tierra del Fuego

Ushuaia

Cabo San Diego

Chapter 17

Cabo de Hornos
(Cape Horn)

0   300 mi

0   300 km

N

city in the world. Many use the city as a jumping-off point for trips to Antarctica or sailing trips around the Cape Horn. As with the Argentine section of Patagonia, this region is outlined in chapter 17.

2 Visitor Information

IN THE U.S.   The Argentina Government Tourist Office has offices at 12 W. 56th St., New York, NY 10019 (© **212/603-0443;** fax 212/315-5545), and 2655 Le Jeune Rd., Penthouse Suite F, Coral Gables, FL 33134 (© **305/442-1366;** fax 305/441-7029). For more details, consult Argentina's Ministry of Tourism website (see "Websites of Note," below).

IN CANADA   Basic tourist information can be obtained by the Consulate General of Argentina, 2000 Peel St., Suite 600, Montreal, Quebec H3A 2W5 (© **514/842-6582;** fax 514/842-5797; www.consargenmtl. com); for more details, consult Argentina's Ministry of Tourism website (see "Websites of Note," below).

IN THE U.K.   For visitor information, contact the Embassy of Argentina in London (see "Entry Requirements & Customs," below) or consult Argentina's Ministry of Tourism website (see "Websites of Note," below).

WEBSITES OF NOTE

- **www.embajadaargentina-usa. org**   Up-to-date travel information from the Argentine embassy in Washington, D.C.
- **www.turismo.gov.ar**   This Ministry of Tourism site has travel information for all of Argentina, including a virtual tour of the country's tourist regions, shopping tips, links to city tourist sites, and general travel facts.
- **www.mercotour.com**   A travel site focused on adventure and ecological excursions, with information on outdoor activities in both Argentina and Chile.
- **www.argentinatravel.com**   This promotional site advertises vacation packages, accommodations, transportation, and *estancia* (ranch) stays.

You can also e-mail questions or requests for information to secturusa@turismo.gov.ar.

3 Entry Requirements & Customs

ENTRY REQUIREMENTS

Citizens of the United States, Canada, the United Kingdom, Australia, New Zealand, and South Africa require a passport to enter the country. No visa is required for citizens of these countries for tourist stays of up to 90 days. For more information concerning longer stays, employment, or other types of visas, contact the embassies or consulates in your home country.

IN THE U.S.   Contact the Consular Section of the Argentine Embassy, 1718 Connecticut Ave. NW, Washington, DC 20009 (© **202/238-6460**). Consulates are also located in California (© **213/954-9155**),

Florida (© **305/373-7794**), Georgia (© **404/880-0805**), Illinois (© **312/819-2610**), New York City (© **212/603-0400**), and Texas (© **713/871-8935**). For more information, try www.uic.edu/orgs/argentina.

IN CANADA   Contact the Embassy of the Argentine Republic, Suite 910, Royal Bank Center, 90 Sparks St., Ottawa, Ontario K1P 5B4 (© **613/236-2351;** fax 613/235-2659).

IN THE U.K.   Contact the Embassy of the Argentine Republic, 65 Brooke St., London W1Y 4AH (© **020/7318-1300;** fax 020/7318-1301; seruni@mrecic.gov.ar).

CUSTOMS
WHAT YOU CAN BRING INTO ARGENTINA

Travelers entering Argentina can bring personal effects—including clothes, jewelry, and professional equipment—without paying duty. In addition, they can bring in 21 liters of alcohol, 400 cigarettes, and 50 cigars duty free.

WHAT YOU CAN TAKE HOME

Returning **U.S. citizens** who have been away for at least 48 hours are allowed to bring back, once every 30 days, $400 worth of merchandise duty-free. You'll be charged a flat rate of 4% duty on the next $1,000 worth of purchases. Be sure to have your receipts handy. On mailed gifts, the duty-free limit is $100. You cannot bring fresh foodstuffs into the United States; tinned foods, however, are allowed. For more information, contact the **U.S. Customs Service,** 1300 Pennsylvania Ave. NW, Washington, DC 20229 (© 877/287-8867) and request the free pamphlet *Know Before You Go.* It's also available on the Web at www.customs.gov. (Click on "Traveler Information," then "Know Before You Go.")

For a clear summary of **Canadian** rules, write for the booklet *I Declare,* issued by the **Canada Customs and Revenue Agency** (© 800/461-9999 in Canada, or 204/983-3500; www.ccra-adrc.gc.ca). Canada allows its citizens a C$750 exemption, and

you're allowed to bring back duty free one carton of cigarettes, one can of tobacco, 40 imperial ounces of liquor, and 50 cigars. In addition, you're allowed to mail gifts to Canada valued at less than C$60 a day, provided they're unsolicited and don't contain alcohol or tobacco (write on the package "Unsolicited gift, under $60 value"). All valuables should be declared on the Y-38 form before departure from Canada, including serial numbers of valuables you already own, such as expensive foreign cameras. *Note:* The $750 exemption can only be used once a year and only after an absence of 7 days.

U.K. citizens returning from a non-EU country have a customs allowance of 200 cigarettes; 50 cigars; 250 grams of smoking tobacco; 2 liters of still table wine; 1 liter of spirits or strong liqueurs (over 22% volume); 2 liters of fortified wine, sparkling wine, or other liqueurs; 60cc (ml) perfume; 250cc (ml) of toilet water; and £145 worth of all other goods, including gifts and souvenirs. People under 17 cannot have the tobacco or alcohol allowance. For more information, contact **HM Customs & Excise,** Passenger Enquiry Point, 2nd Floor Wayfarer House, Great South West Road, Feltham, Middlesex, TW14 8NP (© 0181/910-3744; from outside the U.K. 44/181-910-3744), or consult its website at www.open.gov.uk.

4 Money

CASH & CURRENCY

The official Argentine currency is the **peso,** made up of 100 **centavos.** Money is denominated in notes of 2, 5, 10, 20, 50, and 100 pesos and coins of 1, 2, and 5 pesos and 1, 5, 10, 25, and 50 centavos. Argentina ended its parity with the dollar in January 2002. At the time this book went to press,

the exchange rate was fluctuating at 3 to 4 pesos to the dollar, with inflation running at approximately 30%.

Prices have fallen across the board with the peso's devaluation, and Argentina has become a bargain for foreign visitors. Often, prices are only half what they were before the economic crisis. Prices quoted in this book continue to be quoted in dollars only, but realize that high inflation and volatile exchange rates will limit their accuracy. Prices in Buenos Aires are typically higher than in the rest of the country.

EXCHANGING MONEY

U.S. dollars are widely accepted in Buenos Aires and can be used to pay taxis, hotels, restaurants, and stores. (In fact, many ATMs in Buenos Aires dispense U.S. dollars as well as pesos.) Keep some pesos on hand, however, because you might run into spots where you'll need them. You'll find that U.S. dollars are less useful in rural areas (and places to exchange money less common), so plan ahead. You can convert your currency in hotels, *casas de cambio* (money-exchange houses), some banks, and at the Buenos Aires airport. Change American Express traveler's checks in Buenos Aires at **American Express,** Arenales 707 (© **11/4130-3135**). It is difficult to change traveler's checks outside the capital. Therefore, I recommend that you carry sufficient pesos (or purchase traveler's checks in pesos) when you venture into small-town Argentina.

ATMS

Traveler's checks are something of an anachronism from the days when people wrote personal checks instead of going to an ATM. Because traveler's checks could be replaced if lost or stolen, they were a sound alternative to filling your wallet with cash at the beginning of a trip.

ATMs (automated teller machines) are easy to access in Buenos Aires and other urban areas, but don't depend on finding them off the beaten path. Typically, they are connected to **Cirrus** (© **800/424-7787;** www. mastercard.com/cardholderservices/ atm) or **PLUS** (© **800/843-7587;** www.visa.com/atms) networks. Check the back of your ATM card to see which network your bank belongs to.

The toll-free numbers and websites will give you specific locations of ATMs where you can withdraw money while on vacation. You can withdraw only as much cash as you need every couple of days, which eliminates the insecurity of carrying around a wad of cash. Many ATMs also accept Visa and MasterCard.

One important reminder: Many banks now charge a fee ranging from 50¢ to $3 whenever non–account holders use their ATMs. Your own bank might also assess a fee for using an ATM that's not one of its branch locations. This means that, in some cases, you'll get charged *twice* just for using your bank card when you're on vacation. And while an ATM card can be an amazing convenience when traveling in another country (put your card in the machine, and out comes foreign currency, at an extremely advantageous exchange rate), banks are also likely to slap you with a "foreign currency transaction fee."

CREDIT CARDS

If you choose to use plastic instead of cash, Visa, American Express, Master-Card, and Diners Club are commonly accepted. However, bargain hunters take note: Some establishments—especially smaller businesses—will give you a better price if you pay cash. Credit cards are accepted at most hotels and restaurants, except for the very cheapest ones. But note that you cannot use credit cards in many taxis or at most attractions (museums, trams, and so on).

You can get **cash advances** off your credit card at any bank, and you don't even need to go to a teller; you can get a cash advance at the ATM if you know your PIN. If you've forgotten your PIN or didn't even know you had one, call the phone number on the back of your credit card and ask the bank to send it to you. It usually takes 5 to 7 business days, although some banks will do it over the phone.

Another hidden expense to contend with: Interest rates for cash advances are often significantly higher than rates for credit card purchases. More importantly, you start paying interest on the advance *the moment you receive the cash.*

5 When to Go

The seasons in Argentina are the reverse of those in the Northern Hemisphere. Buenos Aires is ideal in fall (Mar–May) and spring (Sept–Nov), when temperatures are mild. The beaches and resort towns are packed with vacationing Argentines in summer (Dec–Mar), while Buenos Aires becomes somewhat deserted (you decide if that's a plus or a minus—hotel prices usually fall here in summer). Plan a trip to Patagonia and the southern Andes in summer, when days are longer and warmer. Winter (June–Aug) is the best time to visit Iguazú and the Northwest, when the rains and heat have subsided; but spring (Aug–Oct) is also pleasant, as temperatures are mild and the crowds have cleared out.

CLIMATE   Except for a small tropical area in northern Argentina, the country lies in the temperate zone, characterized by cool, dry weather in the south, and warmer, humid air in the center. Accordingly, January and February are quite hot—often in the high 90s to more than 100°F (35°C–40°C)—while winter (approximately July–Oct) can be chilly.

HOLIDAYS   Public holidays are January 1 (New Year's Day); Good Friday; May 1 (Labor Day); May 25 (First Argentine Government); June 10 (National Sovereignty Day); June 20 (Flag Day); July 9 (Independence Day); August 17 (Anniversary of the Death of General San Martín);

October 12 (Día de la Raza); December 8 (Immaculate Conception Day); and December 25 (Christmas).

FESTIVALS & SPECIAL EVENTS   Several holidays and festivals are worth planning a trip around; the best place to get information for these events is through your local Argentine tourism office (see "Visitor Information," above). **Carnaval (Mardi Gras),** the week before the start of Lent, is celebrated in many towns in Argentina, although to a much lesser extent than in neighboring Brazil. In Salta, citizens throw a large parade, including caricatures of public officials and "water bomb" fights. The **Gaucho Parade** takes place in Salta on June 16, with music by folk artists and gauchos dressed in traditional red ponchos with black stripes, leather chaps, black boots, belts, and knives.

Inti Raymi (Festival of the Sun) takes places in towns throughout the Northwest the night before the summer solstice (June 20) to give thanks for the year's harvest. **Día de Independencia (Independence Day)** is celebrated in Tucumán on July 9. **Exodo Jujeño (Jujuy Exodus)** takes place August 23 and 24, when locals reenact the exodus of 1812. The **Batalla de Tucumán (Battle of Tucumán)** celebrates Belgrano's victory over the Spanish on September 24. And the **Fiesta Provincial del Turismo (Provincial Tourist Festival)** takes place in December in Puerto Iguazú.

6 Health & Insurance

HEALTH

Argentina requires no vaccinations to enter the country, except for passengers coming from countries where cholera and yellow fever are endemic. Some people who have allergies can be affected by the pollution in the city and the high level of pollen during spring. Because motor vehicle crashes are a leading cause of injury among travelers, walk and drive defensively. Avoid nighttime travel if possible and always use a seat belt.

Most visitors find that Argentine food and water is generally easy on the stomach. Water and ice are considered safe to drink in Buenos Aires. Be careful with street food, especially in dodgy neighborhoods of Buenos Aires and in cities outside the capital.

ALTITUDE SICKNESS If you visit the Andes Mountains, beware of **altitude sickness.** Altitude sickness, known as *soroche* or *puna,* is a temporary yet often debilitating affliction that affects about a quarter of travelers to the northern Altiplano, or the Andes at 2,427m (7,872 ft.) and up. Nausea, fatigue, headaches, shortness of breath, and sleeplessness are the symptoms, which can last from 2 to 5 days. If you feel as though you've been affected, drink plenty of water, take aspirin or ibuprofen, and avoid alcohol and sleeping pills. To prevent altitude sickness, acclimatize your body by ascending gradually to allow time for your body to adjust to the high altitude.

AUSTRAL SUN The shrinking ozone layer in southern South America has caused an onset of health problems among the citizens who live there, including increased incidents of skin cancer and cataracts. If you are planning to travel to Patagonia, keep in mind that on "red alert" days (typically Sept–Nov), it is possible to burn in *10 minutes.* If you plan to be outdoors, you'll need to protect yourself with strong sunblock, a long-sleeved shirt, a wide-brimmed hat, and sunglasses.

MALARIA & OTHER TROPICAL AILMENTS The **Centers for Disease Control and Prevention** (**www.cdc.gov**) recommends that travelers to northwestern Argentina take malaria medication, but I have not heard of any incidents of malaria. Cholera has appeared from time to time in the Northwest, but such tropical diseases do not seem to be a problem in the sultry climate of Iguazú.

WHAT TO DO IF YOU GET SICK AWAY FROM HOME

The medical facilities and personnel in Buenos Aires and the other urban areas in Argentina are very professional and comparable to United States standards. Argentina has a system of socialized medicine, where basic services are free. Private clinics are inexpensive by Western standards. If you worry about getting sick away from home, you may want to consider **medical travel insurance** (see the section on travel insurance below). In most cases, however, your existing health plan will provide all the coverage you need. Be sure to carry your identification card in your wallet.

TRAVEL INSURANCE

Check your existing insurance policies before you buy travel insurance to cover trip cancellation, lost luggage, medical expenses, or car-rental insurance. You're likely to have partial or complete coverage. But if you need some, ask your travel agent about a comprehensive package. The cost of travel insurance varies widely, depending on the cost and length of your trip, your age and overall health, and the type of trip you're taking. Insurance for extreme sports or adventure travel, for example, will cost more than coverage for a cruise. Some insurers provide packages for specialty vacations, such as skiing or backpacking. More dangerous activities may be excluded from basic policies.

And keep in mind that in the aftermath of the terrorist attacks of

September 11, 2001, a number of airlines, cruise lines, and tour operators are no longer covered by insurers. *The bottom line:* Always, always check the fine print before you sign on; more and more policies have built-in exclusions and restrictions that may leave you out in the cold if something does go awry.

For information, contact one of the following popular insurers:

- **Access America** (② 866/807-3982; www.accessamerica.com)
- **Travel Guard International** (② 800/826-4919; www.travelguard.com)
- **Travel Insured International** (② 800/243-3174; www.travelinsured.com)
- **Travelex Insurance Services** (② 888/457-4602; www.travelexinsurance.com)

TRIP-CANCELLATION INSURANCE (TCI)

There are three major types of trip-cancellation insurance—one, in the event that you pre-pay a cruise or tour that gets canceled, and you can't get your money back; a second, when you or someone in your family gets sick or dies, and you can't travel (but beware that you may not be covered for a pre-existing condition); and a third, when bad weather makes travel impossible. Some insurers provide coverage for events such as jury duty; natural disasters close to home, such as floods or fire; even the loss of a job. A few have added provisions for cancellations due to terrorist activities. Always check the fine print before signing on, and don't buy trip-cancellation insurance from the tour operator that may be responsible for the cancellation; buy it only from a reputable travel insurance agency. Don't overbuy. You won't be reimbursed for more than the cost of your trip.

MEDICAL INSURANCE

Most health insurance policies cover you if you get sick away from home—but check, particularly if you're insured by an HMO. With the exception of certain HMOs and Medicare/Medicaid, your medical insurance should cover medical treatment—even hospital care—overseas. However, most out-of-country hospitals make you pay your bills upfront, and send you a refund after you've returned home and filed the necessary paperwork. Members of **Blue Cross/Blue Shield** can now use their cards at select hospitals in most major cities worldwide (② **800/810-BLUE** or www.bluecares.com for a list of hospitals).

Some credit cards (American Express and certain gold and platinum Visas and MasterCards, for example) offer automatic flight insurance against death or dismemberment in case of an airplane crash if you charged the cost of your ticket.

If you require additional insurance, try one of the following companies:

- **MEDEX International,** 9515 Dereco Rd., Timonium, MD 21093-5375 (② **888/MEDEX-00** or 410/453-6300; fax 410/453-6301; www.medexassist.com).
- **Travel Assistance International** (② **800/821-2828;** www.travelassistance.com), 9200 Keystone Crossing, Suite 300, Indianapolis, IN 46240 (for general information on services, call the company's Worldwide Assistance Services, Inc., at ② **800/777-8710**).

The cost of travel medical insurance varies widely. Check your existing policies before you buy additional coverage. Also, check to see if your medical insurance covers you for emergency medical evacuation: If you have to buy a one-way same-day ticket home and forfeit your nonrefundable round-trip ticket, you may be out big bucks.

7 Specialized Travel Resources

FOR TRAVELERS WITH DISABILITIES

Argentina is not a very accessible destination for travelers with disabilities. Four- and five-star hotels in Buenos Aires often have a few rooms designed for travelers with disabilities—check with the hotel in advance. But once you get out of the city, services dry up pretty quickly.

Fortunately, there are several organizations in the United States that can help.

AGENCIES/OPERATORS

- **Flying Wheels Travel** (© 507/451-5005; www.flyingwheels travel.com) offers escorted tours and cruises that emphasize sports and private tours in minivans with lifts.
- **Access Adventures** (© 716/889-9096), an agency based in Rochester, New York, offers customized itineraries for a variety of travelers with disabilities.
- **Accessible Journeys** (© 800/TINGLES or 610/521-0339; www.disabilitytravel.com) caters specifically to slow walkers and wheelchair travelers and their families and friends.

ORGANIZATIONS

- **The Moss Rehab Hospital** (© 215/456-9603; www.moss resourcenet.org) provides friendly, helpful phone assistance through its **Travel Information Service.**
- **The Society for Accessible Travel and Hospitality** (© 212/447-7284; fax 212/725-8253; www.sath.org) offers a wealth of travel resources for all types of disabilities and informed recommendations on destinations, access guides, travel agents, tour operators, vehicle rentals, and companion services. Annual membership costs $45 for adults, $30 for seniors and students.
- **The American Foundation for the Blind** (© 800/232-5463; www.afb.org) provides information on traveling with Seeing Eye dogs.

PUBLICATIONS

- **Mobility International USA** (© 541/343-1284; www.miusa. org) publishes *A World of Options,* a 658-page book of resources, covering everything from biking trips to scuba outfitters, and a biannual newsletter, *Over the Rainbow.* Annual membership is $35.
- **Twin Peaks Press** (© 360/694-2462) publishes travel-related books for travelers with special needs.
- *Open World for Disability and Mature Travel* magazine, published by the Society for Accessible Travel and Hospitality (see above), is full of good resources and information. A year's subscription is $13 ($21 outside the U.S.).

FOR SENIORS

Argentines treat seniors with great respect, making travel for them easy. Discounts are usually available; ask when booking a hotel room or before ordering a meal in a restaurant. **Aerolíneas Argentinas** (© 800/333-0276 in the U.S.; www.aerolineas. com.ar) offers a 10% discount on fares to Buenos Aires from Miami and New York for passengers 62 and older; companion fares are also discounted. Both **American** (© 800/433-7300; www.americanair.com) and **United** (© 800/241-6522; www.united.com) also offer discounted senior fares.

Members of **AARP** (formerly known as the American Association of Retired Persons), 601 E St. NW, Washington, DC 20049 (© 800/424-3410 or 202/434-2277; www. aarp.org), get discounts on hotels, airfares, and car rentals. AARP offers members a wide range of benefits, including *AARP: The Magazine* and a monthly newsletter. Anyone over 50 can join.

The Alliance for Retired Americans, 8403 Colesville Rd., Suite 1200, Silver Spring, MD 20910 (© **301/ 578-8422;** www.retiredamericans. org), offers a newsletter six times a year and discounts on hotel and auto rentals; annual dues are $13 per person or couple. *Note:* Members of the former National Council of Senior Citizens receive automatic membership in the Alliance.

AGENCIES/OPERATORS

- **Grand Circle Travel** (© **800/ 221-2610** or 617/350-7500; fax 617/346-6700; www.gct.com) offers package deals for the 50-plus market, mostly of the tour-bus variety, with free trips thrown in for those who organize groups of 10 or more.
- **Elderhostel** (© **877/426-8056;** www.elderhostel.org) arranges study programs for those aged 55 and over (and a spouse or companion of any age) in the United States and in more than 80 countries around the world. Most courses last 5 to 7 days in the U.S. (2–4 weeks abroad), and many include airfare, accommodations in university dormitories or modest inns, meals, and tuition.
- **Interhostel** (© **800/733-9753;** www.learn.unh.edu/interhostel), organized by the University of New Hampshire, also offers educational travel for seniors. On these escorted tours, the days are packed with seminars, lectures, and field trips, with sightseeing led by academic experts. **Interhostel** takes travelers 50 and over (with companions over 40), and offers 1- and 2-week trips, mostly international.

PUBLICATIONS

- *The Book of Deals* is a collection of more than 1,000 senior discounts on airlines, lodging, tours, and attractions around the country; it's available for $9.90 by calling © **800/460-6676.**
- *101 Tips for the Mature Traveler* is available from Grand Circle Travel (see above).
- *The 50+ Traveler's Guidebook* (St. Martin's Press).
- *Unbelievably Good Deals and Great Adventures That You Absolutely Can't Get Unless You're Over 50* (Contemporary Publishing Co.).

FOR GAY & LESBIAN TRAVELERS

Argentina remains a very traditional, Catholic society, and is fairly closed minded about homosexuality. Buenos Aires is more liberal than the rest of the country; in particular, the Rosario neighborhood is gay- and lesbian-friendly.

The International Gay & Lesbian Travel Association (IGLTA) (© **800/ 448-8550** or 954/776-2626; fax 954/ 776-3303; www.iglta.org) links travelers up with gay-friendly hoteliers, tour operators, and airline and cruise-line representatives. It offers monthly newsletters, marketing mailings, and a membership directory that's updated once a year. Membership is $200 yearly, plus a $100 administration fee for new members.

AGENCIES/OPERATORS

- **Above and Beyond Tours** (© **800/397-2681;** www.above beyondtours.com) offers gay and lesbian tours worldwide and is the exclusive gay and lesbian tour operator for United Airlines.
- **Now, Voyager** (© **800/255- 6951;** www.nowvoyager.com) is a San Francisco–based gay-owned and -operated travel service.

- Olivia Cruises & Resorts (© 800/631-6277 or 510/655-0364; http://oliviatravel.com) charters entire resorts and ships for exclusive lesbian vacations all over the world.

PUBLICATIONS

- *Out and About* (© 800/929-2268 or 415/644-8044; www.out andabout.com) offers guidebooks and a newsletter 10 times a year packed with solid information on the global gay and lesbian scene.
- *Spartacus International Gay Guide* and *Odysseus* are good, annual English-language guidebooks focused on gay men, with some information for lesbians. You can get them from most gay and lesbian bookstores, or order them from **Giovanni's Room** bookstore, 1145 Pine St., Philadelphia, PA 19107 (© **215/ 923-2960;** www.giovannisroom. com).
- *Gay Travel A to Z: The World of Gay & Lesbian Travel Options at Your Fingertips,* by Marianne Ferrari (Ferrari Publications; Box 35575, Phoenix, AZ 85069) is a very good gay and lesbian guidebook series.

FOR WOMEN TRAVELERS

Female beauty is idealized in Argentina, and women seem constantly on display—both for each other and for Argentine men. Any looks and calls you might get are more likely to be flirtatious than harassing in nature. If you seek to avoid unwanted attention, don't dress skimpily (as many Porteñas do) or flash jewelry. Women should not walk alone at night.

FOR STUDENTS

Student discounts are very common in Argentina, but usually only if one has appropriate ID. **STA Travel** (© **800/781-4040** in the U.S., 020/ 7361-6144 in the U.K., or 1300/360-960 in Australia; www.statravel.com) specializes in affordable airfares, bus and rail passes, accommodations, insurance, tours, and packages for students and young travelers, and issue the **International Student Identity Card (ISIC).** This is the most widely recognized proof that you really are a student. As well as getting you discounts on a huge range of travel, tours, and attractions, it comes with a 24-hour emergency help line and a global voice/fax/e-mail messaging system with discounted international telephone calls. Available to any full-time student over 12, it costs $22.

8 Getting There

BY PLANE

Argentina's main international airport is **Ezeiza Ministro Pistarini (EZE)** (© **11/4480-9538**), located 42km (26 miles) outside Buenos Aires. You will be assessed a departure tax of approximately $24 upon leaving the country. For flights from Buenos Aires to Montevideo (in Uruguay), the departure tax is $5. Passengers in transit and children under 2 are exempt from this tax. However, visitors are advised to verify the departure tax with their airline or travel agent, as the exact amount changes frequently.

I have listed below the major airlines that fly into Argentina from North America, Europe, and Australia. They include Argentina's national airline, **Aerolíneas Argentinas** (© **800/333-0276** in the U.S., 0810/222-86527 in Buenos Aires, or 1800/22-22-15 in Australia; www. aerolineas.com.ar); **American Airlines** (© **800/433-7300** in the U.S., or 11/4318-1111 in Buenos Aires; www.americanair.com); **United Airlines** (© **800/241-6522** in the U.S., or 0810/777-8648 in Buenos Aires;

www.ual.com); **Air Canada** (© **888/ 247-2262** in Canada, or 11-4327-3640 in Buenos Aires; www.aircanada. ca); **British Airways** (© **0845/773-3377** in the U.K., or 11/4320-6600 in Buenos Aires); and **Iberia** (© **0845/ 601-2854** in the U.K., or 11/4131-1000 in Buenos Aires).

FLYING FOR LESS: TIPS FOR GETTING THE BEST AIRFARE

Passengers within the same airplane cabin are rarely paying the same fare for their seats. Passengers who can book their ticket long in advance, who don't mind staying over Saturday night, or who are willing to travel on a Tuesday, Wednesday, or Thursday after 7pm usually pay a fraction of the full fare. Here are a few easy ways to save.

1. Check your newspaper for advertised discounts or call the airlines directly and ask if any **promotional rates** or **special fares** are available. You'll almost never see a sale during peak travel times (Dec–Feb). If your schedule is flexible, ask if you can secure a cheaper fare by staying an extra day or by flying midweek. (Many airlines won't volunteer this information.) If you already hold a ticket when a sale breaks, it might even pay to exchange your ticket, which usually incurs a $50 to $75 charge.

   Note, however, that the lowest-priced fares are often nonrefundable, require advance purchase of 1 to 3 weeks and a certain length of stay, and carry penalties for changing dates of travel.

2. **Consolidators,** also known as bucket shops, are a good place to find low fares. Consolidators buy seats in bulk from the airlines, then sell them back to the public at prices below even the airlines' discounted rates. Their small,

boxed ads usually run in the Sunday travel section at the bottom of the page. Before you pay, however, ask for a confirmation number from the consolidator, then call the airline itself to confirm your seat. Be prepared to book your ticket with a different consolidator; there are many to choose from if the airline can't confirm your reservation. Also be aware that bucket shop tickets are usually nonrefundable or rigged with stiff cancellation penalties, often as high as 50% to 75% of the ticket price. (In addition, many airlines won't grant frequent-flier miles on consolidator tickets.)

   STA Travel (© 800/781-4040; www.statravel.com) caters especially to young travelers, but its bargain-basement prices are available to people of all ages. **Travel Bargains** (© 800/AIR-FARE; www.1800airfare.com) was formerly owned by TWA but now offers the deepest discounts on many other airlines, with a 4-day advance purchase. Other reliable consolidators include **Fly-Cheap.com** (www.1800flycheap. com); **TFI Tours International** (© 800/745-8000 or 212/736-1140), which serves as a clearinghouse for unused seats; or "rebators" such as **Travel Avenue** (© 800/333-3335 or 312/876-1116) and the **Smart Traveller** (© 800/448-3338 in the U.S., or 305/448-3338), which rebate part of their commissions to you.

3. **Look into courier flights.** Companies that hire couriers use your luggage allowance for their business baggage; in return, you get a deeply discounted ticket. Flights are often offered at the last minute, and you might have to arrange a pretrip interview to make sure you're right for the job.

Now Voyager, open Monday through Friday from 10am to 5:30pm and Saturday from noon to 4:30pm (✆ 212/431-1616), flies from New York. Now Voyager also offers non-courier discounted fares, so call the company even if you don't want to fly as a courier.

4. **Surf the Net and save.** It's possible to get some great deals on airfare, hotels, and car rentals via the Internet. Grab your mouse and surf before you take off; you could save a bundle on your trip. Always check the lowest published fare, however, before you shop for flights online.

Of course, we're a little biased, but we think **Frommers.com** is an excellent travel-planning resource. You'll find indispensable travel tips, reviews, destination information, monthly vacation giveaways, and online booking. Full-service sites like **Travelocity** (www.travelocity.com) and **Microsoft Expedia** (www.expedia.com) offer domestic and international flight booking; hotel and car-rental reservations; late-breaking travel news; and personalized "fare watcher" e-mails that keep you posted on special deals for preselected routes.

5. **You've got mail.** Most major airlines offer a free e-mail service known as **E-Savers,** via which they'll send you their best bargain airfares on a regular basis. Once a week (usually Wed) or whenever a sale fare comes up, subscribers receive a list of discounted flights to and from various destinations, both international and domestic. *Here's the catch:* These fares are usually available only if you leave the very next Saturday (or sometimes Fri night) and return on the following Monday or Tuesday. It's really a service for the spontaneously inclined and travelers looking for a quick getaway. For instance, American often has good last-minute deals on flights from the United States to Buenos Aires. *One caveat:* You'll get frequent-flier miles if you purchase one of these E-saver fares, but you can't use miles to buy the ticket.

If the thought of all that surfing and comparison shopping gives you a headache, try **Smarter Living** (www.smarterliving.com). Sign up for its newsletter service, and every week you'll get a customized e-mail summarizing the discount fares available from your departure city. Smarter Living tracks more than 15 different airlines, so it's a worthwhile time-saver. Another excellent way to take advantage of several Internet travel-booking services at once is to use **Qixo** (www.qixo.com). Qixo is a search engine that offers real-time airfare price comparisons for some 20 online booking sites (such as Travelocity) at once.

9 Getting Around

BY PLANE

The easiest way to travel Argentina's vast distances is by air. **Aerolíneas Argentinas** (see above) connects most cities and tourist destinations in Argentina, including Córdoba, Jujuy, Iguazú, and Salta. Its competitors, **LAPA** (✆ 0810/777-5272 in Buenos Aires; www.lapa.com.ar) and **Southern Winds** (✆ 0810/777-7979), serve roughly the same routes. Please note that, at press time, LAPA was going through bankruptcy and its future was uncertain. By American standards, domestic flights within Argentina are expensive. In Buenos Aires, domestic flights and flights to Uruguay (see chapter 9) travel out of **Jorge Newbery Airport** (℃ **11/4514-1515**), 15 minutes from downtown.

If you plan to travel extensively in Argentina, consider buying the **Airpass Visit Argentina,** issued by Aerolíneas Argentinas. You must purchase the pass in your home country; it cannot be purchased once you are in Argentina. This pass offers discounts for domestic travel in conjunction with your international Aerolíneas Argentinas ticket. Purchase between one and three flight coupons (1 coupon for each flight) for $300. Up to five additional coupons can be purchased for $125 each. If you arrive in Argentina on an eligible airline other than Aerolíneas Argentinas, the price for the first three coupons is $400, with each additional coupon costing $165. For more information, contact the Aerolíneas office in your home country or try **www.aerolineas.com.ar**.

BY BUS

Argentine buses are comfortable, safe, and efficient. They connect nearly every part of Argentina, as well as bordering countries. In cases where two classes of bus service are offered (*común* and *diferencial*), the latter is more luxurious. Most long distance buses offer toilets, air-conditioning, and snack/bar service. Bus travel is usually considerably cheaper than air travel for similar routes. In almost every instance, I believe travelers would prefer a more expensive 2-hour flight to a 20-plus-hour bus ride (see chart below). But taking a long-distance bus in South America is a singular cultural experience, so you might find it time well spent.

Among the major bus companies that operate out of Buenos Aires are **La Veloz del Norte** (℃ **11/4315-2482**), serving destinations in the Northwest, including Salta and Jujuy; **Singer** (℃ **11/4315-2653**), serving Puerto Iguazú as well as Brazilian destinations; and **T.A. Chevallier** (℃ **11/4313-3297**), serving Bariloche.

Sample Times & Fares for Travel in Argentina from Buenos Aires

From Buenos Aires to	Length of bus trip	Cost of a one-way bus ticket	Length of plane trip	Cost of a one-way plane ticket
Bariloche	23 hr.	$76	2¼ hr.	$100–$220
Puerto Iguazú	21 hr.	$50	2 hr.	$90–$220
Salta	22 hr.	$80	2 hr.	$110–$220

BY CAR

Argentine roads and highways are generally in good condition, with the exception of some rural areas. Most highways have been privatized and charge nominal tolls. In Buenos Aires, drivers are aggressive and don't always obey traffic lanes or lights. Wear your seat belt, as required by Argentine law. U.S. driver's licenses are valid in greater Buenos Aires, but you need an Argentine or international license to drive in most other parts of the country. Fuel is expensive at about $1 per liter (or $4 per gal.). A car that uses gasoil (as the name implies, a hybrid fuel of gas and oil) is the cheaper option fuel-wise, about 15% cheaper than regular unleaded gasoline.

The **Automóvil Club Argentino (ACA),** Av. del Libertador 1850 (℃ **11/4802-6061**), has working arrangements with international automobile clubs. The ACA offers numerous services, including roadside assistance, road maps, hotel and

Finding an Address

In Argentina and Chile, as in many South American countries, not all addresses have street numbers. This is especially true in rural areas. You'll know there's no number if the address includes the abbreviation "s/n," which stands for *sin número* (without number).

camping information, and discounts for various tourist activities.

CAR RENTALS Many international car-rental companies operate in Argentina with offices at airports and in city centers. Here are the main offices in Buenos Aires for the following agencies: **Hertz,** Paraguay 1122 (② **800/654-3131** in the U.S., or 11/4816-8001 in Buenos Aires); **Avis,** Cerrito 1527 (② **800/230-4898** in the U.S., or 11/4300-8201 in Buenos Aires); **Dollar,** Marcelo T. de Alvear 523 (② **800/800-6000** in the U.S., or 11/4315-8800 in Buenos Aires); and **Thrifty,** Av. Leandro N. Alem 699 (② **800/847-4389** in the U.S., or 11/4315-0777 in Buenos Aires). Car rental is expensive in Argentina, with standard rates beginning at about $90 per day for a subcompact with unlimited mileage (ask for any special promotions, especially on weekly rates). Check to see if your existing automobile insurance policy (or a credit card) covers insurance for car rentals; otherwise, purchasing insurance should run you an extra $15 a day.

BY TRAIN

Argentina's railroad network is very limited. There are trains from Buenos Aires to Bariloche and to Mar del Plata, but they are neither as comfortable nor as convenient as buses. One train service stands out, however. The tourist train called *Tren a las Nubes* **(Train to the Clouds)** begins in Salta and cuts an unforgettable swath through the Andes in Argentina's Northwest. The trip lasts approximately 14 hours and costs $100 per person. For more information, call ② **387/431-4984** in Salta, or ② 11/4311-8871 in Buenos Aires, consult www.trenubes.com.ar (a Spanish-language site), or see chapter 5 for more information.

10 The Active Vacation Planner

Argentina encompasses so many climate zones, with such a wide variety of terrain, that it is a haven for outdoor activities of all kinds. There are numerous hiking and climbing opportunities in the Northwest. Activities around Iguazú Falls range from easy hiking along the waterfall circuits and on San Martín Island to speed rafting along the river and trekking into the jungle. And of course, Argentine Patagonia is home to more kayaking, climbing, and trekking than you could possibly fit in one lifetime. Below, I have listed some recommended tour operators specializing in outdoor-themed vacations in Argentina.

ORGANIZED ADVENTURE TRIPS The advantages of traveling with an organized group are plentiful, especially for travelers who have limited time and resources. Tour operators take the headache out of planning a trip, and they iron out the wrinkles that invariably pop up along the way. Many tours are organized to include guides, transportation, accommodations, meals, and gear (some outfits will even carry gear for you, for example, on trekking adventures). Independent travelers tend to view organized tours as antithetical to the joy of discovery, but leaving the details to someone else does free up substantial time to concentrate on something else. Besides, your traveling companions are likely to be kindred souls interested in similar things.

Remember to be aware of what you're getting yourself into. A 5-day trek in the remote Patagonian wilderness may look great on paper, but are you physically up to it? Tour operators are responsible for their clients' well-being and safety, but that doesn't let you off the hook in terms of personal responsibility. Inquire about your guide's experience, safety record, and insurance policy. Remember, no adventure trip is 100% risk free.

RECOMMENDED OPERATORS

The following U.S.-based adventure operators offer solid, well-organized tours, and they are backed by years of experience. Most of these operators are expensive, a few are exorbitant (remember that prices do not include airfare), but that usually is because they include luxury accommodations and gourmet dining. Most offer trips to hot spots like Patagonia, and operators with trips to that region are listed here for both Argentina and Chile.

- **Abercrombie & Kent,** 1520 Kensington Rd., Oak Brook, IL 60521 (℗ **800/323-7308;** www. abercrombiekent.com), is a luxury tour operator that offers a "Patagonia: A Natural Playground" trip that heads from Buenos Aires to Ushuaia for a 3-day cruise around Tierra del Fuego, followed by visits to Torres del Paine park, Puerto Varas, and Bariloche. Cost is $6,980 per person, double occupancy. This trip also features a 4-day extension to Iguazú Falls.
- **Butterfield and Robinson,** 70 Bond St., Toronto, Canada M5B 1X3 (℗ **800/678-1147;** www. butterfieldandrobinson.com), is another gourmet tour operator, with a walking-oriented, 10-day trip to Patagonia starting in El Calafate, Argentina, and finishing in Punta Arenas, Chile. In between, travelers visit national parks Los Glaciares and Torres del Paine, with visits to the Perito Moreno glacier and lodging in fine lodges and ranches. Cost is $5,975 per person, double occupancy.
- **Mountain-Travel Sobek,** 6420 Fairmount Ave., El Cerrito, CA 94530 (℗ **888/MTSOBEK** or 510/527-8100; fax 510/525-7718; www.mtsobek.com), are the pioneers of organized adventure travel, and they offer trips that involve a lot of physical activity. One of their more gung-ho journeys traverses part of the Patagonian Ice Cap in Fitzroy National Park for 21 days; a more moderate "Patagonia Explorer" mixes hiking with cruising. Prices run from $1,500 to $3,000 and more. Sobek always comes recommended for their excellent guides.
- **Backroads Active Vacations,** 801 Cedar St., Berkeley, CA 94710-1800 (℗ **800/GO-ACTIVE** or 510/527-1555; www.backroads. com), offers a biking tour through the lake districts of Chile and Argentina, with stops in Villa La Angostura and San Martín de los Andes; an afternoon of rafting is included. There's also a hiking trip through the same region, and a 9-day hiking trip in Patagonia that begins in El Calafate and travels between the two countries. Guests lodge in luxury hotels and inns. Costs run from $3,798 to $5,298.
- **Wilderness Travel,** 1102 Ninth St., Berkeley, CA 94710 (℗ **800/ 368-2794** or 510/558-2488; www.wildernesstravel.com), offers a more mellow sightseeing/day hiking tour around Patagonia, including Los Glaciares, Ushuaia, El Calafate, and Perito Moreno Glacier. The trip costs $4,495 to $5,095, depending on the number of guests (maximum 15).

- **Wildland Adventures,** 3516 NE 155th St., Seattle, WA 98155 (② **800/345-4453** or 206/365-0686; www.wildland.com), offers a few adventure tours of Argentina. The "Salta Trek Through Silent Valleys" tour takes in Salta, Jujuy, and the Andean plain. Two Patagonia tours are offered: "Best of Patagonia," which concentrates on Argentine Patagonia (including Península Valdés, Río Galle-gos, Perito Moreno, and Ushuaia); and "Los Glaciares Adventure," which visits El Calafate, Fitzroy National Park, and Perito Moreno Glacier, among others. Accommodation ranges from hotels to camping to rustic park lodges. Ecotourism is an integral part of Wildland tours. Prices start at $1,380 for the 8-day Salta tour and continue upwards of $3,000 for the 2-week Patagonia trip.

 FAST FACTS: Argentina

American Express Offices are located in Buenos Aires, Bariloche, Salta, San Martín, and Ushuaia. In Buenos Aires, the Amex office is at Arenales 707 (② **11/4130-3135**).

Business Hours Banks are open weekdays from 10am to 3pm. Shopping hours are weekdays from 9am to 8pm and Saturday from 9am to 1pm. Shopping centers are open daily from 10am to 8pm. Some stores close for lunch.

Climate See "When to Go," earlier in this chapter.

Currency See "Money," earlier in this chapter.

Documents See "Entry Requirements & Customs," earlier in this chapter.

Driving Rules In cities, Argentines drive exceedingly fast and do not always obey traffic lights or lanes. Seat belts are mandatory, although few Argentines actually wear them. When driving outside the city, remember that *autopista* means motorway or highway, and *paso* means mountain pass. Don't drive in rural areas at night, as cattle sometimes overtake the road to keep warm and are nearly impossible to see.

Drugstores Ask your hotel where the nearest pharmacy *(farmacia)* is; they are generally ubiquitous in city centers, and there is always at least one open 24 hours. In Buenos Aires, the chain Farmacity is open 24 hours, with locations at Lavalle 919 (② **11/4821-3000**) and Av. Santa Fe 2830 (② **11/4821-0235**). Farmacity will also deliver to your hotel.

Electricity If you plan to bring a hair dryer, radio, travel iron, or any other small appliance, pack a transformer and a European-style adapter because electricity in Argentina runs on 220 volts. Note that most laptops operate on both 110 and 220 volts. Luxury hotels usually have transformers and adapters available.

Embassies These are all in Buenos Aires: **U.S. Embassy,** Av. Colombia 4300 (② 11/4774-5333); **Australian Embassy,** Villanueva 1400 (② 11/4777-6580); **Canadian Embassy,** Tagle 2828 (② 11/4805-3032); **New Zealand Embassy,** Carlos Pellegrini 1427, 5th Floor (② 11/4328-0747); **United Kingdom Embassy,** Luis Agote 2412 (② 11/4803-6021).

Emergencies The following emergency numbers are valid throughout Argentina. For an **ambulance,** call ℂ **107;** in case of **fire,** call ℂ **1100;** for **police** assistance, call ℂ **101.**

Information See "Visitor Information," earlier in this chapter.

Internet Access Cybercafes have begun to pop up on seemingly every corner in Buenos Aires and are found in other cities as well, so it won't be hard to stay connected while in Argentina. Access is reasonably priced (usually averaging $1–$2 per hr.) and connections are reliably good.

Mail Airmail postage for a letter 7 ounces or less from Argentina to North America and Europe is $1. Mail takes on average between 10 and 14 days to get to the U.S. and Europe.

Maps Reliable maps can be purchased at the offices of the **Automóvil Club Argentino,** Av. del Libertador 1850, in Buenos Aires (ℂ **11/4802-6061** or 11/4802-7071).

Safety Petty crime has increased significantly in Buenos Aires as a result of Argentina's economic crisis. Travelers should be especially alert to pickpockets and purse snatchers on the streets and on buses and trains. Violent crime has increased in the suburbs of the capital and in Buenos Aires Province. Tourists should take care not to be overly conspicuous, walking in pairs or groups when possible. Avoid demonstrations, strikes, and other political gatherings. In Buenos Aires, do not take taxis off the street. You should call for a radio-taxi instead. Take similar precautions when traveling in Argentina's other big cities.

Smoking Smoking is a pervasive aspect of Argentine society, and you will find that most everyone lights up in restaurants and clubs. Most restaurants do, however, provide no-smoking sections.

Taxes Argentina's value added tax (VAT) is 21%. You can recover this 21% at the airport if you have purchased local products totaling more than 70 pesos (per invoice) from stores participating in tax-free shopping. Forms are available at the airport.

Telephone The country code for Argentina is **54.** When making domestic long-distance calls in Argentina, place a 0 before the area code. For international calls, add 00 before the country code. Direct dialing to North America and Europe is available from most phones. International, as well as domestic, calls are expensive in Argentina, especially from hotels (rates fall 10pm–8am). Holders of AT&T credit cards can reach the money-saving **USA Direct** from Argentina by calling toll-free ℂ **0800/555-4288** from the north of Argentina or 0800/222-1288 from the south. Similar services are offered by **MCI** (ℂ **0800/555-1002**) and **Sprint** (ℂ **0800/555-1003** from the north of Argentina, or 0800/222-1003 from the south).

Public phones take either phone cards (sold at kiosks on the street) or coins (less common). Local calls cost 20 centavos to start and charge more the longer you talk. Telecentro offices—found everywhere in city centers—offer private phone booths where calls are paid when completed. Most hotels offer fax services, as do all telecentro offices. Dial **110** for directory assistance (most operators speak English) and **000** to reach an international operator.

Time Argentina does not adopt daylight saving time, so the country is 1 hour ahead of Eastern Standard Time in the United States in summer and 2 hours ahead in winter.

Tipping A 10% tip is expected at cafes and restaurants. Give at least $1 to bellboys and porters, 5% to hairdressers, and leftover change to taxi drivers.

Water In Buenos Aires, the water is perfectly safe to drink. But if you are traveling to more remote regions of Argentina, it's best to stick with bottled water for drinking.

Buenos Aires

The elegance of Europe and the spirit of South America live side by side in Buenos Aires. Founded by immigrants along the shores of the Rio de la Plata, Buenos Aires built its identity on Spanish, Italian, and French influences. Take a walk through neighborhoods like Recoleta and Belgrano, for example, and you'll be convinced you're still in the Old World. Even Porteños, as residents of Buenos Aires are called, characterize themselves as more European than South American.

If Buenos Aires has a European face, its soul is intensely Latin. This is a city where the sun shines brightly, where people speak passionately, where family and friendship still come first. It is a city where locals go outside to interact, lining the streets, packing cafe terraces, and strolling in parks and plazas.

While exploring Buenos Aires, you will find a city of contradictions. Great wealth exists alongside considerable poverty. The economy has continued to falter, but hotels and restaurants remain inexplicably busy. Porteños seem self-assured, although the population is intensely image-conscious and uncertain about the future. And although Buenos Aires defines Argentina, it has little to do with the rest of the country. All these elements demonstrate the complexity of a city searching for identity among its South American and European influences.

This search has become more prominent as ordinary Argentines reel from the country's economic meltdown of late 2001. Middle class citizens watched their savings disappear in the wake of sharp currency devaluations, ending the peso's decade-long parity with the dollar and with it the illusion that Argentina was a rich nation. Weekend shopping, eating out, clubbing, and traveling to other countries—routine for many Porteños in the 1990s—ceased to be possible for everyone but the very rich. Homelessness, malnutrition, and street crime rose as a result of ongoing economic troubles, and foreign travelers must exercise greater caution than they did in the past. But one of the few up-sides of the country's financial woes, besides the fact that Argentina is a much, much cheaper country to visit now, is an increased recognition among Argentines that tourists provide oxygen for the economy. Do not let Argentina's economic situation keep you away: Buenos Aires remains a fascinating and welcoming city to visit.

1 Essentials

GETTING THERE

BY PLANE International flights arrive at **Ezeiza International Airport** (© **11/4480-0224**), located 34km (21 miles) west of downtown Buenos Aires. You can reach the city by shuttle or *remise* (private, unmetered taxi); you will see official stands with set fares in the airport once you clear Customs. Taxis from the airport to the center of town cost about $11 to $15.

> **Tips** **A Great Travel Agency**
>
> **Rotamund** is by far the most professional company we found in Buenos Aires, offering personalized, efficient service, including airline bookings, hotel/car/vacation package reservations, travel insurance, English-speaking guides, and more for travel throughout Argentina. They're located at Av. Roque Sáenz Peña 846, Piso 2 and 3 (Floors 2 and 3), 1035 Buenos Aires (© **11/1321-5100;** www.rotamund.com).

Domestic airlines and flights to Uruguay use **Jorge Newbery Airport** (© **11/ 4514-1515**), located only 15 minutes from downtown. Taxis and *remises* cost $5 to $10 to the city center. At both airports, only take officially sanctioned transportation and do not accept transportation services from any private individuals. **Manuel Tienda León** (© **11/4314-3636**) is the most reliable transportation company, offering buses and *remises* to and from the airports.

BY BUS   The **Estación Terminal de Omnibus,** Av. Ramos Mejía 1680 (© **11/ 4310-0700**), located near Retiro Station, serves all long-distance buses.

BY CAR   In Buenos Aires, travel by *subte* (subway), *remise,* or radio-taxi (radio-dispatched taxis, as opposed to street taxis) is easier and safer than driving yourself. Rush-hour traffic is chaotic, and parking is difficult. If you do rent a car, park it at your hotel and leave it there.

CITY LAYOUT

Although Buenos Aires is a huge city, the main tourist neighborhoods are concentrated in a small, comparatively wealthy section near the Río de la Plata. The "microcenter" of the city extends from Plaza de Mayo to the south and Plaza San Martín to the north, and from Plaza del Congreso to the west and Puerto Madero to the east. The neighborhoods of San Telmo, La Boca, Puerto Madero, Recoleta, and Palermo surround the microcenter. The city layout is fairly straightforward; *avenidas* signify two-way avenues, *calles* are one-way streets, and *diagonales* cut streets and avenues at 45-degree angles. Each city block extends 100m (328 ft.), and building addresses indicate the distance on that street.

The **microcenter** includes Plaza de Mayo (the political and historic center of Buenos Aires), Plaza San Martín, and Avenida 9 de Julio (the widest street in the world). Most commercial activity is focused here, as are the majority of hotels and restaurants. Next to the microcenter, the riverfront area called **Puerto Madero** boasts excellent restaurants and nightlife as well as new commercial areas. Farther south, **La Boca, Monserrat,** and **San Telmo** are the historic neighborhoods where the first immigrants arrived and *milonga* and tango originated.

The city's most strikingly European neighborhood, **Recoleta,** offers fashionable restaurants, cafes, and evening entertainment amid rich French architecture. It's home to the city's cultural center as well as the Recoleta Cemetery, where key personalities such as Evita are buried. To the northwest, **Palermo** is a neighborhood of parks, mansions, and gardens—perfect for a weekend picnic. Another similarly wealthy neighborhood, **Belgrano,** lies farther west.

STREET MAPS   Ask the front desk of your hotel for a copy of "The Golden Map" and "QuickGuide Buenos Aires" to help you navigate the city.

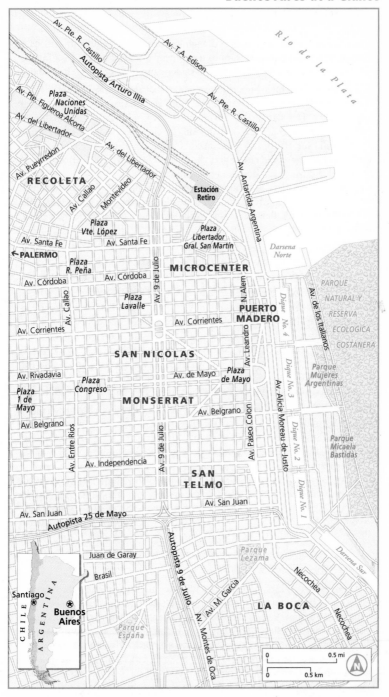

GETTING AROUND

The Buenos Aires metro—called the *subte*—is the fastest, cheapest way to get around. Buses are also convenient, though less commonly used by tourists. Get maps of metro and bus lines from tourist offices and most hotels. (Ask for the "QuickGuide Buenos Aires.") All metro stations and most bus stops have maps.

BY METRO   Five *subte* lines connect commercial and tourist areas in the city Monday through Saturday from 7am to 8pm and Sunday and holidays from 8am to 8pm. The flat fare is 70 *centavos* (25¢), with tickets purchased at machines or windows at every station. You can also buy a *subte pass* for 7 pesos ($2.30), valid for 10 trips. See the inside back cover of this guide for a map. Although the *subte* is the fastest and cheapest way to travel in Buenos Aires, it gets crowded during rush hour and hot in summer.

Neither the Recoleta nor Puerto Madero neighborhoods have *subte* access. Most of Puerto Madero, however, can be reached via the L.N. Alem *subte*. (It's a 5- to 20-min. walk, depending on which dock you're going to.)

BY BUS   There are 140 bus lines operating in Buenos Aires 24 hours a day. The minimum fare is 75 *centavos* and goes up depending on distance traveled. Pay your fare inside the bus at an electronic ticket machine, which accepts coins only. Many bus drivers, provided you can communicate with them, will tell you the fare for your destination and help you with where to get off.

BY TAXI   Like busy bees, thousands of black-and-yellow cabs crowd the streets of Buenos Aires. Fares are relatively inexpensive, with an initial meter reading of 1.22 pesos increasing 15 centavos every 200m (218 yd.) or each minute. *Remises* and radio-taxis are much safer than street taxis and only a bit more expensive (see the "Traveling by Taxi" box below). To request a taxi by phone, consider **Taxi Premium** (© 11/4374-6666), which is used by the Four Seasons Hotel, or **Radio Taxi Blue** (© 11/4777-8888) contracted by the Alvear Palace Hotel.

BY CAR   Driving in Buenos Aires is like warfare: Never mind the lane, disregard the light, and honk your way through traffic. It's far safer, and cheaper, to hire a *remise* or radio-taxi with the help of your hotel or travel agent. If you must drive, international car-rental companies rent vehicles at both airports.

CAR RENTALS   Rental cars are available from **Hertz** (© 800/654-3131 in the U.S.), Paraguay 1122 (© 11/4815-6789); **Avis** (© 800/230-4898 in the U.S.), Cerrito 1527 (© 11/4326-5542); **Dollar** (© 800/800-6000 in the U.S.), Marcelo T. de Alvear 523 (© 11/4315-8800); and **Thrifty** (© 800/847-4389 in the U.S.), Av. Leandro N. Alem 699 (© 11/4315-0777).

✔ *Tips* Traveling by Taxi

At the risk of sounding repetitive, we strongly recommend that if you need a taxi, you only take a *remise* or radio-taxi that has been called in advance. Do not take taxis off the streets or contract with private individuals for transportation. There has been a sharp increase in the number of robberies by street taxi drivers since the economic crisis began. *Remises* are only marginally more expensive than taxis, but far safer. Most hotels have contracts with *remise* companies, and will be happy to call one for you. You should also call for a cab from restaurants, museums, and so on (see above for numbers).

ON FOOT   Buenos Aires is a walker's city. The microcenter is small enough to navigate by foot, and you can connect to adjacent neighborhoods by catching a taxi or using the *subte*. Plazas, parks, and pedestrian walkways are omnipresent in the city center.

VISITOR INFORMATION

Obtain tourist information for Argentina from the **Tourism Secretariat of the Nation,** Av. Santa Fe 883 (© **0800/555-0016,** or 11/4312-1132). It is open weekdays from 9am to 5pm, but the toll-free information line remains open daily from 8am to 8pm. There are branches at Ezeiza International Airport and Jorge Newbery Airport as well, open daily from 8am to 8pm.

The central office of the **City Tourism Secretariat,** responsible for all visitor information on Buenos Aires, is located at Av. Sarmiento 1551, on the fifth floor (© **11/4372-3612** or 11/4313-0187), and is open weekdays from 9am to 5pm. Additional city tourism branches, which have maps and hotel, restaurant, and attraction information, are found at J. M Ortiz and Quintana in Recoleta, Galerías Pacífico, Puerto Madero, the central bus terminal, and Caminito. Most are open Monday through Friday from 10am to 5pm. The center on Caminito in La Boca is open weekends only, usually Saturday and Sunday from 10am to 5pm.

 FAST FACTS: Buenos Aires

American Express The enormous American Express building is located next to Plaza San Martín, at Arenales 707 (© **11/4312-1661**). The travel agency is open Monday through Friday from 9am to 6pm; the bank is open Monday through Friday from 9am to 5pm. In addition to card-member services, the bank offers currency exchange (dollars only), money orders, check cashing, and refunds.

Area Code The area code for Buenos Aires is **11**. The country code for Argentina is **54**.

Business Hours Banks are generally open weekdays 10am to 3pm. Shopping hours are Monday through Friday from 9am to 8pm and Saturday from 10am to midnight. Shopping centers are open daily from 10am to 10pm. Some stores close for lunch.

Currency Exchange Changing money has become more difficult as a result of the economic crisis, with long queues in front of banks and exchange houses and occasional limits on the amount of money you can change or withdraw. Because the exchange rate now varies on a daily basis, it is best to withdraw smaller amounts at a time. Although American dollars are often accepted in major hotels and businesses, you will need Argentine pesos for ordinary transactions. Credit cards are widely used, although some businesses have suspended credit card services during periods of the economic crisis. It's easiest to change money at the airport, your hotel, or an independent exchange house rather than an Argentine bank. Traveler's checks can be difficult to cash: **American Express** (see above) offers the best rates on its traveler's checks and charges no commission. It offers currency exchange for dollars only. ATMs are plentiful in Buenos Aires, but you should only use those in secure, well-lit locations. You can withdraw pesos only, no dollars. You can have money wired to **Western Union,** Av. Córdoba 917 (✆ **0800/800-3030**).

Embassies/Consulates See "Fast Facts: Argentina" in chapter 2.

Emergencies For an **ambulance,** call ✆ **107;** in case of **fire,** call ✆ **100;** for **police** assistance, call ✆ **101;** for an English-speaking hospital, call **Clínica Suisso Argentino** (✆ **11/4304-1081**). The **tourist police** (✆ **11/4346-5770**) is located at Av. Corrientes 436.

Language Shops, hotels, and restaurants are usually staffed by at least one or two fluent English speakers, and many people speak at least a few words of English.

Post Office You never have to venture more than a few blocks to find a post office, open weekdays from 10am to 8pm and Saturday until 1pm. The main post office, or *Correo Central,* is at Av. Sarmiento 151 (✆ **11/ 4311-5040**).

Safety Crime in Buenos Aires—especially pickpocketing, robberies, and car thefts—has increased sharply in recent years as the economy has collapsed, although it's generally safe to walk around Recoleta, Palermo, and the microcenter both day and evening. Some tourist areas deemed safe by day, like San Telmo, La Boca, and Monserrat, should be avoided at night. Tourists should take care not to be overly conspicuous, walking in pairs or groups when possible. Do not flaunt expensive possessions, particularly jewelry. Avoid demonstrations, strikes, and other political gatherings. Most importantly, do not take taxis off the street. You should call for a radio-taxi or *remise* instead.

Taxes The 21% sales tax, or VAT, is already included in the sales price. Foreign tourists are entitled to a VAT tax return for purchases over 70 pesos, but you must request a refund check at the time of purchase from participating shops (the shop should display a "Global Refund" logo). Before departing the country, present these refund checks (invoices) to Customs, and then your credit card will be credited for the refund or you will be mailed a check.

Taxis See "Getting Around," earlier in this chapter.

Telephone Unless you are calling from your hotel (which will be expensive), the easiest way to place calls in Buenos Aires is by going to a branch of *telecentro,* the country's telecommunications company, found on nearly every city block. Private booths allow you to place as many calls as you like, after which you pay an attendant. A running meter gives you an idea what the call will cost. Most *telecentros* also have fax and Internet machines.

There are some coin-operated public phones in Buenos Aires, but most require a calling card, available at kiosks. Local calls, like all others, are charged by the minute. Dial ✆ **110** for information, ✆ **000** to reach an international operator. To dial another number in Argentina from Buenos Aires, dial the area code first, then the local number. *Note:* If you call someone's cellular phone in Argentina, the call is also charged to you, and can cost over $1 per minute.

Tipping A 10% tip is common at cafes and restaurants.

2 Where to Stay

Hotels in Buenos Aires often fill up in high season, so book ahead. The best hotels are found in Recoleta and the microcenter; the Hilton in Puerto Madero is close to the center. Recoleta is more scenic and not quite as noisy as the microcenter. Prices listed below are rack rates in high season; discounts are almost always available for weekends and low season, and may even be available in high season. Most hotels charge about $5 a night for valet parking. (Self-parking is not really an option; we definitely do *not* recommend trying to park on the street.)

Buenos Aires accommodations have improved in recent years, following a series of renovations among many of the city's government-rated four- and five-star hotels. All five and most four star hotels in Buenos Aires offer in-room safes, cable TV, direct dial phones with voice mail, and in-room modem access. Five star hotels also offer twice-daily maid service with nightly turndown. Most hotels in this chapter are designated four or five stars.

As a result of the currency devaluation, some hotels cost two to three times less than they did before December 2001. However, certain hotels are charging higher rates for foreigners than Argentines, and for overseas versus local bookings. Because of this volatility, we've quoted prices in dollars only. Contact the hotel beforehand and get a confirmed rate in writing.

PUERTO MADERO

There are no convenient metro stops to this neighborhood.

EXPENSIVE

Hilton Buenos Aires ★★   The Hilton opened in mid-2000 as the first major hotel and convention center in Puerto Madero. The Hilton lies within easy walking distance of some of the best restaurants in Buenos Aires, and is an excellent choice for steak and seafood gourmands. The strikingly contemporary hotel—a sleek silver block hoisted on stilts—features a seven-story atrium with more than 400 well-equipped guest rooms and an additional number of private residences. Spacious guest rooms offer multiple phone lines, walk-in closets, and bathrooms with separate showers and baths. Those staying on the executive floors receive complimentary breakfast and have access to a private concierge. Next to the lobby, El Faro restaurant serves California cuisine with a focus on seafood. The hotel has an impressive on-site pool and fitness center, and the staff can also arrange access to golf, tennis, and other recreational activities. Although the Hilton is not the city's most intimate hotel, it is one of the newest and best-regarded, with an excellent location in fashionable Puerto Madero.

Av. Macacha Güemes 351. ✆ 11/4891-0000. Fax 11/4891-0001. www.buenos.hilton.com. 418 units. From $150 double; from $300 suite. AE, DC, MC, V. **Amenities:** Restaurant; bar; modern gym facility with open-air pool deck and a service of light snacks and beverages; concierge; business center and secretarial services; room service; babysitting; dry cleaning; laundry service; executive floors; 2 ballrooms; exhibition center. *In room:* TV, dataport, minibar, hair dryer, safe.

RECOLETA

There are no convenient metro stops to this neighborhood.

VERY EXPENSIVE

Alvear Palace Hotel ★★★   Located in the center of the upscale Recoleta district, the Alvear Palace is the most exclusive hotel in Buenos Aires and one of

Buenos Aires Accommodations & Dining

DINING ◆

Broccolino **22**
Cabaña las Lilias **7**
Café Tortoni **6**
Café Victoria **39**
Catalinas **13**
Clark's **42**
Club Español **5**
De Olivias I Lustres **45**
El Mirasol **33**
Filo **17**
Galani **32**
Katrine **10**
La Biela **38**
La Bourgogne **37**
La Brigada **2**
La Casa de
   Esteban de Lucas **1**
La Chacra **24**
Las Nazarenas **19**
Le Sud **30**
Ligure **29**
Lola **41**
Massey **44**
Morizono **15**
Petit Paris Café **27**
Piegari **34**
Plaza Grill **18**
Primera Plana **35**
Restaurante y Bar
   Mediterraneo **4**
Sorrento del Puerto **9**

ACCOMMODATIONS ■

Alvear Palace **37**
Amerian Buenos Aires
   Park Hotel **12**
Aspen Towers **25**
Bell Air Hotel **31**
Best Western Embassy **23**
Caesar Park **36**
Claridge Hotel **11**
Etoile Hotel **40**
Four Seasons **32**
Hilton Buenos Aires **8**
Holiday Inn Express **14**
Hotel Crillon **28**
Hotel Nogaro **3**
Howard Johnson's **21**
InterContinental **4**
Loi Suites Esmeralda **26**
Loi Suites Recoleta **43**
Marriott Plaza Hotel **18**
Meliá Confort
   Buenos Aires **16**
Park Tower **20**
Sheraton **20**
Sofitel **30**

Padre Mujica

Estación
Retiro ⊠ Ⓒ

Av. del Libertador

Darsena
Norte

ⓘ Information
⊠ Post office
·····Ⓐ Subway

0   0.25 mi
0   0.25 km

PARQUE NATURAL
Y RESERVA ECOLÓGICA
COSTANERA

Av. Antártida Argentina

Av. Ramos Mejía

San Martín

Av. E. Madero

20

Florida

19

Plaza
Libertador
Gral.
San Martín
18 18

17   16

Av. Maipú

Ⓒ 27
ⓘ
M.T. de Alvear

26

21
⊠

25

Paraguay
Av.

Córdoba

15

14

13

12

MICROCENTER

23 22

Viamonte

11

San Martín

Lavalle

PUERTO
MADERO

Av. de los Italianos

24

Tucumán
Florida
Malpú

Esmeralda

Ⓒ

Av. Corrientes

Ⓑ

Sarmiento

25 de Mayo

Ⓑ

Av. Leandro N. Alem

Reconquista

Av. Rosales

9

Av. Macacha
Guemes

8

Parque
Mujeres
Argentinas

Suipacha

Tte. Gral. J.D. Perón

Av. de la Rabida

Av. Alicia Moreau

de Justo

Ⓑ
Ⓓ Ⓒ
⊠

Av. Pte. Roque Saenz Peña
(Diagonal Norte)

Plaza Ⓐ
de Mayo

ⓘ
Ⓓ

Balcarce

7

SAN NICOLAS

C. Pellegrini

Bartolome Mitre

Ⓐ
Ⓔ

Defensa

Av. Ing. Huergo

Libertad

Cerrito

Rivadavia

Ⓐ ⊠
Hipolito Yrigoyen

Bolivar

Moreno

Av. Paseo Colón

Azopardo

Rivadavia
Av. de Mayo

Ⓐ

6

Ⓒ

Alsina

Peru

Av. Belgrano

Santiago del Estero

Salta

Lima

5

4 4

MONSERRAT

Venezuela

Mexico

San José

Av. 9 de Julio

Bernardo de Irigoyen

Ⓒ

3

Ⓔ

Chacabuco

Piedras

Chile

Belgrano

Av.

Av. Independencia

⊠

Pte. Luis Saenz Peña

Tacuari

SAN
TELMO

2

1

Balcarce

Ⓒ

Estados Unidos

Plaza
Dorrego

Ⓔ

Carlos Calvo

Humberto Iº

Av. San Juan

Autopista 25 de Mayo

Av. Independencia

the top hotels in the world. European by design, the Alvear reflects the Belle Epoque era in which it was created, combining Empire- and Louis XV–style furniture with exquisite French decorative arts. The illustrious guest list has included names like Antonio Banderas, Donatella Versace, the Emperor of Japan, and Warren Christopher, to name a few. Recently renovated guest rooms combine luxurious comforts, such as chandeliers, Egyptian cotton linens, and silk drapes, with modern conveniences such as touch-screen telephones that control all in-room functions. All the individually decorated rooms come with personal butler service, cellphones, fresh flowers and fruit baskets, and daily newspaper delivery. Large marble bathrooms contain Hermès toiletries, and most have Jacuzzi baths. The formal hotel provides sharp, professional service, and the excellent concierge staff goes to great lengths to accommodate guest requests. The Alvear Palace is home to one of the best restaurants in South America (**La Bourgogne,** p. 57), and also offers an excellent, if expensive, Sunday brunch and afternoon tea in L'Orangerie.

Av. Alvear 1891, 1129 Buenos Aires. ⒸⒸ **11/4808-2100.** Fax 11/4804-0034. www.alvearpalace.com. 210 units, including 85 "palace" rooms and 125 suites. From $410 double; from $475 suite. Rates include luxurious buffet breakfast. AE, DC, MC, V. **Amenities:** 2 restaurants; bar; small health club; spa; concierge; elaborate business center; shopping arcade; room service; massage service; dry cleaning; laundry service; private butler service. *In room:* A/C, TV, dataport, minibar, hair dryer, safe.

Four Seasons Hotel ★★★ *Kids*   In 2002, the Four Seasons took over what was already one of the city's most luxurious properties. There are two parts to this landmark hotel—the 12-story "Park" tower housing the majority of the guest rooms, and the turn-of-the-last-century French-rococo "La Mansión" with seven elegant suites and a handful of private event rooms. A French-style garden and a pool separate the two buildings, and there's a well-equipped health club offering spa treatments. The hotel's restaurant, **Galani** (p. 58), serves excellent Mediterranean cuisine in a casual environment. Spacious guest rooms offer atypical amenities like walk-in closets, wet and dry bars, stereo systems, and cellphones. Large marble bathrooms contain separate bathtubs and showers. People staying on the club floors enjoy exclusive check-in and check-out, additional in-room amenities including a printer, fax machine, and Argentine wine, and complimentary breakfast and evening cocktails. The attentive staff will assist you in arranging day tours of Buenos Aires, as well as access to golf courses, tennis, boating, and horseback riding. Kids receive bedtime milk and cookies.

Posadas 1086/88, 111 Buenos Aires. Ⓒ **11/4321-1200.** Fax 11/4321-1201. www.fourseasons.com/ buenosaires. 165 units, including 49 suites (7 suites in La Mansión). $250 double; from $300 suite. AE, DC, MC, V. **Amenities:** Restaurant; lobby bar; heated outdoor pool; exercise room; health club; sauna; concierge; multilingual business center; room service; massage service; babysitting; dry cleaning; laundry service. *In room:* A/C, TV/VCR, dataport, minibar, hair dryer, safe.

EXPENSIVE

Caesar Park ★ *Overrated*   This classic hotel sits opposite Patio Bullrich, the city's most exclusive shopping mall. Guest rooms vary in size and amenities, but all have been tastefully appointed with fine furniture and elegant linens, marble bathrooms with separate bathtubs and showers, and entertainment centers with TVs and stereos. Larger rooms come with a fresh fruit basket on the first night's stay. The art collection in the lobby and on the mezzanine is for sale, and there are a few boutique shops on the ground level. Although the hotel, part of a larger international chain, is a member of The Leading Hotels of the World, service is formal and not particularly warm.

Posadas 1232/46, 1014 Buenos Aires. 🕿 **11/4819-1100.** Fax 11/4819-1121. www.caesar-park.com. 170 units. $180 double; from $400 suite. Buffet breakfast included. AE, DC, MC, V. Free valet parking. **Amenities:** Restaurant; 2 bars; small fitness center with indoor pool and sauna; concierge; business center; room service; dry cleaning and laundry service. *In room:* A/C, TV, dataport, minibar, hair dryer, safe.

Loi Suites ★★   Part of a small local hotel chain, the new Loi Suites Recoleta is a contemporary hotel with spacious rooms and personalized service. A palm-filled garden atrium and covered pool adjoin the lobby, which is bathed in various shades of white. Breakfast and afternoon tea are served in the "winter garden." Although the management uses the term "suites" rather loosely to describe rooms with microwaves, sinks, and small fridges, the hotel does in fact offer some traditional suites in addition to its more regular studio-style rooms. Loi Suites lies just around the corner from Recoleta's trendy restaurants and bars, and the staff will provide information on city tours upon request.

Vicente López 1955, 1128 Buenos Aires. 🕿 **11/5777-8950.** Fax 11/5777-8999. www.loisuites.com.ar. 112 units. From $200 double; from $300 suite. Rates include buffet breakfast. AE, DC, MC, V. Parking $4. **Amenities:** Restaurant; indoor pool; exercise room; sauna; small business center; limited room service; dry cleaning and laundry service. *In room:* A/C, TV, dataport, minibar, fridge, hair dryer, safe.

MODERATE

Etoile Hotel ★ *Value*   Located in the heart of Recoleta, steps away from the neighborhood's fashionable restaurants and cafes, the 14-story Etoile is an older hotel with a Turkish flair. It's not as luxurious as the city's other five-star hotels, but it's not as expensive either—making it a good value for Recoleta. Colored in gold and cream, guest rooms are fairly large—although they're not really "suites," as the hotel describes them. Executive rooms have separate sitting areas, large tile-floor bathrooms with whirlpool baths, and balconies. Rooms facing south offer balconies overlooking Plaza Francia and the Recoleta Cemetery.

Roberto M. Ortiz 1835, 1113 Buenos Aires. 🕿 **11/4805-2626.** Fax 11/4805-3613. www.etoile.com.ar. 96 units. $80 double; from $115 suite. Rates include buffet breakfast. AE, DC, MC, V. Free parking. **Amenities:** Restaurant; rooftop health club with indoor pool; exercise room; concierge; executive business services; room service; dry cleaning; laundry service. *In room:* A/C, TV, minibar, hair dryer.

MONSERRAT
MODERATE

Inter-Continental ★★★   The Inter-Continental is one of the capital's newer five-star hotels. Despite its modernity, this luxurious tower hotel was built in one of the city's oldest districts, Monserrat, and decorated in the Argentine style of the 1930s. The marble lobby is colored in beige and apricot tones, with handsome furniture and antiques inlaid with agates and other stones. The lobby's Café de las Luces, in which you might catch a glimpse of an evening tango performance, resembles the colonial style of the famous Café Tortoni. The **Restaurante y Bar Mediterráneo** (p. 60) serves healthy, gourmet Mediterranean cuisine. Stop by the Brasco & Duane wine bar for an exclusive selection of Argentine vintages. Guest rooms continue the 1930s theme, with elegant black woodwork, comfortable king beds, marble-top nightstands, large desks, and black and white photographs of Buenos Aires. Marble bathrooms have separate showers and bathtubs and feature extensive amenities.

Moreno 809, 1091 Buenos Aires. 🕿 **11/4340-7100.** Fax 11/4340-7119. www.buenos-aires.interconti.com. 312 units. $110 double; from $210 suite. AE, DC, MC, V. Metro: Moreno. **Amenities:** Restaurant; wine bar; lobby bar; health club with an indoor pool; exercise room; massage service; sauna; concierge; business center; room service; dry cleaning; laundry service; executive floors; sun deck. *In room:* A/C, TV, dataport, minibar, hair dryer, safe.

INEXPENSIVE

Hotel Nogaro ★ *Finds*   Hotel Nogaro's grand marble staircase leads to a variety of guest rooms noteworthy for their comfort and quietness. Deluxe rooms boast hardwood floors and high ceilings, and small but modern bathrooms with whirlpool tubs in the suites. Standard rooms, while smaller, are pleasant too, with red carpeting, large closets, and a bit of modern art. The hotel is a good bet for people who want to stay slightly outside the city center, although you should not walk in Monserrat at night. The staff will arrange sightseeing tours, upon request.

Av. Julio A. Roca 562, 1067 Buenos Aires. ✆ 11/4331-0091. Fax 11/4331-6791. www.nogarobue.com.ar. 140 units. From $40 double; from $45 suite. Rates include buffet breakfast. AE, DC, MC, V. Metro: Monserrat. **Amenities:** Restaurant; business center; room service; babysitting; laundry service. *In room:* A/C, TV, minibar.

MICROCENTER
VERY EXPENSIVE

Marriott Plaza Hotel ★★★   The historic Plaza was the grande dame of Buenos Aires for most of the 20th century, and the Marriott management has maintained much of its original splendor. (The hotel still belongs to descendants of the first owners from 1909.) The intimate lobby, decorated in Italian marble, crystal, and Persian carpets, is a virtual revolving door of Argentine politicians, foreign diplomats, and business executives. The veteran staff offers outstanding service, and the concierge will address needs ranging from executive business services to sightseeing tours. Although the quality of guest rooms varies widely (some still await renovation), all are spacious, well-appointed, and now include cellphones. Twenty-six overlook Plaza San Martín, some with beautiful bay windows. The **Plaza Grill** (p. 61) remains a favorite spot for a business lunch and offers a reasonably priced multi-course dinner menu, as well. The hotel's health club is one of the best in the city.

Calle Florida 1005, 1005 Buenos Aires. ✆ 11/4318-3000. Fax 11/4318-3008. www.marriott.com. 325 units. $300 double; from $400 suite. Rates include buffet breakfast. AE, DC, MC, V. Valet parking $23. Metro: San Martín. **Amenities:** 2 restaurants; cigar bar; excellent health club with outdoor pool; exercise room; sauna; concierge; business center; salon; room service; massage service; dry cleaning; laundry service. *In room:* A/C, TV, minibar, coffeemaker, hair dryer, safe.

Park Tower Buenos Aires (The Luxury Connection) ★★★   One of the most beautiful, and expensive, hotels in Buenos Aires, the Park Tower is connected to the Sheraton next door. The hotel combines traditional elegance with technological sophistication and offers impeccable service. Common areas as well as private rooms feature imported marble, Italian linens, lavish furniture, and impressive works of art. The lobby, with its floor-to-ceiling windows, potted palms, and Japanese wall screens, contributes to a sense that this is the Pacific Rim rather than South America. Tastefully designed guest rooms are equipped with 29-inch color TVs, stereo systems with CD players, and cellphones. Guests also have access to 24-hour private butler service. The hotel boasts three restaurants, including Chrystal Garden serving refined international cuisine, El Aljibe cooking Argentine beef from the grill, and Cardinale offering Italian specialties. The lobby lounge features piano music, a cigar bar, tea, cocktails, and special liquors.

Av. Leandro N. Alem 1193, 1104 Buenos Aires. ✆ 11/4318-9100. Fax 11/4318-9150. www.luxurycollection. com/parktower. 181 units. From $400 double. AE, DC, MC, V. Metro: Retiro. **Amenities:** 3 restaurants; snack bar; piano bar; 2 pools; putting green; 2 lighted tennis courts; fitness center with gym; wet and dry saunas; concierge; business center and secretarial services; room service; massage therapy; dry cleaning; laundry service. *In room:* A/C, TV/VCR, minibar, hair dryer, safe.

Sofitel ★★★   The Sofitel opened in late 2002, the first in Argentina. This classy French hotel near Plaza San Martín joins two seven-story buildings to a 20-story neoclassical tower dating from 1929, with a glass atrium lobby bringing them together. The lobby resembles an enormous gazebo, with six ficus trees, a giant iron and bronze chandelier, an Art Nouveau clock, and Botticcino and black San Gabriel marble filling the space. Adjacent to the lobby you will find an elegant French restaurant, **Le Sud** (p. 61), and the early-20th-century-style Buenos Aires Café. The cozy library, with its grand fireplace and dark woods, offers guests an enchanting place to read outside their rooms. These rooms vary in size, mixing modern French decor with traditional Art Deco styles; ask for one of the "deluxe" rooms or suites if you're looking for more space. Rooms are light-filled with beiges, yellows, and blacks; beautiful marble bathrooms have separate showers and bathtubs and feature Roger & Gallet amenities. Rooms above the eighth floor enjoy the best views, and the 17th floor suite, *L'Appartement*, covers the whole floor. Many of the staff members speak Spanish, English, and French.

Arroyo 841/849, 1007 Buenos Aires. © **11/4909-1454.** Fax 11/4909-1452. www.sofitel.com. 144 units. From $240 double; from $340 suite. AE, DC, MC, V. **Amenities:** Restaurant; cafe; bar; indoor swimming pool; fitness center; concierge; business center; room service; laundry service. *In room:* A/C, TV, dataport, minibar, hair dryer, safe.

EXPENSIVE

Amerian Buenos Aires Park Hotel ★★ *Finds*   Without question one of the finest four-star hotels in the city, the modern Amerian is a good bet for tourists as well as business travelers. The warm atrium lobby looks more like California than Argentina, and the highly qualified staff offers personalized service. Sound-proof rooms are elegantly appointed with wood, marble, and granite, and all boast comfortable beds, chairs, and work areas. The Argentine-owned hotel is just blocks away from Calle Florida, Plaza San Martín, and the Teatro Colón.

Reconquista 699, 1003 Buenos Aires. © **11/4317-5100.** Fax 11/4317-5101. www.amerianhoteles.com.ar. 152 units. $200 double; from $260 suite. Rates include buffet breakfast. AE, DC, MC, V. Metro: Florida. **Amenities:** Restaurant and pub; exercise room; sauna; concierge; business center; room service; dry cleaning and laundry service. *In room:* A/C, TV, minibar.

Meliá Confort Buenos Aires ★★   Within easy walking distance of Plaza San Martín and Calle Florida, the new Meliá Confort is among the best of the city's four-star hotels. Spacious guest rooms colored in soft earth tones feature overstuffed chairs, sound-proof windows, and marble bathrooms. Large desks, two phone lines, and available cellphones make this a good choice for business travelers. The staff offers friendly, relaxed service. The Meliá has a small Spanish restaurant and bar.

Reconquista 945, 1003 Buenos Aires. © **11/4891-3800.** Fax 11/4891-3834. www.solmelia.com. 125 units. $230 double; from $270 suite. Rates include buffet breakfast. AE, DC, MC, V. Metro: San Martín. **Amenities:** Restaurant; bar; exercise room; concierge; business services; room service; dry cleaning and laundry service. *In room:* A/C, TV, dataport, minibar, hair dryer, safe.

Sheraton Buenos Aires Hotel and Convention Center ★   The enormous Sheraton houses one of the main convention centers of Buenos Aires. Situated in the heart of the business, shopping, and theater district, it's an ideal location for business travelers and tourists. Guest rooms are typical of a large American chain—well-equipped, but lacking in charm. What the hotel lacks in intimacy, however, it makes up for in the wide range of services offered to guests. It shares three restaurants with the neighboring Park Tower Buenos Aires (The Luxury Collection), and its "Neptune" pool and fitness center is the best in the city.

Av. San Martín 1225, 1104 Buenos Aires. ℂ **11/4318-9000.** Fax 11/4318-9353. www.sheraton.com. 741 units. $260 double; from $360 suite. AE, DC, MC, V. Metro: Retiro. **Amenities:** 3 restaurants; snack bar; piano bar; 2 pools; putting green; 2 lighted tennis courts; fitness center with gym; wet and dry saunas; concierge; activities desk; car-rental desk; business center; shopping arcade; salon; room service; massage therapy; babysitting; dry cleaning; laundry service. *In room:* A/C, TV, minibar, hair dryer, safe.

MODERATE

Aspen Towers ★★ Built in 1995, the Aspen Towers is one of the city's newer and more refined hotels. Its 13-floor tower is contemporary in design, with a light-filled atrium lobby, elegant restaurant, and inviting rooftop pool. Guest rooms are small but classically decorated, with faux-antique furniture and soft-colored linens. All rooms feature marble bathrooms with whirlpool baths— something you're unlikely to find anywhere in the city at this price. The hotel is popular with Brazilians, Chileans, and Americans, and lies within easy walking distance of downtown's attractions.

Paraguay 857, 1057 Buenos Aires. ℂ **11/4313-1919.** Fax 11/4313-2662. www.aspentowers.com.ar. 105 units. $135–$175 double. Rates include buffet breakfast. AE, DC, MC, V. Metro: San Martín. **Amenities:** Restaurant; cafe; rooftop pool; exercise room; sauna; concierge; business center; room service; dry cleaning; laundry service. *In room:* A/C, TV, minibar.

Claridge Hotel ★ While no longer the capital's most luxurious hotel, the Claridge remains among the most well-known. The grand entrance with its imposing Roman columns and the elegant lobby with its English hunt-club theme seem far removed from the bustling city life outside. Wood paneling, wrought-iron lamps, and dark furniture lend the hotel a sense of tranquillity. Even the staff seems more relaxed, although service remains attentive and professional. Guest rooms are spacious, tastefully decorated, and equipped with all the amenities expected of a five-star hotel. The Claridge restaurant offers a good-value menu with carefully prepared international food and an inviting breakfast buffet. Because it occasionally hosts conventions, the Claridge can become very busy.

Tucumán 535, 1049 Buenos Aires. ℂ **11/4314-7700.** Fax 11/4314-8022. www.claridge.com.ar. 165 units. $190 double; from $290 suite. Rates include buffet breakfast. AE, DC, MC, V. Metro: Florida. **Amenities:** Restaurant; bar; health club with a heated outdoor pool; exercise room; sauna; concierge; business center; room service; massage service; dry cleaning; laundry service. *In room:* A/C, TV, minibar, safe.

Holiday Inn Express ★ This new Holiday Inn Express enjoys a great location next to Puerto Madero. Although there is no room service, concierge, or bellhops, the hotel is friendly, modern, and inexpensive. Guest rooms have large, firm beds, ample desk space, and 27-inch cable TVs; half of them boast river views. Coffee and tea are served 24 hours, and the buffet breakfast is excellent.

Av. Leandro N. Alem 770, 1057 Buenos Aires. ℂ **11/4311-5200.** Fax 11/4311-5757. www.holiday-inn.com. 116 units. From $140 double. Children under 18 stay free in parent's room. Rates include buffet breakfast. AE, DC, MC, V. Metro: L.N. Alem. **Amenities:** Deli; exercise room; whirlpool; sauna; business center. *In room:* A/C, TV.

Loi Suites Esmeralda ★ *Kids* Previously a Comfort Inn, this Loi Suites (part of a small local chain) lies 3 blocks from Plaza San Martín and the pedestrian walking street, Calle Florida. Spacious rooms can accommodate up to six people, making this a good choice for families traveling with children. Renovated in 2001, rooms are decorated in soft whites with kitchenettes and microwaves, and all come with cellphones. The hotel also offers complimentary access to a gym and swimming pool located off property. A more upscale (5-star) Loi Suites is in Recoleta.

Marcelo T. de Alvear 842, 1058 Buenos Aires. ✆ **11/4131-6800.** Fax 11/4131-6888. 103 units. $120 double; $205 suite. Rates include buffet breakfast. AE, DC, MC, V. Metro: San Martín. **Amenities:** Restaurant; bar; room service; laundry service. *In room:* A/C, TV, dataport, minibar, safe.

INEXPENSIVE

Bel Air Hotel ⭐ *Finds*   Opened in late 2000, the inexpensive and intimate Bel Air is as close as Buenos Aires comes to having a boutique hotel. Although the lobby and building's exterior are more extravagant than the rooms, guests can look forward to comfortable, quiet accommodations. Superior rooms are bigger than standards and only slightly more expensive, while suites have separate sitting areas. Certain rooms contain showers only (no tubs). Next to the lobby, Bis-a-Bis restaurant and bar features window-side tables, great for people-watching along the fashionable Arenales Street. The majority of the hotel's guests hail from Peru, Chile, and Columbia. The hotel provides airport transfer, upon request.

Arenales 1462, 1061 Buenos Aires. ✆ **11/4021-4000.** Fax 11/4816-0016. www.hotelbelair.com.ar. 76 units. $40 double; from $50 suite. Rates include buffet breakfast. AE, DC, MC, V. No parking. Metro: San Martín. **Amenities:** Restaurant; bar; gym; business services; room service; dry cleaning; laundry service. *In room:* A/C, TV, dataport, minibar.

Best Western Embassy *Kids*   Although the owners may be exaggerating when they call this an "all-suites" hotel, guest rooms (available in 5 categories) do have kitchenettes. Some also have separate living areas and bedrooms, and rooms facing Avenida Córdoba come with balconies. Renovated in 1998, the hotel is convenient and comfortable, offering decent if limited service. Don't be alarmed by the talking elevators.

Av. Córdoba 860, 1054 Buenos Aires. ✆ **11/4322-1228.** Fax 11/4322-2337. www.bestwestern.com. 80 units. From $62 double. Rates include buffet breakfast. AE, DC, MC, V. Metro: Lavalle. **Amenities:** Cafe; fitness room; sauna; business center; room service; laundry service. *In room:* A/C, TV, minibar, hair dryer.

Hotel Crillon ⭐   This 50-year-old French-style hotel enjoys an outstanding location adjacent to Plaza San Martín, next to some of the city's best sights and shops. Having recently completed a renovation, the Crillon has become more comfortable, with guest rooms refitted with nicer furniture and better linens. A business center, racquetball and squash courts, gym, and sauna have been added. The hotel is popular with European and Brazilian business travelers, and offers high-tech conveniences such as wireless Internet access and cellphones. Deluxe rooms enjoy views of calles Santa Fe and Esmeralda; the suites (with Jacuzzis) overlook Plaza San Martín. Stay away from interior rooms, which have no views. The hotel staff is extremely helpful.

Av. Santa Fe 796, 1059 Buenos Aires. ✆ **11/4310-2000.** Fax 11/4310-2020. www.hotelcrillon.com.ar. 96 units. $50–$70 double; $80 suite. Rates include buffet breakfast. AE, DC, MC, V. Metro: San Martín. **Amenities:** Restaurant; bar; business services; concierge; room service; dry cleaning; laundry service. *In room:* A/C, TV, wireless Internet access, minibar, hair dryer, safe.

Howard Johnson ⭐⭐ *Value*   Having taken over from Courtyard by Marriott, this new Howard Johnson's is an excellent choice for business travelers who don't require many special services. It has a great location off Calle Florida near Plaza San Martín, although there is no direct street access to the hotel (making it cumbersome to get to if you have lots of luggage). Guest rooms resemble studio apartments, with king- or queen-size beds, sleeper chairs, large desks and dressers, and well-appointed bathrooms. Each room has two phones, and local calls and Internet use are free—a rarity in Buenos Aires. There's a small, airy cafe adjacent to the lobby, but room service is not offered. There are four function rooms available for business and social events.

Calle Florida 944, 1005 Buenos Aires. © **11/4891-9200**. Fax 11/4891-9208. www.hojoar.com. 77 units. $75 double. Rates include buffet breakfast. AE, DC, MC, V. Metro: San Martín. **Amenities:** Restaurant; business services; laundry service. *In room:* A/C, TV, minibar, hair dryer, safe.

3 Where to Dine

Buenos Aires offers world-class dining, with a variety of Argentine, Italian, and international restaurants. With the collapse of the peso, fine Argentine dining has become marvelously inexpensive, as well. You've heard that Argentine beef is the best in the world; *parrillas* (grills) serving the choicest cuts are ubiquitous. Many kitchens have an Italian influence, and you'll find pasta on most menus. The city's most fashionable neighborhood for eating out is Las Cañitas in Old Palermo, also called "Palermo Hollywood." A row of excellent Argentine and ethnic restaurants, shops, and bars teem with young, hip Porteños. Additional top restaurants line the docks of Puerto Madero—with the majority focused on seafood. The microcenter and Recoleta offer many outstanding restaurants and cafes as well. Cafe life is as sacred to Porteños as it is to Parisians.

Porteños eat breakfast until 10am, lunch between noon and 2:30pm, and dinner late—usually after 9pm. Many restaurants require reservations, particularly on weekends. Executive lunch menus are offered most places at noon, but dinner menus are "a la carte." There is sometimes a small "cover" charge for bread and other items placed at the table. In restaurants that serve pasta, the pasta and its sauce are priced separately. Standard tipping is 10% in Buenos Aires, more for exceptional service. When paying by credit card, you will often be expected to leave the *propina* (tip) in cash, since many credit card receipts don't provide a place to include it. Many restaurants close between lunch and dinner, and remain closed on Monday nights.

To locate the following restaurants, see the map on p. 48.

PUERTO MADERO

There are no convenient metro stops to this neighborhood.

EXPENSIVE

Cabaña las Lilas ★★★ ARGENTINE   Widely considered the best *parrilla* in Buenos Aires, Cabaña las Lilas is always packed. The menu pays homage to Argentine beef, which comes from the restaurant's private *estancia* (ranch). The table "cover"—which includes dried tomatoes, mozzarella, olives, peppers, and delicious garlic bread—nicely whets the appetite. Clearly, you're here to order steak: The best cuts are the rib eye, baby beef, and thin skirt steak. Order sautéed vegetables, grilled onions, or Provençal-style fries separately. Service is hurried but professional; ask your waiter to match a fine Argentine wine with your meal. And make reservations well in advance.

Alicia Moreau de Justo 516. © **11/4313-1336**. Reservations recommended. Main courses $8–$12. AE, DC, V. Daily noon–midnight. Metro: L.N. Alem.

Katrine ★★★ INTERNATIONAL   One of the top dining choices in Buenos Aires, Katrine (named after the restaurant's Norwegian chef-owner) serves exquisite cuisine. Yet for such an exclusive restaurant, the dining room is surprisingly loud and festive. You won't go wrong with any of the menu choices, but a couple of suggestions include marinated salmon Scandinavian-style, followed by shrimp with vegetables and saffron, or thinly sliced beef tenderloin with portobello mushrooms, onions, and a cabernet sauvignon reduction. All of the pasta dishes are excellent, too. Katrine's modern dining room and outdoor terrace overlook the water. Service is outstanding.

Av. Alicia Moreau de Justo 138. ℂ **11/4315-6222.** Reservations recommended. Main courses $8–$15. AE, DC, MC, V. Mon–Fri noon–3:30pm and 8pm–midnight; Sat 8pm–12:30am; closed Sun. Metro: L.N. Alem.

MODERATE

Sorrento del Puerto ★★ ITALIAN   The only two-story restaurant in Puerto Madero enjoys impressive views of the water from both floors. When the city decided to reinvigorate the port in 1995, this was one of the first five restaurants opened (today, there are more than 50). The sleek modern dining room boasts large windows, modern blue lighting, and tables and booths decorated with white linens and individual roses. The outdoor patio accommodates only 15 tables, but the inside is enormous. People come here for two reasons: great pasta and even better seafood. Choose your pasta and accompanying sauce: seafood, shrimp scampi, pesto, or four cheeses. The best seafood dishes include trout stuffed with crabmeat, sole with a Belle Marnier sauce, Galician-style octopus, paella Valenciana, and assorted grilled seafood for two. A three-course menu with a drink costs $7. Sorrento has a second location in Recoleta at Posadas 1053 (ℂ **11/4326-0532**).

Av. Alicia Moreau de Justo 430. ℂ **11/4319-8731.** Reservations recommended. Main courses $5–$9. AE, DC, MC, V. Mon–Fri noon–4pm and 8pm–1am; Sat 8pm–2am; closed Sun. Metro: L.N. Alem.

RECOLETA

There are no convenient metro stops in this neighborhood.

EXPENSIVE

La Bourgogne ★★★ FRENCH   The only Relais Gourmand in Argentina, Chef Jean Paul Bondoux serves the finest French and international food in the city. *Travel and Leisure* rated La Bourgogne the number one restaurant in South America, and *Wine Spectator* gave it the distinction of being one of the "Best Restaurants in the World for Wine Lovers." Decorated in elegant pastel hues, the formal dining room serves the city's top gourmands. To begin your meal, consider a warm *fois gras* scallop with honey wine sauce, or perhaps the succulent *ravioli d'escargots.* Examples of the carefully prepared main courses include *chateaubriand béarnaise,* roasted salmon, veal steak, and lamb with parsley and garlic sauce. The kitchen's fresh vegetables, fruits, herbs, and spices originate from Bondoux's private farm. Downstairs, **La Cave** offers a slightly less formal dining experience, with a different menu but from the same kitchen as La Bourgogne. Wine tastings are offered Thursdays in the restaurant's wine cellar; contact La Bourgogne directly for details.

Av. Alvear 1891 (Alvear Palace Hotel). ℂ **11/4805-3857.** Reservations required. Jacket and tie required for men. Main courses $7–$12. Free valet parking. AE, DC, MC, V. Mon–Fri noon–3pm and 8pm–12am; Sat 8pm–12am; closed Sun. Closed Jan.

Lola ★★ *Overrated* INTERNATIONAL   Among the best-known international restaurants in Buenos Aires, Lola recently completed a makeover, turning its dining room into one of the city's brightest and most contemporary. Caricatures of major personalities adorn the walls, and fresh plants and flowers give Lola's dining room a spring-like atmosphere. A French-trained chef offers creative dishes such as chicken fricassee with leek sauce, grilled trout with lemon grass butter and zucchini, and beef tenderloin stuffed with Gruyère cheese and mushrooms. The chef will prepare dishes for those with special dietary requirements. Although Lola remains among the city's most famous restaurants, some feel that its quality has slipped in recent years due to a number of management changes.

Roberto M. Ortiz 1805. 🕐 **11/4804-5959** or 11/4802-3023. Reservations recommended. Main courses $7–$12. AE, DC, MC, V. Daily noon–4pm and 7pm–1am.

MODERATE

El Mirasol ★★ ARGENTINE   One of the city's best *parrillas,* El Mirasol serves thick cuts of fine Argentine beef. Your waiter will guide you through the selection of cuts, among which the rib eye, tenderloin, sirloin, and ribs are most popular. El Mirasol serves steaks as their own featured item, with potatoes, vegetables, and other accoutrements appearing only as separate side-dish orders. The best dessert is an enticing combination of meringue, ice cream, whipped cream, *dulce de leche,* walnuts, and hot chocolate sauce. The wine list pays tribute to Argentina malbec, syrah, merlot, and cabernet sauvignon. El Mirasol, which is frequented by business executives and government officials at lunch and a more relaxed crowd at night, remains open throughout the afternoon (a rarity in a city where most restaurants close between lunch and dinner).

Posadas 1032. 🕐 **11/4326-7322.** Reservations recommended. Main courses $5–$10. AE, DC, MC, V. Daily noon–2am.

Galani ★★ MEDITERANNEAN   This elegant but informal bistro inside the spectacular Four Seasons Hotel serves Mediterranean cuisine with Italian and Asian influences. The executive lunch menu includes an antipasto buffet with seafood, cold cuts, cheese, and salads, followed by a main course and dessert. From the dinner menu, the aged Angus New York strip makes an excellent choice, and all grilled dishes come with béarnaise sauce or *chimichurri* (a thick herb sauce) and a choice of potatoes or seasonal vegetables. Organic chicken and fresh seafood join the menu, along with a terrific selection of desserts. Live harp music often accompanies meals, and tables are candlelit at night. Enjoy an after-dinner drink in Le Dôme, the split-level bar adjacent to the lobby featuring live piano music and occasional tango shows.

Posadas 1086 (Four Seasons Hotel). 🕐 **11/4321-1234.** Reservations recommended. Main courses $5–$8. Fixed-price lunch $10. AE, DC, MC, V. Daily 7–11am, noon–3pm, and 8pm–1am.

Piegari ★★ ITALIAN   Piegari has two restaurants located across the street from each other; the more formal focuses on Italian dishes, and the other (Piegari Vitello e Dolce) specializes in steaks and desserts. Both restaurants are good, but visit the main Piegari for outstanding Italian cuisine, with an emphasis on seafood and pastas. Homemade spaghetti, seafood risotto, pan pizza, veal scallops, and black salmon ravioli are just a few of the mouth-watering choices. Huge portions are made for sharing, and an excellent Argentine wine list accompanies the menu. If you decide to try Piegari Vitello e Dolce instead, the best dishes are the short rib roast and the leg of Patagonian lamb.

Posadas 1042. 🕐 **11/4328-4104.** Reservations recommended. Main courses $7–$15. AE, DC, MC, V. Daily noon–3:30pm and 7:30pm–12am.

INEXPENSIVE

Café Victoria ★ CAFE   Perfect for a relaxing afternoon in Recoleta, the cafe's outdoor patio is surrounded by flowers and shaded by an enormous tree. Sit and have a coffee or enjoy a complete meal. The three-course express lunch menu offers a salad, main dish, and dessert, with a drink included. Afternoon tea with pastries and scones is served daily from 4 to 7pm. The cafe remains equally popular in the evening, when live music serenades the patio and there's excellent people-watching. This is a great value for the area—the Recoleta Cemetery and cultural center are located next door.

Roberto M. Ortiz 1865. ℂ 11/4804-0016. Main courses $3–$5. AE, DC, MC, V. Daily 7:30am–11:30pm.

Clark's ✪ INTERNATIONAL   The dining room here is an eclectic mix of oak, yellow lamps, live plants, and deer antlers. A slanted ceiling descends over the English-style bar with a fine selection of spirits; in back, a 3m (10-ft.) high glass case showcases a winter garden. Booths and tables are covered with green-and-white checkered tablecloths and are usually occupied by North Americans. Specialties include tenderloin steak with goat cheese, sautéed shrimp with wild mushrooms, and sole with a sparkling wine, cream, and shrimp sauce. There are a number of pasta and rice dishes, as well. A large outside terrace attracts a fashionable crowd in summer.

Roberto M. Ortiz 1777. ℂ 11/4801-9502. Reservations recommended. Main courses $4–$8. AE, DC, MC, V. Daily noon–3:30pm and 7:30pm–12am.

La Biela ✪✪✪ CAFE   Originally a small sidewalk cafe opened in 1850, La Biela earned its distinction in the 1950s as the rendezvous choice of race car champions. Black and white photos of these Argentine racers decorate the huge dining room. Today, artists, politicians, and neighborhood executives (as well as a fair number of tourists) all frequent La Biela, which serves breakfast, informal lunch plates, ice creams and crepes. The outdoor terrace sits beneath an enormous 19th-century Gum tree opposite the church of Nuestra Señora del Pinar. It is said that you have not seen Buenos Aires until you stop for a coffee or whisky at La Biela, and indeed this thoroughbred Argentine has become one of the city's cultural landmarks. Sip an espresso and watch the crowd.

Quintana 600. ℂ 11/4804-0449. Main courses $3–$5. V. Daily 7am–3am.

Primera (1ra) Plana *Value* PIZZA/SNACKS   Located in the part of Recoleta known as "La Recova de Posadas," Primera Plana is an inviting spot for a quick meal or drink on the outdoor terrace. The restaurant takes its name from a newspaper published in Buenos Aires decades ago: The restaurant's entire decor reflects front pages of the country's numerous periodicals. Come for one of the delicious pizzas or try the inexpensive lunchtime buffet. Order a large pizza and get a free beer with it. The salads are also large and tasty.

Posadas 111. ℂ 11/4326-4499. Main courses $2–$4. AE, MC, V. Daily 7am–2am (weekends until 3am).

PALERMO
MODERATE

De Olivas i Lustres ✪✪ MEDITERRANEAN   Located in Palermo Viejo, this magical restaurant is one of our favorites in Buenos Aires. The small, rustic dining room displays antiques, olive jars, and wine bottles, and each candlelit table is individually decorated—one resembles a writer's desk, another is sprinkled with seashells. The reasonably priced menu celebrates Mediterranean cuisine, with light soups, fresh fish, and sautéed vegetables the focus. The breast of duck with lemon and honey is mouthwatering; there are also a number of *tapeos*—appetizer-size dishes. For about $9 each, you and your partner can share 15 such dishes brought out individually (a great option provided you have at least a couple of hours). Open only for dinner, this romantic spot offers soft, subtle service.

Gascón 1460. (11/4867-3388. Reservations recommended. Main courses $3–$5; fixed-price menu $8. AE, V. Mon–Sat 7:30pm–1:30am. Metro: Scalabrini Ortiz.

Novecento ★★★ INTERNATIONAL   With a sister restaurant in SoHo, Novecento was one of the pioneer restaurants of Palermo's Las Cañitas neighborhood. Fashionable Porteños pack the New York–style bistro by 11pm, clinking wine glasses under a Canal Street sign or opting for the busy outdoor terrace. Waiters rush to keep their clients happy, with dishes like salmon carpaccio and steak salad. The pastas and risotto are mouth-watering, but you may prefer a steak *au poivre* or a chicken brochette. Other wonderful choices include filet mignon, grilled Pacific salmon, and penne with wild mushrooms. Top it off with an Argentine wine. This is *the* place to see and be seen if you're out for a bite.

Báez 199. (11/4778-1900. Reservations recommended. Main courses $4–$7. AE, DC, MC, V. Daily 8pm–2am, Sunday brunch 8am–noon. Metro: Olleros.

MONSERRAT
MODERATE

Club Español ★★ SPANISH   This Art Nouveau Spanish club, with its high, gilded ceiling and grand pillars, bas-relief artwork, and original Spanish paintings, boasts the most magnificent dining room in Buenos Aires. Despite the restaurant's architectural grandeur, the atmosphere is surprisingly relaxed and often celebratory; don't be surprised to find a table of champagne-clinking Argentines next to you. Tables have beautiful silver place settings, and tuxedo-clad waiters offer formal service. Although the menu is a tempting sample of Spanish cuisine—including the paella and Spanish omelets—the fish dishes are the best.

Bernardo de Yrigoyen 180. (11/4334-4876. Reservations recommended. Main courses $4–$8. AE, DC, MC, V. Daily noon–4pm and 8pm–midnight. Metro: Lima.

Restaurante y Bar Mediterráneo ★★ MEDITERRANEAN   The Inter-Continental Hotel's exclusive Mediterranean restaurant and bar were built in colonial style, resembling the city's famous Café Tortoni. The downstairs bar, with its hardwood floor, marble-top tables, and polished Victrola playing a tango, takes you back to Buenos Aires of the 1930s. A spiral staircase leads to the elegant restaurant, where subdued lighting and well-spaced tables create an intimate atmosphere. Mediterranean herbs, olive oil, and sun-dried tomatoes are among the chef's usual ingredients. Carefully prepared dishes might include shellfish bouillabaisse; black hake served with ratatouille; chicken casserole with morels, fava beans, and potatoes; or duck breast with cabbage confit, wild mushrooms, and sautéed apples. Express menus (ready within minutes) are available at lunch.

Moreno 809. (11/4340-7200. Reservations recommended. Main courses $6–9. AE, DC, MC, V. Daily 7–11am, 11:30am–3:30pm, and 7pm–midnight. Metro: Moreno.

MICROCENTER
EXPENSIVE

Catalinas ★★★ MEDITERRANEAN/INTERNATIONAL   Since 1979, Galician-born Ramiro Rodríguez Pardo has impressed gourmands from Argentina and abroad, his kitchen defined by culinary diversity and innovation. The colorful yet classic dining room—adjacent to the Lancaster hotel—has three open salons, each painted by one of Argentina's most famous "plastic" artists: Polesello, Beuedit, and Rovirosa. A Venetian crystal chandelier shines on the center dining room, created by the same artist who arranged the chandeliers in the lobby of New York's Plaza Hotel. Tables are large, decorated with white linens, fresh flower arrangements, and porcelain. A three-course, prix-fixe menu, including two bottles of Argentina's finest wines, is offered at lunch and dinner—an excellent value for such an elegant restaurant. The menu changes seasonally but always includes impeccable lobsters, T-bone steaks, and steaks of Patagonian tooth fish. Pardo's grilled lamb chops are famous throughout Argentina.

Reconquista 850. ✆ **11/4313-0182.** Reservations recommended. Main courses $7–$10; fixed-price menu $15. AE, DC, MC, V. Mon–Fri noon–3pm and 8pm–1am; Sat 8pm–1am. Closed Sun. Metro: San Martín.

Le Sud ★★ FRENCH/MEDITERANNEAN   Executive Chef Thierry Pszonka earned a gold medal from the National Committee of French Gastronomy and gained experience at La Bourgogne before opening this gourmet restaurant in the new Sofitel Hotel. His simple, elegant cooking style embraces spices and olive oils from Provence to create delicious entrees, such as the stewed rabbit with green pepper and tomatoes, polenta with Parmesan and rosemary, and spinach with lemon ravioli. Le Sud's dining room offers the same sophistication as its cuisine, a contemporary design with chandeliers and black marble floors, tables of Brazilian rosewood, and large windows overlooking Calle Arroyo. Following dinner, consider a drink in the adjacent wine bar.

Arroyo 841/849 (Sofitel Hotel). ✆ **11/4131-0000.** Reservations recommended. Main courses $10–$20. AE, DC, MC, V. Daily 6:30–11am, 12:30–3pm, and 7:30pm–12am. Metro: San Martín.

Plaza Grill ★★ INTERNATIONAL   For nearly a century, the Plaza Grill dominated the city's power-lunch scene, and it remains the first choice for government officials and business executives. The dining room is decorated with dark oak furniture, 90-year-old Dutch porcelain, Indian fans from the British Empire, and Villeroy & Boch china place settings. Tables are well-spaced, allowing for intimate conversations. Order a la carte from the international menu or off the *parrilla*—the steaks are perfect Argentine cuts. Marinated filet mignon, thinly sliced and served with gratinéed potatoes, is superb. The "po parisky eggs" form another classic dish—two poached eggs in a bread shell topped with a rich mushroom-and-bacon sauce. The restaurant's wine list spans seven countries, with the world's best Malbec coming from Mendoza.

Marriott Plaza Hotel, Calle Florida 1005. ✆ **11/4318-3070.** Reservations recommended. Main courses $7–$10. AE, DC, MC, V. Daily noon–4pm and 7pm–midnight. Metro: San Martín.

MODERATE

Broccolino ★ ITALIAN   Taking its name from New York's Italian immigrant neighborhood—notice the Brooklyn memorabilia filling the walls and the mural of Manhattan's skyline—this casual trattoria near Calle Florida is popular with North Americans (Robert Duvall has shown up 3 times). Many of the waiters speak English, still a rarity in much of the city, and the restaurant has a distinctly New York feel. Three small dining rooms are decorated in quintessential red-and-white checkered tablecloths, and the smell of tomatoes, onions, and garlic fills the air. The restaurant is known for its spicy pizzas, fresh pastas, and above all its sauces (*salsas* in Spanish). The restaurant also serves 2,000 pounds per month of baby calamari sautéed in wine, onions, parsley, and garlic.

Esmeralda 776. ✆ **11/4322-7652.** Reservations recommended. Main courses $3–$5. No credit cards. Daily noon–4pm and 7pm–1am. Metro: Lavalle.

La Chacra ⭐ ARGENTINE   Your first impression will be either the stuffed cow begging you to go on in and eat some meat, or the open fire spit grill glowing through the window. Professional waiters clad in black pants and white dinner jackets welcome you into what is otherwise a casual environment, with deer horns and wrought-iron lamps adorning the walls. Dishes from the grill include sirloin steak, T-bone with red peppers, and tenderloin. Barbecued ribs and suckling pig call out from the open-pit fire, and there are a number of hearty brochettes. Steaks are thick and juicy. Get a good beer or an Argentine wine, to wash it all down.

Av. Córdoba 941. ℂ **11/4322-1409.** Main courses $4–$6. AE, DC, MC, V. Daily noon–1:30am. Metro: San Martín.

Las Nazarenas ⭐ ARGENTINE   This is not a restaurant, an old waiter will warn you; it's an *asador*. More specifically, it's a steakhouse with meat on the menu, not a pseudo-*parrilla* with vegetable plates or some froufrou international dishes for the faint of heart. You have two choices: cuts grilled on the *parrilla*, or meat cooked on a spit over the fire. Argentine presidents and foreign ministers have all made their way here. The two-level dining room is handsomely decorated with cases of Argentine wines and abundant plants. Service is unhurried, offering you plenty of time for a relaxing meal.

Reconquista 1132. ℂ **11/4312-5559.** Reservations recommended. Main courses $4–$6. AE, DC, MC, V. Daily noon–1am. Metro: San Martín.

Ligure ⭐⭐ *Finds* FRENCH   Painted mirrors look over the long rectangular dining room, which since 1933 has drawn ambassadors, artists, and business leaders by day and a more romantic crowd at night. A nautical theme prevails, with fishnets, dock ropes, and masts decorating the room; captain's wheels substitute for chandeliers. Portions are huge and meticulously prepared—an unusual combination for French-inspired cuisine. Seafood options include the Patagonian tooth fish sautéed with butter, prawns, and mushrooms, or the trout glazed with an almond sauce. If you're in the mood for beef, the chateaubriand is outstanding, and the *bife de lomo* (filet mignon) can be prepared seven different ways (pepper sauce with brandy is delightful, and made at your table).

Juncal 855. ℂ **11/4393-0644** or 11/4394-8226. Reservations recommended. Main courses $4–$6. AE, DC, MC, V. Daily noon–3pm and 8–11:30pm. Metro: San Martín.

INEXPENSIVE

Café Tortoni ⭐⭐⭐ *Moments* CAFE   This historic cafe has served as the artistic and intellectual capital of Buenos Aires since 1858, with guests such as Jorge Luis Borges, Julio de Caro, Cátulo Castillo, and José Gobello. Waiters gaze over the cafe's antique tables and their occupants with sphinxlike serenity, just as the eyes of the great poets whose photographs line the walls have watched so many come and go. Come in for coffee, or even a simple meal (the food is not the point), and feel Argentine history surround you. The Tortoni is a cultural tradition; there are a number of social events here, including evening tango shows.

Av. de Mayo 825. ℂ **11/4342-4328.** Main courses $3–$7. AE, DC, MC, V. Mon–Thurs 8am–2am; Fri–Sat 8am–3am; Sun 8am–1am. Metro: Av. de Mayo.

Filo ⭐ *Finds* PIZZA   Popular with young professionals, artists, and anyone looking for cause to celebrate, Filo presents its happy clients with mouthwatering pizzas, delicious pastas, and potent cocktails. The crowded bar has occasional live music, and tango lessons are offered downstairs a few evenings per week.

San Martín 975. (© 11/4311-0312. Main courses $2–$5. AE, MC, V. Daily noon–4pm and 8pm–2am. Metro: San Martín.

Morizono ★ (Value) JAPANESE   A casual Japanese restaurant and sushi bar, Morizono offers such treats as dumplings stuffed with pork, shrimp and vegetable tempuras, salmon with ginger sauce, and a variety of sushi and sashimi combination platters. Morizono also has locations in Palermo at Paraguay 3521 (© 11/4823-4250) and Lacroze 2173, in Belgrano (© 11/4773-0940).

Reconquista 899. (© 11/4314-0924. Reservations recommended. Main courses $3–$6. AE, DC, MC, V. Mon–Fri 12:30–3:30pm and 8pm–midnight; Sat 8pm–1am. Closed Sun. Metro: San Martín.

Petit Paris Café ★ SNACKS/AFTERNOON TEA   Marble-top tables with velvet upholstered chairs, crystal chandeliers, and bow tie–clad waiters give this cafe a European flavor. Large windows look directly onto Plaza San Martín, placing the cafe within short walking distance of some of the city's best sights. The menu offers a selection of hot and cold sandwiches, pastries, and special coffees and teas. Linger over your coffee as long as you like—nobody will pressure you to move.

Av. Santa Fe 774. (© 11/4312-5885. Main courses $2–$4. AE, DC, MC, V. Daily 7am–2am. Metro: San Martín.

SAN TELMO
MODERATE

La Brigada ★★★ ARGENTINE   The best *parrilla* in San Telmo is reminiscent of the pampas, with memorabilia of gauchos (Pampas cowboys) filling the restaurant. White linen tablecloths and tango music complement the atmosphere, with an upstairs dining room that faces an excellent walled wine rack. The professional staff makes sure diners are never disappointed. Chef-owner Hugo Echevarrieta, known as *el maestro parrillero,* carefully selects meats. The best choices include the *asado* (short rib roast), *lomo* (sirloin steak, prepared with a mushroom or pepper sauce), baby beef (an enormous 850g/30 oz., served for 2), and the *mollejas de chivito al verdero* (young goat sweetbreads in a scallion sauce). The Felipe Rutini merlot goes perfectly with baby beef and chorizo. Service is outstanding.

Estados Unidos 465. (© 11/4361-5557. Reservations recommended. Main courses $4–$8. AE, DC, MC, V. Daily noon–3pm and 8pm–12am. Metro: Constitución.

INEXPENSIVE

Casa de Esteban de Luca ★ ARGENTINE   This historic house, once inhabited by Argentina's beloved poet and soldier Esteban de Luca (who wrote the country's first national anthem, the *Marcha Patriótica*), was built in 1786 and declared a National Historic Monument in 1941. Today, it's a popular restaurant serving pasta and meat dishes. Come on Thursday, Friday, or Saturday night after 9pm for the fun-spirited piano show.

Calle Defensa 1000. (© 11/4361-4338. Main courses $4–$6. AE, DC, MC, V. Tues–Sun noon–4pm and 8pm–1am. Metro: Constitución.

4 What to See & Do

Buenos Aires is a wonderful city to explore and fairly easy to navigate. The most impressive historical sites surround Plaza de Mayo, although you will certainly experience Argentine history in neighborhoods such as La Boca and San Telmo, too. Don't miss a walk along the riverfront in Puerto Madero, or an afternoon

Buenos Aires Attractions

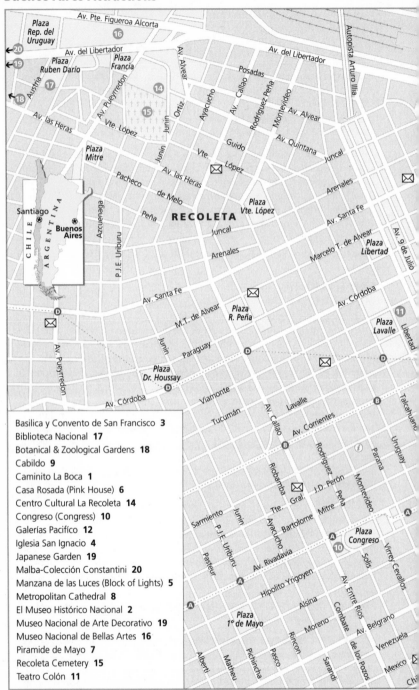

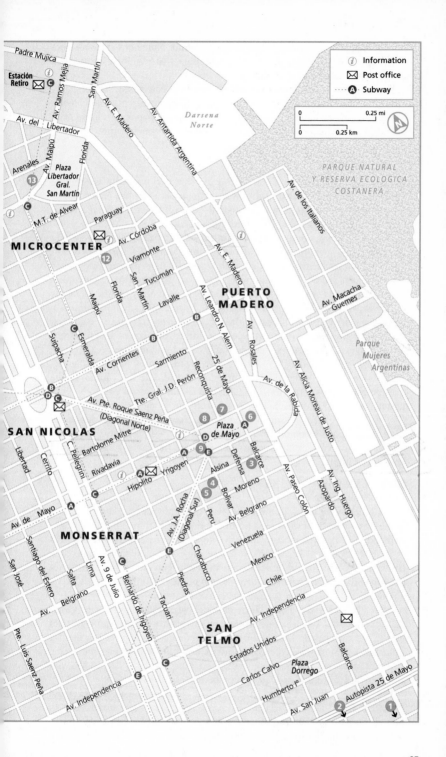

Information
Post office
Subway

Estación Retiro

Padre Mujica
San Martín
Av. Ramos Mejía
Av. E. Madero
Av. Antártida Argentina

Darsena Norte

0   0.25 mi
0   0.25 km

PARQUE NATURAL
Y RESERVA ECOLÓGICA
COSTANERA

Av. del Libertador
Arenales
Av. Maipú
Florida
Plaza Libertador Gral. San Martín
M.T. de Alvear
Paraguay

MICROCENTER
Av. Córdoba
Viamonte
Tucumán
San Martín
Lavalle
Florida
Maipú
Esmeralda
Suipacha

Av. Leandro N. Alem
Av. E. Madero

PUERTO MADERO

Av. de los Italianos

Parque Mujeres Argentinas

Av. Rosales
Av. Alicia Moreau de Justo
Av. de la Rábida

Av. Corrientes
Sarmiento
Tte. Gral. J.D. Perón
Reconquista
25 de Mayo

SAN NICOLAS
Av. Pte. Roque Saenz Peña
(Diagonal Norte)
Bartolome Mitre
Libertad
Cerrito
C. Pellegrini
Rivadavia
Hipolito Yrigoyen

Plaza de Mayo
Balcarce
Defensa
Alsina
Moreno
Bolívar
Perú
Av. Belgrano
Av. Paseo Colón
Azopardo
Av. Ing. Huergo

Av. de Mayo
MONSERRAT
Santiago del Estero
San José
Salta
Lima
Av. Belgrano
Pte. Luis Saenz Peña
Av. 9 de Julio
Bernardo de Irigoyen
Av. J.A. Rocha
(Diagonal Sur)
Chacabuco
Piedras
Tacuarí
Venezuela
Mexico
Chile
Av. Independencia

SAN TELMO
Estados Unidos
Carlos Calvo
Humberto Iº
Plaza Dorrego
Balcarce
Av. Independencia
Av. San Juan
Autopista 25 de Mayo

13 12 8 7 6 3 9 4 5 2 1

among the plazas and cafes of Recoleta or Palermo. Numerous sidewalk cafes offer respite for weary feet, and there's good public transportation to carry you from neighborhood to neighborhood.

Your first stop should be one of the city tourism centers (see "Visitor Information," earlier in this chapter) to pick up a guidebook, city map, and advice. You can also ask at your hotel for a copy of "The Golden Map" and "QuickGuide Buenos Aires" to help you navigate the city and locate its major attractions.

NEIGHBORHOODS TO EXPLORE
LA BOCA

La Boca, on the banks of the Río Riachuelo, developed originally as a trading center and shipyard. Drawn to the river's commercial potential, Italian immigrants moved in, giving the neighborhood the distinct flavor it maintains today. La Boca is most famous for giving birth to the tango.

At the center of La Boca lies the **Caminito** ★★★, a pedestrian walkway (and a famous tango song) that is both an outdoor museum and a marketplace. Surrounding the cobblestone street are shabby metal houses painted in dynamic shades of red, yellow, blue, and green, thanks to designer Benito Quinquela Martín. Today, many artists live or set up their studios in these houses. Along the Caminito, art and souvenir vendors work side by side with tango performers—this is one place you won't have to pay to see Argentina's great dance. Sculptures, murals, and engravings—some with political and social themes—line the street. This Caminito "Fine Arts Fair" is open daily from 10am to 6pm.

To catch an additional glimpse of La Boca's spirit, walk 4 blocks to the corner of Calles Del Valle Iberlucea and Brandsen. **Estadio de Boca Juniors**—the stadium for Buenos Aires's most popular *club de fútbol* (soccer club), the Boca Juniors—is here. Go on game day, when street parties and general debauchery take over the area. For information on football (soccer) games, see the *Buenos Aires Herald* sports section. Use caution in straying too far from the Caminito, however, as the less patrolled surrounding areas can be unsafe. *Caution:* **Avoid La Boca at night.**

SAN TELMO

Buenos Aires's oldest neighborhood, San Telmo originally housed the city's elite. When yellow fever struck in the 1870s—aggravated by substandard conditions in the area—the aristocrats moved north. Poor immigrants soon filled the neighborhood, and the houses were converted to tenements, called *conventillos*. In 1970, the city passed regulations to restore some of San Telmo's architectural landmarks. With new life injected into it, the neighborhood has taken on a bohemian flair, attracting artists, dancers, and numerous antiques dealers 7 days a week.

After Plaza de Mayo, **Plaza Dorrego** is the oldest square in the city. Originally the site of a Bethlehemite monastery, the plaza is also where Argentines met to reconfirm their Declaration of Independence from Spain. On Sunday from 10am to 5pm, the city's best **antiques market** ★★★ takes over the square. You can buy leather, silver, handicrafts, and other products here along with antiques, and tango and *milonga* dancers perform on the square.

San Telmo is full of tango clubs; one of the most notable is **El Viejo Almacén** ★ (at Independencia and Balcarce). An example of colonial architecture, it was built in 1798 and was a general store and hospital before its reincarnation as the quintessential Argentine tango club. Make sure to go back for a

Evita Perón: Woman, Wife, Icon

Eva Duarte de Perón, widely known as Evita, captured the imagination of millions of Argentines because of her social and economic programs for the working classes. A mediocre stage and radio actress, she married Colonel Juan Perón, a widower, in 1945 and helped in his charismatic presidential campaign.

Once Perón took office, she created the Eva Perón Foundation, which redirected funds traditionally controlled by Argentina's elite to programs benefiting hospitals, schools, elderly homes, and various charities. In addition, she raised wages for union workers, established nationwide religious education, and successfully fought for women's suffrage. When Evita died of cancer in 1952, the working classes tried (unsuccessfully) to have her canonized. She is buried next to Juan Perón in the Recoleta Cemetery, one of the only bodies allowed there from a non-elite family.

You will find that even today there is considerable disagreement among Argentines over Evita's legacy. Members of the middle and lower classes tend to see her as a national hero, while many of the country's upper classes believe she stole money from the wealthy and used it to embellish her own popularity.

show at night (see "Buenos Aires After Dark," later in this chapter). If you get the urge for a beginner or refresher tango course while you're in San Telmo, look for signs advertising lessons in the windows of clubs.

PALERMO

Palermo is a neighborhood of parks filled with magnolias, pines, palms, and willows, where families picnic on weekends and couples stroll at sunset. Designed by French architect Charles Thays, the parks take their inspiration from London's Hyde Park and Paris's Bois de Boulogne. Take the metro to Plaza Italia, which lets you out next to the **Botanical Gardens** ✿ (✆ 11/4831-2951) and **Zoological Gardens** ✿ (✆ 11/4806-7412), open dawn to dusk. Stone paths wind their way through the botanical gardens, where a student might escape hurried city life to study on a park bench. Flora from throughout South America fills the garden, with over 8,000 plant species from around the world represented. Next door, the city zoo features an impressive diversity of animals, including indigenous birds and monkeys, giant turtles, orangutans, and a polar bear and brown bear habitat.

Parque Tres de Febrero ✿✿, a 1,000-acre paradise of trees, lakes, and walking trails, begins just past the Rose Garden off Avenida Sarmiento. In summer, paddleboats are rented by the hour. Nearby, small streams and lakes meander through the **Japanese Garden** ✿✿ (✆ 11/4804-4922; open daily 10am–6pm; admission $1), where children can feed the fish (*alimento para peces* means "fish food") and watch the ducks. Small wood bridges connect classical Japanese gardens surrounding the artificial lake. A simple restaurant offers tea, pastries, sandwiches, and a few Japanese dishes such as sushi and teriyaki chicken.

RECOLETA

The city's most exclusive neighborhood, La Recoleta wears a distinctly European face. Tree-lined avenues lead past fashionable restaurants, cafes, boutiques, and galleries, many housed in French-style buildings. Much of the activity takes place along the pedestrian walkway Roberto M. Ortiz, and in front of the Cultural Center and Recoleta Cemetery. This is a neighborhood of plazas and parks, a place where tourists and wealthy Argentines spend their leisure time outside. Weekends bring street performances, art exhibits, fairs, and sports.

The **Recoleta Cemetery** ★★★ (no phone), open daily from 10am to 5pm, pays tribute to some of Argentina's historical figures and is a lasting place where the elite can show off its wealth. Once the garden of the adjoining church, the cemetery was created in 1822 and is the oldest in the city. You can spend hours wandering the grounds that cover 4 city blocks, adorned with works by local and international sculptors. More than 6,400 mausoleums form an architectural free-for-all, including Greek temples and pyramids. The most popular site is the tomb of Eva "Evita" Perón, which is always heaped with flowers and letters from adoring fans. To prevent her body from being stolen (as it once was in 1955), she has been buried in a concrete vault 8.1m (27 ft.) underground. Many other rich or famous Argentines are buried here as well, including a number of Argentine presidents of the 20th century, various literary figures, and heroes of the war for independence. As any Argentine will tell you, it's important to live in Recoleta while you're alive, but even more important to remain here in death. How to get a space? You're in luck if your family already owns a plot; otherwise, you can buy space for about $20,000 per square meter—if someone is willing to sell. Guided tours of the cemetery take place the last Sunday of each month at 2:30pm from the cemetery's entrance.

Adjacent to the cemetery, the **Centro Cultural Recoleta** ★ (p. 77) holds permanent and touring art exhibits along with theatrical and musical performances. Designed in the mid–18th century as a Franciscan convent, it was reincarnated as a poorhouse in 1858, serving that function until becoming a cultural center in 1979. The first floor houses an interactive children's science museum where it is "forbidden not to touch." Next door, Buenos Aires Design Center features shops specializing in home decor.

PLAZA DE MAYO

Juan de Garay founded the historic core of Buenos Aires, the Plaza de Mayo, in 1580. The plaza's prominent buildings create an architectural timeline: the Cabildo, Pirámide de Mayo (Pyramid of May), and Metropolitan Cathedral are vestiges of the colonial period (18th and early 19th c.), while the seats of national and local government reflect the styles of the late 19th and early 20th century. In the center of the plaza, you'll find palm trees, fountains, and benches. Plaza de Mayo remains the political heart of the city, serving as a forum for protests. The mothers of the *desaparecidos,* victims of the military dictatorship's war against leftists, have demonstrated here since 1976. You can see them march every Thursday afternoon at 3:30pm.

The Argentine president, whose actual residence is located in a suburb, goes to work every day at the **Casa Rosada (Pink House)** ★★★. It is from a balcony of this mansion that Eva Perón addressed adoring crowds of Argentine workers. You can watch the changing of the guard in front of the palace every hour on the hour, and around back is a small museum (© **11/4344-3802**) with information on the history of the building and of the nation. It's open Monday through Friday from 10am to 6pm; admission is free.

The original structure of the **Metropolitan Cathedral** ★★ (© 11/4331-2845) was built in 1745; it was given a new facade with carvings telling the story of Jacob and his son Joseph and was designated a cathedral in 1836. Inside lies a mausoleum containing the remains of General José de San Martín, South American liberator regarded as the "Father of the Nation." (San Martín fought successfully for freedom in Argentina, Peru, and Chile.) The tomb of the unknown soldier of Argentine independence is also here.

The **Cabildo** ★, Bolívar 65 (© 11/4334-1782), was the original seat of city government established by the Spaniards. Completed in 1751, the colonial building proved significant in the events leading up to Argentina's declaration of independence from Spain in May 1810. Parts of the Cabildo were demolished to create space for Avenida de Mayo and Diagonal Sur. The remainder of the building was restored in 1939 and is worth a visit, although the small museum inside is not particularly interesting (museum open Tues–Fri 12:30pm-7pm, Sun 2pm–6pm; admission $1). The Cabildo is the only remaining public building dating back to colonial times.

A striking neoclassical facade covers the **Legislatura de la Ciudad (City Legislature Building),** at Calle Perú and Hipólito Yrigoyen, which houses exhibitions in several of its halls. The building's watchtower has more than 30 bells. In front of the Legislatura, you'll see a bronze statue of Julio A. Roca, considered one of Argentina's greatest presidents.

Farther down Calle Perú stands the enormous **Manzana de las Luces (Block of Lights)** ★★, Calle Perú 272, which served as the intellectual center of the city in the 17th and 18th century. This land was granted in 1616 to the Jesuits, who built **San Ignacio**—the city's oldest church—still standing at the corner of calles Bolívar and Aslina. San Ignacio has a beautiful altar carved in wood with Baroque details. Also located here is the **Colegio Nacional de Buenos Aires (National School of Buenos Aires).** Argentina's best-known intellectuals have gathered and studied here, and the name "block of lights" recognizes the contributions of the National School's graduates, especially in achieving Argentina's independence in the 19th century. Tours are usually led on Saturday and Sunday at 3 and 4:30pm and include a visit to the Jesuits' system of underground tunnels, which connected their churches to strategic spots in the city (admission $2). In addition to weekend tours, the Comisión Nacional de la Manzana de las Luces organizes a variety of cultural activities during the week, including folkloric dance lessons, open-air theater performances, art expositions, and music concerts. Call © 11/4331-9534 for information.

PUERTO MADERO

Puerto Madero became Buenos Aires's first major gateway to trade with Europe when it was built in 1880. But by 1910, the city had already outgrown the port. The Puerto Nuevo (New Port) was established to the north to accommodate growing commercial activity, and Madero was abandoned for almost a century. Urban renewal saved the original port in the 1990s with the construction of a riverfront promenade, apartments, and offices. Bustling and businesslike during the day, the area attracts a fashionable, wealthy crowd at night. It's lined with elegant restaurants serving Argentine steaks and fresh seafood specialties, and there is a popular cinema showing Argentine and Hollywood films.

PLAZA SAN MARTIN AND SURROUNDING AREA

Plaza San Martín ★★, a beautiful park at the base of Calle Florida in the Retiro neighborhood, acts as the nucleus of what's considered the city's *microcentro*. In summer months, Argentine businesspeople flock to the park on their lunch hour, loosening their ties, taking off some layers, and sunning for a while amidst the plaza's flowering jacaranda. A monument to General José de San Martín towers over the scene. The San Martín Palace, one of the seats of the Argentine Ministry of Foreign Affairs, and the elegant Plaza Hotel face the square.

Calle Florida ★★★ is the main pedestrian thoroughfare of Buenos Aires and a shopper's paradise. The busiest section, extending south from Plaza San Martín to Avenida Corrientes, is lined with boutiques, restaurants, and record stores. You'll find the upscale Galerías Pacífico fashion center here (see "Shopping," below).

Avenida Corrientes ★ is a living diary of Buenos Aires's cultural development. Until the 1930s, Avenida Corrientes was the favored hangout of tango legends. When the avenue was widened in the mid-1930s, it made its debut as the Argentine Broadway. Today, Corrientes, lined with cinemas and theaters, pulses with cultural and commercial activity day and night.

MUSEUMS

Note that several of these museums are in the Recoleta area, which has no metro stations.

El Museo Histórico Nacional (National History Museum) ★★　Argentine history from the 16th through the 19th century comes to life in the former Lezama family home. The expansive Italian-style mansion houses 30 rooms with items saved from Jesuit missions, paintings illustrating clashes between the Spaniards and Indians, and relics from the War of Independence against Spain. The focal point of the museum's collection is artist Cándido López's series of captivating scenes of the war against Paraguay in the 1870s.

Calle Defensa 1600. © 11/4307-1182. Free admission. Tues–Sun noon–6pm. Closed Jan. Metro: Constitución.

Malba–Colección Constantini ★★★　The stunning Museo de Arte Latinoamericano de Buenos Aires (Malba), which vaguely resembles New York's Museum of Modern Art, houses the private art collection of Eduardo Constantini. One of the most impressive collections of Latin American art anywhere, temporary and permanent exhibitions showcase names like Antonio Berni, Pedro Figari, Frida Kahlo, Cândido Portinari, Diego Rivera, and Antonio Siguí. Many of the works confront social issues and explore questions of national identity. In addition to the art exhibitions, Latin films are held Tuesday through Sunday at 2pm and 10pm. This wonderful museum, which opened in late 2001, is located in Palermo.

Av. Figueroa Alcorta 3415. © 11/4808-6500. Admission $1. Free admission Wed. Wed–Mon noon–8pm. Closed Tues.

Museo Nacional de Arte Decorativo (National Museum of Decorative Art) ★　French architect Rene Sergent, who designed some of the grandest mansions in Buenos Aires, envisioned and developed this museum. The building's 18th-century French design provides a classical setting for the diverse decorative styles represented within. Breathtaking sculptures, paintings, and furnishings round off the collection. The **Museo de Arte Oriental (Museum of Eastern Art)** displays art, pottery, and engravings on the first floor of the building.

Av. del Libertador 1902. © 11/4801-8248. Admission $1. Mon–Fri 2–8pm; Sat–Sun 11am–7pm.

Museo Nacional de Bellas Artes (National Museum of Fine Arts) ★★
This building that formerly pumped the city's water supply metamorphosed into Buenos Aires's most important art museum in 1930. The museum contains the world's largest collection of Argentine sculptures and paintings from the 19th and 20th centuries. It also houses European art dating from the pre-Renaissance period to the present day. The collections include notable pieces by Renoir, Monet, Rodin, Toulouse-Lautrec, and van Gogh.
Av. del Libertador 1473. ☎ 11/4803-0802. Free admission. Tues–Sun 12:30–7:30pm.

OTHER ATTRACTIONS
Among the other attractions is the **Café Tortoni,** long a meeting place for Porteño artists and intellectuals. For a dining review, see p. 62, and for information on the cafe's tango shows, see p. 78.

Basílica y Convento de San Francisco (San Francisco's Church and Convent) ★   The San Roque parish is one of the oldest in the city. A Jesuit architect designed the church in 1730, but a final reconstruction in the early 20th century added a German baroque facade, along with statues of Saint Francis of Assisi, Dante, and Christopher Columbus. Inside, you'll find a tapestry by Argentine artist Horacio Butler along with an extensive library.
Calle Defensa and Alsina. ☎ 11/4331-0625. Free admission. Hours vary. Metro: Plaza de Mayo.

Biblioteca Nacional (National Library) ★   Opened in 1992, this modern architectural oddity stands on the land of the former Presidential Residence in which Eva Perón died. With its underground levels, the library's 13 floors can store up to 5 million volumes. Among its collection, the library stores 21 books printed by one of the earliest printing presses, dating from 1440 to 1500. Visit the reading room—occupying two stories at the top of the building—to enjoy an awe-inspiring view of Buenos Aires. The library also hosts special events in its exhibition hall and auditorium.
Calle Aguero 2502. ☎ 11/4807-0885. Free admission. Weekdays 9am–9pm; weekends noon–8pm.

Congreso (Congress) ★   The National Congress towers over Avenida de Mayo, its occupants theoretically keeping a watchful eye on the president's Casa Rosada down the street. The capitol building, built in 1906, combines elements of classical Greek and Roman architecture and is topped with an immense central dome modeled after its counterpart in Washington, D.C. Today, the building cannot accommodate the entire congressional staff, some of whom have spilled over into neighboring structures.

Plaza Congreso was designed in 1910 to frame the congress building and memorialize the centennial of a revolutionary junta that helped overthrow Spanish rule in Argentina. Stroll around the square and its surroundings to see a number of architectural landmarks, theaters, sidewalk cafes, and bars.
Plaza Congreso. Not open to the public. Metro: Congreso.

Teatro Colón (Colón Theater) ★★★   Buenos Aires's golden age of prosperity gave birth to this luxurious opera house, which has hosted Luciano Pavarotti, Julio Bocca, Maria Callas, Plácido Domingo, Arturo Toscanini, and Igor Stravinsky. The project took close to 80 years to complete, but the result is spectacular. The majestic building, completed in 1908, combines a variety of European styles, from the Ionic and Corinthian capitals and French stained-glass pieces in the main entrance to the Italian marble staircase and French furniture, chandeliers, and vases in the Golden Hall. In the main theater—which seats

2,500 in orchestra seats, stalls, boxes, and four rises—an enormous chandelier hangs from the domed ceiling painted by Raúl Soldi. The theatre's acoustics are world-renowned. In addition to hosting visiting performers, the Colón has its own philharmonic orchestra, choir, and ballet company. Opera and symphony seasons last from April to early December. **Guided tours,** which let you view the main theater, backstage, and costume and stage design workshops, take place hourly between 11am and 3pm weekdays and from 9am to noon Saturday. Call ☎ 11/4378-7130 for information.

Calle Libertad 621 or Calle Toscanini 1180. ☎ 11/4378-7100. Admission $5. Metro: Tribunales.

SPECTATOR SPORTS & OUTDOOR ACTIVITIES

GOLF   Argentina has more than 200 golf courses. Closest to downtown are **Cancha de Golf de la Ciudad de Buenos Aires,** Av. Torquist 1426 and Olleros (☎ 11/4772-7261), 10 minutes from downtown with great scenery and a 71-par course; and **Jockey Club Argentino,** Av. Márquez 1700 (☎ 11/4743-1001), in San Isidro, which offers two courses (71 and 72 par) designed by Allister McKenzie.

HORSE RACING   Over much of the 20th century, Argentina was famous for its thoroughbreds. It continues to send prize horses to competitions around the world, although you can watch some of the best right here in Buenos Aires. Races take place at two tracks: **Hipódromo de San Isidro,** Av. Márquez 504 (☎ 11/4743-4010), and **Hipódromo Argentino de Palermo,** Av. del Libertador 4205 (☎ 11/4778-2839), in Palermo. Check the *Buenos Aires Herald* for race information.

POLO   Argentina has won more international polo tournaments than any other country, and the **Argentine Open Championship,** held late November through early December, is the world's most important polo event. There are two seasons for polo: March through May and September through December, held at the **Campo Argentino de Polo,** Avenida del Libertador and Avenida Dorrego (☎ 11/4576-5600). Tickets can be purchased at the gate. Contact the **Asociación Argentina de Polo,** Hipólito Yrigoyen 636 (☎ 11/4331-4646 or 11/4342-8321), for information on polo schools and events. **La Martina Polo Ranch** (☎ 11/4576-7997), located 37 miles (60km) from Buenos Aires near the town of Vicente Casares, houses more than 80 polo horses, as well as a guesthouse with a swimming pool and tennis courts.

SOCCER   One cannot discuss soccer in Argentina without paying homage to Diego Armando Maradona, Argentina's most revered player and one of the sport's great (if fallen) players. Any sense of national unity dissolves when Argentines watch their favorite clubs—River Plate, Boca Juniors, Racing Club, Independiente, and San Lorenzo—battle on Sunday. Passion for soccer could not run hotter, and you can catch a game at the **Estadio Boca Juniors,** Brandsen 805 (☎ 11/4362-2260), in San Telmo, followed by raucous street parties. Ticket prices start at $10 and can be purchased in advance or at the gate.

5 Shopping

Porteños like to consider their city one of the fashion capitals of the world. Although the wealthiest Argentines still fly to Miami for their wardrobes, Buenos Aires boasts many of the same upscale stores you would find in New York or Paris. Do not expect to find a city full of indigenous textiles and crafts as you would elsewhere in Latin America; Hermès, Louis Vuitton, Versace, and Ralph Lauren are more on the mark in wealthy districts like Recoleta or Palermo. The European boutiques also sell much better quality clothes than their Argentine counterparts, with the exception of furs, wool, and some leather goods, which are excellent across the country.

STORE HOURS & SHIPPING

Most stores are open weekdays from 9am to 8pm and Saturday from 9am until midnight, with some still closing for a few hours in the afternoon. You might find some shops open Sunday along Avenida Santa Fe, but few will be open on Calle Florida. Shopping centers are open daily from 10am to 10pm.

Certain art and antiques dealers will crate and ship bulky objects for an additional fee; others will tell you it's no problem to take that new sculpture directly on the plane. If you don't want to take any chances, contact **UPS** at 🕾 **800/ 222-2877** or **Federal Express** at 🕾 **810/333-3339.** Whatever your purchase, keep your receipts for invoices over 70 pesos; you should be able to get a refund of the 19% tax (VAT) when you leave the country.

GREAT SHOPPING AREAS

MICROCENTER   Calle Florida, the pedestrian walking street in the microcenter, is home to wall-to-wall shops from Plaza San Martín past Avenida Corrientes. The **Galerías Pacífico** mall is located at Calle Florida 750 and Avenida Córdoba (🕾 **11/4319-5100**), with a magnificent dome and stunning frescoes painted by local artists. Over 180 shops are open Monday through Saturday from 10am to 9pm and Sunday from noon to 9pm, with tango shows held on weekends at 8pm. As you approach Plaza San Martín, you find a number of well-regarded shoe stores, jewelers, and shops selling leather goods.

RECOLETA   Avenida Alvear is Argentina's response to the Champs-Elysées, and—without taking the comparison too far—it is indeed an elegant, Parisian-like strip of European boutiques and cafes. Start your walk from Plaza Francia and continue from Junín to Cerrito. Along Calle Quintana, French-style mansions share company with upscale shops. Nearby **Patio Bullrich,** Av. del Libertador 750 (🕾 **11/4814-7400**), is one of the city's best malls. Its 69 elegant shops are open daily from 10am to 9pm.

AVENIDA SANTA FE   Popular with local shoppers, Avenida Santa Fe— which the city tourist office likens to Madrid's Gran Vía—offers a wide selection of clothing stores and more down-to-earth prices. You will also find bookstores, ice-cream shops, and cinemas. The **Alto Palermo Shopping Center,** Av. Santa Fe 3253 (🕾 **11/5777-8000**), is another excellent shopping center, with 155 stores open daily from 10am to 10pm.

SAN TELMO & LA BOCA   These neighborhoods offer excellent antiques as well as arts and crafts celebrating tango. Street performers and artists are omnipresent. Both should be visited during the day and avoided at night.

OUTDOOR MARKETS

The **antiques market in San Telmo** 🎯, which takes place every Sunday from 10am to 5pm at Plaza Dorrego, is a vibrant, colorful experience. As street vendors sell their heirlooms, singers and dancers move amid the crowd to the music of tangos and *milongas.* Among the 270-plus vendor stands, you will find antique silversmith objects, porcelain, crystal, and other antiques.

   Plaza Francia's Fair, at avenidas del Libertador and Pueyrredón, offers ceramics, leather goods, and arts and crafts amidst street musicians and performers. It's held Sunday from 9am to 7pm.

SHOPPING A TO Z

Almost all shops in Buenos Aires accept credit cards. However, you will often get a better price if you offer to pay with cash. You won't be able to use credit cards at outdoor markets.

ANTIQUES

Throughout the streets of San Telmo, you will find the city's best antiques shops; don't miss the antiques market that takes place all day Sunday at Plaza Dorrego (see "Outdoor Markets," above). There are also a number of fine antiques stores along Avenida Alvear in Recoleta, including a collection of boutique shops at **Galería Alvear,** Av. Alvear 1777.

Galería El Solar de French   Built in the early 20th century in a Spanish colonial style, this is where Argentine patriot Domingo French lived. Today, it's a gallery, with antiques shops and photography stores depicting the San Telmo of yesteryear. Calle Defensa 1066. Metro: Constitución.

Pallarols   Located in San Telmo, Pallarols sells an exquisite collection of Argentine silver and other antiques. Calle Defensa 1015. ℂ 11/4362-5438. Metro: Constitución.

ART GALLERIES

Galería Ruth Benzacar   This avant-garde gallery, in a hidden underground space at the start of Calle Florida next to Plaza San Martín, hosts exhibitions of local and national interest. Among the best-known Argentines who have appeared here are Alfredo Prior, Miguel Angel Ríos, Daniel García, Graciela Hasper, and Pablo Siguier. Calle Florida 1000. ℂ 11/4313-8480. Metro: San Martín.

FASHION & APPAREL

Most Argentine clothing stores do not offer the same quality as European names. You will find the city's top fashion stores along Avenida Alvear and Calle Quintana in Recoleta, including **Gianni Versace** (Av. Alvear 1901), **Polo Ralph Lauren** (Av. Alvear 1780), and **Emporio Armani** (Av. Alvear 1750).

Ermenegildo Zegna   The famous Italian chain sells outstanding suits and jackets made of light, cool fabrics. If you've landed in Buenos Aires without your suit, this is among your best options. Av. Alvear 1920. ℂ 11/4804-1908.

Escada   You can find casual and elegant selections of women's clothing combining quality and comfort in this boutique shop. Av. Alvear 1516. ℂ 11/4815-0353.

JEWELRY

The city's finest jewelry stores are in Recoleta and inside many five-star hotels. You can find bargains on gold along Calle Libertad, near Avenida Corrientes.

Cousiño Jewels   Located along the Sheraton hotel's shopping arcade, this Argentine jeweler features a brilliant collection of art made of the national stone, the rhodochrosite, or Inca Rose. In the Sheraton Buenos Aires Hotel, Av. San Martín. ℂ 11/4318-9000. Metro: Retiro.

H.Stern   This upscale Brazilian jeweler, with branches in major cities around the world, sells an entire selection of South American stones, including emeralds and the unique imperial topaz. It's the top jeweler in Latin America. Branches in the Marriott Plaza (ℂ 11/4318-3083) and the Sheraton (ℂ 11/4312-6762).

LEATHER

Argentina is famous for its leather—particularly raw leather—and there are a number of excellent shops in Buenos Aires selling everything from clothing, wallets, and purses to luggage, saddles, and shoes. You can usually find better values here than abroad, but do pay close attention to the quality of craftsmanship—especially in lesser-known stores—before making your purchase.

Tips **Shopping Tip**

Most antiques stores will come down 10% to 20% from the listed price if you try to bargain.

Casa López Widely considered the best *marroquinería* (leather goods shop) in Buenos Aires, Casa López sells an extensive range of Argentine leather products. There is also a shop in the Patio Bullrich Mall. Marcelo T. de Alvear 640. ℰ **11/4312-8911.** Metro: San Martín.

El Nochero All the products sold at El Nochero are made with first-rate Argentine leather and manufactured by local workers. Shoes and boots, leather goods and clothes, and native silverware (including *mates*) decorate the store. Posadas 1245, in the Patio Bullrich Mall. ℰ **11/4815-3629.**

Louis Vuitton The famous Parisian boutique sells an elite line of luggage, purses, and travel bags. It's located alongside Recoleta's most exclusive shops. Av. Alvear 1751. ℰ **11/4813-7072.**

Rossi & Caruso This store offers the best leather products in the city and is the first choice for visiting celebrities—the king and queen of Spain and Prince Philip of England among them. Products include luggage, saddles and accessories, leather and chamois clothes, purses, wallets, and belts. There is another branch in the Galerías Pacífico mall. Av. Santa Fe 1601. ℰ **11/4811-1965.** Metro: Bulnes.

WINE SHOPS

Argentine wineries, particularly those in Mendoza and Salta, produce some excellent wines. Stores selling Argentina wines abound, and three of the best are **Grand Cru,** Av. Alvear 1718; **Tonel Privado,** in the Patio Bullrich Shopping Mall; and **Winery,** which has branches at L.N. Alem 880 and Av. Del Libertador 500, both downtown.

6 Buenos Aires After Dark

From the Teatro Colón (Colón Theater) to dimly lit tango salons, Buenos Aires offers an exceptional variety of nightlife. Porteños eat late and play later, with theater performances starting around 9pm, bars and nightclubs opening around midnight, and no one showing up until after 1am. Thursday, Friday, and Saturday are the big going-out nights, with the bulk of activity in Recoleta, Palermo, and Costanera. Summer is quieter because most of the town flees to the coast.

Performing arts in Buenos Aires are centered on the highly regarded Teatro Colón, home to the National Opera, National Symphony, and National Ballet. In addition, there are nearly 40 professional theaters around town (many located along Av. Corrientes between 9 de Julio and Callao and in the San Telmo and Abasto neighborhoods) showing Broadway- and off-Broadway-style hits, Argentine plays, and music reviews, although most are in Spanish. Buy tickets for most productions at the box office or through **Ticketmaster** (ℰ **11/4321-9700**). The **British Arts Centre,** Suipacha 1333 (ℰ **11/4393-0275**), offers productions in English.

> ## *Moments* Tango: Lessons in the Dance of Seduction & Despair
>
> It seems impossible to imagine Argentina without thinking of tango, its greatest export to the world. Tango originated with a guitar and violin toward the end of the 19th century and was first danced by working-class men in La Boca, San Telmo, and the port area. Combining African rhythms with the *habanera* and *candombe,* it was not the sophisticated dance you know today—rather, the tango originated in brothels and was accompanied by obscene lyrics.
>
> Increasing waves of immigrants helped the tango make its way to Europe, however, and the dance was internationalized in Paris. With a sense of European approval, Argentine middle and upper classes began to accept the newly refined dance as part of their cultural identity, and the form blossomed under the extraordinary voice of Carlos Gardel, who brought tango to Broadway and Hollywood, and is nothing short of legendary among Argentines. Astor Piazzola further internationalized the tango, elevating it to a more complex form incorporating classical elements.
>
> Tango may be played by anywhere from two musicians to a complete orchestra, but a piano and *bandoneón*—an instrument akin to an accordion—are usually included. If there is a singer, the lyrics might come from one of Argentina's great poets, such as Jorge Luis Borges, Homero Manzi, or Horacio Ferrer. The dance itself is improvised rather than standardized, although it consists of a series of long walks and intertwined movements, usually in eight-step. In the tango, the man and woman glide across the floor as an exquisitely orchestrated duo with early flirtatious movements giving way to dramatic leads and heartfelt turns.

For current information on after-dark entertainment, consult the *Buenos Aires Herald* (in English) or any of the major local publications. The "QuickGuide Buenos Aires" also has information on shows, theaters, and nightclubs.

THE PERFORMING ARTS
OPERA, BALLET & CLASSICAL MUSIC

Luna Park   Once the home of international boxing matches, the Luna is the largest indoor stadium in Argentina and hosts the biggest shows and concerts in Buenos Aires. Many of these are classical music concerts, and the National Symphonic Orchestra often plays here. Av. Corrientes and Bouchard. ✆ **11/4311-1990.** Metro: L.N. Alem.

Teatro Colón   Known across the world for its impeccable acoustics, the Colón has attracted the world's finest opera performers—Luciano Pavarotti, Julio Bocca, Maria Callas, Plácido Domingo, and Arturo Toscanini among them. Opera season runs from April to November, and the Colón has its own philharmonic orchestra, ballet, and choir companies. The main theater seats 2,500. Calle Libertad 621. ✆ **11/4378-7100.** Metro: Tribunales.

Learning to dance the tango is an excellent way for a visitor to get a sense of what makes the music—and the dance—so alluring. Entering a tango salon—called a *salon de baile*—can be intimidating for the novice. The style of tango danced in salons is more subdued than "show tango." Most respectable dancers would not show up before midnight, giving you the perfect opportunity to sneak in for a group lesson, offered at most of the salons starting around 8 or 9pm. They usually cost between $1 and $3 for an hour; you can request private instruction for between $10 and $20 per hour, depending on the instructor. In summer, the city of Buenos Aires promotes tango by offering free classes in many locations. Visit the nearest tourist information center for updated information.

For additional advice on places to dance and learn tango, get a copy of *B.A. Tango* or *El Tangauta*, the city's dedicated tango magazines. One of the best spots to learn is **Gricel,** La Rioja 1180 (© **11/4957-7157**), which offers lessons Monday through Friday at 8pm and opens its doors to the city's best dancers on Saturday and Sunday nights. **La Galería,** Boedo 722 (© **11/4957-1829**), is open Thursday, Saturday, and Sunday and attracts excellent dancers, many of whom compete professionally. **Ideal,** Suipacha 384 (© **11/4326-1081**), is open Monday, Wednesday, and Friday. The dancers here come in all ages and have varied abilities. Ongoing evening lessons are also offered at the **Academia Nacional de Tango,** Av. de Mayo 833 (© **11/4345-6968**), which is an institute rather than a tango salon.

THEATERS & EXHIBITIONS

The city's best theater takes place at the **Teatro Nacional Cervantes,** Calle Libertad 815 (© **11/4816-4224**). **Teatro Opera,** Av. Corrientes 860 (© **11/4326-1335**), has been adapted for Broadway-style shows. The **Teatro Municipal General San Martín,** Av. Corrientes 1530 (© **0800/333-5254**), has three theaters offering drama, comedy, ballet, music, and children's plays. In Recoleta, **Teatro Coliseo,** Marcelo T. de Alvear 1125 (© **11/4816-5943**), puts on classical music productions. **Teatro Presidente Alvear,** Av. Corrientes 1659 (© **11/4374-6076**), features tango and other music shows. The majority of foreign and national music concerts are held at the **Teatro Gran Rex,** Av. Corrientes 857 (© **11/4322-8000**).

Centro Cultural Recoleta (Recoleta Cultural Center) The distinctive building—originally designed as a Franciscan convent—hosts Argentine and international art exhibits, experimental theater works, occasional music concerts, and an interactive science museum for children. The Hard Rock Cafe is located behind the Cultural Center. Junín 1930. © **11/4803-1041.**

THE CLUB & MUSIC SCENE
TANGO CLUBS

In Buenos Aires, you can *watch* the tango or *dance* the tango. You'll have many opportunities to see the dance during your visit: Tango and *milonga* dancers frequent the streets of La Boca and San Telmo, some hotels offer tango shows in their lobbies and bars, and tango salons blanket the city. The most famous (besides Café Tortoni) are in San Telmo and combine dinner and show. Have a radio-taxi or *remise* take you to San Telmo, La Boca, or Barracas at night, rather than taking the metro or walking.

Café Tortoni   High-quality yet inexpensive tango shows are held in the back room of the Café Tortoni and do not include dinner. There is a show every day except Tuesday at 9pm. Av. de Mayo 829. ℂ 11/4342-4328. Metro: Plaza de Mayo.

El Querandí   Some people swear that El Querandí offers the best package in the city—a good meal of Argentine beef and wine with an excellent tango show. Open Monday through Saturday, dinner begins at 8:30pm followed by the show at 10:15pm. Perú 302. ℂ 11/4345-0331.

El Viejo Almacén   The most famous of the city's tango salons, the Almacén offers what some consider the city's most authentic performance. Shows involve traditional Argentine-style tango (many other shows feature international-style tango). Sunday through Thursday shows are at 10pm; Friday and Saturday shows are at 9:30 and 11:45pm. Dinner is served each night before the show starts (guests may opt for dinner-show or show only). Transportation is offered from some downtown hotels. Independencia and Balcarce. ℂ 11/4307-6689.

Esquina Carlos Gardel   One of the city's newest tango spots, Esquina Carlos Gardel lies in the same location where "Chanta Cuatro"—a restaurant where Carlos Gardel used to dine with his friends—was located. The luxurious old-time dining room features high-tech acoustics and superb dancers, creating a wonderful tango environment. Doors open at 8pm. Carlos Gardel 3200. ℂ 11/4876-6363.

Recoleta Tango   Opened in December 2002, this small, intimate tango bar next to the Alvear Palace Hotel is reminiscent of a tango salon of the 1940s. Dancers interact with members of the audience in what is destined to become one of the city's sleekest shows. Dinner-shows begin at 8pm. Bring your dancing shoes! Av. Alvear 1885. ℂ 11/4808-0600.

Señor Tango   This enormous theater is more akin to a Broadway production hall than a traditional tango salon, but the dancers are fantastic and the owner, who clearly loves to perform, is a good singer. The walls are decorated with photos of what appear to be every celebrity who's ever visited Buenos Aires—and all seem to have made it to Señor Tango! Diners choose between steak, chicken, or fish for dinner and, despite the huge crowd, the food quality is commendable. Have dinner or come only for the show (dinner is at 8:30pm; shows start at 10pm). Vieytes 1653. ℂ 11/4303-0212.

OTHER DANCE CLUBS

Dancing in Buenos Aires is not just about tango; the majority of the younger population prefers salsa and European beats. Of course, nothing in life changes quite so fast as the "in" discos, so ask around for the latest hot spots. The biggest nights out are Thursday, Friday, and Saturday. Here are some of the hottest clubs as this book went to press: **Opera Bay,** Cecilia Grierson 225 in Puerto Madero, boasts the top spot among the city's clubs, attracting an affluent and fashionable crowd. Built along the waterfront and resembling the Sydney opera house, Opera Bay features an international restaurant, tango show, and disco. The city's best salsa dancers head to **Salsón,** Av. Alvarez Thomas 1166 (© **11/4637-6970**), which offers lessons on Wednesday and Friday at 9pm. In Palermo, **Buenos Aires News,** Av. del Libertador 3883 (© **11/4778-1500**), is a rocking late-night club with Latin and European mixes. **Tequila,** Costanera Norte and La Pampa (© **11/4788-0438**), is packed every night. There are a number of popular discos nearby, as well. The most popular gay and lesbian club is **Amerika,** Gascón 1040 (© **11/4865-4416**), which has three floors of dance music and all-you-can-drink specials on Friday and Saturday.

THE BAR SCENE

There is no shortage of popular bars in Buenos Aires, and Porteños need little excuse to party. The following are only a few of many bars and pubs worthy of recommendation.

Chandon Bar   This intimate champagne lounge serves bottles and flutes of Chandon, produced in both France and Argentina. Located in Puerto Madero adjacent to some of the city's best restaurants, Chandon is perfect for a before- or after-dinner drink. Light fare is offered as well. Av. Alicia Moreau de Justo 152. © **11/4315-3533.** Metro: L.N. Alem.

Gran Bar Danzon   A small intimate bar, Danzon attracts a fashionable crowd. An excellent barman serves exquisite cocktails, and a small selection of international food is offered as well. Smart, relaxing lounge music is played at night. Libertad 1161. © **11/4811-1108.**

Henry J. Beans   A favorite of the expat-American community and visiting foreigners, this casual Recoleta bar serves burgers, sandwiches, and nachos, along with cocktails and beer. Old Coca-Cola ads, Miller and Budweiser neon signs, and model airplanes hang from the ceilings. The waiters do occasional impromptu dances, and the place is packed after midnight. There are a number of other popular restaurants, bars, and discos along Junín. Junín 1749. © **11/4801-8477.**

The Kilkenny   This trendy cafe-bar is more like a rock house than an Irish pub, although you will still be able to order Guinness, Kilkenny, and Harp draft beers. Packed with both locals and foreigners, you are as likely to find people in suits and ties as in jeans and T-shirts. The Kilkenny offers happy hour from 6 to 8pm and live bands every night after midnight; it stays open until 5am. A new whisky bar has opened on the first floor. Marcelo T. de Alvear 399. © **11/4312-9179** or © 11/4312-7291. Metro: San Martín.

Plaza Bar   Nearly every Argentine president and his cabinet have come here, as well as visiting celebs such as the queen of Spain, the emperor of Japan, Luciano Pavarotti, and David Copperfield. The English-style bar features mahogany furniture and velvet upholstery, where guests can sip martinis and smoke Cuban cigars. Tuxedo-clad waiters recommend a fine selection of whiskies and brandies. Marriott Plaza Hotel, Calle Florida 1005. © **11/4318-3000.** Metro: San Martín.

Plaza Dorrego Bar ⭐   Representative of a typical Porteño bar from the 19th century, Plaza Dorrego displays portraits of Carlos Gardel, antique liquor bottles in cases along the walls, and anonymous writings engraved in the wood.

Feel Like a Movie?

Buenos Aires has over 250 movie theaters showing Argentine and international films. One of the best is the 16-theater **Village Recoleta,** V. López and Junín (℗ **11/4805-2220**). There are also cinemas at the **Alto Palermo,** Av. Santa Fe 3251 (℗ **11/4827-8000**), and **Galerías Pacífico,** Calle Florida 753 (℗ **11/4319-5357**), shopping malls. Most films are American and shown in English with Spanish subtitles, but some are Argentine films, which are not subtitled. Check the *Buenos Aires Herald* for current film listings. Every April, Buenos Aires hosts an international **independent film festival** (www.bafilmfest.com).

Stop by on Sunday, when you can catch the San Telmo antiques market on the plaza in front. Calle Defensa 1098. ℗ **11/4361-0141.** Metro: Constitución.

The Shamrock The city's best-known Irish pub is somewhat lacking in authenticity; you're more likely to hear hot Latin rhythms than soft Gaelic music here. That said, it remains hugely popular with both Argentines and foreign visitors, and is a great spot to begin the night. Rodríguez Peña 1220. ℗ **11/4812-3584.** Metro: Callao.

7 A Side Trip from Buenos Aires: Mar del Plata

400km (248 miles) south of Buenos Aires

Argentina's most popular beach resort is a sleepy coastal town until mid-December, when Porteños flock here through March for summer vacation. Although not as luxurious as Uruguay's Punta del Este—the beach favorite of many jet-setting Argentines—Mar del Plata is closer to Buenos Aires and far cheaper to reach. Its long, windy coastline offers crowded tan-bodied beaches and quieter seaside coves, as well as beautiful landscapes further inland leading to the Pampas. Within Mar del Plata, a number of high-rise developments, products of the Perón era, sadly have replaced much of the city's earlier charm. However, some of the magnificent French-style residences, which housed Argentina's summer elites in the early 20th century, have been meticulously preserved as museums. Mar del Plata offers excellent nightlife in summer, when independent theater companies from Buenos Aires travel to this seaside resort and nightclubs open their doors to passionate Latin party-goers.

ESSENTIALS

GETTING THERE You can reach Mar del Plata by plane, bus, car, train, or boat. The airport lies ten minutes from downtown and is served by **Aerolíneas Argentinas** (jets) and **Aerovip** (prop planes). The RN2 is the main highway from Buenos Aires; it takes about 4 to 5 hours to drive to Mar del Plata. More than 50 bus companies link the city with the rest of the country. Buses to Buenos Aires, which leave from the central bus terminal at Alberti 1602 (℗ **223/451-5406**), are comfortable and cost under $15 each way. A train also connects Mar del Plata with Buenos Aires and is only slightly more expensive than buses. Purchase tickets at the train station, located at Avenida Luro and Italia (℗ **223/475-6076**). Bus and train trips also take about 4 to 5 hours.

VISITOR INFORMATION The **Centro de Información Turística,** Bulevar Marítimo P.P. Ramos 2270, at the Casino building (℗ **223/495-1777**), has a knowledgeable, helpful staff offering maps and suggested itineraries. It is open daily from 10am to 5pm (until 8pm in summer). There is also a branch at the airport. You can visit their website at www.mardelplata.gov.ar.

GETTING AROUND   La Rambla marks the heart of the city, the seaside walk in front of the Casino and main city beach. Farther south, the Los Tronces neighborhood houses the city's most prominent residences as well as Playa Grande (the main beach), the Sheraton hotel, and the Mar del Plata Golf Club. Mar del Plata has 47km (29 miles) of Atlantic coastline, so if you plan to leave your hotel you'll need to take a taxi or rent a car. **Avis** (© **223/470-2100**) rents cars at the airport.

WHAT TO SEE & DO

People come first and foremost to Mar del Plata for the beaches, the best of which is **Playa Grande.** A long cluster of cliffs and dunes lead to more serene southern beaches. With long, slow breaks, **Waikiki** is the best spot for surfing. The coastline is nice, but you should not come expecting to find the Caribbean—the Atlantic remains fairly cold, even during summer. Once you've brushed off the sand, visit the **fishing harbor,** where hundreds of red and yellow boats unload their daily catches. The harbor houses a colony of 800 male sea lions that come to bathe on the rocky shores. Next to the colony, there's an ugly but intriguing boat graveyard, where rusty boats have been left to rest. The harbor also offers the town's best seafood restaurants. In the Los Tronces neighborhood, **Villa Victoria,** at Matheu 1851 (© **223/492-0569**) showcases the early-20th-century summer house—all of which came from England—of a wealthy Argentine writer, Victoria Ocampo. Some of Argentina's greatest authors have stayed here, including Jorge Luis Borges. In summer, musical and theatrical performances are held in the gardens. Nearby, **Villa Ortiz Basualdo,** Av. Colón 1189 (© **223/486-1636**), resembles a Loire castle and is decorated with exquisite Art Nouveau furniture from Belgium. In the same neighborhood, the **Museo del Mar,** Av. Colón 1114 (© **223/451-9779**), shelters a collection of 30,000 seashells. Twenty minutes from the city center, **De los Padres Lake and Hills** is a picturesque forest with wide parks surrounding the lake, perfect for an afternoon picnic. Nearby, the **Zoo el Paraíso,** Ruta 266, Km 16.5 (© **223/463-0347**), features a wonderful collection of flora and fauna, including plants and trees from all over Argentina as well as lions, pumas, monkeys, llamas, and other animals. For information on surfing, deep-sea fishing, mountain biking, horseback riding, trekking, and other adventure sports, contact the tourism office.

WHERE TO STAY

Sheraton ★★   It may not be the most modern Sheraton, but it is the city's best hotel by far. Built on a golf course, the Sheraton faces the ocean and is a quick hop to Mar del Plata's best beach, Playa Grande. The fishing harbor is also just down the road. A full-scale heath club leads out to the beautiful pool, next to which is a small outdoor cafe. Rooms are light-filled and well-equipped; suites have Jacuzzi tubs. The staff will help you arrange outdoor activities, including a tee-time, upon request.

Alem 4221. 7600 Mar del Plata. © **0800/777-7002,** or 223/499-9000. Fax 223/499-0009. 193 units. $110 double with city view; $130 double with ocean view. Rates include buffet breakfast. AE, DC, MC, V. **Amenities:** Restaurant; bar; health club with heated outdoor pool; golf; concierge; business center; room service; massage service; dry cleaning and laundry service. *In room:* A/C, TV, minibar, hair dryer, safe.

WHERE TO DINE

La Marca ★★ ARGENTINE   A few times a year, the chefs cook an entire cow for a mesmerized dining room. The rest of the year, La Marca simply acts as the town's best *parrilla,* serving thick rump steaks, tenderloins, barbecued ribs of beef, flanks, and every other cut of meat you can think of. The tender filet mignon with mushroom sauce is delicious. Pork chops, sausages, sweetbread, black pudding, and other delights are on the menu as well. An extensive salad bar allows you to eat something other than protein. Service is polite and unhurried. Try the *dulce de leche* before you go.

Almafuerte 253. (✆ 223/451-8072. Main courses $3–$6. AE, DC, MC, V. Daily noon–3pm and 8:30pm–1am.

MAR DEL PLATA AFTER DARK

Nightlife follows closely behind beaches as Mar del Plata's biggest draw. In summer, theater companies leave Buenos Aires to perform in this coastal resort; ask the tourism office for a schedule of performance times and places. The city's most popular bars are located south of Plaza Mitre. The best dance clubs are along Avenida Constitución, 3km (2 miles) from downtown, including **Chocolate,** Constitución 4451 (✆ 223/479-4848). The other top clubs are: **Divino Beach,** Paseo Costanero Sur Presidente Illia (✆ 223/467-1506), **Go!,** Av. Constitución 5780 (✆ 223/479-6666), and **Sobremonte,** Av. Constitución 6690 (✆ 223/479-7930). **Amsterdam,** Castilli 3045 (✆ 15/527-8606), is the best gay disco. **Coyote,** Av. Constitución 6670 (✆ 223/479-7930), is a favorite local bar that breaks into salsa and merengue as the night goes on.

4

Iguazú Falls

A dazzling panorama of cascades whose power overwhelms the sounds of the surrounding jungle, Las Cataratas del Iguazú (Iguazú Falls) refers to the spectacular canyon of waterfalls fed by the Río Iguazú. Declared a World Heritage Area by UNESCO in 1984, these 275 waterfalls were shaped by 120 million years of geological history and form one of earth's most unforgettable sights. Iguazú Falls are shared by Argentina and Brazil and are easily accessible from nearby Paraguay. Excellent walking circuits on both the Argentine and Brazilian sides allow visitors to peek over the tops of or stare at the faces of raging sheets of water, some with sprays so intense it seems as though geysers have erupted from below. Although a five-star hotel overlooking the falls exists in both the Argentine and Brazilian national parks, visitors looking for less expensive accommodations often stay in the towns of Puerto Iguazú in Argentina or Foz do Iguaçu in Brazil.

While Iguazú is best known for its waterfalls, consider including the surrounding subtropical jungle in your itinerary (see "Behind the Falls & into the Iguazú Jungle," below). Here, *cupay* trees (South American hardwoods) tower over the various layers of life that compete for light, and the national park is known to contain 200 species of trees, 448 species of birds, 71 species of mammals, 36 species of reptiles, 20 species of amphibians, and more than 250 species of butterflies. Spray from the waterfall keeps the humidity levels over 75%, leading to a tremendous growth of epiphytes (plants that grow on other plants without taking nutrients from their hosts). Iguazú's climate also provides for the flowering of plants year-round, lending brilliant color to the forest.

You can visit the waterfalls on your own, but you will most certainly need a tour operator to explore the jungle. Allow at least 1 full day to explore the waterfalls on the Argentine side, another to visit the Brazilian side, and perhaps half a day for a jungle tour.

1 Puerto Iguazú

1330km (825 miles) NE of Buenos Aires

This sedate town serves as the main base from which to explore Iguazú National Park, 18km (11 miles) away. It is smaller and safer than its Brazilian counterpart, Foz do Iguaçu, and the hotels and restaurants here are inexpensive and commendable. Foz do Iguaçu offers better nightlife, however.

ESSENTIALS
GETTING THERE
BY PLANE Aerolíneas Argentinas (© 3757/420-194) and **LAPA** (© 3757/420-390) fly daily from Buenos Aires to **Aeropuerto Internacional Cataratas**

del Iguazú; the trip takes 1½ hours. Round-trip fares range from about $100 to $300, depending on whether any specials are offered. Catch a taxi or one of the shuttle buses from the airport to town, a 20-minute drive.

BY BUS   The fastest bus service from Buenos Aires is with **Vía Bariloche** (© 011/4315-4456 in Buenos Aires), which takes 16 hours for $75 one-way. Less expensive but longer (21 hr.) are **Expreso Singer** (© 011/4313-3927 in Buenos Aires) and **Expreso Tigre Iguazú** (© 011/4313-3915 in Buenos Aires).

VISITOR INFORMATION

In Puerto Iguazú, obtain maps and park information from the **Parque Nacional** office at Victoria Aguirre 66 (© 3757/420-722), open Monday through Friday from 8am to 2pm. For information on the town, contact the **municipal tourist office,** at Victoria Aguirre and Brañas (© 3757/420-800). It's open daily from 8am to 8pm. Visitor information is also available near the national park entrance (see below).

In Buenos Aires, get information about Iguazú from **Casa de la Provincia de Misiones,** Av. Santa Fe 989 (© 011/4322-0686), open Monday through Friday from 10am to 5pm.

GETTING AROUND

El Práctico local buses run every 45 minutes from 7am to 8pm between Puerto Iguazú and the national park, and cost less than $1. **Parada 10** (© 3757/421-527) provides 24-hour taxi service. You can rent a car at the airport, although this is much more a luxury than a necessity. Within both Puerto Iguazú and the national park, you can easily walk.

VISITING THE NATIONAL PARK

Your first stop will likely be the **visitor center,** where you can get maps and information about the area's flora and fauna. Recently opened are a new, environmentally friendly visitor center 1km (½ mile) from the park entrance (next to the parking lot), and new footbridges for the waterfall circuits. Next to the visitor center, you will find a restaurant, snack shops, and souvenir stores. A natural gas train takes visitors to the path entrance for the Upper and Lower Circuits and to the footbridge leading to the Devil's Throat (footpaths remain open for walkers, but the walk to Devil's Throat is about 3km/1¾ miles). The visitor center is staffed with a number of English-speaking guides, available for individual and private tours—you may opt to see the falls on your own or with an experienced local guide. There is an $8 entrance fee for non-Argentines to enter the national park, which includes the train ride. The national park is open from 8am to 7pm in summer, and until 6pm in winter.

The two main paths to view the waterfalls are the **Circuito Superior (Upper Circuit)** 🐦 and the **Circuito Inferior (Lower Circuit)** 🐦, both of which begin within walking distance of the visitor center. There's a small snack shop near the beginning of the trails. The Upper Circuit winds its way along the top of the canyon, allowing you to look down the falls and see the area's rich flora, including cacti, ferns, and orchids. The Lower Circuit offers the best views, as magnificent waterfalls come hurtling down before you in walls of silvery spray. The waterfalls are clearly marked by signs along the way.

The best time to walk the **Upper Circuit** is early in the morning or late in the afternoon, and rainbows often appear near sunset. This .9km (½-mile) path

The Iguazú Falls Region

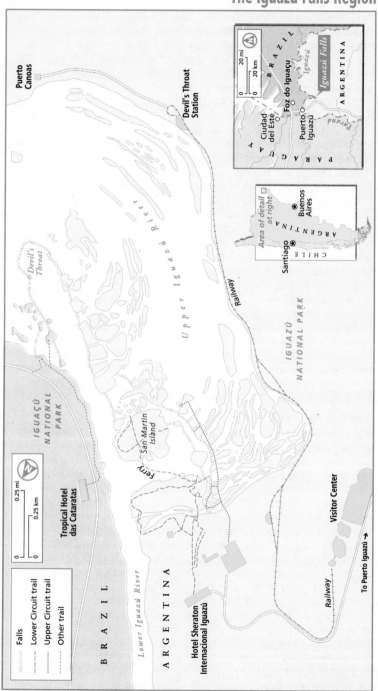

Puerto Canoas

Devil's Throat Station

Inset map:

20 mi
20 km

B R A Z I L

Iguazú Falls

Foz do Iguaçu

Ciudad del Este

Puerto Iguazú

A R G E N T I N A

P A R A G U A Y

Paraná

Area of detail at right

Buenos Aires

A R G E N T I N A

C H I L E

Santiago

Main map:

Devil's Throat

Upper Iguazú River

Railway

IGUAZÚ NATIONAL PARK

IGUAÇU NATIONAL PARK

San Martin Island

Ferry

Tropical Hotel das Cataratas

0   0.25 mi
0   0.25 km

BRAZIL

Lower Iguazú River

ARGENTINA

Hotel Sheraton Internacional Iguazú

Visitor Center

Railway

To Puerto Iguazú →

Legend:

Falls
Lower Circuit trail
Upper Circuit trail
Other trail

takes 1 to 2 hours, starting at the viewing tower and leading past **Dos Hermanos (Two Brothers), Bossetti, Chico (Small), Ramírez,** and **San Martín** (the park's widest) falls. You can come right to the edges of these falls and look over them as they fall as far as 60m (200 ft.) below. Along your walk, you can also look across to San Martín Island and the Brazilian side, and you'll pass a number of small streams and creeks.

The 1.8km (1 mile) **Lower Circuit** takes 2 hours to walk, leading you first past **Lanusse** and **Alvar Núñez** falls, then along the Lower Iguazú River past the raging **Dos Mosqueteros (Two Musketeers)** and **Tres Mosqueteros (Three Musketeers)** falls. The trail winds its way toward **Ramírez, Chico,** and **Dos Hermanos** falls. Here, you'll find an inspiring view of the **Garganta del Diablo (Devil's Throat)** and **Bossetti** falls. From the Salto Bossetti, a small pathway leads down to a small pier where you can catch a free boat to **San Martín Island.**

Once on the island, climb the stairs and walk along clearly marked trails for remarkable views of the surrounding *cataratas*—to the left, you see the enormous **Garganta del Diablo, Saltos Brasileros (Brazilian Falls),** and **Ventana;** to the right, you overlook the mighty **Salto San Martín,** which sprays 30m (100 ft.) high after hitting the river below. This panoramic view looks out at dozens of falls forming an arch before you. San Martín Island also has a small, idyllic beach perfect for sunbathing and swimming.

Garganta del Diablo is the mother of all waterfalls in Iguazú, visible from vantage points in both the Brazilian and Argentine parks. Cross the walking bridge to the observation point, at the top of Garganta del Diablo: The water is calm as it makes its way down the Iguazú River, then begins to speed up as it approaches the gorge ahead. In front of you, Mother Nature has created a furious avalanche of water and spray that is the highest waterfall in Iguazú and one of the world's greatest natural spectacles. You might want to bring a raincoat—you *will* get wet.

TOUR OPERATORS

The area's main tour operator is **Iguazú Jungle Explorer** (© 3757/421-696), located both inside the national park and in the Sheraton International Iguazú. This company offers a "Nautical Adventure" ($9) that visits the falls by inflatable raft, an "Ecological Tour" ($5) that takes you to Devil's Throat and lets you paddle rubber boats along the Upper Iguazú Delta, and the *Gran Aventura* (Great Adventure) tour ($20). This last tour begins with a 8km (5-mile) safari ride along the Yacoratia Path, the original dirt road that led through the forest and on to Buenos Aires. During the ride, you'll view the jungle's extensive flora and might catch a glimpse of some of the region's indigenous wildlife (see "Behind the Falls and into the Iguazú Jungle," below). You will then be let off at Puerto Macuco, where you hop into an inflatable boat with your tour group and navigate 6.5km (4 miles) along the lower Iguazú River, braving 1.6km (1 mile) of rapids as you approach the falls in Devil's Throat Canyon. After a thrilling and wet ride, the raft lets you off across from San Martín Island—from there, catch a free boat to this island with excellent hiking trails and a small beach for swimming and sunbathing. You can combine the Ecological Tour and Great Adventure by buying a full-day Pasaporte Verde ($23).

If you want to arrange a private tour for your specific interests, the best outfit is **Explorador Expediciones,** with offices in the Sheraton International Iguazú and in Puerto Iguazú at Puerto Moreno 217 (© 3757/421-632). The guides are experts on life in the Iguazú jungle.

Behind the Falls & into the Iguazú Jungle

Dawn in Iguazú brings the first rays of light through the forest canopy, as orchids, butterflies, frogs, lizards, parrots, and monkeys wake and spread color and life through the forest. Binoculars in hand, step softly into this wonderland, where most sounds are masked by the roar from the falls.

You see parakeets long before entering the jungle. Their green bodies and loud song make them easy to spot; macaws, parrots, and toucans are other feathered residents. Look and listen carefully for the great dusky swift, which nests near the waterfalls, and the great kiskadee, whose family name—*Tyrannidae*—tells much about this yellow-breasted bird's hunting prowess. Look below the canopy to observe other flying wonders of the park—an enormous population of butterflies. Brilliant blue flyers known as morpho butterflies flit between deciduous trees and above lines of leaf-cutter ants, along with beautiful red, black, and yellow species of butterflies.

It's close to impossible to walk through the park without running across some of the area's indigenous reptiles. The ubiquitous tropidurus lizards, which feed on bird eggs, scamper everywhere, while colorful tree frogs hop and croak the nights away. Larger and rarer creatures, such as the 1.5m (5-ft.) long tegu lizard and the caiman, a crocodile-like reptile, are discovered only by the patient and persistent visitor.

Warm-blooded creatures share the forest as well. Coatis—aardvark-like mammals that travel in groups searching for insects and fruit—are frequent and fearless visitors to the trails. Swinging above the footpaths are brown capuchin monkeys, whose chatter and gestures make them seem more human than most primates. The predators of this warm-blooded group range from vampire bats to endangered jaguars and pumas. Stay on the walking paths and, when in the jungle, with your tour operator.

An array of subtropical flora surrounds Iguazú's resident animals and insects. Bamboo, ficus, fig, and ancient rosewood trees—up to 1,000 years old—are but a few of the trees that grow near the river and compete for light, and there is a proliferation of epiphytes (plants growing on others) such as bromeliads, güembés, and orchids. In fact, 85 species of orchid thrive in the park, mostly close to the damp and well-lit waterfalls.

WHERE TO STAY

Peak season for hotels in Iguazú extends through January and February (summer holiday), and also includes July (winter break), Semana Santa (Holy Week, the week before Easter), and long weekends. On the Argentine side, the Sheraton International Iguazú is the only hotel inside the national park; the rest lie in Puerto Iguazú, 18km (11 miles) away. You can usually find discounts in the off-season.

EXPENSIVE

Hotel Cataratas ★★ *Kids*   Although it's not located next to the falls, Hotel Cataratas deserves consideration for its excellent service, from the helpful receptionists to the meticulous housekeepers. None of the stuffiness you sometimes feel at luxury hotels is evident. Despite the hotel's unimpressive exterior, rooms are among the most modern and spacious in the area—especially the 30 "master rooms" that feature two double beds, handsome wood furniture, colorful artwork, large bathrooms with separate toilet rooms, in-room safes, and views of the pool or gardens (these rooms are only slightly more than the standard rooms—called "superior"—and the staff is often willing to offer promotional rates). The hotel's many facilities, including outdoor pool, spa, tennis and volleyball courts, putting green, playroom, and gymnasium make this a great choice for families. The Cataratas restaurant offers a fine selection of regional and international dishes, and you can dine inside or out. The hotel lies 4km (2½ miles) from the center of Puerto Iguazú and 17km (11 miles) from the national park entrance. Bus service is available.

Ruta 12, Km 4, 3370 Misiones. © **3757/421-100.** Fax 3757/421-090. www.hotelcataratas.com.ar. 111 units. $100 double; from $150 suite. Rates include buffet breakfast. AE, DC, MC, V. **Amenities:** Restaurant; outdoor pool; tennis court; putting green; spa; Jacuzzi; sauna; game room; concierge; conference room; secretarial services; room service; massage; laundry service; twice-daily maid service. *In room:* A/C, TV, minibar, hair dryer, safe.

Sheraton Internacional Iguazú ★★   Once the famous Internacional Cataratas de Iguazú, the Sheraton enjoys a magnificent location inside the national park. Guests have little need to leave the resort, a self-contained paradise overlooking the falls. The hotel lies only steps from the Upper and Lower Circuit trails, and half of the guest rooms have direct views of the water (the others have splendid views of the jungle). The only drawback to the rooms is that they are fairly standard Sheraton decor. There are three restaurants, including the stunning Garganta del Diablo that peers over the Devil's Throat and serves outstanding, if pricy, international dishes. The hotel also offers numerous daytime activities, including swimming, golf, tennis, shopping, and access to national park tour operators. If you're making the trip all the way to Iguazú, you should seriously consider staying inside the national park at this hotel.

Parque Nacional Iguazú, 3370 Misiones. © **0800/888-9180** local toll free, or 3757/491-800. Fax 3757/491-848. www.sheraton.com. 180 units. $170 double with jungle view; $210 double with view of waterfalls; from $350 suite. Rates include buffet breakfast. AE, DC, MC, V. **Amenities:** 3 restaurants; outdoor pool; 2 tennis courts; fitness center; concierge; car rental; conference rooms; shopping; room service; babysitting; laundry service. *In room:* A/C, TV, minibar, hair dryer, safe.

MODERATE

Hotel Saint George ★ *Finds*   A modest hotel in the heart of Puerto Iguazú, the Saint George features colorful rooms with single beds, an inviting pool surrounded by lush vegetation, and a commendable international restaurant that serves tasty fish from the local river. The friendly and enthusiastic staff will answer questions about the national park and help arrange tours if requested.

Av. Córdoba 148, 3370 Puerto Iguazú. © **3757/420-633.** Fax 3757/420-651. 56 units. $30 double. Rate includes buffet breakfast. AE, DC, MC, V. **Amenities:** Restaurant; pool. *In room:* A/C, TV, minibar.

INEXPENSIVE

Los Helechos *Value*   Los Helechos is a great bargain for those seeking comfortable, inexpensive accommodations in Puerto Iguazú. Located in the city center, this intimate hotel offers simple rooms, many of which surround a plant-filled courtyard and offer a sense of sleeping near the jungle.

Paulino Amarante 76, 3370 Puerto Iguazú. (C)/fax **3757/420-338**. 54 units. $10 double. AE, DC, MC, V. **Amenities:** Restaurant; bar; pool. *In room:* A/C, TV (in some rooms).

WHERE TO DINE

Dining in Puerto Iguazú is casual and inexpensive, provided you're looking for a meal outside your hotel. Argentine steaks, seafood, and pasta are common on most menus. The Sheraton, inside the national park, has the area's best restaurant.

EXPENSIVE

Garganta del Diablo ★★ INTERNATIONAL   Located inside the national park at the Sheraton Internacional Iguazú, this inspiring restaurant serves excellent international and regional dishes. Open for nearly 25 years, the restaurant is best known for its magnificent view of the Devil's Throat. Enjoy a romantic table for two overlooking the falls, and consider the grilled *suribí* (a mild fish from the river in front of you) or *bife de chorizo* (a New York strip steak).

Parque Nacional Iguazú. (C) **3757/491-800**. Main courses $8–$12. AE, DC, MC, V. Daily noon–3 and 7–11pm.

INEXPENSIVE

El Charo *Finds* ARGENTINE   El Charo is a shambles of a restaurant: Its sagging roof is missing a number of wood beams, pictures hang crooked on the walls, and the bindings on the menus are falling apart. Consider it part of the charm. The casual, cozy restaurant offers cheap, delicious food and is tremendously popular with both tourists and locals. Among the main dishes, you'll find breaded veal, sirloin steaks, pork chops, catfish, and items from the *parrilla* (grill). There are also salads and pastas such as ravioli and cannelloni.

Av. Córdoba 106. (C) **3757/421-529**. Main courses $2–$3. No credit cards. Daily 11am–1am.

La Rueda ★ *Finds* ARGENTINE   Nothing more than a small A-frame house with an outdoor patio, La Rueda is a delightful place to eat. Despite the casual atmosphere, tables have carefully prepared place settings, waiters are attentive and friendly, and the food—served in large portions—is very good. The diverse menu features pasta, steaks, and fish dishes. Try the *serubi brochette,* a local whitefish served with bacon, tomatoes, onions, and peppers, served with green rice and potatoes.

Av. Córdoba 28. (C) **3757/422-531**. Main courses $2–$4. No credit cards. Daily noon–4pm and 7pm–1am.

PUERTO IGUAZU AFTER DARK

Puerto Iguazú offers little in the way of nightlife, although the major hotels—including the Sheraton and Hotel Cataratas—often have live music and other entertainment during peak seasons. Try **La Reserva,** a popular bar-restaurant, or **La Baranca** ((C) **3757/423-295**), a pub with nightly live music. Both are located next to each other at Avenida Tres Fronteras and Costanera. **Casino Iguazú,** Ruta 12, Km 1640 ((C) **3757/498-000**), attracts a well-dressed Argentine and Brazilian crowd and is open weekdays from 2pm to 5am and 24 hours on weekends. Foz do Iguaçu, on the Brazilian side, offers more evening entertainment than Puerto Iguazú (see "Foz do Iguaçu After Dark," below).

2 The Brazilian Side: Foz do Iguaçu

A visit to the Brazilian side of Iguazú Falls affords a dazzling perspective of the waterfalls. Although the trails here are not as extensive as on the Argentine side, the views are no less spectacular. In fact, many people find Brazil's unobstructed panoramic view of Iguazú Falls even more inspiring.

If you decide to stay on the Brazilian side, the Tropical das Cataratas Hotel and Resort (see "Where to Stay," below) is a spectacular hotel at the foot of the national park, overlooking the falls. Alternatively, you could stay in Foz do Iguaçu—the Brazilian counterpart to Puerto Iguazú. Foz is a slightly larger town 25km (16 miles) from Iguaçu National Park with numerous hotels, restaurants, and shops (along with a slightly larger incidence of poverty and street crime).

ESSENTIALS
GETTING THERE
BY PLANE   Varig (© 045/523-2111) and **Vasp** (© 045/523-2212) fly from Rio de Janeiro and other major Brazilian cities to Foz do Iguaçu Airport. The airport lies 11km (7 miles) from Foz do Iguaçu. Public buses make frequent trips to the national park and into town for a small fee.

FROM THE ARGENTINE SIDE   Crossing the border is fairly easy (make sure you bring your passport). The most convenient way to get from the Argentine to the Brazilian side is by taxi (about $25 round-trip). Buses are considerably less expensive, but less convenient, too. **Tres Fronteras** and **El Práctico** buses make the half-hour trip to Foz do Iguaçu 15 times per day ($1) from the Puerto Iguazú bus terminal; to visit the national park, ask the bus driver to let you off just after the border check, then catch the national park bus.

BY CAR   To avoid border hassles and international driving issues, it's best to take a bus or taxi to the Brazilian side.

VISITOR INFORMATION
Foz do Iguaçu's **municipal tourism office,** at Praça Getúlio Vargas (© 045/ 523-8581), is open weekdays from 7am to 11pm. **Teletur** (© 0800/451-516) is a toll-free information service.

SEEING THE BRAZILIAN SIDE OF THE FALLS
The national park entrance to the **Cataratas do Iguaçu** is at Km 17, Rodovía das Cataratas, and the entrance fee is $3. Park your car or get off the bus here and pay your entry fee; private vehicles (except for taxis and guests of the Tropical) are not allowed in the park. From here, you board a shuttle bus bound for the falls. The waterfall path begins just in front of the Tropical das Cataratas Hotel and Resort, which is 11km (7 miles) from the national park entrance (if you are taking a taxi, have your driver bring you directly to the Tropical das Cataratas Hotel and jump onto the trail from here). You will catch your first sight of the falls from a small viewpoint at the foot of the hotel lawn, from which the path begins. The trail zigzags down the side of the gorge and trundles along the cliff face for about 2km (1¼ miles) past **Salto Santa María, Deodoro,** and **Floriano** falls. There are, in fact, 275 separate waterfalls with an average drop of 60m (197 ft.). The last catwalk plants you directly in front of the awesome **Garganta do Diablo (Devil's Throat)** and, once again, you will get wet (there's a small store in front where you can buy rain gear and film). Back on the main trail, a tower beckons visitors to take an elevator to the top for an even broader panoramic view of the falls. The circuit takes about 2 hours.

WHERE TO STAY

As with the hotels on the Argentine side, peak season is January and February (summer holiday), July (winter break), Semana Santa (Holy Week, the week before Easter Sunday), and all long weekends. Rates are often substantially discounted in the off-season.

EXPENSIVE

Bourbon Foz do Iguaçu ★★★ *Kids*   A beautiful resort hotel, the Bourbon is located 2.5km (1½ miles) out of town on the road to the falls. All rooms are beautifully appointed; standard rooms in the original wing have light colors and look out over the front of the hotel, while superior rooms have verandas with views over the pool and lawn. The newer wing houses master suites with modern furnishings and huge windows. But don't count on spending a lot of time in your room; the real draw of the Bourbon is its leisure space. There's a 1.25km (2-mile) trail in the woods behind the hotel; keep an eye out for toucans, parakeets, and the colorful butterflies in the aviary. The vast outdoor pool area includes three large pools, one especially for children with lots of play equipment. In high season, activity leaders organize all-day children's activities in the pool or in the Tarzan house, tucked away in the forest.

Rodovía das Cataratas, Km 2.5, Foz do Iguaçu, 85863-000 PR. ⓒ **0800/451-010** or 045/523-1313. www. bourbon.com.br. 311 units. Standard, Superior, or Master double R$275–R$320 (US$138–US$160). Extra person R$80–R$100 (US$40–US$50). Bus: Parque Nacional or Cataratas. **Amenities:** 3 restaurants; huge pool complex (3 outdoor pools, 1 small indoor pool); outdoor tennis courts lit for evening play; sauna; children's programs; game room; tour desk; concierge; car rental; business center; shopping arcade; salon; room service; massage; laundry service; nonsmoking rooms. *In room:* A/C, TV, dataport (master suites only), minibar, fridge, hair dryer, safe.

Tropical das Cataratas ★★   The Portuguese colonial hotel (called Hotel das Cataratas for most of its existence), built in 1958 and ideally located in the Brazilian national park, is a UNESCO-declared national heritage site. The meticulously kept pink and white buildings on a cliff above the Brazilian falls have hosted an impressive list of princes and princesses, presidents and ministers, artists and celebrities. The hotel is often fully booked, but if you can get a reservation, its spacious corridors and quiet courtyards promise a relaxing vacation. Deluxe and superior rooms, fitted with two-poster beds, granite or marble-top tables, and hardwood floors, are far better than standard rooms; make sure you ask for one that's been refurbished so you don't get stuck with a 50-year-old bathroom. Only the Presidential suite has direct views of the falls; other rooms stare at trees. The trail to the Brazilian falls is just steps from the hotel entrance; when there's a full moon, magical night hikes are arranged. An in-house tour operator arranges ecological tours through the national park and shopping excursions to nearby Paraguay. The hotel has two commendable restaurants serving Brazilian and international food. Restaurante Itaipu is the more formal choice, while the outdoor Ipe Bar & Grill offers evening entertainment. Although the national park closes to the public after 7pm, people wanting to come for dinner at the hotel can get a special after-hours pass at the park entrance.

Parque Nacional do Iguaçu, Foz do Iguaçu, 85863-000 PR. ⓒ **0800/150-006** or 045/521-7000. www. tropicalhotel.com.br. 200 units. R$260–R$300 (US$130–US$150) double superior; R$320–R$380 (US$160–US$180) double deluxe. Children under 10 stay free in parent's room. AE, DC, MC, V. Take the road to Iguaçu Falls, go straight towards the gate, do not turn left into the visitor's area. Identify yourself at the gate. Reservations recommended. **Amenities:** 2 restaurants; bar; large outdoor pool; tennis court; game room; tour desk; concierge; business center (24-hr. Internet access); shopping arcade; salon; room service; laundry service. *In room:* A/C, TV, minibar, fridge, hair dryer, safe.

MODERATE

Continental Inn ★★ *(Finds)*   Recently renovated, the Continental Inn is a real gem. All rooms have been redone and are quite comfortable, but the suites are truly outstanding, well worth the extra money. The regular suites have beautiful hardwood floors, modern blond-wood furniture, a separate sitting area, a desk, a table, and a bathroom with a large round tub. The best rooms in the house are the master suites: hardwood floors, king-size bed, fancy linens, a large desk, separate sitting area, walk-in closet, and a bathroom with Jacuzzi tub and a view over the city of Iguaçu. The amenities are top-notch, too: large pool with children's play area, sauna, and game room with video games. Rooms for travelers with disabilities are available.

Av. Paranà 1089, Foz do Iguaçu, 85852-000 PR. © 045/523-5000. www.continentalinn.com.br. 113 units (102 rooms showers only). R$135 (US$66) double; R$175 (US$88) suite; R$225 (US$113) master suite. In low season 30% discount. Children under 5 stay free in parent's room, over 5 R$30 (US$15) extra. AE, DC, MC, V. **Amenities:** Restaurant; large pool; exercise room; sauna; game room with video arcade; car rental; business center; room service; laundry service. *In room:* A/C, TV, dataport, minibar, fridge, hair dryer, safe.

WHERE TO DINE

You will find a number of pleasant restaurants in Foz do Iguaçu. **Avenida Brasil,** a main artery of town, is a good place to start for food stalls, coffee bars, and hearty homestyle Brazilian fare.

EXPENSIVE

Restaurante Itaipu—Tropical das Cataratas ★ BRAZILIAN   The best *feijoada* (a Brazilian black bean dish) in town is served here, on Saturday afternoon of course, in the elegant colonial-style Tropical restaurant. A large feast is put out, with white rice, *farofa* (manioc meal), fried banana, green cabbage, orange slices, and all the *feijoada* you can eat. The big clay dishes of beans and meat are clearly labeled (a vegetarian version is also available). Desserts are sweet and rich; try the various caramelized fruits with coconut.

In the Tropical das Cataratas Hotel, Km 28, Parque Nacional do Iguaçu. © 045/574-1688. Main courses R$16–R$42 (US$8–US$21). AE, DC, MC, V. Daily 11:30am–2pm and 6–11pm. *Feijoada* is served Sat 11:30am–3pm. No public transit, easiest combined with a visit to the falls; the park shuttle leaves you in front of the Tropical.

MODERATE

Clube Maringá ★ SEAFOOD   One of the most popular seafood restaurants for locals is Clube Maringá. It can be a bit tricky to find, on a dead-end road that leads to the Brazilian marker across from Argentina and Paraguay. The food is excellent. The menu is all fish and mostly local. Try the *piapara* fish grilled in a banana leaf or the barbequed *dourado.* Other dishes include *surubi* sautéed in butter, tilapia skewers, cod pastries, and *surubi a milanesa* (breaded and fried). Even the *sashimi* is made with local tilapia and piapara.

Av. Dourado (just off Av. General Meira s/n, by the Policia Militar). © 045/527-3472. Main courses R$22–R$34 (US$11–US$17). MC, V. Mon–Sat 5–10pm. Call ahead for lunch hours; these vary by season. A taxi is recommended.

FOZ DO IGUAÇU AFTER DARK

The best bars and clubs line Avenida Jorge Schimmelpfeng. Try **Tass Bier and Club,** Av. Jorge Schimmelpfeng 450 (© **045/523-5373**), which acts as a pub during the week and disco on weekends. The **Teatro Plaza Foz,** BR (National Rd.) 277, Km 726 (© **045/526-3733**), offers evening folkloric music and dance shows celebrating Brazilian, Argentine, and Paraguayan cultures.

5

The Northwest

Far removed from the urban noise of Buenos Aires, Argentina's Northwest feels like a different country altogether. Here you'll find a land rich in history, influenced by an age of pre-Hispanic civilization—a place more culturally similar to Chile and Bolivia (which border the region) than to the federal capital. The Northwest's wildly diverse terrain ranges from the cold peaks of the Andes to the subtropical air of the fertile valleys. You will approach a different pace of life among the old country houses and farms scattered across the land.

The Northwest incorporates one of Argentina's oldest settled regions, inhabited largely by Quechuan Indians, an Inca-influenced tribe that descended from Peru in 1450. The Spaniards arrived in the early 16th century under explorers Pizarro and Diego de Almagro and colonized the area with forts in Salta, San Salvador de Jujuy, Tucumán, and San Luis. The Diaguita tribes (living here before the Quechuans arrived) were agricultural people whom the Spaniards forced into slavery while extending their empire into the New World. Archaeological sites throughout the region reveal traces of pre-colonial life, including Indian settlements with terraced irrigation farming in the subtropical valleys.

EXPLORING THE REGION

The most fascinating way to discover the Northwest is aboard the **Tren a las Nubes (Train to the Clouds)** ⭐, an all-day trip that takes you from Salta toward the Chilean border, climbing through breathtaking Andean landscapes and on to the magnificent La Puña Desert. For more, see the box "Riding the Train to the Clouds," below.

Even if you don't find time for that 15-hour locomotive adventure, you'll still witness the rich history and flavor of the Northwest in its principal towns of **Salta** and **San Salvador de Jujuy.** Keep your eyes open for cultural festivals or religious celebrations to glimpse just how alive the Northwest's traditions remain. Three days at a minimum and 5 days on the outside should allow you to thoroughly experience the flavor of the region. The easiest way to visit the Northwest is to rent a car, take a bus, or hire a tour guide.

1 Salta

90km (56 miles) S of San Salvador de Jujuy

One of Argentina's largest provinces, Salta is bordered by Chile, Bolivia, and Paraguay and is characterized by vastly diverse terrain, ranging from the fertile valley of the provincial capital to the polychrome canyons of Cafayate and the desolate plateau of La Puña. The provincial capital, also called Salta, sits in the Lerma valley with an eternal springlike climate, a town boasting Argentina's best-preserved colonial architecture. Wandering its narrow streets and charming plazas, you will get a sense of how Salta has existed for centuries—quiet, gracious, and reserved. Salta loses its quietude during *Carnaval* (Mardi Gras), when thousands of Salteños come out for a parade of floats celebrating the region's history; water balloons are also tossed from balconies with great aplomb. Without doubt, the Tren a las Nubes is Salta's main attraction (see the box "Riding the Train to the Clouds," below.)

ESSENTIALS
GETTING THERE
I don't recommend making the long-distance drive to Argentina's northwest; it's safer and much easier to either fly or take the bus.

BY PLANE   Flights land at **Aybal Airport,** Ruta Nacional 51 (© **387/424-2904**), 10km (6 miles) from the city center. **Aerolíneas Argentinas** (© **0810/222-86527**), **Southern Winds** (© **0810/777-7979**), and **LAPA** (© **0810/777-5272**) fly from Buenos Aires. Flights from Buenos Aires cost between $55 and $100 each way, depending on the season and availability. A shuttle bus travels between the airport and town for about $1 one-way; a taxi into town will run about $3.

BY BUS   The **Terminal de Omnibus,** or central bus station, is at Avenida H. Yrigoyen and Abraham Cornejo (© **387/431-5227**). Buses arrive from Buenos Aires (22 hr., $25) and travel to San Salvador de Jujuy (2½ hr., $2) and other cities in the region. **Chevalier** and **La Veloz del Norte** are the main bus companies.

VISITOR INFORMATION
The tourism office, **Secretaría de Turismo de Salta,** Buenos Aires 93 (© **387/431-0950** or 431-0640; www.turismosalta.gov.ar), will provide you with maps and information on dining, lodging, and sightseeing in the region. It can also help you arrange individual or group tours. It's open weekdays 8am to 9pm and weekends 9am to 8pm. In Buenos Aires, obtain information about Salta from the **Casa de Salta en Bs. As.,** Sáenz Pena 933 (© **011/4326-2426**).

FAST FACTS: SALTA
Currency Exchange   Exchange money at the airport, at **Dinar Exchange,** Mitre and España (© **387/432-2600**), or at **Banco de La Nación,** Mitre and Belgrano (© **387/431-1909**).

Emergency   Dial © **377/431-9000** for police, © **377/421-2222** for fire.

Hospital   Saint Bernard Hospital, Dr. M. Boedo 69 (© **387/421-4926**).

Tour Operators   Arrange a tour of the region with **Saltur Turismo,** Caseros 525 (© **387/421-2012**). The tourist office can also recommend English-speaking tour guides.

GETTING AROUND
Salta is small and easy to explore by foot. The **Peatonal Florida** is Salta's pedestrian walking street—a smaller version of Calle Florida in Buenos Aires—where most of the city's shops are. The main sites are centered on **Plaza 9 de Julio,** where a monument to General Arenales stands in the center and a beautiful baroque cathedral stands at its edge. Built in 1858, the **Catedral** is considered Argentina's best-preserved colonial church. All the other attractions—except the **Salta Tram** and the **Tren a las Nubes**—are within easy walking distance.

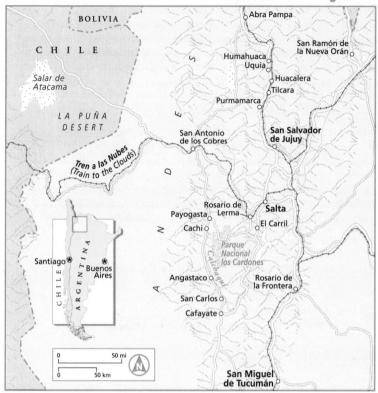

RENTING A CAR **Rent a Truck 4×4 and Car,** Buenos Aires 1 Local 6 Caseros 489 (© **387/431-0740**), has subcompacts and four-wheel drives. **Hertz** is at Caseros 374 (© **387/421-7553**) and **Avis** is at the airport (© **387/424-2289**). Following the currency evaluation, cars have become more affordable to rent here, ranging from $30 to $40 per day.

SEEING THE SIGHTS

Most museums in the Northwest don't have formal admission fees; instead, they request small contributions, usually $1 or less.

El Cabildo   First erected in 1582 when the city was founded, the Cabildo has since reinvented itself a number of times. The latest town hall was completed in 1783 and is typical of Spanish construction—two levels and a tower built around interior patios. The building houses the **Museo Histórico del Norte (Historic Museum of the North),** with 15 exhibition halls related to the Indian, colonial, and liberal periods of Salteño history. Here you will see religious and popular art, as well as works from the Jesuit period and from Upper Peru.

Caseros 549. © **387/421-5340.** Museum open Tues–Sat 9:30am–1:30pm and 3:30–8:30pm; Sun 9:30am–1:30pm.

Iglesia San Francisco (San Francisco Church) 🏛️🏛️ Rebuilt in 1759 after a fire destroyed the original building, the Iglesia San Francisco is Salta's most prominent postcard image. The terra-cotta facade with its 53m (174-ft.) tower and tiered white pillars was designed by architect Luis Giorgi. The belfry—the tallest in the Americas—holds the *Campaña de la Patria,* a bronze bell made from the cannons used in the War of Independence's Battle of Salta. A small museum exhibits a variety of 17th- and 18th-century religious images.

Córdoba and Caseros. No phone. Daily 8am–noon and 4–8pm.

Museo Histórico José Evaristo Uriburo 🏛️ José Evaristo Uriburo's family, who produced two of Argentina's presidents, bought this simple adobe house with a roof of reeds and curved tiles in 1810. An entrance from the street leads directly to the courtyard, characteristic of homes of this era. Exhibits include period furniture and costumes, as well as documents and objects belonging to the Uriburos and General Arenales.

Caseros 179. 🕿 387/421-5340. Tues–Sat 9:30am–1:30pm and 3:30–8:30pm; Sun 9:30am–1:30pm.

Museo Provincial de Bellas Artes de Salta (Museum of Fine Arts) 🏛️ Colorfully decorated tapestries and other regional works fill this 18th-century Spanish house, which houses a permanent collection of colonial art upstairs and religious and contemporary art downstairs. Noteworthy pieces include a portrait of Francisco de Uriburo by Spanish painter Joaquín Sorolla y Bastida and a painting of Salta by Italian Carlo Penutti.

Florida 20. 🕿 387/421-4714. Mon–Fri 8:30am–12:30pm and 4:30–8:30pm; Sat 9am–7pm.

San Bernardo Convent 🏛️🏛️ This is the oldest religious building in Salta, declared a Historical National Monument in 1941. It's worth a walk by to admire the city's most impressive example of colonial and indigenous art (only Carmelite nuns are allowed to enter). The entrance was carved from a carob tree by aborigines in 1762.

Caseros near Santa Fe.

Teleférico (Salta Tram) 🏛️ This Swiss-made cable car has been in operation since 1987 and takes tourists to the top of San Bernardo Hill, 300m (1,000 ft.) over Salta. There is not much to do other than enjoy the panoramic view of the Lerma valley and grab a snack at the casual restaurant. If you miss the last tram, a cheap taxi will return you to the city center.

At the intersection of avenidas H. Yrigoyen and San Martín. 🕿 387/431-0641. Admission $3 adults, $2 children. Daily 10am–7:45pm.

WHERE TO STAY
EXPENSIVE

Gran Hotel Presidente 🏛️🏛️ The best hotel in Salta has attractive guest rooms splashed in rose and apple green with comfortable white tile bathrooms. The hotel's modernity stands in stark contrast to other accommodations in Salta: The chic lobby features black and white marble with Art Deco furniture and leopard-skin upholstery. The international restaurant can be seen on the upstairs mezzanine, and the Presidente has a great spa with a heated indoor pool, sauna, fitness room, and solarium.

Av. de Belgrano 353, 4400 Salta. 🕿/fax 387/431-2022. 96 units. $101 double; $185 suite. Rates include buffet breakfast. AE, DC, MC, V. **Amenities:** Restaurant; indoor pool; fitness room; sauna; room service; dry cleaning; laundry service; solarium; meeting rooms. *In room:* A/C, TV, minibar, hair dryer, safe.

Riding the Train to the Clouds

The **"train to the clouds"** is one of the world's great railroad experiences—a breathtaking ride that climbs to 4,220m (13,842 ft.) without the help of cable tracks. The journey takes you 434km (269 miles) through tunnels, turns, and bridges, culminating in the stunning La Polvorilla viaduct. You will cross magnificent landscapes, making your way from the multicolored Lerma valley through the deep canyons and rugged peaks of the Quebrada del Toro and on to the desolate desert plateau of La Puña. The train stops at the peak, where your tour guide (there's one in each car) will describe the region's topography and check that everyone is breathing fine and not suffering from altitude sickness. In the small town of San Antonio de los Cobres, you'll have a chance to buy handicrafts, ponchos, and other textile goods from the indigenous people. The 14½-hour ride includes a small breakfast, lunch (additional), and folkloric show with regional music and dance. A restaurant, post office, communications center, and infirmary are among the first-class passenger cars. The ride makes for a fascinating experience, but be prepared for a very long day.

The ticket office for *Tren a las Nubes* (Train to the Clouds) is at Caseros 431 (© **387/431-4984**). The train operates April to November and departs Salta's General Belgrano Station most Saturdays at 7:10am and returns that night at 9:50pm, making one stop. The cost is $95, not including lunch.

Portezuelo Hotel ★★ The Portezuelo Hotel stands on top of Cerro San Bernardo, a hill just outside the city center. Local artwork decorates the lobby, adjacent to which is Santana—Salta's most elegant restaurant, boasting panoramic views of the Lerma valley (see "Where to Dine," below). Guest rooms have A-frame ceilings and simple wood decor; expect to sleep peacefully since you're away from downtown. At $10 more, VIP rooms are slightly larger than standard ones and have work desks and safe deposit boxes.

Av. Turística 1, 4400 Salta. © **387/431-0104.** Fax 387/431-4654. www.portezuelohotel.com. 63 units. From $35 double; from $55 suite. Rates include buffet breakfast. AE, DC, MC, V. **Amenities:** Restaurant; bar; outdoor pool; concierge; room service; laundry service. *In room:* A/C, TV, minibar, hair dryer, safe.

MODERATE

Hotel Salta ★ Popular with Europeans, this neoclassical hotel sits in the heart of Salta—next to Plaza 9 de Julio—and makes a good base from which to explore the city. Opened in 1890, it is hardly the most modern accommodation you'll find, but the hotel's wood balconies and arabesque carvings, peaceful courtyard, refreshing pool, and beautiful dining room considerably increase its appeal. At $10 more, "A" rooms are larger than standard rooms and have bathtubs, as opposed to just showers. The staff will arrange horseback riding, golf, and other outdoor activities upon request.

Buenos Aires 1, 4400 Salta. ©/fax **387/431-0740.** www.hotelsalta.com. 97 units. From $35 double; from $65 suite. Rates include buffet breakfast. AE, DC, MC, V. **Amenities:** Restaurant; bar; pool; sauna; small business center; room service; laundry service. *In room:* A/C, TV, fridge.

INEXPENSIVE

Victoria Plaza   If your purpose in Salta is sightseeing rather than hotel appreciation, then the Victoria Plaza should do just fine. Rooms are stark and simple but also clean, comfortable, and cheerfully maintained. Those on the seventh floor and above enjoy better views for a few dollars more. The hotel has an excellent location next to the main plaza, the cabildo (town hall), and the cathedral. The cafeteria-like restaurant is open 24 hours, and the hotel offers free airport transfers.

Zuviría 16, 4400 Salta. ℂ/fax **387/431-8500**. www.usuarios.arnet.com.ar/vplaza. 96 units. From $20 double. Rates include buffet breakfast. AE, DC, MC, V. **Amenities:** Gym; sauna; meeting room; laundry service; free airport transfer. *In room:* A/C, TV, fridge.

WHERE TO DINE

The Northwest has its own cuisine influenced by indigenous cooking. *Locro* (a corn and bean soup), *humitas* (a sort of corn and goat cheese soufflé), tamales (meat and potatoes in a ground corn shell), empanadas (a turnover filled with potatoes, meat, and vegetables), *lechón* (suckling pig), and *cabrito* (goat) occupy most menus. Traditional Argentine steaks and pasta dishes usually are available too. In addition to the locations listed below, the Mercado Central, at Florida and San Martín, has a number of inexpensive eateries serving regional food.

MODERATE

Café van Gogh ★★ CAFE   "Our mission is to make everyone feel at home, no matter where they're from," says one staff member, who proudly displays a collection of coffee cups from Argentina, Europe, and North America. The cheeky cafe, surrounded by little white lights on the outside and decorated with van Gogh prints inside, serves pizzas, sandwiches, meats, hot dogs, and empanadas. Come evening, the cafe-turned-bar becomes the center of Salta nightlife, with live bands playing Wednesday through Saturday after midnight. Café van Gogh is also a popular spot for breakfast.

España 502. ℂ **387/431-4659**. Main courses $2–$3. AE, DC, MC, V. Mon–Thurs 7am–2am; Fri–Sat 24 hr.; Sun 7am–1am.

El Solar del Convento ★★ ARGENTINE   Ask locals to point you to Salta's best "typical" restaurant—the word used to describe places serving traditional Argentine fare—and they won't hesitate with their answer. The former Jesuit convent has long been an outstanding *parrilla* (grill) serving quality steaks (the mixed grill for 2 is a deal at $3) and regional specialties like empanadas, tamales, and *humitas*. The 10-page menu also includes beef brochettes, grilled salmon, chicken with mushrooms, and large, fresh salads. There are two dining rooms connected by an A-frame thatched roof, and a medieval-style chandelier hangs from the front ceiling. Red and green tables give the restaurant an aura of Christmas, and the atmosphere is indeed festive: Even late on a Sunday night, expect the restaurant to be packed.

Caseros 444. ℂ **387/439-3666**. Main courses $2–$4. AE, DC, MC, V. Daily 11am–3pm and 8pm–midnight.

Jockey Club ★★ INTERNATIONAL   Come here for refined dining in the city center. The Jockey Club's small dining rooms feature stone floors, rose-colored tablecloths, soft lighting, and jazz playing in the background. The menu is light and healthy: The trout stuffed with shrimp is the best choice on the menu, but we also recommend the chicken with vegetables and the beef Wellington.

Av. de Belgrano 366. ℂ **387/431-5612**. Reservations recommended. Main courses $3–$6. AE, DC, MC, V. Daily noon–3:30pm and 8:30pm–1am.

Restaurante del Portezuelo Hotel ★★ REGIONAL   This restaurant, in the Portezuelo Hotel, is Salta's most elegant. The intimate dining room, with large windows overlooking the Lerma valley, is decorated with regional artwork and tables topped with white linens and silver candles. You won't go wrong with any of the creative entrees, such as trout stuffed with shrimp and cheese, sirloin steak with scalloped potatoes, or grilled chicken with mustard and tarragon. The restaurant also serves regional specialties like *locro, pastel de choclo* (corn-and-meat pie), empanadas, *humitas,* and tamales. Jazz music occasionally accompanies dinner, and you might consider a table on the veranda in warm weather.

Av. Turística 1. © 387/431-0104. Reservations recommended. Main courses $3–$6. AE, DC, MC, V. Daily noon–3pm and 8pm–1am.

Santana ★★ INTERNATIONAL   This is one of the few international restaurants in Salta with a classic rather than rustic style. The enticing menu features chicken with white-wine cream sauce, lobster with chimichurri sauce, and homemade ravioli with various cheeses. There is a rich selection of Argentine wines; ask for a bottle from San Juan or Mendoza.

Mendoza 208. © 387/432-0941. Reservations recommended. Main courses $3–$5. AE, DC, MC, V. Daily noon–3:30pm and 8pm–midnight.

Viejo Jack II ★★ *Kids* *Value* ARGENTINE   An inexpensive local *parrilla* frequented by locals, Viejo Jack II (Viejo Jack I is at Av. Virrey Toledo 145) serves succulent steaks and fresh pastas. Kids have access to a play area, as well.

Av. Reyes Católicos 1465. © 387/439-2802. Main courses $2–$4. DC, MC, V. Daily noon–3:30pm and 8:30pm–1am.

2 A Driving Tour of the Calchaquíes Valley via Cachi & Cafayate

The landscape surrounding Salta resembles the southwestern United States, with polychromatic hills keeping watch over the Lerma valley. Tobacco, tropical fruits, and sugar cane are the main agricultural products, and you will see tobacco "ovens" off the side of the road (Marlboro grows Virginia tobacco here through a subsidiary). Heading south from Salta on Ruta Nacional 68 for 38km (24 miles) will bring you to **El Carril,** which is a typical small town of the valley, with a central plaza and botanical garden displaying 70% of the region's flora.

Although you can reach **Cafayate** more quickly by continuing south on Ruta Nacional 68, it is far more interesting to go west on Ruta Provincial 33 for about 2.7km (1½ miles) after El Carril. You'll come across **Cabaña de Cabras, La Flor del Pago** (© 387/684-3960), one of the principal goat farm and cheese factories in Argentina. Ducks, geese, and hundreds of goats roam the scenic property, and there is a small dining room and cheese shop in the proprietors' home where you can sample the delicious chèvre. (The kind owners will prepare a multi-course lunch or dinner with advance reservations.)

While the region surrounding El Carril is characterized by dense vegetation, the land quickly becomes dry as you climb Ruta Provincial 33 toward **Piedra del Molino (Mill Rock).** The road narrows from pavement to dirt 10km (6 miles) west of El Carril—watch closely for oncoming cars. A small shrine to Saint Raphael (a patron saint of travelers) indicates your arrival at Mill Rock (3,620m/11,873 ft.) and the entrance to **Parque Nacional los Cardones,** a semi-arid landscape filled with cacti, sage, and limestone rock formations.

Ten kilometers (6 miles) before Cachi lies **Payogasta,** an ancient Indian town on the path of the Inca Road that once connected an empire stretching from Peru. **Cachi** (see below) is another pre-colonial village worth a visit for its Indian ruins. From Cachi, take Ruta Nacional 40 south past Brealito to Molinos, a 17th-century town of adobe homes and dusty streets virtually unchanged from how it must have appeared 350 years ago. Continuing south, consider stopping 9km (5½ miles) before Angastaco at the **Estancia Carmen** (© **368/15693005**), which boasts spectacular views of the Calchaquíes valley and its long mountain canyon. Between 9am and 6pm you can visit the ranch's Inca ruins, rent horses, and peek inside the private church in back, where two 300-year-old mummies rest in peace.

Continue south on Ruta Nacional 40 to **Angastaco**—this may be a good place to spend the night. **Hostería Angastaco,** Avenida Libertad (© **3868/15639016**), lies 1km (about ½ mile) west of the village and is popular with European travelers. The simple hotel offers live folkloric music each evening. The staff will help arrange regional excursions and horseback riding. From Angastaco to San Carlos, you will pass the **Quebrada de las Flechas (Arrows Ravine)** with stunning rock formations that appeared in *The Empire Strikes Back.* People often stop their cars at the side of the road and climb a bit. Jesuits settled in **San Carlos,** and the church is a national historic monument. **Cafayate** (see below) marks the southern end of this circuit.

Return to Salta along Ruta Nacional 68 heading north, which takes you through the **Río Calchaquíes valley** and on to the **Quebrada del Río de las Conchas (Canyon of the River of Shells).** Among the most interesting crimson rock formations you should stop at are the Garganta del Diablo (Devil's Throat), El Anfiteatro (the Ampitheater), and Los Castillos (the Castles), which are all indicated by road signs. Salta is 194km (120 miles) from Cafayate along Ruta Nacional 68, and it shouldn't take more than a few hours to drive.

CACHI

Home of the Chicoanas Indians before the Spaniards arrived, Cachi is a tiny pueblo of about 5,000 people, interesting for its Indian ruins, colonial church, and archaeological museum. The Spanish colonial **church,** built in the 17th century and located next to the main plaza, has a floor and ceiling made from cactus wood. The **archaeological museum** is the most impressive museum of its kind in the Northwest, capturing the influence of the Incas and Spaniards on the region's indigenous people. Located next to the main plaza, its courtyard is filled with Incan stone engravings and pre-Columbian artifacts. Wall rugs, ponchos, and ceramics are sold at the **Centro Artesanal,** next to the tourist office, on the main plaza (the people of Cachi are well respected for their weaving skills, and the ponchos they sell are beautiful). **La Paya,** 10km (6 miles) south of Cachi, and **Potrero de Payogasta,** 10km (6 miles) north of Cachi, hold the area's most important archaeological sites.

GETTING THERE   Cachi lies 157km (97 miles) west of Salta on Ruta Provincial 33. **Empresa Marcos Rueda** offers two buses daily from Salta; the trip takes 5 hours and costs $5.

VISITOR INFORMATION   You can pick up maps, excursion information, and tips on restaurants and hotels at the **Oficina de Turismo,** Avenida General Güemes (© **3868/491053**), open Monday through Saturday from 9am to 8pm.

WHERE TO STAY

Hostal La Paya ★   Opened in 2000 on a 19th-century *estancia* (ranch), this rustic inn looks out to the Calchaquíes valley and is a quiet place to walk, read, and relax. Guest rooms have adobe walls and wood beam ceilings, llama-wool rugs, and mattresses laid on stone frames. You can have your meals here if you like—all the produce (except the meat) comes from this farm. The owners will also arrange excursions to the nearby mountains, valley, and river upon request.

8km (5 miles) from Cachi, on RN 40 to Molinos. ℂ/fax **3868/491139**. 10 units. From $48 double. Rates include breakfast. No credit cards. **Amenities:** Restaurant; pool; outdoor excursions.

WHERE TO DINE

Confitería y Comedor del Sol REGIONAL   When you walk into this village restaurant, locals are likely to cease their conversations and stare for a minute. Not to worry—they will quickly return to their business once you sit down; many are engaged in the afternoon's current soap opera. The menu is simple, consisting of pastas, *milanesas* (breaded meat cutlets), empanadas, and tamales. This is a great place to have lunch on your way to Molinos.

Ruiz de los Llanos. ℂ **387/156055149**. Main courses $1–$3. No credit cards. Daily 8am–1am.

CAFAYATE

Cafayate is a picturesque colonial town nestled in the Río Calchaquíes valley and famous for its wine production. Popular with Argentine tourists, Cafayate's streets are lined with baroque-style houses built in the late 19th century. The main tourist attractions, in addition to the two major vineyards just outside town, are the Regional and Archaeological Museum and the Museum of Grapevines and Wine (see below). You can find regional arts and crafts of excellent quality at shops surrounding the main plaza.

GETTING THERE   Cafayate lies 194km (120 miles) southwest of Salta on Ruta Nacional 68. **Empresa El Indio** (ℂ **387/432-0846**) offers three buses daily from Salta; the trip takes 3½ hours and costs about $5.

VISITOR INFORMATION   The **tourist office** (ℂ **3868/421470**) is located on the main plaza and provides maps, bus schedules, and lodging recommendations. Open hours are Monday through Saturday from 10am to 6pm.

SEEING THE SIGHTS

Most museums in this area are free or request a small donation, usually no more than $1.

Bodegas Etchart ★★★   This is one of the region's most important vineyards, producing 6,000 bottles of wine per hour—including Chardonnay (for which this bodega is best known), cabernet sauvignon, Torrontes, and Malbec. The bodega exports its wine to more than 30 countries. One-hour guided tours and wine tastings are offered Monday through Friday from 8am to noon and 3 to 6pm, and Saturday from 8am to noon.

Finca La Rosa, 3km (2 miles) from Cafayate on Ruta Nacional 40. ℂ **3868/421310**.

Michel Torino Bodega La Rosa ★★   This medium-sized bodega, opened since 1892, produces roughly 10 million liters of wine per year (10,000 bottles per hour), with Malbec (a dry red), cabernet sauvignon, merlot, chardonnay, and "Michael Torino" Torrontes (a Riesling-like white) the main products. The Don David reserve is the vineyard's top selection. Guided tours in Spanish only are offered Monday through Thursday from 8am to 5pm, and Friday from 8am to 4pm. The bodega also has a small guesthouse with charming rustic rooms.

Finca La Rosa, 2 miles (3km) from Cafayate on Ruta Nacional 40. No phone. Hours vary.

Museo de Vitivinicultura (Museum of Grapevines and Wine) ★★ Part of the Bodega Encantada winery, this museum tells the story of grape-growing and wine-making in and around Cafayate. The 19th-century building houses old-fashioned machinery and more modern equipment, as well as agricultural implements and documentary photographs.

Ruta Nacional 40, at Av. General Güemes. © 3868/421125. Weekdays 10am–1pm and 5–9pm.

Museo Regional y Arqueológico Rodolfo Bravo (Regional and Archaeological Museum ★ This small museum displays ceramics, textiles, and metal objects discovered over a 66-year period by Rodolfo Bravo. These archaeological finds celebrate the heritage of Diaguita-Calchaquíes and Incan tribes in the region and cover a period between the 4th and 15th centuries.

Colón 191. © 3868/421054. Hours vary.

WHERE TO STAY

Gran Real This modest hotel has quiet rooms with simple furnishings. These rooms, some with great mountain views, are considerably more enticing than the gloomy downstairs cafe. Popular with Argentine visitors, the Gran Real also has a pool and barbecue area. Service is friendly.

Av. General Güemes 128, 4427 Cafayate. © 3868/421231. Fax 3868/421016. hotelgranreal@hotmail.com. 35 units. From $20 double. MC, V. **Amenities:** Restaurant; pool. *In room:* A/C, TV.

WHERE TO DINE

La Carreta de Don Olegario ★ REGIONAL This is the best restaurant on the main plaza. The large dining room lacks elegance but has an authentic selection of regional dishes, including *cabritos* (young goat). Service is unhurried, so plan to enjoy a leisurely lunch or dinner if you come here. Folkloric shows take place in the evenings.

Av. General Güemes 20. © 3868/421004. Main courses $2–$3. DC, MC, V. Daily noon–3pm and 8–11pm.

3 San Salvador de Jujuy

1,620km (1,004 miles) NW of Buenos Aires, 90km (56 miles) N of Salta

The regional capital of Jujuy, San Salvador—commonly called Jujuy—was established by the Spaniards in 1592 as their northernmost settlement in Argentina. In 1812 during the wars of independence, General Belgrano evacuated residents of the city before Spanish troops arrived—an event celebrated each July known as *éxodo jujeño* (Jujuy Exodus). The well-preserved colonial town is smaller than Salta and doesn't have a great deal to offer, although there are a few interesting museums and a beautiful cathedral surrounding Plaza Belgrano. The Indian market across from the bus terminal offers a good sense of daily life here, with many vendors dressed in traditional costumes selling food, indigenous crafts, and textiles. Jujuy is also the best base from which to explore the Quebrada de Humahuaca (Humahuaca Gorge), which extends to the north (see "Driving the Quebrada de Humahuaca [Humahuaca Gorge]," below). The circuit includes the Cerro de los Siete Colores (Hill of the Seven Colors), the artists' haven Tilcara, and La Garganta del Diablo (Devil's Throat) gorge.

ESSENTIALS

GETTING THERE   Jujuy's airport (📞 388/491-1109) is 35km (22 miles) from town. **Aerolíneas Argentinas** (📞 0810/222-86527) and **LAPA** (📞 0810/777-5272) fly from Buenos Aires. Flights from Buenos Aires cost between $50 and $150, depending on the season and availability.

The **Terminal de Omnibus,** or main bus station, is located at Dorrego and Iguazú (📞 388/422-1375). Buses arrive from Buenos Aires and travel to Salta, Tucumán, Catamarca, and other cities in the region. **Empresa Balut** (📞 387/432-0608) makes the 2½-hour trip to Humahuaca (see "Driving the Quebrada de Humahuaca [Humahuaca Gorge]," below), as well as to other cities throughout the region.

If you opt to rent a car, there are a few independent companies located at the airport.

VISITOR INFORMATION & FAST FACTS   The **regional visitor center** is located at Urquiza 354 (📞 388/424-9501), in the old train station. It is open weekdays from 7am to 9pm and weekends from 9am to 9pm.

You can arrange regional tours at **Grafitti Turismo,** Belgrano 601 (📞 388/423-4033). They will change money here, too.

Citibank, located at the corner of España and Balcare, has a 24-hour ATM and change machine. The bank is open weekdays from 9am to 2pm.

GETTING AROUND   Easy to explore on foot, Jujuy is more compact than Salta, and its major attractions can be visited in a few hours. The bulk of commercial activity takes place around **Plaza Belgrano,** where the Casa de Gobierno, the cabildo (town hall), and the cathedral are located. Built in 1750, the **Catedral** has a baroque pulpit carved in wood by the indigenous people and should not be missed. Shopping in Jujuy is concentrated along **Calle Belgrano.**

SEEING THE SIGHTS

Most museums in this area are free or request a small donation, usually no more than $1.

Catedral (Cathedral) ⭐   Successor to an earlier cathedral dating from the 17th century, this updated version, built in 1763, salvaged the original gold pulpit characteristic of Spanish baroque. The cathedral towers over Plaza Belgrano, where a pottery market takes place during the day.

West side of Plaza Belgrano. No phone. Daily 8am–noon and 5–8:30pm.

Museo Arqueológico Provincial (Provincial Archaeological Museum) ⭐⭐   Archaeological finds represent over 2,500 years of life in the Jujuy region, including a 2,600-year-old ceramic goddess, a lithic collection of arrowheads, the bones of a child from 1,000 years ago, and two mummified adults. Objects from the Yavi and Humahuaca cultures are also exhibited.

Lavalle 434. 📞 388/422-1315. Daily 9am–noon and 3–8pm.

Museo Histórico Provincial (Provincial Historical Museum) ⭐   This was the house in which General Lavalle was killed in 1841, and the large door through which he was shot is on display, right next to an enormous bust of the Argentine hero. Other exhibits include war materials and documents used during the 25-year struggle for independence in Jujuy.

Lavalle 252. 📞 388/422-1355. Mon–Fri 8am–12:30pm and 4–8pm; Sat–Sun 9am–1pm and 4–8pm.

WHERE TO STAY

Accommodations in the Northwest have become more reasonably priced following the peso's devaluation, but their quality has not improved much. The places we list are the best you will find, but in many cases that's not saying much. Yet you're here to see the sights, not to linger in the confines of your hotel. Note that accommodations in San Salvador quickly fill up in July during the *éxodo jujeño* (Jujuy Exodus) celebration.

Altos de la Viña ★★ *Kids* This is the best hotel in Jujuy, located on a hill 3km (2 miles) from the city center. A wealth of outdoor activities on the sprawling property include volleyball, miniature golf, tennis, and swimming in the outdoor pool. Half of the guest rooms have balconies with terrific views of the city; bathrooms have phones, hair dryers, and good amenities. The best rooms are "VIPs" (only $15 more)—they feature classic furniture, impressive woodwork, and linens decorated with country French colors. The hotel has an excellent restaurant and a very friendly staff.

Av. Pasquini López 50, 4600 Jujuy. © 388/426-2626. www.hotelaltosdelavina.com.ar. 70 units. From $95 double; $120 suite. Breakfast included. AE, DC, MC, V. **Amenities:** Restaurant; outdoor pool; massage; tennis; volleyball; children's games; room service; babysitting; laundry service. *In room:* A/C, TV, minibar.

Augustus Hotel Don't expect too much from this simple hotel, located on Jujuy's one shopping street. Standard rooms have uninspiring red carpet, small bathrooms, and twin beds. For only a few dollars more, "VIP" rooms are slightly larger and have better furniture and air-conditioning. This is your best option if the other hotels we recommend are already booked.

Calle Belgrano 715, 4600 Jujuy. © 388/423-0203. Fax 388/423-0209. augustus@cooteplal.com.ar. 81 units. From $25 double; $40 suite. Rates include buffet breakfast. AE, DC, MC, V. **Amenities:** Snack bar; small business center; sauna. *In room:* A/C, TV.

Jujuy Palace Hotel ★ If lobbies are any indication of a hotel's quality, then the modern and comfortable furnishings you'll find upon entering the Jujuy Palace prove that the management is committed to maintaining a good face. Guest rooms have been remodeled to make them more inviting. They are clean, small, and sparsely decorated—definitely overpriced, though. The hotel is centrally located in front of the cathedral.

Calle Belgrano 1060, 4600 Jujuy. ©/fax 388/423-0433. jpalace@imagine.com.ar. 52 units. $30 double; $40 suite. Rates include buffet breakfast. AE, DC, MC, V. **Amenities:** Restaurant; gym; sauna; room service. *In room:* A/C, TV.

WHERE TO DINE

Chung King ★ REGIONAL Despite the misleading name, Chung King is a longtime regional favorite in Jujuy, serving *humitas,* tamales, empanadas, and *picante de pollo* and *pollo al ajillo* (both local chicken and vegetable dishes). The restaurant doubles as a peña on Saturday evenings, with local artists performing traditional Northwestern dances. A pizzeria is located next door.

Alvear 627. © 388/422-8142. Main courses $2–$6. AE, DC, MC, V. Daily 11:30am–4pm and 7pm–3am.

Need a Break?
Heladería Pinguino, Belgrano 718 (© **388/422-7247**), has 50 flavors of ice cream and frozen yogurt to cool you down. The small cafe is open daily from 9am to midnight.

Krysys ★ *Finds* REGIONAL   A giant Coke sign outside marks the entrance to Jujuy's best *parrilla,* serving juicy Argentine steaks. The international menu also has a number of pasta and chicken selections as well, and the trout is excellent. This is a festive restaurant, where locals come to celebrate good times and special occasions.

Balcarce 272. ✆ **388/423-1126.** Main courses $2–$4. AE, DC, MC, V. Daily noon–3:30pm and 8pm–2am (Sun only for lunch).

La Royal Confitería SNACKS   One of the few places you can eat any time of day, La Royal offers pizzas, empanadas, sandwiches, and other light snacks. An old grandfather clock ticks along undisturbed by the modern American rock playing over speakers. Black-and-white photos of American actors decorate the walls of this casual but popular cafeteria, which is also packed at breakfast.

Calle Belgrano 766. ✆ **388/422-6202.** Main courses $2–$3. MC, V. Daily 7:30am–midnight.

Manos Jujeñas ★ *Value* REGIONAL   Tables are normally packed at this delightful restaurant specializing in regional dishes like empanadas, *humitas,* and tamales. The small, two-level dining room is decorated with local crafts and costumes, and soft Andean music plays in the background. You will have an excellent and very inexpensive meal here: Consider the trout from the nearby Yala River, or one of the homemade pastas served weekends only. A tall glass of orange juice is only a peso. When it's crowded, be prepared to wait a bit for your food.

Senador Pérez 222. ✆ **388/422-2366.** Main courses $2–$3. No credit cards. Mon–Sat noon–3pm and 8pm–2:30am (Sun only for lunch).

Restaurante del Hotel Altos de la Viña ★★ INTERNATIONAL   This is as elegant as Jujuy gets. You'll have to leave the city center to reach this hilltop hotel restaurant, with splendid views of the town below. Folkloric groups occasionally serenade the dining room at dinner, and there are candlelit tables outside in summer. The extensive menu focuses on seafood and homemade pastas: The *trucha rellena*—trout stuffed with shrimp, mushrooms, cognac, and white wine—is among the best choices, as are the pastas, *humitas,* and empanadas. Plan to stay for a long meal, as you'll want to linger over one of the mouthwatering desserts.

Av. Pasquini López 50. ✆ **388/426-2626.** Reservations recommended. Main courses $3–$5. AE, DC, MC, V. Daily 11am–3pm and 7:30pm–midnight.

4 Driving the Quebrada de Humahuaca (Humahuaca Gorge)

For the first 30 or 40 minutes as you head north on Ruta Nacional 9 from San Salvador de Jujuy, undulating hills reveal fields rich with tobacco and corn and expose the rural economy of Argentina's Northwest. Quechuan women wearing colorful ponchos walk with babies strapped to their backs while horses, cows, and goats graze on the surrounding vegetation. Look closely and you might spot a gaucho charging after his herd.

As you climb along the Río Grande to Purmamarca, 71km (44 miles) from the region's capital, the land becomes increasingly dry and gives way to striking rock formations. When you arrive at the junction of Ruta Provincial 52 and Ruta Nacional 9, head west for a few kilometers to reach the small colonial hamlet. Framing Purmamarca like a timeless painting, the **Cerro de los Siete Colores (Hill of the Seven Colors)** reflects its beauty onto the pueblo's quiet streets and dusty adobe homes. Try to arrive early—9am is best—when the morning sun shines brightly on the hill's facade and reveals its tapestry of colors.

Heading back to Ruta Nacional 9 and continuing 20km (12 miles) north, you will arrive at the artist's haven of **Tilcara,** with a pre-Hispanic fortress called a *pucará.* Here you will find spectacular panoramic views of the Humahuaca valley as well as a trapezoid-shaped monument marking the Tropic of Capricorn. To visit **La Garganta del Diablo (Devil's Throat)**—a steep gorge with a small walkway leading along the rock's edge—leave Ruta Nacional 9 and head east of Tilcara for a short distance. Be careful walking here, as there is only a small rope separating you from the depths below.

Continue north along Ruta Nacional 9, where you will pass the small adobe villages of Huacalera and Uquia. About 42km (26 miles) north of Tilcara lies **Humahuaca,** a sleepy yet enchanting village of only a couple of thousand Indian residents. Its relaxed pace will make Buenos Aires seem light years away. Note that at an elevation of 2,700m (9,000 ft.), you will feel a little out of breath here, and nights are quite cold. Although the nearby Inca ruins of **Coctaca** are best explored with a tour guide, you can visit them on your own or with a taxi ($5 round-trip, including driver wait time) by following a dirt road about 10km (6 miles) out of Humahuaca. Coctaca is a large Indian settlement that the Spaniards discovered in the 17th century. Although the ruins are hard to distinguish from the rocks and debris, you can make out outlines of the terraced crop fields for which the Incas were famous. The site is surrounded by cactus and provides excellent photo opportunities.

From San Salvador de Jujuy, you can travel this circuit by bus or by car. If you decide you'd like to stay the night in Humahuaca (126km/78 miles north of San Salvador), a simple but hospitable option is the **Posta del Sol,** Martín Rodríguez at San Martín (© **388/499-7157**), which will arrange horseback and 4×4 excursions into the surrounding area. Otherwise, the Humahuaca circuit can easily be completed in a day.

6

Córdoba

Situated in the center of Argentina, Córdoba's diverse regional landscapes range from undulating hills and forest mountains to water-filled valleys and long green plains. Córdoba is both the capital of this province and the intellectual heart of the nation, its colonial buildings comprising the country's most important historic heritage. Allow for at least one or two days to visit the old city, where you will discover Córdoba's Jesuit roots and university tradition. Then get out and explore the mountains, which you can do in a day trip or turn into a longer retreat.

The core of Córdoba's tourist area is the Punilla Valley, peacefully set between the Sierras Chicas to the north and east and the Sierras Grandes to the west. The valley is filled with reservoirs created by the Cosquín and San Antonio rivers, and the San Roque reservoir in Villa Carlos Paz attracts water-lovers with sailing, swimming, windsurfing, and other lake activities. The sleepier village of La Falda to the north attracts a slower-paced crowd longing for quiet and fresh mountain air. Adventure companies in both towns arrange horseback riding, trekking, and camping in the surrounding mountains, as well as driving tours to the province's many estancias and colonial sights.

1 Córdoba

713km (442 miles) NW of Buenos Aires; 721km (447 miles) NE of Mendoza

Córdoba, Argentina's second largest city with 1.3 million inhabitants, was created as a stop for Spaniards traveling between Peru and the Atlantic coast. It was founded in 1573 by Jerónimo Luis de Cabrera, who honored his wife's family by naming this South American city after their Spanish home. The Jesuits arrived at the end of the 16th century, opening Córdoba's university in 1613 and financing their projects by establishing six large estancias throughout the region. Today you can follow the "road of the Jesuit estancias" by arranging a tour with a local travel agent.

Built at the bottom of what is essentially a hole, Córdoba was once plagued by flooding. As a result, a small stream called La Cañada was created with walls around it to capture the water, and today La Cañada is one of the city's symbols. Moving into downtown, Córdoba's most important historical sights line up around Plaza San Martín, including the Cabildo, cathedral, Marqués de Sobre Monte's residence, and the Jesuit Block. The Manzana Jesuítica, as it is called in Spanish, developed not just as a place of worship, but also as an intellectual and cultural center that produced Argentina's top doctors and lawyers. It includes the Jesuit churches, the university, and a prestigious secondary school. In 2000, it was declared a UNESCO World Heritage Site and became a historic museum. The city still serves as an intellectual center, although the economic crisis and dispersion of universities throughout the country has lessened some of Córdoba's luster.

ESSENTIALS

GETTING THERE

BY PLANE Córdoba is most easily reached by air, and there are numerous daily flights from Buenos Aires. **Aeropuerto Internacional Ing. Ambrosio Taravella** (also called Pajas Blancas; © **351/434-8390**) sits 11km (7 miles) outside town. **Aerolíneas Argentinas** (© **0810/222-86527**), **Southern Winds** (© **0810/777-7979**), and **LanChile** (© **351/475-9555**), operate here, with flights to Buenos Aires, Mendoza, and Santiago de Chile. **LAPA** currently offers sporadic service, but the company's future is uncertain. Taxis from the airport to downtown cost between $3 and $4.

BY BUS The **Terminal de Omnibus,** or central bus station, is located at Bulevar Perón 380 (© **351/433-1980**). Numerous companies serve destinations throughout Argentina. Travel times to Buenos Aires are approximately 10 hours, Mendoza 12 hours, Villa Carlos Paz 1 hour, and La Falda 2 hours. Promotions are constantly being offered and companies change their prices frequently; I recommend you check with the tourism office or directly with the bus station before booking your ticket.

BY CAR The drive from Buenos Aires takes approximately 10 hours on the RN9, which is a good road.

VISITOR INFORMATION Córdoba's **Centro de Información Turística,** in the Cabildo (© **351/428-5856**), offers limited hotel and restaurant information and has small city maps. It's open daily from 8am to 9pm in summer, with shorter hours in winter. There are also branches at the airport and bus station. The **provincial tourist board,** located at Tucumán 360 (© **351/434-1545**), is open daily from 8am to 2pm.

GETTING AROUND

The old city of Córdoba is easily explored by foot, with 24 blocks of pedestrian walking streets located near the Cabildo. The heart of the old city spreads out around Plaza San Martín, situated in the southeast quadrant of Córdoba. Most of the historical sights lie in this area. Avenida Colón, which becomes Avenida Olmos, is the city's main street. As a general rule, you should not walk alone in big cities at night. In Córdoba, this is especially true anywhere along the river.

Driving is difficult in the city, and parking almost impossible downtown. If you do rent a car, try **Hertz,** at Pajas Blancas airport (© **351/4475-0581**). Cheaper, but less known, is **AI Rent a Car,** Entre Ríos 70 (© **351/422-4867**). City buses are cheap and abundant, but only *cospeles*—80¢ tokens available at kiosks around town—are accepted. In Córdoba, taxis are colored bright yellow, while the safer and similarly priced *remises* (private, unmetered taxis) are colored light green.

FAST FACTS: CORDOBA

Area Code 351.

ATMs/Currency Exchange ATMs and currency exchange houses have been plagued by long lines and limited cash since the beginning of the economic crisis. Two reliable exchange houses are **Maguitur** at 25 de Mayo 122 and **Barujel** at Rivadavia 97. There is also an exchange booth at the airport. **Citibank** is located at 25 de Mayo and Rivadavia.

Emergency For a **medical** emergency, dial © **107;** for **police,** dial © **101** or **351/428-7000;** in case of **fire,** dial © **100.**

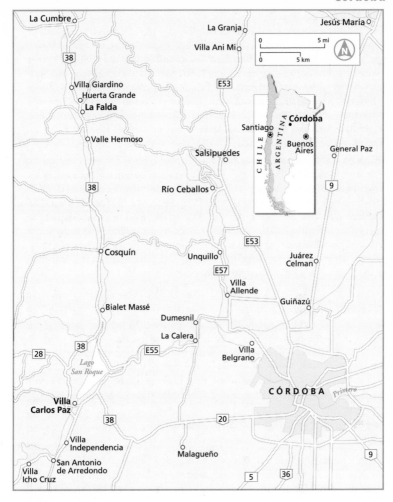

Hospital   The **Hospital de Urgencias** (emergency hospital; ✆ **351/421-5008**), is located at Catamarca and Salta.

Internet Access   **Telefónica,** with a branch on almost every corner downtown, provides Internet access for less than $1 per hour.

Pharmacy   **Farmacia Virtual,** 27 de Abril 99 (✆ **351/411-1101**), is open daily until midnight.

Post Office   The main post office, **Correo Argentino,** is located at Av. General Paz 201.

Seasons   Córdoba can be visited anytime of year, although you should expect hot temperatures and big crowds in January and February, and fairly cold temperatures June through August. In addition to peak summer season, tourist destinations also fill up during Easter week.

WHAT TO SEE & DO

City bus tours operated by **Córdoba City Tour** (© 351/424-6605) explore the main tourist spots. The tour lasts 1½ hours, visiting 40 sights. The double-decker red buses leave from Plaza San Martín, and you should go to the tourist office or call directly for departure times. The tour costs $3. The tourism office also arranges 2-hour **walking tours** of the city departing at 9:30am and 4:30pm, which cost $2. Call in advance to arrange a tour in English (© 351/428-5600). In addition to the sights listed below, an excellent antiques and handicrafts fair, **Feria Artesanal del Paseo de las Artes,** opens at Achaval Rodríguez and La Cañada on Saturdays and Sundays (3–10pm in winter, 6–11pm in summer).

Plaza San Martín and the Cabildo ★   The 4-century-old plaza orients the city, with General San Martín facing the direction of Mendoza (from which his army crossed into Chile and later Peru to liberate them from Spanish rule). Exhibitions, fairs, and impromptu markets are frequent events on the plaza. The **Cabildo** stands on the Plaza's west side. During the military dictatorship of the late 1970s and early 1980s, the Cabildo functioned as police headquarters and was used, as acknowledged by a small sign along Pasaje Santa Catalina, as a clandestine detention, torture, and death center. Today the Cabildo is a friendlier place, used mainly for cultural exhibitions and events.

The Cabildo is located at Deán Funes and Independencia. © 351/428-5856.

Catedral ★   Construction of the cathedral, situated next to the Cabildo, began in 1577 and took nearly 200 years to complete. No wonder then that the structure incorporates such an eclectic mix of styles, heavily influenced by baroque. On each of the towers next to the bells, you will see Indian angels created by—and in the image of—indigenous people of this region. The dome was painted by Emilio Carrafa, one of Córdoba's best-remembered artists. Visitors are free to enter the church, but should respect the Masses that take place at various times during the day.

Independencia 72, at Plaza San Martín. © 351/422-3446. Hours vary.

Manzana Jesuítica ★★★   The Jesuit Block, which includes the Society of Jesus's Church, the Domestic Chapel, the National University of Córdoba, and the National School of Monserrat, has been the intellectual center of Argentina since the early 17th century. Today, the entire complex is a historic museum, although the churches still hold Masses, the cloisters still house priests, and the schools still enroll students. You can enter the Compañía de Jesús, the university patio, and the Colegio Nacional de Monserrat free of charge, and if you pay $1 you can also visit the Domestic Chapel and the Hall of Graduates.

The **Domestic Chapel** was completed in 1668, used throughout much of its history for private Masses and religious studies of the Jesuits. Having practiced their building skills on the Domestic Chapel, the Jesuits finished the main church, called the **Compañía de Jesús,** in much the same style in 1676. Built in the shape of a Latin cross, the Compañía de Jesús is the oldest church in Argentina. Its nave was designed by a Belgian shipbuilder in the shape of an inverted hull, which was the best way to make use of the short wood beams available for construction at the time. The dome is all wood—no iron is found anywhere—and the beams remain fastened with raw cowhide. The gilded altarpiece was carved in Paraguayan cedar, indicative of baroque design. At each of the church's wings stands a chapel, one of which has often been used for university graduation ceremonies.

In 1613, the Jesuits founded the **National University of Córdoba,** the oldest university in Argentina and one of the continent's longtime academic centers. With most of the university (including the medical and law schools) having moved elsewhere in the city, the majority of rooms now form part of the historic museum. You can visit the Hall of Graduates, the main university library, and the exquisite Jesuit library holding roughly 1,000 books dating back to the 17th century. The books are in Latin, Greek, and Spanish, and there's a complete Bible from 1645 written in seven languages. Many of the original books in the library disappeared when the Jesuits were first expelled from the Americas, but some are slowly returning from Buenos Aires, where they were hiding.

The Jesuit library leads to the **National College of Monserrat,** which opened in 1687 and quickly became one of the country's top public secondary schools. Walking around the cloisters, you can see the classrooms as well as exhibits of early science machines used for mechanics, electronics, magnetics, color, and sound. During the academic year, you will also find students at work here.

Obispo Trejo 242. (© 351/433-2075. Free admission to most sites; $1 to see Domestic Chapel and Hall of Graduates. Tues–Sun 9am–1pm and 4–8pm. Guided tours at 10, 11am, 5, and 6pm.

Museo Histórico Provincial Marqués de Sobre Monte ★★   The largest colonial house to survive intact in Argentina, this historical museum was used as the 18th-century home and office of the first Spanish governor of Córdoba. Completed in 1772, the house showcases the town's early colonial history. The governor's commercial and office rooms were downstairs, with the more intimate family rooms upstairs. An amazing collection of period furniture fills the bedrooms; public spaces display religious paintings, military uniforms, a rifle collection, early saddles and other leatherwear, plus an 18th-century chamber organ.

Rosario de Santa Fé. (© 351/433-1661. Admission $1. Tues–Sun 9am–1pm and 3–7pm.

OUTDOOR ACTIVITIES

A number of tour and adventure companies offer excursions into the Sierras de Córdoba, where it is possible to hike, mountain bike, horseback ride, hang-glide, and fish. Try **Estación Uno** (© 354/349-2924), **Explorando Sierras de Córdoba** (© 354/343-7901), or **Aventur** (© 351/474-4595), all of which offer discovery tours into the mountains and overnight camping trips as well. To visit the province's Jesuit estancias, you should contact the tourist office or a local travel agent, such as **Stylo Viajes,** Chacabuco 321 (© 351/424-6605).

WHERE TO STAY

Córdoba offers a wide variety of hotels, with no stellar choices directly downtown. Hotels sometimes charge different prices for foreigners than Argentines, so make sure you confirm the price before you book. Prices listed below do not include the 19% tax. Parking is usually free for hotel guests.

Holiday Inn ★★ *Value*   One of the city's best hotels, this new Holiday Inn is similar in quality but substantially less expensive than the Sheraton. Okay, there's definitely less marble, but the service is comparable. The hotel lies between the airport and downtown, next to a large shopping complex and near the posh neighborhood of Cerro de las Rosas. Standard rooms are colorful, bright, and airy, with slightly larger rooms on the executive floor. The gorgeous pool is complemented by a fitness center, sauna, and state-of-the-art massage facility. The helpful staff will arrange airport transfer, regional excursions, and sports activities upon request. You'll need to take a taxi or *remise* to the city center, located about 10 minutes away. The hotel also functions as a convention center.

Centro Comercial Libertad: Fray Luis Beltrán and M. Cardenosa, 5008 Córdoba. ℂ **351/477-9100.** Fax 351/ 477-9101. www.holidayinncba.com.ar. 144 units. $40 double; from $60 suite. Rates include buffet breakfast. AE, DC, MC, V. **Amenities:** Restaurant; bar; heated outdoor pool; fitness center; sauna; business center; room service; babysitting; dry cleaning; laundry service. *In room:* A/C, TV, minibar, hair dryer, safe.

Sheraton ★★ Just outside the city center next to a fashionable shopping mall, this five-star Sheraton is widely considered Córdoba's best hotel. Elevators shoot up the center of the 16-floor atrium lobby, which is decorated with rose-colored marble, California palms, and paintings by national artists. Spacious, well-appointed guest rooms have marble tables and desks, large bathtubs, and views of either the city or mountains. Service is first rate, although the hotel gets crowded when its convention center is booked. The restaurant is fairly standard, offering a la carte or buffet dining, but the piano bar is good evening fun. The Sheraton offers the most extensive list of amenities of any hotel in Córdoba.

Av. Duarte Quirós 1300, 5000 Córdoba. ℂ **351/526-9000.** Fax 351/526-9150. www.sheraton.com/cordoba. 188 units. $180 double; $350 suite. Rates include buffet breakfast. AE, DC, MC, V. **Amenities:** Restaurant; piano bar; heated outdoor pool; fitness center; sauna; tennis court; business center; room service; dry cleaning; laundry service. *In room:* A/C, TV, minibar, hair dryer, safe.

Windsor Hotel & Tower ★ This centrally located hotel is the best of hotel choices near Plaza San Martín, having added a new tower with modern, comfortable rooms. Ask for a room in this tower, rather than in the "classic" section. King-bed rooms are larger than those with two twins. Also new are the rooftop pool, fitness room, and sauna. The fifth floor Oxford restaurant enjoys an impressive view of the city, with good international cuisine. Piano music fills the lobby after 9pm, and the hotel staff will organize city tours and mountain excursions.

Buenos Aires 214, 5000 Córdoba. ℂ/fax **351/422-4012.** www.windsortower.com. 82 units. $40 double; $80 suite. Rates include buffet breakfast. AE, DC, MC, V. **Amenities:** 2 restaurants; piano bar; small outdoor pool; fitness center; sauna; business center; room service; dry cleaning; laundry service. *In room:* A/C, TV, minibar, hair dryer, safe.

WHERE TO DINE

The restaurants listed below are located downtown. Dining choices are actually very limited in this area, with many places closed on Sunday and Monday (if you find yourself downtown on either of those days, try the **Patio Olmos** shopping center, Av. Vélez Sársfield at Bulevar San Juan, which has open restaurants). The city's more upscale establishments are located in the fashionable **Cerro de las Rosas** neighborhood, a 15-minute drive northwest of downtown.

Elegon's ★★ *Finds* ARGENTINE President Sarmiento once said that Córdoba has more churches than houses, and it is from Elegon's seventh-floor perspective that his words seem most true. This unpublicized restaurant inside the Colegio de Escibanos has panoramic windows overlooking the cathedral, Basílica Santo Domingo, Santa Catalina de Siena Church, Teresa's Church and Convent, and the Manzana Jesuítica. With only a dozen tables and a couch, the dining area resembles a small European tearoom. Open solely during the day, your lunchtime choices are a *milanesa* (the best choice, topped with ham, cheese, and tomatoes) or a beefsteak. You can also come for tea or coffee.

Obispo Trejo 104, 7th floor. ℂ **351/423-2912.** Reservations suggested. Main courses $3–$4. No credit cards. Weekdays 8am–5pm.

La Alameda *(Value* ARGENTINE   The city's best empanada shop is decorated with jokes posted all over its walls. This very casual eatery with wood benches for tables serves food typical of Argentina's Northwest, including *locro, humitas,* and of course a selection of empanadas. Food is quick, cheap, and no-nonsense. Post a joke before you leave.

Obispo Trejo 170. *(℃* 156/562-757. Main courses $1–$3. No credit cards. Mon–Sat noon–5am; Sun 8pm–5am.

Mandarina *(Finds* ITALIAN   This eclectic and not altogether sane bar-restaurant, located along the pedestrian walkway Obispo Trejo, is a cornucopia of surreal and occasionally sexual artwork. The city's cultural crowd comes for salads, pizzas, calzones, and pastas, and later for wines, whiskies, and wacky cocktails. Freshly baked breads and jams prepared with fresh fruits add to Mandarina's credentials.

Obispo Trejo 171. *(℃* 351/426-4909. Main courses $2–$4. No credit cards. Mon–Sat 11am–3:30pm and 8:30pm–12am.

CORDOBA AFTER DARK

The **Cabildo** serves as a cultural center, with occasional evening events. **Teatro Libertador San Martín,** Vélez Sársfield 365 (*℃* **351/433-2319**), is the city's biggest theater hosting mostly musicals and concerts. The smaller **Teatro Real,** San Jerónimo 66 (*℃* **351/433-1669**), presents more traditional theater. You can pick up current theater, comedy, and special events information in the "Espectáculos" section of the daily paper, *La Voz del Interior.* **El Arrabal,** Belgrano 899 at Fructuoso Rivera (*℃* **351/460-2990**), hosts excellent tango, milonga, salsa, and folkloric shows most nights. One of the best bars is **Rock & Fellers,** Av. Hipólito Yrigoyen 320 (*℃* **351/424-3960**), which serves typical American food and has '60's style rock 'n' roll music. Happy hour takes place weekdays from 7 to 9pm. The most popular disco is **Carreras,** Avenida Cárcano and Piamonte (*℃* **156/762-767**), found in the Chateau Carreras neighborhood where a number of other upscale discos are located. The rest of the city's nightlife is concentrated along Bulevar Guzmán in the north of the city and in Nueva Córdoba along Avenida Hipólito Yrigoyen.

2 Villa Carlos Paz

36km (22 miles) W of Córdoba

A quick getaway from Córdoba, Villa Carlos Paz surrounds the picturesque Ebalse San Roque. Although it's actually a reservoir, vacationing Cordobese and Porteño families treat San Roque like a lake, swimming, sailing, and windsurfing in its gentle waters. Year-round, people come to Carlos Paz to enjoy outdoor activities by day and partying by night, with disco-bound buses transporting the youth of Córdoba back and forth. The city of 40,000 inhabitants really comes alive in January and February, when more than 200,000 tourists visit each month. Live theater, comedy shows, music, and dancing fill the night air, and no one seems to sleep. Yet you don't have to be a nocturnal animal to enjoy Villa Carlos Paz, and quiet lakeside resorts offer a more serene alternative.

ESSENTIALS

GETTING THERE   The N20 is a fast, new highway (with a 1 peso toll) that goes directly from Córdoba to Villa Carlos Paz. The drive takes no more than 40 minutes except on Sunday evenings, when Cordobese vacationers return home from the mountains. Bus transportation to Villa Carlos Paz is frequent and reliable. Public bus companies running to and from Córdoba in about 50 minutes are **El Serra** and **Ciudad de Córdoba,** both costing under $1. **Fero Bus** and **Caru** travel slightly faster but less often and cost about $1. **Chevallier** buses to Buenos Aires take about 10 hours.

VISITOR INFORMATION The local **tourism office,** adjacent to the bus station at San Martín 400 (© **351/421-624** or **0810/888-2729**), is open in summer from 7am to 9pm and winter from 7am to 11pm. The staff provides information on hotels, restaurants, and tourist circuits around the city.

GETTING AROUND Villa Carlos Paz is small and easily explored by foot. The city is safe to walk in, although as in other places you should not walk alone at night. In summer, two buses dressed as trains offer city tours, including **Tren de Turismo La Porteñita y del Ensueño** (© **351/431-692**) and **Trencito Turismo Lago San Roque** (© **351/421-521**). You can call directly for departure times and points, or ask at the tourism office. If you want to rent a car, various rental agencies are located at the bus station.

WHAT TO SEE & DO

There are no special sights in the city, save a 7m (22 ft.) high cuckoo clock that for no good reason has become the city's symbol. Daytime activities focus on the lake and excursions into the surrounding hills. Although it's not clear why the city allows so many water activities in what is actually a reservoir, swimming, sailing, windsurfing, trout fishing, and—at least for now—jet skiing are all possible. Villa Carlos Paz is also well positioned for the many driving circuits that explore the Punilla Valley and go into the mountains. These include treks to waterfalls, Jesuit ruins, and mountain estancias. Check with **El Rosario** (© **351/451-257**) or one of the other tourist agencies open at the bus station.

WHERE TO STAY

Hipocampus Resort ★★ *Finds* A bumpy back road leads to this hidden retreat, a white colonial house that resembles an old Spanish mission. Its two pools sit perched on a cliff overlooking the lake, and each of the guest rooms has a balcony with a beautiful water view. Rooms are uniquely decorated, and many have hardwood floors and colorful linens. Bathrooms are small with showers only, however. The hotel offers a cozy fireside sitting room, as well as a small library and TV area. The restaurant serves regional dishes as well as afternoon tea, and the gracious staff makes this feel more like a B&B than a hotel. Excursions, horseback riding, and hiking trips can be arranged at reception.

Calle Brown 240, 5152 Villa Carlos Paz. © **351/421-653.** www.hipocampusresort.com. 50 units. $50 double. Rate includes buffet breakfast. AE, DC, MC, V. **Amenities:** Restaurant; 2 outdoor pools; kids' pool; sauna; gym; mini golf. *In room:* A/C, TV, fridge, hair dryer, safe.

Portal del Lago Hotel ★ A striking wood-frame lobby leads directly out to the main pool and spacious grounds bordering the lake. The hotel forms a half-moon shape along the banks, and most of the rooms have water views. Brick walls and dark woods give you the sense of being deep in the mountains, and there are many sitting areas for relaxing. Guest rooms vary in size, although bathrooms are small; some rooms have two levels and multiple beds to accommodate families. A warm therapeutic pool, sauna, and gym are on the top floor, and a lake-view restaurant extends along the mezzanine of the lobby. The hotel houses a convention center and can become crowded in summer months. The hotel's many stairs prevent access to those with disabilities.

Gdor. Alvarez, at J.L. Cabrera, 5152 Villa Carlos Paz. (℃ **351/424-931**. Fax 351/424-932. www.portal-del-lago.com. 110 units. $55 double. Rate includes buffet breakfast. AE, DC, MC, V. **Amenities:** Restaurant; bar; 3 outdoor pools; sauna; gym; room service. *In room:* A/C, TV, safe.

WHERE TO DINE

Let's just say that fine dining is not the reason people come to Villa Carlos Paz. However, there are a number of good, casual eateries in the center. The two best *parrillas* in town are **Carilo,** Yrigoyen 44 (℃ **351/431-346**) and **La Volanta,** San Martín 1262 (℃ **351/422-954**). The latter is easy to spot—look for loud green and yellow paint and the carriage sitting on the roof. For excellent Italian dishes, try **Il Gato Trattoria,** at Libertad and Belgrano (℃ **351/439-500**), but be prepared to wait a while for the pastas and pizzas, which are made to order.

VILLA CARLOS PAZ AFTER DARK

Many young—and even not so young—people come to Villa Carlos Paz from Córdoba for drinking and dancing, and some of the discos arrange private caravans from the city. Expect a late night out—dancing begins after 2am and continues past dawn. By far, the most famous disco is **Keop's,** R.S. Peña and Seneca (℃ **351/433-553**), with **Zebra Restobar Disco,** Bernardo D'Elia 150 (℃ **351/427-130**), placing second. For something tamer, visit the **Punta Hidalgo** piano bar at the corner of Uruguay and Hidalgo (℃ **351/421-127**). **Casino Carlos Paz** is located at Liniers and Uruguay (℃ **351/425-772**).

3 La Falda

81km (50 miles) NW of Córdoba

An excellent base from which to explore the Punilla, La Falda (literally, "lap of the mountain") lies between the Valle Hermoso (Beautiful Valley) and the Sierras Chicas. Argentines come here for rest and relaxation, not wild entertainment. Crisp, clean air, wonderful hikes, and quiet hotels are the draw. The city's main tourist site is the once-prestigious (now decrepit) Hotel Edén that entertained international celebrities in the early 20th century.

ESSENTIALS

GETTING THERE   Frequent buses travel from both Córdoba and Villa Carlos Paz, the most comfortable of which is **TranSierras** (℃ **351/424-666**). If you are driving, you have the option of first going to Villa Carlos Paz and then on to La Falda via the N38, or you can bypass Carlos Paz by taking the new A73, which branches off from the N20 a few miles before Carlos Paz. The trip takes 2 hours from Córdoba.

VISITOR INFORMATION   The **tourist office** is located inside the old train station at Av. Buenos Aires 50 (℃ **351/423-007**). Open daily from 8am to 11pm, it provides city and regional maps as well as hotel, restaurant, and tourist information.

GETTING AROUND   You can walk around the small center, but you will probably want to hire a driver, rent a car, or sign up with a tour operator to explore the Sierras Chicas (although you can always hike). La Falda's main road is Avenida Edén, which extends from the town center to the old Hotel Edén.

WHAT TO SEE & DO

You are here first and foremost to relax. Once that's accomplished, visit the once prestigious **Hotel Edén** (east end of Av. Edén), which during the first half of the

20th century hosted the likes of Albert Einstein, the Duke of Savoy, two presidents of Argentina, and the country's high society. The hotel quickly fell out of favor after World War II because its owners had been Nazi sympathizers. Boarded up by 1960, the castle-like hotel was left to ruin and the insides have been completely gutted, although amazingly the entrance fountain still operates. Guided tours are offered daily between 10am and 6pm, and there's a bar adjacent to the ghost lobby with pictures of the grand old dame in its day. Outside the city, various adventure agencies offer horseback riding, trekking, mountainbiking, hang-gliding, and 4×4 excursions into the Sierras Chicas. Contact **Purehuek Turismo Aventura,** Av. Edén 338 (② **351/423-690**). You might also considering taking an inexpensive taxi (all taxis are inexpensive here) towards La Cumbre, where numerous handicrafts shops and stands dot the artesian road.

WHERE TO STAY

Hostal L'Hirondelle ⚐   Never mind the term "hostal"; in this case it's an architectural distinction rather than a reference to a budget traveler's dormitory. The house looks like a French chalet, surrounded by gardens and the Sierras Chicas. Each individually decorated room takes a poet's name, as a tribute by the owner to his poet son. On the second floor, Walt Whitman enjoys a corner view of the pool, courtyard, and nearby mountains. French prints and old bottles and spices decorate the long wood dining room, where guests enjoy half-board (breakfast and dinner) in summer months. Breakfast includes tea, croissants, fruit, cereal, homemade sweets, and fresh juice. For city folks unaccustomed to clear, starry nights, the owner has set up a telescope for celestial viewing. The staff will help you arrange outdoor activities, including hiking and horseback riding, as well as airport transfer upon request.

Av. Edén 861, 5172 La Falda. ② **351/422-825.** hostallhirondelle@digitalcoop.com.ar. 21 units. $88 double in summer including ½-board; ½ that price in winter with breakfast only. AE, DC, MC, V. **Amenities:** Restaurant; outdoor pool; video and game room; babysitting; laundry. *In room:* TV.

WHERE TO DINE

La Parrilla de Raúl ⚐ ARGENTINE   A popular *parrilla* with a distinctive family atmosphere, Raúl's menuless system works like this: First, help yourself to the salad bar, an assortment of mixed vegetable dishes, cabbages, stuffed eggs, candied sweet potatoes, and other delights. As you finish your salad, the first meat course will land on your plate, likely a tender slice of pork with a *cerveza* (yes, beer) sauce. Next comes thick *chorizo* and a rich piece of *morcilla* (blood pudding). No stopping here, *costilla* (a beef rib) is next. Ready for more? Following the rib is *matambre,* another delicious morsel of beef. At this point you can politely request that they stop bringing you meat, or you can wave on more. Request a large soda, and they will bring you a 1.25 liter bottle to help wash it all down. Finish your meal with a trip to the dessert bar, an enticing table of flans, fruits, creams, and the obligatory *dulce de leche.* Then go hit the gym.

Av. Buenos Aires 111. ② **351/421-662.** Main courses $3–$4. No credit cards. Daily noon–3pm and 8:30pm–midnight.

7

Mendoza

"**A**nd so you are traveling to the land of *sol y vino*," my taxi driver says with a smile, capturing the two great temptations of a region showered with sun and flowing with wine. Boasting nearly 300 annual days of sun and three-fourths of the nation's wine production, Mendoza seems destined for the distinction of Napa South. Few might imagine, however, that the sweet, voluptuous grapes coloring the province grow on inhospitable desert land brought to life only through a vast network of irrigation canals dating back to the Incas. The canals extend not just through the diverse vineyards but also into the streets of Mendoza itself. This picturesque city lies at the heart of the Cuyo, the name of the region that comprises the provinces of Mendoza, San Juan, and San Luis. It was founded in 1561 by Spanish colonialists, and retains an idyllic serenity that has carried over from centuries past.

Los Caminos del Vino refers to the seven wine roads that wind their way through the most important wine producing zones of Mendoza. You should spend at least 1 or 2 days exploring Mendoza—discovering the old city, visiting the plazas, and wandering about Parque General San Martín—before heading for the wine route. Choose your own pace when touring

the bodegas (wineries); two or three visits are possible in half a day. Keep in mind that the bodegas, which offer free tours with tastings, are open only on weekdays. But a journey into the magnificent mountains is possible anytime, and the best circuit is Alta Montaña, which follows parts of the old Inca trail and Andes railroad to the border with Chile. Travelers are best off choosing Mendoza as their base for exploring the region, although small lodgings and *fincas* (private homes opened to guests) dot the province.

Mendoza offers a wealth of outdoor activities, ranging from Class III, IV, and V white-water rafting in the Mendoza River to horseback riding, mountain biking, and trekking in the Andes. Tour operators in Mendoza will arrange an itinerary according to your choice, from part-day outings to multiple-day excursions. Las Leñas is a world-class ski resort in the south of the province—playground of Porteños escaping the capital for a snowy retreat—while Los Penitentes offers decent runs closer to Mendoza. For the bold and the brave, Aconcagua Mountain provides an irresistible challenge, its 6,960m (22,829 ft.) towering above all other peaks in the Western Hemisphere. With a good bit of endurance, money, and time on your hands, the mountain can be conquered.

1 Mendoza

710km (440 miles) NW of Buenos Aires; 721km (447 miles) SW of Córdoba

Mendoza is an artificial oasis. It receives no more than 5 days of rain per year; the tree-lined boulevards, plazas with trickling fountains, and enormous city park exist thanks to a centuries' old roadside canal system. Ask a local what she likes best about Mendoza, and she is likely to tell you *"La tranquilidad,"* the tranquillity of what must be Argentina's loveliest city. You'll want to linger about these streets and parks before rushing to the countryside, where a seductive journey along Los Caminos de Vino (see "Touring the Wineries," below) awaits.

ESSENTIALS
GETTING THERE

BY PLANE   Mendoza's international airport, **Francisco Gabrielli** (© 261/ 520-6000) lies 8km (5 miles) north of town on R40. **Aerolíneas Argentinas** (© 0810/222-86527), **Southern Winds** (© 0810/777-7979), and **LanChile** (© 261/425-7900) operate here, with flights to Buenos Aires, Córdoba, and Santiago de Chile. LAPA offers sporadic service, but the company's future is uncertain.

BY BUS   The **Terminal del Sol** (© 261/431-3001), or central bus station, lies in the department of Guaymallén, just east of central Mendoza. Buses travel to Buenos Aires (12–14 hr., $18), Córdoba (12 hr., $9), Santiago de Chile (6 hr., $9), Las Leñas (7 hr., $5), and other cities throughout the region. **Chevallier** (© 261/431-0235), **Expreso Uspallata** (© 261/438-1092), and **Andesmar** (© 261/431-0585) are the main bus companies.

BY CAR   The route from Buenos Aires is a long (10 hr.) but easy drive on either the RN7 or RN8. Mendoza is more easily reached by car from Santiago, Chile, along the RN7, although the 250km (155-mile) trek through the Andes can be treacherous (and requires chains) in winter.

VISITOR INFORMATION   Mendoza's **Subsecretaría Provincial de Turismo,** Av. San Martín 1143 (© 261/420-2357), is open daily from 9am to 9pm. The helpful staff will provide you with tourist information on the entire province, including maps of the wine roads and regional driving circuits. **Municipal tourist offices,** called Centros de Información, are located at Garibaldi near San Martín (© 261/423-8745), 9 de Julio 500 (© 261/449-5185), and Las Heras 340 (© 261/429-6298). Open daily from 9am to 9pm, they provide city maps, hotel information, and brochures of tourist activities. You will find small visitor information booths at the airport and bus station, as well. Information and permits for Aconcagua Provincial Park are available at the **Centro de Informes del Parques,** located in Mendoza's Parque San Martín (© 261/420-5052). Permits to climb to the summit cost $200. In addition, several websites offer useful tourist information: www.turismo.mendoza.gov.ar, www.aconcagua.mendoza.gov.ar, www.culturamendoza.com.ar, and www. mendoza.com.ar.

GETTING AROUND   You can easily explore central Mendoza by foot, although you will want to hire a driver or rent a car to visit the wine roads and tour the mountains. Taxis and *remises* (private, unmetered taxis) are inexpensive: drivers cost no more than $10 per hour. Travelers should be wary of walking alone, especially at night. Although traditionally one of Argentina's safest cities, Mendoza has experienced an increase in crime resulting from the economic crisis. Have your hotel call a *remise* or radio-taxi, rather than flagging a taxi down on your own. For a *remise,* try **La Veloz Del Este** (© 261/423-9090), **Mendozar** (© 261/431-3689), or **Remises-Transporte** (© 261/429-8734). For a taxi, call **Radiotaxi** (© 261/437-1111).

America Online Keyword: Travel

Booked seat 6A, open return.

Rented red 4-wheel drive.

Reserved cabin, no running water.

Discovered space.

With over 700 airlines, 50,000 hotels, 50 rental car companies and
5,000 cruise and vacation packages, you can create the perfect getaway for you. Choose the car, the room, even the ground you walk on.

Travelocity.com
A Sabre Company
Go Virtually Anywhere.

Book your air, hotel, and transportation all in one place.

Hotel or hostel? Cruise or canoe? Car? Plane? Camel? Wherever you're going, visit Yahoo! Travel and get total control over your arrangements. Even choose your seat assignment. So. One hump or two? travel.yahoo.com

powered by
COMPAQ

YAHOO!
Travel

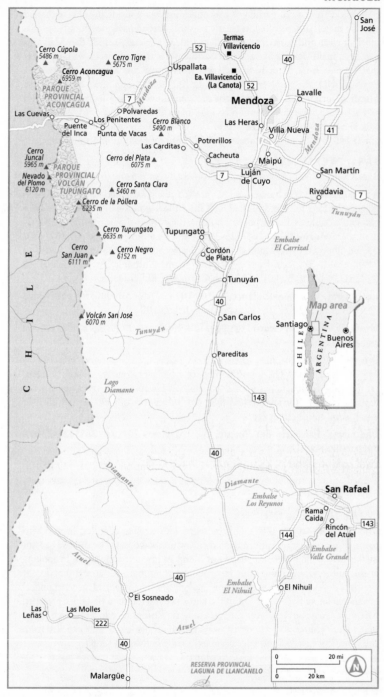

If you do rent a car, parking is easy and inexpensive inside the city, with paid parking meters and private lots clearly marked. Easy to navigate, the city spreads out in a clear grid pattern around Plaza Independencia. Avenida San Martín is the city's main thoroughfare, Paseo Sarmiento is the pedestrian walking street that extends from Plaza Independencia to Avenida San Martín, and Avenida Emilio Civit is the posh residential avenue leading to the entrance of Parque San Martín. Outside the city, road signs are sometimes missing or misleading and you should pay careful attention to road maps. Both **Avis** (© 261/447-0150) and **Hertz** (© 261/448-2327) rent cars at Mendoza's airport. Expect to pay about $40 per day for a compact car with insurance and unlimited mileage.

FAST FACTS: MENDOZA

Area Code   261. The country code for Argentina is **54.**

ATMs/Currency Exchange   ATMs and currency exchange houses have been plagued by long lines and limited cash since the beginning of the economic crisis. Two reliable exchange houses, both at the corner of San Martín and Catamarca, are **Maguitur** (© 261/425-3405) and **Cambio Santiago** (© 261/420-0277). They are open Monday through Friday from 8:30am to 1pm and 5 to 8:30pm and Saturday from 9:30am to 1pm. **Citibank,** Av. Sarmiento 20 (© 261/49-6519) has an ATM with Cirrus and PLUS access.

Emergency   For an **ambulance,** dial © 107 or 261/428-0000; for **police,** dial © 101 or 261/423-8710; in case of **fire,** dial © 100.

Hospital   Hospital Central (© 261/428-0600) is near the bus station at Salta and Alem.

Internet Access   Internet access in most places costs a meager 1 or 2 pesos (35¢–65¢) per hour. There are a number of cybercafes along Avenida Sarmiento; try **Mundo Internet,** Sarmiento 107 (© 261/420-3795), open daily from 8:30am to 1am. **Official Telefónica** and **Telecentro** offices, located all over town, also offer Internet use.

Pharmacy   **Farmacia del Puente,** Av. Las Heras 201 (© 261/425-9209), operates 24 hours.

Post Office   The main post office, **Correo Argentino** (© 261/429-0848), located at the corner of Avenida San Martín and Colón, is open weekdays from 8am to 8pm.

WHAT TO SEE & DO

Museo Fundacional ★★   This museum, located 3km (2 miles) from downtown, displays what remains of the old city, which was ravaged by the 1861 earthquake. Chronicling the early history of Mendoza, the museum begins by looking at the culture of the indigenous Huarpes and continues with an examination of the city's development through Spanish colonization to independence. An underground chamber holds the ruins of the aqueduct and fountain that once provided Mendoza's water supply. Near the museum, the **Ruinas de San Francisco** represent a Jesuit church and school that were used until the Jesuits were expelled from the continent in 1767 and later occupied by the Franciscan Order.

Videla Castillo between Beltrán and Alberdi. © 261/425-6927. Admission $1. Tues–Sat 8am–8pm; Sun 3–8pm.

Museo Histórico General San Martín ★   Adjacent to the "Alameda," a beautiful promenade under white poplars, the San Martín Library and Museum stands in the spot where General San Martín had hoped to make his home. The museum's small collection of artifacts pays homage to Argentina's beloved hero, who prepared his liberation campaigns from Mendoza.

Remedios Escalada de San Martín 1843. ✆ **261/425-7947**. Admission $1. Weekdays 9am–1pm.

Parque General San Martín ★★★   Almost as big as the city itself, this wonderful park, designed in 1896 by Carlos Thays (who also designed the Palermo parks in Buenos Aires), extends over 350 hectares (865 acres) with 17km (11 miles) of idyllic pathways and 300 species of plants and trees. A tourist office, located near the park's main entrance, provides information on all park activities, which include walking, jogging, bicycling, boating, horseback riding (outside the park's perimeters), and hang-gliding. A national science museum and zoo (open daily 9am–6pm) are located inside the park, and you can also camp here. The best hike leads to the top of Cerro de la Gloria, which offers a panoramic view of the city and surrounding valley, as well as a bronze monument to the men who liberated Argentina, Chile, and Peru. You can hang-glide from the top of the other hill, Cerro Arco.

Main entrance at Av. Emilio Civit and Bologne sur Mer. Free admission. Always open.

Plaza Independencia ★★   The Plaza marks the city center, a beautiful square with pergolas, fountains, frequent artesian fairs, and cultural events. Following the 1861 earthquake, the new city was rebuilt around this area. Four additional plazas, San Martín, Chile, Italia, and España, are located 2 blocks off each corner of Independence Square. Surrounding the square you will find the Julio Quintanilla Theater, the National School, the Independencia Theater, the Provincial Legislature, and the small Modern Art Museum.

Art Museum. ✆ **261/425-7279**. Admission $1. Mon–Sat 9am–1pm and 4–9pm.

TOURING THE WINERIES

Less commercialized than their European and American counterparts, Mendoza's wineries are free to visit and easily accessible along wine roads known locally as Los Caminos del Vino. These roads are as enticing as the wine itself, weaving and winding through tunnels of trees to vast dry valleys dominated by breathtaking views of the snowcapped Andes. Some roads climb as high as 1,524m (5,000 ft.) in the High Zone surrounding the Mendoza River, while others lead to lower-level vineyards in the south. Mendoza's wine region is divided into four zones: the High Zone, Mendoza East, Uco Valley, and Mendoza South. Different wine roads branch out through these zones and can be driven in part or total, allowing you to tour as many of Mendoza's bodegas as you like. There are presently 552 functioning wineries, 80 of which formally offer tours.

The **High Zone** that surrounds the Mendoza River includes Luján de Cuyo and parts of Las Heras, Guaymallén, Luján and Maipú. This first zone is best regarded for its production of Malbec, although cabernet sauvignon, Chenin, merlot, chardonnay, and Syrah are all bottled as well. Many of the bodegas in this zone lie within one hour's drive of Mendoza. The **Mendoza East Region** is the second zone, comprised of Junín, Rivadavia, San Martín, Santa Rosa, and La Paz. This is the province's largest wine producing area, where vineyards irrigated by the Tumuyán and Mendoza rivers harvest Malbec, merlot, Sangiovese, and Syrah, among others. South of Mendoza, the **Uco Valley Region,** including Tunuyán, Tupungato, and San Carlos, produces excellent Malbec, Semillon

The Story of Mendoza's Wine

Blessed by rich sunlight and a panorama of snow-filled mountains, Mendoza dominates Argentina's winemaking industry and is one of the most successful wine regions on earth. Surrounding the beautiful city of Mendoza and lying just to the east of the towering Andes, the province accounts for over 70% of the nation's wine production and is the world's sixth largest producer of grapes.

The Spanish began cultivating Mendoza's wild American vines in the 16th century, and wine production soon dominated the region's economy. They were able to harvest this semiarid land—which receives little natural rainfall—by using a vast irrigation system originally developed by the Incas and extended by the Huarpes, indigenous people from the region. A series of artificial irrigation ditches and canals divert water from the Mendoza, Diamante, Tunuyán, and Atuel rivers, which fill as snow melts in the Andes to nourish the land.

The development of Mendoza's wine industry ebbed and flowed. Wine production stalled in the late eighteenth century as Spain restricted grape growing to prevent competition with its colonies. The industry was renewed following national independence, as European experts introduced French grapevine stocks and wineries to the region. However, the earthquake of 1861 destroyed most of the existing wineries, and it was not until the opening of a railroad in 1884 that wine production resumed on a significant scale. The railway brought with it many of the founding families of today's wineries, who carried new

(a white), and Torrontés (another white, more common in Salta). Allow at least two hours to reach here. The final zone is the **Mendoza South Region,** between San Rafael and General Alvear. Fed by the Atuel and Diamante rivers, its best varieties are Malbec, Bonarda, and cabernet sauvignon. You will need at least a day to visit this region.

Throughout your drive you will stumble upon wineries old and new, some producing on a large scale and exporting internationally, others small and focused on the local market. It is difficult to say which bodegas excel over others, as each has its own focus and success. Among some of the best-known are Bodega Catena Zapata (Luján), which is a boutique winery of the larger Bodegas Esmeralda; Chandon (Luján), a subsidiary of France's Moet & Chandon; Salentein (Tunuyán); Norton (Luján); López (Maipú); Nieto Senetiner (Luján); Bodega Jacques et Francoise Lurton (Tunuyán); Etchart (Luján); Finca La Cilia (San Carlos); and Cavas de Weinert (Luján). Close to Mendoza in neighboring Maipú, Bodega La Rural has a small winery museum that exhibits Mendoza's earliest wine production methods. Another excellent winery close to town is Dolium, one of the only bodegas producing underground to allow for natural cooling. As at most bodegas, a tasting follows a tour of the laboratory and winery, and there is little pressure to buy. As Italian owner Mario Giadorou proudly states, "We offer an institutional show, not a sales show."

You can pick up a map of the wine routes, as well as information on individual bodegas, from any of the tourist offices. Each February, the wine season winemaking techniques and varietals from Italy, France, and Spain. Yet a series of economic crises plagued the industry in the first half of the 19th century, and Mendoza's wines seldom made it farther than the common Argentine table. Some of the wines were so low in quality that soda water was needed to help wash them down, a tradition that continues in some places today (although no longer because of poor quality).

In the past decade, wine from Mendoza has finally reached beyond the common table to the international stage. Argentina's National Wine Growing Institute has regulated the wine industry and spearheaded quality improvements, increasingly focusing on the international market. New production techniques, state-of-the-art machinery, advanced irrigation processes, and better grape varieties have combined to bring Mendoza international acclaim. The region's dry, sandy soil, low humidity, and rich sun combine to create wines of high alcohol content and rich fruity character, the most important of which is Malbec, characterized by a powerful fruit bouquet with sweet, dense tannins. Mendocine vineyards grow numerous other varietals, including cabernet sauvignon, Syrah, Barbera, chardonnay, and sauvignon blanc. At press time, some of the top choices were Angelina Zapata Malbec 1997, Doña Paula Malbec 1999, Bramare Malbec 1999, Conbos Malbec 1999, Nieto Senetiner Bonarda 2000, and Alta Vista Alto 1999 (80% Malbec, 20% Cabernet).

culminates with the **Fiesta Nacional de la Venimia (National Wine Harvest Festival),** which includes a parade, folk dancing, and coronation of the festival's queen. March 2003 is expected to bring the best harvest season in 18 years due to ideal weather conditions and improved grape quality, giving Argentines a much-needed reason to celebrate.

OUTDOOR ACTIVITIES

HIKING   Huentata, Las Heras 680, Mendoza (© **261/425-3108**), arranges single or multiple-day hiking trips. Two-hour treks offered by **Argentina Rafting Expediciones,** Ruta 7 s/n, 5549 Potrerillos (© **262/448-2037**), extend from Potrerillos to the waterfall at la Quebrada del Salto, where rappelling is possible. The 2-hour trek costs $10, while a full-day hike with lunch included runs $20.

HORSEBACK RIDING   Juan Jardel (© **262/448-3030**) offers horseback riding trips of various lengths and also coordinates with Argentina Rafting Expediciones. A day trip involving rafting in the morning and horseback riding in the afternoon can easily be arranged. **Argentina Rafting Expediciones** (see above) and **Ríos Andinos,** Ruta 7 Km 64, 5549 Potrerillos (© **261/431-6074**), offer 2-hour horseback rides for $13.

MOUNTAIN BIKING   In February, cyclists from around the world participate in **La Vuelta Ciclista de Mendoza,** a mini–Tour de France around Mendoza province. **Argentina Rafting Expediciones** (see above) and **Ríos Andinos** (see above) offer 2-hour mountain bike adventures for $12.

SKIING   The best place to ski, not just in Argentina but also in South America, is **Las Leñas** (see box, later in this chapter). Closer to Mendoza, the small resort of **Los Penitentes** (see "The Alta Montaña Driving Circuit," below) offers 23 downhill slopes and cross-country skiing. **Portillo** is a much larger and better-equipped ski resort just on the other side of the Chilean border. Just 80km (50 miles) south, **Vallecitos** is the smallest and closest ski resort to Mendoza, but can be difficult to reach in heavy snow conditions. Obtain information on the province's ski areas from Mendoza's **Subsecretaría Provincial de Turismo** (see "Essentials," earlier in this chapter).

WHITE-WATER RAFTING   Mendoza offers the best white-water rafting in Argentina, and during the summer months when the snow melts in the Andes and fills the Mendoza River, rafters enjoy up to Class IV and V rapids. Rafting is possible year-round, but the river is colder and calmer in winter months. Potrerillos, 53km (33 miles) west of Mendoza, has two professional tour operators offering half-day, whole-day, and 2-day trips on the Mendoza River, with direct transfers provided from Mendoza. These are **Argentina Rafting Expediciones** (see above) and **Ríos Andinos** (see above). Be sure to bring an extra pair of clothes and a towel, because you are guaranteed to get soaked. Children under 12 are not allowed to raft. Argentina Rafting has a small restaurant and bar where you can eat and defrost following your soaking in the river. Rafting starts at $12 for one hour, and both agencies also offer kayaking ($14 for 1 hr., single or double kayaks available), horseback riding, trekking, and mountain biking. The 2-day, 60km (37-mile) rafting trip is a Class III–IV excursion offered November through April. It costs $60 and includes all meals, camping gear, and transfer from Mendoza.

SHOPPING

On Friday, Saturday, and Sunday, an outdoor **handicrafts market** takes place during the day on Plaza Independencia. Regional shops selling handicrafts, leather goods, gaucho paraphernalia, and mate are located along Avenida Las Heras, two of which are **Las Veñas,** Av. Las Heras 399 (© 261/425-0498) and **Los Andes,** Av. Las Heras 445 (© 261/425-6688). More mainstream stores line Avenida San Martín. The city's best shopping mall is **Palmares Open Mall,** located on Ruta Panamericana 2650 in Godoy Cruz (© 261/413-9100). Most shops close from 1 to 4pm each day for siesta. You can also buy Mendocine wines at many shops, the least expensive costing no more than a few dollars a bottle and premiums going for $25 to $80. The Park Hyatt, Chile 1124 (© 261/441-1234), has an excellent wine shop, with a knowledgeable sommelier.

WHERE TO STAY

Mendoza has recently opened a few new hotels, which have substantially boosted the city's lodging quality. However, after the Park Hyatt, the level of hotel service quickly drops and the star classification posted at local accommodations is not reliable. In addition to the hotels listed below, a couple up-and-coming, modestly priced accommodations worth looking into are the **Microtel,** outside the city center at Acc. Sur and Lamadrid (© 261/432-0503) and a new bed and breakfast called **Quinta Rufino,** Rufino Ortega 142 (© 261/420-4696). Prices quoted are for high season, which in Mendoza is February through March, July, and September through November. Hotel rates are often discounted 15 to 20% in the off season. Prices listed below do not include the 21% tax.

EXPENSIVE

Park Hyatt Mendoza ★★★   Peering majestically over the Plaza de la Independencia, the Park Hyatt opened in 2001 after restoring the original facade of the 19th-century Plaza Hotel and building a seven-floor tower for guest rooms. Sweeping columns of granite and stone showcase the lobby, and an impressive collection of Mendocino art pays tribute to local culture. A landscaped courtyard separates different sections of the hotel, leading past water fountains and an outdoor dining area to a warm, inviting pool. Guest rooms could stand to lose a bit of the wood paneling, but are nevertheless spacious and contemporary. Fluffy duvets and feather pillows blanket the beds, and white marble bathrooms have separate bathtubs and showers with crystal washbasins. Kaua Spa deserves special mention because of its uniqueness: A professional team of masseurs from Bangkok give wonderful Thai massages, and the spa incorporates Mendocino wines in a variety of its body treatments (for example, shampoo based on wine acids or grape-seed oil body lotion). A well-equipped fitness room, Jacuzzi, sauna, and steam bath are here too. Hotel guests benefit from frequent cultural events, ranging from jazz and music shows to Spanish festivals and flamenco dances. Some events take place in Bistro M (see "Where to Dine," below), an excellent international restaurant boasting South America's first open kitchen. Bar Uvas is the city's premier wine bar, and the Regency Casino is Mendoza's try at Las Vegas. Many guests are from Buenos Aires and Chile, the latter taking advantage of favorable exchange rates across the border.

Chile 1124, 5500 Mendoza. Ⓒ **261/441-1234.** Fax 261/441-1235. www.mendoza.park.hyatt.com. 186 units. $145 double; from $175 suites. Rates include a beautiful buffet breakfast. AE, DC, MC, V. **Amenities:** Restaurant; wine bar; sports bar; heated outdoor pool; nearby golf; excellent health club and spa; concierge; business center; room service; babysitting; dry cleaning; laundry service. *In room:* A/C, TV, minibar, hair dryer safe.

MODERATE

Hotel NH Cordillera ★   The Spanish hotel chain NH caters to business travelers, and this Mendoza property is no different. Opened in late 2002, the NH has four floors of crisp, compact rooms, half of which face Plaza San Martín. The staff describes the hotel's style as minimalist, which fairly well describes their approach to service, as well. Yet the NH stands heads and shoulders above the city's other self-proclaimed four-star hotels, and guest rooms offer every modern convenience. Stay here because of the hotel's newness and central location, but don't expect many thrills.

Av. España 1324, 5500 Mendoza. Ⓒ **261/441-6464.** Fax 261/441-6450. www.nh-hotels.com. 105 units. $50 double; from $60 suites. Rates include small buffet breakfast. AE, DC, MC, V. **Amenities:** Restaurant; limited room service; Internet access. *In room:* A/C, TV, minibar, hair dryer, safe.

Park Suites Apart Hotel ★   A stylish new hotel 2 blocks from Plaza Independencia, the Park Suites attracts business people during the week and tourists on weekends. Single rooms are called "suites," ranging in size from junior to grand, while those with more than one room are called "apartments," accommodating up to six people. All have hardwood floors, kitchenettes, firm mattresses, stereo systems, and light, modern decor, although bathrooms are on the small size. Ask for a room with a mountain view. The staff is small, but friendly.

Mitre 753, 5500 Mendoza. Ⓒ **261/413-1000.** Fax 261/413-1019. www.parksuitesmza.com.ar. 56 units. Double $50 and up. Rates do not include breakfast. AE, DC, MC, V. **Amenities:** Restaurant; bar; pool; sauna; fitness room. *In room:* A/C, TV, minibar, fridge, hair dryer, safe.

WHERE TO DINE
EXPENSIVE

Bistro M ★★ INTERNATIONAL An international restaurant with French overtones, Bistro M created the first open kitchen in South America. Busy chefs attend to the wood-burning oven while crisp waiters attend to you; the most interesting dishes include marinated goat with *chimichurri* (chile and garlic sauce), grilled trout with artichokes and tomato slices, and veal spareribs. A spiral staircase climbs past a two-floor wine gallery housing over 2,500 selected regional wines, some of which are available by the glass. The sommelier will help guide you towards selection, but don't be surprised if you're steered towards a Malbec. At $60 a bottle, the Alta Vista "Alta 1999" is an exquisite, if expensive, choice. Bistro M has large windows looking out to Plaza Independencia, and an outdoor terrace opens in warm weather. Cultural events, such as a Mexican festival or a Spanish flamenco, are occasionally offered on weekend nights.

Park Hyatt Hotel, Chile 112. 📞 261/441-1234. Reservations recommended. Main courses $9–$15. AE, DC, MC, V. Daily 6:30–11am, 12:30–3:30pm, and 8pm–midnight.

1884 ★★★ INTERNATIONAL Francis Mallman has created Mendoza's top restaurant inside Bodega Escorihuela, known among other things for housing the biggest wine barrel in the province. Using fine Argentine meats and fresh local produce, his carefully presented cuisine combines his Patagonian roots with his French culinary training. Dishes are prepared with matching wine selections, with Malbec and Syrah topping the list. You can easily combine a tour of the bodega, which also has an art gallery, in the same visit. Tours are offered weekdays, every hour from 9:30am to 3:30pm.

Belgrano 1188, Godoy Cruz. 📞 261/424-2698. Reservations recommended. Main courses $9–$15. AE, DC, MC, V. Daily 6:30–11am, 12:30–3:30pm, and 8pm–midnight.

MODERATE

Don Mario ★★ ARGENTINE Next door to La Marchigiana, Don Mario serves the best Argentine steaks in town. Don't let the soothing country house atmosphere fool you—this is a serious Argentine *parrilla*. The *bife de chorizo* (strip steak) served *a punto* (medium rare) is the top selection, but any of the meats are outstanding. The "Don Mario brochette" includes sirloin, chicken, tomatoes, onions, and peppers on one delicious skewer. Non–meat eaters can choose from pizza, pasta, or one of the fish dishes. Two shelves of Mendoza wines beg to be disturbed, and the expert waitstaff will help guide you to a selection.

Palmares Open Mall. 📞 261/439-4838. Main courses $4–$6. AE, DC, MC, V. Daily noon–3pm and 8pm–midnight.

La Marchigiana ★★ ITALIAN Known to nearly everyone in town, Maria Theresa arrived from Italy in 1950 to open what's become Mendoza's top Italian kitchen. The restaurant's own history book details 50 years of experience in Mendoza and reveals some of the recipes of its famed homemade pastas. Octopus-like chandeliers hang from the familial A-frame dining room, where guests can easily hear the creative voices of the kitchen. You could start with a seasonal salad, but I recommend a hearty bowl of minestrone sprinkled with fresh Parmesan. Spaghetti, tagliatelli, ravioli, cannelloni, and lasagna are among the pasta choices, with a diverse selection of sauces to choose from (mushrooms in a light Provençal sauce being one). Never mind the North American tradition of drinking white wine with your pasta; a polite waiter is sure to steer you towards a *vino* *tinto* (red wine). Three pages of meat and fish follow on the menu, but you well may not have room after the minestrone and pasta. An extensive selection of desserts seals the menu—maybe a rich ricotta with chocolate pudding? The restaurant has a second location at Av. España 1619 (© **261/423-0751**).

Palmares Open Mall. © **261/439-1961**. Main courses $3–$5. AE, DC, MC, V. Daily noon–3pm and 8pm–midnight.

INEXPENSIVE

Estancia La Florencia *Value* ARGENTINE   This casual eatery pays homage to the legendary gaucho, and its two levels mimic a traditional estancia. Ask one of the waiters, none of whom is under 50, for a recommended plate and he is likely to tell you, *"Una comida sin carne no es comida"* (a meal without meat isn't a meal). So choose one of the many varieties of steaks, the *lomo* being the most tender, or order a half grilled chicken served with a lemon slice. Just remember that a plate of meat is a plate of meat, uncorrupted by green vegetables or anything but potatoes (usually fries). Other accouterments must be ordered separately. Food is served promptly and without fanfare, and the bill may be one of the lowest you will ever find.

Sarmiento and Perú. © **261/429-9117**. Main courses $2–$4. AE, DC, MC, V. Mon–Wed noon–5pm and 8pm–2am; Thurs–Sun noon–2am.

MENDOZA AFTER DARK

Mendoza nightlife is substantially more subdued than in Buenos Aires or Córdoba, but there is still a fair selection of bars and nightclubs that capture a night owl's attention. Thursday through Sunday are the biggest nights, with people getting started around midnight. The Park Hyatt Mendoza **Bar Uvas,** Chile 1124 (© **261/441-1234**), begins a bit earlier and offers a complete selection of Mendocine wines, with jazz and bossa nova groups playing most nights. Wine tastings are offered every Thursday at 9pm. **Apeteco,** at San Juan and Barraquero, has live music and dancing most nights. The city's best bars line Aristides Villanueva street in the center of town, and many people begin here with a drink before heading to a disco along Ruta Panamericana, located roughly 10km (6 miles) from the town center. **Runner** and **El Diablo** are the top discos in this area. There are a few tango bars in Mendoza, two of which are **C'Gastón** at Lavalle 35 (© **261/423-0986**) and **Abril Café,** at Las Heras 346 (© **261/ 420-4224**). For you gamblers, the **Regency Casino,** Chile 1124 (© **261/ 441-1234**), is substantially better than the Casino Provincial, offering blackjack, roulette, poker, and slots. Table bets are $1 to $50.

2 The Alta Montaña Driving Circuit

Climbing the mountains on the way to the Chilean border, this excellent driving circuit leads past the magnificent vineyards of Mendoza to breathtaking vistas of the Andes. It is an all-day excursion (it would take at least 5 hr. with no stops) that leads past the Uspallata Valley up to nearly 3,000m (9,843 ft.) at Las Cuevas and the entrance of Aconcagua Park. There are two routes you can take: The easier drive takes you past Potrerillos on the RN7—a small area along the Mendoza River popular for its white-water rafting—while a more challenging drive (due to winding dirt roads) takes you through the gorgeous natural-springs town of Villavicencio. (We recommend you go Villavicencio on the way and return via Potrerillos on the RN7.) Whichever route you choose, the roads come together in Uspallata, where the circuit continues to Las Cuevas on the RN7.

You can do this tour on your own, but it is easier with a driver who knows the roads. Note that a 4×4 is preferable, although not obligatory, for the route to Villavicencio. Expect temperatures to drop by about 15 degrees Fahrenheit as you climb the mountains.

HEADING TO USPALLATA VIA VILLAVICENCIO

Although it takes a couple hours longer than heading straight north on RN7, driving the R52 takes you to the natural springs of Villavicencio, the source of Argentina's well-known mineral water. Leaving Mendoza to the north through Las Heras, you'll be driving on the old international road to Chile. After 34km (21 miles) you'll pass the **Monumento Canota,** the spot where Generals San Martín and Las Heras split to confront the Spanish at different fronts in 1817. After Canota, you will begin to climb the Villivicencio Valley, and by 40km (25 miles) the road turns to gravel and becomes winding (the road here is known locally as the Caracoles de Villavicencio, or "the snails of Villavicencio"). A small **ranger station** at 50km (31 miles) offers information on the Villavicencio natural reserve, including sources of the mineral water and the region's flora and fauna. Eagles, condors, pumas, mountain cats, foxes, ostriches, guanacos, flowering cacti, and many plants and trees occupy the area.

VILLAVICENCIO

French-owned Danone purchased the rights to this land and its mineral water, and it is working hard to preserve the integrity of the springs. This explains why the **Hotel Termas Villavicencio,** frequented by Argentina's high society until its closing in 1980, has not reopened. Yet the lush gardens of the Normandy-style hotel, seen on the label of Villavicencio bottles, can still be toured by foot. Perched against the foothills with oaks and poplars, trickling streams, and wild flowers surrounding it, the hotel location represents a little paradise in the Andes. A small chapel, opened in 1941, lies just behind it. Next to the hotel, you can stop at the Hostería Villavicencio for lunch or a drink.

THE USPALLATA VALLEY

Continuing along the R52, you will follow the path that San Martín used for his liberation campaign. The dirt road zigzags its way up the canyon, dotted with silver mines exploited by the Spaniards in the 18th century. When you get 74km (46 miles) from Mendoza, you will have climbed to the 3,000m (9,843-ft.) summit. From here, you have a magnificent view of Aconcagua and the mountains, and the road begins to improve.

The road from the summit to Uspallata is a breathtaking 28km (17-mile) drive through the **Uspallata Valley.** You will descend into the valley through a small canyon, and when the valley emerges it must be one of the most beautiful sights in Argentina. The polychromatic mountains splash light off Aconcagua to your left and the "Tiger Chain" ahead, with occasional clouds painting shadows on some mountains and allowing sun to pour light on others. The curious rock formations surrounding you were filmed for the dramatic setting of *Seven Years in Tibet,* starring Brad Pitt. Just before you arrive in Uspallata, 2km (1 mile) north of town, you will see **Las Bovedas**—peculiar egg-shaped mud domes built in the 18th century to process gold and silver for the Spaniards.

HEADING TO USPALLATA VIA POTRERILLOS

This drive is significantly easier than the route through Villavicencio, taking you along the RN7 through the Precordillera mountains. Potrerillos is a small stop along the Río Mendoza, where tour companies arrange white-water rafting, horseback riding, and trekking. **Argentina Rafting Expediciones** (see "Outdoor Activities" under "Mendoza," earlier in this chapter) operates a small restaurant and bar off the RN7. The drive continues 49km (30 miles) alongside the Mendoza River directly to Uspallata.

USPALLATA

With only 3,500 inhabitants, Uspallata is a pretty sleepy place. But this small Andean town offers a variety of outdoor activities and makes an excellent base from which to explore the mountains. You can obtain limited visitor information from the **tourist information booth,** open daily from 9:30am to 8:30pm and located at the corner of RN7 and R52. Gustavo Pizarro is the area's best tour guide, and his **Pizarro Expediciones,** Ruta 7 (© **262/442-0261**), organizes horseback riding, mountain biking, climbing, and white-water rafting. If you want to stop for lunch while doing the Circuito Alta Montaña, do it in Uspallata, the last real town before the Chilean border.

WHERE TO STAY & DINE

Hotel Valle Andino ⭐   Given the town's limited selection of hotels, this is probably the best choice. The hotel's greatest merit is its beautiful grounds stretching towards the Andes. A true mountain retreat, the dimly lit wood lodge is popular with backpackers and hiking groups, and the staff can organize horseback riding trips from the hotel. Rooms are stark but modern, some accommodating up to five people. The recreation room has a fireplace and pool table.

Ruta 7 s/n. © 262/442-0033. www.hotelguia.com/hoteles/valleandino. 26 units. $25 double. Rate includes breakfast. No credit cards. **Amenities:** Restaurant; bar; indoor pool.

La Estancia de Elias ARGENTINE   A simple, friendly *parrilla* across from the Shell station, La Estancia de Elias is less touristy than other restaurants located along RN7. The empanadas are fresh and fluffy, and the *bife de chorizo* is enormous. There are also salads and pastas, or you could try the grilled *chivito* (goat), which is the specialty of the region. Heck, it's cheap enough you could probably order one of each.

Ruta 7, Km 1146. © 262/442-0165. Main courses $1–$4. No credit cards. Daily 9am–2am.

HEADING TO ACONCAGUA FROM USPALLATA

Continuing along the RN7, you'll drive through the wide U-shaped valley carved from ancient glaciers and loaded with minerals like iron, sulfur, talc, and copper. As you climb the canyon, you will see the first signs of the atrophying **Andes railway** to your left, an old narrow track from 1902 that lifted an

---

Las Cuevas: An Argentine Ghost Town

The final stop before the Chilean border, Las Cuevas (about 8km/5 miles from Parque Provincial Aconcagua) was a railroad town abandoned over two decades ago when the train stopped working. All around this area, you will see where huge boulders have crushed through railroad guards, designed to protect the train from fearsome avalanches. In addition to the abandoned building in Las Cuevas, you will also find the ruins of 18th-century snow shelters used for colonial travelers crossing the border. At 3,000m (9,840 ft.) above sea level, this chilly ghost town marks the peak of your excursion.

Hitting the Slopes in Las Leñas

One of South America's top ski destinations with more slopes than any single resort in the Americas, Las Leñas boasts 64km (40 miles) of runs, excellent snow, and typically small crowds. The summit reaches 3,430m (11,253 ft.), with a 1,230m (4,035-ft.) vertical drop. There are 30 runs, with approximately 8% set aside for beginners, 22% for intermediates, and 70% for advanced skiers. The resort's 11 lifts can transport up to 9,200 skiers per hour, which is far more capacity than the town has in accommodations. Consequently, you seldom have to wait in line to get to the top.

Las Leñas attracts wealthy Porteños as well as international skiers, and it has an active nightlife in winter. Snow season runs from June to mid-October. In summer, Las Leñas offers mountain biking, trekking, rafting, and fishing, and hotel prices drop significantly. The resort is most easily reached by taking a 90-minute flight from Buenos Aires to Malargüe, followed by a 1-hour bus to Las Leñas (68km/42 miles). Alternatively, you can travel by car or bus from Mendoza, which is a 4- to 5-hour drive (399km/248 miles).

While maybe not quite the five-star hotel the sign proclaims, **Pisces Club Hotel** ★★ is by far the best place to stay in Las Leñas. Many people arriving at the hotel, as elsewhere in Las Leñas, come on weeklong ski packages. Well-equipped rooms accommodate up to three people, and the stay includes breakfast and dinner. Following a day of skiing, the hotel provides hot drinks and warming by the fireplace, and the indoor pool, Jacuzzi, and sauna should re-invigorate the remaining cold parts of your body. The hotel also offers ski instruction and children's activities, as well as adult activities in the casino and nightclub.

Las Leñas lies in the southwest of Mendoza province, near the city of Malargüe and close to the Chilean border. To drive from Mendoza, take the RN40 to the PR 222. One tour operator offering packages from the United States is **Holidaze Ski Tours,** www.holidaze.com. In Buenos Aires, try **Rotamund,** Av. Roque Sáenz Peña 846, Piso 2, Buenos Aires (✆ 4321-5100; www.rotamund.com).

early-20th-century steam train up the mountains. The railroad was abandoned in 1980 due to a political dispute between Chile and Argentina and has never been reopened. When you get 20km (12 miles) from Uspallata, you'll come to **Puente Pichueta,** a stone bridge over the Pichueta River that was commissioned by Fernando VII in 1770 to allow messengers to travel from Argentina to Chile. The road leading to the bridge forms part of the old Inca trail.

LOS PENITENTES

About 165km (102 miles) past Mendoza, you will hit **Los Penitentes,** a small resort for downhill and cross-country skiing. It was named after a nearby mountain whose tall narrow peaks resemble a cathedral, a sort of mountain in penitence. There are 23 slopes accommodating all ski levels, as well as a ski school for instruction. Keep in mind, however, that **Portillo** is a much larger and better-equipped ski resort just on the other side of the Chilean border. If you decide to stay in Los Penitentes, **Ayelan,** Ruta 7, Km 165 (© **261/427-1123**), sits across the street from the ski resort with basic rooms looking towards the mountains. Doubles cost roughly $60 including breakfast, and the rustic dining room serves quality regional dishes (although the selection is limited).

PUENTE DEL INCA

Puente del Inca is a natural stone bridge used by the Incas to cross the Río de las Cuevas; it's about 6km (4 miles) past Los Penitentes. Under the bridge you will see the remains of an old spa that once belonged to a hotel. That hotel was destroyed in an avalanche but, in what many consider a miracle, the adjacent church went unscathed. Natural hot springs still flow through here, and you can don your bathing suit and take a dip. Near the spa, vendors sell handicrafts.

PARQUE PROVINCIAL ACONCAGUA

Just after Puente del Inca, you will come to the entrance of **Aconcagua Provincial Park.** At 6,960m (22,829 ft.), Cerro Aconcagua is the highest peak, not just in South America, but also in the entire Western Hemisphere. From RN7, you can see the summit on clear days. To enter the park, however, you must first obtain a permit from the park's "attention center" called Edificio Cuba (© **261/425-2031**) inside Mendoza's Parque San Martín. The location for where to buy permits changes periodically, so you should check with Mendoza's tourism office for additional details. Two-day, 7-day, and 20-day permits are available. With one of the shorter-duration permits, you can hike to the base camps without climbing to the summit. Those hoping to reach the top must buy a 20-day permit, which costs $200 (including emergency medical insurance). The climb is not technically difficult, but it demands strength and endurance. The south face, which gets little sun, is the most treacherous climb. The normal route is along the west side. You can get more information by checking the following website: www.aconcagua.com.

After visiting the park, we recommend you continue on to Las Cuevas (see box below). Return to Mendoza via Potrerillos on the RN7.

8

The Argentine Lake District

The Lake District is Argentina's premier vacation destination, a ruggedly beautiful jewel of a region characterized by snowcapped mountains, waterfalls, lush forest, the area's namesake lakes, and trout-filled, crystalline rivers. The region stretches from north of Junín de los Andes to the south of Esquel, incorporating small villages, ranches, several spectacular national parks, and the thriving city of Bariloche. Visitors here often liken the Lake District to Alpine Europe, as much for the landscape as for the clapboard architecture influenced by Swiss and German immigration. Although it is considered part of Patagonia, the Lake District has little in common with its southern neighbors, especially now that increased migration from cities such as Buenos Aires continues to urbanize the region.

The allure of the Lake District is that it offers something for everyone year-round, from hiking to biking, fishing to hunting, sightseeing to sunbathing, summer boating to winter skiing. The region is also well known for its food—venison, wild boar, trout, smoked cheeses, wild mushrooms, sweet marmalades, chocolates, and more. Tourism is the principal economic force here, which means that prices soar as the swarming masses pour into this region from mid-December to early March and during the month of July. We highly recommend that you plan a trip during the off season, especially in November or April, when the weather is still pleasant, although it is possible to escape the crowds even during the middle of summer.

Considering the enormous, flat pampa that separates Buenos Aires from the Lake District, and the region's proximity to the international border with Chile, many visitors opt to include a trip to Chile's Lake District while here. (For more on Chile's Lake District, see chapter 14.) This can be done by boat aboard the popular "Lake Crossing" through Puerto Blest to Lago Todos los Santos near Ensenada, or by vehicle. For general information about this region on the Web, try **www.interpatagonia.com**.

EXPLORING THE REGION

In this chapter, we have focused on the most scenic and accessible destinations in the Lake District: San Carlos de Bariloche (usually called simply Bariloche), Villa La Angostura, and San Martín de los Andes. This coverage includes the area's many national parks as well as driving tours and boat trips that take in the best of the stunning lakeside scenery. The best way to view this region is to base yourself in one of these towns and strike out and explore the surrounding wilderness. All of the towns described in this chapter offer enough outdoor and sightseeing excursions to fill 1 or even 2 weeks, but 4 to 5 days in one location is ample time for a visit. An interesting option for travelers is to make a detour into Chile via the lake crossing from Bariloche, or to organize a boat-bus combination that loops from Bariloche and Villa La Angostura in Argentina, then crosses the border into Chile and stops in Puyehue, continuing on south to

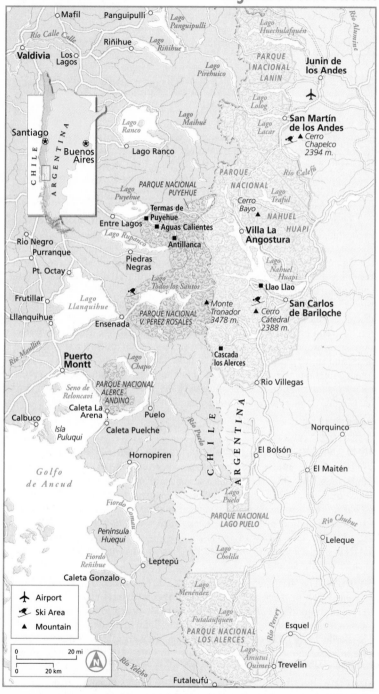

Mafil
Panguipulli
Lago Panguipulli
Río Calle Calle
Río Aluminé
Riñihue
Lago Riñihue
Lago Huechulafquén
Valdivia
Los Lagos
Lago Pirehuico
PARQUE NACIONAL LANIN
Junín de los Andes
✈
Lago Maihué
Lago Lolog
Lago Ranco
Lago Lacar
San Martín de los Andes
🎿 ▲ *Cerro Chapelco 2394 m.*
Santiago ✹
CHILE
ARGENTINA
Buenos Aires ✹
Lago Ranco
PARQUE NACIONAL *NAHUEL*
Río Calefú
PARQUE NACIONAL PUYEHUE
Lago Traful
Cerro Bayo ▲
NAHUEL
Lago Puyehue
Termas de Puyehue ■
■ Aguas Calientes
Villa La Angostura
HUAPI
Entre Lagos
Lago Rupanco
Rio Negro
Purranque
▲ Antillanca
Piedras Negras
Pt. Octay
Lago Nahuel Huapi
■ Llao Llao
Frutillar
Lago Todos los Santos
🎿
🎿
Lago Llanquihue
San Carlos de Bariloche
Llanquihue
Ensenada
PARQUE NACIONAL V. PEREZ ROSALES
▲ *Monte Tronador 3478 m.*
▲ *Cerro Catedral 2388 m.*
Río Maullín
Puerto Montt
Lago Chapo
■ *Cascada los Alerces*
Río Villegas
Seno de Reloncaví
PARQUE NACIONAL ALERCE ANDINO
CHILE
ARGENTINA
Caleta La Arena
Puelo
Norquinco
Calbuco
Isla Puluqui
Caleta Puelche
El Bolsón
El Maitén
Hornopiren
Golfo de Ancud
Lago Puelo
PARQUE NACIONAL LAGO PUELO
Río Chubut
Fiordo Comau
Leleque
Península Huequi
Lago Cholila
Fiordo Reñihue
Leptepú
Caleta Gonzalo
Lago Menéndez
Esquel
Lago Futalaufquen
✈ Airport
🎿 Ski Area
▲ Mountain
Río Percey
PARQUE NACIONAL LOS ALERCES
0   20 mi
0   20 km
Lago Amutui Quimei
Trevelin
Río Yelcho
Futaleufú

Puerto Varas or Puerto Montt, then crossing back into Argentina and Bariloche via the Lake Crossing. Another option is to cross from San Martín de los Andes to Pucón, Chile. All this takes some intricate planning; see chapter 14 for more information.

1 San Carlos de Bariloche (★(★

1,621km (1,005 miles) SW of Buenos Aires; 180km (112 miles) S of San Martín de los Andes

San Carlos de Bariloche, or simply Bariloche, is the winter and summer playground for vacationing Argentines and the second most-visited destination in the country. The city sits in the center of Nahuel Huapi National Park and is fronted by an enormous, irregularly shaped lake of the same name. Bariloche's grand appeal are the many outdoor activities, sightseeing drives, boat trips, great restaurants, and shopping opportunities here. Visitors could occupy themselves for a week regardless of the season.

The city itself embodies a strange juxtaposition: an urban city plopped down in the middle of beautiful wilderness. Unfortunately, Argentine migrants fleeing Buenos Aires, an ever-growing tourism industry, and 2 decades of unchecked development have left a cluttered mess in what once was an idyllic mountain town. Bits and pieces of the charming architecture influenced by German, Swiss, and English immigration are still in evidence. But visitors to Bariloche are sometimes overwhelmed by the hodgepodge of ugly apartment buildings, clamorous discos, and the crowds that descend on this area, especially from mid-December until the end of February and during ski season in July. Yet drive 10 minutes outside town, and you'll once again be surrounded by thick forests, rippling lakes, and snowcapped peaks that rival those found in alpine Europe. If you're looking for a quiet vacation, you'd be better off lodging outside the city center, on the road to the Llao Llao Peninsula or in the town of Villa La Angostura (see later in this chapter). On the flip side, Bariloche offers a wealth of services.

ESSENTIALS
GETTING THERE
BY PLANE The **Aeropuerto Bariloche** (© 02944/426162) is 13km (8 miles) from downtown. Buses to the city center are timed with the arrival of flights, and can be found outside at the arrival area; some are run by the airlines themselves. A taxi costs about $7. **Aerolíneas Argentinas/Austral,** Quaglia 238 (© 02944/422425;** www.aerolineasargentinas.com), has three daily flights from Buenos Aires and in summer operates three weekly flights from El Calafate. **LAPA,** Villegas 121 (© 02944/423714), serves Buenos Aires with one daily flight while **LADE,** Quaglia 238 #8 (© 02944/423562), serves small destinations in the area such as San Martín and Esquel.

BY BUS The **Terminal de Omnibus** (© 02944/432860) is at Av. 12 de Octubre 2400; there are a dozen companies that serve most major destinations in Argentina and Chile. **TAC** (© 02944/431521) has three daily arrivals from Buenos Aires and daily service from El Bolsón, Esquel, Mendoza, and Córdoba. **Vía Bariloche** (© 02944/435770) has three daily arrivals from Buenos Aires (the trip lasts about 20 hr.), and one daily trip from Mar del Plata. **Andesmar** (© 02944/422140) has service from Mendoza, Río Gallegos, and Neuquén, and service from Osorno, Valdivia, and Puerto Montt in Chile. In addition, there's a daily service from San Martín de los Andes via the scenic Siete Lagos (Seven Lakes) route (only during the summer); from Villa La Angostura, try **Ko-Ko** (© 02944/423090). For more on the Siete Lagos route, see chapter 14.

ACCOMMODATIONS ■
Hostería la Pastorella **9**
Hotel Aconcagua **7**
Hotel Edelweiss **8**
Hotel Huemel **5**
Hotel Nevada **16**
Hotel Panamericano **6**
Hotel Tres Reyes **20**
La Caleta Bungalows **3**
Llao Llao Hotel & Resort **1**
Residencial Piuké **19**
Villa Huinid **3**

DINING ◆
Casita Suiza **12**
Caza y Pesca **21**
Días de Zapata **11**
El Boliche de Alberto **14**
El Patacón **4**
Familia Weiss **18**
Friends **17**
Jauja Restaurante **13**
La Marmite **15**
Los Cesares **2**

ATTRACTIONS ●
Museo de la Patagonia **10**

BY CAR Bariloche can be reached from San Martín via several picturesque routes. The 200km (124-mile) scenic Siete Lagos route from San Martín de los Andes follows routes 234-231-237 (not recommended when it's raining, as the dirt roads turn to mud); the 160km (99-mile) Paso Córdoba takes routes 234-63-237; the longest, yet entirely paved (unlike the other routes described), 260km (161-mile) Collón Curá route follows routes 234-40-237 and is recommended for night driving or when the weather is crummy. To get to El Bolsón, follow Route 258 south; continue down 40 to get to Esquel. To cross into Chile, take the Puyehue Pass via Route 231 (through Villa La Angostura); during periods of heavy snowfall, chains are required.

TRAVELING BY BOAT TO CHILE **Catedral Turismo** offers a spectacular journey to the Lake District in Chile that operates as a boat-and-bus combination that terminates in Lago Todos los Santos near Ensenada and Puerto Varas. If you're planning to visit Chile, this is a superb option that really allows you to take in the beauty of the Andes and the volcanoes, rivers, and waterfalls in the mountain range; however, this journey is not recommended on days with heavy rain. The trip can be done in 1 long day or in 2 days, with an overnight in the Hotel Peulla in Chile (see Parque Nacional Vicente Pérez Rosales, in chapter 14, for more information). The trip costs $120 per person for the boat trip, and an average of $75 double for an overnight at the Hotel Peulla. Book at any travel agency or from Catedral Turismo's offices in Bariloche at Moreno 238 (© **02944/425443; www.crucedelagos.cl**).

GETTING AROUND

BY FOOT   The city is compact enough to explore by foot. However, most visitors spend just a few hours touring the city, and instead use Bariloche as a base to explore surrounding areas.

BY CAR   A rental car is how most savvy travelers visit this area; you'll want one here if you're staying outside the city center and also to drive through the region's sinuous roads that pass through exceptionally scenic landscapes, such as the Circuito Chico. All travel agencies offer excursions to these areas, which is another option. Rental agencies, including Budget, Dollar, Hertz, and Avis, have kiosks at the airport, and many downtown offices: **Budget** at Mitre 106 (© **02944/422482**), **AI Rent a Car** at Av. San Martín 235 (© **02944/422582**), **Dollar** at Villegas 285 (© **02944/430333**), **Hertz** at Quaglia 165 (© **02944/434543**), **Baricoche Rent A Car** at Moreno 115 (© **02944/427638**), **Localiza** at Av. San Martín 463 (© **02944/424767**), and **A Open Rent a Car** at Mitre 171 #15 (© **02944/426325**).

When navigating the streets of Bariloche, do not confuse two streets with similar names: V.A. O'Connor runs parallel to the Costanera, and J. O'Connor bisects it.

VISITOR INFORMATION

The **Secretaría de Turismo,** in the stone-and-wood Civic Center complex between calles Urquiza and Panzoni (© **02944/426784;** securismo@bariloche.com.ar), has general information about Bariloche, and it is an indispensable source for accommodation listings, especially during the high season. It also operates an information stand in the bus terminal. It's open Monday through Friday from 8am to 9pm, Saturday and Sunday from 9am to 9pm. For information about lodging and attractions surrounding Bariloche, try the **Secretaría de Turismo de Río Negro,** Av. 12 de Octubre 605, at the waterfront (© **02944/426644**); it's open Monday through Friday from 9am to 2pm.

A good website for all sorts of up-to-date travel information is www.bariloche.org.

The **Club Andino Bariloche,** Av. 20 de Febrero 30 (© **02944/422266;** fax 02944/424579; transitando@bariloche.com.ar), provides excellent information about hiking, backpacking, and mountaineering in the area. They sell maps and provide treks, mountain ascents, and ice walks led by guides from the Club Andino, as well as rafting, photo safaris, and horseback rides; open daily from 9am to 1pm and 6 to 9pm during winter, daily from 8:30am to 3pm and 5 to 9pm during summer. For general info about **Nahuel Huapi National Park,** head to the park's headquarters in the Civic Center (© **02944/424111**), open Monday through Friday from 8:30am to 12:30pm.

⌒ *Tips* Taking a Car Into Chile

If you're hoping to do a Lake District circuit combining both the Argentine and Chilean lake districts, be warned that you'll need additional insurance and written permission from the car-rental agency to take the vehicle across the border. We suggest using Avis rental car for these trips as it's the only company that has offices in numerous towns in both countries and can offer road-side assistance and get a replacement car to you quickly if you run into any problems.

FAST FACTS: BARILOCHE

Banks/Currency Exchange   Most banks exchange currency, including **Banco de Galicia,** at Moreno and Quaglia (*☎ 02944/427125*), or **Citibank,** Mitre 694 (*☎ 02944/436301*). Try also **Cambio Sudamérica,** Mitre 63 (*☎ 02944/434555*).

Hospital   Hospital Privado Regional, 20 de Febrero 594 (*☎ 02944/423074*).

Internet Access   Internet cafes are opening at a dizzying rate; chances are there'll be one right by your hotel. If not, try **Cybermac Café,** Rolando 217, #12 (no phone), or **Net & Cappuccino,** Quaglia 220 (*☎ 02944/426128*).

Laundry   Marva Lavematic, San Martín 325 (*☎ 02944/426319*); or **Lavematic,** Beschtedt 180 (*☎ 02944/433022*).

Pharmacy   Angel Gallardo at A. Gallardo 701 (*☎ 02944/427023*), **Zona Vital** at Moreno and Rolando (*☎ 02944/420752*) or **Nahuel** at Moreno 238 (*☎ 02944/422490*).

Police   For emergencies, dial **101.** For other matters call *☎ 02944/423434.*

Post Office   The central post office (no phone) is in the Civic Center, next to the tourist office.

WHAT TO SEE & DO IN BARILOCHE

Bariloche's **Civic Center,** Avenida Juan Manuel de Rosas and Panzoni, is a charming stone-and-wood complex that houses most municipal offices and tourism services, such as the information center and national park headquarters. The complex, built in 1940, was inspired by the architecture of Bern, Switzerland. Here you'll find the **Museo de la Patagonia Perito Moreno** (*☎ 02944/422309*), open Tuesday through Friday from 10am to 12:30pm and 2 to 7pm, Monday from 10am to 1pm; closed Sunday. Admission is $1. The museum has five salons dedicated to the natural science, history, and ethnography of the Bariloche region. The well-tended displays here are intriguing, notably the stuffed and mounted local fauna, such as *pudú* (miniature deer), puma, condor, and more. The second floor has displays of Mapuche artifacts, such as weapons, art, and jewelry, and other artifacts from the colonial period. A small gift shop sells postcards, books, and crafts.

SHOPPING   You'll find everything and anything along Bariloche's main street, Mitre, including shops selling souvenirs and Argentine products such as *mate* (tea) gourds and leather goods. For the region's famous smoked meats and cheese, and other regional specialties such as trout paté, try the renowned **Familia Weiss** at Mitre 360 (*☎ 02944/424829*) or **Del Turista** at Av. San Martín 252 or Mitre 239 (no phone). Del Turista also has an enormous array of chocolates and candy, as do other confectioneries up and down Calle Mitre, such as **Abuela Goye** at Mitre 258 (*☎ 02944/423311*) and Quaglia 221 (*☎ 02944/422276*); **Bari** at Mitre 339 (*☎ 02944/422305*); **Mexicana** at Mitre 288 (*☎ 02944/422505*); and **Mamuschka** at Mitre 216 (*☎ 02944/423294*). Stop by the visitor center for a map of Avenida Bustillo and the Llao Llao Peninsula, along which are dozens of shops selling regional specialties. Note that food items such as smoked meats wrapped in plastic are generally not permitted outside Argentina.

TOUR OPERATORS

A plethora of travel agencies offer everything under the sun along the streets of Bariloche. Most tours do not include lunch, and some charge extra for a bilingual guide. The best of the lot include **Catedral Turismo** at Moreno 238 (② **02944/ 425443**), with a wide variety of land excursions to El Bolsón, Cerro Tronador, and circuit sightseeing routes. **Tom Wesley Viajes de Aventura** at Mitre 385 (② **02944/435040**) specializes in horseback riding, but offers everything else too, even sightseeing tours and an adventure camp. **Cumbres Patagonia,** Ville-gas 222 (② **02944/423283;** cumbres@bariloche.com.ar), has easy sightseeing trips and more adventurous excursions, including trekking, fishing, and 4×4 trips. Also try **Ati Viajes** at V.A. O'Connor 335 (② **02944/426782**), **Barlan Travel** at Mitre 340 #68 (② **02944/426782**), or **Viajes Danneman** at Mitre 86 (② **02944/428793**).

PARQUE NACIONAL NAHUEL HUAPI ✸✸

Nahuel Huapi is Argentina's oldest and most popular national park, offering just about everything for any interest or physical level. The park surrounds the city of Bariloche, and its headquarters are downtown in the Civic Center (see "Visitor Information," above). The park's main feature is the 3,500m (11,480-ft.) extinct volcano **Tronador (Thunderer),** named for the rumbling produced by ice falling from the mountain's peak. But the park is also known for the glacial-formed Lake Nahuel Huapi and its lovely forested peninsulas and waterways that often provoke comparison to the channels of southern Patagonia or the fjords of Norway. Dur-ing summertime visitors can take part in day hikes or backpacking trips along one of the park's several trails or boat out to one of the lake's islands.

There are also plenty of other outdoor activities such as rafting, horseback rid-ing, and fishing, and during the winter the park's other dominant peak, **Cerro Catedral,** is a popular ski resort. Easy access to all regions of the park make Nahuel Huapi popular with visitors seeking mellower activities, such as sight-seeing drives and cable cars to magnificent lookout points. The following infor-mation is for all attractions within Nahuel Huapi and around Bariloche.

THE ROAD TO THE LLAO LLAO PENINSULA ✸✸✸

The Cerro Campanario provides possibly the best lookout point in the region, with exceptional views of Nahuel Huapi and Perito Moreno lakes, as well as the ravishing beauty of the Llao Llao Peninsula and the peaks surrounding it. The lookout point is accessed by a 7-minute cable car ride located 17km (11 miles) outside Bariloche on the road to Llao Llao, meaning you'll have to arrange transportation with a tour, drive a rental car, or take a bus. Or you can inquire about transfer shuttles from downtown at the Cerro Campanario cable car com-pany's Bariloche office. There's also a restaurant with panoramic views. The office is at Belgrano 41 #B (② **02944/427274**), and is open daily from 9am to noon and 2 to 6pm; the cost for the cable car is $4.

The Cerro Campanario is along a popular, 60km (37-mile) drive around the Llao Llao Peninsula, commonly known as the **Circuito Chico.** This drive offers spectacular views of Nahuel Huapi and Perito Moreno lakes and the snow-capped peaks of Cerro Otway and Catedral that tower over them. The drive begins 18km (11 miles) from Bariloche on Avenida Bustillo, which changes into Route 237, loops around the peninsula as Route 77 and meets back at Route 237 and eventually Bustillo, all the while meandering through dense forest and picturesque bays with outstanding lookout points. Visitors will find *parrilla* (grill) and fondue-style restaurants along the way, as well as the world-renowned **Llao Llao Hotel & Resort** (see later in this chapter). Stop by the visitor center to pick up a detailed Circuito Chico map highlighting restaurants and shops along the way. Again, most tour operators offer this excursion.

CERRO OTTO ★★

Walk, bike, drive, or ride a cable car to the top of **Cerro Otto** for sweeping views of Lake Nahuel Huapi, the Llao Llao Peninsula, and the high peaks of Catedral and Tronador, as well as for an assortment of diversions, including paragliding, trekking, rock climbing, and, during the winter, skiing and dog-sledding. The road up to Cerro Otto takes visitors through a thick forest of pine, beech, and *alerce* (larch) populated with charming chalets. To walk (2–3 hr.) or bike, take Avenida Los Pioneros for about 1km (about ½ mile) and follow the signs to Cerro Otto. Or take the free shuttle bus that leaves from Mitre and Villegas; it runs daily, every hour, from 10:30am to 4:30pm. The **cable car** (*©* **02944/441035**) costs $8 per person and runs January through February and July through August daily from 9:30am to 6pm; the rest of the year it runs daily from 10am to 6pm. Atop the summit you'll also find a revolving restaurant (*©* **02944/441035**). About a 20-minute walk from the restaurant there's a cafe run by the **Club Andino** (see "Visitor Information," earlier in this chapter).

A DRIVING TOUR: CERRO TRONADOR, LOS ALERCES WATERFALL & VENTISQUERO NEGRO

This wonderful, full-day excursion takes visitors through lush forest and past hidden lakes such as the picturesque Lago Mascardi, waterfalls, and beaches to a trail head that leads to the face of the Ventisquero Negro (Black Glacier). You'll need a vehicle to drive the 215km (133-mile) round-trip road, including a detour to the Cascada Los Alerces (Los Alerces Waterfall); it's 170km (105 miles) without the detour. Plan to stop frequently at the various lookout points along the road. Most tour agencies offer this excursion for about $12 to $14 per person.

Leaving Bariloche on Onelli Street headed south, continue along Route 258 toward El Bolsón, passing Lake Gutierrez and several teahouses and smokeries that sell regional specialties. After about 35km (22 miles), you'll reach Villa Mascardi. From here it is possible to take a full-day sailing excursion aboard the *Victoria II* that takes riders across Lake Mascardi to the Hotel Tronador for lunch, followed by a bus ride up the valley to Pampa Linda and Los Ventisqueros for a trail walk. Visitors return the same way. This excursion can be booked at any travel agency and usually includes transportation from Bariloche leaving at 9am and returning at 8pm (Nov–Mar only), or you can leave directly from the dock if you have your own vehicle. The cost, including transportation from Bariloche, is $15 per person.

If you're not taking the sailing excursion, continue past Villa Mascardi, and take the road that branches off to the right. At the Río Manso bridge a road heads left to the Los Alerces Waterfall. A 300m (984-ft.) walk takes you to a vista point looking out at the waterfall. After doubling back, you reach the bridge again, where you head left, continuing along the shore of Lake Mascardi until reaching the Hotel Tronador. The charming log cabin hotel, built in 1929 by a Belgian immigrant family, is backed by high peaks and makes a good spot for lunch. The road continues up the valley of the Río Manso Superior, winding through alpine scenery until arriving at Pampa Linda and eventually ending at a stunning cirque (a steep valley containing a lake) draped with vegetation and waterfalls. From here there's a trail that leads to the Black Glacier, named for the debris that colors the ice at its terminus. Return to Bariloche the same way you came.

BOAT EXCURSIONS

There are several boat excursions available from Puerto San Carlos or Puerto Pañelo at Llao Llao. Cost fluctuates between $7 and $16 per person; to obtain exact prices for any of the following trips and make a reservation, stop by any travel agency, or call ℂ **02944/426109** for more information.

An enjoyable full-day excursion takes you to **Isla Victoria** and the **Bosque Arrayanes** (see also "Villa La Angostura," later in this chapter) by boat from Puerto San Carlos or Puerto Pañuelo. The excursion begins with a 30-minute sail to Isla Victoria, where passengers can disembark for a walk through a conifer forest or ascend to a lookout point atop Cerro Bella Vista via chair lift. The second stop is Península Quetrihué and the Bosque Arrayanes, famous for its concentration of the unusual terra cotta–colored *arrayán* tree. These handsome trees (which are really bushes) have an odd, slick trunk that is cool to the touch. From Puerto Pañuelo to Isla Victoria, trips leave at 10am and return at 5:30pm; from Puerto San Carlos, trips leave at 9am and return at 6:30pm.

There are also boat trips to **Puerto Blest.** These excursions sail through classic fjords and exuberant vegetation known as the Valdivian Forest, until reaching Puerto Blest. From this point there is an optional bus ride to Laguna Frías followed by a boat ride to Puerto Frías, then back to Puerto Blest. The return trip to Puerto Pañuelo includes a stop at Los Cántaros waterfall. There is a restaurant at Puerto Blest, or you can bring a picnic lunch. The trips are very crowded in the summer. From Puerto Pañuelo, trips to Puerto Blest leave at 10am and return at 5pm; trips from Puerto San Carlos leave at 9am and return at 6pm.

The new sailing trip to the well-organized, auto-guided trail at **Isla Huemul** gives visitors a chance to walk through native forest and visit a now-abandoned nuclear fusion study center. There are six sailings daily from Puerto Pañuelo; the round-trip journey takes 3 hours.

OUTDOOR ACTIVITIES

BIKING   Mountain bike rental and information about bike trails and guided trips in Nahuel Huapi are available from **Bike Way** at V.A. O'Connor 867 (ℂ **02944/424202**), **Bariloche Mountain Bike** at Gallardo 375 (ℂ **02944/ 462397**), and **Dirty Bikes** at V.A. O'Connor 681 (ℂ **02944/425616**).

FISHING   This region provides anglers with excellent fly-fishing on the Manso, Traful, and Machico rivers, and trolling on Lake Nahuel Huapi for introduced species such as brown trout, rainbow trout, and landlocked salmon. You can pick up information and fishing licenses at the **Club Caza y Pesca** on the coast at Onelli and Avenida 12 de Octubre (ℂ **02944/421515**), open Monday through Friday from 9am to 1pm, or the office of the Parque Nacional Nahuel Huapi in the Civic Center. The **Patagonia Fly-Shop** and its owner-guide Ricardo Ameijeiras offer great fly-fishing expeditions, multiple-day programs in lodges, and day tours with bilingual guides. They can be found at Quichahuala 200 (ℂ **02944/441944;** flyshop@bariloche.com.ar). Tour agencies such as **Cumbres Patagonia,** at Villegas 222 (ℂ **02944/423283**), offer half-day and full-day fly-casting and trolling fishing excursions.

HIKING   The Nahuel Huapi National Park has a well-developed trail system that offers day hikes, multiple-day hikes, and loops that connect several backcountry *refugios,* some of which offer rustic lodging. The national park office in the Civic Center provides detailed maps and guides to difficulty levels of trails. Another great source for information is the **Club Andino,** at Av. 20 de Febrero 30 (ℂ **02944/422266;** www.clubandino.com.ar), which also has trails, guided trekking, ice walks, and climbing trips on Cerro Tronador.

HORSEBACK RIDING   Horseback rides in various areas of the park are offered by **Tom Wesley Viajes de Aventura** at Mitre 385 (ℂ **02944/435040**), which also has a kid-friendly adventure camp. Rides cost an average of $8 for 2 hours and $12 for 3 hours. **Cumbres Patagonia** at Villegas 222 (© **02944/ 423283**) has trips to Fortín Chacabuco for $15 per half day and $22 per full day, including lunch.

RAFTING   Various companies offer river rafting on the Río Manso in both Class III and Class IV sections, either half-day or full-day trips. The average cost for a half day is $22 to $25 and full day, $30 to $38. Easier floats down the Class I Río Limay are also available, for about $12 for a half day. Excursions include all equipment, transportation, and a snack or lunch (full-day trips). Try **Cumbres Patagonia** at Villegas 222 (© **02944/423283**), **Transitando lo Natural** at Mandisoví 72 (© **02944/423918**), or **Rafting Adventure** at Mitre 161 (© **02944/432928**).

SKIING & SNOWBOARDING   Bariloche's main winter draw is the ski resorts at Cerro Catedral. The resort is divided in two, with separate tickets for Robles and Catedral (it's possible to buy a more expensive ticket accepted by both resorts). Robles's bonus is that it is typically less crowded, with excellent open bowl skiing. Catedral offers more advanced lift services, but its runs are usually packed. Lift tickets cost $10 to $15 for adults and $6 to $10 for kids, depending on high and low seasons. Bariloche suffers from a continually ascending snowline level, so the bottom portion is often patchy or bald. Both resorts are well liked by families and beginners for their abundance of intermediate terrain, but there's plenty of advanced terrain, too.

The season runs from about June 15 to September 30. Every August the resorts host the **National Snow Party,** with torchlight parades and other events (contact the Catedral ski resort for more information). The bustling Villa Catedral is at the base of the resorts with a jumble of shops, rental stores, and several lodging options. **Alp Apart Hotel** has fully furnished apartments for two to six guests, with lodging and ticket combinations that run about $60 to $80 per person, per evening (© **02944/460105;** alp_uno@bariloche.com.ar). **Cabañas Autu Pukem** has cabins for six to eight guests; consult them directly for prices (© **02944/460074;** norconde@ciudad.com.ar).

WHERE TO STAY

If you're looking for luxury, you'll find the most options along the main road outside town that runs parallel to the lake and leads to the Llao Llao Peninsula. The larger hotels in the city (such as the Panamericano) tend to cater to tour groups and aren't especially luxurious or service oriented, but their advantage is location; staying in town puts you steps from the many excellent restaurants and shops in this tiny metropolis in the mountains. If you're planning to rent a car, then by all means stay outside the city and drive in at your convenience.

A handful of hotels in and around Bariloche are owned by unions and offer discounts to members. These hotels, such as Argentina Libre, Curu Leuvu, Puente Perón, and the larger hotels on Avenida Bustillo toward Llao Llao, including the Amancay and Panamericano (not to be confused with the Panamericano that's downtown), can take on a clubby workers' atmosphere not usually desired by most visitors. Avoid completely hotels owned by the several tour groups that bring thousands of energetic teens to Bariloche from June to December every year (these hotels are identifiable by the blue logo AUSTONIA). A few hotels are subcontracted to lodge students, such as the Hotel Bella Vista. During the high season (Dec 15–Feb 28 and Easter week), prices double. Many hotels consider the months of July and August to be mid-season, with mid-range prices to match, but some hotels charge high-season rates (July is especially busy).

The cheapest rates are from March 1 to June 30 and September 1 to December 15. Dates vary; inquire before booking and always ask for promotions or discounts for multiple-day stays.

WITHIN THE CITY CENTER
Expensive

Hotel Edelweiss ⓖ★   This hotel offers reliable service and huge double bedrooms, and is a solid choice in downtown Bariloche in this price category (but don't expect much luxury). Double superiors come with two full-size beds, bay windows, and lake views, as do the suites. The double standards are smaller, with a single full-size bed or two twins and a view of a building in the back, but they are just as comfortable and $10 cheaper. All rooms and bathrooms have recently been updated. The design is pleasant but very run-of-the-mill for a hotel that deems itself a five-star. The suites deserve mention for their gargantuan size, with separate living areas and small bars; suite bathrooms have hydromassage tubs. There is an aging penthouse pool with glass walls affording views of Lake Nahuel Huapi. The lounge area has polished floors, leather couches, and fresh flowers; there's also a computer with Internet access available for a nominal fee. The hotel offers several attractive packages and promotional rates, so be sure to ask when making your reservations.

Av. San Martín 202, San Carlos de Bariloche. ⓒ 02944/426165; in the U.S. 800/207-6900; in the U.K. 08705/300-200; in Australia 800/221-176. Fax 02944/425655. www.edelweiss.com.ar. 100 units. $95–$160 double superior; from $170 suite. Rates include buffet breakfast. AE, DC, MC, V. Valet parking. **Amenities:** 2 restaurants; bar; indoor pool; sauna; room service; game room. *In room:* TV, minibar, safe.

Hotel Nevada   Centrally located and welcoming with an appealing mint green and wood facade, the Nevada underwent a complete renovation in 1993, a date it now posts in large numbers outside in contrast to its real age, 1952, when it was one of the few hotels in the city. The hotel is billed as traditional although its rooms and lobby are slick and modern. A cream-and-maroon restaurant/lounge has a bar offset with pillars painted to appear marble, and there is often loud music playing in the background. The rooms are agreeable, with varnished wood paneling, but are average-size for the price. Two rooms can be connected to make an apartment, but there isn't really any advantage, apart from giving parents an open door to their kids' bedroom. For $10 to $15 more, you can book a brighter double superior with a tiny seating area and large windows that overlook the street. Most guests are South American and traveling individually so you get less of the busloads of tourists traveling on package tours here.

Rolando 250, San Carlos de Bariloche. ⓒ 02944/522778. Fax 02944/527914. www.nevada.com.ar. 81 units. $65–$105 double standard; from $115 junior suite. Rates include continental breakfast. AE, DC, MC, V. **Amenities:** Restaurant; lounge; sauna; room service; laundry service. *In room:* TV, minibar.

Hotel Panamericano ⓖ★ *Overrated*   The Hotel Panamericano has long coasted on its reputation as one of Bariloche's premier accommodations, boasting a casino, a lake view, a range of amenities, and a downtown branch of the popular El Patacón restaurant (see "Where to Dine," later in this chapter). Its five-star rating is exaggerated, however, especially when compared to rivals such as the Llao Llao Hotel & Resort (see below). The rooms are spacious and comfortable, but the design needs a face-lift and everything seems rather aging and tired. The lake views are available only above the fifth floor; in fact, the hotel rarely books rooms on the bottom floors unless they're hosting a convention, although they have plenty of tour groups that fill the hotel year-round. The back rooms face an ugly building, but are cheaper. The junior suites are quite nice, and really a better deal than the regular suites—although just a tad smaller, they come with plant-filled balcony patios and outdoor table and chairs, as well as a fireplace and a living area setup the staff will arrange to your liking. A double comes with two full-size beds or a king. Inside the lobby, a faux waterfall trickles in the background, and a bar/lounge regularly has live piano music. There is a steamy penthouse pool and a glass-enclosed exercise room where you can work out while savoring the lake view; a personal trainer is on hand to offer special ski-oriented workouts in the winter. The hotel has another 100 or so rooms and a casino on the other side of the street, connected by an aerial walkway.

Av. San Martín 536, San Carlos de Bariloche. ©/fax 02944/425846. www.panamericanobariloche.com. 306 units. $110 double; from $185 suite. Rates include buffet breakfast. AE, DC, MC, V. Valet parking. **Amenities:** 2 restaurants; lounge; bar; indoor pool; exercise room; sauna; room service; massage; laundry/dry cleaning service. *In room:* TV, minibar, coffeemaker.

Moderate

Hotel Tres Reyes   Located directly on the Costanera, just a few minutes' walk from the civic center, this venerable hotel is often overlooked, but it's difficult to understand why. It has a tremendous amount of stark, Scandinavian style preferred by the Belgian immigrant who built the hotel in 1950, and perhaps that does not appeal to everyone. Nevertheless, the hotel has been superbly maintained, with architectural details such as wood ceilings and beechwood paneling, and the vast lounge area has dozens of chairs and a velvet couch to sink into while you gaze out over the lake. The backyard has a path that meanders through a pleasant garden. All the rooms have been renovated within the past year, with new bedding, paint, curtains, and carpet, and all are warm and come with sparkling bathrooms. Lake-view rooms are more expensive, but they might not be as desirable as loud traffic speeds by well into the night. During the 1960s, the hotel's red leather bar was the "in" spot for Bariloche's fashionable set, and it hasn't been altered in the slightest. The service is very friendly.

Av. 12 de Octubre 135, San Carlos de Bariloche. © 02944/426121. Fax 02944/424230. www.hoteltres reyes.com. 75 units. $52–$92 double garden view; $64–$112 lake view; from $96 suite. Rates include continental breakfast. AE, DC, MC, V. **Amenities:** Restaurant; bar; room service; laundry service. *In room:* TV, safe.

Inexpensive

Hostería La Pastorella   This cozy little hotel was one of the first in Bariloche, built in the 1930s. Its gingerbread style hearkens back to the German family who first ran the establishment. The Pastorella is entirely comfortable, with a dining area and a sunny lounge and bar that open up onto a lush garden. The rooms are a bit tired, but for the price they're a good value. Some rooms have an extra seating area, although the funny futon-like chairs do nothing to beckon you to take a seat. Try to get a room that looks out over the garden. The hotel is run by a friendly Argentine couple who have recently installed a sauna ($3 extra). Note that this hotel does not accept children.

Belgrano 127, San Carlos de Bariloche. © 02944/424656. Fax 02944/525984. lapastorella@bariloche.com.ar. 12 units. $20–$35 double. Rates include continental breakfast. AE, MC, V. **Amenities:** Bar; sauna.

Hotel Aconcagua *Value*   This small, well-kept but older hotel is one of the best values in Bariloche. The establishment runs like clockwork, a carry-over from the German immigrant who built the hotel and whose design influence can be found throughout the lobby and lounge area. The rooms are nothing to go wild over, with average beds and a late 1960s design, but a few have lake views, and doubles with a full-size bed are spacious (doubles with 2 twins are not, however). The bathrooms are aging but impeccable; the showers do not have stalls, just a shower curtain. Within the lounge is a cowhide bar with leatherette chairs surrounding a fireplace. The included "American" breakfast is quite good, and the dining area is pleasant and sunny. The receptionists are friendly and try hard to help with directions; but be patient as they don't speak much English.

Av. San Martín 289, San Carlos de Bariloche. © **02944/424718.** Fax 02944/424719. aconcagua@ infovia.com.ar. 32 units. $18–$30 double. Rates include continental breakfast. AE, MC, V. **Amenities:** Lounge; room service. *In room:* TV.

OUTSIDE THE CITY CENTER, ON THE ROAD TO THE LLAO LLAO PENINSULA
Very Expensive

Llao Llao Hotel & Resort ★★★ *Kids*   The internationally renowned Llao Llao Hotel & Resort is one of the finest hotels in Latin America, as much for its magnificent location as its sumptuous, elegant interiors and refined service. Situated on a grassy crest of the Llao Llao Peninsula and framed by rugged peaks, this five-star hotel was modeled after the style of Canadian mountain lodges, taking cues such as cypress and pine-log walls, stone fireplaces, antler chandeliers, and barn-size salons. This is the place to spend the night if you're willing to splurge for a special evening. The hotel was first built in 1938, but burned to the ground and was rebuilt again in 1939; since its inception it has been scrupulously maintained. A driveway winds up to the hotel where a discreet security guard monitors traffic: The hotel tries to keep gawkers at a distance, although visitors may come for a drink, afternoon tea, or a meal. The lounge has glossy wood floors carpeted with Oriental rugs, coffee-colored wicker furniture, and soft lights, and is the site of frequent teas and special appetizer hours. The nearby Club House has a daily tea from 4 to 7pm.

From the lobby, every turn leads to another remarkable room, including a "winter garden" cafe whose expansive glass walls look out onto a large patio, the hotel's golf course, and Lake Nahuel Huapi beyond. A monumental hallway adorned with paintings from local artists leads to the rooms, all of which have been decorated in a rustic country design and come with gleaming white bathrooms—nice, but the style is not as exceptional as one would expect from a hotel of this caliber. Standard rooms are comfortable but quite small; superior suites are split into bedroom and living areas and come with a wraparound deck and fireplace; there's also a lovely two-bedroom cabin with a splendid view of Lake Moreno. The hotel has a handful of unadvertised inside standard double rooms that come without a view. Those are reserved for drop-ins who inquire at reception for the cheapest accommodations (no prior reservations accepted for these rooms). There's a new spa with treatment rooms affording breathtaking lake and mountain views. Included in the price of the rooms is a myriad of daily activities from watercolor painting classes for adults to games and events for kids.

The hotel's fine-dining restaurant, Los Cesares, is the best in the Bariloche area (see "Where to Dine," below) and the business center has free Internet access available for registered guests.

Av. Bustillo, Km 25. © **02944/448530.** Fax 02944/445789. Reservations (in Buenos Aires): © 11/4311-3434; fax 11/4314-4646. www.llaollao.com. 159 units. $160–$402 double; $318–$1,365 suite; $378–$531 cottage. Rates include buffet breakfast. AE, DC, MC, V. **Amenities:** 2 restaurants; bar; lounge; small indoor heated pool; on-property golf course; tennis courts; exercise room; fabulous spa; Jacuzzi; extensive watersports equipment; children's center; video arcade; tour and car-rental desk; business center; shopping arcade; salon; room service; massage; babysitting; laundry/dry cleaning service. *In room:* TV, safe.

Expensive

La Cascada Hotel ⭐ La Cascada's prize feature is a lovely garden with a frothing waterfall that gives the hotel its name. The property has an uneven style but is comfortable and pleasant, and its location 6km (4 miles) from town ensures a quiet connection with nature. The hotel has hosted its share of luminaries, notably Argentine ex-president Carlos Ménem and more recently Sarah Ferguson, the Duchess of York. The hotel seems like someone's stately home. Although the property was totally renovated in 1988, many design details hearken back to the hotel's founding in 1950, such as the Scandinavian-style dining area and the classic English "Imperial" suites. Each guest room and common area seems to come from a different school of design, such as the early '80s purple disco or the country-style, wood-walled standard doubles with gingham bedspreads. The "Gris" suites are perhaps the best in the hotel; fresh, clean interiors feature two glass-enclosed nooks and an abundance of sunlight. A double with a lake view costs $20 more than rooms with a view of the surrounding vegetation. Doubles have bay windows and a few have king-size beds, but you'll have to ask for one. Outside is a grassy slope that leads to a private beach, and there is a short nature trail that winds around the hotel's 3-hectare (7-acre) property. A taxi to town costs about $2.

Av. Bustillo, Km 6. © 02944/441088. Fax 02944/441076. www.lacascada.com. 25 units. $110–$130 double; from $180 suite. Rates include full breakfast. AE, DC, MC, V. **Amenities:** Restaurant; bar; heated indoor pool; exercise room; sauna; game room. *In room:* TV, safe.

Villa Huinid ⭐⭐ *Finds* The country-style, luxurious cabins and suites that make up the newer and very modern Villa Huinid, 2.5km (1½ miles) from the city center, are top-notch choices for travelers looking for independent accommodations outside town. The complex faces the lake, where it has a private beach, and is backed by a thick forest with a walking trail. Each cabin is handcrafted of knotty cypress, with stone fireplaces, lovely decks with a full-size barbecue, and a handsome decor of floral wallpaper, plaid bedspreads, craftsy furniture, and other accents such as dried flowers and iron lamps. The units come as four-, six- and eight-person *cabañas* with fully stocked kitchens and cozy living areas; however, there are also five suites with minibar and coffeemaker, but no kitchen or separate seating area. The suites might seem a bit lonely as there is no lobby to relax in. All accommodations come with daily maid service. The bathrooms are sumptuous, with wooden sinks and hydromassage baths, and the cabins come with one and a half bathrooms. The service provided by the gracious owners of the Villa Huinid is one of this hotel's highlights, as are the property's well-manicured grounds, which are offset by a trickling stream that meanders through the property. Behind the rooms are several aromatic gardens and a dense forest. A full-service luxury hotel annex (with bar, restaurant, and guest rooms) is being built in this forest and should be operational in mid-2003; until then expect a little bit of construction noise and inquire as to the status of the building when you make your reservations. The Huinid has its own transfer van to get you into town when you need to or to the ski areas in winter.

Av. Bustillo, Km 2.5. ©/fax 02944/5235234. www.villahuinid.com.ar. 18 units. $53–$90 suite; $90–$152 2-person *cabaña*. AE, DC, MC, V. **Amenities:** Laundry service. *In room:* TV, fridge, coffeemaker, safe.

Moderate

La Caleta Bungalows *Value* These two- to seven-person bungalows are a deal for those seeking the independence of kitchen facilities and a location close to town, without actually being in it. Run by an amicable British expatriate, the rooms are not the most luxurious on the shore, but they are entirely comfortable and have knockout views of Nahuel Huapi. Each bungalow is nestled among winding, flower-filled walkways, and the principal room has a large dining table and a basic, open kitchen. The interiors are made of white stucco and feature a combination of one full-size bed and bunk beds, depending on the size. The bedrooms that sit behind the dining area have large, one-way mirrored windows that allow guests to see out toward the view. Each unit comes with a central fireplace. La Caleta has a private beach across the road, and the owner has a wealth of tourist information and offers excursions. Downtown is a 25-minute walk or $1 taxi ride away.

Av. Bustillo, Km 5.7, San Carlos de Bariloche. ©/fax **02944/441837.** bungalows@bariloche.com.ar. 13 units. $22–$72 *cabaña* for 2. No credit cards. **Amenities:** Tour desk. *In room:* TV, kitchen.

Inexpensive

Huemel *Value Kids* This wood and stone lodge sits right on the edge of a cliff, affording magnificent views of the lake from most of its expansive public areas. A 100-year-old cypress tree towers over the entire structure. Originally built in the late 1940's, the rambling building has seen several additions including a restaurant and lounge on the lower floor, closer to the water, where you feel as if you're aboard a ship heading out to sea. Rooms are very basic, with white bedspreads, wooden shelves, and tiny clean bathrooms. Many of the rooms have a window looking directly out onto the water; though beware that some have only partial lake views. Ask to see the room, if possible, before accepting it. This is the best bargain in Bariloche for budget accommodations with lake views so be sure to make your reservations early if you're arriving during the high season. On the flip side, during the low season a single room can go for as low as $11 including both tax and breakfast, so do not hesitate to bargain.

Av. Bustillo 1500, San Carlos de Bariloche. ©/fax **02944/424066.** Huemel@bariloche.com.ar. 78 units. $21–$33 double. Rates include continental breakfast. No credit cards. **Amenities:** Restaurant; bar; lounge; game room; laundry service. *In room:* TV.

WHERE TO DINE

The best restaurants are located on the road to the Llao Llao Peninsula. El Patacón and Los Cesares are the region's top restaurants. Unlike hotels, however, the restaurants in downtown Bariloche are an excellent value and if you're not staying in town, you'll probably find yourself coming here to dine. The best value in Patagonia might very well be the El Boliche de Alberto Steakhouse where you can get a tender cut of Argentine steak, salad, and potatoes for less than $6. For value and quality, Bariloche restaurants are quite superb. Service, however, is not the highlight here. We've found the starred restaurants below to offer the best over-all service, quality, and variety in the city. But remember to be patient with the waitstaff at the rest of the establishments listed below, and always allow plenty of time for lunch (2 hr.) and dinner (3 hr.).

WITHIN THE CITY CENTER
Moderate

Casita Suiza SWISS The Casita Suiza lives up to its name with a menu of Swiss dishes such as smoked pork, sauerkraut, and apple strudel, but it also offers a wide variety of international meat and fish dishes. The restaurant is owned by the children of Swiss immigrants; the owner's mother still bakes fresh cakes and tarts daily using old family recipes. The Casita Suiza's ambience is slightly more cozy than its competitor, the Rincón Suiza, and the service is impeccable. Fondues are an excellent value at $6 per person. If you're interested in a diner-participation meal, choose instead the *pierrade,* a platter of various meats, sauces, and potatoes that you grill at the table, for $7 per person. Call ahead to see if they're open for lunch as their daytime hours are erratic.

Quaglia 342. ℂ 02944/426111. Main courses $4–$7. AE, DC, MC, V. Daily 8pm–midnight.

Caza y Pesca REGIONAL   Like the name ("Hunting and Fishing") suggests, this panoramic restaurant on the waterfront has a hunting lodge atmosphere with rough-hewn interiors made of knotty cypress tree trunks, a crackling fireplace, and deer antler chandeliers. The chef here whips up tasty regional specialties and international dishes such as trout in garlic, tomatoes, and wine; salmon ravioli; or steak with a pepper sauce, but the restaurant also makes a suitable spot for a drink and an appetizer platter. The restaurant has great views during the day and a warm, candle-lit ambience in the evening, at least until around 11pm when they drop a giant TV screen and begin playing music videos and concerts.

Av. 12 de Octubre and Onelli. ℂ 02944/435963. Main courses $4–$6. AE, MC, V. Daily 7pm–2am year-round; Nov–Feb open for lunch daily 11am–4pm.

Días de Zapata MEXICAN   Bariloche's only Mexican restaurant is surprisingly good. You'll find the usual tacos, fajitas, and nachos on the menu, but you'll also find dishes that stay true to Mexican cooking, such as chicken *mole* (a spicy sauce made with chocolate), Veracruz conger eel, and spicy enchiladas. Every evening from 7 to 9pm the restaurant has a happy hour, with buy-one-get-one-free drinks. The warm brick walls and Mexican folk art make for a cozy atmosphere; the service is very friendly, too.

Morales 362. ℂ 02944/423128. Reservations recommended for dinner on weekends. Main courses $3–$5. MC, V. Daily noon–3pm and 7pm–midnight.

Familia Weiss ⚅ *Kids* *Value* REGIONAL   The Weiss family is well known all over the region for their outstanding smoked meats and cheeses, which they've been selling from their shop at Mitre 360 for decades. They've also run a tiny restaurant up the street for years, and in 2000 they opened this new restaurant near the waterfront that is so architecturally unique you really should at least stop in for one of the locally brewed beers and to view the handsome interiors. The decor includes cypress trunks that form pillars rising from a mosaic floor also made of cypress. Each wall is a patchwork of wood, brick, and ceramic, except the front area, which has large picture windows looking out onto the lake. Details such as papier-mâché lamps and folk art lend character.

As for the food, there's a lot on offer here, all very good. Start off with an appetizer of the smoked meats, seafood, and cheese the Familia Weiss is known for. There's cheese and beef fondue with five dipping sauces, large leafy salads, stewed venison with spaetzle, grilled meats with fresh vegetables, homemade pastas, local trout served with ratatouille, and much, much more. A good wine list and a kid's menu make the Familia Weiss hard to beat.

Corner of Palacios and V.A. O'Connor. ℂ 02944/435789. Main courses $2.50–$4.50. AE, DC, MC, V. Daily 11:30am–1am.

Jauja ⚅⚅ REGIONAL   Jauja is one of the best restaurants in Bariloche, both for its extensive menu and woodsy atmosphere. You'll find just about everything on offer here, from regional to German-influenced dishes, including grilled or stewed venison, goulash with spaetzle, stuffed crepes, homemade pastas, barbecued meats, and trout served 15 different ways. The semi-casual dining area is made entirely of wood, with wooden tables and lots of glass, plants, basket lamps, and candles. A glass-and-wood wall divides smoking and nonsmoking sections. The Jauja's fresh salads and desserts are quite good, especially the poached pears and apple mousse. Food is available to go.

Quaglia 366. ℂ **02944/422952**. Main courses $3.50–$4.50. AE, MC, V. Daily 11:30am–3pm and 7:30pm–midnight.

La Marmite SWISS   La Marmite is very similar to the Casita Suiza; it's not as cozy in the evening but there's more on the menu. The Swiss-inspired decor includes ruby-red tablecloths and carved wooden beams stained black and stenciled with flowers. The menu offers fondue ($8–$10 for 2) and *raclette,* but the main dishes are a better bet, especially regional specialties such as hunter's hare stew or wild boar steeped in burgundy wine with mushrooms. You'll also find grilled tenderloin beef and exquisite tarts and cakes.

Mitre 329. ℂ **02944/423685**. Main courses $3–$6. AE, DC, MC, V. Daily noon–3:30pm and 7:30–11:30pm.

Inexpensive

El Boliche de Alberto ★★ *Value* STEAKHOUSE   If you're in the mood for steak, this is your place. El Boliche de Alberto is our favorite *parrilla* in Bariloche, and everyone else's too, it seems. Some regulars have been coming back for 20 years and some make the crossing from Chile to have an inexpensive delicious meal here. The quality of meat is outstanding, and the prices are extremely reasonable. The menu is brief: several cuts of beef, chicken, and sausages, with salads and side dishes such as french fries. The dining area is unpretentious and brightly lit, with wooden tables. The charismatic owner, Alberto, has plastered an entire wall with photos of regulars and luminaries who have paid a visit, along with notes thanking him for a wonderful meal. Alberto will usually take your order. A typical *bife de chorizo* steak is so thick you'll need to split it with your dining partner; if you're alone, they can do a half order for $2. The Boliche de Alberto has a very good pasta restaurant at Elflein 163 (ℂ **02944/431084**).

Villegas 347. ℂ **02944/431433**. Main courses $3.50–$4. AE, MC, V. Daily noon–3:30pm and 8pm–midnight.

El Mundo PIZZERIA   El Mundo serves up crispy pizza in more than 100 varieties, as well as empanadas, pastas, and salads. There are so many kinds of pies on offer that the menu gets a little overwhelming. The pasta is fresh, and they deliver. A large seating area makes El Mundo a good spot for groups.

Mitre 759. ℂ **02944/423461**. Main courses $2.50–$5. AE, DC, MC, V. Daily noon–midnight.

Friends *Kids* CAFE   Friends is worth a mention more than anything because it is open 24 hours a day and is popular with families with kids. The cafe is embellished with hundreds of antique toys and trinkets, which hang from the ceiling and fill every corner. The menu serves grilled meats and fish, crepes, sandwiches, soups, and salad. There's also pan-fried trout served several different ways and a huge selection of rich, sugary desserts, too.

Corner of Mitre and Rolando. ℂ **02944/423700**. Main courses $1.75–$4. AE, MC, V. Daily 24 hr.

Tips **Don't Count on Credit**

With the financial situation in Argentina so precarious, some restaurants are forced to "suspend" use of their credit card machines for days or weeks at a time. Always carry enough cash to pay for your lunch or dinner just in case the restaurant has stopped accepting credit cards.

OUTSIDE THE CITY CENTER/ON THE ROAD TO THE LLAO LLAO PENINSULA
Expensive

El Patacón ★★ *Finds* ARGENTINE/REGIONAL   This superb restaurant is a 7km (4-mile) drive from the city center. El Patacón's unique architecture and mouth-watering cuisine are so appealing that it was chosen as the dining spot for Bill Clinton and Argentina's Carlos Ménem during a presidential meeting several years back, a fact the restaurant is more than happy to advertise. The building is made of chipped stone inlaid with polished, knotty tree trunks and branches left in their natural shape, which form zany crooked beams and pillars. The tables and chairs were handcrafted from cypress driftwood also kept in its natural form.

Start your meal with a platter of five provolone cheeses served crispy warm off the grill, and follow it with venison ravioli or goulash, trout in a creamy leek sauce with puffy potatoes, wild boar in wine, or mustard chicken. There is also a *parrilla* with grilled meats and daily specials, and a bodega with an excellent selection of wines. The restaurant recently inaugurated an adjoining bar, a fascinating, medieval-style lounge with iron chandeliers and a tremendous fireplace with a tree-trunk mantel. If you're staying in the city center you can opt to dine at the downtown branch of this restaurant, located at the Hotel Panamericano (see "Where to Stay," earlier in this chapter) where the menu is identical but the decor is not nearly as enticing as this location's.

Av. Bustillo, Km 7. ✆ 02944/442898. Reservations recommended on weekends. Main courses $5–$11. AE, DC, MC, V. Daily noon–3pm and 8pm–midnight.

Los Cesares ★★★ *Moments* PATAGONIAN FINE DINING   This enchantingly romantic restaurant offers the only fine dining experience in the Bariloche area. Located in the luxurious Llao Llao Hotel & Resort (see "Where to Stay," earlier), the refined and slightly formal setting comes complete with fireplace, antiques, white tablecloths, and ultra-comfortable chairs with armrests. The restaurant prides itself on using the highest quality ingredients grown locally— from wild game for the main courses to the wild berries for dessert. Specialties include grilled venison with blackberry sauce, almond-crusted local trout (from the nearby lake), and a good selection of Argentine steaks. The excellent wine list features many regional wines for under $15. Service is superb, and when you finally get the bill, you'll be pleasantly surprised at how affordable it really is for such an exquisite place.

Av. Bustillo, Km 25. In the Llao Llao Hotel & Resort. ✆ 02944/448530. Reservations required. Main courses $8–$18. AE, DC, MC, V. Daily 7:30–11:30pm.

BARILOCHE AFTER DARK

Bariloche is home to a handful of discos catering to the 20- to 30-year-old crowd. These discos adhere to Buenos Aires nightlife hours, beginning about midnight to 12:30am, with the peak of the evening at about 3 or 4am. The cover charge is usually $3 to $4 per person, and often women enter for free. Try **Roket** at J.M. de Rosas 424 (✆ **02944/431940**) or **Cerebro** at J.M. de Rosas 405 (✆ **02944/424965**). The Hotel Panamericano runs Bariloche's **Casino** at Av. San Martín 570 (✆ **02944/425846**), open from 9am to 5am. The Casino hosts live shows every evening. Guests must be over 18 years old; entrance is free. The local cinema can be found at Moreno 39 (✆ **02944/422860**).

2 Villa La Angostura ★★

81km (50 miles) N of Bariloche; 44km (27 miles) E of the Chilean border

Villa La Angostura (Narrow Village) takes its name from the slender isthmus that connects the town's center with the Quetrihué Peninsula. The town was founded in 1934 when it was a collection of simple farmers with small plots of land. These farmers were eventually usurped by out-of-towners who chose this lovely location for their summer homes. Increased boating activity, the paving of the road to Bariloche, increased tourism with Chile (whose border crossing is just 20 min. from town), and the inauguration of several exclusive hotels and a handful of bungalow complexes has converted Villa La Angostura into a popular tourist destination—although the tiny enclave still sees only a fraction of visitors to the region, unlike Bariloche. This picturesque village is for visitors seeking to get away from the crowds. Most lodging options are tucked away in the forest on the shore of the Lake Nahuel Huapi, providing beautiful views and quiet surroundings. Like Bariloche, Villa La Angostura is located within the borders of Parque Nacional Nahuel Huapi.

GETTING THERE **By Plane** For airport and flight information, see "Getting There," under Bariloche. To get to Villa La Angostura from the airport, take a taxi or transfer service (about $45–$50). The drive takes about an hour.

By Bus **Algarrobal Buses** (© 02944/494360) leave for Villa La Angostura from Bariloche about every 3 hours from 8am to 9pm, from the Terminal de Omnibus. The trip takes about 1½ hours.

VISITOR INFORMATION **The Secretaría de Turismo** is at Av. Siete Lagos 93 (© 02944/494124), open daily from 8am to 8pm. It offers accommodation listings and prices, and information about excursions around the area. For information about Nahuel Huapi National Park or Parque Nacional Bosque Arrayanes, try the **Bosques y Parques Provinciales Oficína de Turismo** at the pier (© 02944/494157), open Monday through Friday from 11am to 4pm, Wednesday until 2pm, Saturday and holidays from 2:30 to 5pm; closed Sunday.

WHAT TO SEE & DO

PARQUE NACIONAL BOSQUE ARRAYANES ★

The Parque Nacional Bosque Arrayanes is home to the only two *arrayán* forests in the world (although the *arrayán* can be found throughout this region, including in Chile), one of which can be visited at the tip of Península Quetrihué. This fascinating bush grows as high as 20m (66 ft.) and to the untrained eye looks like a tree, with slick cinnamon-colored trunks that are cool to the touch. They are especially beautiful in the spring when in bloom.

The peninsula itself offers a pleasant, 24km (15-mile) round-trip moderate hiking and biking trail to the *arrayán* forest. Most visitors either walk (2–3 hr.) or bike (1–2 hr.) half of the trail and boat to or back from the park; you can also take the boat both ways (trip time 2½ hr.). **Paisano** (© 02944/494459) has an 18-passenger launch with a cafeteria and daily trips leaving at 3pm. They offer four to five trips during the summer depending on demand; cost for adults is $8 round-trip, kids 6 to 12, $5 round-trip; $5 for all ages one-way. **Bettanso Excursiones** has a 50-person boat with daily departures at 2:30pm, and six to seven trips during the summer for the same price as Paisano (© 02944/495024). Bettanso also offers excursions to Isla Victoria and Puerto Blest, a trip that is described in "Boat Excursions," above.

OTHER OUTDOOR ACTIVITIES

BIKING   Ian Bikes, Topa Topa 102 (© **02944/495047;** ianbikes@ hotmail.com), has a large selection of rental bikes for $1 per hour, $4 up to 6 hours, and $5 for a full day. They also supply trail information.

FISHING   Anglers typically head to the renowned Río Correntoso for rainbow and brown trout, reached just before crossing the bridge just outside town on Ruta Nacional 231, from the Siete Lagos road. **Banana Fly Shop,** at Arrayanes 282 (© **02944/494634**), sells flies and gear, and they have information and can recommend guides. You may pick up a **fishing license** here or at the Bosques y Parques Provinciales office at the port (© **02944/494157**); open Monday through Friday from 11am to 4pm, Wednesday until 2pm, Saturday and holidays from 2:30 to 5pm; closed Sunday.

SKIING   Villa La Angostura is home to a little gem of a ski resort, **Cerro Bayo,** located about 9km (5½ miles) from downtown. It's a smaller resort than the one at Cerro Catedral, but the crowds are thinner and the view is wonderful—for those reasons we almost prefer it. There are 250 skiable acres, with 40% of the terrain intermediate and about 35% advanced. To get to it, you'll need to take a long lift from the base up to the summit; during the summer this same chair lift provides access to an excellent short hike and lookout point. Cerro Bayo has ski and snowboard rental and instruction; the season runs from mid-June to mid-September, although it can get fairly patchy toward the end of the season.

To get to Cerro Bayo, ask your hotel to arrange transportation or hire a taxi for the short ride. Tickets are $6 to $10 for adults, $4 to $6 for kids, depending on the season. Kids under 6 and adults over 65 ski free. There are also half-day tickets, 3-day tickets, and weekly passes. For more information, call © **02944/ 494189** or visit www.laangostura.com/cerrobayo.

WHERE TO STAY

Hostal Las Nieves ★★ (Value)   The very friendly and energetic Marita Miles owns and runs this lovely lodge located 5 minutes from the center of town behind exquisitely manicured gardens (Marita is an avid gardener and has won many awards for her landscaping). The rooms are rustic, simple, and comfortable, with white-washed walls, red checkered bedspreads, and handmade wooden side tables. The gleaming bathrooms are small but adequate. Apartments are on the upper level and come with kitchenettes, slanted roofs, and wood furniture, including a pair of charming cypress chairs in each unit. There's an outdoor pool in the lovely back garden and overlooking the front garden there's a lounge with a roaring fireplace where you can order drinks from the bar. The ample breakfast buffet is served from 8am onwards (until the last guest has been served), and the restaurant serves both lunch and dinner in high season.

Av. Siete Lagos 980. ©/fax 02944/494573. www.lasnieves.com. 12 units. $23–$43 double; from $34–$57 apt. Rates include buffet breakfast. MC, V. **Amenities:** Restaurant; bar; lounge; heated outdoor pool; sauna; massage. *In room:* TV, fridge (in apts only).

La Posada ★ (Kids) (Finds)   This attractive country inn packs a punch with a magnificent view of the rippling waters of Lago Nahuel Huapi from its west-facing rooms. La Posada's cozy country decor features plaid and oak-wood furnishings. The junior suites don't seem any larger than the doubles. Doubles that face the lake come with bay windows, and are substantially better than those that don't, but this might not matter if you plan to spend the entire day outdoors. The beds are very comfortable, and the decor handsome, with striped furnishings and wooden ceilings. Outside, a terraced walkway leading through the award-winning garden to the dock has tables and lounge chairs set among fragrant flowers. Another walkway leads to the hotel's outdoor pool overlooking the lake. The hotel has its own private dock, and during the summer sets out kayaks and small boats for guests; in the evening, the dock is lit up with twinkling lights. The hotel is near the Río Correntoso, which offers excellent fishing.

Ruta Nacional 231. © **02944/494368.** Fax 02944/494450. www.hosterialaposada.com. 20 units. $66–$94 double with view; $46–$79 double without view; $66–$112 suite. Rates include continental breakfast. AE, MC, V. Closed June. **Amenities:** Restaurant; lounge; bar; small heated outdoor pool; Jacuzzi; room service; laundry. *In room:* TV, safe.

Las Balsas ✪ *Overrated* Unfortunately, this pleasant country inn's service has been in decline recently. Part of the Relais & Châteaux group, this hideaway sits directly on the shore of Lago Nahuel Huapi, with its own private dock, spa, and superb gourmet restaurant (see below). While the location is ideal, service is non-existent and rooms are far too small to warrant more than a speedy overnight stay. That said, all the rooms do come with views of the lake and the evening sunset, and each is thematically different, from romantic to folksy. But there's hardly room to open a suitcase or move around without bumping into the wall or the bed. A nice touch are the peek-a-boo windows in the extra-small bathrooms, leading to views of the room and the lake. There's also a cozy attic loft (read: really tiny) popular with honeymooning couples. If you really want to spend the night here, you should splurge for a suite. Ask for the upstairs unit, which comes with polished wood floors, larger-than-king-size beds, rectangular desks with fax and stereo, bathrooms nearly as large as the standard doubles, and wraparound floor-to-ceiling windows that allow the sun to cascade in.

Downstairs, the lounge area abounds with couches and chairs to sink into for reading, gazing at the roaring fire, or enjoying conversation among guests. Next door, a minimalist river rock–and–wood "spa" has an exquisite indoor/outdoor heated pool separated by a wall of windows, and a massage room built like a temple of relaxation. This is one of the few Relais & Châteaux hotels to welcome children, and although kids are required to dine upstairs, they usually love it, as the room doubles as a play/TV area. There's also a computer with free Internet access for guests. The hotel offers inflatable rafts, paddle boats, and kayaks to guests, as well as a fleet of mountain bikes. The only regretful thing about Las Balsas (other than the size of the rooms) is that for such expensive lodgings, the customer service is lacking; we wish the hotel staff could match the courteous and attentive service at the restaurant. Only then will this place shine again.

Bahía Las Balsas. ©/fax **02944/494308.** www.lasbalsas.com.ar. 15 units. $200 double; $250 suite. Rates include continental breakfast. AE, MC, V. **Amenities:** Exquisite restaurant; lounge; bar; indoor/outdoor heated pool; sauna; watersports equipment; room service; massage; laundry service.

WHERE TO DINE

There are many *parrillas* and cafes on the town's sole main street. The best, however, are on side streets or a few minutes' drive from town. Note that some restaurants are unable to use their credit card machine for days or weeks at a time due to the precarious financial situation in Argentina—always carry enough cash to cover your meals, just in case.

La Macarena ✪ CONTEMPORARY ARGENTINE Don't be fooled by the semi-casual atmosphere at La Macarena—the food is divine. Chef Pablo Tejeda whips up a creative take on regional cooking, with mouth-watering cuisine such as polenta with a ragout of wild mushrooms, venison goulash, and rack of lamb steeped in merlot and sautéed vegetables. His recipe for wild hare in a sauvignon blanc sauce was chosen as northern Patagonia's representative dish in the Certamen Nacional Cucarón cooking competition in 2000. There's also fresh pasta with a choice of 10 different sauces, as well as several Chinese and Mexican dishes.

Cerro Bayo 65. © **02944/495120.** Main courses $3.50–$6. MC, V. Tues–Sun noon–3pm and 8–11:30pm.

Las Balsas ★★ *Moments* PATAGONIAN/INTERNATIONAL   A 10-minute drive from town, this enchanting restaurant is on the ground floor of the Las Balsas Inn (see "Where to Stay," above) and boasts large picture windows overlooking the lake. There are only a few tables here and both the quality of the food and the service are top-notch. The menu changes daily, but always includes three courses for $15. Using only local ingredients, the Chef seamlessly blends together Patagonian and International cuisines to create dishes such as the deer carpaccio with whipped cream cheese or the local greens served with a delicate fresh raspberry dressing. For a main course, trout from the lake is always available and usually a wild game dish such as venison, wild boar, or guanaco (a Patagonian animal similar to the llama), grilled and served with a side such as pureed garbanzo and quinoa. Desserts are exquisite—try the stewed cherries and strawberries with homemade vanilla ice cream and a chocolate brownie. The wine list is extensive and offers regional wines for under $20. Las Balsas is not easy to find; be sure to ask for detailed directions when making reservations.

Bahía Las Balsas. ©/fax **02944/494308.** Reservations required. Fixed-price menu only, $15 for 3 courses. AE, MC, V. Daily 8–10:30pm.

Parrilla Cancahue ★ *Value* STEAKHOUSE   Two kilometers out of town you'll find this gem of a place, opened in the fall of 2002. It's a very basic and very good Argentine steakhouse that is steadily gaining a local following. In the large unassuming dining room with large windows and tables with checkered tablecloths, the menu is short and simple: Several different kinds of salads and several different kinds of steak grilled the way you like it. The bife de chorizo is excellent here and, at $2.50 per order, is an incredible bargain. There's also grilled chicken, if you prefer, and homemade french fries. Order a house red wine to accompany your meal and a mixed salad and you'll walk away paying less than $7 per person, plus tip.

Av. Siete Lagos 727. © **02944/494922.** Main courses $3–$5. No credit cards. Daily 12:30–4pm and 8:30pm–midnight. Closed Wed in low season.

Rincón Suiza SWISS/REGIONAL   This little restaurant comes with all the usual trappings of a Swiss-style restaurant, from Alpine interiors to a menu offering everything from fondue to pork chops with sauerkraut. The owner, a Swiss descendant, strives to "rescue the traditional flavors of the Swiss and regional Argentine kitchens." Also on the menu are venison marinated in beer and served with spaetzle, lamb brochettes, and a trout dish served with sauces of capers, Roquefort cheese, and almonds. Some of the richest, most flavorful items on the menu are the desserts, including the *Torta Rincón Suiza* made of chocolate, peaches, and cream, as well as the apple strudel.

Av. Arrayanes 44. ©/fax **02944/494248.** Main courses $4–$6. AE, MC, V. Daily noon–3pm and 8–11:30pm. Apr–Sept closed Wed.

Waldhaus SWISS/REGIONAL   If you think the Rincón Suiza has gone overboard with the Swiss theme, try this little restaurant, whose gingerbread eaves, notched furniture, and woodsy location will make you feel like you're dining in the Black Forest. The location 6km (4 miles) from downtown makes the Waldhaus less convenient than the Rincón Suiza, but the food is slightly better here. There are nightly specials, and typical menu offerings include wild mushroom soup, beef fondue, venison marinated in burgundy wine, and typical Tyrolean dishes such as spaetzle with ham.

Ruta Nacional 231, Km 61. ℂ **02944/495123.** Main courses $3.50–$6. MC, V. Daily noon–3:30pm and 8pm–midnight.

3 San Martín de los Andes ★★

1,640km (1,017 miles) SW of Buenos Aires; 200km (124 miles) N of San Carlos de Bariloche

San Martín de los Andes is a charming mountain town of 15,000 nestled on the tip of Lago Lácar between high peaks. The town is considered the tourism capital of the Neuquen region, a claim that's hard to negate considering the copious arts and crafts shops, gear rental shops, restaurants, and hotels that constitute much of downtown. San Martín has grown considerably in the past 10 years, but thankfully hasn't succumbed to the whims of developers as Bariloche has, owing to city laws that limit building height and regulate architectural styles. The town is quieter than Bariloche, and decidedly more picturesque, thanks to its timber-heavy architecture and Swiss Alpine influence. San Martín overflows with activities, from biking to hiking to boating to skiing, but it is also very popular for hunting and fishing, and some do come just to relax. The tourism infrastructure here is excellent, with every lodging option imaginable (except the ultra-luxurious) and plenty of great restaurants.

ESSENTIALS
GETTING THERE
BY PLANE Aeropuerto Internacional Chapelco (ℂ 02972/428388) sits halfway between San Martín and Junín de los Andes (see later in this chapter), and therefore serves both destinations. **Aerolíneas Argentinas/Austral,** Capitán Drury 876 (ℂ 02972/427003), has one to two flights daily from Buenos Aires. **LADE,** Av. San Martín 915 (ℂ 02972/427672), has seasonal service to Buenos Aires and Bariloche. A taxi to San Martín costs about $6; there are also transfer services available at the airport for $2 per person. A taxi to Junín de los Andes costs $5; transfer services are $2 per person. By Mich Rent a Car and Avis both have auto rental kiosks at the airport.

BY BUS The **Terminal de Omnibus** is at Villegas and Juez del Valle (ℂ 02972/427044). Daily bus service to San Martín de los Andes from Buenos Aires (a 19-hr. trip) is offered by **El Valle** (ℂ 02972/422800). **Ko-Ko Chevalier** (ℂ 02972/427422) also offers service to and from Buenos Aires, and serves Villa La Angostura and Bariloche by the paved or by the scenic Siete Lagos route. **Centenario** (ℂ 02972/427294) has service to Chile, and also offers daily service to Buenos Aires; Villarrica- and Pucón-bound buses leave Monday through Saturday, and those for Puerto Montt, Tuesday through Thursday. **Albus** (ℂ 02972/428100) has trips to Bariloche via the Siete Lagos route (about 3 hr.). Bus service can vary due to season, and it's best to evaluate a coach's condition and services before buying a ticket, especially for trips to and from Buenos Aires.

BY CAR San Martín de los Andes can be reached from San Carlos de Bariloche following one of three routes. The popular 200km (124-mile) Siete Lagos route takes Routes 234-231-237, and sometimes closes during the winter. The 160km (99-mile) Paso Córdoba route takes Routes 234-63-237; the longest, yet entirely paved 260km (161-mile) Collón Curá route follows routes 234-40-237. If driving at night, take the paved route. To get to Neuquén (420km/260 miles), take Routes 234-40-22. From Chile, take the Tromen Pass (132km/82 miles from Pucón) to Route 62, taking you to Route 234 and through Junín de los Andes; note that a large portion of this route is on unpaved roads.

GETTING AROUND
San Martín is compact enough to explore by foot. For outlying excursions, tour companies can arrange transportation. **Avis** car rental has an office at Av. San Martín 998 (© **02972/427704;** fax 02972/428500) as well as a kiosk at the airport; **ICI Rent-A-Car** is at Villegas 590 (© **02972/427800**); **Nieves Rent-A-Car** is at Villegas 725 (© **02972/428684**); **Localiza/El Claro** is at Villegas 977 (© **02972/428876**); and **By Mich Rent a Car** is at Av. San Martín 960 (© **02972/427997**) and at the airport.

Note that two main streets have similar names and can be confusing: Perito Moreno and Mariano Moreno.

VISITOR INFORMATION
San Martín's excellent **Oficina de Turismo** offers comprehensive accommodation listings with prices and other tourism-related info, and the staff is friendly and eager to make your stay pleasurable. They can be found at Rosas and Avenida San Martín at the main plaza and are open Monday to Sunday 8am to 11pm (©/fax **02972/427347** and 02972/427695). The **Asociación Hotelero y Gastronomía** (© **02972/427166**) also offers lodging information, including photographs of each establishment. It's open Monday through Sunday from 9am to 1pm and 3 to 7pm, and during high season Monday through Sunday from 9am to 10pm, but this service is not as efficient as the Oficina de Turismo.

A new website chock-full of valuable information is www.sanmartin delosandes.com.

FAST FACTS: SAN MARTIN DE LOS ANDES
Banks/Currency Exchange **Andina International** at Capitán Drury 876 exchanges money; banks such as **Banco de la Nación** at Av. San Martín 687, **Banco de la Provincia Neuquén** at Belgrano and Obeid, and **Banco Río Negro** at Perito Moreno and Elordi have automatic tellers and money exchange. All banks are open Monday through Friday from 10am to 3pm.

Emergency Dial **107.**

Hospital **Hospital Regional Ramón Carrillo** is at Avenida San Martín and Coronel Rodhe (© **02972/427211**).

Laundry **Marva** at Capitán Drury and Villegas (© **02972/428791**); **Laverap Plus** at Villegas 972 (© **02972/427500**); **Lácar** at Elordi 839 (© **02972/427317**).

Police For emergencies, dial **101.** The federal police station is at Av. San Martín 915 (© **02972/428249**); the provincial police station is at Belgrano 635 (© **02972/427300**).

Post Office **Correo Argentino** is at the corner of General Roca and Coronel Pérez (© **02972/427201**).

Telephone & Internet The fastest computers are at **Cooperativa Telefónica** at Capitán Drury 761; open from 9am to 11pm, where you can also make phone calls. Half an hour of Internet use costs $1.10.

WHAT TO SEE & DO

San Martín de los Andes is heavily geared toward tourism, and accordingly its streets are lined with shops selling arts and crafts, wonderful regional specialties such as smoked meats and cheeses, outdoor gear, books and more. Visitors will find most of these shops on **Avenida San Martín** and **General Villegas.** For regional specialties and/or chocolates try **Ahumadero El Ciervo,** General Villegas 724 (© **02972/427450**); **El Turista,** Belgrano 845 (© **02972/428524**); or **Su Chocolate Casero,** Villegas 453 (© **02972/427924**). For arts and crafts try **Artesanís Neuquinas,** J.M. de Rosas 790 (© **02972/428396**).

San Martín is a mountain town geared toward outdoor activities. If you're not up to a lot of physical activity, take a stroll down to the lake and kick back on the beach. Alternatively, rent a bike and take a slow pedal around town. Pack a picnic lunch and head to Hua Hum (described below).

TOUR OPERATORS & TRAVEL AGENCIES

Both **Tiempo,** Av. San Martín 950 (©/fax **02972/427113;** tiempopatagonico@ usa.net), and **Pucará,** Av. San Martín 943 (© **02972/427218;** pucara@smandes. com.ar), offer similar tours and prices, and also operate as travel agencies for booking plane tickets. Excursions to the village Quila Quina, via a sinuous road that offers dramatic views of Lago Lácar, cost $6; a longer excursion including Chapelco and Arrayán is $8. Excursions to the hot springs Termas de Lahuenco are $10; scenic drives through the Siete Lagos route are $10 (to Villa La Angostura) and $12 (to Bariloche). A gorgeous circuit trip to Volcán Lanín and Lago Huechulafquén goes for $10. Tours do not include lunch, which must be brought along or arranged ahead of time.

OUTDOOR ACTIVITIES

BIKING San Martín is well suited for biking, and shops offer directions and maps. Bike rentals are available at **Enduro Kawa & Bikes** at Belgrano 845 (© **02972/427093**), **HD Rodados** at Av. San Martín 1061 (© **02972/427345**), and **Mountain Snow Shop** at Av. San Martín 861 (© **02972/427728**).

BOATING **Naviera Lácar & Nonthué** (© **02972/428427**) at the Costanera and main pier offers year-round boat excursions on Lago Lácar. A full-day excursion to Hua Hum includes a short navigation through Lago Nonthué. The cost is $12 adults, $6 kids 6 to 12 and seniors, plus park entrance fees; there's a restaurant in Hua Hum, or you can bring a picnic lunch. Naviera also operates a ferry service to the beautiful beaches of Quila Quina (which are packed in the summer) for $4 adults, $3 kids 6 to 12 and seniors. Naviera also rents kayaks for $2 per hour.

To raft the Hua Hum River, get in contact with Tiempo Tours or Pucará (see "Tour Operators & Travel Agencies," above).

FISHING INFORMATION & LICENSES **Jorge Cardillo Pesca** at General Roca 636 (© **02972/428372;** cardillo@smandes.com.ar) is a well-stocked fly-fishing shop that organizes day and overnight fishing expeditions to the Meliquina, Chimehuín, and Malleo rivers, among other areas. The other local fishing expert is **Alberto Cordero** (© **02972/421453;** acordero@smandes. neuquen.com.ar), who will arrange fishing expeditions around the area. He speaks fluent English; for more information visit his website at www.ffandes.com. You can pick up a fishing guide at the **Oficina Guardafauna** at General Roca 849 (© **02972/427091**).

MOUNTAINEERING   Víctor Gutiérrez and his son Jano Gutiérrez are the top climbing and mountaineering guides in the region (Víctor has more than 40 years' experience), and offer climbing and orientation courses, ascents of Volcán Lanín and Volcán Domuyo, and treks, climbs and overnight trips in Lanín and Nahuel Huapi national parks. Both have cellphones; Víctor can be reached at ℭ **02944/15-61-0440;** victorg11@latinmail.com. Jano can be reached at ℭ **02944/15-63-3260;** janoclif@latinmail.com; both speak passable English.

SKIING   The principal winter draw for San Martín de los Andes is **Cerro Chapelco,** one of the premier ski resorts in South America. Just 20km (12 miles) outside town, Cerro Chapelco is known for its plentiful, varying terrain and great amenities. Although popular, the resort isn't as swamped with skiers as Bariloche is. The resort sports one gondola (which takes skiers and visitors to the main lodge), five chair lifts, and five T-bars. The terrain is 40% beginner, 30% intermediate, and 30% advanced/expert. Chapelco offers excellent, bilingual ski instruction, ski and snowboard rental, and special activities such as dog-sledding. The resort has open-bowl skiing and tree skiing, and numerous restaurants. To get here without renting a car, ask your hotel to arrange transportation or hire a *remise* (private taxi).

To drive to the resort from town, follow Ruta 234 south along Lago Lácar; it's paved except for the last 5km (3 miles). Lift tickets are quite reasonable, and vary from low to high season. A 3-day ticket runs $19 to $45 for adults, and $16 to $29 for kids. During the summer the resort is open for hiking and sightseeing, with lift access. For more information, call ℭ **02972/427460** or visit www.sanmartindelosandes.com. The road is usually passable, but you may need chains during heavy snowfall; check before heading up to the resort.

WHERE TO STAY

What is lacking in San Martin is a luxury hotel. Although there are plenty of excellent *hosterías* and *cabañas,* if it's luxury you're looking for, you'd be better off spending the bulk of your time in the Bariloche area. This is a very laid back, outdoorsy town and its hotels reflect that.

MODERATE

La Cheminée 𝔊 ★   Warm, attentive service and snug accommodations make La Cheminée a top choice, which is why so many foreign travel groups book a few nights here. The Alpine-Swiss design popular in San Martín is in full swing here, with carved and stenciled woodwork and other touches that have been meticulously well-maintained. Spacious rooms are carpeted and feature wood ceilings and a pastel, country design with thick cotton floral bedspreads and striped wallpaper. The room they call a double *hogar* includes a fireplace for $8 more. The best room is the top-floor unit with wood-beamed ceilings. The bathrooms are rather small in all units. The fern-filled lobby's wooden floors are softened by fluffy rugs, and the walls are adorned with oil paintings rendered by local artists; there's even a small gallery with paintings for sale. The hotel is known for its delicious breakfast, adding trout paté, caviar, and fresh bread to the usual offerings; a restaurant also serves lunch and dinner. It's conveniently located, but a block away from the hubbub. Ask for multiple-day discounts. Although this hotel has stopped accepting credit cards this may change if the financial situation improves in Argentina; inquire when making reservations.

General Roca and Mariano Moreno, San Martín de los Andes. ℭ **02972/427617.** Fax 02972/427762. www.hosterialacheminee.com.ar. 19 units. $43–$64 double. Rates include full breakfast. No credit cards. **Amenities:** Restaurant; lounge; bar; outdoor pool; Jacuzzi; sauna; room service; laundry service. *In room:* TV, minibar.

Le Chatelet   Le Chatelet's spacious bedrooms, charming Swiss design, and full-service amenities are its strength. The classically designed lobby/lounge area is not as cozy as those in other hotels, but the bedrooms are wonderful, with fireplaces and queen-size beds. All rooms have wooden ceilings, triangular windows, lace curtains, and a tremendous amount of walking room; suites are twice the size of doubles. There's free use of VCRs, and the hotel stocks a video and book library in the lobby. The suites come with CD players. The location is 2 blocks from downtown on a quiet residential street, and there's a grassy, enclosed backyard with an outdoor pool. Le Chatelet often offers ski and summer package deals; inquire when making a reservation. They'll also help you organize excursions. An abundant breakfast is served each morning; the restaurant sports a roaring fire in the evenings and makes a good place to unwind after a day of outdoor activity. Internet access is available for registered guests.

Villegas 650, San Martín de los Andes. ℂ **02972/428294.** www.hotellechatelet.com. 32 units. $67–$114 double; $80–$130 suite. Rates include full breakfast. No credit cards. **Amenities:** Lounge; outdoor pool; exercise room; sauna; game room; room service; laundry service. In room: TV.

Le Village   This Alpine Swiss–style hotel is similar to La Cheminée and Le Chatelet in design, and is popular during the off season for its slightly lower prices. The ambience leans toward family style; the staff is extremely friendly, knowledgeable, and eager to help you plan activities. Rooms are average-size and carpeted; a few come with a small balcony. There are several lounge areas, including a reading area and library, felt-covered game table, and TV/VCR. Le Village also has five *cabañas* with queen and twin beds and spacious living areas, although they are not particularly bright. Also, *cabañas* for six mean two will sleep on a sofa bed in the living room. All guests have use of the sauna. An ample breakfast features specialties such as deer and trout and comes served in a pleasant eating area. There is also a *quincho*, a separate barbecue/dining area for groups; guests are allowed to throw dinners for friends not staying at the hotel. There's also a computer for guest use, with 1 hour free Internet access.

General Roca 816, San Martín de los Andes. ℂ/fax **02972/427698.** www.hotellevillage.com.ar. 23 units, 5 *cabañas.* $30–$63 double; $44–$76 *cabaña* for 4. Rates include full breakfast. AE, MC, V. **Amenities:** Restaurant; bar; sauna; room service; library; game room. In room: TV, minibar.

Patagonia Plaza *(Overrated*   San Martín's only full service four-star hotel feels like a bland, generic motel. Although the public areas are expansive with lots of windows overlooking the street, there's a feeling that everything is fading already. Rooms are comfortable and fairly modern with colorful bedspreads and large windows overlooking the street. Bathrooms are sparkling clean and adequate. There's a small indoor heated pool and sauna and an ample breakfast buffet every morning. This is a good place for a hassle-free overnight stay just steps from all the shops and restaurants, but don't expect much luxury or charm.

Av. San Martín and Rivadavia. ℂ **02972/422280.** Fax 02972/422284. 78 units. $65–$110 double. Rates include buffet breakfast. AE, DC, MC, V. **Amenities:** Restaurant; bar; lounge; indoor heated pool; sauna; tour desk; limited room service; massage; laundry service. In room: TV.

Rincón de los Andes *(Kids*   Rincón de los Andes is part of the timeshare operation Interval, but rents many of its apartments to travelers who are not part of the program. The sizeable resort abuts a steep, forested mountain slope, and is recommended both for the smartly decorated apartments and the wealth of activities offered—especially for families. Set up like a town house complex and centered on a large, airy restaurant with outdoor deck, the apartments range in size to accommodate two to eight guests. All come with fully stocked kitchens and spacious bedrooms. The new units are set up for two guests. One features a large living room and kitchen; the neighboring unit has a breakfast nook and kitchenette. You can connect the two to form a larger apartment. The grassy grounds include a driving range and paddle court, and there's a heated pool in a glass-enclosed building. The complex is about a 5-block walk to downtown.

Juez de Valle 611, San Martín de los Andes. (C) **02972/428583.** www.rinconclub.com.ar. 100 units. Apts $59–$93 double. AE, MC, V. **Amenities:** Restaurant; lounge; indoor pool; sauna; game room; tour desk; room service; massage; laundry service. *In room:* TV, kitchen.

INEXPENSIVE

Hostería Anay *Value*   A convenient location, economical price, and simple yet comfortable accommodations make the Anay a good value in San Martín. The rooms come with a double bed or two twins, and there are triples and apartments for four and five guests. All rooms come with wooden ceilings and ruby-red bedspreads, a lamp here and there, and nothing else, and all are clean and neat. The bathrooms are older, yet they have huge showers (no bathtubs). Downstairs, the lobby has a large fireplace, a felt-covered game table, and plenty of plants. The sunny, pleasant eating area is a nice spot for breakfast. The hotel is owner-operated, with direct and professional service.

Capitán Drury 841, San Martín de los Andes. (C)/fax 02972/427514. anay@smandes.com.ar. 15 units. $18–$22 double. Rates include continental breakfast. No credit cards. **Amenities:** Lounge; limited room service; babysitting; laundry service. *In room:* TV.

Hostería del Chapelco   Just about every kind of unit is available at this *hostería,* including new hotel rooms and *cabañas,* and cheaper, older duplex and A-frame units. Although it sits on the lakeshore, the rooms do not benefit from the view, but a bright lobby takes advantage of the location with giant picture windows. The hotel rooms and the six attached *cabañas* are spanking new, with stark, modern furnishings and tile floors; the *cabañas* have open living/kitchen areas. The duplex units are more economical, but they feel like family rumpus rooms, and the interiors could use new carpet and fresh paint. Las Alpinas houses the oldest units, six small but decent A-frame detached *cabañas.* The wood and whitewashed walls of the hotel are pleasant, but lend little character to the place. The lobby's fireside chairs and wraparound banquette are a nice place to watch the rippling lake. Quality, size, and character of the units differ, so it's best to view all of them if you have the opportunity to do so before booking.

Almirante Brown 297, San Martín de los Andes. (C) **02972/427610.** Fax 02972/427097. 14 units, 22 *cabañas.* $16–$19 double. AE, MC, V. **Amenities:** Bar; limited room service. *In room:* TV, microwaves (in *cabañas* only).

Hostería La Casa de Eugenia *Finds*   Built in 1927, this lovely old building with bright blue trim used to house the local Historical Society; now it's a bed and breakfast. The charming living room with its large fireplace, piano, and colorful sofas leads to five bedrooms, named by color. The *verde* (green) has a skylight keeping it bright throughout the day; all the rooms come with comfortable beds with down comforters, gleaming white bathrooms, and little else. Breakfast is served in the bright dining room overlooking a small park, and the friendly managers can help you plan excursions in and around San Martín.

Colonel Díaz 1186. (C) **02792/427206.** www.lacasadeeugenia.com.ar. 5 units. $20–$34 double. Rates include continental breakfast. No credit cards. **Amenities:** Lounge; room service. *In room:* No phone.

Hostería La Posta del Cazador *★*   The *hostería* that bills itself as "the only lodge with a view of the lake" actually affords views to only half the guests; the other half have a view of a leafy parking lot. Either way, proximity to the lakeshore is a bonus during the summer months, and the street on which the hotel sits is quiet and wooded. La Posta del Cazador (The Hunting Lodge) comes with the de rigueur deer antlers and the like, but it feels more like a castle thanks to an enormous circular iron chandelier, a floor-to-ceiling stone fireplace, stained glass, and walls adorned with battle swords and crosses-of-arms. Rooms are slightly cramped, but they are exceptionally clean and comfortable with wood furniture and flowery bedspreads; interiors feature wavy white plaster walls, dark wood, and chiffon curtains. The *hostería* is owner-run and patrolled by a friendly cat. The breakfast features homemade breads and pastries.

Av. San Martín 175, San Martín de los Andes. (℃/fax **02972/427501**. www.postadelcazador.com.ar. 19 units. $23–$35 double. Rates include full breakfast. AE, DC, MC, V. **Amenities:** Bar; lounge. *In room:* TV.

La Raclette   The design of this appealing hotel is a cross between Morocco and Switzerland—molded white stucco interiors set off by carved wooden shutters and eaves. It might also be described as a Hobbit House—anyone over 1.8m (6 ft.) tall might have to stoop, the ceilings upstairs are so low. On a quiet street, La Raclette has a cozy seating area and a bar and restaurant downstairs. The public areas and the rooms have nooks and crannies and a haphazard design; lots of charisma, but slightly cramped (especially the attic apartments), and the beds are nothing more than thick foam mattresses. The hotel exudes a lot of warmth in the evening, but the service can be harried and distracted during the day.

Coronel Pérez 1170, San Martín de los Andes. (℃/fax **02972/427664**. aspen@smandes.com.ar. 9 units. $18–$24 double. MC, V. **Amenities:** Restaurant; bar. *In room:* TV.

Residencial Italia   This little hotel, run by a sweet, elderly woman, is simple and kept scrupulously clean; indeed, it is doubtful you'll find a speck of dust anywhere. It's a good value, given that the double price does not fluctuate during the year. Rooms are modestly decorated in 1950s style; downstairs rooms are slightly darker—book the sunnier upstairs double or one of the two apartments. The apartments are for four and six people, with fully stocked kitchens, and both have large dining tables. There's a tiny eating area for breakfast (for guests only). The sole single room is not recommended due to its Lilliputian size. In the spring and summer, beautiful roses frame the *residencial.*

Coronel Pérez 799 (at Obeid), San Martín de los Andes. (℃ **02972/427590**. 7 units. $22 double. Rates include full breakfast. No credit cards. **Amenities:** Laundry. *In room:* TV.

CABAÑAS

There are over three dozen *cabaña* complexes in San Martín, ranging from attached units to detached A-frames. The quality varies somewhat; generally, the real difference between each is size, so always ask if a cabin for four means one bedroom and two fold-out beds in the living room. *Cabañas* are a great deal for parties of four to six, as they're usually less expensive and come with small kitchens. During the off season, couples will find reasonably priced *cabañas;* however, many places charge a full six-person price during the high season.

On the upscale end (with doubles priced at around $20 during low season and high season at $70) try the following: **Claro del Bosque** ✿, Belgrano 1083 (℃ **02972/427451;** fax 02972/428434; www.clarodelbosque.com.ar;), is a Swiss Alpine–style building tucked away at the end of a street on a wooded lot. The managers are very friendly and accommodating. If they're full here (which they frequently are) they also operate a brand new complex of charming apartments nearby, **Appart Niwen** ✿, G. Obeid 640 (℃ **02972/425888;**

www.niwen.com.ar), with similar accommodations and rates, though a tad less charming than the *cabañas* above.

If you'd like to get out of town, try **Paihuén's** beautiful stone-and-mortar, attached *cabañas* in a forested lot at Ruta Nacional 234, Km 48 (✆/fax **02972/ 428154;** www.paihuen.com.ar). **Aldea Misonet,** Los Cipreses 1801 (✆/fax **02972/421821;** aldeamisonet@smandes.com.ar), has wood-and-stone attached units that sit at the edge of town; some units look out onto a gurgling stream, as does a pleasant terrace. **Terrazas del Pinar,** Juez de Valle 1174 (✆/fax **02972/429316;** www.7lagos.com/terrazasdelpinar), is near the lakeshore, and it has a children's play area.

Cabañas with doubles ranging from a low-season price of $14 to $38 in the high season include the following: **El Ciervo Rojo,** Almirante Brown 445 (✆/fax **02972/427949;** cabanaselciervorojo@smandes.com.ar), has nice, wooden cabins; cheaper units have open second-story sleeping areas. **Del Lácar,** Coronel Rohde 1144 (✆/fax **02972/427679;** cabanasdellacar@smandes.com.ar), has several large, detached wooden cabins. **Las Rosas,** Almirante Brown 290 (✆/fax **02972/422002;** lrosas@ciudad.com.ar), has pretty whitewashed units half a block from the shore. **Hostería del Chapelco** and **Le Village** both offer *cabañas* in addition to their regular hotel rooms (see "Where to Stay," above).

The newest *cabañas* in town opened in the summer of 2002 on the edge of town and are extremely charming with lots of local wood, fireplaces, modern kitchens, a barbecue area and a new pool under construction: **Cabañas Arique** ★ (✆ **02972/429262;** www.arique.com). Cabins are $15 to $37 double, $20 to $46 for four people.

WHERE TO DINE

San Martín has several excellent restaurants. For sandwiches and quick meals, try **Peuma Café** at Av. San Martín 851 (✆ **02972/428289**); for afternoon tea and delicious cakes and pastries, try **La Casa de Alicia** at Capitán Drury 814, #3 (✆ **02944/616215**).

EXPENSIVE

Avataras ★ *Finds* INTERNATIONAL   Exceptionally warm, friendly service and a marvelous variety of international dishes from Hungary to China to Egypt make this restaurant an excellent, if slightly expensive, choice in San Martín. The chefs, youngish transplants from Buenos Aires, whip up exquisite items, such as Indian lamb curry, wild boar with juniper berry sauce, Malaysian shrimp sambal, and filet mignon with four-pepper sauce. The appetizer menu features Scandinavian gravlax and Caribbean citrus shrimp. What stands out, however, is Avataras's willingness to please its guests. Although they officially do not serve dinner until 8:30pm, give them 15 minutes' notice and they'll open earlier for parties as small as two (they'll also open for lunch if you call ahead). The decor includes light beechwood, ferns, Japanese paper lanterns, and an acoustic ceiling made of beige linen. There are smoking and nonsmoking sections; the restaurant even sells cigars, which diners may smoke on the premises. Avataras sometimes hosts live jazz music.

Teniente Ramayón 765. ✆ **02972/427104**. Reservations recommended. Main courses $7–$15. AE, DC, MC, V. Daily 8:30pm–midnight.

MODERATE

La Pierrade ★★ *Finds* INTERNATIONAL   This brand new restaurant opened in the fall of 2002 and is the town's most modern and sleek eatery. A giant stone fireplace and a long bar can be found on the ground floor and there are two cozy dining areas on the floor above. Soothing and romantic lighting gives the place a very relaxing atmosphere. Fluffy red pillows are strewn around the fireplace so you can unwind with your pre-dinner drink. Once you've been seated, the young waitstaff will take extra-good care of you. Begin with the very unusual rabbit pudding with green salad and dried tomatoes, a delicate deer carpaccio, or a tasting of Patagonian patés; then move on to the exquisite pumpkin cannelloni with a mushroom ragout or the grilled steak encrusted in sesame seeds and served with tomato and basil risotto. There's usually also a fish or shrimp specialty, along with a choice of wild game. For dessert, the tiramisu is divine, and so is the homemade ice cream. You can round out your evening with a Cuban cigar from the restaurant's collection and a glass of Argentine port.

Mariano Moreno and Villegas. ℂ 02972/421421. Reservations recommended. Main courses $3–$5. No credit cards. Daily 8pm–1am.

La Reserva ✦✦ *(Moments* ARGENTINE   This lovely stone and wood house has recently been transformed into one of the most romantic restaurants in Patagonia with a stone fireplace, elegant cloth-covered tables, soothing music, and superb service. La Reserva is run by the talented chef Rodrigo Toso, who is influenced by many ethnic cuisines while using mostly Patagonian ingredients. Begin with a cold glass of Argentine champagne to go with an order of tapas—a tasting of cheeses and dried meats. Then move on to grilled trout fresh from the nearby lake, tender venison with fresh berry sauce, or chicken breast stuffed with feta cheese and herbs. There are excellent regional wines for under $10 a bottle, and the desserts, a selection of homemade fruit tarts and ice creams, are divine.

Belgrano 940. ℂ **02972/428734.** Reservations recommended. Main courses $4–$8. AE, DC, MC, V. Daily noon–3pm and 8pm–midnight.

La Tasca ✦ REGIONAL   La Tasca is a solid choice for its fresh, high-quality cuisine and extensive wine offerings. Regional specialties are the focus, such as venison flambéed in cognac and blueberries, saffron trout, and raviolis stuffed with wild boar. All meats are hand-picked from local ranches by the chef-owner, and the organic cheese is made at a German family farm. Mushroom lovers will savor the fresh, gourmet varieties served with appetizers and pasta. Appetizer platters are a specialty here. The cozy restaurant is festooned with hanging hams, bordered with racks of wine bottles, and warmed by a few potbellied iron stoves. It's a bit too bright for a romantic dinner, but great for families as they have several large tables.

Mariano Moreno 866. ℂ **02972/428663.** Reservations recommended. Main courses $5–$8. AE, MC, V. Daily noon–3:30pm and 7pm–1am.

INEXPENSIVE

El Tata Jockey *(Value* PARRILLA/PASTA   This semi-casual restaurant is popular for its grilled meats and pastas at reasonable prices. It's possible to order a *parrilla* of assorted barbecued meats and sausages for two; the price is $5 for enough food for three diners. The homemade pastas are also a good bet, as is the trout al Jockey, served with seasonal vegetables and a smoked bacon and cream sauce. Owned and operated by a friendly, enthusiastic mountaineer, the restaurant is decorated with photos and tidbits taken from his various exploits around the area; the long, family-style tables have checkered tablecloths. El Tata Jockey also offers special menus for groups.

Villegas 657. ℂ **02972/427585.** Main courses $2.50–$5. No credit cards. Daily noon–2:30pm and 8pm–midnight.

La Costa del Pueblo (*Kids*) INTERNATIONAL   A lake view and an extensive menu with everything from pastas to *parrilla* make this restaurant a good bet. The establishment operated as a cafe for 20 years until new owners expanded to include a dozen more tables, a cozy fireside nook, and a children's eating area separate from the main dining room, complete with mini tables and chairs. La Costa offers good, homemade pasta dishes such as cannellonis stuffed with ricotta and walnuts, grilled meats and dishes, pizzas, and sandwiches. There's also a kid's menu and vegetarian sandwiches. The restaurant is also a good spot for a cold beer and an appetizer platter of smoked cheeses and venison while watching the lake lap the shore. Service can be really slow.

Av. Costanera and Obeid. © 02972/429289. Main courses $2–$4.50. No credit cards. Daily 11am–1am.

La Nonna Pizzería PIZZA   La Nonna's pizza, calzones, and empanadas are so good, they're sold packaged and ready-to-bake at the supermarket. Toppings unfortunately run the repetitive gamut of ham and onion, ham and pineapple, ham and hearts of palm, but there are a few deviations, such as anchovy, Roquefort, and Parmesan and, oddly enough, mozzarella with chopped egg. There are also specialty regional pizzas with trout, wild boar, and deer, and calzones with fillings such as chicken, mozzarella, and bell pepper. La Nonna also delivers.

Capitán Drury 857. © 02972/422223. Pizzas $1.50–$2.50 small, $2–$4 large. No credit cards. Daily noon–3:30pm and 7:30pm–midnight.

Pura Vida VEGETARIAN   San Martín's only vegetarian restaurant serves a few chicken and trout dishes too (the curried chicken is excellent). The vegetarian offerings are not really extensive, but what they offer is fresh and good. This homespun, tiny restaurant has about seven tables, and features meatless dishes such as vegetable chop suey, soufflés, soy and eggplant *milanesas* (breaded filets), and rich flan. Pura Vida serves substantial slices of vegetable-and-egg tarts, and salads can be ordered for an additional price. Pastas are not only homemade, but are made from scratch the moment you order, which can mean a long wait.

Villegas 745. © 02972/429302. Main courses $2–$5. No credit cards. Daily 12:30–3:30pm and 8:30pm–midnight.

4 Junín de los Andes

41km (25 miles) N of San Martín de los Andes

The tiny town of Junín de los Andes does not hold much interest unless you're a fly-fishing fanatic. The sport has caught on so well here that now even the street signs are shaped like fish. Junín is spread out in a grid pattern, a fertile little oasis along the shore of the Río Chimehuín, surrounded by dry pampa. You'll pass through Junín if you're crossing into Argentina from the Pucón area in Chile.

ESSENTIALS
GETTING THERE   By Plane   See "Getting There" under "San Martín de los Andes," earlier in this chapter.

By Bus   Ko-Ko Chevalier (© 02972/427422) has service from San Martín de los Andes and Buenos Aires. Koko also has service to Lago Huechulafquen.

GETTING AROUND   Most visitors find that the only real way to get around is to rent a car, especially if you've come to fly-fish. Car-rental agencies can be found at the airport and in San Martín (see "Getting Around" under "San Martín," earlier).

VISITOR INFORMATION The **Secretaría Municipal de Turismo** is located at Padre Milanesio 596 (© **02972/491160**); it's open daily from 8am to 9pm, from 8am to 11pm during the summer.

WHAT TO SEE & DO

Puerto Canoa is the central entrance to the splendid **Parque Nacional Lanín,** 30km (19 miles) from Junín. Here, you'll find a 30-minute interpretive trail and the departure spot for catamaran excursions across Lago Huechulafquen, which looks out onto the snowcapped, conical Volcán Lanín. Río Chimehuín begins at the lake's outlet and offers outstanding fishing opportunities. There are several excellent hiking and backpacking trails in the area, as well as a few rustic back-country huts; you can pick up information at the ranger station at Puerto Canoa. If you're in San Martín de los Andes, stop by the park's headquarters, the **Intendencia Parque Nacional Lanín,** Emilio Frey 749 (© **02972/427233**).

Visitors can book a tour or rent a car for the 132km (82-mile) drive to the hot springs **Termas de Epulafquen,** winding through volcanic landscape and past Lake Curruhue. For tours, try Huiliches Turismo, Padre Milanesio 570, Local B (© **02972/491670**), or ask at the visitor center.

FISHING INFORMATION & LICENSES Licenses can be obtained at the **Tourism Office,** the office of the Guardafauna (© **02972/491277**), open Monday to Friday 8am to 3pm; The Fly Shop (Pedro Illera 378; © **02972/491548**); Bambi's Fly Shop (Juan Manuel de Rosas 320; © **02972/491167**); or Patagonia Fly Fishing (Laura Vicuña 135; ©/fax **02972/491538**).

WHERE TO STAY & DINE

There are a few lodges that specialize in fly-fishing, such as the **Hostería de Chimehuín** at Suarez and Avenida 21 de Mayo, on the shore of the Chimehuín River (© **02972/491132**; $9 double). Accommodations are basic, including rooms with balconies and apartments, but the atmosphere is friendly and homey and there's a good breakfast. An excellent fly-fishing lodge is the **San Humberto Lodge,** located on a privately owned stretch of the Malleo River (© **02972/491238**), which charges $65 for a double. The San Humberto consists of six chalets with twin beds, units that are separate from an enormous rustic lodge. The restaurant is excellent and so are the fishing guides. **Cerro los Pinos,** Brown 420 (© **02972/427207**), is a charming family ranch with close access to the Chimehuín River. Doubles are $8 to $22; they'll arrange a fishing guide. Dining options are limited here; try the **Ruca Hueney** at Milanesio 641 (© **02972/491113**), which serves pasta dishes and, of course, trout.

9

Uruguay

The second-smallest nation in South America, Uruguay is a little place that makes a big impression. With an impressive living standard, high literacy rate, large urban middle class, and excellent social services—including the best medical care system in South America—it has become a model for other developing countries in the region. Despite its homogeneous population (mostly of European descent), Uruguay reveals splendid contrasts.

This is a land of dusty colonial towns and sparkling beach resorts, of rough-and-ready gauchos and subtle artists and festive plazas. Uruguay is a place where soccer *(fútbol)* is worshipped without reserve, where the sun shines brightly and the air stays warm, where few question the dignity of their homeland. And despite the economic troubles of recent years, Uruguay remains a proud and peaceful nation.

1 The Regions in Brief

Uruguay's origins as a country rest firmly in Europe; the indigenous people inhabiting the region were displaced by the colonizing Portuguese and Spanish in the late 17th and early 18th centuries. Montevideo is the cultural heartland of the country, a place where you will discover the bold accomplishments of Uruguay in music, art, and literature. Among the internationally accomplished Uruguayan artists are Pedro Figari, who inspired a school of painters; José Enrique Rodó, Uruguay's famed essayist from the early 20th century; and Mauricio Rosencof, the politically active playwright from recent decades. Outside the capital, pastureland and rolling hills draw your attention to a softer, quieter life. But this rural lifestyle stops at the coast, where world-class resorts centered on **Punta del Este** lure the continent's rich and famous.

2 Planning Your Trip to Uruguay

VISITOR INFORMATION

The Internet is an excellent source of information on Uruguay. Try **www.turismo.gub.uy** or **www.uruguaynatural.com** for official visitor information. Additional countrywide tourist information can be found at www.visit-uruguay.com.

The Uruguayan embassy in your home country is a good source of information. At **www.embassy.org/uruguay**, the Uruguayan embassy site in Washington, D.C., you'll find a description of tourist activities in Montevideo, Punta del Este, and Uruguay's northwest, as well as travel tips and a hostel list.

ENTRY REQUIREMENTS & CUSTOMS

Citizens of the United States, the United Kingdom, Canada, and New Zealand need only a passport to enter Uruguay (for tourist stays of up to 90 days). Australian citizens must get a tourist visa before arrival.

Telephone Dialing Info at a Glance

Uruguay's national telephone company is called ANTEL. You can buy a telephone card from any kiosk or ANTEL *telecentro* location. You can also make domestic and international calls from telecentro offices, but international calls are very expensive, especially during peak hours.

- **To place a call from your home country to Uruguay,** dial the international access code (011 in the U.S., 0011 in Australia, 0170 in New Zealand, 00 in the U.K.) plus the country code (598), plus the city or region area code (for example, Montevideo 2, Punta del Este 42, Colonia del Sacramento 11) followed by the number. For example, a call from the United States to Montevideo would be 011+ 598+2+000+0000.
- **To place a domestic long-distance call within Uruguay,** dial a 0 before the area code, then the local number.
- **To place a direct international call from Uruguay,** dial the international access code (00), plus the country code of the place you are dialing, plus the area code and the number.
- **To reach an International Long Distance Operator,** dial ✆ 000-410 for **AT&T;** ✆ 000-412 for **MCI;** ✆ 000-417 for **Sprint.**

A helpful Customs information guide for Uruguay can be found at **www.euro-trans.com/customs/uruguay.asp**.

URUGUAYAN EMBASSY LOCATIONS

In the U.S.: 2715 M St. NW, 3rd Floor, Washington, DC 20007 (✆ **202/331-1313;** fax 202/331-8142; www.embassy.org/uruguay).

In Canada: 130 Albert St., Suite 1905, Ottawa, ON K1P 5G4 (✆ **613/234-2727;** fax 613/233-4670; www.iosphere.net/~uruott).

In the U.K.: 140 Brompton Rd., 2nd Floor, London SW3 1HY (✆ **207/589-8835**).

MONEY

The official currency is the **Uruguayan peso** (designated NP$, $U, or simply $); each peso is comprised of 100 **centavos.** Uruguayan pesos are available in $10; $20; $50; $100; $200; $500; $1,000; and $5,000 notes; coins come in 10, 20, and 50 centavos, and 1 and 2 pesos. The Uruguayan currency devalued by half in July 2002, and the exchange rate as this book went to press was approximately 27 pesos to the dollar. The value of the peso fluctuates greatly with inflation, so all prices in this chapter are quoted in U.S. dollars.

WHEN TO GO

The best time to visit Uruguay is October through March, when the sun shines and temperatures are mild. Punta del Este overflows with tourists from Argentina in summer; if you're seeking a more relaxed time to visit the beaches of the coast, consider going between October and December.

Average temperatures are spring 62°F (17°C), summer 73°F (23°C), autumn 64°F (18°C), and winter 53°F (12°C). (Remember that seasons are reversed from the Northern Hemisphere.)

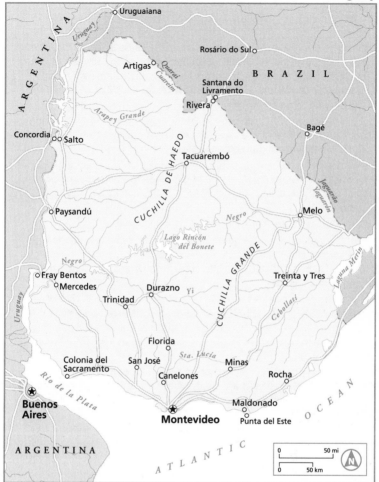

GETTING THERE

International flights land at **Carrasco International Airport** (☏ **02/604-0386**), located 19km (12 miles) from downtown Montevideo. A taxi to downtown costs about $15. Uruguay's national carrier is **Pluna,** Colonia and Julio Herrera (☏ **0800/118-811** or 02/604-4080), serving domestic and international destinations. **United** (☏ **800/247-6522** in the U.S., 02/902-4630 in Uruguay) and **American** (☏ **800/433-7300** in the U.S., 02/916-3929 in Uruguay) offer connecting service from the United States. **Aerolíneas Argentinas** (☏ **02/901-9466**) connects Buenos Aires and Montevideo; the flight takes 50 minutes.

Punta del Este has its own international airport; the majority of flights arrive from Buenos Aires. From Montevideo, the easiest way to reach Colonia and Punta del Este is by bus (see "Getting There" under "Montevideo" and "Punta del Este," below).

FAST FACTS: **Uruguay**

American Express In Montevideo, American Express Bank is located at Rincón 477, 8th Floor (☎ 02/916-0000). **Turisport Limitada** acts as an agent of American Express Travel Services in Uruguay. Hours for the Montevideo location, Calle San José 930 (☎ **02/902-0829;** fax 02/902-0852), are Monday through Friday from 9am to 5pm.

ATMs ATMs on the Cirrus network are widely available in Montevideo and Punta del Este. If you travel to Colonia or elsewhere outside these cities, you should bring Uruguayan pesos.

Business Hours In general, businesses stay open Monday through Friday from 9am to 6:30 or 7pm, with a 2-hour break for lunch around noon. Retail outlets keep similar hours and are usually open a half day on Saturday as well.

Customs See "Entry Requirements & Customs," above.

Electricity Electricity in Uruguay runs on 220 volts, so bring a transformer and adapter along with any electrical appliances. Note that most laptops operate on both 110 and 220 volts. Some luxury hotels may supply transformers and adapters.

Embassies & Consulates United States Embassy, Lauro Muller 1776, Montevideo 11100 (☎ **02/408-7777**); British Embassy, Marco Bruto No. 1073, P.O. Box 16024, Montevideo 11300 (☎ **02/622-3630**); Canadian Embassy, Edificio Torre Libertad, Plaza Cagancha 1335, Office 1105, Montevideo 11100 (☎ **02/902-2030**).

Emergencies The general **emergency** number is ☎ **911.** Outside Montevideo, dial 02/911 to connect with Montevideo Central Emergency Authority. The following numbers also work: **police** ☎ **109; ambulance** ☎ **105; fire** department ☎ **104.**

Holidays New Year's Day (Jan 1), Día de los Reyes (Jan 6), Carnaval (the days leading up to Ash Wednesday), Easter, Desembarco de los 33 Orientales (Apr 19), Labor Day (May 1), Batalla de las Piedras (May 18), Natalicio de José Gervasio Artigas (June 19), Jura de la Constitución (July 18), Independence Day (Aug 25), Día de la Raza (Columbus Day; Oct 12), Día de los Difuntos (Nov 2), and Christmas (Dec 25).

Internet Access Many hotel business centers have Internet access, as do the guest rooms in five-star hotels. See "Internet Access" under "Fast Facts: Montevideo," below, for a listing of cybercafes in town.

Restrooms It's permissible to use the toilets in restaurants and bars without patronizing the establishment; offer a nice smile on the way in. Nobody should bother you unless they're having a bad day.

Safety Uruguay is one of the world's safest countries, although petty crime in Montevideo has risen in recent years. Outside the capital, cities and beach resorts such as Punta del Este are considered safe. Travelers visiting Uruguay are advised to take common-sense precautions and avoid demonstrations or protests.

Taxes Value-added tax is called *IVA* in Spanish. IVA is 14% for hotels and restaurants and 24% for general sales tax; the tax is almost always included in your bill.

Telephones See "Telephone Dialing Info at a Glance," above.

Time Zone Uruguay is 1 hour ahead of Eastern Standard Time. (4pm in New York is 5pm in Uruguay.)

Water Locals swear that the drinking water in Uruguay is perfectly healthy; in fact, Uruguay was the only country in the Americas to escape the cholera pandemic of the early 1990s. If you are concerned, stick with bottled water (*agua mineral sin gas* in Spanish).

3 Montevideo

Montevideo, the southernmost capital on the continent, is home to half the country's population. Born on the banks of the Río de la Plata, Montevideo first existed as a fortress of the Spanish Empire and developed into a major port city in the mid–18th century. European immigrants, including Spanish, Portuguese, French, and British, influenced the city's architecture, and a walk around the capital reveals architectural styles ranging from colonial to Art Deco. Indeed, the richness of Montevideo's architecture is unrivaled in South America.

Although Montevideo has few must-see attractions, its charm lies in wait for the careful traveler. A walk along La Rambla, stretching from the Old City to the neighborhood of Carrasco, takes you along the riverfront past fishermen and their catch to parks and gardens where children play and elders sip *mate* (a tea-like beverage). Restaurants, cafes, bars, and street performers populate the port area, where you will also discover the flavors of Uruguay at the afternoon and weekend Mercado del Puerto, or Port Market. Many of the city's historic sites surround Plaza Independencia and can be visited in a few hours.

ESSENTIALS

GETTING THERE

BY PLANE   To get to Montevideo by plane, see "Getting There & Getting Around," above. A taxi or *remise* (private, unmetered taxi) from the airport to downtown costs about $15.

BY BOAT OR HYDROFOIL   **Buquebús,** Calle Río Negro 1400 (© **02/916-8801**), operates three to four hydrofoils per day between Montevideo and Buenos Aires; the trip takes about 2½ hours and costs less than $100 round-trip. Montevideo's port is about 1.5km (1 mile) from downtown. If you have taken a ferry to Colonia del Sacramento, you can get connecting bus service to Montevideo.

BY BUS   **Terminal Omnibus Tres Cruces,** General Artigas 1825 (© **02/409-7399**), is Montevideo's long-distance bus terminal, connecting the capital with cities in Uruguay and throughout South America. Buses to Buenos Aires take about 8 hours. **COT** (© **02/409-4949**) offers the best service to Punta del Este, Maldonado, and Colonia.

For roadside emergencies or general information on driving in Uruguay, contact the **Automóvil Club de Uruguay,** Av. Libertador 1532 (© **02/902-4792**), or the **Centro Automovilista del Uruguay,** E.V. Haedo 2378 (© **02/408-2091**).

ORIENTATION

Montevideo is surrounded by water on three sides, a testament to its earlier incarnation as an easily defended fortress for the Spanish Empire. The Old City begins near the western edge of Montevideo, found on the skinny portion of a peninsula between the Rambla Gran Bretaña and the city's main artery, Avenida 18 de Julio. Look for the Plaza Independencia and the Plaza Constitución to find the center of the district. Many of the city's museums, theaters, and hotels reside in this historic area, although a trip east on Avenida 18 de Julio reveals the more modern Montevideo with its own share of hotels, markets, and monuments. Along the city's long southern coastline runs the Rambla Gran Bretaña, traveling 21km (13 miles) from the piers of the Old City past Parque Rodó and on to points south and east, passing fish stalls and street performers along the way.

GETTING AROUND

It's easy to navigate around the center on foot or by bus. Safe, convenient buses crisscross Montevideo if you want to venture outside the city center (for less than $1 per trip). Taxis are safe and relatively inexpensive, but can be difficult to hail during rush hour. One recommended company is **Remises Carrasco** (© 09/ 440-5473). To rent a car, try **Thrifty** (© 02/204-3373).

VISITOR INFORMATION

Uruguay's **Ministerio de Turismo** is at Av. Libertador 1409 and Colonia (© 02/ 908-9105). It assists travelers with countrywide information and is open daily from 8am to 8pm in winter, from 8am to 2pm in summer. There's also a branch at Carrasco International Airport and Tres Cruces bus station. The **municipal tourist office,** Explanada Municipal (© 1950), offers city maps and brochures of tourist activities and is open weekdays from 11am to 6pm, weekends from 10am to 6pm. It also organizes cultural city tours on weekends.

FAST FACTS: MONTEVIDEO

Area Code   The country code for Uruguay is **598;** the city code for Montevideo is **2.**

ATMs   ATMs are plentiful; look for **Bancomat** and **Redbrou** banks. Most have access to the Cirrus network.

Currency Exchange   To exchange money, try **Turisport Limitada** (the local Amex representative), San José 930 (© 02/902-0829); **Gales Casa Cambiaria,** Av. 18 de Julio 1046 (© 02/902-0229); or one of the airport exchanges.

Hospital   The **British Hospital** is located at Av. Italia 2420 (© 02/487-1020) and has emergency room services.

Internet Access   Internet cafes appear and disappear faster than discos, but you won't walk long before coming across another spot in the city center. Reliable cybercafes include **El Cybercafé,** Calle 25 de Mayo 568; **Arroba del Sur,** Guayabo 1858; and **El Cybercafé Softec,** Santiago de Chile 1286. Average cost is $2 per hour of usage.

Post Office   The main post office is at Calle Buenos Aires 451 (© 0810/444- CORREO) and is open weekdays from 9am to 6pm.

Safety   Although Montevideo remains very safe by big city standards, street crime has risen in recent years. Travelers should avoid walking alone, particularly at night, in Ciudad Vieja, Avenida 18 de Julio, Plaza Independencia, and the vicinity around the port. Take a taxi instead.

WHAT TO SEE & DO

Catedral ✿   Also known as Iglesia Matriz (Matriz Church), the cathedral was the city's first public building, erected in 1804. It houses the remains of some of

Montevideo

ATTRACTIONS ●
Cathedral **3**
El Cabildo **4**
Museo de Arte
Contemporaneo **10**
Museo Municipal
de Bellas Artes
"Juan Manuel Blanes" **12**
Palacio Salvo **8**
Palacio Taranco **2**
Teatro Solís **5**

ACCOMMODATIONS ■
Belmont House **14**
Days Inn **13**
Holiday Inn **7**
Plaza Victoria Hotel **6**
Sheraton Montevideo **15**

DINING ◆
Arcadia **5**
El Fogón **11**
El Viejo y El Mar **16**
Las Brasas **9**
Río Alegre **1**

ⓘ Information

Uruguay's most important political, religious, and economic figures, and is distinguished by its domed bell towers.

Calle Sarandí at Ituzaingó. Free admission. Mon–Fri 8am–8pm.

El Cabildo (Town Hall) ⭐ Uruguay's constitution was signed in the old town hall, which also served as the city's jailhouse in the 19th century. Now a museum, the Cabildo houses the city's historic archives as well as maps and photos, antiques, costumes, and artwork.

Juan Carlos Gómez 1362. © 02/915-9685. Free admission. Tues–Sun 2:30–7pm.

Museo de Arte Contemporáneo (Museum of Contemporary Art) ⭐ Opened in 1997, this museum is dedicated to contemporary Uruguayan art and exhibits the country's biggest names. To promote cultural exchange across the region, a section of the museum has been set aside for artists who hail from various South American countries.

Av. 18 de Julio 965, 2nd Floor. © 02/900-6662. Free admission. Daily noon–8pm.

Museo Municipal de Bellas Artes "Juan Manuel Blanes" (Municipal Museum of Fine Arts) ⭐ The national art history museum displays Uruguayan artistic styles from the beginning of the nation to the present day. Works include oils, engravings, drawings, sculptures, and documents. Among the great Uruguayan artists exhibited are Juan Manuel Blanes, Pedro Figari, Rafael Barradas, José Cúneo, and Carlos Gonzales.

Av. Millán 4015. © 02/336-2248. Free admission. Tues–Sun 2–7pm.

Palacio Salvo (Salvo Palace) ⭐ Often referred to as the symbol of Montevideo, the Salvo Palace was once the tallest building in South America. Although its 26 stories might not impress you, it remains the city's highest structure.

Plaza Independencia.

Palacio Taranco (Taranco Palace) ⭐ Now the decorative arts museum, the Taranco Palace was built in the early 20th century and represents the trend toward French architecture during that period. The museum displays Uruguayan furniture, draperies, clocks, paintings, and other cultural works.

Calle 25 de Mayo 379. © 02/915-1101. Free admission. Tues–Sat 10am–6pm.

Plaza Independencia ⭐⭐ Originally the site of a Spanish citadel, Independence Square marks the beginning of the Old City and is a good point from which to begin your tour of Montevideo. An enormous statue of General José Gervasio Artigas, father of Uruguay and hero of its independent movement, stands in the center. His ashes are displayed in a mausoleum under the monument.

Bordered by Av. 18 de Julio, Florida, and Juncal.

Teatro Solís ⭐⭐ Montevideo's main theater and opera house, opened in 1852, completed an extensive renovation a few years back. It hosts Uruguay's most important cultural events and is the site of the **Museo Nacional de Historia Natural (National Museum of Natural History).**

Calle Buenos Aires 652. © 02/916-0908. Free admission. Museum Mon–Fri 2–6pm.

SHOPPING

Shopping in Montevideo is concentrated in a few downtown shops and in three major shopping centers. In Uruguayan stores, expect to find leather goods, jewelry, and local crafts and textiles—including sweaters, cardigan jackets, ponchos, coats, and tapestries made of high-quality wool. International stores carry American and European products. Montevideo's most fashionable mall is the **Punta Carretas Shopping Center,** Calle Ellauri and Solano, next to the new Sheraton hotel. Downtown, the **Montevideo Shopping Center,** Av. Luis Alberto de Herrera 1290, is the city's original mall with more than 180 stores and a 10-screen theater. **Portones de Carrasco,** avenidas Bolivia and Italia, is another recommended shopping center in the Carrasco neighborhood.

MARKETS The **Villa Biarritz fair** at Parque Zorilla de San Martín-Ellauri takes place Saturday from 9:30am to 3pm and features handicrafts, antiques, books, fruit and vegetable vendors, flowers, and other goodies. The **Mercado del Puerto (Port Market)** ⭐ opens afternoons and weekends at Piedras and Yacaré, letting you sample the flavors of Uruguay, from small empanadas to enormous barbecued meats. Saturday is the best day to visit. **Tristán Narvaja,** Avenida 18 de Julio in the Cordón neighborhood, is the city's Sunday flea market (6am–3pm), initiated more than 50 years ago by Italian immigrants. **De la Abundancia/Artesanos** is a combined food and handicrafts market. It takes place Monday through Saturday from 10am to 8pm at San José 1312.

WHERE TO STAY

Montevideo's hotel infrastructure is improving, and hotel rates have fallen since the currency devalued in July 2002. Prices are jacked up during Carnaval time in February and when major conventions come to town, however. A 14% tax will be added to your bill. Parking is included in the rates of most Uruguay hotels.

EXPENSIVE

Belmont House ⭐⭐⭐ (Finds) A boutique hotel in Montevideo's peaceful Carrasco neighborhood, Belmont House offers its privileged guests intimacy and luxury. Small elegant spaces with carefully chosen antiques and wood furnishings give this the feeling of a wealthy private home. Beautiful guest rooms feature two- or four-poster beds, rich, colorful linens, and marble bathrooms with small details like towel warmers and deluxe toiletries. Many of the rooms feature balconies overlooking the pretty courtyard and pool, and two of the rooms have Jacuzzis. Belmont House is a skip and a jump away from the beach, golf, and tennis. Gourmands will find an excellent international restaurant, afternoon tea, and a *parrilla* (grill) open weekends next to the pool. The gracious staff assists guests with outdoor activities and local itineraries.

Av. Rivera 6512, 11500 Montevideo. ⓒ **02/600-0430.** Fax 02/600-8609. www.belmonthouse.com.uy. 28 units. $155 double; from $170 suite. Rates include gourmet breakfast. AE, DC, MC, V. **Amenities:** Restaurant; tearoom; bar; beautiful outdoor pool; discounts for tennis and golf; small fitness center; sauna; business center; babysitting; laundry service; dry cleaning. *In room:* A/C, TV, minibar, hair dryer.

Radisson Montevideo Victoria Plaza Hotel ⭐⭐ The Victoria Plaza has long been one of Montevideo's top hotels. The European-style hotel stands in the heart of the financial district and makes a good base from which to do business or explore the capital. Its convention center and casino also make it the center of business and social activity. Ask for a room in the new tower, built in 1995, which houses spacious guest rooms and executive suites with classic French-style furnishings and panoramic city or river views. The busy hotel has a large, multilingual staff that attends closely to guest needs. Inquire about weekend spa packages. Plaza Victoria is famous for its casino, with French roulette tables, blackjack, baccarat, slot machines, horse races, and bingo. There are two lobby bars, in addition to the casino bars. **Arcadia** (see "Where to Dine," below) on the 25th floor is the city's most elegant dining room.

Plaza Independencia 759, 11100 Montevideo. ℂ **02/902-0111.** Fax 02/902-1628. www.victoriaplaza.com. 254 units. $170 double; from $190 suite. Rates include breakfast at rooftop restaurant. AE, DC, MC, V. **Amenities:** Restaurant; cafe; 2 bars; excellent health club with skylit indoor pool; fitness center; aerobics classes; Jacuzzi; sauna; concierge; travel agency; business center with high-speed Internet access; room service; massage service; dry cleaning; laundry service; executive floors. *In room:* A/C, TV, dataport, minibar, hair dryer, safe.

Sheraton Montevideo ★★ Opened in 1999, the Sheraton Montevideo has replaced Plaza Victoria as Montevideo's most luxurious hotel. A walkway connects the hotel to the Punta Carretas Shopping Center, one of the city's best malls. Spacious guest rooms have imported furniture, king-size beds, sleeper chairs, marble bathrooms, 25-inch televisions, and works by Uruguayan artists. Choose between views of the Río de la Plata, Uruguay Golf Club, or downtown Montevideo, with views from the 20th through 24th floors being the most impressive. Rooms on the top two executive floors feature Jacuzzis and individual sound systems. Hotel service is excellent, particularly for guests with business needs. The main restaurant, Las Carretas, serves Continental cuisine with a Mediterranean flair—don't miss the dining room's spectacular murals by contemporary Uruguayan artist Carlos Vilaro. Next door, the lobby bar is a popular spot for casual business meetings and afternoon cocktails.

Calle Víctor Soliño 349, 11300 Montevideo. ℂ **02/710-2121.** Fax 02/712-1262. www.sheraton.com. 207 units. From $175 double; from $200 suite. Rates include buffet breakfast. AE, DC, MC, V. **Amenities:** Restaurant; bar; indoor pool; deluxe health club with fitness center; sauna; concierge; car-rental desk; business center and secretarial services; room service; massage service; babysitting; laundry service; dry cleaning; executive floors; emergency medical service. *In room:* A/C, TV, dataport, minibar, hair dryer, safe.

MODERATE

Holiday Inn ★ This colorful Holiday Inn is actually one of the city's best hotels, popular with tourists and business travelers. It's situated in the heart of downtown, next to Montevideo's main square. A bilingual staff greets you in the marble lobby, which is attached to a good restaurant and bar. Guest rooms have simple, contemporary furnishings typical of an American chain. Because the hotel doubles as a convention center, it can become very busy.

Colonia 823, 11100 Montevideo. ℂ **02/902-0001.** Fax 02/902-1242. www.holidayinn.com.uy. 137 units. From $88 double. Rates include buffet breakfast. AE, DC, MC, V. **Amenities:** Restaurant; bar; heated indoor pool; fitness center; sauna; business center; room service; laundry service; dry cleaning. *In room:* A/C, TV, minibar, safe.

INEXPENSIVE

Days Inn Obelisco *Value* This modern Days Inn caters to business travelers looking for good-value accommodations. The hotel is located next to the Tres Cruces bus station and not far from downtown or the airport. Rooms are comfortable and modern, if not overly spacious. Free local calls are permitted.

Acevedo Díaz 1821, 11800 Montevideo. ℂ **02/400-4840.** Fax 02/402-0229. www.daysinn.com. 60 units. From $40 double. Rates include buffet breakfast. AE, DC, MC, V. **Amenities:** Coffee shop; small health club; business center; room service. *In room:* A/C, TV, minibar, hair dryer.

WHERE TO DINE

Restaurants in Montevideo serve steak—just as high quality as Argentine beef—and usually include a number of stews and seafood selections as well. You will find the native barbecue, in which beef and lamb are grilled on the fire, in any of the city's *parrilladas.* Sales tax on dining in Montevideo is a whopping 23%. There's usually a table cover charge, called the *cubierto,* as well—usually about $1 per person.

MODERATE

Arcadia ★★ *Moments* INTERNATIONAL   Virgil and Homer wrote that Arcadia was a quiet paradise in ancient Greece; this elegant restaurant atop the Plaza Victoria is a quiet paradise and the best restaurant in Montevideo. Tables are nestled in semiprivate nooks with floor-to-ceiling bay windows. The classic dining room is decorated with Italian curtains and crystal chandeliers; each table has a fresh rose and sterling silver place settings. Creative plates such as terrine of pheasant marinated in cognac are followed by grilled rack of lamb glazed with mint and garlic, or duck confit served on a thin strudel pastry with red cabbage.

Plaza Independencia 759. © 02/902-0111. Main courses $6–$10. AE, DC, MC, V. Daily 7pm–midnight.

El Fogón ★ URUGUAYAN   This brightly lit *parrillada* and seafood restaurant is popular with Montevideo's late-night crowd. The extensive menu includes calamari, salmon, shrimp, and other fish, as well as generous steak and pasta dishes. Food here is inexpensive and prepared with care. The express lunch menu comes with steak or chicken, dessert, and a glass of wine. Giant mirrors covering the walls give you an opportunity to inspect yourself; the large painting of two horses and a deserted wagon might spark a new table conversation.

San José 1080. © 02/900-0900. Main courses $5–$9. AE, DC, MC, V. Daily noon–4pm and 7pm–1am.

El Viejo y el Mar ★ SEAFOOD   Resembling an old fishing club, El Viejo y el Mar is located on the riverfront near the Sheraton hotel. The bar is made from an abandoned boat, while the dining room is decorated with dock lines, sea lamps, and pictures of 19th-century regattas. You'll find every kind of fish and pasta on the menu, and the restaurant is equally popular for evening cocktails. An outdoor patio is open most of the year.

Rambla Gandhi 400. © 02/710-5704. Main courses $5–$7. MC, V. Daily noon–4pm and 8pm–1am.

Las Brasas ★★ URUGUAYAN   Hillary Clinton once visited this restaurant; a picture of her with the staff hangs proudly on the wall. This casual *parrillada* resembles one you'd find in Buenos Aires—except that this restaurant also serves an outstanding range of *mariscos* (seafood) such as the Spanish paella or *lenguado Las Brasas* (a flathead fish) served with prawns, mushrooms, and mashed potatoes. From the *parrilla*, the *filet de lomo* is the best cut—order it with Roquefort, mustard, or black pepper sauce. The restaurant's fresh produce is displayed in a case near the kitchen.

San José 909. © 02/900-2285. Main courses $5–$8. AE, DC, MC, V. Daily 11:45am–3:30pm and 7:30pm–midnight.

INEXPENSIVE

Río Alegre ★ *Value* SNACKS   This casual, inventive lunch stop specializes in quick steaks off the grill. Ribs, sausages, and most cuts of beef are cooked on the *parrilla* and made to order. Río Alegre is a local favorite because of its large portions, good quality, and cheap prices. Order a tall beer to wash it all down.

Calle Pérez Castellano and Piedras, at the Mercado del Puerto, Local 33. © 02/915-6504. Main courses $2–$3. No credit cards. Daily 11am–3pm.

MONTEVIDEO AFTER DARK

As in Buenos Aires, nightlife in Montevideo means drinks after 10pm and dancing after midnight. For earlier entertainment, ask at your hotel or call the **Teatro Solís,** Calle Buenos Aires 652 (© **02/916-0908**), the city's center for opera, theater, ballets, and symphonies, for performance information. **SODRE,** Av. 18 de

Julio 930 (℃ **02/901-2850**), is the city's "Official Radio Service," which hosts classical music concerts from May to November. Gamblers should head to the **Plaza Victoria Casino,** Plaza Independencia (℃ **02/902-0111**), a fashionable venue with French roulette tables, blackjack, baccarat, slot machines, horse races, and bingo. It opens at 2pm and keeps going through most of the night. **Mariachi,** Gabriel Pereira 2964 (℃ **02/709-1600**), is one of the city's top bars and discos, with live bands or deejay music Wednesday to Sunday after 10pm. **Café Misterio,** Costa Rica 1700 (℃ **02/600-5999**), is another popular bar, while **New York,** Calle Mar Artico 1227 (℃ **02/600-0444**), mixes a restaurant, bar, and dance club under one roof and attracts a slightly older crowd. Montevideo's best tango clubs are **La Casa de Becho,** Nueva York 1415 (℃ **02/400-2717**), where composer Gerardo Mattos Rodríguez wrote the famous "La Cumparsita," and **Cuareim,** Zelmar Michelini 1079, which offers both tango and *candombe,* a lively dance indigenous to the area. La Casa de Becho is open Friday and Saturday after 10:30pm; Cuareim, Wednesday, Friday, and Saturday after 9pm. The tourist office can give you schedule information for Montevideo's other tango salons.

4 A Side Trip to Colonia del Sacramento

242km (150 miles) W of Montevideo

The tiny gem of Colonia del Sacramento, declared a World Heritage City by UNESCO, appears untouched by time. Dating from the 17th century, the old city boasts beautifully preserved colonial artistry down its dusty streets. A leisurely stroll into the **Barrio Histórico (Historic Neighborhood)** leads under flower-laden windowsills to churches dating from the 1680s, past exquisite single-story homes from Colonia's time as a Portuguese settlement, and on to local museums detailing the riches of the town's past. The Barrio Histórico contains brilliant examples of colonial wealth and many of Uruguay's oldest structures. A mix of lovely shops and delicious cafes makes the town more than a history lesson.

ESSENTIALS
GETTING THERE
Many people make Colonia a day trip from Buenos Aires. The easiest way to reach Colonia from Buenos Aires is by ferry. **FerryLíneas** (℃ **02/900-6617**) runs a fast boat that arrives in 45 minutes and a slower 3-hour bus. **Buquebús** (℃ **02/916-1910**) also offers two classes of service. Prices range from $10 to $35 each way.

Colonia can also easily be visited from Montevideo, and is a good stopping-off point if you're traveling between Buenos Aires and Montevideo. **COT** (℃ **02/409-4949** in Montevideo) also offers bus service from Montevideo and from Punta del Este.

VISITOR INFORMATION
The **Oficina de Turismo,** General Flores and Rivera (℃ **052/27000** or 052/27300), is open daily from 8am to 8pm. Speak with someone at the tourism office to arrange a guided tour of the town.

WHAT TO SEE & DO
A WALK THROUGH COLONIA'S BARRIO HISTORICO
Your visit to Colonia will be concentrated in the **Barrio Histórico (Old Neighborhood),** located on the coast at the far southwestern corner of town. The sites,

which are all within a few blocks, can easily be visited on foot in a few hours. Museums and tourist sites are open daily (except Tues–Wed) from 11:30am to 5:45pm. For less than $1, you can buy a pass at the Portuguese or Municipal museum that will get you into all the sites.

Start your tour at **Plaza Mayor,** the principal square that served as the center of the colonial establishment. To explore Colonia's Portuguese history, cross the Calle Manuel Lobo on the southeastern side of the plaza and enter the **Museo Portugués (Portuguese Museum),** which exhibits European customs and traditions that influenced the town's beginnings. Upon exiting the museum, turn left and walk to the **Iglesia Matriz (Matriz Church),** among the oldest churches in the country and an excellent example of 17th-century architecture and design.

Next, exit the church and turn left to the **Ruinas Convento San Francisco (San Francisco Convent Ruins).** Dating from 1696, the San Francisco convent was once inhabited by Jesuit and Franciscan monks, two brotherhoods dedicated to preaching the gospel to indigenous people. Continue up Calle San Francisco to the **Casa de Brown (Brown House),** which houses the **Museo Municipal (Municipal Museum).** Here, you will find an impressive collection of colonial documents and artifacts, a must-see for history buffs.

For those with a more artistic bent, turn left on Calle Misiones de los Tapes and walk 2 blocks to the **Museo del Azulejo (Tile Museum),** a unique museum of 19th-century European and Uruguayan tiles housed in a gorgeous 300-year-old country house. Then stroll back into the center of town along Calle de la Playa, enjoying the shops and cafes along the way, until you come to the **Ruinas Casa del Gobernador (House of the Viceroy Ruins).** The House of the Viceroy captures something of the glorious past of the city's 17th- and 18th-century magistrates, when the city's port was used for imports, exports, and smuggling. Complete your walk with a visit to the **UNESCO–Colonia** headquarters, where exhibits on the city's newly acquired Historic Heritage of Humanity status will place your tour in the larger context of South American history.

WHERE TO STAY & DINE

Few people stay in Colonia, preferring to make a day trip from Buenos Aires or a stop along the way to Montevideo. If you'd rather get a hotel, however, your best bets are the colonial-style **Hotel Plaza Mayor,** Calle del Comercio 111 (✆ **052/23193**), and **Hotel La Misión,** Calle Misiones de los Tapes 171 (✆ **052/26767**), whose original building dates from 1762. Both hotels charge from $90 for a double. For dining, **Mesón de la Plaza,** Vasconcellos 153 (✆ **052/24807**), serves quality international and Uruguayan food in a colonial setting, while **Pulpería de los Faroles,** Calle Misiones de los Tapes 101 (✆ **052/ 25399**), in front of Plaza Mayor, specializes in beef and bean dishes and homemade pasta.

5 Punta del Este

140km (87 miles) E of Montevideo

Come late December, Punta del Este is transformed from a sleepy coastal village into a booming summer resort. For 2 months, there seem to be more Porteños (as residents of Buenos Aires are called) in "Punta" than in Buenos Aires itself. Without a doubt, this coastal strip that juts into the southern Atlantic is the favorite summer getaway for Argentines, a resort with beautiful white-sand beaches and perfect swimming, world-class hotels and restaurants, and an inexhaustible list of outdoor activities—including golf, tennis, horseback riding, biking, bird-watching, and numerous watersports. The shopping here is world class, you'll have no problem finding an excellent restaurant for dinner, and nightlife in Punta del Este beats just about anywhere else in South America in summer.

ESSENTIALS
GETTING THERE
BY PLANE   International flights arrive at **Aeropuerto Internacional de Laguna del Sauce,** 24km (15 miles) east of Punta del Este. **Pluna** (℃ **0800-118-881** or **042/490-101**), **LAPA** (℃ **042/559-338**), and **Aerolíneas Argentinas** (℃ **042/444-343**) fly between Buenos Aires and Punta. The flight takes 50 minutes. A taxi or *remise* from the airport into town will run about $14.

BY BUS   The **Terminal de Buses Punta del Este,** Rambla Artigas and Calle Inzaurraga (℃ **042/489-467**), has buses connecting to Montevideo, Colonia, and other cities throughout Uruguay. **COT** (℃ **042/486-810,** or 02/409-4949 in Montevideo) offers the best service to Montevideo. The trip takes 1½ to 2 hours and costs about $15 round-trip.

BY CAR   From Montevideo, you can reach Punta in 1½ hours by taking Route 1 east past Atlántida and Piriápolis to the turnoff for Route 93.

ORIENTATION
Punta del Este is both the name of the famous resort city and the broader region taking in Punta Ballena and Maldonado. The Rambla Artigas is the coastal road that winds its way around the peninsula past the enticing beaches (see "Outdoor Activities," below). Avenida Gorlero is the main street running through the center of Punta, where you find most of the restaurants, cafes, and boutiques.

GETTING AROUND
If you want to explore the region by car, you can visit **Avis** at the airport (℃ **042/559-065**) or at Calle 31 and Calle Gorlero (℃ **042/442-020**). **Budget** also has a branch at the airport. **Hertz** rents cars at the airport (℃ **042/559-032**) and in the Conrad Hotel (℃ **042/492-109**).

VISITOR INFORMATION
The **Oficina de Turismo** is at Parada 24 (℃ **042/230-050**), and is open daily from 9am to 10pm (shorter hours in winter). You should also be able to obtain visitor information from your hotel staff and from the **Centro de Hoteles y Restaurantes de Punta del Este,** Plaza Artigas on Avenida Gorlero (℃ **042/440-512**).

WHAT TO SEE & DO
OUTDOOR ACTIVITIES
In Punta itself, the main beaches are **Playa Mansa** (on the Río de la Plata) and **Playa Brava** (on the Atlantic). The two beaches are separated by a small peninsula only a few blocks wide. **La Barra del Maldonado,** a small resort 5km (3 miles) east of Punta del Este, also boasts clean, beautiful beaches.

In summer, you will find vendors offering watersports from parasailing and windsurfing to water-skiing and snorkeling on both Playa Mansa and Playa Brava. For boating or fishing expeditions, contact the **Yacht Club Punta del Este,** Puerto de Punta del Este (℃ **042/441-056**).

Golf courses include **Club de Golf** (℃ **042/482-127**) in Punta itself, and **Club del Lago** (℃ **042/578-423**) in Punta Ballena. Horseback riding can be arranged through **Hípico Burnett,** Camino a La Laguna, Pinares 33 (© **042/ 230-375**). Tennis fans should call **Médanos Tennis,** Avenida Mar del Plata and Avenida Las Delicias (© **042/481-950**).

SHOPPING

Punta has world-class shopping, with Uruguayan shops and European boutiques lining **Calle Gorlero,** the principal street bisecting this resort town. **Punta Shopping Mall,** Avenida Roosevelt at Paradas 6 and 7, has 100 stores on three levels and a 12-screen cinema. A weekend crafts market takes place from 5pm to midnight at Plaza Artigas.

WHERE TO STAY

Prices listed below are for summer peak season and are often half that in the off season. Christmas Eve to New Year's Eve is the busiest, most expensive week. Reserve well ahead of your visit, as all of Buenos Aires seems to flee to Punta del Este during summer vacation. Parking is free and available at all hotels in Punta.

VERY EXPENSIVE

Conrad Resort & Casino ★★★   The spectacular Conrad dominates social life in Punta del Este. It's the first choice of the international jet set that descends on this Atlantic resort in summer. The hotel's elegance stands in stark contrast to the city's other hotels, and guests look as though they've dressed for an afternoon on Rodeo Drive rather than the beach. Luxurious rooms have terraces overlooking Playa Mansa and Playa Brava, and the professional staff is highly attentive to guest needs. Personal trainers can assist you with your favorite sport, from tennis to golf to horseback riding. The outdoor pool and gardens are gorgeous, and there's an excellent health club for the truly motivated. The Conrad's casino and showrooms are focal points for Punta nightlife.

The Conrad offers nonstop entertainment, from fashion shows and Las Vegas–style reviews to music, dance, and magic shows. Open 24 hours, the enormous casino features 450 slots and 63 tables for baccarat, roulette, blackjack, poker, dice, and fortune wheel. There are five restaurants, from refined dining to poolside barbecues. Two excellent beaches are located in front of the resort.

Parada 4, Playa Mansa, 20100 Punta del Este. © **042/491-111.** Fax 042/489-999. www.conrad.com.uy. 302 units. From $300 double (high season). AE, DC, MC, V. **Amenities:** 5 restaurants; temperate-water pool; golf; 2 lit tennis courts; deluxe health club with fitness center; sauna; concierge; business center and secretarial services; room service; massage; laundry service; dry cleaning; executive floors; water-skiing; scuba diving; horseback riding. *In room:* A/C, TV, dataport, minibar, hair dryer, safe.

EXPENSIVE

L'Auberge ★★   This exclusive boutique hotel lies in the quiet residential neighborhood of Parque de Golf, 2 blocks from the beach. Formerly an 18th-century water tower, the hotel houses beautiful guest rooms decorated with antiques and a dedicated staff committed to warm, personalized service. The staff can help you arrange horseback riding, golf, tennis, or other outdoor sports in the surrounding parks. The sophisticated resort has an elegant European tearoom overlooking the gardens, famous for its homemade waffles. An evening barbecue is offered by the pool.

Barrio Parque del Golf, 20100 Punta del Este. © **042/482-601.** Fax 042/483-408. www.lauberge.com.uy. 40 units. From $160 double; from $350 suite. Rates include continental breakfast. AE, DC, MC, V. **Amenities:** Outdoor pool; golf; tennis court; fitness center; spa; concierge; business center and secretarial services; room service; babysitting; laundry service; dry cleaning; barbecue; garden; horseback riding. *In room:* TV, minibar, hair dryer, safe.

MODERATE

Best Western La Foret ⭐ *(Kids)*   Opened in 2000, La Foret offers spacious guest rooms 1 block from Playa Mansa. The amenities are impressive given the price, and the hotel is a nice option for families (children under 17 stay free, and there's a children's playground and babysitting services). There's also a good international restaurant and coffee shop, with a multilingual staff.

Calle La Foret, Parada 6, Playa Mansa, 20100 Punta del Este. ℂ 042/481-004. Fax 042/481-004. www.best western.com. 49 units. From $70 double. Rates include buffet breakfast. AE, DC, MC, V. **Amenities:** Restaurant; bar/lounge; pool; tennis; hot tub; sauna; concierge; business services; babysitting; playground. *In room:* TV, minibar, dataport, hair dryer, safe.

Days Inn Punta del Este ⭐⭐ *(Value)*   Opened in 1999, this atypical Days Inn sits on the waterfront. It's an excellent value for its location, featuring simple but modern rooms, many with ocean views. The Conrad Resort & Casino is next door, along with restaurants, cinemas, and excellent beaches. This is the best midrange hotel in Punta.

Rambla Willman, Parada 3, Playa Mansa, 20100 Punta del Este. ℂ 042/484-353. Fax 042/484-683. www.daysinn.com. 38 units. From $105 double, including buffet breakfast. AE, DC, MC, V. **Amenities:** Bar/lounge; indoor heated and outdoor pool; room service; babysitting; laundry services. *In room:* TV, minibar, dataport, hair dryer, safe.

WHERE TO DINE

Punta's dining scene is seasonal, with restaurants packed in summer and fairly dead in winter. Restaurant hours vary depending on the season, and some establishments close altogether from April to October.

EXPENSIVE

La Bourgogne ⭐⭐⭐ *(Moments)* FRENCH   Jean-Paul Bondoux is the top French chef in South America, splitting his time between La Bourgogne in Punta del Este and its sister restaurant in Buenos Aires (p. 57). You'll have an unforgettable dining experience at this Relais & Châteaux member. Traditional main courses such as rack of lamb, breast of duck, rabbit with mustard sauce, and veal cutlet are the chef's favorites, while fresh vegetables, fruits, herbs, and spices from the owner's private farm accentuate the menu. Delicious French bread, baked in-house, is available for takeout from the restaurant's small bakery. Ask for a table inside the elegant dining room or amid the jasmine-scented garden. Service is impeccable, as is the wine list featuring French and South American labels.

Pedragosa Sierra (Maldonado). ℂ 042/482-007. Main courses $15–$25. AE, DC, MC, V. Open for lunch and dinner. Closed Mar 31–Oct 15.

MODERATE

Andrés ⭐⭐ INTERNATIONAL   This father-son establishment enjoys an excellent reputation across the board. Its setting along the Rambla, with most tables outside, makes for a perfect summer night out. Dishes, ranging from grilled meats to baked fish and fresh vegetable soufflés, are prepared with considerable care. Service is friendly and professional; ask for assistance matching a South American wine with your meal.

Edificio Vanguardia, Parada 1. ℂ 042/481-804. Main courses $8–$15. AE, MC, V. Open Dec–Mar Thurs–Sun.

Lo de Tere ⭐⭐ *(Finds)* URUGUAYAN   This cozy establishment has a staff that makes you feel at home, offering graceful, cheerful service. Lo de Tere sits right on the water, with a beautiful view of the harbor. The specialties are fresh fish and pasta, which vary depending on the catch and the chef's inspiration. The restaurant transforms from festive and relaxed at lunch to more refined at dinner. Three-course menus are available for $16 to $32.

Rambla del Puerto and Calle 21. © **042/440-492.** Main courses $6–$15. AE, DC, MC, V. Summer daily 12:30–6pm and 9pm–3am; winter daily noon–3:30pm and 8pm–midnight.

Yacht Club Uruguayo ✪ URUGUAYAN   This popular restaurant, with tables inside and on the outdoor terrace, looks across the water to Gorriti Island. The dining room's marine theme prepares you for an evening of seafood, with octopus, hake, and swordfish among the favorites. Waiters, dressed in proud white shirts, offer attentive service.

Rambla Artigas and Calle 8. © **042/441-056.** Main courses $8–$20. AE, DC, MC, V. Summer daily noon–2am; winter daily noon–3:30pm and 7:30pm–midnight.

INEXPENSIVE

Los Caracoles ✪ (Value) URUGUAYAN   The town's most recommended *parrillada* also serves excellent seafood, including Spanish-style paella. A good salad bar accompanies the hearty selection of meats and fish, and there are a number of homemade pastas to choose from as well. Packed with 70 tables, the rustic dining room is casual and boisterous.

Calle Gorlero 20. © **042/440-912.** Main courses $4–$7. AE, DC, MC, V. Summer daily noon–6pm and 8pm–3am; winter daily noon–4pm and 7pm–1am.

PUNTA DEL ESTE AFTER DARK

The **Conrad Resort & Casino,** Parada 4, Playa Mansa (© **042/491-111**), is the focal point for evening entertainment in Punta, featuring Las Vegas–style reviews and other music, dance, and magic shows—sometimes around the torch-lit swimming pools. The enormous 24-hour casino has 450 slots and 63 tables for baccarat, roulette, blackjack, poker, dice, and fortune wheel.

Bars and discos come and go with considerable frequency in Punta. The concierge at Conrad Resort & Casino (see "Where to Stay," above) is a good source for what's hot in town. The best bar is **Moby Dick,** located at Rambla de la Circunvalación (© **042/441-240**), near the yacht harbor. Punta's bronzed Latin bodies then make their way to **Gitane** and **La Plage** (© **042/484-869**), two discos next to each other on Rambla Brava, Parada 12. The Conrad Hotel's own disco, **La Boite,** is another upscale club free for hotel guests and $10 to enter for outsiders (this $10 can be redeemed for chips in the casino).

10

Planning Your Trip to Chile

Pristine landscapes and an improved tourism infrastructure have made Chile, especially Patagonia and the Lake District, a hot destination for international travelers. A well-defined high season dictates price jumps in lodging and more, leaving the question, when should you go? *Where* should you go? What level of value can you expect? The following information should answer all the questions you might encounter when planning your trip to Chile.

1 The Regions in Brief

Chile's lengthy, serpentine shape incorporates nearly every kind of landscape and temperate zone imaginable. (In fact, the only zone not found in mainland Chile is tropical.) From tip to tail, Chile stretches 4,635km (2,880 miles). Conversely, traveling from the Pacific Coast to the border of Argentina in the Andes takes an average of only 3 hours. Most of Chile is sandwiched between the Pacific Ocean and the Andes, but despite that common geographical trait, the scenery changes so dramatically from north to south that it is often hard to believe it's all within the same country. For our purposes, we've divided Chile into four broad regions: the North, the Central Valley, the Lake District, and Patagonia.

NORTHERN CHILE   This region claims the world's driest desert, a beautiful "wasteland" set below a chain of purple and pink volcanoes and high-altitude salt flats. The most popular destinations here, including the Atacama Desert, sit at altitudes of 2,000m (6,560 ft.) and up. The extreme climate and the geological forces at work in this region have produced far-out land formations and superlatives such as the highest geyser field in the world. The earth here is parched, sun-baked, and unlike anything you've ever seen, but it gives relief through many of its tiny emerald oases, such as San Pedro de Atacama. See chapter 13.

SANTIAGO & CENTRAL CHILE
The central region of Chile, including Santiago and its environs, features a mild, Mediterranean climate. Many North American visitors say that this region reminds them of California. This is Chile's breadbasket, with fertile valleys and rolling fields that harvest a large share of the country's fruit and vegetables; it also is the site of world-famous Chilean wineries. Santiago's proximity to ski resorts, beach resorts, and the idyllic countryside with its campestral and ranching traditions and colonial estates offers a distinct variety of activities that make the Central Valley an excellent destination. See chapter 11 and chapter 12.

LAKE DISTRICT   Few destinations in the world rival the magnificent scenery of Chile's Lake District, and for that reason it's the most popular destination for foreigners visiting Chile. This region is packed with a chain of conical, snowcapped volcanoes, glacier-scoured valleys, several national parks, thick groves of native

Chile

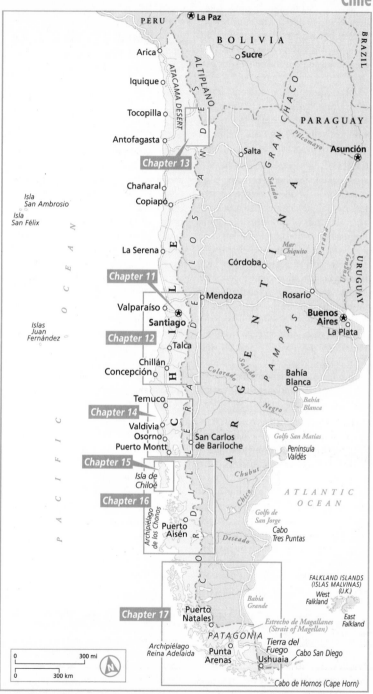

PERU

La Paz

BOLIVIA

Arica

Sucre

Iquique

Tocopilla

Antofagasta

Salta

PARAGUAY

Asunción

Chapter 13

Chañaral

Copiapó

Isla San Ambrosio

Isla San Félix

La Serena

Córdoba

Chapter 11

Valparaíso

Mendoza

Rosario

Buenos Aires

La Plata

Santiago

Chapter 12

Talca

Chillán

Concepción

Colorado

Salado

Bahía Blanca

Negro

Bahía Blanca

Islas Juan Fernández

PAMPAS

ARGENTINA

GRAN CHACO

Pilcomayo

Salado

Mar Chiquito

Uruguay

Paraná

URUGUAY

ATACAMA DESERT

ALTIPLANO

ANDES

CORDILLERA DE LOS ANDES

Temuco

Chapter 14

Valdivia

Osorno

Puerto Montt

San Carlos de Bariloche

Golfo San Matías

Península Valdés

Chapter 15

Isla de Chiloé

Chubut

Chapter 16

Archipiélago de los Chonos

Puerto Aisén

Chico

Deseado

ATLANTIC OCEAN

Golfo de San Jorge

Cabo Tres Puntas

PACIFIC OCEAN

Chapter 17

Puerto Natales

Bahía Grande

FALKLAND ISLANDS (ISLAS MALVINAS) (U.K.)

West Falkland

East Falkland

Archipiélago Reina Adelaida

PATAGONIA

Punta Arenas

Estrecho de Magallanes (Strait of Magellan)

Tierra del Fuego

Ushuaia

Cabo San Diego

Cabo de Hornos (Cape Horn)

| 0 | | 300 mi |
| 0 | | 300 km |

N

forest, hot springs, jagged peaks, and, of course, many shimmering lakes. Temperatures during the summer are idyllic, but winter is characterized by months of drizzling rain. It's an outdoor-lover and adventure-seeker's paradise, especially in Pucón and Puerto Varas, offering biking, hiking, kayaking, rafting, fly-fishing, and more, but it is also a low-key destination for those who just want to kick back and enjoy the marvelous views. See chapter 14.

CHILOE   The island of **Chiloé** is as attractive for its emerald, rolling hills, and colorful wooden churches as it is for the unique culture that developed after 300 years of geographic isolation. During this period, a religion based on a mix of Catholicism and native customs created a strong belief in mythical figures; at the same time the island's cuisine, speech, and architectural style developed differently from that of mainland Chile. Beautiful fishing hamlets and views that stretch from the Pacific to the Andes make for fine sightseeing drives, and Chiloé National Park offers ample opportunity for hiking along the island's untamed coastal rainforest. See chapter 15.

THE   CARRETERA   AUSTRAL Across the sound from Chiloé sits Chile's "frontier" highway, commonly known as the **Carretera Austral,** a dirt road that stretches nearly 1,000km (620 miles) from Puerto Montt in the north to beyond Coyhaique in the south. Along the way, this relatively new road passes through virgin territory visited by few travelers: tiny villages separated by thick, untouched rainforest, rugged peaks that rise from crystal-clear lakes, and more waterfalls

than one can reasonably count. This could be one of Chile's best-kept secrets. See chapter 16.

PATAGONIA   Also known as the **Magallanes Region,** this dry, arid region at the southern end of the continent has soared in popularity over the past 5 years, drawing visitors from all over the world to places such as Torres del Paine National Park in Chile and Argentina's Perito Moreno Glacier. We've grouped both Argentina and Chile in one Patagonia chapter because the majority of travelers visit destinations in both countries when here. Patagonia is characterized by vast, open pampa, the colossal Northern and Southern Ice Fields and hundreds of mighty glaciers, the jagged peaks of the Andes as they reach their terminus, beautiful emerald fjords, and wind, wind, wind. Getting here is an adventure—it usually takes 24 hours if coming directly from the United States or Europe. But the long journey pays off in the beauty and singularity of the region. Cruise the fjords, walk across a glacier, stroll through frontier-like immigrant towns such as Puerto Natales, and, without a doubt, visit Chile's national jewel, Torres del Paine. For more, see chapter 17.

TIERRA DEL FUEGO   Even more south than the Deep South, this archipelago at the southern extremity of South America is, like Patagonia, shared by both Chile and Argentina. The main island, separated from the mainland by the Strait of Magellan, is a triangle with its base on the Beagle Channel. See chapter 17 for more information.

2 Visitor Information

You'll find a municipal tourism office in nearly every city and a **Sernatur (National Tourism Board)** office in major cities. The quality of service and availability of maps and brochures

varies from office to office. A good place to begin your research is Sernatur's helpful website at **www.serna tur.cl,** which has general regional information in Spanish and English.

Recommended Websites for Chile

In addition to the following websites, each major tourist destination has its own complete site, some of which are very good. Try **www.pucon.com**, **www.chiloe.cl**, **www.sanpedroatacama.com**, **www.puntaarenas.cl**, and **www.puertovaras.cl**.

- **www.visit-chile.org** The Corporación Promoción Turística offers a site featuring general information in English about Chile, including travel and information about hotels, restaurants, and tour companies, many of whom have paid to join their association (most top businesses are members). Good overall view of top sites in Chile.

- **www.chiptravel.com** This comprehensive site is run by a group of expats in Santiago. It offers great travel ideas and information, but it is not religiously updated. The informed reviews and essays are especially enlightening. Good first-timer's guide to history, politics, and cultural issues.

- **www.gochile.cl** Well-designed and chock-full of information, this site includes city and national park descriptions and information about tour packages. This site is run by the for-profit tour operator gotolatin.com, and they can book reservations for car rental and hotels.

- **www.turistel.cl** This popular Chilean tour guide series has a website, and although it is in Spanish, you can download complete route maps of Chile by clicking on *mapas ruteras.* These maps are more detailed than maps found on www.visit-chile.org.

- **www.chilevinos.com** Every aspect of the Chilean wine industry is covered at this excellent website, such as winemaker and winery profiles, grape-growing updates, a glossary, chat room, and online ordering—but it is entirely in Spanish. Try a general site such as **www.winespectator.com** for travel ideas in the wine country or information about which Chilean wines are a best buy.

- **www.chileaustral.com** and **www.portalpatagonia.com** This is your one-stop site for Chilean Patagonia, with listings of virtually everything—even land for sale. Links take you to the independent Web pages of businesses such as hotels, restaurants, tour operators, clubs, news and media . . . the list goes on.

- **www.samexplo.org** The South American Explorer's Club produces an excellent website that includes up-to-date information about health and political crises, as well as frequently asked questions, travelogues, and catalogs and books for sale.

- **www.pablovalenzuela.com** One of Chile's top photographers, his website featuring stunning photos of various landscapes celebrates the beauty of Chile.

Outside of Chile, you won't find a tourism promotion board, but Chile's consulates do provide printed material and visitor information. Other helpful sites are listed above.

3 Entry Requirements & Customs

ENTRY REQUIREMENTS

Citizens of the United States, Canada, the United Kingdom, Australia, and New Zealand need a valid passport to enter Chile. Most visitors are unaware that Chile charges a steep **reciprocity fee** for citizens of some countries when they arrive at the Santiago airport before passing through customs. The U.S. recently upped the fee for Chileans seeking a U.S. tourist visa to $100, so now Chile has responded by charging visitors from the U.S. $100. Visitors from Australia pay $33 and visitors from Canada pay $55. New Zealanders do not pay a fee, nor do visitors from the U.K. The entrance fee must be paid in cash and in U.S. dollars only. This fee is levied only to tourists entering by plane, not crossing the border by vehicle, and the one-time charge is good for the life of your passport, so keep the stub stapled on a page in your passport for future visits. Before entering Chile, you'll need to fill out a tourist card that allows visitors to stay for 90 days. You'll need to present this tourist card to Customs when leaving the country, so don't lose it. Also, many hotels waive Chile's 18% sales tax applied to rooms when the guest shows this card and pays with U.S. dollars. The easiest (and free) way to renew your 90-day stay is to cross the border and return. However, for $100, tourist cards can be renewed (for another 30 days) at the **Extranjería,** Moneda 1342 in Santiago (© 2/550-2400), open

Monday through Friday from 8:30am to 3:30pm, or at any Gobernación Provincial office in the provinces.

LOST DOCUMENTS

If you lose your tourist card outside Santiago, any police station will direct you to the Extranjería police headquarters for that province (usually the nearest principal city). In Santiago, go to the **Policía Internacional,** Departamento Fronteras, General Borgoña 1052 (© 2/737-1292), open Monday through Friday from 8:30am to 12:30pm and 3 to 6pm. If you lose your passport, contact your embassy for a replacement. If you are an American, you can only get a passport replacement at the U.S. embassy in Santiago, Av. Andrés Bello 2800 (© 2/232-2600), which is open Monday through Friday from 8:30am to 5pm. The fee is $60. It is imperative that you carry a photocopy of your passport with you and another form of ID to facilitate the process.

CUSTOMS

Any travel-related merchandise brought into Chile, such as personal effects or clothing, is not taxed. Visitors entering Chile may also bring in no more than 400 cigarettes, 500 grams of pipe tobacco, or 50 cigars, and 2.5 liters of alcoholic beverages per adult. Please see "Entry Requirements & Customs" in chapter 2 for information about what you're allowed to take home with you.

4 Money

CASH & CURRENCY

The unit of currency in Chile is the **peso.** The value of the peso has slowly declined over the past few years and is, at press time, 700 pesos to the U.S. dollar. During the past year it has fluctuated between 750 pesos and 650 pesos, offering travelers with dollars an inexpensive vacation. Bills come in

denominations of 500, 1,000, 2,000, 5,000, 10,000, and 20,000. There are currently five coins in circulation, in denominations of 1, 5, 10, 50, and 100; however, it's rare to be issued 1 peso or even 5. In slang, Chileans often call 1,000 a *luca,* as in, "it cost me *cinco luca*" (5,000).

Chile levies a steep, 18% **sales tax** on all goods and services called *IVA (Impuesto al Valor Agregado)*. Foreigners are supposedly exempt from the IVA tax when paying in dollars for hotel rooms, car rentals, and some tourism-oriented shops; however, you might find this is not the case with inexpensive hotels. Always verify if the price quoted to you is without IVA. The prices given in this book are listed in dollars (adjusted per a 700-pesos-to-the-dollar rate), due to the ambiguous nature of the IVA tax.

EXCHANGING MONEY

Dollars and traveler's checks can be exchanged at a *casa de cambio* (money-exchange house) for a small charge, and they are generally open from 9am to 6pm Monday through Friday (closing 1–3pm for lunch), and Saturday until 1pm. A *casa de cambio* can be found near the center of every major city, but note that they are scarce in small towns. Some banks exchange money, although most charge a steep fee. Hotels have laughably poor exchange rates, so avoid changing money at one if possible. By far the best exchange rates are given when retrieving money from an **ATM,** identifiable by the name "Redbanc" posted on a maroon and white sticker. These Redbancs use a variety of networks, including Cirrus and Plus, as well as Visa and MasterCard. Really, the ATM card has replaced the **traveler's check** as the preferred way to deal with money when abroad, but be sure to investigate your bank's policies as to whether they charge a fee for each withdrawal. Also, you might consider traveling with an ATM card and a few traveler's checks in U.S. dollars as a backup in the event of a lost or stolen card. American Express sells traveler's checks online at **www.americanexpress**, or by calling ℭ **800/221-7282.**

CREDIT CARDS

Most hotels and restaurants in Chile accept credit cards such as Visa, MasterCard, Diners Club, and American Express. In the event of a lost or stolen credit card, call the following numbers (in Santiago): Visa/Master-Card at ℭ **2/631-7003,** American Express at ℭ **800/361002,** and Diner's Club at ℭ **800/220220.**

5 When to Go

High season for Chilean, Brazilian, and Argentine vacationers is during the summer from December 15 to the end of February, as well as the month of July and during Holy Week (Semana Santa), the week preceding Easter Sunday. The sheer volume of travelers to popular destinations such as Pucón or Viña del Mar during the high season is overwhelming. If that weren't enough, consider that hotels nearly double in price, and some businesses quietly jack up their prices in anticipation of the masses who come with money to burn. If being in Chile from December to February during the peak of the austral summer is still what you'd prefer, book a room *well* in advance. Or you can do as most North American and Europeans do and come from late September to early December for the spring bloom, or from March to mid-May when the trees turn color; both seasons have pleasant weather and the views are less crowded. In fact, it's preferable to be in the extreme regions of Chile during these "off seasons." In northern regions, such as San Pedro de Atacama, the searing heat is a killer. In the deep south, the fierce Patagonian wind blows from October to April, but is most consistent in December and January.

CLIMATE

Chile's tremendous length incorporates a variety of climates, and in many areas there are microclimates, pockets of localized weather that can completely alter the vegetation and landscape of a small area. As well, weather and temperature can vary greatly the short distance from Andes to the coast.

The northern region of Chile is home to the driest desert in the world. Summer temperatures from early December to late February in this region can top 100°F (38°C), then drop dramatically at night to 30°F (–1°C). Winter days, from mid-June to late August, are crisp, but sunny and pleasant, but as soon as the sun drops it gets bitterly cold. Along the coast, the weather is mild and dry, ranging from 60°F to 90°F (16°C–32°C).

The central zone that stretches to Puerto Montt has seasons that are better defined. Temperatures in this region range from 32°F to 55°F (0°C–13°C) in the winter, and 60°F to 95°F (16°C–35°C) during the summer. Santiago and the Central Valley feature a more Mediterranean climate, whereas the Carretera Austral and the Lake District are home to very wet winters, especially in the regions around Valdivia and Puerto Montt.

Below Puerto Montt, temperatures drop the farther you travel south. The Patagonia region is unpredictable with its weather patterns, especially during the summer. The Magellanic Region sees extraordinary, knockout windstorms that can reach upwards of 120kmph (74 mph), and it's not unusual to experience heavy rain during the summer. The windiest months are from mid-December to early February, but it can hit any time between October and April. Winters are calm, with irregular snowfall and temperatures that can dip to 5°F.

HOLIDAYS

Chile's major celebrations are Christmas, New Year's, Easter week, and Independence Day (Sept 18), the latter of which can carry on for days and

days of dancing, drinking, and military parades. During official holidays, Chilean towns can take on the appearance of a ghost town. Transportation services might be reduced in some areas, government offices, banks, and the majority of stores and markets close.

National and local elections bring about a virtual standstill from midnight to midnight as Chileans cast their obligatory votes. Alcohol is not sold on this day.

The following are official holidays: **January 1** (New Year's Day), **Semana Santa** (Holy Week, but just Good Friday is considered a holiday), **May 1** (Labor Day), **May 21** (remembrance of the War of the Pacific victory), **June 29** (Corpus Christi), **August 15** (Asunción de la Virgen), **September 11** (commemoration of the 1973 military coup), **September 18** and **19** (Independence Day and Armed Forces Day), **October 12** (Día de la Raza), **November 1** (All Saint's Day), **December 8** (Feast of the Immaculate Conception), and **December 25** (Christmas).

CALENDAR OF EVENTS The following are some of Chile's major events and festivals that take place during the year. For 1 week in early **February,** the city of Castro in Chiloé hosts a celebration of the culture, history, and mythical folklore that makes the island unique, including regional cooking, in the **Festival Costumbrista Chilote** (see chapter 15). During late **February,** Viña del Mar hosts its gala **Festival de la Canción,** or the Festival of Song, that showcases Latin American performers during a 5-day festival of concerts held in the city's outdoor amphitheater (see "Viña del Mar," chapter 12). The spectacle draws thousands of visitors to an already packed Viña del Mar, so plan your hotel reservations accordingly. In **mid-February,** Valdivia hosts a grand, weeklong event called the **Semana Valdiviana.** A variety of maritime-theme activities, contests, expositions, and more takes place during the week, but the highlight takes place the third Saturday of February, the **Noche Valdiviana,** when the Río Valdivia fills with festively decorated boats and candles, and the skies fill with fireworks. This is a very crowded event, and advance hotel reservations are essential (see chapter 14). Between **March and mid-April,** Chilean wineries celebrate the grape harvest with a **Festival de Vendimia,** with food, winemaking exhibitions, grape-crushing, and more. Each winery celebrates according to the date of its harvest (the farther south, the later the date), so call ahead for each winery's exact festival date (see "The Wineries of the Central Valley," in chapter 12, for contact information). The **first Sunday after Easter** is the **Fiesta del Cuasimodo,** an event typically held throughout central Chile, in which *huaso* cowboys parade through the streets, accompanied by Catholic priests who often pay visits to the infirm and disabled. On **May 29,** fishermen celebrate the **Fiesta de San Pedro** in towns along the coast of Chile, to bring about good fortune, weather, and bountiful catches. Fishermen decorate their boats, light candles, arm themselves with an image of their patron saint, and drift along the coast. A great place to check out this event is in Valparaíso. **July 16** sees the celebration of the **Virgen del Carmen,** the patron saint of the armed forces. On this day, military parades take place throughout the country, especially near Maipú, where O'Higgins and San Martín defeated Spanish forces in the fight for independence. Chile's rodeo season kicks off on Independence Day, **September 18,** and culminates with a championship in the city Rancagua around late March or early April. There are a variety of rodeo dates throughout the Central Valley, but September 18 and the championships are festivals in their own right, with food stalls, lots of *chicha* (a fermented fruit cider) drinking and traditional *cueca* dancing. Contact the Federación de Rodeos in Santiago at ℂ/fax **2/699-0115,** or stop by its office at Moneda 1045, #1302 for a schedule of rodeos throughout Chile.

6 Health & Insurance

HEALTH

Chile poses few health risks to travelers. There are no diseases such as malaria or dysentery, so no special vaccinations are required. In fact, there are no poisonous plants or animals in Chile to worry about, either. Nevertheless, standard wisdom says that travelers should drop in the doctor's office for tetanus and hepatitis boosters.

DIARRHEA & INTESTINAL PROBLEMS Few visitors to Chile experience anything other than run-of-the-mill traveler's stomach in reaction to unfamiliar foods and any microorganisms in them. Chile's tap water is clean and safe to drink; however, a small percentage of travelers

with delicate stomachs report having experienced intestinal upsets from tap water. You'll often hear that the water has a "high mineral content," but by and large most experience nothing at all. Bottled mineral water is widely available throughout Chile if you'd rather not take any chances.

Chile's love of shellfish has its consequences, and each year there are a dozen reports of intoxication due to the *marea roja,* or "red tide." This toxic alga poisons shellfish and is due to a rise in the temperature of the sea. Your chances of intoxication by the *marea roja* are nil, unless you plan to collect shellfish yourself and are oblivious to the signs posted by the government

> **Tips** **A Drinking Water Caution**
>
> Do not under any circumstances drink tap water while in San Pedro de Atacama (see chapter 13). It contains trace amounts of arsenic.

that caution you otherwise. All fish and shellfish in restaurants and markets are safe.

ALTITUDE SICKNESS Altitude sickness, known as *soroche* or *puna*, is a temporary yet often debilitating affliction that affects about a quarter of travelers to the northern *altiplano,* or the Andes at 2,400m (7,872 ft.) and up. Nausea, fatigue, headaches, shortness of breath, and sleeplessness are the symptoms, which can last from 2 to 5 days. If you feel as though you've been affected, drink plenty of water, take aspirin or ibuprofen, and avoid alcohol and sleeping pills. To prevent altitude sickness, acclimatize your body by breaking the climb to higher regions into segments.

AUSTRAL SUN The shrinking ozone layer in southern Chile has caused an onset of health problems among the citizens who live there, including increased incidents of skin cancer and cataracts. Last year the ozone hole opened *completely* for several days in the southern town Punta Arenas—the first time it had ever happened. If you are planning to travel to Patagonia, keep in mind that on "red alert" days (typically Sept–Nov), it's possible to burn in *10 minutes.* If you plan to be outdoors, you need to protect yourself with sunblock, a long-sleeved shirt, a wide-brimmed hat, and sunglasses.

WHAT TO DO IF YOU GET SICK AWAY FROM HOME
Medical attention in private hospitals and clinics throughout Chile is up to international standards, but you may find limited or nonexistent service in tiny villages. *Clínicas* are always better than a town's general hospital; in fact, some general hospitals are downright appalling. Most health insurance policies cover incidents that occur in foreign countries; check to see if yours does, and be sure to gather all receipts and information so that you can make a claim back home. The cost of medicine and treatment is expensive, but most hospitals and pharmacies accept credit cards. Many doctors, especially in Santiago, speak basic English; for a list of English-speaking doctors, call your embassy.

PHARMACIES Chile is rife with pharmacies, and you'll find them in odd locations, such as shopping malls and gas stations—and, strangely enough, they always seem to be packed with ailing clientele. Many stay open 24 hours a day, and a few chains will deliver for a small fee. Chilean pharmacies sell numerous kinds of prescription drugs over the counter, including antibiotics and birth control pills.

INSURANCE
Please see "Health & Insurance," in chapter 2, for information on traveler's insurance.

7 Specialized Travel Resources

For more information on general resources for travelers with special needs, see chapter 2.

FOR TRAVELERS WITH DISABILITIES There are relatively few wheelchair-accessible buildings in Chile, apart from supermarkets and major hotels, which come equipped with ramps and wide doorways. It's best to call ahead and inquire about an establishment's facilities, or check out its website, which will often tell you if any of the rooms are accessible.

FOR SENIORS   Seniors traveling in Chile are often given discounts for attractions such as museums (seniors here are called *tercera edad,* or "third age"). Probably the most interesting and well-respected senior organization is **Elderhostel,** 75 Federal St., Boston, MA 02110-1941 (© **800/426-8056;** www.elderhostel.org), which offers cultural and educational trips to Chile with themes such as "Land of Poets" and "Wine for the New Millenium."

FOR GAY & LESBIAN TRAVELERS   Gays and lesbians visiting Chile will most likely not encounter any prejudice or outward intolerance. However, public displays of affection between same sexes are rare, even in metropolitan cities such as Santiago. In general, attitudes, especially those of Chilean men, toward gays and lesbians are not very liberal, owing in part to the Catholic, conservative nature of their society. Homosexual relationships have only recently been declared officially legal, and many gays and lesbians are not actively open about their orientation outside their own circles.

The best source for information is the website **www.gaychile.com**, a resource directory that covers gay issues and provides information about travel, gay-oriented businesses and bars, employment, and more.

FOR FAMILIES   Chile is family-friendly, and parents will not have a problem finding lodging suitable for kids. Many hotels feature playgrounds, swimming pools, child care, and attached rooms or space for additional beds. Some larger resort hotels even arrange activities for kids. Parents might consider renting an apart-hotel or a *cabaña* (found in resort areas), which are self-catering units with living areas and kitchens; they are frequently less expensive. Many hotels

offer discounts or grant a free stay for kids traveling with parents, so be sure to inquire when making a reservation.

FOR WOMEN TRAVELERS   Women traveling in Chile will not encounter harassment other than a sporadic catcall or a few taps on the car horn. More than anything, Chilean men tend to stare intensely, which can be annoying or make some women feel uncomfortable. Staring back or ignoring the situation usually works. Hitchhiking is a well-accepted form of transportation in Chile, and you will occasionally see a woman hitchhiking on her own, especially on country lanes with poor public transportation. Although hitchhiking in Chile is safer than in most countries, exercise judgment if contemplating hitchhiking solo. A lift up to a ski resort or into a national park that does not have public transportation will probably result in nothing more than a free ride, but longer trips up and down the Panamericana Highway are best undertaken aboard one of the country's cheap and plentiful long-distance buses.

FOR STUDENTS   Many Chilean businesses and hostels recognize the International Student Identity Card issued by **Council Travel** (© **800/2-COUNCIL;** www.counciltravel.com). The card offers discounts and a 24-hour help line for travel emergencies to anyone 25 and under and to full-time teachers. Their **Council Travel** agencies, located in most major cities, offer rock-bottom prices for flights. **The Council on International Educational Exchange (CIEE)** (© **800/40-STUDY;** www.ciee.org) offers semester and yearlong study and work programs in Santiago and Valparaiso. **American Youth Hostels,** P.O. Box 37613, Washington, DC 20013-7613 (© **202/783-6161;** www.hiayh.org), offers a directory of youth hostels around South America and other travel-related publications.

8 Getting There

BY PLANE

Several major airlines serve Santiago's Arturo Merino Benítez airport with nonstop flights from Miami, Atlanta, New York, Dallas–Fort Worth, and sometimes Los Angeles. Turbulent times in the airline industry mean that fares can vary wildly depending on the time of year, departure location, and price wars that periodically break out. Most flights are red-eyes. For some money-saving tips, see "Flying for Less: Tips for Getting the Best Airfare" in chapter 2.

THE MAJOR AIRLINES The following airlines serve Chile from the United States and Canada (where noted). Registering at each airline's website allows you to receive up-to-date information about special fares and promotions. **LanChile** (© **800/735-5526;** www.lanchile.com), the country's national air carrier, has direct flights to Santiago from New York and Los Angeles, and nonstop from Miami. LanChile offers last-minute deals on their website that are announced every Wednesday, with rock-bottom, but heavily restricted, fares from Miami to Santiago. **American Airlines** (© **800/433-7300;** www.aa.com) has daily nonstop flights from Miami and Dallas–Fort Worth, with connections from Vancouver, Toronto, and Montréal. **Delta** (© **800/221-1212;** www.delta.com) offers nonstop daily flights from Atlanta. Costa Rica's **Lacsa** airline, of the parent company Taca (© **800/535-8780;** www.taca.com), has flights from San Francisco, Los Angeles, New York, or Miami.

LanChile (© **1293/596607** in the U.K.; www.lanchile.com) serves London to Santiago via Madrid, in partnership with Iberia and British Airways, or try booking directly with **Iberia** (© **800/772-4642** in the U.S., or 020/7830-0011 in London; www.iberia.com). **Air France** (© **0845/0845 111;** www.airfrance.com/uk) has two to five daily flights from London to Santiago via Paris.

Qantas (© **13 13 13** in Australia, or 9/357-8900 in New Zealand; www.qantas.com) works in conjunction with LanChile, offering three flights per week from Sydney and Auckland to Santiago. **Aerolíneas Argentinas** (© **1800/222-215** in Australia, or 0800/650-881 in New Zealand; www.aerolineas.com.ar) has two weekly direct flights from Sydney and Auckland to Buenos Aires, Argentina, with a connecting flight to Santiago aboard LanChile.

BY CRUISE SHIP

There are now quite a few 11- to 15-day cruises that sail around the Cape Horn, beginning in Buenos Aires and ending in Valparaíso, Chile, or vice versa, and usually with a stop in Montevideo, Uruguay. Ports of call include Chile's Puerto Montt, Puerto Chacabuco, and Punta Arenas; Argentina's Ushuaia, Puerto Madryn, and sometimes the Falkland Islands. Keep in mind that like all cruises, you are treated to an exceptionally brief view of each port of call; however, sailing through the southern region's fjords can often be quite stunning. Several cruise operators that provide this trip are **Norwegian Cruises** (© **800/327-7030;** www.ncl.com), **Celebrity Cruises** (© **800/722-4951;** www.celebrity-cruises.com), **Silverseas Cruises** (© **800/722-9955;** www.silversea.com) and **Princess Cruises** (© **800/PRINCESS;** www.princesscruises.com). Most offer the Cape Horn trip in both directions, and some add-on stops in northern Chile and Brazil.

9 Getting Around

BY PLANE

The drawn-out geography of Chile makes flying the most reasonable way to get around: Even flying from Santiago to Punta Arenas takes about 3½ hours. LanChile is now the only airline with domestic service in Chile, and their domestic line is called Lan-Express (© **800/735-5526** in the U.S., LAN-2000 in Santiago, and 600/LAN-2000 outside of Santiago; www.lanchile.com). LanChile flies to all major cities including Arica, Iquique, Calama, Antofagasta, Concepción, Temuco, Valdivia, Osorno, Puerto Montt, Coyhaique, and Punta Arenas. Some smaller towns can be reached by air taxi; see individual chapters for information.

LanChile offers foreigners a **Visit Chile Pass** good for three flights within the country. The price is $250 if you choose LanChile as your international carrier, and $60 for any additional flights; the cost is $350 if you use another carrier to Chile, and $80 for each additional flight. A maximum of six flights is permitted per Visit Chile Pass. Travelers have a maximum of 1 month to use the tickets, and you must start using them within 14 days of your arrival. LanChile requires travelers to book their routes when buying, but they allow date and time changes. A pass can only be purchased before arriving to Chile, directly from LanChile or a travel agent.

BY BUS

Traveling by bus is very common in Chile, and there are many companies to meet the demand. Fortunately, most Chilean buses are clean and efficient and a good way to travel shorter distances, from Santiago to Valparaíso, for example. Think long and hard before booking a 30-hour ride to the desert north, or any comparable distance; it's an excruciatingly long time to be on the highway.

If you decide to travel for more than a few hours by bus, it helps to know your options. Standard buses go by the name *clásico* or *pullman* (no relation to the giant bus company Pullman). An *ejécutivo* or *semi-cama* is a little like business class: lots of legroom, and seats that recline farther. At the top end of the scale is the *salón cama,* which features seats that fold out into beds. A *salón cama* is an excellent way to get to a region like the Lake District, as riders sleep all night and arrive in the morning. Fares are typically inexpensive, and seats fill up fast, so buy a ticket as far in advance as possible. Ask what is included with your fare, and whether they serve meals or if they plan to stop at a restaurant along the way.

BY CAR

Travelers seeking the independence to explore at their own pace might consider renting a car. Weekly rates for a compact or intermediate-size car, rented from and returned to the Santiago airport, average about $180 to $350; a van will cost an average of $475 to $700 per week. You can either book ahead of time or book once you arrive at the Santiago airport. Most major American rental car companies have offices in Chile, which are listed

Finding an Address

In Argentina and Chile, as in many South American countries, not all addresses have street numbers. This is especially true in rural areas. You'll know there's no number if the address includes the abbreviation "s/n," which stands for *sin número* (without number).

under the appropriate chapter for each company's location. To make a reservation from the United States, call **Alamo** (© 800/GO-ALAMO; www.alamo.com), **Avis** (© 800/230-4898; www.avis.com), **Budget** (© 800/472-3325; www.budget.com), **Dollar** (© 800/800-4000; www.dollar.com), or **Hertz** (© 800/654-3001; www.hertz.com). If renting once you're already in Chile, don't overlook a few of the local car-rental agencies for cheaper prices; you sometimes find better value with the smaller operations. *Remember to request the special paperwork needed for border crossings if you plan to visit Argentina.* These documents might cost an additional fee of up to $75.

To rent a car, you need to bring your current driver's license; car-rental agencies and the police will accept an international driver's license, but it is not mandatory. Be forewarned that in Chile, the police, or *carabineros,* are allowed to stop motorists without reason, which they frequently do under the guise of "control." They usually just ask to see your driver's license, and then let you pass through their checkpoint.

Driving in Chile is fairly straightforward. Drivers use their indicators constantly to signal where they're going, and you should too, even if there's no one close to you. On the highway, car and especially truck drivers signal to show that it's safe ahead to pass, but don't put your entire faith in the other driver's judgment, and give yourself ample space, as many drivers tend to speed. Right turns on red are forbidden unless otherwise indicated. It's simply auto chaos in the confines of Santiago, with congested streets and speedy, aggressive drivers—*especially* bus drivers. Outside Santiago, especially on roads off the Panamericana Highway, your major concern will be keeping an eye out for the occasional farm animal grazing near the road. The Panamericana underwent a huge

expansion and modernization program over the past few years, and drivers will find periodic tollbooths along the highway and at some highway exits. Tolls, or *peajes,* range from 40¢ to $5. Few roads off the Panamericana are paved, and the condition of unpaved roads can be smoothly graveled or horrible washboard and Swiss cheese, conditions demanding that you drive very, very slowly. Gasoline is called *bencina,* and Chile sells both the leaded and unleaded varieties; unleaded gas is sold in varying grades as 93, 95, and 97.

The **Automóvil Club de Chile** offers services, including emergency roadside service, to its worldwide members. For more information, contact their offices in Santiago at Av. Andrés Bello 1863 (© 2/431-1000; www.aclub.cl). **Copec,** the popular gas station chain, now sells Automapa's *Rutas de Chile* road maps at most of their larger stations. **Sernatur** might have road maps, but don't count on it. **Turistel** guidebooks, which are sold at most bookstores and a few kiosks on popular intersections, are in Spanish but provide detailed road maps, city maps, and visitor information—you can even download and print them from their website **www.turistel.cl** before you leave for your trip. Car-rental agencies provide emergency road service. Be sure to obtain a 24-hour number before leaving with your rental vehicle.

BY FERRY

A superb way to get around the southern regions of Chile is by ferry. **Navimag** offers a trip that leaves from Puerto Montt and cruises along the shore of the Carretera Austral; the other is an exceptionally popular 3-day trip through the fjords from Puerto Montt to Puerto Natales, or vice versa, stopping along the way at Puerto Eden. This is not a luxury liner, but it's not bad either, and the

A Note on Hitchhiking

Hitchhiking is common in Chile and mostly carried out along country roads with infrequent public transportation. In fact, you often see fed-up Chileans hitchhiking from a bus stop, especially in the southern regions of Chile. Hitchhiking is popular with students, workers, families, elderly folks without cars—in short, *everyone*. You stand a good chance of being picked up near the entrances to national parks or ski resorts. Hitching is never entirely recommended for obvious reasons, but if you feel comfortable with your ride, you might consider it.

views are breathtaking. There's also **Skorpios,** which offers more upscale 4- and 7-day cruises aboard one of their three boats from Puerto Montt or Puerto Chacabuco, stopping at Castro and Quellón in Chiloé before or after the Laguna San Rafael Glacier. **Transmarchilay** is comparable in quality to Navimag, and they provide most ferry service around the gulf south of Puerto Montt. **Andina del Sud** provides countless visitors with a picturesque cruise across the emerald Lago Todos los Santos in Vicente Pérez Rosales National Park near Puerto Varas, and they also connect with the company Cruce de Lagos, which continues across Lago Nahuel Huapi to Bariloche, Argentina. The brand-new **Mare Australis** offers absolutely superb one-way and round-trip cruises from Punta Arenas to Ushuaia. For more information, see "Ferry Journeys Through the Fjords to Laguna San Rafael," near the end of chapter 16, and chapter 17.

10 Spanish-Language Programs

Spanish-language programs are not only an excellent way to pick up the local tongue, they are also indispensable introductions to Chilean culture for visitors who choose to stay with a host family. There are a fair amount of good options, and if the following two don't meet your needs, or if you're looking for something outside of Santiago, try checking **www.studyabroad.com** or **www.spanishinlatinamerica.com**.

- **Bridge-Linguatec,** Los Leones 439, Providencia, Santiago (© **800/724-4210** in the U.S., or 2/233-4356 in Santiago; fax 2/234-1380; www.bridgelinguatec.com), has received praise for its intensive private tutoring and group programs (3–8 students) for all levels. Classes run 4 to 6 hours per day, and there is an 8-hour per day "immersion" program. A 2-week group course for 4 hours per

day, including classes, homestay, and first set of books costs $985. Four hours of private lessons per day, for 1 week, costs $850. Note that it charges a $95 registration fee and books are extra after the first set. Contact the company for cheaper rates if you already have your own lodging or plan to look for lodging elsewhere. Bridge-Linguatec offers excursions and university credit, and it serves professional executives as much as students.

- **Latin Immersion Language Network,** Tomás Andrew 074, Providencia, Santiago (© **866/577-8693** in the U.S., or 2/635-4776 in Santiago; www.latinimmersion.com). This program offers group lessons (5 or fewer students) for 20 hours per week, with a 2-week minimum. The program organizes homestays, independent courses for special topics such as business or law, and Chile-Argentina combination programs. Group classes are $280 for 2 weeks; a homestay with meals is an additional $300 for 2 weeks. Private lessons are $440 for 2 weeks, instruction only.

11 Tips on Accommodations

Chile's high season is from December 15 to the end of February, Easter week, and, in resort areas, the month of July. Hotels generally heed these blocks of time, but the start and end dates could vary slightly, and they might charge a "mid-season" rate during November and March. Rates during the high season are often sky-high in resort areas such as Pucón or Viña del Mar; however, reasonable or downright cheap accommodations can be had the rest of the year. Some hotels drop their prices by as much as 50% in the off season. **Price ranges listed in hotel write-ups reflect low to high season;** for example, $50 to $75 double would mean $50 from March to November and $75 from December to February. Always verify high-season dates with your hotel.

The past few years have been stagnant for the hotel industry in Chile, and many establishments are maintaining or even dropping prices in an effort to draw in business. The prices listed in this book are **rack rates,** that is, a hotel's standard rate offered to guests who simply walk in off the street. Hotels might be willing to offer a special price for multiple-day stays during the high season, but during the low season you're almost guaranteed they'll drop the price, so don't be afraid to ask when making a reservation. Some hotels might also be offering a promotion or package deal that you're not aware of, so inquire about that, too.

Almost every hotel in Chile includes **breakfast** in the price. In fact, of all the hotels I've seen throughout Chile, only about five did not, and I've stated this in the hotel's review. Expect a continental breakfast at inexpensive and moderately priced hotels and an "American" or buffet breakfast at larger, four- and five-star hotels.

ROOM RATES

Price categories in this guide are listed according to **Very Expensive,** $125 and up; **Expensive,** $80 to $125; **Moderate,** $40 to $80; and **Inexpensive,** under $40. All prices are for double occupancy, and Moderate to Very Expensive hotel prices shown do not include the 18% IVA tax (inexpensive hotels rarely accept dollars, always including the IVA tax in their set prices).

HOTEL OPTIONS

HOTELS & *HOSTERIAS* An *hostería* is a hotel attended by its owner, typically found in a country setting. The Chilean tourism board rates hotels using one to five stars, but the system is dubious because it concentrates too much on a checklist of services and amenities that may or may not be important to a guest. For example, a luxurious nature lodge that caters to fly-fishermen might receive three stars because it chooses not to equip its rooms with TV or because it does not offer 24-hour room service.

APART-HOTEL The amalgam is exactly what it implies: an "apartment-hotel," or a hotel room with an additional living area and kitchen. Found primarily in Santiago and other large cities, they offer a wider range of services than a *cabaña*. Some are bargains for their price and the independence they give their occupants, and they come with maid service. However, some are nothing more than a hotel room with a kitchenette tucked into a random corner.

CABAÑAS *Cabañas* are a great lodging option. They are commonly found in resort areas and are popular with families and travelers seeking an independent unit. Each establishment will have between two and ten *cabañas* on its property, some hidden in wooden groves and some in a more "suburban" atmosphere. They resemble cabins or chalets and range from bare bones to deluxe, although all come with fully equipped kitchens and most have maid service. During the high season, owners sock it to couples, who must pay a full-cabin price (usually 6 people), but low-season deals at some places can be negotiated down to $30 for two.

RESIDENCIALES & HOSTELS These lodging options are for budget travelers. *Residenciales* are private homes whose owners rent out rooms, and they range from simple, clean rooms with a private or shared bathroom to ugly flats with creepy bathrooms. In towns that see more tourists, a hostel can be a hip and very comfortable place run by foreigners or Chileans, typically from Santiago. Some hostels are private homes that use their living area as a common area, and some of them can be very comfortable.

12 The Active Vacation Planner

Chile is a veritable paradise for adventure and active travel, offering a tremendous diversity of activities such as trekking through lush forests and rugged peaks, kayaking blue lakes, rafting white water, mountain biking country lanes and desert canyons, horseback riding and skiing in the Andes, ascents to the top of smoking volcanoes . . . the list is endless.

There are several ways to go about planning an active vacation in Chile. Several full-service lodges have popped up throughout the country that offer limited or all-inclusive packages that include transportation, guides, and equipment.

ORGANIZED ADVENTURE TRIPS

The advantages of traveling with an organized group are plentiful, especially for travelers who have limited time and resources. Tour operators take the headache out of planning a trip, and they iron out the wrinkles that invariably pop up along the way. The language is less of a barrier when you have a guide to translate for you, and a guide can interpret the culture and history of Chile and the natural surroundings of your destination. Many tours are organized to include guides, transportation, accommodations, meals, and gear (some outfitters even carry gear for you—for example, on trekking adventures). Independent travelers tend to view organized tours as antithetical to the joy of discovery, but leaving the details to someone else does free up substantial time to concentrate on something else. Besides, your traveling companions are likely to be kindred souls interested in similar things.

Be careful of tour operators who try to pack 20 people or more into a trip. The personal attention just isn't there, nor is that bit of breathing room you might find yourself needing after a week on the road. Also, be sure you know what you're getting yourself into. A 5-day trek through a national park might look great on paper, but are you physically up to it? Tour operators are responsible for their clients' well-being and safety, but that doesn't let you off the hook in terms of your own personal responsibility. Inquire about your guide's experience, safety record, and insurance policy. Remember, no adventure trip is 100% risk-free.

A Select Tour of Chile's Vineyards

Chile's top wine-growing valleys are the Maipo (near Santiago), Aconcagua, Rapel, Curicó, Maule, and Colchagua. The practice of "tasting" Chilean wine has been slow to catch on, but each year more and more wineries open their doors to the public for tours. The first three wineries listed below are close to Santiago; others require a full-day or overnight excursion, meaning you must join a tour or rent a car. The Chilean tour companies **Cocha Tours** (© **2/464-1000**; www.cocha.com) and **ACE Turismo** (© **2/335-6550**) can plan day visits or multiple-day tours to visit several wineries, as can the American company **Avalon Tours** (© **949/673-7376**; www.avalon-tours.com). Trips usually include tours of the surrounding countryside and the superb Museum of Colchagua, or the pottery-producing village Pomaire.

- **Cousiño-Macul** (Peñalolen, near Santiago; © **2/284-1011**; www.cousino macul.cl). If you have time to visit just one winery while in Chile, make it the Cousiño-Macul. This winery is more traditional than eating empanadas on Sunday; in fact, the first vines in Chile were planted here in 1546. The beautiful estate and its lush, French-designed gardens are as impressive as the winery's Antiguas Reservas traditional red, and it's just a cab ride away from Santiago.
- **Concha y Toro** (Pirque, near Santiago; © **2/853-0042**; www.conchay toro.com). Chile's most popular winery produces the lion's share of wines, from inexpensive table reds to some of Chile's priciest cabernet sauvignons, as well as Chile's top traditional red Don Melchior. Like Cousiño Macul, the winery itself is part of the attraction, with gardens large enough to require eight full-time gardeners, and antique bodegas whose interiors are part of your tour. Concha y Toro is also close enough to Santiago to get there by cab.
- **Viña Santa Rita** (Buin, near Santiago; © **2/362-2100**; www.santa rita.com). Santa Rita offers tours but no wine tasting—still, don't

U.S.-BASED ADVENTURE TOUR OPERATORS

These companies offer solid, well-organized tours, and they are backed by years of experience. Most of these operators are expensive, and a few are exorbitant (remember that prices do not include airfare), but that usually is because they include luxury accommodations and gourmet dining. Most offer trips to hot spots like Patagonia, and operators with trips to that region are listed here for both Argentina and Chile.

- **Abercrombie & Kent,** 1520 Kensington Rd., Oak Brook, IL 60521 (© **800/323-7308;** www.abercrombiekent.com), is a luxury tour operator that offers a variety of trips for people of different abilities and interests. They also recently opened an office in Santiago. Their 15-day, all-inclusive tour "Chile, Land of Fire and Ice" takes visitors to Buenos Aires, on a cruise from Ushuaia to Punta Arenas, trekking in Torres del Paine, and then to the Puerto Varas and finally Santiago, for prices starting at $6,850 per person, double occupancy. Custom tours are available as well.

write off this winery, because its restaurant (where you *can* sample their wines) and estate are truly above par. Also, should you decide to spend the night, their former estate house has been converted into an elegant inn, and it is the ideal lodging option for those who want to be close to Santiago without being in it. About a 1-hr drive from Santiago or the airport, it makes for a pleasant day trip and a good base for exploring the Central Valley.

- **Veramonte** (Casablanca, near Valparaíso; 𝄞 **3/274-2421;** www.vera monte.com). The Casablanca region is relatively new to winemaking, yet it is an ideal location for growing chardonnay and sauvignon blanc grapes. One slick new winery has invested heavily in Casablanca's potential with a state-of-the-art facility capable of crushing 75 tons of grapes per day. The winery prides itself on its "Napa Valley-style" wine-tasting facilities, with a service-oriented staff and an impressive tasting room with a soaring rotunda and glass walls that let you peek into the barrel caves below. The winery makes for a perfect stop on the road from Santiago to Valparaíso.

- There is a wine route in the Colchagua Valley that encompasses some of Chile's up-and-coming wineries such as Viña Bisquertt and Viu Manent. Sernatur offers a guide to this route in its "Wine Circuits of Chile" brochure. You can rent a car and visit these wineries at your own pace or hire a tour company (mentioned above) to take you there. Check at Sernatur to see if an organized tour of the Colchagua Valley is back up and running, leaving from the plaza in the town Santa Cruz. Every March, wineries organize the Fiesta de la Vendimia, a festival that celebrates the grape harvest, with tastings and wine-making demonstrations.

- **Butterfield and Robinson,** 70 Bond St., Toronto, Canada M5B 1X3 (𝄞 **800/678-1147;** www. butterfield.com), is another gourmet tour operator that offers a walking-oriented, 10-day trip to Patagonia starting in El Calafate, Argentina, and finishing in Punta Arenas, Chile. In between, travelers visit the national parks Los Glaciares and Torres del Paine, with visits to the Perito Moreno Glacier and lodging in fine lodges and ranches. Cost is $5,650 per person, double occupancy.

- **Mountain-Travel Sobek,** 6420 Fairmount Ave., El Cerrito, CA 94530 (𝄞 **888/MTSOBEK** or 510/527-8100; fax 510/525-7718; www.mtsobek.com), are the pioneers of organized adventure travel, and they offer trips that involve a lot of physical activity. One of their more gung-ho journeys is an ascent of the Western Hemisphere's highest mountain, Aconcagua (a 22-day adventure); or try a 10-day rafting adventure down the Futaleufú River; or a more moderate Patagonia Explorer that mixes hiking with cruising. Prices run from $1,500 to $3,000 and more. Sobek always comes recommended for its knowledgeable guides.

- **Backroads Active Vacations,** 801 Cedar St., Berkeley, CA 94710-1800 (© **800/GO-ACTIVE** or 510/527-1555; www.backroads. com), offers a biking tour through the lake districts of Chile and Argentina, with stops in Puerto Varas and the Llao Llao Peninsula; an afternoon of rafting is included. There's also a hiking trip through the same region, and a 9-day hiking trip in Patagonian Chile and Argentina. Guests lodge in luxury hotels and inns. Costs run from $3,798 to $4,998.

- **Wilderness Travel,** 1102 Ninth St., Berkeley, CA 94710 (© **800/368-2794** or 510/558-2488; www.wildernesstravel.com), offers a mellower sightseeing/day hiking tour and a more involved hiking/sea kayaking tour around Patagonia, including Torres del Paine; a hiking tour through the Futaleufú River area; cruises to Easter Island; and hiking in Fitz Roy National Park. The hiking trip around Patagonia costs $4,295 to $4,595, depending on the number of guests (maximum 15).

- **Wildland Adventures,** 3516 NE 155th St., Seattle, WA 98155 (© **800/345-4453** or 206/365-0686; www.wildland.com), offers several adventure tours of Chile: trekking in Patagonia, sea kayaking in Chiloé and Tierra del Fuego, and an 11-day overview tour that stretches from the Atacama Desert down to Torres del Paine National Park. Accommodations range from hotels to camping to rustic park lodges. Ecotourism is an integral part of Wildland tours. Prices start at $695 for a 4-day kayaking tour

and continue to upward of $3,000 for a 2-week Patagonia trip.

- **REI Adventures,** P.O. Box 1938, Sumner, WA 98390 (© **800/622-2236;** www.rei.com/travel), offers multi-sport and trekking adventures in the Lake District and Patagonia, including a 10-day journey in both Chile and Argentina that features mountain biking, hiking, and rafting for $2,095 per person, with lodging in comfortable *hosterías.* Their Patagonia trekking trip features camping and lodging in hotels.

- **PowderQuest Tours** (© **888/565-7158** toll-free in the U.S., or 804/285-4961; www.powderquest. com) offers complete ski and snowboard tour packages that take guests to a variety of ski resorts in both Chile and Argentina, and they offer free-ride and heliski camps. Each group has a maximum of 8, and their guides are highly trained and can take skiers and snowboarders farther into the backcountry. Prices range from $1,795 to $2,595 per person for 9- to 16-day trips.

CHILEAN TOUR AGENCIES

Chilean tour agencies typically offer a wider variety of tours in Chile—after all, they operate within their own country. The following active travel operators are good bets.

- **Cascada Expediciones,** Orrego Luco 040, Providencia, Santiago (© **2/234-2274;** fax 2/233-9768; www.cascada-expediciones.com), offers a very wide variety of active trips around Chile but is particularly active in Cajón de Maipo, where the company is based. Activities include rafting, kayaking, mountaineering, horseback riding, trekking in Torres del Paine, 1- to multiple-day climbing trips, and more.

- **Altué Expediciones,** Encomenderos 83, 2nd floor, Las Condes, Santiago (© **2/233-6799**), is a well-organized, excellent Chilean outfitter that specializes in kayaking and rafting. Altué offers kayak trips around the island of Chiloé and the Andean fjords, horseback riding on the Army of Liberation trail through the Andes, rafting the Futaleufú, hiking in the Lake District, climbing the Ojos del Salado, and more.

OTHER GENERAL-INTEREST TOUR OPERATORS & PACKAGE DEALS

- **PanAmerican Travel,** 320 E. 900 S., Salt Lake City, UT 84111 (© **801/364-4359** or 800/364-4300; fax 801/364-4330; www.panam-tours.com), an excellent company that arranges custom trips for its clients for most destinations in Chile. PanAmerican is the operator for LanChile Vacations, and can package great deals.
- **2000 Latin Tours,** 9300 S. Dixie Hwy., Miami, FL (© **800/254-**7378; www.gotolatintours.com) is a leader in travel to Chile and run by Chileans themselves in the U.S. This company can plan just about any kind of trip imaginable, or simply book hotels, car rentals, tours, and more.
- **Discover Chile Tours,** 5755 Blue Lagoon Dr., Suite 190, Miami, FL 33126 (© **800/826-4845** or 305/266-5827; www.discoverchile.com), is another excellent resource, offering complete trip planning and set packages, custom tours, and low-cost deals on transportation. Also run by Chilean natives from their office in the U.S.
- **Ladatco Tours,** Aviation Ave. #4C, Coconut Grove, FL 33133 (© **800/327-6162;** www.ladatco.com), organizes dozens of set and custom tours in all regions of Chile, including theme-oriented tours such as wine tasting, fly-fishing, glaciers, and more. Ladatco has operated as a Central and South America tour operator for 30 years.

 FAST FACTS: Chile

Business Hours Banks are open Monday through Friday from 9am to 2pm, and are closed on Saturday and Sunday. Commercial offices close for a long lunch hour, which can vary from business to business. Generally, hours are Monday through Friday from 10am to 7pm, closing for lunch around 1 or 1:30pm and reopening at 2:30 or 3pm.

Cameras/Film Most types of film are available in Chile, as are print-developing services. Slide-developing services are almost nonexistent except in Santiago. The best in the country is **Tecnología Uno** at Av. Santa María 0120, Providencia, Santiago (© 2/200-0482; www.tecnologiauno.com).

Currency Exchange See "Money," earlier in this chapter.

Electricity Chile's electricity standard is 220 volts/50Hz. Electrical sockets have two openings for tubular pins, not flat prongs, so you'll need a plug adapter available from most travel stores.

Embassies/Consulates The only United States representative in Chile is the **U.S. Embassy** in Santiago, located at Av. Andrés Bello 2800 (© 2/232-2600). The **Canadian Embassy** is at Nuevo Tajamar 481, Piso 12 (© 2/362-9660). The **British Embassy** can be found at El Bosque Norte 0125

(ⓒ 2/370-4100). The **Australian Embassy** is at Gertrudis Echenique 420 (ⓒ 2/228-5665); the **New Zealand Embassy** is at Av. El Golf, Office 703 (ⓒ 2/290-9802).

Emergencies Obviously you'll want to contact the staff if something happens to you in your hotel. Otherwise, for a **police** emergency, call ⓒ **133.** For **fire,** call ⓒ **132.** To call an **ambulance,** dial ⓒ **131.**

Internet Access No matter where you are in Chile, chances are there is an Internet station, either in a cafe or at the telephone centers CTC or Entel. Most hotels have their own Internet service; if they don't, they'll be able to point out where to find one. Expect to pay $2 to $4 per hour.

Language Spanish is the official language of Chile. Many Chileans in the tourism industry and in major cities can speak basic English, but don't count on it. Try to learn even a dozen basic Spanish phrases before arriving; there are several excellent phrasebooks on the market and they will facilitate your trip tremendously.

Liquor Laws The legal drinking age in Chile is 18. Alcohol is sold every day of the year, except during elections.

Police Police officers wear olive-green uniforms and are referred to as *carabineros* or colloquially as *pacos*. Dial ⓒ **133** for an emergency. To file a robbery or crime report you'll need to file a *constancia* or a *denuncia*.

Restrooms Most establishments, apart from upscale hotels and restaurants, will ask that you deposit used toilet paper in a wastebasket and not in the toilet itself, because of poor plumbing.

Safety Santiago is probably the safest major city in South America. Serious violent crime is not unheard of, but it's not common either. A visitor's principal concern will be pickpockets, tire slashers, and vandals, but even then your chances of being a victim are rare.

Taxes See "Cash & Currency" under "Money" earlier in this chapter.

Telephone Each carrier has its own prefix, which you must dial when placing national and international long distance calls. Telephone centers use their own prefix, and there is a list of prefixes in telephone booths—all offer virtually the same rates. The prefixes are CTC (188), Entel (123), BellSouth (181), and Chilesat (171) among others. To place a collect call, dial a prefix and then 182 for an operator. The country code for Chile is 56. A local phone call requires 100 pesos, and better rates are had with a phone card sold from kiosks, but verify that a particular company's phone card works with any phone and not only with its own public phone. Cellular phones are prefixed by 09, and are more expensive to call. To reach an **AT&T** operator while in Chile, dial ⓒ **800/800-288.** The access numbers for **MCI** are ⓒ **800/207-300** (using CTC) and ⓒ **800/360-180** (using Entel). The access number for **Sprint** is ⓒ **800/360-777.**

Time Chile is 4 hours behind Greenwich mean time from the first Saturday in October until the second Saturday in March; the country is 6 hours behind during the rest of the year.

Tipping Diners leave a 10% tip in restaurants. In hotels, tipping is left to the guest's discretion. Taxi drivers are not tipped.

11

Santiago

Santiago, one of South America's most sophisticated cities, is a thriving metropolis that's home to five million people, or nearly a third of Chile's entire population. On a clear day, Santiago's main attraction is its spectacular location at the foot of the snowcapped Andes, which rise majestically over the city's eastern limits. It's a breathtaking sight, but the opportunity to view it in its glory is not common due to a dense layer of smog that shrouds the city. The smog is at its eye-burning worst in the winter

Nevertheless, Santiago is an intriguing city, and there's certainly plenty to see and do here. It is the historic, economic, and cultural center of Chile, and its restaurants, art centers, and theaters are the best in the country. It also makes a convenient base for exploring a number of great destinations outside the city limits— including beaches, ski resorts, and wineries. If you're planning a visit to Chile, you'll inevitably spend at least 1 night here on your way into or out of the country, but if you have the time you should try to spend 2 or 3 days here, more if you plan to visit those outlying areas.

The city is a curious mix of old and new; a glitzy glass skyscraper towers over a 200-year-old stone building, and a charming cobblestone street dead-ends at a tacky 1970s shopping gallery. Some neighborhoods look as though they belong to entirely different cities.

1 Orientation

ESSENTIALS
GETTING THERE

BY PLANE   Santiago's **Comodoro Arturo Merino Benítez Airport** (© 2/ **690-1900**) is served by the Chilean national carrier LanChile, as well as by most major international carriers. This relatively new international airport has several restaurants and a number of shops. Once you pass through Customs, there is a small **currency exchange** kiosk, but it is recommended that you exchange larger sums downtown at a bank for better rates. Men in olive jumpsuits at the arrival area and the outdoor departure curb work as airport bellhops, and they will jump in and try to assist you with your luggage for a 45¢ to 75¢ tip; if you're okay on your own, just shoo them away with a *"No, gracias."*

Depending on traffic, your Santiago destination, and how you get there, the city can be reached in 20 minutes to an hour. When making hotel reservations, ask about transfers because most hotels offer private car or van pickup for around $20; some offer the service for free. A **taxi** to Santiago costs between $10 and $18; negotiate the price beforehand. Official taxi drivers await passengers at the exit gate, and cheaper, unofficial drivers who have just dropped passengers off wait just outside the airport's doors. The next cheapest option is one of the several minivan **transfers** that charge from $4 to $6, such as Delfío or Tour Express; their desks are at the arrival area. You can also make a reservation for a transfer service to pick you up for the return trip to the airport. Keep in mind that your transfer might stop several times for other passengers before arriving at your destination. Cheaper yet are **bus** services that depart from the far ends of the arrival curb and drop passengers downtown, from where they can take the metro or a taxi. The blue bus Centropuerto leaves every 15 to 30 minutes from 7am to 11:30pm, and drops passengers at Los Héroes metro station on the main avenue Alameda. Tur Bus has a bus that leaves every 30 minutes from 6am to 12:30pm, dropping passengers off at Moneda 1529, near San Martín, a couple of blocks from the Moneda metro station.

BY BUS   There are three principal **bus stations** in Santiago. The station for international arrivals and departures to and from destinations in southern Chile is **Terminal Santiago,** also known as **Terminal Sur,** Alameda 3850 (© **2/376-1755;** Metro: Universidad de Santiago). The **Terminal Alameda** next door at Alameda 3712 is the terminal for the Pullman and Tur Bus companies, two well-respected, high-quality services. For departures to northern and central Chile, you'll go to **Terminal San Borja,** Alameda 3250 (© **2/776-0645;** Metro: Estación Central). The smaller **Terminal Los Héroes,** Tucapel Jiménez 21 (© **2/420-0099;** Metro: Los Héroes), has service to a variety of destinations in both northern and southern Chile.

BY TRAIN   Santiago is serviced by two train lines from the south (from Temuco and Chillán), both of which leave from the giant Estación Central at Alameda 3170. Trains to Chillán leave five times a day; the fare is $11 and the trip is about 4½ hours. For Temuco, there is one train, which leaves nightly at 9:30pm and arrives at 9:30am. Fares are $11 for tourist class, or $14 for salon class, with reclining seats. For schedules and train information, check out the Spanish-only website www.efe.cl or check with your travel agent or hotel for a reservation.

VISITOR INFORMATION

There are several outlets offering information about Santiago and Chile in general, such as the main office of Chile's **National Tourism Service (Sernatur),** which can be found at Av. Providencia 1550 (© **2/731-8300;** www.sernatur.cl). Hours are Monday through Friday from 9am to 6:30pm, Saturday from 9am to 2pm, closed Sunday (Metro: Manuel Montt). Sernatur also has an information center at the airport near the Duty Free shop that is open daily from 8:30am to 9pm (© **2/601-9230**). Sernatur has a bilingual staff, but is plagued by inconsistent service and often depleted of brochures after the high season in March. Be sure to ask for a brochure if you don't see what you want because they are usually hidden, especially the booklet guides to the wine country, national parks, beaches, and camping. Another option is the **Oficina de Turismo,** located in the Casa Colorada at Merced 860 (Mon–Fri 10am–6pm; © **2/632-7783;** www.ciudad.cl/turismo). The Oficina de Turismo offers brochures about Santiago and its nearby destinations only; be sure to pick up a copy of their *Historical Heritage of Santiago: A Guide for Tourists.* A private concession operates a good tourism **kiosk** conveniently located at the intersection between Paseo Ahumada and Paseo Huérfanos pedestrian walkways in the city center; the kiosk provides brochures and relevant information, and you can book city tours there. The **Yellow Pages** have detailed maps of the entire city of Santiago.

CITY LAYOUT

Santiago incorporates 32 *comunas,* or neighborhoods, although most visitors will find they spend their time in just a few of these neighborhoods. **Downtown,** or *el centro,* is the thriving financial, political, and historic center of Santiago,

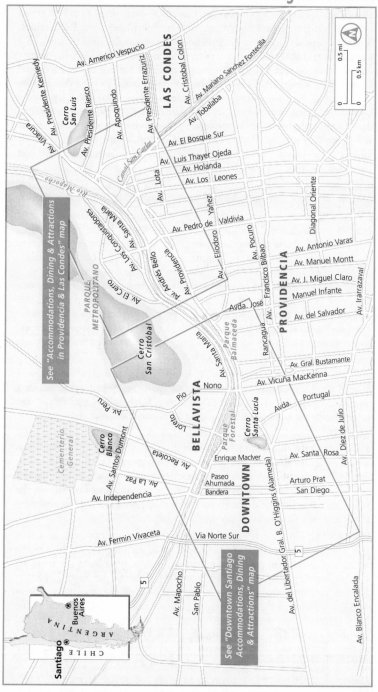

See "Accommodations, Dining & Attractions in Providencia & Las Condes" map

See "Downtown Santiago Accommodations, Dining & Attractions" map

LAS CONDES

PROVIDENCIA

BELLAVISTA

DOWNTOWN

Parque METROPOLITANO

Cementerio General

Cerro San Cristóbal

Cerro Blanco

Cerro Santa Lucia

Parque Forestal

Parque Balmaceda

Río Mapocho

Canal San Carlos

Av. Americo Vespucio

Av. Presidente Kennedy

Av. Vitacura

Cerro San Luis

Av. Presidente Riesco

Av. Apoquindo

Av. Presidente Errazuriz

Av. Cristobal Colon

Av. Mariano Sanchez Fontecilla

Av. Tobalaba

Av. El Bosque Sur

Av. Luis Thayer Ojeda

Av. Holanda

Av. Los Leones

Av. Lota

Av. Pedro de Valdivia

Av. Eliodoro Yañez

Av. Providencia

Av. Andrés Bello

Av. Los Conquistadores

Av. Santa María

Av. El Cerro

Av. Pocuro

Av. Francisco Bilbao

Diagonal Oriente

Av. Antonio Varas

Av. Manuel Montt

Av. J. Miguel Claro

Manuel Infante

Av. del Salvador

Av. Irarrazaval

Avda. José

Rancagua

Av. Santa María

Av. Gral. Bustamante

Av. Vicuña MacKenna

Avda. Portugal

Av. Diez de Julio

Nono

Pio

Loreto

Av. Recoleta

Av. Peru

Cerro Santa Lucia

Enrique MacIver

Paseo Ahumada

Bandera

Av. Santa Rosa

Arturo Prat

San Diego

Av. Santos Dumont

Av. La Paz

Av. Independencia

Av. Fermin Vivaceta

Via Norte Sur

Av. Mapocho

San Pablo

Av. del Libertador Gral. B. O'Higgins (Alameda)

Av. Blanco Encalada

0   0.5 mi
0   0.5 km

ARGENTINA

Buenos Aires

CHILE

Santiago

although it has been losing clout as more and more companies opt to locate their offices in burgeoning neighborhoods, such as **Providencia** and **Las Condes.** These two upscale, attractive neighborhoods are residential areas centered on a bustling strip of shopping galleries, restaurants, and office buildings. In comparison, *el centro* appears older and often scruffier. Farther east sit the residential communities **Ñuñoa** and **La Reina,** which offer few attractions and therefore little interest to the visitor. Santiago is bisected by the muddy Río Mapocho, a brown stream that alternately rushes or trickles down from the Andes and is bordered through downtown and Providencia by the grassy Parque Forestal. On one side of the Mapocho rises the hill Cerro San Cristóbal, a large, forested park with lookout points over the city. Below the hill is the artists' and actors' neighborhood **Bellavista,** which is popular for its fashionable bars and restaurants.

2 Getting Around

BY METRO   Cheap, clean, and efficient, the Metro is the preferred mode of intercity transportation. There are three Metro lines. Line 1 runs from Providencia to west of downtown along the Alameda; this is the most convenient trajectory that will take you to most major attractions. Line 2 runs from Cal y Canto (near the Mercado Central) to Lo Ovalle (convenient for Palacio Cousiño). Line 5 runs from La Florida to Baquedano, with a stop in the Plaza de Armas. There are two fares, 40¢ and 50¢ depending on the time of day (fares are posted in the ticket window). Visitors can buy a *boleto valor,* for peak times, or a *boleto multiviaje,* for travel during slower hours; both cost $4.70. The *valor* is worth 10 trips, the *multiviaje* is worth 12. The Metro runs from 6am to 10:30pm. The Metro is very safe, but normal precautions against pickpockets should be taken.

BY BUS   City buses, or *micros,* are tricky in Santiago because there aren't any printed route maps available. A particular bus route might be mapped out on a sign inside the bus, but you have to guess its general path by reading the sign posted inside the windshield highlighting its principal destinations.

BY TAXI   Taxis are identifiable by their black exterior and yellow roof; there's also a light in the corner of the windshield that displays a taxi's availability. Taxis are plentiful and moderately priced. Drivers do not expect tips, but you might find it convenient to round off a fare rather than grapple with change. Do not confuse taxis with *colectivos,* which are similar in appearance but without the yellow roof. They are local, shared taxis with fixed routes that are too confusing to the average visitor to merit taking a ride.

BY RENTAL CAR   It is totally unnecessary to rent a car in Santiago unless you plan to drive to any of the peripheral areas, such as Viña del Mar or the Andes—and even then public transportation, such as direct buses and transfers, is very convenient. If you must have a car, be forewarned that driving in Santiago can be a hair-raising experience due to maniacal, swerving buses; drivers who do not confine their cars to one lane; and absolutely phenomenal traffic jams, especially between 5:30 and 7:30pm. The commuter gridlock is dreadful anywhere around Santiago but especially bad in Providencia and Las Condes.

Car Rentals   At the airport you'll find most international rental agencies, such as **Alamo** (© 2/225-3061), **Avis** (© 600/601-9966), **Budget** (© 2/362-3200), **Dollar** (© 2/202-5510), **Econorent** (© 600/200-0000), **Hertz** (© 2/420-5222), local agency **Rosselot** (© 800/201 298), and **Thrifty** (© 2/225-6328). All agencies also have downtown or Providencia offices.

Driving Hints Chileans use their horn and their indicators habitually to warn other motorists or advise them of their next move. Right turns on red lights are forbidden unless otherwise indicated. Ask your rental car company for a list of rules you may be unfamiliar with.

Parking Most hotels offer parking on their own property or in a nearby lot. Parking downtown is difficult during weekdays, although you should be able to find an above-ground or underground lot, called an *estacionamiento,* by driving around. Santiago has begun metering busy streets in Providencia and Bellavista, which is done by an official meter maid who times and charges drivers. Chile is also home to a peculiar phenomenon known as parking *cuidador,* where unofficial, freelance meter maids stake out individual blocks and watch your car for you while you go about your business. You're expected to give them whatever change you have (15¢–75¢) when you leave your space. *Cuidadores* can be aggressive if you decide not to pay them.

ON FOOT With a map in hand, Santiago is fairly easy to figure out, especially if you stick close to major streets. The problem with walking in Santiago is that busy avenues are a loathsome mess, with screeching buses expelling huge, gray plumes of exhaust into the already polluted air. Saturday and Sunday afternoons are typically calmer days for a stroll, and the summer usually blesses its residents with cleaner air. You might consider taking shorter walks or at least breaking periodically in a quiet museum or park. Pedestrians should be alert at all times and should not stand on curbs, as buses roar by dangerously close to sidewalks. Also, drivers do not always give the right of way to pedestrians, and therefore you should get across the street as quickly as possible.

 ***FAST FACTS:* Santiago**

American Express The American Express office is at Av. Isidora Goyenechea 3621, Piso 10 (© **2/350-6700**; open Monday through Friday from 9:30am to 5pm; for 24-hour bilingual service © **800/361002**).

Banks Open from 9am to 2pm, closed on Saturday and Sunday. ATMs are referred to as "RedBancs" and can be identified by the maroon-and-white logo sticker. These machines accept Cirrus, PLUS, Visa, and MasterCard. RedBancs can also be found in most gas stations and pharmacies.

Business Hours Commercial offices close for a long lunch hour, which can vary from business to business. Generally, hours are Monday through Friday from 10am to 7pm, closing for lunch between 1 and 1:30pm and reopening between 2:30 or 3pm. Most stores are open from 10am to 2pm on Saturday and closed Sunday.

Currency Exchange All major banks exchange currency, but only a few, such as Citibank, do so without charging commission. Downtown Citibank branches can be found at Ahumada 40, Huérfanos 770, Teatinos 180, and La Bolsa 64. Your best bet for rates are at one of the *casas de cambio* (money-exchange houses). In downtown, there are numerous exchange houses on Agustinas between Ahumada and Bandera. In Providencia, exchange houses are around Avenida Pedro de Valdivia and Avenida Providencia. Exchange houses are generally open Monday through Friday from 9am to 2pm and 4 to 6pm, Saturday from 9am to 1 or 2pm.

Emergencies For a **police** emergency, call **133**. For **fire,** call **132**. To call an **ambulance,** dial **131**.

Hospital The American Embassy can provide a list of medical specialists in Santiago. The best hospitals in Santiago are private: **Clínica Las Condes** at Lo Fontecilla 441 (© 2/210-4000), **Clínica Alemana** at Vitacura 5951 (© 2/212-9700), and **Clínica Indisa** at Av. Santa María 01810 (© 2/362-5555).

Internet Access Virtually every hotel and commercial center in Santiago has Internet access. In Providencia, try **Cyber Café Internet** at Pedro de Valdivia 037 (© 2/233-3083) or **Cafetería Las Urbinas** at Las Urbinas 31 (© 2/232-8303). In downtown, try **Sicosis Pub** near the Palace of Fine Arts at José Miguel de la Barra 544 (© 2/632-4462), or **Sonnets Internet Café** at Londres 43 (no phone).

Language See "Language" under "Fast Facts: Chile" in chapter 10.

Pharmacies **Farmacias Ahumada** branches are open 24 hours a day, and there are dozens of locations. Try the one at the corner of Ahumada and Huérfanos streets; along Avenida Providencia between Pedro de Valdivia and Suecia or at El Bosque 164, in Las Condes; call © 2/222-4000 for information and ordering.

Police See "Police" under "Fast Facts: Chile" in chapter 10.

Post Office The main post office is on Plaza de Armas (Mon–Fri 8:30am–7pm, Sat 8:30am–1pm). There are other branches at Moneda 1155 in downtown and Av. 11 de Septiembre 2239 in Providencia.

Safety See "Safety" under "Fast Facts: Chile" in chapter 10.

Taxes See "Cash & Currency" under "Money" in chapter 10.

Telephone Santiago's area code is **2**; cellular numbers are prefixed by **09**. The country code for Chile is **56**. Tourists are offered cheaper rates from phone centers than from their hotels. The centers are predominately run by Entel (at Morandé between Huérfanos and Compañía) and Telefónica CTC Chile (found inside the Metro stations Universidad de Chile and Moneda, and in Providencia at the Mall Panorámico at Av. 11 de Septiembre 2155). Most phone centers have fax service and Internet access.

3 Where To Stay

Santiago accommodations are a mixed bag, and price is not always the best indicator of quality. Also, bear in mind that your opinion of Santiago can easily be shaped by the neighborhood you're staying in. Many lodging options costing in the $80 to $100 range from nondescript, uninspiring hotels to B&Bs in renovated mansions. Downtown is the obvious choice if proximity to major sites of interest is what's important to you, but keep in mind that an efficient metro quickly links visitors with areas such as Providencia and Las Condes. If price is a factor, you'll find the most economical lodging downtown. Parking at Santiago hotels is free unless otherwise indicated in the review.

DOWNTOWN SANTIAGO
VERY EXPENSIVE

Hotel Carrera ★★★ This grande dame of Santiago hotels has during its 60 years become part of the city's legacy; its history and old-fashioned splendor make it one of the more unique choices in the city. Built between 1937 and 1940, and for decades the social center of Santiago's elite, the building's lobby features crystal chandeliers from Bohemia and an enormous glass mural depicting the arrival of the Spanish to the New World. The hotel sits directly on the Plaza Constitución. All rooms have a richly textured English decor with classic floral and striped wallpaper, Oriental carpets, and heavy drapes. Standard doubles are called deluxe rooms, and the remodeled fifth and sixth floor "Carrera Club" executive rooms are larger and come complete with marble sinks and mahogany furniture. Rooms facing the neighboring Ministerio de Hacienda can be dark; brighter rooms with a "park view" face the plaza. A highlight at the Carrera is its glitzy rooftop pool. Competition has forced the Carrera to drop prices, and now even the deluxe executive rooms go for just $170 a night.

The hotel's three restaurants are all worth a visit even if you're not staying at the hotel. The Copper Room Bar is a cozy spot for a cocktail.

Teatinos 180. © **2/698-2011.** Fax 2/672-1083. www.carrera.cl. 305 units, 26 suites. $140 deluxe; $170 Carrera Club junior suite; $360 suite. AE, DC, MC, V. Metro: Estación Moneda. **Amenities:** 3 restaurants; bar; outdoor pool; racquetball court; gym; sauna; whirlpool tub; concierge; business center; gift and floral shops; salon; room service; massage; babysitting; laundry service; photo service; conference rooms. *In room:* A/C, minibar, TV.

Hotel Fundador ★★   The Fundador is similar to the Plaza (see below) in its classic decor, though ever-so-slightly less elegant. But the attractive, English-style rooms are comfortable and bright, and its wonderful swimming pool is housed in a sunny penthouse. The hotel also has a great central location on a quiet street in the charming París-Londres neighborhood. Many doubles come with two full-size beds instead of twins; inquire before booking. The Fundador expanded 4 years ago and renovated every one of its older guest rooms. The suites are compact but exceptionally cozy; all come with cherrywood armoires to separate the bedroom from a sitting area. Adjoining the lobby is a wood-and-leather-walled bar that's a nice place to hole up in for a drink.

Paseo Serrano 34. © **2/387-1200.** Fax 2/387-1300. www.hotelfundador.cl. hotelfundador@hotelfundador.cl. 150 units. $170 double; $200 junior suite. AE, DC, MC, V. Metro: Univ. de Chile. **Amenities:** 2 restaurants; bar; indoor pool; gym; sauna; business center; gift shop; room service; babysitting; laundry service; conference rooms; valet parking. *In room:* A/C, minibar, TV.

Hotel Plaza San Francisco ★★   This elegant hotel with its clubby design offers smart service, impeccable rooms, and a central location. The decor is traditional and the interior lighting dark, with low, wood ceilings supported by pillars, richly colored fabric wallpaper, and Oriental rugs. Relax in the lobby to the sound of the tinkling indoor fountain, or enjoy the Bar Bristol's all-you-can-drink happy hour from 6 to 9pm. Guest rooms are spacious, with sparkling bathrooms and classic furniture. The hotel is conveniently located on busy Avenue Alameda, but you won't hear the din of traffic due to double-paned windows. The hotel has a wine shop and an indoor pool hidden downstairs in a windowless room. Apart from executives, plenty of travelers choose the Plaza when visiting Santiago, including the Dalai Lama, who has stayed here twice.

Alameda 816. © **2/639-3832.** Fax 2/639-7826. www.hotelsanfrancisco.cl. 160 units. $120 double; $140 double superior; $210 junior suite; $300 executive suite. AE, DC, MC, V. Metro: Univ. de Chile. **Amenities:** Award-winning restaurant; bar; indoor pool; gym; whirlpool; concierge; LanChile office; business center; room service; massage; laundry service; art gallery. *In room:* A/C, TV, minibar.

MODERATE

Apart-Hotel Carlton   This no-frills hotel is boxier and older than the Foresta or Riviera; however, the rooms are neat and crisp and their 1950s and '60s

Downtown Santiago Accommodations, Dining & Attractions

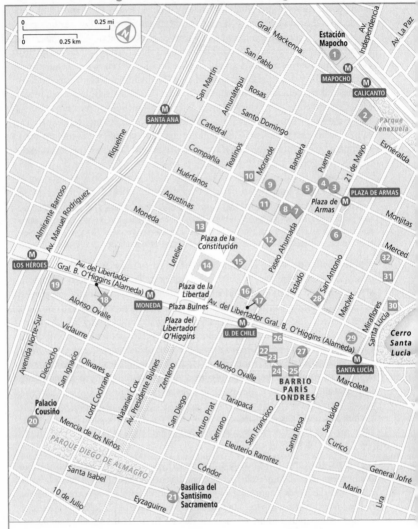

ACCOMMODATIONS ■
Apart Hotel Carlton **30**
City Hotel **10**
Hotel Carrera **13**
Hotel Club Presidente **44**
Hotel Foresta **33**
Hotel Fundador **22**
Hotel París **25**
Hotel Plaza San Francisco **26**
Hotel Riviera **31**

Hotel Vegas **23**
Residencial Londres **24**

DINING ◆
Bar Nacional **12**
Confitería Torres **18**
Don Vitorino **34**
El Novillero **15**
Gatopardo **35**
Govindas **7**
Kintaro **38**

Le Due Torri **28**
Les Assassins **37**
Mercado Central **2**
Squadritto **36**
27 de Nueva York **17**

ATTRACTIONS ●
Basílica de la Merced **32**
Basílica del Santísimo
   Sacramento **21**
Biblioteca Nacional **29**

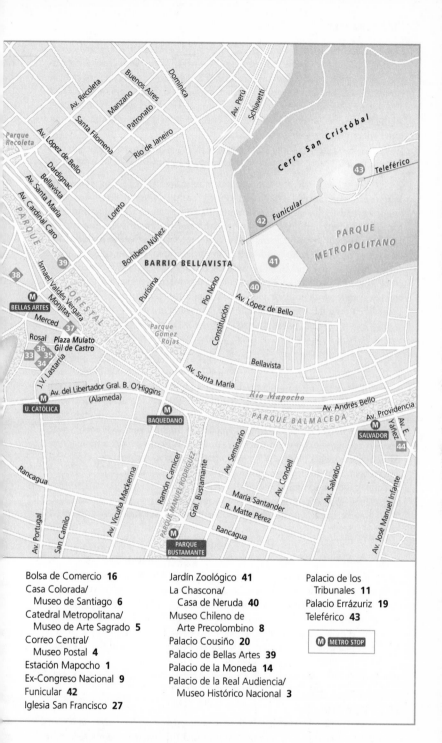

furniture has been fitted with fresh gingham slipcovers. It is highly recommended that guests opt for one of the suites, which come with older but complete kitchenettes and fairly large common areas; those facing the street have sunny terraces and are really worth requesting because the gloomier doubles face a parking garage and are not as much of a value. The hotel is slowly renovating all the bathrooms. Although the Carlton is as simple as it gets, it sits on a quaint, quiet street near the Cerro Santa Lucía.

Máximo Humbster 574. ℂ **2/638-3130.** Fax 2/638-2930. 33 units, 22 suites. $34 double; $40 suite with kitchenette. AE, DC, MC, V. Parking $4.50 per day. Metro: Santa Lucía. **Amenities:** Restaurant; bar. *In room:* TV.

Hotel Foresta ★ If you can get past the dungeon-like lobby, the Hotel Foresta offers comfortable, spacious rooms, a rooftop restaurant with panoramic windows, and leafy views of Cerro Santa Lucía. It is an excellent location both for the neighborhood's beautiful architecture and its proximity to downtown. Doubles, specifically a "matrimonial," that face Calle Subercaseaux are large enough to be junior suites, and each room is decorated with an eclectic mix of furniture—one room has floral bedspreads, the next, jade-colored wallpaper and smoked glass tables. It's an older hotel, and its funkiness makes for a fun place to stay. Singles with interior views are disappointingly dark and cramped. A plant-filled restaurant serves Chilean fare, and there is a bar.

Victoria Subercaseaux 353. ℂ **2/639-6261** or 2/639-4862. Fax 2/632-2996. 35 units. $31 double; $37 junior suite. AE, DC, MC, V. Metro: Santa Lucía. **Amenities:** Restaurant; bar. *In room:* A/C, TV, minibar.

Hotel Riviera ★ This hotel is a great deal for its reasonable prices and convenient downtown location—but you'll need to request a room on the sixth, seventh or eighth floor because the hotel is on a busy corner and traffic noise can be too much (except on weekends). Try for an eighth-floor suite, which is the same price as a double. The Riviera is located near a wealth of attractions and overlooks a pretty plaza and the Santa Lucía hill. Bright corner rooms have wide, floor-to-ceiling windows and the suite on the top floor has a panoramic view. Although somewhat older, the Riviera is freshly painted and updated every year, and its Spanish decor features textured walls and iron chandeliers. There's a small restaurant for breakfast and snacks near the lobby.

Miraflores 106. ℂ **2/633-1176.** Fax 2/633-5988. www.rivierahotel.cl. 40 units. $40 double; $40 suite. AE, DC, MC, V. Metro: Santa Lucía. **Amenities:** 24-hr. restaurant; bar; room service; laundry service. *In room:* A/C, TV, safe.

Hotel Vegas The Hotel Vegas overlooks a cobblestone street in an antique stone mansion in the charming París-Londres neighborhood. The price is economical, but rooms can be drab, especially if you end up with one of the rooms with interior light. Rooms in the back are sunnier, but they don't have the street view. Dark-wood paneling, diamond-paned yellow windows with heavy shutters, iron chandeliers, and '70s-style furniture set the atmosphere. The price and the age of the hotel make for bathrooms that look a little tired and carpet that's a bit thin, but they're all generally neat and clean, the service is friendly, and the location is convenient for sightseeing and museums.

Londres 49. ℂ **2/632-2514.** Fax 2/632-5084. www.hotelvegas.net. 20 units. $55 double. AE, DC, MC, V. Metro: Univ. de Chile. **Amenities:** 24-hr. restaurant; bar; laundry service. *In room:* A/C, TV.

INEXPENSIVE

City Hotel This 1925 relic has needed an update for many years, and it's surprising given the beauty of its stone exterior that the owners have not seen fit to do so. A hint of the old-world charm still shines through somehow, perhaps because of the manual elevator, creaky floors, and heavy room keys. It's an interesting place to spend the night if you don't mind spartan accommodations, and the price is right. Rooms are fairly spacious, and the beds and the bathrooms a bit battered, but clean. The location near the Plaza de Armas is ideal if you're looking to be in the thick of things, and there's an adjoining restaurant that harks back to the same era, with dark wood and iron banisters.

Compañía 1063. (C) **2/695-4526.** Fax 2/695-6775. 72 units. $33 double; $43 quad. AE, DC, MC, V. Metro: Plaza de Armas. **Amenities:** Restaurant; bar; laundry service. *In room:* TV.

Hotel París *Value* This is another good budget hotel with a central location and, in the case of the hotel's newer annex, charming antique interiors. Budget backpackers from all over the world bunk in the older annex, but you really need to be a backpacker to not mind the simplicity and worn-out look of the rooms. Pay a little extra here and opt for a room in what's referred to as the Hotel Nuevo París, where rooms are quieter and include oriental rugs and mahogany molding. A few of these rooms even come with a glass-enclosed alcove or tiny outdoor terrace; they are the same price and worth asking for. Continental breakfast costs $2.

París 813. (C) **2/664-0921.** Fax 2/639-4037. carbott@latinmail.com. 40 units. $26 double new wing; $23 double. AE, DC, MC, V. Parking across the street, $3–$5 per day. Metro: Univ. de Chile. **Amenities:** Cafe; laundry service. *In room:* TV (not all rooms).

Residencial Londres *Value* Residencial Londres is simply the best choice for travelers on the cheap in Santiago and is, accordingly, wildly popular in the summer—make reservations well in advance. There are four floors of basic rooms that wrap around an interior patio; some rooms have French doors that open onto Calle París. Residencial Londres is stuffed with antiques; some rooms come with armoires, tables, and chairs. The mattresses are thin-ish foam, and lighting can be a bare bulb hanging from the ceiling, but the furnishings and architecture make up the difference. Golden light floats through the lobby in the afternoon, and there's a TV lounge off to the side. The hotel is frequented more by backpackers and younger travelers, and many use the interior terrace to dry tents and store bicycles. A toast-and-coffee breakfast is available for $1.

Londres 54. (C)/Fax **2/638-2215.** 25 units. $21 double with private bathroom; $19 double with shared bathroom. No credit cards. Metro: Univ. de Chile. *In room:* No phone.

PROVIDENCIA
VERY EXPENSIVE

The Park Plaza The Park Plaza is easily confused with the Plaza Hotel downtown, and indeed their styles are quite similar. This exclusive brick hotel also caters predominately to traveling executives and diplomats, although its discreet location tucked away on Calle Lyon in Providencia is more tranquil. The Park Plaza is a boutique hotel designed in the European style, with classic furniture and rich fabrics; adjoining the lobby is a small restaurant serving excellent French cuisine. All rooms have plenty of space and good light. The hotel is conveniently located near shops and a block from the Metro, but what really stands out is the Park Plaza's impeccable service. The Park Plaza has a second hotel around the corner, the **Park Suite Apartments** (Lota 2233; $100 1-bedroom, $180 2-bedroom), with 20 fully furnished guest rooms featuring spacious kitchenettes and living areas. Prices for these apartments are reduced for multiple-day stays.

Ricardo Lyon 207. (C) **2/372-4000.** Fax 2/233-6668. www.parkplaza.cl. 104 units. $150 standard double; $250 junior suite. Parking available. Metro: Los Leones. **Amenities:** Restaurant; bar; indoor pool; city tours and transfers to tennis and golf courts; gym; sauna; business center; room service; babysitting; laundry service; Internet. *In room:* A/C, TV, minibar, hair dryer, safe.

Sheraton Santiago *★★*   The gala Sheraton Santiago offers more room sizes and amenities than are possible to list in this description, especially since they added on the San Cristóbal Tower with conference centers and luxury executive rooms. The Sheraton sits apart from the city, facing the Río Mapocho and backing the Cerro San Cristóbal mountain; psychologically you're cut off from the city, but it's just 5 blocks from downtown Providencia. Anything over the 10th floor offers spectacular views. The rooms at the Sheraton vary according to their location within the hotel, but all are well appointed with the same high-quality linens and attractive furnishings. The new executive guest rooms and suites in the Tower complex are truly top-notch; each floor has its own butler, and there's a private lounge for breakfast or tea on the 21st floor. The Neptune Pool & Fitness Center is unbelievable, with a turquoise pool surrounded by murals and softly lit by skylights. With its crystal chandeliers and marble floors, the Sheraton is all about glamour whereas the Park Plaza is low-key elegance. Take note that the entire Sheraton can be sold out for a week at a time due to visiting conventioneers. Call or check their website for promotions.

Av. Santa María 1742. ⓒ **800/335-3535** in the U.S., or 2/233-5000. Fax 2/234-1066. www.sheraton.cl. 379 units. $125 double standard; $155 executive suite; San Cristóbal Tower: $190 executive double, $450 suite. AE, DC, MC, V. Metro: Pedro de Valdivia. **Amenities:** 3 restaurants; bar; outdoor and indoor pools; tennis courts; sauna; whirlpool; concierge; travel agency; rental car agency; business center; shopping gallery; salon and barber; massage; babysitting; laundry service. *In room:* A/C, TV, minibar, hair dryer, safe.

EXPENSIVE

Four Points Sheraton *★*   The Four Points has rooms that cost far less than the Santiago Sheraton (see above), but offer the same standard amenities. A bland exterior is virtually indistinguishable from the office buildings that surround it, but the location ensures quiet evenings. The hotel is a safe bet for anyone used to American chains: prompt, professional service and an attractive, shabby-chic design that nevertheless feels store-bought. The rose and cream decoration gives off warmth in the rooms, and along with simple yet fine furnishings creates an exceptionally comfortable place to spend the night. Corner suites come with walk-in closets. A great detail here is the rooftop pool and solarium.

Santa Magdalena 111. ⓒ **2/244-3344.** Fax 2/244-2442. www.starwood.com/fourpoints. 128 units. $110 double. AE, DC, MC, V. Metro: Los Leones. **Amenities:** Restaurant; bar; outdoor pool; gym; sauna; whirlpool; business center; room service; laundry service. *In room:* A/C, TV, minibar, coffeemaker.

Hotel Orly *★★ (Finds*   This irresistible boutique hotel is one of my favorites in Santiago, and it is close to absolutely everything. The Orly is housed in a renovated mansion with French-influenced architecture. The lobby has a few nooks with reading lights for relaxing and a small, glass-covered patio; there's also a bar and an eating area for breakfast. The interiors are white and accented with contemporary art and glowing light. Room sizes vary; doubles come with two twins or a full-size bed and are of average size; singles are claustrophobic. All rooms have desks, and suites have a sitting area within the same room. If you need peace and quiet, request a room in the back. One of the high points here is the hotel's friendly service.

Av. Pedro de Valdivia 027. ⓒ **2/231-8947.** Fax 2/252-0051. www.orlyhotel.com. 30 units, 2 suites. $77–$98 double; $100–$124 suite. AE, DC, MC, V. Metro: Pedro de Valdivia. **Amenities:** Cafe; bar; laundry service. *In room:* A/C, minibar, TV.

Los Españoles *★*   Los Españoles is part of the Best Western chain, although it has been independently run by the same family for 26 years, and the owners

Accommodations, Dining & Attractions in Providencia & Las Condes

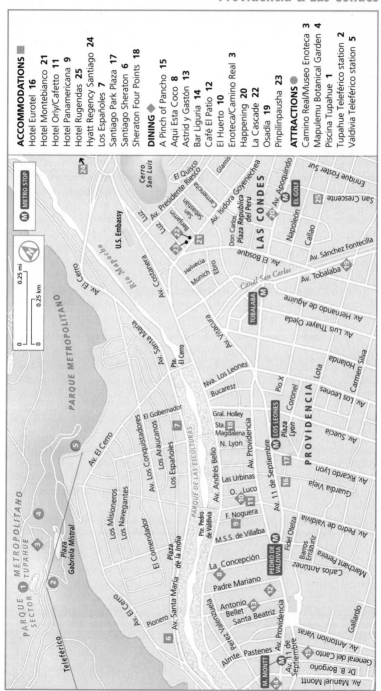

ACCOMMODATIONS ■
Hotel Eurotel **16**
Hotel Montebianco **21**
Hotel Orly/Cafetto **11**
Hotel Panamericana **9**
Hotel Rugendas **25**
Hyatt Regency Santiago **24**
Los Españoles **7**
Santiago Park Plaza **17**
Santiago Sheraton **6**
Sheraton Four Points **18**

DINING ◆
A Pinch of Pancho **15**
Aqui Esta Coco **8**
Astrid y Gastón **13**
Bar Liguria **14**
Café El Patio **12**
El Huerto **10**
Enoteca/Camino Real **3**
Happening **20**
La Cascade **22**
Osadia **19**
Pinpilinpausha **23**

ATTRACTIONS ●
Camino Real/Museo Enoteca **3**
Mapulemu Botanical Garden **4**
Piscina Tupahue **1**
Tupahue Teleférico station **2**
Valdivia Teleférico station **5**

want guests to feel as though they are in their own homes. The rooms are sized differently and laid out in a maze. Top floor suites have attached terrace patios, and all rooms are comfortable, modern, and neat. A restaurant/bar near the lobby serves a good breakfast, and the hotel will arrange airport transportation. This is a good hotel for travelers seeking dependable, familiar comfort, and for that reason it is popular with Americans. It sits beside the Mapocho River in a quiet residential area, and is a 10-minute walk to the commercial center of Providencia and the closest Metro station.

Los Españoles 2539. © 2/232-1824. Fax 2/233-1048. www.bestwestern.com. 48 units, 2 suites. $65 double; $75 suite. AE, DC, MC, V. Metro: Pedro de Valdivia. **Amenities:** Restaurant; bar; sauna; whirlpool; business center; room service; babysitting; laundry service. In room: A/C, TV, minibar, hair dryer.

MODERATE

Eurotel   The Eurotel is a European-style hotel frequented by French travelers; the owners themselves are French. It's in the hub of Providencia, near shopping and transportation, and is part of the Best Western chain. The Eurotel added 35 new units last year, and they are really worth asking for as the decoration is lighter and brighter than the '80s-style rooms in the older wing (dark furniture, low light, and smoked-glass furnishings). Standards are called executives, and junior suites come with a sitting area and desk; there are also five apartments, each with two bedrooms and a kitchenette, that go for $125. The restaurant is particularly agreeable, with a cheery atmosphere and a daily changing menu.

Guardia Vieja 285. ©/fax 2/251-6111. www.eurotel.com. 60 units. $59–$80 double. AE, DC, MC, V. Metro: Los Leones. **Amenities:** Restaurant; bar; concierge; business center; babysitting; laundry service. In room: A/C, TV, minibar, hair dryer, iron, safe.

Hotel Club Presidente ★ *Value*   The Hotel Club Presidente is one of the best values in this category. The rooms here are fresh, tidy, and immensely comfortable, although a little on the small side and slightly dark. The Presidente is a small hotel but doesn't skimp on friendly, professional service. The compact, white foyer is decorated with Peruvian gold mirrors; from here a hall leads to a restaurant and a great patio draped in foliage and serenaded by a bubbling fountain. The hotel is located on a residential street just a 3-minute walk away from the subway, about halfway between Providencia and downtown. This is another hotel that offers airport transfer service, and the price is just unbeatable. The Club Presidente also owns the **Apart-Hotel Club Presidente** in Las Condes at Luis Thayer Ojeda 558 (© 2/233-5652), with double rooms of the same quality as this hotel, plus a full kitchen—a great deal for extended stays in Santiago. Rates for a two-bedroom apartment run from $72 to $83.

Av. Eliodoro Yañez 867. © 2/235-8015. Fax 2/235-9148. www.presidente.cl. 50 units. $44–$50 double. Metro: Salvador. **Amenities:** Restaurant; bar; room service; laundry service. In room: A/C, TV, minibar.

Hotel Panamericana Providencia ★★ *Kids*   Perhaps the best feature of the Panamericana (formerly Hotel Aloha) is its outdoor pool, surrounded by greenery and fronted by a seating area covered by a white fabric awning with curtains. It's such a refreshing, tranquil place that you almost won't believe you're on a busy street in Providencia. The lobby entrance crosses a trickling pond shrouded in leafy plants, viewable from the inside thanks to glass panels. The rooms are identical, and all are smartly furnished, colorful, and filled with natural light, as is the rest of the hotel. Prices include a buffet breakfast at the hotel's full-service restaurant, which also offers a menu primarily of seafood, pastas, and meat. The Panamericana frequently offers weekend deals.

Francisco Noguera 146. © **2/233-2230**. Fax 2/233-2230. www.panamericanahoteles.cl. 66 units. $75 double; $105 suite. AE, DC, MC, V. Metro: Pedro de Valdivia. **Amenities:** Restaurant; bar; outdoor pool; city tours. *In room:* A/C, TV, minibar.

LAS CONDES
VERY EXPENSIVE

Hyatt Regency Santiago ★★★   In 1992, the Hyatt brought a whole new concept in five-star luxury to Santiago: 310 spacious, opulent rooms, hip restaurants, a plethora of services, and sky-high prices. The Hyatt is a 24-story atrium tower with two adjacent wings and four glass elevators that whisk guests up to their split-level rooms and terraced suites. Inside it feels as spacious as an airport hanger. Unfortunately, for this reason the Hyatt can't help feeling somewhat antiseptic, a fact exacerbated by bland, uniform brown stone interiors. Nevertheless, guests are usually wowed by this behemoth and always rave about the flawless service provided by the staff. The palm-and-fern–fringed pool and fully staffed gym are superb. The Hyatt's standard rooms are accented with weathered blond wood and richly colored furnishings. They're as large as average suites, meaning the executive suites are enormous. Guests in suites enjoy their own 16th-floor private lounge for lingering over breakfast and soaking up the spectacular view. All rooms have sumptuous bathrooms. A complete business center rents out computers and cellphones. The lounge hosts daily tea, complete with a buffet of mouth-watering cakes, that is open to the public. You'll always need to take a taxi, because the location at the head of a crazy traffic loop makes it difficult to walk anywhere from here.

Av. Kennedy 4601. © **2/218-1234**. Fax 2/218-3155. www.santiago.hyatt.com. 310 units, 26 suites. $225–$320 double; $375–$670 suite. AE, DC, MC, V. **Amenities:** 3 restaurants; bar; outdoor pool; tennis courts; gym; sauna; whirlpool; concierge; American Airlines office; Hertz car-rental office; business center; shopping arcade; salon; room service; massage; babysitting; laundry service; solarium; valet service; billiards room (suites only). *In room:* A/C, TV, minibar, hair dryer, safe.

EXPENSIVE

Hotel Montebianco ★   This small hotel is a good choice for travelers seeking a Las Condes address with cheaper prices than the Hyatt or the Ritz-Carlton. Located in the midst of restaurant alley in the El Bosque area of Las Condes, the Montebianco has attractively decorated, Mediterranean-style interiors with white stucco walls and a full-service restaurant. The rooms are average-size with large bathrooms, but if you need elbow space, book a Montebianco Pieza suite, which comes complete with a walk-in closet and an attached patio, for an additional $15. One of the perks here is the Montebianco's private minibus, which it uses for city tours, tours to outlying destinations, and airport pickup, all at an extra charge.

Av. Isidora Goyenechea 2911. © **2/232-5034**. Fax 2/233-0420. www.hotelmontebianco.cl. 33 units. $92 Grand double; $105 suite with patio. AE, DC, MC, V. Metro: El Golf. **Amenities:** Restaurant; room service; business center; laundry; city tours. *In room:* A/C, TV, safe.

Hotel Rugendas ★★   The newer Hotel Rugendas is a high-quality choice in Las Condes for its cozy accommodations and excellent amenities that seem too good to be true for the price. Located on a leafy street a few blocks from busy Av. Apoquindo, the hotel is housed in a tall brick building whose top floor is encased with glass; here you'll find a game room with card tables and a billiards table, not to mention a breathtaking view. The Rugendas's state-of-the-art gym is open 24 hours a day, and there is a sauna. Thick, golden curtains and bedspreads, a country decor, and large wooden headboards accent each room. Rooms on the upper floors have great views of the Andes, and a few have terraces. A Tuscan-style restaurant serves wonderful cuisine and an abundant breakfast buffet; there's also outdoor seating under large canvas umbrellas. Professional service and frequent promotions round out this premium hotel.

Callao 3121. ⓒ/fax **2/655-1881.** www.rugendas.cl. 48 units. $145 double. AE, DC, MC, V. Metro: El Golf. **Amenities:** Restaurant; bar; gym; sauna; game room; concierge; business center; laundry. *In room:* A/C, TV, minibar, hair dryer, safe.

Ritz-Carlton Santiago ✦✦✦   Although this book went to press before the Ritz-Carlton's grand opening, it is widely expected to be the finest five-star hotel in the city. Conveniently located near shops, restaurants, and the thriving economic hub of Santiago, the Ritz-Carlton's bland brick exterior belies its handsome interiors. The hotel's lobby, which has a two-story rotunda and floors made of imported marble with a Mediterranean-style black and gold inlay, features a lounge with frequent drink and appetizer service, and there is a plush wine bar. Their Restaurant Mediterráneo has a terrace for outside dining. The guest rooms have been decorated in floral designs in blues, greens, and reds, all made of plush silk and brocade and with custom-made South American furnishings. Club level rooms are accessible only by elevator key and feature upgraded amenities. Of course, the Ritz-Carlton provides noteworthy service, with a multilingual staff and sharp attention to detail. The state-of-the-art gym deserves special mention for its location on the top floor and beneath a tremendous glass dome, offering a spectacular view of the city and the Andes.

El Alcalde 15. ⓒ **800/241-3333** from the U.S., or 2/362-9619. Fax 2/362-9640. www.ritzcarlton.com. 205 units total, 52 Club Level rooms, 15 Executive Suites, 1 Ritz-Carlton suite. Please check website or call for rates. AE, DC, MC, V. Metro: El Golf. **Amenities:** 3 restaurants; bar; indoor rooftop pool; gym; sauna; whirlpool; concierge; car rental; business center; salon; room service; massage; babysitting; laundry service; valet service. *In room:* A/C, TV, minibar, hair dryer, safe.

4 Where To Dine

Santiago's gastronomic scene is currently undergoing a revolution, and hungry diners can expect to find dozens upon dozens of innovative restaurants that serve updated Chilean cuisine. Ethnic restaurants, led by a growing sushi craze, have slowly made their way into the market. Santiago's downtown caters to business folk and most restaurants are open for lunch only. It is possible to eat quite cheaply in the downtown area; most restaurants have a *menú del día* or *menú ejecutivo,* a fixed-price lunch for $4 to $7 that includes an appetizer, main course, beverage or wine, coffee, and dessert. *Autoservicios,* or self-service restaurants, abound, and most restaurants advertise their prices on sandwich boards or on signs posted near the front door. These restaurants are a dime a dozen, and quality is about the same.

Bellavista is perhaps the most popular gastronomic center. This artistic and intellectual haven has bred a mind-boggling number of hip restaurants, from Chilean to Cuban to Mediterranean. A few of the local favorites are listed below, but you could really just stroll the streets until something strikes your fancy. The same could be said for El Bosque Norte in the Las Condes district. Both El Bosque and its parallel street Avenida Isidora Goyenechea are lined door to door with a potpourri of flavorful offerings. Don't forget that most major hotels have outstanding restaurants open to the public. Highlights are the Hyatt's **Anakena** and **Matsuri** restaurants, the Sheraton's **El Cid** restaurant, the Intercontinental's **Bice** restaurant, and the Plaza San Francisco's **Bristol** restaurant. Chile is to seafood what Argentina is to beef; don't miss out on the wonderful varieties it has to offer.

DOWNTOWN

There are a cluster of restaurants around the tiny plaza Mulato Gil de Castro, really your best bet for evening dining if you are staying downtown and don't feel like going far. However, almost everything is closed on Sunday. In addition to restaurants listed below, at the plaza try **La Pérgola de la Plaza** (② 2/639-3604; open Mon–Sun 8am–4pm), a pretty cafe with a good fixed-price lunch menu, or **"R"** (② 2/664-9844; open Mon–Sat 12:30–4:30pm and 7:30pm–1:30am), a cozy spot for wine and conversation. For food to go, try **Chez Henry** on the Plaza de Armas (② 2/696-6612; open daily 9am–11pm). Parking is nearly impossible in this area, so walk or take a cab.

EXPENSIVE

Le Due Torri ★★ ITALIAN   Set back from busy Calle San Antonio, the classic Le Due Torri serves more than 20 kinds of pasta and other Italian favorites, as well as international fish and meat entrees. It offers excellent service and great food to match. For a light lunch, try the vast, colorful antipasto bar that offers one trip around for $10. Walls made of wood and river rock create a warm atmosphere. This is an expensive, semiformal setting that sees many executives during the lunch hours, usually wining and dining clients.

San Antonio 258. ② 2/639-7609. Main courses $7–$15. AE, DC, MC, V. Mon–Fri 12:30–11pm.

Squadritto ★ ITALIAN/INTERNATIONAL   Squadritto is on a charming, leafy street near the Plaza Mulato Gil de Castro, and its Tuscan-style dining room is a preferred setting for businesspeople in the area. It's semiformal, with a warm interior filled with plants and twinkling lights—and a choice restaurant if you're looking for fine cuisine and a special place to dine. The fresh pastas are superb, with items such as salmon ravioli in a bay shrimp sauce, but there's lots else on offer, including grilled fish, beef, chicken seasoned with herbs or a light sauce, and an extensive wine list.

Rosal 332. ② 2/632-2121. Reservations recommended. Main courses $7–$12. AE, DC, MC, V. Daily 1–3pm and 7:30–11pm.

MODERATE

Bar Nacional CHILEAN   This traditional, diner-like restaurant has been a hit with downtown workers for decades, despite being slightly overpriced. Typical Chilean fare is served, such as empanadas, *cazuela* (a hearty chicken soup), and steak and fries, as well as surprisingly good fresh juices. There is a fixed-price lunch, which is typically gone by 3:30pm. The atmosphere is colorful, with a dated interior that serves as a great backdrop for the characters who come in to eat, gossip, and smoke, in no particular order. Although there are two Bar Nacionals (another at Paseo Huérfanos), go to the one on Bandera.

Bandera 317. ② 2/695-3368. Main courses $7–$12; sandwiches $3–$4. DC, MC, V. Mon–Sat 8am–11pm.

Don Vitorino INTERNATIONAL/CHILEAN   This cozy, brick-and-wood restaurant is housed in a 16th-century annex of the neighboring Iglesia de la Veracruz and features a tiny ceramic patio with a bubbling fountain. The Don Vitorino serves simply prepared fish, meat, and homemade pastas: Try the Peri-Peri filet of beef marinated in the chef's 26 secret ingredients, and finish it off with a slice of fresh raspberry cheesecake. A good fixed-price lunch is $7, and offers more than just one option. In the evening, candlelit tables exude romance.

Lastarria 138. ② 2/639-5263. Main courses $9–$14. DC, MC, V. Mon–Thurs 12:30–4pm and 7:30pm–1am; Fri–Sat 12:30–4pm and 7:30pm–2am.

Gatopardo ✦ MEDITERRANEAN/CHILEAN   Tasty nouvelle cuisine has made this restaurant a local favorite. During lunch, executives head over for a fixed-price menu that can include pork loin in herb and curry sauce or for a run through the fresh salad bar, which, with the wine and dessert included, makes $8 seem like a steal. Gatopardo mixes Chilean, Mediterranean, and Bolivian specialties that might include spinach-ricotta ravioli with chopped walnuts in a Roquefort sauce. Bar appetizers are varied, from tacos and quesadillas to steamed mussels. The light, airy interior has mustard-colored walls and an atrium supported by giant oak trunks felled by an earthquake in the south of Chile.

Lastarria 192. ✆ 2/633-6420. Main courses $8–$15. AE, DC, MC, V. Mon–Fri 12:30–3:30pm and 7:30pm–midnight; Sat 7:30pm–1am.

Kintaro ✦ JAPANESE   This very plain, but excellent, Japanese restaurant is a favorite among writers and actors in the area, and serves some of the best sushi in Santiago. The sashimi is wonderfully fresh, and they make creative rolls often made of tuna, which is not found in every sushi bar in Chile. The chef, a native of Japan, is also the owner.

Monjitas 460 ✆ 2/638-2448. Main courses $4–$9. AE, DC, MC, V. Mon–Sat 12:30–3pm and 7:30–11pm.

Les Assassins ✦ FRENCH   Undeniably one of Santiago's most romantic restaurants, this tiny French bistro near the Mulato Gil de Castro plaza has been a downtown favorite for years. The food won't make you say "wow," but the candlelit ambience makes up for it. Expect French classics such as coq au vin and rabbit stew, and a few surprises such as sole in snow crab sauce, and wash it all down with a cold bottle of Chilean chardonnay.

Merced 297. ✆ 2/638-4280. Main courses $6–$8. DC, MC, V. Mon–Fri 12:30–3:30pm and 7pm–11am; Sat 7pm–midnight.

Picada Ana María ✦✦ *Finds* TRADITIONAL CHILEAN   This restaurant is a classic—I always recommend it to diners seeking traditional Chilean food and an old-world ambience. The Picada started out as that: a *picada,* or restaurant that serves inexpensive Chilean snacks, but it soon grew into a full-service restaurant. In a handsome antique home, you'll find typical Chilean cuisine and wild game entrees such as venison, boar and pheasant. The uniqueness of this establishment draws politicians and heavyweight businessmen at lunch, and families on weekends. It is a great place to people-watch. It's close to the Alameda, but on an old, somewhat shabby street, so it's best to take a cab.

Club Hípico 476. ✆ 2/671-3099. Reservations recommended. Main courses $7–$12. AE, DC, MC, V. Mon–Sat noon–4pm and 7pm–midnight.

27 de Nueva York ✦ INTERNATIONAL   Located in the heart of the financial district, the 27 de Nueva York is an ideal place to stop for lunch if you are around the Bolsa de Comercio or Plaza de Armas. A warm, attractive dining area is a favorite with businessmen and women. The restaurant serves grilled meats, fish, and salads, and it also offers an *autoservicio,* or self-serve, restaurant next door, which is recommended if you're in a hurry.

Nueva York 27. ✆ 2/699-1555. Reservations recommended. Main courses $5–$9. AE, DC, MC, V. Mon–Fri 8am–11pm.

INEXPENSIVE

Confitería Torres *Moments* CHILEAN   Confitería Torres is recommended more for the turn-of-the-century ambience than for the food. Once you spy the mirrors fogged black around the edges and droopy chairs, you'll know that this is indeed Santiago's oldest restaurant. Old-timers will rave about the cuisine, but really it's just the same old mix-and-match menu of fries and pan-cooked meat and fish—not bad, but not necessarily exciting, either. Drop in for a look if you're in the neighborhood.

Bernardo O'Higgins 1570. (*C*) 2/698-6220. Main courses $6–$10. AE, MC, V. Daily 10:30am–1am.

El Mercado ★★ *Moments* SEAFOOD   Throughout the Mercado (see "Seeing the Sights," later in this chapter) are restaurants and booths where you can savor traditional favorites such as *paila marina,* a seafood stew cooked with cilantro, *ceviche,* fish cooked in lemon juice, or the much-adored abalone *loco.* It must be said that the food quality is better at other seafood restaurants; what you're here for is the atmosphere. The best-known, easiest to find, and most expensive restaurant here is Donde Augusto; however, several smaller and more economical outfits sit just at the edge of the central market.

Enter on Ismael Valdés Vergara between 21 de Mayo and Puente. No phone. Main course prices vary. AE, DC, MC, V. Sun–Thurs 6am–4pm; Fri 6am–8pm; Sat 6am–6pm. Metro: Cal y Canto.

Govindas VEGETARIAN   This casual Indian restaurant run by Hare Krishnas offers good, inexpensive vegetarian food. It has been very popular for some time now with office workers for its creative Chilean and Indian-influenced dishes, such as curried stir-fry and eggplant pizza. You'll sometimes find crepes stuffed with seasoned vegetables, and there are always soups and sandwiches.

Compañia 1489. (*C*) 2/673-0892. Main courses $2–$5. No credit cards. Mon–Sat 12:30–11pm.

BELLAVISTA
EXPENSIVE

Cocoa ★ PERUVIAN   Don't pass up Peruvian food because you're in Chile. The country's northern neighbors are known for their spicy, flavorful food, and this restaurant is a good place to give it a try. Start with a pisco sour—two's the limit—the "typical" Chilean drink that Peruvians claim originated in their country. Start with a *ceviche* (chopped fish and onion in lemon juice) and follow it with a shrimp-stuffed filet with a bacon and corn sauce, or a *lomo saltado,* beef, onion, pepper and french fries tossed together and guaranteed to ruin your diet. Warm and romantic atmosphere.

Antonio López de Bello 102. (*C*) 2/735-0634. Reservations not accepted. Main courses $6–$11. AE, DC, MC, V. Mon–Fri noon–4pm and 8pm–midnight; Sat 8pm–midnight.

Como Agua Para Chocolate ★★ MEXICAN   This restaurant opened to rave reviews for its innovative Mexican dishes and hip design, including terracotta ceramic floors, an indoor fountain, brass bed frames, and other trimmings influenced by the movie that gave this restaurant its name *(Like Water for Chocolate).* You will find fajitas on the menu, but most dishes reflect authentic and revised traditional Mexican fare rather than Tex-Mex, with exotic entrees such as pheasant in mango sauce. It's a great place to go with friends for the plentiful variety of shared platters.

Constitución 88. (*C*) 2/777-8740. Main courses $11–$18. DC, MC, V. Daily 1–4pm and 8pm–midnight.

San Fruttoso ★★ ITALIAN   After earning acclaim in Asia, Peru, and the United States for his fine Italian restaurants, Roberto Revello moved to Chile and continued to find success with his restaurant San Fruttoso. Elegant dining and superb cuisine are guaranteed within the warm brick walls of this Bellavista favorite. The menu serves up highlights such as risotto, porcini mushrooms, tiramisu, and wild hare tortellini in cream. Expect to find creative takes on fish, meats, and pastas; sharp service; and an extensive wine list.

Mallinkrodt 102. © **2/777-1476.** Main courses $8–$20. AE, DC, MC, V. Mon–Sat 1:15–3:30pm and 8–11:30pm; Sun lunch only 1:15–3:30pm.

MODERATE

Azul Profundo ★★ SEAFOOD   If you love seafood, the "Deep Blue" is the place to come. Salmon, conger eel, swordfish, sea bass, and more come grilled, or *a la plancha* (it comes sizzling out of the kitchen on a cast-iron plate), and are served alone or with tantalizing sauces. Everything on the menu is appealing; therefore, decisions are not easily made, so try getting started with an appetizer of one of eight different kinds of *ceviche*. The cozy, nautical-themed ambience includes a wooden siren hanging from a mock ship's bow, as well as bathroom doors that look like they lead to a sailor's bunk.

Constitución 111. © **2/738-0288.** Main courses $7–$13. DC, MC, V. Daily 1–4pm and 8:30pm–midnight.

Etniko ★★ ASIAN   Etniko is one of Santiago's hippest restaurants, serving Asian-influenced cuisine to the modern beat of house music played by resident DJs. The place is chic, sophisticated, and frequented by Santiago's stylish yuppies. The menu offers a diverse selection, but the mainstay is the 16 varieties of sushi. Also on offer are Japanese tempura and Chinese and Vietnamese stir-frys. The bar is a great place for a cocktail, and there is an extensive wine and champagne menu. Don't expect the place to fill until 10pm.

Constitución 172. © **2/732-0119.** Main courses $7–$14. AE. Reservations recommended. Daily noon–4pm and 8pm–midnight (until 2am Fri–Sat).

Kilometre 11860 ★★ FRENCH BISTRO   The two French wine lovers who own Kilometre came to Chile to sample its varietals and ended up opening this bistro to offer what is possibly the best wine list in town. There are nearly 150 varieties of Chilean wine on the menu, including export varieties you won't find in stores. Each week they choose a special, expensive wine by the glass to try so you won't have to buy an entire bottle. The food includes French staples such as foie gras, baked goat cheese, duck confit, tarte tatin, fish, and meats. Lunch is only available on Friday, when there is a fixed-price menu for $11. The terrific patio has an outdoor seating area and a bar.

Dardignac 0145. © **2/777-0410.** Main courses $10–$17. AE. Mon–Thurs and Sat 8pm–1am; Fri lunch only noon–4pm.

La Tasca MEDITERRANEAN   La Tasca is part restaurant, part cafe, and dinner or lunch may be served at either side from the same menu. The cozy restaurant has long, dark wood tables, wood beams, and white stucco walls; the cafe features tiny, candlelit tables with red tablecloths. The simple Mediterranean dishes include meats and fish seasoned with homemade ingredients, and there is a good selection of wine by the glass. The staff is friendly, and there is jazz piano in the cafe starting at midnight on Saturday.

Purísima 165. © **2/735-3901.** Main courses $5–$9. AE, DC, MC, V. Mon–Fri noon–1:30am; Sat noon–3am.

INEXPENSIVE

Caramaño ★ CHILEAN   They call themselves the "anti-restaurant," and they're probably right. The Caramaño is totally anonymous from the street, and diners used to miss it until they put a sign up this year. Just ring the front bell to enter. Inside, graffiti-scrawled walls are something of a contrast to the tables filled with men and women in suits. Service is casual, and the food classic Chilean: inexpensive and good.

Purísima 257. ⓒ 2/737-7043. Main courses $3–$9. AE, DC, MC, V. Daily 1–4pm and 7pm–12:30am.

Galindo CHILEAN This local favorite is a hit for its cheap prices and its *comida casera:* simple, hearty dishes like your mother used to make—if your mother were Chilean, that is. Virtually any kind of typical meal served in Chilean homes can be found here, including *pastel de choclo* (a ground beef and chicken casserole) and *cazuela* (chicken soup with vegetables). The atmosphere is very casual; in the evening the restaurant serves as a meeting place for writers, artists, and other local folk to share a bottle of wine and good conversation. There's additional seating outside on the sidewalk, and it's open late into the evening.

Dardignac 098. ⓒ 2/777-0116. Main courses $3.50–$9; fixed lunch $5. AE, DC, MC, V. Mon–Sat noon–3am.

PROVIDENCIA

Avenida Suecia in Providencia and the several streets that surround it are commonly referred to as *gringolandia,* or "little America," for its eerie resemblance to a commercial center in the United States. Happy hours and a couple of restaurants serving typical American food, including Cajun, can be found here, but opinions about the neighborhood are mixed. Either way, there are a few gems to be rooted out here, and a few bars good for a nightcap. The best way to find them is to simply head over and take a look.

EXPENSIVE

Aquí Está Coco ★★★ SEAFOOD This one-of-a-kind restaurant not only serves superb seafood, it's also a fun place to dine. Housed in a 140-year-old home with more nooks and crannies than one can reasonably navigate, the restaurant is owned by one charismatic Jorge "Coco" Pacheco, who gave the place its name: "Here's Coco." Jorge traveled the world for 3 years and brought back boxes of crazy knickknacks and a wealth of tantalizing recipes, both of which give Aquí Está Coco its unique flavor. Nearly every kind of seafood is offered, including trout stuffed with crab, hake, swordfish, cod, sea bass, and more, served with sauces such as caper, black butter, or tomato-wine. The appetizers are mouth-watering, such as crab cakes or broiled scallops in a barnacle sauce.

La Concepción 236. ⓒ 2/235-8649. Main courses $9–$16. AE, DC, MC, V. Mon–Sat 1–3pm and 8–10:30pm.

Astrid y Gastón ★★★ INTERNATIONAL/CHILEAN Frequently rated as one of the top five eateries in Santiago, Astrid y Gastón is named for the Peruvian and German couple who own and run this wonderful restaurant with such care. Beyond the outstanding food served here, the service is truly impeccable, and they have an on-site sommelier and a lengthy wine list (for variety, it is tied with Kilometre 11680). The chef uses the finest ingredients, combined so that each plate bursts with flavor and personality; here you'll find French, Spanish, Peruvian, and Japanese influences. Dessert orders are usually placed early, so they can make each one specially. Try the duck salad, the glazed pork, or the tuna filet bathed in a honey sauce.

Antonio Bellet 201. ⓒ 2/650-9125. Reservations required. Main courses $10–$15. AE, DC, MC, V. Mon–Sat 1–3:30pm and 8pm–midnight.

De Cangrejo a Conejo ★★ *Finds* INTERNATIONAL/CHILEAN This modern, fashionable restaurant doesn't have a sign hanging in front, so ring the bell for admittance. The name means "from crab to rabbit," and keeping true to its name this restaurant offers nearly everything imaginable, from lamb chops in wine, to tuna with a ginger/soy sauce, to crab cakes and rabbit tenderloin stew. The huge U-shaped bar is a good place for a drink and conversation, or to grab a quick bite or appetizer. Word of mouth has popularized this restaurant. Try their berry crumble for dessert. Waiters are a bit too cool to provide great service, but the overall atmosphere is lively and enjoyable.

Av. Italia 805. ℃ 2/634-4041. Reservations recommended. Main courses $7–$12. AE, DC, MC, V. Mon–Sat 1–3:30pm and 8pm–midnight.

Enoteca/Camino Real ⭐ (Moments) INTERNATIONAL/CHILEAN There's nothing quite like dining in Santiago with the city lights twinkling at your feet. This restaurant/wine bar and museum is located atop Cerro San Cristóbal, affording sweeping views across the valley and up to the Andes. Smog is an issue if you come for lunch, but even bad air can't mask the thousands of lights at night. The cuisine is good, although one could certainly find more outstanding restaurants in the *barrios* below. What you're here for is the view. The menu serves a wide mix of international cuisine, including beef, chicken, seafood, and pasta. An on-site wine museum and cellar guarantees an excellent selection.

Parque Metropolitano, Cerro San Cristóbal. ℃ 2/232-1758. Main courses $15–$25; fixed lunches/dinners $20. AE, DC, MC, V. Daily 12:30–3:30pm and 8pm–midnight.

MODERATE

Café el Patio ⭐ VEGETARIAN A soothing break from hectic Avenida Providencia, the location at the back of a tranquil little plaza is just one thing that makes this vegetarian restaurant so enjoyable. Fresh salads include Greek, chef, Chinese, and more, and all vegetables come from the owner's organic farm. El Patio offers several seafood dishes as well, such as shrimp and mushroom *ceviche,* all served by good-looking waiters dressed in black. This restaurant is especially nice when jazz musicians play on Thursday and Friday. There are a few tables outside in the dark wood-and-glass-walled patio.

Av. Providencia 1670. ℃ 2/236-1251. Main courses $5.50–$9. DC, MC, V. Mon–Thurs noon–midnight; Fri–Sat noon–1:30am; Sun 12:30–4pm.

El Huerto ⭐ VEGETARIAN Some call the popular El Huerto the best vegetarian restaurant in Santiago, and with reason: The chefs whip up creative, appetizing dishes, from burritos to pasta to Chinese stir-fries. Add one of their fresh apple, raspberry, or peach juices, and it makes for a wonderful meal. Prices have risen slightly recently, and the owners have opened up a more economical cafe, La Huerta, next door (at the left), with a limited but good menu and fixed-price lunch. The softly lit, mellow dining room of El Huerto is a cool place to relax on a summer day.

Orrego Luco 054. ℃ 2/233-2690. Main courses $4–$10. AE, DC, MC, V. Mon–Thurs 12:30pm–midnight; Fri–Sat 12:30pm–1am. Cafe opens at 9am.

A Pinch of Pancho ⭐⭐ NORTH AMERICAN This restaurant serves excellent American-style fare, such as barbecue ribs, Cajun chicken, and Caesar salads, in a rather odd crossover atmosphere between comfortable elegance and American kitsch. The place is hidden behind a white, plant-covered metal fence; you'll see a *Miami Herald* newsstand by the door. Impeccable service and a menu that is 100% recognizable by Americans are the reasons you usually see a few U.S. businessmen having lunch here on weekdays. Don't miss the mouth-watering desserts, even apple pie a la mode.

General de Canto 45. ℃ 2/235-1700. Reservations recommended. Main courses $6–$13. AE, DC, MC, V. Daily 1–3:30pm and 8–11:30pm.

INEXPENSIVE

Bar Liguria ★★ *Finds* CHILEAN BISTRO   This place is one of my favorites in Santiago. It's vibrant and warm and is the "in" spot in Providencia for actors, businesspeople, and young people in the area. It's a great restaurant with tiny alcoves and corners to hide in, and a long wooden bar for dining and drinking. The menu is bistro-style, with about 15 entrees and a selection of soups and sandwiches. The walls are covered with kitsch: movie posters, street signs, pictures of soccer stars, advertisements, and so on. Good service is provided by plentiful waiters in black bow ties. In the evening, the Bar Liguria is tremendously popular, especially for the potent pisco sours, and you might have to wait for a table. It's a great place for outdoor dining, but get here early.

Av. Providencia 1373. © 2/235-7914. Main courses $4–$9. No credit cards. Mon–Wed 10am–noon; Thurs–Sat 10am–2am. Metro: Pedro de Valdivia.

Cafetto CAFE   Cafetto is a nice little cafe to have a snack or meal at any time of the day. It's popular for its creative fixed lunches, which usually sell out before 3pm, and for staying open all day. The menu offers soups, sandwiches, pizzas, pastas, and more, and a bright dining area enclosed in glass.

Av. Pedro de Valdivia 23 © 2/252-0053. Main courses $4–$7. AE, DC, MC, V. Mon–Sat 7am–1am.

LAS CONDES/EL BOSQUE/VITACURA

Around El Bosque and Goyenechea streets you'll find everything and anything, from upscale French cuisine to a fast-food court. If you're looking to spot other gringos like yourself, especially those who live in Santiago, you'll find them at **New York Bagel,** Roger de Flor 2894 (© 2/246-3060), or **Cafe Melba,** Don Carlos 2898 (© 2/232-4546). Cafe Melba is a bustling, friendly restaurant and an excellent spot for lunch—and it serves American-style breakfasts such as eggs Benedict, early too (it opens at 7:30am on weekdays; 8:30 weekends). Their delicious, seasonally changing menu features pastas, salads, meats, and seafood, and there's an Internet cafe and an outdoor seating area. You'll need a cab to reach restaurants in Vitacura but they're well worth seeking out.

EXPENSIVE

Agua ★★★ FUSION   After receiving rave reviews by dozens of critics, not to mention being named one of *Conde Nast Traveler*'s "Best New Restaurants," Agua quickly became the chic place to be seen, and for good reason: the hip, minimalist design of concrete and glass is as fashionable and tasteful as the fusion cuisine. The young chef at Agua has catapulted to culinary fame in Santiago for his creations, such as tuna, either tartare or rolled with king crab and served over an avocado and shrimp relish. Agua is known for its extensive and noteworthy seafood dishes, but dishes such as pork loin stuffed with mushrooms and foie gras are outstanding as well. The wine list is superb.

Nueva Costanera 3467. © 2/263-0008. Reservations recommended. Main courses $8–$15. AE, DC, MC, V. Mon–Sat 1–3:30pm and 8pm–midnight.

Europeo ★★★ CENTRAL EUROPEAN   Europeo, which some consider one of the best restaurants in Santiago, is named for its cuisine: central European–based cuisine expertly prepared by the restaurant's Swiss-born-and-trained chef. In a word, the food is heavenly, and the offer of a more upscale main dining area and a more economical adjoining cafe makes the Europeo suitable for any budget. Foie gras sautéed in a reduction of white wine; leg of lamb in a merlot sauce and served over polenta; and king crab ravioli stand out on the menu, as do the Austrian-style desserts. The cafe, La Brasserie, offers a less-formal ambience and a menu that is not as elaborate as the restaurant's, but of excellent quality nonetheless. It's close to the Hyatt.

Alonso de Córdova 2417. © **2/208-3603**. Reservations recommended for the restaurant. Main courses $10–$15. AE, DC, MC, V. Mon–Sat 12:30–4:30pm and 7–11pm.

Happening ★★ ARGENTINE/CHILEAN   If you're in the mood for steak, this Argentine-owned restaurant (there's another Happening in Buenos Aires) is your place. The grilled meat selection is endless, cooked on an enormous indoor barbecue and served in a refined, attractive ambience. There's also a variety of salads, fish, and pastas to choose from. It's housed on a busy corner in a large, gray building. You can bring your clients here for lunch or enjoy a candlelit dinner in the evening.

Av. Apoquindo 3090. © **2/233-2301**. Reservations recommended. Main courses $7–$13. AE, DC, MC, V. Mon–Sat noon–4pm and 8pm–midnight.

La Cascade ★★ FRENCH   This traditional French restaurant has been on the scene since 1962, drawing Santiago's elite to savor traditional dishes such as coq au vin, duck à l'orange, escargot, and goose liver paté. The menu is varied and includes meat, fowl, and seafood entrees, as well as an extensive wine list. Waiters deliver outstanding personal attention, and the atmosphere is elegant and stylish, with attractive paintings and white linen tablecloths.

Av. Isidora Goyenechea 2930. © **2/232-2798**. Reservations recommended. Main courses $7–$15. AE, DC, MC, V. Mon–Sat noon–4pm and 8pm–midnight.

Osadía ★★★ FUSION   One of Santiago's newest and most unique restaurants, Osadía boasts a fantastical design of semi-demolished brick walls painted white and dripping with candles and spidery lamps that dangle above each white linen table. The food is as out-there as the restaurant's decor, with high-concept blends of flavors and complicated presentations that can often be difficult to figure out how to eat. It's a superb place to dine, elegant yet fun, and they serve exquisite dishes such as rabbit cooked with tarragon and beer and served with spaetzle; crab ravioli with mushroom sauce; and smoked mussels in a cilantro vinaigrette. Save room for dessert.

Tobalaba 477. © **2/232-2732**. Reservations recommended. Main courses $9–$15. AE, DC, MC, V. Mon–Fri 1–4pm and 8pm–midnight and Sat 8pm–midnight.

Pinpilinpausha ★★ SPANISH   The long name means "butterfly" in Basque, the heritage of the Sanz family who has owned this restaurant since the 1940s. Pinpilinpausha operated downtown for 55 years, and though it relocated to Las Condes, the essential menu hasn't deviated too much, and still includes paella. The shellfish, fish, and meat dishes are all excellent, especially the conger eel stuffed with shrimp and served with a tart lemon sauce. The interiors are rustic Mediterranean, with terra-cotta walls and green-and-white checkered tablecloths.

Av. Isidora Goyenechea 2900. © **2/232-5800**. Main courses $10–$15. AE, DC, MC, V. Mon–Sat 12:30–11:30pm; Sun 12:30–4pm.

MODERATE

Akarana ★★ _Finds_ FUSION   Akarana is a welcome new addition to the El Bosque area, opened recently by the owner of the Cafe Melba, who is from New Zealand. She has created a menu that reflects the tastes from her home country, fusing Asian cuisine with New Zealand specialties to create a wonderful feast for the palate. Appetizers include gingery egg rolls and tempura, or try a plate of fresh oysters, served with one of three recipes. Move on to grilled, herbed sea bass with radish puree and aioli, one of their unconventional pizzas, or a steak with portobello mushrooms and Parmesan mashed potatoes. The white interiors are fresh and airy, and the wraparound patio dining area offers undoubtedly the most pleasant outdoor seating in the area.

Reyes Lavalle 3310. © 2/231-9667. Reservations recommended. Main courses $6–$10. AE, DC, MC, V. Daily noon–midnight.

INEXPENSIVE

Tiramisu ✦ PIZZA   Come to Tiramisu for big, thin-crust pizzas baked in a stone oven and served in a delightful atmosphere. With dozens and dozens of combinations from traditional to arugula with shaved Parmesan and artichokes, you'll have a hard time choosing. There are fresh, delicious salads, too, and desserts that of course include tiramisu. Outdoor seating is available. Tiramisu is very popular with the lunch crowd.

Av. Isidora Goyenechea 3141. © 2/335-5135. Main courses $4–$7. AE, DC, MC, V. Mon–Sun 1–4pm and 7pm–midnight.

5 Seeing the Sights

Visitors to Santiago should allow at least 2 or 3 days to get to know the city. But even if you have just 1 day in Santiago, you should be able to pack in a sizeable amount of the city's top attractions, because nearly all attractions lie within a short walk or taxi ride from each other.

The best place to begin is in *el centro,* the city's historic downtown and home to museums, cathedrals, cultural centers, and civic institutions housed within handsome, neoclassical-style buildings. If you enjoy marveling at stately mansions, you'll want to spend a half hour exploring the sinuous streets of the Barrio París-Londres and then head to Calle Dieciocho, a street whose stone palaces convey the wealth of Santiago's elite at the turn of the 20th century.

If you're lucky enough to have a smog-free day, you won't want to miss heading to the top of one of the city's hilltop parks for a sweeping view of the rugged, snowcapped Andes that rise dramatically behind the city. If you have a little more time and just feel like strolling the city streets and watching Santiaguinos go about their daily business, you'll want to spend an afternoon in the residential and commercial neighborhoods of Providencia and Las Condes.

DOWNTOWN HISTORIC & CIVIC ATTRACTIONS
PLAZA DE ARMAS

Begin your tour of Santiago at the **Plaza de Armas** ✦✦✦ (Metro: Estación Plaza de Armas). The plaza was founded by Pedro de Valdivia in 1541 as the civic nucleus of the country, and its importance was such that all distances to other parts of Chile were, and still are, measured from here.

The impressive plaza was surrounded by the Royal Court of Justice (now the Natural History Museum), the Governor's Palace (now the Central Post Office), the Metropolitan Cathedral, and the grand residences of principal conquistadors, including Valdivia himself. In the mid-1800s, the plaza was fitted with gardens and trees, creating a promenade that became a social center for fashionable society. The plaza is not only a wonderful place to sit, relax, or read, but is also a great place to watch the colorful characters milling about—old street photographers with box cameras, men lingering over chess games, shouting religious fanatics, office workers having their shoes shined, young couples strolling hand in hand, and artists hawking paintings.

There are several monuments here: a giant chiseled-stone sculpture dedicated to indigenous peoples; an equestrian statue of Pedro de Valdivia; a monument to the first Chilean Cardinal José María Caro; and *A la Libertad de América,* a marble statue commemorating independence from Spain.

Catedral Metropolitana and Museo de Arte Sagrado ★★   The Metropolitan Cathedral occupies nearly an entire city block, and it is the fifth cathedral to have been erected at this site. The cathedral began construction in 1748 but was completed in 1780 by the Italian architect Joaquín Toesca, who gave the building its neoclassical-baroque facade. Toesca virtually launched his career with this cathedral, and he went on to design many important buildings in colonial Chile, including La Moneda and the Governor's Palace. Tremendous doors made of cypress carved by Jesuits open into three interior naves with pews made of carved wood. The central nave holds the cathedral's ornate alter, brought from Munich in 1912 and made of marble, bronze, and lapis lazuli. Just off the main body of the church is the cathedral's religious museum, the Museo de Arte Sagrado, where you'll find a collection of paintings, furniture, antique manuscripts, and silverwork handcrafted by Jesuits.

Paseo Ahumada, on the west side of the plaza. No phone. Free admission. Mon–Sat 9am–7pm; Sun 9am–noon. Metro: Plaza de Armas.

Correo Central and Museo Postal   The pink, Renaissance-style Central Post Office was built in 1882 on the remains of what was once the colonial Governor's Palace and the post-independence Presidential Palace. After the building succumbed to fire in 1881, workers rebuilt, incorporating several of the old building's walls. In 1908, architect Ramón Feherman added a third floor and a gorgeous, metal-framed glass cupola. On the second floor, you'll find a small museum whose main interest is its stamp collection.

Calle Puente, north side of the plaza. 🕿 2/601-0141. Free admission. Mon–Fri 9am–5pm. Metro: Plaza de Armas.

Palacio de la Real Audiencia/Museo Histórico Nacional ★★★   Palacio de la Real was built between 1804 and 1807 by a student of the architect Toesca who followed his preference for neoclassical design. The building has undergone several transformations, but the facade is still intact. The Palacio functioned for 2 years as a Supreme Court under Spanish rule, and then became the site of the first Chilean congressional session following independence. Today, the Palacio holds the fascinating National History Museum, which displays more than 70,000 items from the colonial period, including antiques, clothing, suits of armor, weapons, home appliances, industrial gadgets, flags, you name it. There is also a collection of money and medallions, including tokens used at salt mines, and an interpretive timeline and photo montage of Chilean history.

Plaza de Armas 951. 🕿 2/681-4095. Admission 80¢ adults, 40¢ kids under 18; free Sun and holidays. Tues–Sat 10am–5:30pm; Sun and holidays 10am–1pm. Metro: Plaza de Armas.

NEAR THE PLAZA DE ARMAS

At the southwest corner of the plaza you'll find **Paseo Ahumada,** which bisects **Paseo Huérfanos** a block away; both are lively pedestrian walkways lined with shops and restaurants. The streets can get frenzied during the lunch hour, but it's a fun spot to watch Santiaguinos go about their business. This is also where you'll find a few of the city's renowned cafes that serve "coffee with legs," meaning waitresses in skimpy ensembles serving ogling businessmen from behind a stand-up bar. **Café Haiti** (© **2/697-1810**) and **Café Caribe** (© **2/639-5041**) are two of the better-known cafes, and because both are fairly tame compared to the raunchier versions with darkened windows, these two cafes are patronized by women as well as men.

Basílica de la Merced ★ One block from the Casa Colorada on Merced at the corner of MacIver sits this intriguing, neo-Renaissance-style church and museum. Built in 1735, the church boasts a magnificent Bavarian baroque pulpit and arched naves. The museum, surprisingly, has an excellent collection of Easter Island art, including wooden Moai sculptures. There are also 78 wood and ivory Christ Child figures, among other religious artifacts.

MacIver 341, corner of Merced. No phone. Admission 75¢ adults, 25¢ students. Tues–Fri 10am–1pm and 3–6pm; Sat 10am–1pm. Metro: Plaza de Armas.

Casa Colorada ★★ The Casa Colorada is a half block from the Plaza de Armas, an antique structure made of stone whose color gives it its name—"The Red House." It's widely regarded as the best-preserved colonial structure in Santiago, built between 1769 and 1779 as a residence for the first president of Chile, Mateo de Toro y Zambrano. Today, the Casa Colorada operates as the Santiago Museum, depicting the urban history of the city until the 19th century. The museum is small and fairly interesting, but is worth the visit to marvel at the architecture and browse through the museum's bookstore. A **visitor center** with information about Santiago is also located in the Casa Colorada.

Merced 860. © **2/633-0723**. Admission 70¢. Tues–Fri 10am–6pm; Sat 10am–5pm; Sun 10am–1pm. Metro: Plaza de Armas.

Ex-Congreso Nacional and Palacio de los Tribunales ★ Two blocks from Plaza de Armas you'll find these two grand civic buildings across the street from each other on Compañía. The ex–Congress Building, with its French neoclassical design and Corinthian pillars, is a handsome edifice inaugurated in 1901. The National Congress convened here until the coup d'état on September 11, 1973, which dissolved Congress; Pinochet eventually moved the Congress to Valparaíso. The dove-white building is surrounded by lush gardens, and is now occupied by a branch of the Ministry of Foreign Affairs. Across the street, the Palace of the Courts of Justice stretches the entire block. The Palace is home to the Supreme Court, the Appeals Court, and the Military Court, and it was the site of the birth of the First National Government Assembly. The building's stern exterior belies the beauty found once you step inside. Leave your ID at the front, and take a stroll through the exquisite hallway whose vaulted metal and glass ceiling runs the length of the building, dappling the walls with light.

Morandé and Compañía. No phone. Palacio: Mon–Fri 1–7pm.

Museo Chileno de Arte Precolombino ★★★ Heading back on Merced and past the plaza to Bandera, you'll find the excellent Chilean Museum of Pre-Columbian Art, housed in the old Royal Customs House that was built in neoclassical design in 1807. This is one of the better museums in Chile, both for its collection of pre-Columbian artifacts and its inviting design. There are more than 1,500 objects on display here, including textiles, metals, paintings, figurines, and ceramics spread through seven exhibition rooms. It's not a stuffy old museum, but a vivid exhibition of indigenous life and culture before the arrival of the Spanish. The material spans from Mexico to Chile, incorporating all regions of Latin America divided into four areas: Mesoamérica, Intermedia,

Andina, and Surandina. Each display is attractively mounted and infinitely absorbing. Downstairs there's a patio cafe and a well-stocked bookstore that also sells music, videos, and reproductions of Indian art, textiles, and jewelry.

Bandera 361. © **2/688-7348.** www.precolombino.cl. Admission $2 adults, free for students, free Sat, Sun, and holidays for everyone. Tues–Sat 10am–6pm; Sun and holidays 10am–2pm. Closed Mon.

PLAZA CONSTITUCION & THE COMMERCE CENTER

The Plaza Constitución, located between streets Agustinas, Morandé, Moneda, and Teatinos, is an expansive plaza used primarily as a pedestrian crossway. It's also the site of the famous **Palacio de la Moneda** ★★, the Government Palace that was first built as headquarters of the Royal Mint (hence its name). The largest building erected by the Spanish government during the 18th century, the Palace was criticized for being too ostentatious, but today it's considered one of the finest examples of neoclassical architecture in Latin America.

Joaquín Toesca, the Italian architect responsible for setting the neoclassical tone of civic buildings in Santiago, directed the design of the Palace until his death in 1799. From 1846 to 1958 it was the official presidential residence, and continued as presidential headquarters until the infamous coup d'état on September 11, 1973, when Pinochet's troops shelled and bombed the building until ex-President Allende surrendered by suicide. The military has since patched up the damage they inflicted.

Try to visit the Palace during the **changing of the guard** ★★, when hundreds of soldiers march in step in front of the Palace, every other day at 10am. Across Alameda is the **Plaza Bernardo O'Higgins.** His remains are buried under the monument dedicated to him in the center of the plaza.

One block from the plaza at Moneda and Bandera is the **Bolsa de Comercio** ★ (© **2/399-3000**), Santiago's stock market exchange, housed in a 1917 national monument building with a beautiful metal dome roof. Inside, traders group around La Rueda (The Wheel), a circular railing where they conduct hectic transactions— you can even watch the action Monday to Friday 10:30 to 11:20am, 12:30 to 1:20pm, and 4 to 4:30pm. The Bolsa de Comercio is a triangular building set among several picturesque, cobblestone streets that make for an intriguing short stroll: New York, La Bolsa, and Club de la Unión.

ATTRACTIONS OFF THE ALAMEDA

Hectic, heavily trafficked Avenida Bernardo O'Higgins is commonly referred to as *la Alameda,* and it's the main artery that runs through downtown Santiago. You'll find some of the city's interesting attractions along this avenue.

Calle Dieciocho and Palacio Cousiño Macul ★   Heading west on Alameda, past the giant Entel tower, will put you at **Calle Dieciocho,** a once-elegant neighborhood of ornate mansions built by wealthy families at the turn of the century. The neighborhood is certainly scruffier these days, but it is possible to picture the area during its heyday. The first few homes are on the corners of Dieciocho and Alameda, including the 1873 Palacio Errázuriz, now home to the Brazilian Embassy; the 1917 Palacio Ariztía; and the Iglesia San Vicente de Paul. These palaces were designed using beautiful European architectural styles.

The crème de la crème is the **Palacio Cousiño,** located several blocks down Calle Dieciocho, today a museum and testament to the obscene wealth of one of Chile's most successful entrepreneurial dynasties, the Goyenechea-Cousiño family. In addition to their well-known wine business and ownership of the Lota coal mines, the family had interests in copper, thoroughbred horses, shipping, and railways. Inside, opulent interiors are lavished with parquet floors, tapestries, ceramics, Bohemian crystal chandeliers, and furniture imported from Europe—along with European craftsmen to handcraft the interiors.

To get here, you'll have to walk (it's 8 blocks from the Plaza Bernardo O'Higgins), take a taxi, or ride the Metro to Estación Toesca. If you're walking back to downtown from here, head through the Parque Diego de Almagro near Palacio Cousiño and turn left up to Alameda via Paseo Bulnes until you reach O'Higgins. At the end of the Parque Diego de Almagro is the grand **Basílica del Santísimo Sacramento,** constructed between 1919 and 1931 and modeled after the church in Montmartre, France. If you've gone this far, you might want to continue to the row of **rare bookstores** located just beyond the church. As mentioned before, however, the neighborhood is a little scrappy, so you may just want to walk back to the Alameda or grab a cab to your next destination.

Dieciocho 438. (C) **2/698-5063.** Admission $2 adults, $1 children under 12. Bilingual tours given Tues–Fri 9:30am–1:30pm and 2:30–5pm; Sat–Sun 9:30am–1:30pm.

Barrio París-Londres ★   This charming, singular neighborhood with its narrow cobblestone streets was built between the 1920s and '30s on the old gardens of the Monastery of San Francisco. The neighborhood consists of small mansions, each with a different facade, that today house artists, students, and cultural centers. The neighborhood was designated a national monument in 1982, and its streets are now pedestrian walkways.

The streets between Prat and Santa Rosa, walking south of Alameda.

Iglesia, Convento y Museo de San Francisco ★★   The Church of San Francisco is the oldest standing building in Santiago, and although this landmark has been renovated over the years, the main structure has miraculously survived three devastating earthquakes. At the altar sits the famous *Virgen del Socorro,* the first Virgin Mary icon in Chile, brought here to Santiago by Pedro de Valdivia. The highlights, however, are the museum and the convent, the latter with its idyllic patio planted with flora brought from destinations as near as the south of Chile and as far away as the Canary Islands. The garden is so serene, you'll find it hard to believe you're in downtown Santiago. The museum boasts 54 paintings depicting the life and death of San Francisco, one of the largest and best-conserved displays of 17th-century art in South America.

Av. Bernardo O'Higgins. (C) **2/638-3238.** Admission to convent and museum $1. Tues–Sat 10am–1pm and 3–6pm; Sun and holidays 10am–2pm.

Biblioteca Nacional   The venerable National Library is housed in a French neoclassical stone building that occupies an entire city block. Inside its handsomely painted interiors are over six million works as well as historical archives and a map room. Don't miss the classic leather and wood splendor of the Jose Medina reading room, with antique books stacked in tiers, leather-topped reading desks, and a giant spinning globe.

Av. Bernardo O'Higgins 651. (C) **2/360-5259.** Mon–Fri 9am–6:30pm; Sat 9am–1pm.

CERRO SANTA LUCIA & PLAZA MULATO GIL DE CASTRO

Cerro Santa Lucía ★★★ is a hilltop park located steps from the Biblioteca Nacional on Alameda and Santa Lucía. It's open daily 9am to 8pm from September to March, 9am to 7pm from April to August; admission is free. The Mapuches called this rocky hill *Huelén* (Curse) until Pedro de Valdivia renamed it Santa Lucía in 1540. In 1872, the area was expanded to create walkways and small squares for the public's entertainment, and now office workers, tourists, couples, schoolchildren, and solitary thinkers can be seen strolling along leafy terraces to the Caupolicán Plaza for a sweeping view of Santiago. The plaza also serves as the site of theater and concerts in the summer.

Continue along the garden walk to Castle Hidalgo, built in 1820 and now an event center. To get to the top, begin at the stone monument staircase on Santa Lucía and O'Higgins, or take the glass elevator up a bit farther on Santa Lucía. Keep an eye open for suspicious characters if you choose to climb up at sunset. At the staircase you'll also find the **Centro de Exposición de Arte,** with a large assortment of Indian-influenced crafts, clothing, and jewelry on display and for sale. Across the street is a bustling crafts and junk market, the **Centro Artesanal de Santa Lucía,** with handicrafts, T-shirts, and more.

Behind the park, at José Victorino Lastarria 307, you'll find the **Plaza Mulato Gil de Castro** (closed Sun). Named for the 18th-century Peruvian Army captain and portrait painter José Gil, who lived in the neighborhood, this quaint plaza is a great place to explore, grab a cup of coffee, or have lunch. The plaza sits in the middle of a historic neighborhood built of beautiful stone mansions and boasts an excellent **Museo de Artes Visuales** ★★ (open Mon–Sun 10:30am–6:30pm, $1.40 admission). The art museum displays an impressive amount of sculptures, photography, and paintings by Chilean artists.

PARQUE FORESTAL

This slender, well-manicured park, built in 1900 and lined with rows of native and imported trees, skirts the perimeter of the Río Mapocho from Vicuña Mackenna at the Metro station Baquedano to its terminus at the Mapocho station. The winding path takes walkers past several great attractions, and makes for a pleasant 1- to 2-hour stroll, especially on a sunny afternoon when the air is clear. If you plan to walk the entire park, try to finish at the Mercado Central for lunch.

Palacio de Bellas Artes ★★ The Palacio de Bellas Artes houses both the Fine Arts and Contemporary Art museums in a regal, neoclassical building inaugurated on the eve of Chile's centennial independence day in 1910. The Palace has a noteworthy glass cupola that softly lights the vast lobby. The importance of the permanent installations in the Fine Arts museum may be debatable (an uneven mix of Chilean and international artists' works since the colonial period), but they occasionally host great temporary exhibitions. The Contemporary Museum features more than 2,000 paintings, sculptures, and other works by well-known Latin American artists.

Parque Forestal, by way of Jose Miguel de la Barra. ⓒ 2/632-7760. Admission Museum of Fine Arts 75¢ adults, 35¢ students; Museum of Contemporary Art 55¢ adults, 30¢ students. Museum of Fine Arts daily 10am–7pm; Museum of Contemporary Art Tues–Fri 11am–7pm, Sat–Sun 11am–2pm.

Mercado Central ★★ Just before reaching the Estación Mapocho, you'll pass the colorful, chaotic world of the Mercado Central. This lively market sells fruits and vegetables, handicrafts, and rows and rows of slippery fish and shellfish displayed on chipped ice. Depending on your perspective, the barking fishmongers and waitresses who harangue you to choose *their* zucchini, *their* sea bass, *their* restaurant, can be entertaining or somewhat annoying. Either way, don't miss it, especially for the market's lofty, steel structure that was fabricated in England and assembled here in 1868; it was originally intended as a gallery for national artists. Try to plan your visit during the lunch hour, for a rich bowl of *caldillo de congrio* (a thick eel soup) or a tangy *ceviche* at one of the many typical restaurants (see "Where to Dine," above).

Vergara and Av. 21 de Mayo. No phone. Daily 7am–3pm. Metro: Cal y Canto.

Estación Mapocho ★ Built in 1912 on reclaimed land formed by the canalization of the Río Mapocho, this behemoth of a building served as the train station for the Santiago–Valparaíso railway. In 1976 it was abandoned, and 15 years later repaired and converted into a cultural center that hosts events such as the yearly International Book Fair. It's worth a stop to admire the tremendous structure, which has a copper roof made of 40 tons of metal, as well as marble and glass. You'll also find a bookstore, restaurants, and theaters.

Bandera and Río Mapocho. ✆ 2/361-1761. www.estacionmapocho.cl. Daily 9am–5pm; other hours according to events.

BARRIO BELLAVISTA & PARQUE METROPOLITANO

These two attractions lie next to one another, so it makes sense to see both in one visit. But here's a word of caution: The extensive views that come with an ascent to the top of Cerro San Cristóbal can be ruined if it is a particularly smoggy day. But if the air is clear, this attraction rates as one of the best in the city, offering a breathtaking panorama of sprawling Santiago and its city limits that stop just short of the craggy Andes.

The Cerro San Cristóbal and its Metropolitan Park rise high above Santiago's bohemian hamlet **Bellavista** ★. One of the more interesting neighborhoods in the city, its streets are lined with trees and colorful antique homes, many of which have been converted into great restaurants and studios for artists and musicians. It's a pleasant place for an afternoon stroll; in the evening, Bellavista pulses to the sound of music pouring from its many discos and bars.

You might begin your visit with a trip to Bellavista's prime attraction, **La Chascona** ★★★ (Fernando Márquez de la Plata 0192; ✆ 2/777-8741). Located near the zoo and the entrance point to the Parque Metropolitano, this is one of three homes once owned by the brilliant, Nobel Prize–winning poet Pablo Neruda. As with Neruda's other two homes, La Chascona was built to resemble a ship, with oddly shaped rooms that wind around a compact courtyard. It's fascinating to wander through Neruda's quirky home and observe his collection of precious antiques and whimsical curios collected during his travels. Neruda's library is especially interesting, and it holds the antique encyclopedia set he purchased with a portion of his earnings from the Nobel Prize. The home is headquarters for the Fundación Pablo Neruda, which provides guided tours. Admission is $2 adults for Spanish tour, $3.25 for English tour, and it's open Tuesday through Sunday from 10am to 1pm and 3 to 6pm.

The **Parque Metropolitano** ★★★ is a 730-hectare (1,803-acre) park and recreation area with swimming pools, walking trails, a botanical garden, a zoo, picnic grounds, restaurants, and children's play areas. It's the lungs of Santiago, and city dwellers use the hill's roads and trails for jogging, biking, or just taking a stroll. The park is divided into two sectors, Cumbre and Tupahue, both of which are accessed by car, cable car, funicular, or foot. In Bellavista, head to the end of Calle Pío Nono to Plaza Caupolicán, where you'll encounter a 1925 **funicular** that lifts visitors up to a lookout point, open Monday through Friday from 10am to 7:30pm, Saturday and Sunday from 10am to 8pm; tickets cost $1.50 adults, $1 children. Along the way, the funicular stops at the **Jardín Zoológico** ★★, open Monday through Sunday from 10am to 6pm; admission is $3 adults, 75¢ children. This surprisingly diverse zoo features more than 200 species of mammals, reptiles, and birds—it's a rather outmoded, sad affair, but fascinating just the same. You will have to restrain yourself when you see kids feeding monkeys cotton candy and Fanta. The lookout point is watched over by a 22m (72-ft.) high statue of the **Virgen de la Inmaculada Concepción,** which can be seen from all over the city. Below the statue is the *teleférico* (**cable car**) that connects the two sections of the park, open Monday through Friday from 11am to 6pm, Saturday and Sunday from 10:30am to 7:30pm. Tickets cost $2.25 adults, $1 children; ticket combinations with the funicular cost $3 adults, $1.50 children. The gondola offers great views while suspended high above the park before arriving at Tupahue, which is the Mapuche name for this hill, meaning "place of God." Here you'll find the **Piscina Tupahue,** an attractive, rock-lined swimming pool (no phone). The pool is open Tuesday through Friday from 10am to 6pm, Saturday and Sunday from 10am to 7pm; admission for adults is $8 Monday through Friday, $9 Saturday and Sunday; children $6 Monday through Friday, $6.50 Saturday and Sunday.

A walk down the road will take you to the **Camino Real** and its wine museum **Museo Enoteca** (② 2/232-1758). The museum is disappointing, but the restaurant is worth the visit for the marvelous views from the dining area and patio (see "Where to Dine," earlier in this chapter). The museum offers a basic wine tasting at a bar that's relatively inexpensive. Nearby is the **Botanical Garden Mapulemu** (no phone). It's open daily from 9am to 6pm; admission is free weekdays, 25¢ weekends. From Tupahue you can either head back on the gondola to Cumbre and the funicular, or take the Valdivia *teleférico* down, which will drop you off at the end of Avenida Pedro de Valdivia. It's also possible to head back down by foot following a road that ends at Avenida Valdivia, passing first by the Plaza Gabriela Mistral. Of course, this trip can be done in the reverse direction, which might be more convenient if you're starting from Providencia or Las Condes.

If you're driving up to the park, you can drive via the Valdivia entrance road that continues at the end of Pío Nono, winding around first to Tupahue, then to Cumbre, or via the road that climbs up from Avenida Pedro de Valdivia. The admission fee for cars is $2 per vehicle—but if you buy two glasses of house red at the Camino Real for $2, they'll give you a voucher for a free entrance. It's also possible to take a taxi up, but you'll need to pay the park entrance fee as well as the fare. The Parque Metropolitano's hours are daily from 8:30am to 9pm.

PARQUE QUINTA NORMAL

If you still can't get enough of museums, take a taxi to the **Parque Quinta Normal,** located at 502 Matucana. This 39-hectare (96-acre) park was first used as an animal breeding site and acclimatization park for imported trees; today, it's home to lawns, a wide variety of non-native trees, and a lagoon with boats. It's also home to the **Museo Nacional de Historia Natural** ⊛ (② 2/680-4600), open Tuesday through Saturday from 10am to 5:30pm, Sunday from noon to 5:30pm; admission is 75¢ adults, 35¢ children under 18. The museum has a fairly interesting collection of stuffed animals and birds, mounted insects, plants, and anthropological exhibits. More worthwhile is the **Artequín Museum** ⊛⊛ at Av. Portales 3530 (② 2/681-8687), open Tuesday through Sunday from 10am to 5pm; admission is $1.25 adults, 50¢ students. The museum is housed in a cast-iron building that was first used as the Chilean exhibition hall at the 1889 Parisian centenary of the French Revolution. The building was taken apart, shipped to Santiago, and reassembled here. The museum strives to introduce visitors to the art world through 120 reproductions of well-known works by artists from Picasso to Monet. Kids love the **Museo de Ciencia y Tecnología** ★ (© 2/ **681-6022**) for its interactive displays. It is open Tuesday through Friday from 10am to 5pm, Saturday and Sunday from 11am to 6pm; admission is $1 adults, 50¢ students. Last, there's the **Museo Ferroviario** (© 2/681-4627), with railway exhibits that include 14 steam engines and railway carriages. It's open Tuesday through Friday from 10am to 5:30pm, Saturday and Sunday from 11am to 5:30pm; admission is $1 adults, 50¢ students.

ESPECIALLY FOR KIDS

The Parque Metropolitano Zoo, Museum of Science and Technology, and Railway Museum described above all appeal to kids. Another place is **Parque Bernardo O'Higgins,** reached by taxi or Metro to Estación Parque O'Higgins. Kid-friendly attractions include **Fantasilandia** (© 2/689-3035); admission is $5.50 adults, $4 children. It's open April through November on Saturday, Sunday, and holidays only, from 11am to 8:30pm; December through March Tuesday through Friday from 2 to 8pm, Saturday and Sunday from 11am to 8pm. It's the largest amusement park in Chile, complete with a roller coaster, toboggan ride, and haunted house. The **Museo de Insectos y Caracoles** (© 2/556-5680) displays more than 1,500 mounted butterflies, beetles, and snails; admission is 25¢ adults, 10¢ children. It's open Monday through Sunday from 10am to 8pm.

ORGANIZED TOURS

Most hotels offer city tours and trips to Viña del Mar and the Andes for an additional price; if not, they'll at least know how to put you in touch with a tour operator. For custom-planned tours, especially of the coast and wineries, try **Ace Turismo** at Don Carlos 949 (© 2/696-0391). Also try **Turismo Cocha** at El Bosque Norte 0430 (© 2/230-1000; fax 2/230-5110; www.cocha.cl) or try **First Premium** at Av. Suecia 734 (© 2/258-2000; www.firstpremium.cl). These agencies offer a wide variety of day tours to ski resorts, coastal towns, wineries, and more. The information kiosk at Paseo Ahumada and Paseo Huérfanos in downtown Santiago organizes city tours.

   CHIP tours (© 2/735-9044; www.chiptravel.cl) offers several general tours including a fascinating look into the Pinochet legacy with its Human Rights Legacy day trip, which takes visitors on bilingual half-day or full-day visits to important sites during the dictatorship. This is an exceptionally worthwhile tour, offering an in-depth look at the most important events in Chile's history.

SPECTATOR SPORTS & RECREATION

GYMS   Try **Fisic** at Tobalaba 607 in Providencia (© 2/232-6641; $8 per visit) or **Bio Acción** at Av. Providencia 065 near the Baquedano Metro station (© 2/ 634-7282; $6 for *each* apparatus used, such as sauna, weights, and so on).

HORSE RACING   Two racetracks hold events on either Saturday or Sunday throughout the year: the recommended **Club Hípico** at Blanco Encalada 2540 (© 2/683-9600) and the **Hipódromo Chile** at Avenida Vivaceta in Independencia (© 2/270-9200). The Hípico's classic event, El Ensayo, takes place the first Sunday in November; the Hipódromo's classic St. Leger, the second week in December. El Ensayo is a sight to be seen, with hundreds of barbecues flaming in the middle of the racetrack.

POOLS   Your best bet is the public pool **Tupahue** atop Cerro San Cristóbal; see "Barrio Bellavista & Parque Metropolitano," above, for details.

SKIING   For information about skiing in the area, see chapter 12.

SOCCER (FOOTBALL)   Top games are held at three stadiums: **Estadio Monumental,** Avenida Grecia and Marathon; **Universidad de Chile,** Camp de Deportes 565 (both are in the Ñuñoa neighborhood); and **Universidad Católica,** Andrés Bello 2782, in Providencia. Check the sports pages of any local newspaper for game scheduling. Though *fútbol* is popular in Chile, fans aren't quite as maniacal as they are in Argentina.

TENNIS   Try one of the 22 courts at **Parque Tenis** at Cerro Colorado 4661, near the Parque Arauco mall in Las Condes (© **2/208-6589**), or **Todo Tenis** at Arturo Pérez Canto 10755 in Las Condes (© **2/311-3790**); fees are around $9 per hour weekdays, $14 evenings and weekends.

6 Shopping

SHOPPING CENTERS
Santiago is home to two American-style megamalls: **Parque Arauco** at Av. Kennedy 5413, open Monday through Saturday from 10am to 9pm, Sunday and holidays from 11am to 9pm; and **Alto Las Condes** at Av. Kennedy 9001, open Monday through Sunday from 10am to 10pm. Both offer hundreds of national brands and well-known international chains, junk-food courts, and multiscreen theaters (Parque Arauco is closer to Providencia). The best way to get to Parque Arauco is by cab (about $4–$5 from Providencia) or take the Metro to Escuela Militar and take a blue "Metro Bus" that will drop you off at the door. Note that weekends are hectic and jam-packed with shoppers.

Throughout Santiago, stores are typically clustered together in *galerías,* labyrinthine mini-malls with dozens of independent shops; you'll find them virtually everywhere. A good example is the **Mall Panorámico** at Avenida Ricardo Lyon and Avenida 11 de Septiembre, with 130 shops and live music on weekends. If you need to find clothing or shoes, you'll find lots of options around Pedro de Valdivia and Providencia and 11 de Septiembre avenues, or just hit the mall. Several blocks away on General Holley, Suecia, and Bucarest streets you'll find more expensive, upscale clothing boutiques. Chile's version of Rodeo Drive is Alonso de Córdova in the Vitacura Neighborhood.

CRAFTS MARKETS
Crafts markets can be found around Santiago either as permanent installations or weekly events. **Las Condes Los Domínicos** at Av. Apoquindo 9085 (no phone), open Tuesday through Sunday and holidays from 10:30am to 7pm (some stalls vary in hours), is a permanent shopping area designed to resemble a colonial village; here you'll find everything from hand knit sweaters to lapis lazuli to arts and crafts to live pheasants. It sits next to the (usually closed) **San Vicente Ferrer de Los Domínicos Church,** built in the 18th century. To get here take a taxi, which will cost $3 to $5 one-way if coming from Providencia.

At Cerro Santa Lucía, on the other side of Alameda, the outdoor market **Feria Santa Lucía** is hard to miss with its soaring billboards and sprawl of stalls hawking clothing, jewelry, and arts and crafts—even some antiques and collectibles. Hours vary, but it's generally open Monday through Saturday (sometimes Sun) from 10am to 7pm. In **Bellavista** on weekends, a crafts fair runs along Calle Pío Nono (akin to Telegraph Ave. in Berkeley, Calif.), where you'll find dozens of booths selling a variety of goods such as jewelry and old records, but it's pretty scrappy and most vendors are do-it-yourselfers with trinkets displayed on fabric laid out on the sidewalk. For antiques fairs, see below.

SHOPPING FROM A TO Z
ANTIQUES

Antiques lovers and collectors should not miss the **Bío Bío Market,** also referred to as the Franklin Market and located—where else?—between Bío Bío and Franklin streets, open Saturday and Sunday 9am to 7pm. Take the Metro to the Franklin station and walk up several blocks through a so-so selection of wares until you reach the antiques area. You'll find an even higher quality selection at **Mapocho;** the red warehouse near Parque de Los Reyes, at the corner of Brasil and Matucana streets, houses dozens of small shops; it's open Saturday and Sunday 9am to 8pm. I furnished my entire apartment with antiques bought here because the price is right. A superb spot in Providencia is at the corner of Calle Bucarest and Avenida Providencia, where dozens of galleries offer paintings, china, furniture, and nearly every knickknack imaginable. If you still haven't found what you want, keep in mind that every Saturday and Sunday—and only in the morning—**Plazas Techadas** at Calle Placer between San Diego and San Francisco opens its doors to antiques buyers. This sector was recently built to house antiques dealers who for 40 years sold their wares at the Bío Bío. This is not a particularly bad neighborhood, but keep an eye open. The Plaza Mulato Gil de Castro on Lastarría street occasionally has a small antiques fair on Saturday and Sunday from about 9am to 5pm.

ARTESANIA

The best one-stop shop for a wide variety of arts & crafts (and an expensive selection of antique collectables) is the Los Domínicos market, or try the open-air market Feria Santa Lucía (see "Crafts Markets," above). **Artesanías de Chile** at the Mapocho Station Cultural Central, open Monday through Friday from 10am to 8pm, Saturday from 10:30am to 1:30pm, is a top place to find a wide variety of artisan goods, including ceramics, lapis lazuli, textiles, baskets, woodwork, and more. **Chile Típico** at Moneda 1025, Local 149 (© **2/696-5504**), open Monday through Friday from 9:30am to 10pm and Saturday from 10am to 2pm, is worth a stop as it sells everything from ceramics to those great wooden stirrups and pinwheel spurs that *huaso* cowboys use. In Providencia, try Artesanía Latina Veracruz at Av. Providencia 2124, Local G and H (© **2/696-5504**), open Monday through Friday from 9:30am to 8pm and Saturday from 10am to 2pm. Many museums have small shops that sell a variety of photo books and arts and crafts, such as the Museo Chileno de Arte Precolombino (see "Seeing the Sights," earlier in this chapter).

BOOKS

Libro sells a diverse and expensive array of English-language magazines, and a smaller assortment of paperbacks at Av. Pedro de Valdivia 039 in Providencia (© **2/232-8839**), open Monday through Friday from 10am to 8pm, Saturday from 10am to 2pm, or downtown at Paseo Huérfanos 1178 inside the Gran Palace Galería (© **2/699-0319**), open Monday through Friday from 9:30am to 7:30pm. **Librería Inglesa,** with shops at Av. Pedro de Valdivia 47 (© **2/231-6270**); Paseo Huérfanos 669, Local 11 (© **2/632-5153**); Vitacura 5950 (© **2/219-2735**); and Av. Providencia 2653, Local 10 (© **2/234-3619**), sells English-language literature, nonfiction, and children's books. In Las Condes, for English-language magazines go to the underground parking garage at Isidora Goyenechea and Carmencita; you'll find a magazine store near the ticket pay window. For the largest selection of books in Spanish, the **Feria Chilena del**

Finds   **Lapis Lazuli, a Gem of a Gift**

Looking for that special something to bring home to your loved ones? Try lapis lazuli, a stone that can be found in only two places in the world: Afghanistan and Chile (although there are also spotty reserves in Russia). The color of lapis ranges from a bright royal blue to a violet-navy blue. Lapis is used primarily for jewelry, but it's also commonly seen in sculptures and even counter tile.

Lapis has been used for 6,500 years, and was considered the most valuable gem until the Middle Ages. The Chinese used lapis for hair ornaments, the Romans carved it into beads, the Greeks recommended it for poisonous snake bites, and the Buddhists thought it encouraged peace of mind. Indigenous peoples, especially the Incas, used lapis to create decorative pieces and jewelry.

The best place to shop for lapis is in the **Bellavista** neighborhood, where a dozen stores are clustered along Calle Bellavista between Pío Nono and Arzobispo Casanova. Here, you'll find jewelry, chess sets, figurines, picture frames, and more, all fabricated from lapis. For fine jewelry and outlandish works, try **PietArt** at Los Conquistadores 2421, near the Providencia neighborhood (© **2/233-6404**), open daily from 9:30am to 7pm, or **Morita Gil** at Los Misioneros 1991 (© **2/232-6853**).

Libro at Paseo Huérfanos 623 (© **2/639-6758**) is your best bet, and it sells local and national maps. It has a smaller branch in Providencia at Santa Magdalena 50 (© **2/232-1422**).

WINE

Don't miss the old-fashioned **Larbos** at Estado 26, downtown Santiago (© **2/639-3434**), open Monday through Saturday from 8am to 10pm, for gourmet foods, wines, and wonderful chocolates. There's a cluster of wine shops in Las Condes, such as the huge **El Mundo de Vino** at Av. Isidora Goyenechea 2931 (© **2/244-8888**), open Monday through Saturday from 10:30am to 8:30pm, Sunday from 10:30am to 8pm, which has a wide selection and a very knowledgeable staff. Also on Avenida Isidora Goyenechea at 2966 is **La Vinoteca** (© **2/334-1987**), open Monday to Friday 9:30am to 8pm, Saturday 11am to 3pm. Around the corner at El Bosque Norte 038 is **Vinópolis** (© **2/335-1345**), open Monday through Saturday from 10am to 10pm, Sunday from 10am to 8pm, with a good selection. Most shops will ship wine for you. Most supermarkets offer a wide selection, and at cheaper prices too.

7 Santiago After Dark

There are plenty of theaters, nightclubs, and bars to keep your evenings busy in Santiago. Residents of Santiago adhere to a vampire's schedule, dining as late as 11pm, arriving at a nightclub past 1am, and diving into bed before the sun rises. But there are many early-hour nighttime attractions if you can't bear late nights. Several newspapers publish daily movie listings and Friday weekend-guide supplements, such as *El Mercurio*'s "Wiken" or *La Tercera*'s "Guía Fin de Semana." Both contain movie, theater, and live music listings and special events.

THE PERFORMING ARTS

Santiago is known for its theater, from large-scale productions to one-person monologues put on at a local cafe. However, it might be difficult to find a production that interests you because newspaper listings typically advertise the title, address, and telephone number, nothing else. Ask around for recommendations, either from the hotel staff or at a visitor information center, such as the kiosk at Paseo Ahumada and Paseo Huérfanos, which typically have complete theater listings and can suggest particular acts.

The following are some of the more well-established theaters in Santiago. Four theaters in Bellavista offer contemporary productions and comedies in an intimate setting: **Teatro Bellavista** at Dardignac 0110 (© 2/735-2395), **El Conventillo** at Bellavista 173 (© 2/777-4164), **Teatro La Feria** at Crucero Exeter 0250 (© 2/737-7371), and **Teatro San Ginés** at Mallinkrodt 76 (© 2/738-2159). As the name implies, the nearby **Teatro La Comedia** at Merced 349 (© 2/639-1523) hosts comedy, but it is better known for cutting-edge productions. In Las Condes, try the **Teatro Apoquindo** at Av. Apoquindo 3384 (© 2/231-3560). The cultural center **Estación Mapocho** at the Plaza de la Cultura s/n (© 2/361-1761) hosts a large variety of theater acts, often concurrently.

If symphony music, ballet, or opera is your thing, you won't want to miss a performance at the historic downtown **Teatro Municipal** at Agustinas 749 (© 2/639-0282). The National Chilean Ballet performs here, with contemporary productions that might be danced to the tunes of tango, Chilean folklore, or Janis Joplin. Visiting orchestras and the Fundación Beethoven play at the **Teatro Oriente** at Avenida Pedro de Valdivia between Avenida Providencia and Avenida Andrés Bello (© 2/251-5321), from May to late September; the ticket and information office can be found at Av. 11 de Septiembre 2214, #66. **Teatro Universidad de Chile** at Av. Providencia 043 (© 2/634-4746) hosts ballet and symphony productions, both national and international, throughout the year.

THE CLUB, MUSIC & DANCE SCENE

Crowd-pulling national and international megabands typically play in the **Estado Nacional** or the **Estación Mapocho.** You'll find listings for these shows in the daily newspaper. If you're looking for something mellower, **Bellavista** is a good bet for jazz, bolero, and folk music that is often performed Thursday through Saturday in several restaurants/cafes. **La Tasca Mediterráneo**'s next-door cafe at Purísima 161 (© 2/735-3901) hosts mostly jazz acts in a cozy atmosphere, but it can get crowded as the night wears on.

Also in Bellavista, there are four similar cozy bars at Antonio López and Mallinkrodt. **La Casa en el Aire** at Antonia López de Bello 0125 (© 2/735-6680) has a great ambience lit by candlelight, and is a relaxing place to enjoy a drink listening to soft live music. Across the street at López de Bello 0126 is **El Perseguidor** (© 2/777-6763), a literary cafe with jazz performances every evening Thursday through Sunday. For salsa dancing, try the **Habana Salsa** at Dominica 142 (© 2/737-1737). Despite the hokey exterior of faux building facades, it's where many salsa fanatics spend their weekend nights. For a younger crowd, head to **Delirio Caribeño**, at Bucarest 117 (© 2/231-8029).

There are dozens of music venues spread across the city, but several are concentrated in the Ñuñoa neighborhood, about a 5- to 10-minute taxi ride from downtown and Providencia. **La Batuta** at Jorge Washington 52 (© 2/274-7096) is a dance club on Saturday; the rest of the week it's a great spot to check out a wide variety of international and national contemporary and folk bands. The atmosphere is underground, but the crowd profile depends on who's playing.

The **Club de Jazz** at José Pedro Alessandri 85 (✆ 2/274-1937) is one of the city's most traditional places (Louis Armstrong once played here), and every Thursday, Friday, and Saturday beginning at 11pm, several excellent bands get together and jam for the audience.

In Providencia, **Tomm** at General Holley 2366 has live music and a changing crowd depending on the music that evening.

Santiago's club scene typically caters to an 18- to 35-year-old crowd, and it all gets going pretty late, from midnight to 6am, on the average. If you like electronica music, you might check out "fiestas" publicized in the weekend entertainment sections of newspapers that list one-night-only raves and live music, or, in Bellavista, try **La Feria** at Constitución 275, in an old theater. **Blondie** at Alameda 2879 (✆ 2/681-7793) is like spending a night in 1985, with an '80s revival scene, and music to match. Harder to get to (semi-long cab ride) but worth the distance is the **Skuba** club in Paseo San Damian (Av. Las Condes 11271; ✆ 2/243-1108), a European-style disco that attracts Chilean jetsetters. **OZ** at Chucre Mansur 6 in Bellavista (✆ 2/737-7066) draws the Chilean yuppie crowd; you'll find a mixed crowd at **Laberinto** at Vicuña Mackenna 915, closer to downtown.

THE BAR SCENE
For the amount of pisco and wine that Chileans drink, bars have strangely never caught on; most bars are also restaurants or cafes by day. Bars that also feature live music can be found in "The Club, Music & Dance Scene," above.

DOWNTOWN
There are several bars near the Plaza Mulato Gil de Castro, such as **Bar Berri** at Rosal 321, a classic old watering hole frequented by locals and college students for its great atmosphere. The **Confitería Torres** at Av. Alameda 1570 (✆ 2/698-6220), the antique cafe by day, fills with younger revelers at night and sometimes features music or dancing. **Sicosis** at José Miguel de la Barra 544 (✆ 2/634-4462), open daily until 3am, is casual and comfy, although there's not much atmosphere. **El Túnel**, at Santo Domingo 439 (✆ 2/639-4914) is an old '70s-style bar and small dance floor popular with 20- and 30-somethings. For a more refined experience, try the **Copper Room** bar at the Hotel Carrera.

PROVIDENCIA
The **Bar Liguria** at Av. Providencia 1373 (✆ 2/235-7914), open to 2am on weeknights, until 5am on weekends, and closed Sunday, is Providencia's happening spot for a drink; it's a restaurant by day and bar by night, but serves snacks practically until closing time. The **Phone Box Pub** at Av. Providencia 1670 (✆ 2/235-9972), open Monday through Thursday until 1am, weekends until 3am, closed Sunday, is good for a pint of brew and a snack. The pub is inside a small plaza off the main drag, and there's outside seating under a trellised roof. In the same plaza is the **Café del Patio** (✆ 2/236-1251), open Monday to Thursday until midnight, Friday and Saturday until 1:30am, a stylish vegetarian restaurant with a great bar, outside seating, and live jazz on weekends.

Xampanyet at General Salvo 115 (✆ 2/235-6175) is recognizable for the rhinoceros head above the door. It's mellow, and serves abundant piscolas to a 20- to 40-year-old crowd. **Cabo Frío** at Manuel Montt 234 (✆ 2/264-1389) is a warm, modern bar with snacks and a sofa. **Santo Remedio** at Roman Díz serves "aphrodisiac" drinks amid a great atmosphere: zinc bar, wooden tables, and an outside terrace. **The Barcelona** restaurant/bar at Santa Beatriz 40 (✆ **2/ 235-6292**) serves drinks and tapas—and nothing else—in a low-lit, warm atmosphere. **Mister Ed** at Av. Suecia 152 (✆ **2/231-2624**), open Monday through Saturday from 6pm to 5am (open Sun during the summer), transforms into a dance hall at 2am with live music, and is frequented by many gringos. Avenida Suecia overflows with revelers of all ages during the weekends—you could just walk the neighborhood until something strikes your fancy, and it's all here: pubs, restaurants, loud clubs, and more. Happy hours are a standby in nearly every bar here.

LAS CONDES

Several restaurants convert into pubs or cocktail lounges in the evening. One of them is **Flannigans's Geo Pub** at Encomenderos 83 (✆ **2/233-6675**), open until midnight on weeknights, 2am on weekends. It's a cozy, contemporary Irish pub with the usual pints on draft that's very popular with an international crowd. **PubLicity** at El Bosque Norte 0155 (✆ **2/246-6414**), open until 1am on weeknights and 3am on weekends, is almost too much of a sensory overload, combining English architecture with urban "publicity," or advertisements. It's very popular with upscale young adults and yuppies, and there is often live music. **Branigan's Pub** at Las Condes 11271 (✆ **2/243-1108**), open Monday through Sunday until 4am, has an intimate atmosphere for enjoying a quiet cocktail, and serves snacks. If it's a summer evening and you're looking for a relaxing place to have a cocktail with a crowd in their 30s and up, try **Zanzíbar** in the multi-restaurant complex Borderío at Av. Escrivá de Balaguer (about a $3 taxi ride from Las Condes; ✆ **2/218-0120**). This Mediterranean/Moroccan restaurant and bar has an outdoor, candlelit terrace on the second floor that has pillows and comfy chairs to kick back in a look at the stars. Excellent snacks and food, too. It's open Monday to Thursday from noon to 1am, Friday and Saturday from noon to 2am, and Sunday from 10am to 6pm.

CINEMAS

Megaplexes such as CineHoyts and Cinemark, with their multiscreened theaters, feature the widest variety of movies and a popular Monday to Wednesday discount price. More avant-garde and independent films can be found in "Cine Arte" theaters, such as **Cine Alameda,** Alameda 139 (✆ **2/664-8842**), or **El Biógrafo,** Lastarria 181 (✆ **2/633-4435**). The entertainment sections of *El Mercurio, La Tercera,* or *El Metropolitán* list titles, times, and locations.

12

Around Santiago & the Central Valley

Some of the most interesting attractions in Chile can be found right outside Santiago. Lush beaches, an eccentric port town, nature preserves, hot springs, wineries, and rolling countryside are a few examples of what's nearby. There's also a mind-boggling array of outdoor activities to be had, including skiing at one of four world-renowned resorts, hiking, rafting, biking, horseback riding, and more. These attractive destinations and excursions are all within several hours' drive from Santiago, which means it is possible to pack a lot of action into just a few days.

EXPLORING THE REGION

Wineries, ski resorts, and coastal communities around Santiago can all be explored on day trips. You might find an overnight stay in Viña del Mar or Valparaíso an attractive option; it will allow for more time for exploring the area. Rental cars are obviously handy, especially if visiting area wineries or taking a drive down the coast. But rental cars are not entirely necessary. Public transportation—minivan shuttles to Santiago's ski resorts, for example—is also available. Transportation aboard frequent, clean coaches from Santiago's downtown bus terminals is a great option for coastal destinations.

1 Viña del Mar

120km (74 miles) NW of Santiago; 8km (5 miles) N of Valparaíso

Viña del Mar is one of Chile's most fashionable beach resorts. The town was founded in 1874 as a weekend retreat and garden residence for the wealthy elite from Valparaíso and Santiago, and it has remained a top beach destination for Santiaguinos ever since. Most simply call the city "Viña"—you'll call it chaos if you come any time between December and late February, when thousands of vacationers descend.

The sight of Viña's attractive homes, manicured lawns, and golden beaches dotted with colorful surfboards is something of a contrast to the ramshackle streets of Valparaíso. There are plenty of fine beaches here, but the Humboldt Current that runs the length of Chile to Antofagasta makes for cold swimming conditions. Whether or not you swim, Viña is a wonderfully relaxing place to spend 1 or 2 days.

The city is divided into two sectors: the downtown and the beachfront. Several downtown locations are desirable for their proximity to the lush Quinta Vergara Park and shops, but it's about a 15-minute walk to the beach from here. The beach is better suited for tourists, with plenty of hotels and restaurants.

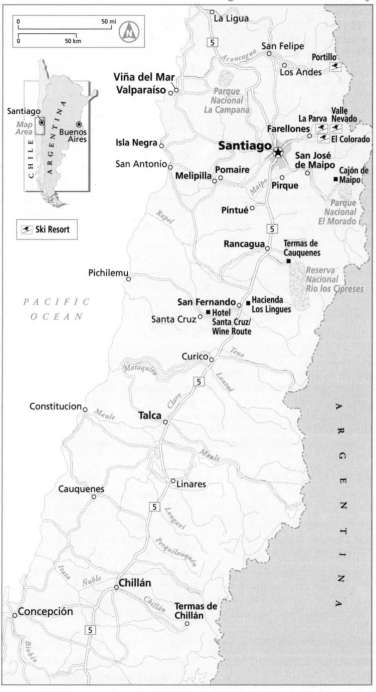

0 50 mi
0 50 km

Map Area

Santiago

Buenos Aires

CHILE
ARGENTINA

⛷ Ski Resort

La Ligua

5

Aconcagua

San Felipe

Portillo ⛷

Los Andes

Viña del Mar
Valparaíso

Parque Nacional La Campana

La Parva ⛷ Valle Nevado ⛷

Farellones ⛷

El Colorado ⛷

Isla Negra

Santiago

San José de Maipo

Cajón de Maipo

San Antonio

Pomaire

Melipilla

Maipo

Pirque

Rapel

Pintué

Parque Nacional El Morado

5

Rancagua

Termas de Cauquenes

Reserva Nacional Rio los Cipreses

Pichilemu

PACIFIC OCEAN

San Fernando

Hacienda Los Lingues

Santa Cruz

Hotel Santa Cruz/ Wine Route

Curico

Teno

Mataquito

Lontué

5

Constitucion

Maule

Claro

Talca

Maule

Linares

Cauquenes

5

Longavi

Perquilauquén

ARGENTINA

Itata

Ñuble

Chillán

Concepción

Chillán

Termas de Chillán

5

Biobío

ESSENTIALS

GETTING THERE   Frequent, comfortable buses leave the Terminal Alameda in Santiago at Alameda O'Higgins 3712 (1 block from Terminal Santiago; Metro: Universidad de Santiago), about every 15 minutes. Tur Bus and Pullman both offer service to and from Viña del Mar, for about $4 each way. The trip takes about 1 hour and 15 minutes, depending on traffic. In Viña you'll disembark at the terminal located at Avenida Valparaíso and Quilpué; it's close to the main plaza, and taxis are available.

VISITOR INFORMATION   The **Oficina de Turismo de Viña** is located on Plaza Vergara, next to the post office near avenidas Libertad and Arlegui (© **800/800830,** toll-free in Chile). Summer hours are Monday through Saturday from 9am to 9pm (closed 2–3pm); off-season hours are Monday through Friday from 10am to 7pm (closed 2–3pm), and Saturday from 10am to 2pm. A helpful staff (including a few who speak basic English) can provide visitors with accommodations information, but without ratings. It's also a good place for information about where to go to rent a temporary apartment.

GETTING AROUND   Viña's beachfront promenade and the lush Quinta Vergara Park are pleasant place to stroll. Driving is easier here than in Valparaíso, but parking is difficult in summer. To get to Valparaíso, take the commuter train "Merval" at Francisco Vergara between Bohn and Alvarez streets. The train runs every 20 minutes from about 6am to 10pm and costs 35¢. In Valparaíso, get off at the final stop, Estación Puerto (next to the visitor center). The Merval is really the best way to get to and from both cities. **Taxis** can be hailed in the street, or your hotel can call one.

SPECIAL EVENTS   During the second or third week of February, Viña plays host to the **Festival de la Canción,** a weeklong event that draws national and international musicians to perform in the outdoor amphitheater in Quinta Vergara Park. It's the largest music festival in Chile, drawing almost 30,000 spectators nightly. The city bursts at the seams during this event, and hotel reservations are imperative. Viña also hosts a **Film Festival** between October 17 and October 25 at the Teatro Municipal. Inquire at the visitor center for more information on both events.

FAST FACTS: VIÑA DEL MAR

Banks   Most major banks can be found on Avenida Arlegui, and although they're open Monday through Friday from 9am to 2pm only, nearly all have ATMs (RedBancs).

Car Rentals   Try **Hertz Rent-A-Car,** Av. Quillota 766 (© **32/381025**) or **Flota Verschae,** Av. Libertad 1045 (© **32/267300**).

Currency Exchange   *Cambios* (money-exchange houses) are open in the summer Monday through Friday from 9am to 2pm and 3 to 8pm, Saturday from 9am to 2pm; in the winter, Monday through Saturday 9am to 2pm and 4 to 7pm, Saturday from 9am to 2pm. Several *cambios* can be found along Avenida Arlegui.

Emergencies   For **police,** dial **133;** for **fire,** dial **132;** and for an **ambulance,** dial **131.**

Hospital   For medical attention, go to **Hospital Gustavo Fricke** on calles Alvarez and Simón Bolívar (© **32/675067,** or for emergencies 32/652328).

WHERE TO STAY
EXPENSIVE

Gala Hotel ⭐ Although not exactly "gala," this hotel's upscale accommodations feature panoramic windows and sensational views—but part of that view is of the dirty river directly below. Room interiors are designed with contemporary wood headboards, floral bedspreads, and watercolor paintings; try to book a corner room for maximum views and sunshine. The marble and brass reception area, at the back of the building, is filled with sculptures and paintings. At the front of the building is a small *galería* with a variety of shops.

Av. Arlegui 273, Viña del Mar. ℂ **32/321500.** Fax 32/689568. galahotel@webhost.cl. 64 units. $130 double; $145 junior suite. AE, DC, MC, V. **Amenities:** Restaurant; bar; pool; gym; sauna; car rental; business center; room service; massage; babysitting; laundry service. *In room:* A/C, TV, minibar.

Hotel del Mar ⭐⭐⭐ This brand-new, five-star hotel is opening as this book goes to press, and will be Viña's most upscale luxury lodging option. The Hotel del Mar is owned by and located next to the casino and overlooks the sea; it's an ideal location close to everything. Double Standard and Superior rooms have balconies and panoramic views of the ocean and the casino gardens, as do all suites. The Salute Health Center sits inside a semicircular building that overlooks the ocean and features a state of the art gym, beauty center, and indoor lap pool. There's also a terrace that overlooks the sea. Lodging includes free entrance to the casino and shows.

Av. San Martín 199. ℂ **600/700-6000.** Fax 32/500601. www.casino.cl. 60 units. $200–$250 double standard; $330–$390 suite. AE, DC, MC, V. Valet parking. **Amenities:** 4 restaurants; bar; indoor pool; gym; sauna; children's game room; business center; room service; massage; babysitting; laundry service; solarium; art gallery. *In room:* A/C, cable TV, DVD and CD player, safe.

Hotel O'Higgins ⭐ This traditional hotel, a stone landmark constructed in the heart of Viña in 1934, has sadly begun to show its age. Minor renovations, including newer hallway carpet and fresh drapes and bedspreads, have improved its image somewhat, but a stale lobby, dark hallways, and worn furniture reveal that the glory days of the O'Higgins are over. Nevertheless, the hotel is still frequented by dignitaries. It's an interesting place to spend the night, if not for its historical appeal then for its downtown location (close to shops but on a noisy plaza), idyllic outdoor pool, and complete services, including two restaurants and the legendary Harry's Bar. Ask to see the accommodations if at all possible as the quality varies from room to room, and those facing the main plaza are nicer than side rooms. Ask for price specials when booking.

Plaza Vergara, Viña del Mar. ℂ **32/882010.** Fax 32/883537. www.panamericanahoteles.cl. 265 units. $70–$80 double; $130 suite. AE, DC, MC, V. **Amenities:** 2 restaurants; bar; disco (Jan–Feb only); outdoor pool; children's activities and disco (Jan–Feb only); car-rental agency; business center; room service; babysitting; laundry service. *In room:* A/C, cable TV, minibar, safe.

Hotel Monterilla ⭐⭐ *(Finds)* This appealing boutique hotel is one of the best in Chile. Warm, personal service and a central location are definite draws, but the chic, contemporary design is what really makes the Monterilla special. The interiors feature white carpet, cushy orange chairs, and walls adorned with colorful postmodern art. The rooms are not huge, but they are elegant and comfortable, and several have kitchenettes. There's a cafe/restaurant that serves snacks and an excellent daily breakfast buffet. A small common area has several sofas for reading or relaxing. The Monterilla is a family-run hotel, and service is friendly and personal. This is a great value, with a convenient location near the beach and the casino.

Dos Norte 65, Plaza México, Viña del Mar. ✆ **32/976950.** Fax 32/683576. www.monterilla.cl. 20 units. $80 double; $90 apt. AE, DC, MC, V. **Amenities:** Cafeteria; bar; office services; laundry service. *In room:* Cable TV, minibar.

Hotel San Martín The San Martín began with a bang in 1958, opening as the only hotel with an ideal beachfront location and later lobbying to bring the casino to town. But the tired interiors are visual proof that this hotel has passed its heyday. It's still a good option for travelers who want to have an up-close view of the crashing waves and still be close to town, but don't book a room without a view—it's not worth it. Some seaview rooms come with sliding doors and a balcony, and they are not necessarily bad, but they do have dated wallpaper and furniture and a slightly musty smell. Service is very professional and there is a large restaurant and piano bar. "Apartment" guest rooms have two bedrooms; suites have a small seating area separated by a curtain.

Av. San Martín 667, Viña del Mar. ✆ **32/689191.** Fax 32/689195. www.hotelsanmartin.cl. 172 units. Seaview $60 double, $125 suite; street view $45 double, $80 suite. AE, DC, MC, V. **Amenities:** Restaurant; bar; gym; sauna; laundry service. *In room:* Cable TV, minibar, safe.

The Oceanic ★★ The Oceanic enjoys a spectacular location on a rocky promontory with dramatic views of Valparaíso and the ocean crashing against the shore. The hotel is warm and friendly and full of places to sit and relax to the soothing sound of the sea. During the summer, the pebbled terrace with its oceanside pool and lounge chairs is the best around. The cozy rooms come with comfortable beds, wooden beams, and rose-colored drapes. (Some have sea views, and some look out to the busy road to Reñaca.) A few "attic" rooms are especially spacious and come with a breakfast nook and great views. The plant-filled restaurant is popular, but the views are a tad more noteworthy than the cuisine. The Oceanic is a short taxi ride away from most restaurants and points of interest.

Av. Borgoño 12925, Viña del Mar. ✆ **32/830006.** Fax 32/830390. www.hoteloceanic.cl. 28 units. $115–$125 seaview double. AE, DC, MC, V. **Amenities:** Restaurant; bar; outdoor pool; sauna; salon; laundry service. *In room:* Cable TV; minibar.

MODERATE

Hotel Albamar ★ The Hotel Albamar offers good value for the price due to its location—near restaurants and a block from the casino and the beach—and its comfortable rooms. The owners have completely renovated a separate building in the back, which I recommend for its ample suites and brand-new furnishings; however, the rooms in the main building are also decent, apart from a few that are quite dark. The "double special" has extra space for a table and chairs and a free-standing shelving unit. The rooms feature a slightly frilly romantic design.

Av. San Martín 419, Viña del Mar. ✆ **32/975274.** Fax 32/970720. www.vinadelmar.cl/albamar. 30 units. $40 double; $50 suite. AC, DC, MC, V. **Amenities:** Cafe; office services; babysitting; laundry service. *In room:* A/C, cable TV, minibar.

Hotel Andalúe The Andalúe sets itself apart from others in its price range with its higher-quality beds. The hotel is actually divided into two different sections across the street from each other, both about the same in terms of design. The furnishings and decoration in the lobby lean a wee bit toward the 1970s. The hotel recently inaugurated its basic "spa," which includes a pool and massage. The casino and beach are just 2 blocks away.

Av. 6 Poniente 124, Viña del Mar. ✆/fax **32/684147.** www.hotelandalue.cl. 42 units. $45 double. AE, DC, MC, V. **Amenities:** Restaurant; bar; heated indoor/outdoor pool; sauna; massage. *In room:* Cable TV.

Hotel Hispano Crisp and clean, the Hotel Hispano has pleasant rooms with large windows looking out onto an atrium patio. The Hispano is a good value in this price range, especially when you factor in its central location close to the Quinta Vergara Park (but not the beach). This is an older, well-kept hotel that has been family-run for 50 years. Rooms come with average, but not uncomfortable, foam beds. There's a lounge and dining area for breakfast. Note that during the Song Festival the Hispano books early, and the surrounding area is very busy. The same goes for the Quinta Vergara Hotel (see below).

Plaza Parroquia 391, Viña del Mar. ℂ **32/685860**. Fax 32/680981. www.hotelhispano.cl. 30 units. $35 double. AE, DC, MC, V. **Amenities:** Cafeteria; bar; office services room service; laundry service. *In room:* Cable TV; safe.

Offenbacher-hof Residencial ★★ Housed in a lovely Victorian building perched high atop Cerro Castillo, the Offenbacker has sweeping views of Viña del Mar and an exquisite patio cafe. Still, it is the friendly German-Chilean owners of the Offenbacker that make this bed-and-breakfast really special. The interiors are older, and in some rooms you might find the furnishings a tad worn, but most rooms are spacious. Each features a different style, from romantic to masculine. The attic rooms are well lit, but slightly smaller. Breakfast is served in the antique dining room downstairs or underneath an umbrella at a patio table outside. You'll be wowed by the view, so be sure to get a room that has one. There's also a sauna, solarium, and hydromassage whirlpool for an extra price.

Balmaceda 102, Cerro Castillo, Viña del Mar. ℂ **32/621483**. Fax 32/662432. residoff@chilesat.net. 15 units. $35–$45 double. AE, DC, MC, V. **Amenities:** Cafe; bar; sauna; laundry service; sightseeing tours. *In room:* Cable TV.

Quinta Vergara This little bubblegum-pink hotel, built around 1910 as a private home, sits at the entrance to the Quinta Vergara Park; several upper rooms look out onto its lush grounds. Some rooms have French windows and ample bathrooms. The Quinta Vergara has the feel of an older bed-and-breakfast, with shirred chiffon curtains and faded floral bedspreads. Service is exceptionally friendly and the location is ideal, although it's a long walk to the beach. A common area has a lived-in look, but the hotel is casual and guests are made to feel like they're in their own home.

Errázuriz 690, Viña del Mar. ℂ **32/691978**. Fax 32/691978. 15 units. $40 double. MC, V. **Amenities:** Office services; laundry services.

WHERE TO DINE

Cap Ducal ★ SEAFOOD This offbeat restaurant hangs from the shore and is built to resemble a ship moored against the cliff. If you're looking for an intimate, candlelit place to dine with a view of the sparkling coastline, this is your place. The focus here is fresh seafood served in both Chilean and international styles. The dishes tend to float a bit in too much sauce, so you might want to order it on the side. One exception is their Congio Oriental, with soy-flavored vegetables. If you're dying to try *erizos*, or sea urchin, this is your chance. You'll need to take a taxi to get here from downtown Viña.

Av. Marina 51. ℂ **32/626655**. Main dishes $6–$9. AE, DC, MC, V. Daily 1pm–midnight.

Diego's Pizzas *Kids* PIZZA Diego's creative, artistic pizzas stand out from Domino's and Pizza Hut down the road for their dozens and dozens of far-out toppings, more than 50 kinds of empanadas, and wonderful, fresh salads. Every pizza has a name; the biggest seller at Diego's is the "Four-Season Pizza," with shrimp, mussels, smoked salmon, razor clams, onion, mozzarella, and tomato.

A few are a little over the top, such as the "Jalapeño" that comes with guacamole and a blob of corn dough, but the majority of the pizzas are very good and are served in a casual, wood-and-tile dining room.

Av. San Martín 636. ✆ 32/689512. Individual pizzas $5–$8; salads $6. AE, DC, MC, V. Open daily 10am–2am.

El Gaucho ☆ STEAKHOUSE/ARGENTINE   Carnivores need only head to El Gaucho for ample servings of just about any kind of meat, served sizzling off the *parrilla* (grill). The Argentine-style, "interiors" appetizers include blood sausage, sweetbreads, and crispy intestines. If that doesn't make your mouth water, try starting with grilled provolone cheese with oregano. El Gaucho serves beef loin, ribs, chicken, sausages, and other grilled items, as well as salads and side dishes. The atmosphere is warm, with lemon-yellow tablecloths, wood floors, and brick walls.

Av. San Martín 435. ✆ 32/693502. Main courses $6–$14. AE, DC, MC, V. Daily 12:30–3:30pm and 7:30–11pm.

Fellini ☆☆ ITALIAN/INTERNATIONAL   The extensive menu at Fellini includes dozens of rich, homemade pastas, fresh seafood, grilled meats served draped in sauces such as Roquefort and cognac, stuffed crepes, vegetarian and low-fat plates, and more. Is it any good? You bet—just ask any of the locals who frequently drop in and greet the owner, who knows most of them by name. Everything is made fresh here, including the bread and the ice cream. The dining area is semi-elegant and warm, and the tables are well appointed.

Av. 3 Norte 88. ✆/fax 32/975742. Main courses $7.50–$11. AE, DC, MC, V. Daily 1–4pm and 7:30pm–midnight.

Las Delicias del Mar ☆☆ SEAFOOD   This Basque-influenced restaurant serves wonderfully sumptuous seafood dishes that are matched by sharp, attentive service. Las Delicias is known for its paella, which is decent, but the fish dishes are really the most savory. This is one of the few Chilean restaurants to actually put time and thought into preparing a dish, and the results are mouth-watering: sea bass, salmon, or conger eel under a rich cream, mushroom, and shrimp sauce topped with Parmesan, or sole stuffed with cheese and prawns. Tangerine-colored walls, leafy plants, and colorful linens make for a warm, comfortable atmosphere.

Av. San Martín 459. ✆ 32/901837. Main courses $10–$12. AE, DC, MC, V. Daily 12:30–4pm and 7:30pm–midnight.

Ristorante San Marco ☆☆ ITALIAN   If you're in the mood for pasta, this is the place to come. San Marco is one of the best restaurants in the area, and has been since it opened its doors in 1957. Everything is made fresh daily here. Most of the pastas are traditional and served with typical sauces, such as bolognese or alfredo, plus more original options like seafood or creamy basil sauce. San Marco offers an extensive list of rich, homemade desserts and a reasonably priced wine list. The simple dining area has wraparound windows festooned with hanging vines and tables draped with white linen tablecloths.

Av. San Martín 597. ✆ 32/975304. Fax 32/884872. Main courses $6–$10. AE, DC, MC, V. Daily noon–4pm and 8pm–midnight.

WHAT TO SEE & DO
BEACHES

The **Playa Caleta Abarca** beach is located in a protected bay near the entrance to Viña del Mar, next to the oft-photographed "flower clock" and the Cerro Castillo. In the northeast, fronting rows of terraced high-rise apartment buildings, you'll find **Playa Acapulco, Playa Mirasol,** and **Playa Las Salinas** (the latter is near the naval base). These beaches all see throngs of vacationers and families in the summer. Beach-lovers might consider heading just north of Viña to **Reñaca**—it's close enough to take a taxi, or grab bus no. 1, 10, or 111 at avenidas Libertad and 15 Norte. Reñaca is *the* in spot, and sees a slightly younger, and sometimes larger, crowd than Viña.

THE TOP ATTRACTIONS

Casino Municipal ★★★   Built in 1930, the Casino Municipal was the most luxurious building in its day and is worth a visit even if you're not a gambler. The interior has been remodeled over time, but the facade has withstood the caprices of many a developer and is still as handsome as the day it opened. Semiformal attire (no T-shirts, jeans, or sneakers) is required to enter the gaming room. The casino also holds temporary art exhibits on the second floor.

Plaza Colombia between Av. San Martín and Av. Perú. ✆ **32/500600** or 32/500700. Admission $6 (charged only to enter game room). Hours vary, but generally: game room daily 6pm–4am (Sun–Thurs winter hours are 6pm–2am); slot machines daily noon–4am; bingo daily 4pm–4am. Weekends open 24 hr.

Museo de Arqueología e Historia Francisco Fonck ★★   This museum boasts a large collection of indigenous art and archaeological items from Easter Island, with more than 1,400 pieces and one of the six Moai sculptures outside Easter Island (the others are in England, the U.S., Paris, Brussels, and La Serena in Chile). There is also a decent archaeological exhibition of Mapuche pieces and other items from the north and central zones of Chile. The Museum of Natural History is on the second floor, featuring birds, mammals, insects, and fossils.

Av. 4 Norte 784. ✆ **32/686753**. Admission $1.60 adults, 30¢ children. Tues–Fri 9:30am–6pm; Sat–Sun 9:30am–2pm.

Museo Palacio Rioja ★   This enormous 1906 Belle Epoque stone mansion is worth a visit for a peek into the lives of the early-20th-century elite in Viña del Mar. Built by Spaniard Fernando Rioja, a banker, and originally spanning 4 blocks, the palace took opulence to a new level, with a stone facade featuring Corinthian columns and a split double staircase. Interiors are made of oak and stone, with enough salons to fit a family of 20. Although a fraction of what it once was, the palm-fringed garden surrounding the house is idyllic.

Quillota 214. ✆ **32/689665**. Admission 60¢ adults, 20¢ children. Tues–Sun 10am–1pm and 3–5:30pm.

Quinta Vergara Park/Museum of Fine Art ★★★   One of the loveliest parks in central Chile, the Quinta Vergara is also home to a large amphitheater that holds Viña's yearly Song Festival as well as the Museum of Fine Art. The Quinta, whose area is naturally fenced in by several steep hills, was once the residence of Portuguese shipping magnate Francisco Alvarez and his wife, Dolores, who created the park, planting a multitude of native and other exotic species. The museum is housed in the ornate **Palacio Vergara,** which was built by Francisco's great-granddaughter, and the collection includes art from the family collection and other works from collectors in Viña.

Near Plaza Parroquia. Museum ✆ **32/252481**. Park: Free admission; open daily 7am–6pm (until 7pm in summer). Museum: Admission 60¢ adults, 30¢ children; open Tues–Sun 10am–2pm and 3–6pm.

2 Valparaíso

115km (71 miles) NW of Santiago; 8km (5 miles) S of Viña del Mar

Valparaíso is Viña del Mar's next-door neighbor, but the two couldn't be more different. This port town is Viña's blue-collar sister, with a history and vibrant culture that speaks strongly of the golden days before the Panama Canal, when every ship on its way around the Cape stopped here for supplies. Valparaíso, with its multicolored jumble of clapboard homes and weathered Victorian mansions, sinuous streets, steep hills, and rollicking seafront bars, is enchanting— although it might not capture you at first. It is a poorer city, and a little rough around the edges. Because of this, Valparaíso can be a little scary to first-time visitors, but give it a chance and allow the city to work its magic on you.

Valparaíso has spawned a generation of international poets, writers, and artists who have found inspiration in the city, including the Nobel prize–winning poet Pablo Neruda, who owned a home here. The bohemian flavor is still going strong, and the city is known for its eccentric and antiquated bars that stay open into the wee hours of the morning. The city is also known for its restaurants, some of which have the most dramatic sea views found anywhere in Chile.

But the real attractions here are losing yourself in the city's streets, viewing the angular architecture of homes and mansions that cling to the hillsides, and especially riding the century-old, clickety-clack *ascensores,* or funiculars, that lift riders to the tops of hills. If you're the type who craves character and culturally unique surroundings, this is your place.

ESSENTIALS

GETTING THERE **By Bus** Frequent, comfortable buses leave the Terminal Alameda in Santiago at Alameda O'Higgins 3712 (1 block from Terminal Santiago; Metro: University de Santiago), about every 15 minutes. Tur Bus and Pullman offer service to and from Valparaíso, with fares running an average of $4 one-way. The trip takes about 1 hour and 15 minutes, depending on traffic. In Valparaíso you'll disembark at the terminal at Avenida Pedro Montt; taxis are available and a good idea at night. Consider buying a round-trip ticket if you plan to travel on weekends or holidays.

By Car To get to Valparaíso from Santiago, take Av. Alameda west until it changes into Ruta Nacional 68. Ten kilometers (6 miles) from the coast, follow the signs to Valparaíso. There is one tollbooth along the way; the toll varies between 1,000 to 3,300 pesos ($1.40–$4.50) depending on the time and day. Valparaíso is 115km (71 miles) northwest of Santiago. Most hotels will arrange parking, and there's a garage on Calle Errázuriz, across from the Plaza Sotomayor. Do not park your car full of belongings on the city street at night.

VISITOR INFORMATION/CITY TOURS There are several **tourist offices** in Valparaíso; the best is at Muelle Prat (© 32/939489), open daily from 10am to 6pm. There's also an information kiosk at the bus station open daily from 8:30am to 5:30pm. **La Hoya del Pacífico** (© 09/533-3681; $11 per person) and **Enlace Tours** (© 32/232313; $13 per person) offer **city tours** in minivans (English-speaking guides are available). Both tours last for 2½ hours and include an ascent up the city's funiculars.

GETTING AROUND Walking is really the only way to see Valparaíso; parking is limited and most attractions lie within a compact area. To get to and from Viña del Mar, take a taxi or, better yet, ride the Merval, a commuter train that runs every 20 minutes from the Estación Puerto (next to Valparaíso's visitor center) and costs about 35¢ to 75¢.

SPECIAL EVENTS Valparaíso's famed **New Year's Pyrotechnic Festival** takes place every December 31, lighting the sky with a spectacular fireworks display. A memorable way to see the show is atop one of the hills, such as Cerro

Valparaíso

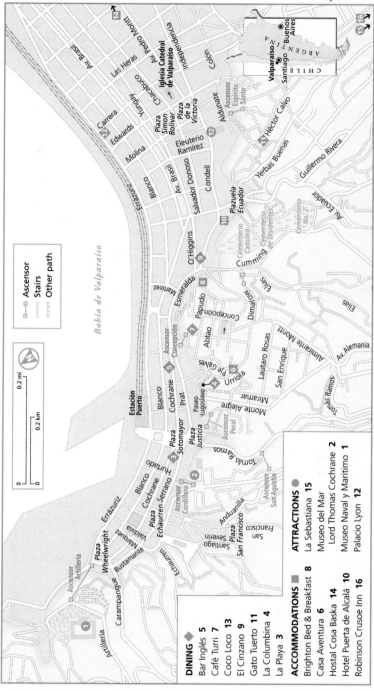

DINING ◆
Bar Inglés **5**
Café Turri **7**
Coco Loco **13**
El Cinzano **9**
Gato Tuerto **11**
La Columbina **4**
La Playa **3**

ACCOMMODATIONS ■
Brighton Bed & Breakfast **8**
Casa Aventura **6**
Hostal Cosa Baska **14**
Hotel Puerta de Alcalá **10**
Robinson Crusoe Inn **16**

ATTRACTIONS ●
La Sebastiana **15**
Museo del Mar
Lord Thomas Cochrane **2**
Museo Naval y Maritimo **1**
Palacio Lyon **12**

Bahía de Valparaíso

Ascensor
Stairs
Other path

0.2 mi
0.2 km

Alegre or Cerro Concepción, or from one of the several boats that offer special excursions around the harbor. Ask at the visitor center at Muelle Prat about making arrangements; reservations need to be made 1 to 2 weeks in advance. Another highlight, during late October, is **Regatta Off Valparaíso,** a traditional Chilean regatta organized by the Arturo Prat Naval Academy, featuring more than 50 competing yachts. Call the tourism office for dates, or check the Valparaíso naval website at www.armada.cl.

WHERE TO STAY

With the exception of one hotel, the bulk of lodgings in Valparaíso take the form of scrappy *residenciales* with shared bathrooms, lumpy beds, and dingy lighting—the reason most travelers choose to lodge in Viña del Mar and visit Valparaíso by day instead.

Brighton Bed & Breakfast ★★ *Moments* This is one of the prettiest places to spend the night in Valparaíso, in spite of the so-so rooms. A big yellow Victorian perched high atop Cerro Concepción, this B&B offers stunning, sweeping views of the harbor and the city center below. Rooms are unremarkable, but the exceptional location more than makes up for it. Because this is a converted home, room sizes vary; try booking the "suite" (really a large double) with a balcony and sea view. There's also a cafe on the first floor with checkered black-and-white floors and two terrace patios—an unbeatable location for lunch or coffee. On weekends, the cafe has live bolero and tango music, and it stays open until 4am. To get here, take the Concepción *ascensor* and go left.

Paseo Atkinson 151–153, Cerro Concepción, Valparaíso. ©/fax **32/223513.** www.brighton.cl. 6 units. $42 double without bathroom; $50 double with bathroom; $57 double with bathroom and sea view. AE, DC, MC, V. **Amenities:** Cafe.

Casa Aventura ★ *Value* This tiny gem of a *hostal* has a central location, clean, attractive interiors, Spanish language courses, and Internet access. With just five rooms (2 triples, 2 with a double bed, and 1 quad), the atmosphere is quiet and intimate, with a sunny living area and couches for just hanging out. The German-Chilean couple who own Casa Aventura opened the *hostal* three years ago, and they typically cater to budget travelers and students who take part in their on-site, optional Spanish courses. If your group doesn't fill the room, you might end up sharing with a stranger. Beds have fluffy down comforters, but the only rooms that are sunny and bright are the two triples. Guests have kitchen and laundry privileges. Casa Aventura also arranges tours in and around Valparaíso, and to places such as La Campana. Spanish courses should preferably be reserved in advance by e-mail; average cost for a private class is $10 per hour, or $14 total for two students.

Pasaje Gálvez 11, Cerro Alegre, Valparaíso. ©/fax **32/755963.** www.backpackerschile.com. 5 units. $9 per person. No credit cards. **Amenities:** Self-service laundry; kitchen facilities.

Hotel Puerta de Alcalá This newer hotel just off busy Avenida Condell is a tad frumpy, but it is comfortable and without a doubt one of the better hotels in the city. Rooms come with soundproof windows and are somewhat dark; however, an on-site restaurant is light and pleasant, due in part to a five-floor atrium that allows sunshine to cascade in. Style isn't a high point here, as boxes of tacky plastic flowers attest; however, service is friendly, and they'll even arrange tours in Valparaíso and to locations as far away as Portillo Ski Resort.

Pirámide 524 (off Av. Condell), Valparaíso. © **32/227478.** Fax 32/745642. www.hotelpuertaalcala.cl. 21 units. $39–$50 double. AE, DC, MC, V. **Amenities:** Restaurant; laundry service; sightseeing tours. *In room:* Cable TV, minibar.

Robinson Crusoe Hotel ★★★ *(Finds)* They don't have a website, nor do they seem to want much publicity, which makes this little bed-and-breakfast the best find in Valparaíso. The Robinson Crusoe is a stylish inn topped with a terrace lounge that offers a knockout view of the city. The inn was once a collection of several run-down homes that the owner, Jorge Henderson, bought, enclosed to form one unit, and topped with glass roofs. He then remodeled the interiors with dark wood, ceramic floors, winding stairways, and walls painted in rich plums and ornamented with arts and crafts and nautical decor. The old-fashioned tall doors, stained glass, and high windows all lend an antique splendor to the inn. The rooftop restaurant/lounge has captivating views of the port and the colorful streets that plummet toward it. An excellent breakfast is another highlight. The hotel is about a 15-minute walk to downtown Valparaíso, and a climb back, so you might find yourself taking a taxi. Close to the Pablo Neruda museum.

Héctor Calvo 389, Valparaíso. ✆ 32/495499. robinsoncrusoeinn@hotmail.com. 14 units. $60–$78 double. AE, MC, DC, V. **Amenities:** Restaurant. *In room:* TV.

WHERE TO DINE
EXPENSIVE

Café Turri ★★★ INTERNATIONAL/CHILEAN Regionally famous, Café Turri is one of the best restaurants in the city. Fine food, gorgeous views, and an attentive waitstaff make this an enjoyable gastronomic experience, especially when it is sunny and you dine on the terrace. Housed in a converted home built a century ago by an English immigrant, the restaurant sits high atop the Cerro Concepción and occupies three floors. Café Turri's specialty is seafood, but they also serve a variety of meat and chicken dishes. The remarkably extensive menu includes sea bass, salmon, congrio, albacore tuna, and more, each cooked 24 different ways, as well as exquisite appetizers and desserts.

Calle Templeman 147 (Cerro Concepción; take the Concepción lift). ✆ 32/259198. Dinner reservations recommended for outdoor seating. Main courses $5–$15. AE, DC, MC, V. Mon–Fri 9am–midnight; Sat–Sun 9am–2am.

La Columbina ★★★ *(Moments)* INTERNATIONAL/CHILEAN This terrific restaurant occupies three floors of a beautiful Victorian building and includes a tearoom with stained-glass windows and a panoramic view; a restaurant/pub with parquet floors and a pretty terrace shaded by striped awnings; and a more formal dining area with linen tablecloths, antiques, and smartly dressed waiters. The antique building is an old servants' quarters for the nearby Palacio Baburizza. In the evening, the pub offers an additional menu of appetizers, including Mexican and Thai platters, as well as excellent, artfully prepared entrees, such as filet mignon marinated in dark beer and fresh herbs. Wood-burning stoves, sumptuous views, a colorful, amicable staff, and live jazz, tango, and bolero music on Friday and Saturday make for a great atmosphere.

Pasaje Apolo 91–77. ✆ 32/236254. Main courses $5–$10. No credit cards. Tues–Sat 9am–4pm, 4–8pm (tearoom only) and 8pm–midnight (Fri–Sat until 2am); Sun–Mon 9am–4pm.

MODERATE

Bar Inglés CHILEAN So-so food and a slightly overpriced menu do not make the Bar Inglés a great value, but the old-world atmosphere merits a visit, especially to sidle up to the long oak bar for a coffee or beer. The ambience is early 1900s, with antique tile floors, wooden pillars and walls, and tables draped with white linen. Smaller items such as sandwiches are usually fairly good, but main courses are too simple for the asking price. Still, the Bar Inglés remains a local favorite among businessmen, who spend long lunches pounding out deals.

Entrance on Cochrane 851 or Blanco 870. © **32/214625**. Main courses $7–$11. No credit cards. Mon–Fri 9am–midnight.

Caleta Portales ★★ SEAFOOD   This is yet another seafood restaurant, but the newly renovated Caleta Portales deserves special mention. It has been consistently rated as the best seafood restaurant in town, notably because they serve fresh-from-the-sea fish and shellfish—however, some dishes, such as their Congrio Portales, tend to be drowned in sauce or not prepared to the height of one's expectations. Nevertheless, most items are reasonably tasty. Try their Albacore tuna with a light caper sauce, or the salmon with a garlic and shrimp sauce, or any of their appetizers, including an excellent *ceviche* (chopped fish and onion in lemon juice). It's a bit of a walk, so take a taxi if you're in Cerro Alegre or Concepción.

Caleta Portales s/n (at Av. España and Av. Phillippi). © **32/625814**. Main courses $6–$11. AE, DC, MC, V. Daily noon–midnight.

Coco Loco ★★ SEAFOOD   This port version of the well-known Santiago seafood restaurant features two floors—one of which is a *giratorio,* a revolving dining area underneath a glass dome that allows diners to appreciate all the splendor of Valparaíso. The restaurant is more upscale than its companions along the port, and it doesn't have that old-world Valparaíso ambience. Nevertheless, the Coco Loco offers a good menu of grilled, poached, and fried fish served with tasty sauces, and a range of hot appetizers that typically feature shellfish. There are also beef and chicken dishes available.

Blanco 1781, 22nd floor. © **32/227614**. Main courses $6–$16. AE, DC, MC, V. Daily noon–4pm and 8–11pm (until midnight Fri–Sat).

Gato Tuerto ★★ SEAFOOD/INTERNATIONAL   This restaurant is housed within the vividly painted lemon yellow and blue Victorian that hovers over Plaza Victoria. The Gato Tuerto doesn't merit any special culinary awards, but the ambience is wonderful, due to the view and the service. The menu serves about 20 dishes from a dozen different countries, ranging from Moroccan to Thai to Indonesian, such as Nasi Goreng, a dish with shrimp, red pepper, squash, and almonds, served with rice.

Héctor Calvo 205 (Espíritu Santo Funicular). © **32/593156**. Main courses $5–$8. AE, DC, MC, V. Daily noon–midnight.

INEXPENSIVE

El Cinzano ★ *Moments* CHILEAN   Since 1896 this classic restaurant has been the popular hangout for poets, intellectuals and musicians, who come for latenight *chorrillanas,* a Valparaíso specialty of steak, eggs, onions, and french fries tossed together and heaped on a platter. Waiters in smart black jackets and bow ties serve typical Chilean seafood fare and grilled meats, as well as their other specialty: *vino arreglado,* or "fixed" wine with strawberry, peach, or *chirimoya* (custard apple). The Cinzano frequently hosts dinner dances on the second floor, and tango singers serenade customers on weekends.

Aníbal Pinto 1182. © **32/213043**. Main courses $3.50–$8. AE, DC, MC, V. Daily 10am–1am (until 4:30am Thurs–Sat).

La Playa ★ CHILEAN   Founded in 1903, this traditional bar serves up cheap Chilean lunches and even cheaper *picoteos* (appetizer platters) and beer in the evening; it converts into a pub after 10pm. The long oak bar, wooden floors, marine memorabilia, and gigantic mirrors rescued from the Seven Mirrors brothel offer old Valparaíso charm. The food is standard Chilean fare, such as crab soup and filet mignon *a la pobre* (topped with fried eggs and onions), and on Thursday, Friday, and Saturday, there's live jazz, rock, and blues music starting at 1:30am. On Monday evenings La Playa holds live poetry readings. This is the epicenter of late-night life, and can get packed after midnight.

Serrano 568. (C) 32/594262. Main courses $3–$7. MC, V. Mon–Wed 10am–2am; Thurs–Sat noon–5:30am.

WHAT TO SEE & DO

La Sebastiana ✦✦✦   La Sebastiana is one of poet Pablo Neruda's three charming homes that have since been converted into museums honoring the distinguished Nobel Laureate's work and life. La Sebastiana is exceptionally enjoyable because the staff allow visitors to wander about freely without an accompanying guide.

There are self-guiding information sheets in a variety of languages that explain the significance of important documents and items on display, as well as Neruda's whimsical collection of eccentric knickknacks culled from his journeys through the Americas and abroad. Despite being terrified of sailing, Neruda was fascinated by the sea, and he fashioned his homes to resemble boats, complete with porthole windows. A cultural center has been built below the house, with a gallery and a gift shop.

The walk from Plaza Victoria is a hike, so you might want to take a taxi. From Plaza Ecuador, there's a bus, Verde "D." Or you might opt to take **La Cintura (The Waist),** a bus route that takes riders up and down and around the snaking streets of Valparaíso and eventually stops a block or so from Neruda's house (be sure to tell the driver that's your final destination because the bus continues on). To take this route, board Bus Verde "O" at Plaza Echaurren near the Customs House (La Aduana).

Calle Ferrari 692. (C) 32/256606. Admission $2.50 adults, $1.25 students. Mar–Dec Tues–Fri 10:30am–2pm and 3:30–6pm, Sat–Sun 10:30am–6pm; Jan–Feb Tues–Sun 10:30am–6pm; closed Mon.

Museo de Historia Natural ✦✦ *Kids*   This museum is housed in the grand Palacio Lyon, a 50-room palace that was built as a residence in 1881. The museum holds a collection of 27,000 pieces related to the natural history of the region and beyond, including Easter Island. The museum opens with a vast display of shells and continues with eight rooms devoted to flora and fauna, as well as an interesting collection of the coins used as barter at the nitrate mines of Chile's north. The museum updated itself a bit last year, and removed the oddball items such as a two-headed baby, much to everyone's dismay.

Av. Condell 1546. (C) 32/257441. Admission $1 adults, 50¢ students and seniors; Wed and Sun free. Tues–Sat 10am–1pm and 2–6pm; Sun 10am–2pm.

Museo de Mar Thomás Cochrane ✦   High atop Cerro Cordillera sits Lord Cochrane's Museum of the Sea inside the old residence of Juan Mouat, who built the house in 1841 in colonial style with all the trimmings, including its own observatory. Now it houses a display of model ships once owned by Lord Cochrane. If the theme doesn't interest you, the dramatic view will.

Calle Merlet 195 (via the Ascensor Cordillera). (C) 32/213124. Free admission. Tues–Sun 10am–6pm.

Museo Naval y Marítimo ✦✦   This fascinating museum merits a visit even if you do not particularly fancy naval and maritime-related artifacts and memorabilia. The museum is smartly designed and divided into four salons: the War of Independence, the War against the Peru-Bolivia Confederation, the War against Spain, and the War of the Pacific. Each salon holds interesting artifacts, such as antique documents, medals, uniforms, and war trophies. Of special note is the Arturo Prat room, with artifacts salvaged from the *Esmeralda,* a ship was sunk during the War of the Pacific.

Paseo 21 de Mayo, Cerro Artillería. ℂ **32/283749.** Admission 90¢ adults, 35¢ kids under 12. Tues–Sun 10am–5:30pm.

WALKING TOUR	FROM THE PORT TO THE HEIGHTS OF VALPARAISO

Start:	Muelle Prat, Visitor Center.
Finish:	Ascensor Concepción or Calle Esmeralda.
Time:	1 to 3 hours.
Best Times:	Saturday and Sunday are less hectic, but begin after 10am when everything opens.

① Muelle Prat/Visitor Center

Begin at the visitor center at Muelle Prat. You might consider taking a 75¢ "cruise" aboard one of the many fishing skiffs and launches that ferry visitors around the Valparaíso harbor for 20 minutes. Just head toward the dock—an eager skipper will find you. One company, **Maite** (ℂ **09/238-2832**), offers a harbor tour every day at 11am in January and February, and on-call throughout the rest of the year. Prices depend on the number of passengers, and daily journeys are about $2–$5 for 1 hour. To rent the entire boat for 3 to 50 passengers, for 1 hour, costs $115.

Head away from the pier and cross Errázuriz to reach:

② Plaza Sotomayor

This plaza acted as the civic center of Valparaíso until 1980. At the plaza's entrance you'll encounter the **Monument to the Heroes of Iquique,** under which the remains of Prat, Condell, and Serrano, heroes of the War of the Pacific, are buried. To the right of the plaza sits the Navy Command Headquarters, built in 1910 and once used as the seat of the provincial government and the presidential summer residence.

To the left of the plaza, next to the Palacio de Justicia, ride the Ascensor Peral (ca. 1902) for 10¢ to the top of Cerro Alegre and there you'll find:

③ Paseo Yugoslavo

This pleasant terrace walkway was built by Pascual Baburizza in 1929 and named in honor of his heritage.

Continue along the terrace until you pass:

④ Palacio Baburizza

This 1916 home was built for the nitrate magnate Ottorino Zanelli, and later became the home of Baburizza until his death in 1941. It now houses the city's Fine Arts Museum, a collection of 19th- and 20th-century Chilean and European paintings, including paintings of Valparaíso by Rugendas and Somerscales, and occasional expositions of local modern works (ℂ **32/252481;** open Tues–Sun 10am–6pm; free admission).

Continue along Paseo Yugoslavo, past the La Columbina restaurant. The road curves to the right around a tiny plaza; follow it until you reach Calle Alvaro Besa. Take Alvaro Besa as it winds down the hill, or take the shortcut down Pasaje Bavestrello, a cement stairway at the left. Continue until you reach Calle Urriola, which you'll cross, then walk up 20m (22 yd.) and turn left into another stairway, Pasaje Gálvez. The narrow walkway twists and turns, passing the colorful facades of some of the most striking homes in Valparaíso. At Calle Papudo, climb the stairway and turn left into:

⑤ Paseo Gervasoni

This pleasant walkway, lined with stately, 19th-century mansions, looks out onto the port of Valparaíso.

Legend:
- ▭—▭ Ascensor
- ▦ Stairs
- ▭▭▭ Other path
- - - - Walking Tour route

1 Muelle Prat/Visitor's Center
2 Plaza Sotomayor
3 Paseo Yugoslavo
4 Palacio Baburizza
5 Paseo Gervasoni
6 Casa Mirador de Lukas
7 Anglican Church of St. Paul
8 Paseo Atkinson

At the end of the walkway, you'll find Café Turri, an idyllic place for lunch or coffee. First you might want to check out:

6 Casa Mirador de Lukas

The museum displays a permanent exhibition of hundreds of illustrations made by Renzo Pecchenino, a wonderful cartoonist and satirist for the newspaper *El Mercurio* (© **32/221344**; Tues–Sun 11am–8pm; admission 70¢). It is possible to end the walking tour here and descend via Ascensor Concepción, but I recommend that you keep walking.

Continue around Gervasoni until you reach Papudo. You take a detour here 2 blocks up Calle Templeman to visit the:

7 Anglican Church of St. Paul

Built in 1858, this unadorned church was not officially recognized until 1869, when the Chilean government repealed a law banning religions other than Catholicism. The church houses a grand organ donated by the British in 1901 in honor of Queen Victoria. You can hear this magnificent instrument at work at 12:30pm every Sunday.

Double back to Calle Papudo, head southeast (turning right if returning from the church) until reaching:

8 Paseo Atkinson

At the entrance to Paseo Atkinson, you'll pass a Lutheran church, built in 1897 and housing the antique organ (ca. 1855) that was once played in the Anglican Church. Paseo Atkinson is another breathtaking pedestrian walkway, bordered by antique homes featuring the zinc facades and guillotine windows popular with the British in the early 20th century. Continue down the pedestrian stairway until you reach Calle Esmeralda, and the end of the walk. You can also descend by doubling back and riding the Ascensor Concepción to Calle Prat.

OTHER SHORT WALKS

THE PORT NEIGHBORHOOD Begin at the **Customs House (Aduana),** the grand, colonial American–style building built in 1854 and located at the north of town at Plaza Wheelwright at the end of Cochrane and Calle Carampangue. To the right you'll find the **Ascensor Artillería,** built in 1893 (and it shows); it costs 10¢. The wobbly contraption takes visitors to the most panoramic pedestrian walkway in Valparaíso, **Paseo 21 de Mayo.** Don't miss the view of the port from the gazebo. Follow the walkway until reaching the **Museo Naval y Marítimo** (described in "What to See & Do," above). To return, double back and descend via the *ascensor,* or head down the walkway that begins at the cafe, and take a left at Calle Carampangue.

PLAZA VICTORIA/MUSEO A CIELO ABIERTO/LA SEBASTIANA (PABLO NERUDA'S HOUSE) Plaza Victoria is the prettiest plaza in Valparaíso. In the late 1880s, it was the elegant center of society; the grand trees, trickling fountain, and sculptures imported from Lima recall that era's heyday.

From the plaza, head south on Calle Molina to Alduante for the **Open Air Museum,** which features more than 20 murals painted on cement retainer and building walls along winding streets. Begin at the steep stairway at Calle Alduante and turn left at Pasaje Guimera, and left again at the balcony walkway that leads to **Ascensor Espíritu Santo** (you can ride the funicular up and backtrack this route, walking down). Continue along Calle Rudolph until reaching Calle Ferrari. It's possible to walk up Ferrari to number 692 and **La Sebastiana,** Pablo Neruda's old house (described in "What to See & Do," above), although it's a bit of a hike. Head down Ferrari all the way to Edwards and Colón. Note that the Open Air Museum runs through an interesting but grubby, somewhat rough neighborhood, and for that reason might not appeal to everyone.

VALPARAISO AFTER DARK

Valparaíso is famous for its nightlife, especially its bohemian pubs and bars where poets, writers, tango aficionados, sailors, university students, and just about everyone else spend hours drinking, dancing, and socializing well into the early morning hours. In fact, most restaurants and bars do not adhere to a set closing hour, but instead close "when the candles burn down."

Most places serve snacks, especially bars and pubs that operate as restaurants by day. **Cinzano,** facing Plaza Aníbal Pinto on Calle Esmeralda (© **32/213043**), hosts dinner dances and spotlights tango music and singers in an early-20th-century ambience. **La Columbina** (© **32/236254**) is frequented by the 30-and-up crowd for its comfortable ambience, live jazz and bolero music, and view of the glittering lights of Valparaíso that spread out below; take a cab or the funicular Ascensor Peral and walk down Paseo Yugoslavo.

Bars and nightspots keep popping up on Calle Errázuriz and include **La Piedra Feliz,** Errázuriz 1054 (© **32/256788**), which has wooden floors, a dance floor, and a normally tranquil atmosphere—until they fire up live music in the evening from Tuesday through Sunday. **La Cueva del Chivato,** Errázuriz 1152 (© **32/758160**), plays live music amid a chaotic ambience, including a disco with good electronic music. There's also the more traditional **Roland Bar,** Errázuriz 1152 (© **32/235123**); or for salsa or merengue, try **Puerto Bahía,** Errázuriz 1090 (no phone).

Calle Ecuador has lost its rank as the in spot, but it's still a popular area, especially among the 20- to 30-year-old crowd. Try **Liverpool,** Ecuador 130 (© **32/610109**), probably the nicest spot with live music and a relaxed atmosphere;

there's also **Bar Emile Dubois,** Ecuador 144 (© **32/213486**), an offbeat bar/disco whose name is an homage to the first person to die under capital punishment in Chile, and where drinks come with names like "strangulation."

3 Excursions Outside Valparaíso & Viña del Mar

ISLA NEGRA

125km (78 miles) W of Santiago

The coast south of Valparaíso is dotted with small towns, many of which are summer and weekend retreats for Santiago residents. However, at Isla Negra, visitors will find a tiny village and Pablo Neruda's third, and most interesting, home. Isla Negra, which means Black Island, is not an island but a promontory. There are several good cafes and restaurants here, such as the **Café del Poeta** (located within the museum) and the **Hostería La Candela,** making for a pleasant half-day trip. Hostería La Candela is a nice little hotel should you decide to spend the evening here (Calle de la Hostería 67; © **32/461254;** www.candela.cl). The coastal strip has been declared a Zona Típica (Heritage Zone) to preserve the area from becoming overrun by multistoried apartment buildings. You can get here from Valparaíso **by bus** with the company Pullman (© **32/224025**), which leaves every 20 minutes from the bus terminal, until 10pm. To get here **by car,** you'll need to drive back out toward Santiago on Ruta 68 until you see the sign for Algarrobo and the road back toward the coast. Isla Negra is south of Algarrobo.

Casa Pablo Neruda ★★★ *(Moments*   This was Neruda's favorite home, and it's the best preserved of his three houses. It's packed full of books by his favorite authors and the whimsical curios, trinkets, and toys he collected during his travels around the world, including African masks, ships in bottles, butterflies, and more. You can see the home by guided (bilingual) tour only, which lasts about 40 minutes. This is a fascinating and very enjoyable half-day trip if you combine it with lunch and a stroll down the beach.

Costanera of Isla Negra. © **35/461284**. Admission $4. Summer Tues–Sun 10am–8pm; winter Tues–Fri 10am–2pm and 3–6pm; Sat, Sun, and holidays 10am–8pm.

PARQUE NACIONAL LA CAMPANA

Chile is home to the southernmost species of palm tree in the world, the Palma Chilena *(Jubaea chilensis).* The palms grow very slowly and live as long as 800 years. They were almost harvested to extinction for their sap, which was used to make *miel de palma,* which is much like pancake syrup. Chilean Palms have been planted in parks in London and California, but you can see hundreds of them here at La Campana National Park, about 43km (27 miles) from Viña del Mar.

The park also offers surprisingly extensive views, such as from the lookout point on Cerro La Campana that allows hikers to view the Andes on one side and the Pacific on the other. Charles Darwin stood at this very spot to admire the view in 1834, claiming that Chile could be seen "as in a map." There are three sectors in the park, each with separate entrances: Palmar de Ocoa, Granizo, and Cajón Grande. There is an easy walk in the Cajón Grande sector, and a longer, 3-hour climb in the Granizo sector. The Granizo sector is the park's main entrance, and here you'll find a park ranger station with information (© **33/442922**).

Palmar de Ocoa is where you really get to view the sea of thick palms. This section of the park can be reached by road, or by foot from the Sector Granizo (which is really a full-day trip that is best done as a backpack trip). There is a

6km (3½-mile) trail here to a waterfall. To get here by car, take Ruta 5 north through Llaillay and take the turn-off to Los Maitenes and Palmar de Ocoa. There is no bus service to this sector.

The park is open daily June through August from 8am to 7pm, and September through May from 8am to 6pm (© **33/442922;** www.parquelacampana.cl). Admission is $2.50 adults and $1 children, and it costs an additional $8.50 to camp. **Buses Golondrina** leaves from Santiago's San Borja Terminal every 30 minutes (© **2/778-7082**) and arrives at San Francisco de Limache—from here you take a *colectivo* (shared taxi). Due to changing service, ask at the visitor centers in Valparaíso or Viña del Mar for information about tours and transportation to La Campana. By car from Santiago, take Ruta 68 through Casablanca, then head right toward Villa Alemana and then Limache.

4 Cajón de Maipo

San Alfonso is 65km (40 miles) E of Santiago

Cajón de Maipo is part *huaso* (a cowboy from the central valley), part artist's colony, part small-town charm tucked into a valley in the foothills of the Andes. From Santiago it's less than 1 hour to the heart of the Cajón, the reason so many city denizens come to exchange the city smog and cement for the area's rugged, pastoral setting of towering peaks, freshly scented forest slopes, and the roar of the Maipo River as it descends along its route to the sea.

The highlight of this area is **El Morado National Park** (see "Attractions & Activities," below), but it is certainly not a requisite destination. Cajón de Maipo offers a wide array of outdoor activities, such as rafting, horseback riding, hiking, climbing, and more, but it also offers a chance to linger over a good lunch or picnic, stroll around the area, and maybe even lay your head down for the night in one of the charming little *cabañas* that line the valley.

The well-paved road through this valley follows the trajectory of the Maipo River. Along the way you'll pass dozens of stalls set up by locals who sell fresh bread, honey, *kuchen* (a dense cake), empanadas, and chocolate to passers-by.

Then you'll pass the tiny hamlets of Vertientes and San José de Maipo, the principal city of the area, founded in 1792 when silver was discovered in the foothills. The colonial adobe homes and 18th-century church still surround the traditional plaza in the center of town. Continuing southeast the road curves past San Alfonso and eventually reaches a police checkpoint where drivers register before continuing on the dirt road to El Morado. It is about a 2-hour drive to El Morado, due to the condition of the dirt portion of the road past San Gabriel.

ESSENTIALS

GETTING THERE **By Bus** Blue and white buses leave daily from the Metro station at Parque O'Higgins in Santiago (line 2) to San José de Maipo about every 15 minutes from 6am to 11:30pm, and every half hour for San Alfonso. If you're going to El Morado, you need to catch a local bus in the Cajón de Maipo. Your hotel should be able to arrange a private minivan tour to Cajón de Maipo, or, to do it at your own leisure, rent a car.

By Car The route to Cajón de Maipo is fairly straightforward, but it's possible to miss the turn-off if you're not paying attention. Head south on Avenida Los Leones in Providencia. The road will change its name to España, then Macul. Continue through the neighborhood of La Florida, and take a left at the fork at Puente Alto. If you are downtown, following Vicuña Mackenna street will take you directly there. Take a map and plan on weekend traffic. If you plan to go to El Morado, note that there is a police checkpoint where drivers must show their documents, including a passport.

WHERE TO STAY

Cascada de las Animas ★★ *Kids*   This tourism center is run by the bohemian Astorga-Moreno family, long-time residents who own a tremendous amount of acreage outside San Alfonso, part of which is used for excursions, and 80 campground and picnic sites scattered about a lovely, wooded hillside. What is really special here, however, are their log cabins, set amid sylvan, leafy surroundings and uniquely built with carved wood details. The cabins are rustic, but snug and comfortable, with fully equipped kitchens and wood-burning stoves. There's an outdoor swimming pool, and a wonderful trail for a day hike. They offer kayaking, rafting, and horseback riding excursions, and there is a full-service restaurant. The owners also offer meditation, healing programs, and a women's spiritual retreat. Unfortunately, the service is consistently lackluster and can often be excruciatingly slow.

San Alfonso s/n, San Alfonso. ⓒ 2/861-1303. www.cascadadelasanimas.cl. 8 units. $57 *cabaña* for 3; $100 *cabaña* for 8. No credit cards. **Amenities:** Restaurant; outdoor pool; guided activities.

La Bella Durmiente ★★ *Kids*   Located at the end of a steep dirt road, these fairy-tale *cabañas* seem as if they've jumped out of the tale "Sleeping Beauty," which is what the name means—but the word *durmiente* also refers to the thick wooden railroad planks used to build these quaint cabins. Each *cabaña* is distinct, and all are handcrafted from wood and stucco and nestled among a grove of trees that surround a small restaurant and pool. The style is rustic but refined; two, including the cozy honeymoon cabin, have sunny patios. There are cabins for two to six guests; the latter is especially nice, with a large dining area. If you don't want to cook, you can opt for full pension. Maid service comes only with the full pension price (an additional $10 per person).

Calle Los Maitenes 115, San Alfonso. ⓒ 2/861-1525. www.labelladurmiente.cl. 5 units. $50 double, $7 each additional person. No credit cards. **Amenities:** Restaurant; outdoor pool; organized excursions. *In room:* TV.

Piedra Luna ★   Piedra Luna is a set of *cabañas* within one large building, somewhat like a rustic, wood-and-stone condominium unit. It's just across the road from La Bella, and although it's not as charming, the couple who own and run the establishment strive to make you feel like part of the family. The *cabañas* are decent, with comfy beds and large windows; two have mountain views. The simple kitchens don't exactly inspire you to cook. *Cabañas* meant for four are ridiculously tight; go for a six-person *cabaña* instead. There is a large living area with tables, a couch, and large-screen TV. The English- and German-speaking owners can often be found here, and they are always up for a good chat.

Calle Los Maitenes 100, San Alfonso. ⓒ/fax 2/861-1542. www.piedraluna.cl. 5 units. *Cabañas:* $65 for 4; $43–$57 for 2, $57 for 6. No credit cards. **Amenities:** Organized excursions.

WHERE TO DINE

Casa Bosque ★★★ *Kids* STEAKHOUSE   If you don't eat at Casa Bosque, stop here anyway to admire the fabulously outlandish architecture. The local artist who designed Casa Bosque has left his mark on many buildings in Cajón de Maipo, but none as dramatically as here: polished, raw tree trunks are kept in their natural shape, forming madcap doorframes, ceiling beams, and pillars; oddly shaped windows and stucco fill in the gaps. It's pure fantasy, and adults will love it as much as kids. Casa Bosque is a *parrilla,* and it serves delicious grilled beef, chicken, and sausages from a giant indoor barbecue, which you can pair with fresh salads, creamy potatoes, or a grilled provolone cheese, along with a few vegetarian dishes. During the weekend lunch hour, this restaurant can get pretty packed, mostly with families. There's live music every Friday after 11pm; the restaurant sometimes closes for events.

Camino el Volcán 16829. (℃) 2/871-1570. Main courses $5.50–$12. AE, DC, MC, V. Mon–Thurs 12:30–6pm; Fri–Sat 12:30pm–midnight; Sun 12:30–8pm.

Cascada de las Animas ⊕ CHILEAN/VEGETARIAN Cascada serves a simple menu of Chilean and vegetarian dishes, but what's really special here is the idyllic location vertiginously high above the Maipo River. For the best view, grab a table outside on the sunny deck. The menu offers a plentiful variety of dishes, including pastas, meats, and seafood. Vegetarian dishes include tofu sautéed with vegetables and soy sauce and served on a bed of rice. It's best to come outside the lunch hour because service is laughably bad when the waiters get overwhelmed. Often you'll find music and dancing in the evening.

Just past San Alfonso, turn right at sign. (℃) 2/861-1303. Main courses $5–$10; sandwiches $2–$5. No credit cards. Sun–Thurs 9am–8pm; Fri–Sat 9am–midnight.

La Petite France ⊕ *Finds* FRENCH BISTRO The walls of La Petite France, with its Edith Piaf posters and ads for French products, are pure French kitsch. The locals love it, and you will too. Since opening 2 years ago, La Petite's cuisine has drawn in diners with a menu that successfully blends French bistro classics with flavorful Chilean and international dishes. Menu highlights include filet mignon in a puff pastry with Roquefort sauce, and turkey breast stuffed with almonds, plums, and apples in a cactus sauce. Of course, there's also paté, escargot, and Croque Monsieur. During tea time, mouthwatering desserts are laid out enticingly across a long table: tarte tatin, crème brûlée, and chocolate layer cake are just a few choices. It's a pretty spot for outdoor dining.

Camino el Volcán 16096. (℃) 2/861-1967. Main courses $5–$8. AE, DC, MC, V. Tues–Sun noon–midnight, kitchen closed 6–7pm.

Trattoria Calypso ⊕⊕ ITALIAN Owned and operated by a Genovese family who immigrated to this region nearly a decade ago, Trattoria Calypso serves wonderful homemade pastas and stone oven–baked pizzas (pizzas are served Sat only). Everything is made using organic and local farm ingredients, such as the delicious mozzarella bought from a family in Cajón de Maipo and smoked here at the restaurant. Pastas include raviolis, cannelloni, fungi fettuccine, and pesto lasagna, but you might want to nibble an antipasti platter with fresh focaccia bread. The cozy restaurant has indoor and outdoor seating at wooden tables; the staff gives a warm welcome to all who pass through the doors. It's open Thursday through Sunday only, but if you're in the area during one of these days, don't miss a stop here.

Camino el Volcán 9831. (℃) 2/871-1498. Main courses $7.50–$9. AE, DC, MC, V. Thurs–Sun 12:30–10pm.

ATTRACTIONS & ACTIVITIES
EL MORADO NATIONAL PARK This 3,000-hectare (7,410-acre) park is 90km (56 miles) from Santiago. It takes its name from the sooty-colored rock of the Morado mountain (*morado* means "purple," "dark," or "bruised"). The views at El Morado are impressive, and a great spot to take in all this beauty is the attractive, gingerbread-style mountain lodge **Refugio Alemán at Lo Valdés.**

Pomaire Pottery

If you love ceramic pottery, Pomaire is your place. Pomaire is a small, dusty village 65km (40 miles) west of Santiago. Its main street (almost the only street here) overflows with shops selling vases, funny little figurines, decorative pieces and pots, plates, and other kitchen crockery—all at reasonable prices.

To get to Pomaire, you can rent a car or take **Buses Melipilla,** which has several daily trips from the San Borja Terminal in Santiago at Alameda O'Higgins 3250. The bus will leave you at the end of the road to Pomaire, where you'll have to take a *colectivo,* or shared taxi, into town. To get here by car, take the Panamericana Highway to the turnoff for the Ruta 78 to San Antonio, follow the highway until you see the sign for Pomaire 3km (2 miles) before Melipilla. Any of the tour companies listed in chapter 10 can arrange a visit. Note that Pomaire is pretty much shut down on Monday, and weekends are crowded.

The *refugio* (cabin) serves a tasty fixed-price lunch and dinner, and you can eat out on the deck while gazing out at the snowcapped peaks. Refugio Alemán has clean, bunk-bed–style accommodations should you decide to spend the night. Unfortunately, their telephone number changes or does not work frequently. Check with Sernatur or your hotel for the current number. Per-person rates are $30; full-board rates are $50.

You'll find the Conaf park ranger hut at **Baños Morales.** The park is open daily October through April from 8:30am to 6pm, and costs $2 to enter. There is an 8km trail that varies between easy and intermediate terrain, eventually passing by an alpine lake and a glacier with a view of the profile of the El Morado mountain. This is a good day hike (about 6 hr. average round-trip), and there is a place to camp near the lake. The raggedy little village of Baños Morales features several hot spring pools open daily from 8:30am to 8pm during the summer and from 10am to 4pm April through September, but in truth they are not particularly inviting, and are packed during the peak of summer. There are more hot springs at **Termas de Colina,** rock pools located in an outstanding Alpine setting, with fascinating clay pools. To get there by car, continue past Lo Valdés up a semi-paved/dirt road for about 12km. If you don't have a car, try **Manzur Expediciones** (© 2/777-4284), which has trips on Wednesday, Saturday, and Sunday. Call for more information. These hot springs can get crowded during weekends. There are also transport services to Termas de Colina at Baño Morales. Admission is $5 per adult, $2.25 kids.

RAFTING Rafting the Maipo River is very popular among Santiaguinos and foreigners alike. Although the season runs from September to April, the river really gets going from November to February, when rafters can expect to ride Class III and IV rapids. Two reliable companies offer half-day rafting excursions: **Cascada de las Animas** (© 2/861-1303; www.cascadadelasanimas.cl) arranges rafting trips from its tourism complex (see "Where to Stay," earlier in this chapter) in San Alfonso, but it's best to reserve beforehand. Another highly respected outfitter is **Altué Expediciones,** in Santiago, Encomenderos 83 (© 2/232-1103; www.altue.com).

HORSEBACK RIDING Visitors to El Morado can rent horses with a guide at Baños Morales or Termas de Colina (see "El Morado National Park," above) for about $6 to $15 per person, depending on group size and duration. The best horseback ride, however, is a half day with Cascada de las Animas through its own private chunk of the Andes (see above). This ride is suitable for families. Cascada offers multiple-day horseback trips, including a 12-day Andes cross.

For multiple-day horseback trips through this region of the Andes (with themes such as "Following Darwin's Footsteps"), try **Altué Expediciones** (see above), or **Ace Turismo** (© 2/335-6309).

5 The Wineries of the Central Valley

The international popularity of Chilean wine has soared over the past decade. Chileans often brag about their industry, claiming a wine tradition that stretches back to the days of the Spanish conquest.

But wine production didn't really take off until the late '70s, when Spaniard Miguel Torres introduced modern techniques that revolutionized the industry. Chileans nevertheless have been slow to appreciate finer wines, and consequently many winegrowers export the bulk of their product to Europe and the United States. French and American companies such as Châteaux Lafite and Robert Mondavi have formed partnerships with vineyards in Chile, taking advantage of cheaper land prices and ideal growing conditions to produce wine that can now compete with wine-growing regions such as Napa Valley.

Many "classic" wineries can be found within 35km (20 miles) of Santiago, south toward the Central Valley, close enough to take a radio-taxi. Prominent wine-growing valleys outside Santiago limits that you will hear of are the Aconcagua, Maule, or Curicó, yet it is the Rapel Valley and its smaller Colchagua Valley that offer the best full-day/overnight wine-tasting trip, including the organized Ruta del Vino. For wineries in the Colchagua Valley (3 hr. from Santiago), rent a car or join a bilingual tour. **Ace Turismo** specializes in custom-made wine country and culture trips (© 2/335-6309; www.aceturismo.cl), or try **Chip Tours,** with a variety of day tours to the Maipo and Colchagua Valley (© 2/735-9044; www.chiptravel.cl). Nearly all the travel agencies listed in chapter 11, "Santiago," offer day trips and/or transportation.

Concha y Toro ★★ Located at the southeastern edge of Santiago, this winery is the largest and best known—it's sort of the Gallo winery of Chile. It was founded by mining magnate Francisco Subercaseaux and expanded in 1883 by his nephew Don Melchor Concha y Toro, who imported European vines and built grand wine cellars. Don Melchor also enlisted the help of Gustave Renner to design a magnificent 24-hectare (59-acre) garden to surround the winery and his beautiful, stately manor house.

Today the grounds, including tranquil ponds, grand old trees, roses, and a riot of colorful flowers, are maintained by eight full-time gardeners. A visit to Concha y Toro includes a tour of the garden and the original bodega, ending in a well-designed tasting room where you can taste and purchase wine. Note that this is a very popular winery. To get here by car, take Avenida Vicuña Mackenna to Puente Alto, head right and cross the Maipo River toward Pirque until you're at Av. Virginia Subercaseaux 210; a taxi or minivan transfer is another option. Concha y Toro requires reservations 4 days in advance, but it's worth a call to see if they can squeeze you in if you haven't planned that far ahead.

Av. Virginia Subercaseaux 210, Pirque. (© 2/821-7069. www.conchaytoro.com. Tours in English Mon–Fri 11:30am and 3pm, Sat 10am and noon. Tours in Spanish Mon 10:30am and 4pm, Fri 10:30am and 3:30pm, Sat 11am. Reservations required. Tour is $4, but you take your wineglass with you.

Cousiño Macul ★★★ *Moments* If you visit just one of Chile's traditional wineries, make it this one. Cousiño-Macul's vineyard does not produce the top competing wine in Chile, but the estate is extraordinarily beautiful and affords a glimpse into the opulence that defined Chile's elite families during the late 19th century. The vineyard's history stretches back to 1546, when Juan Jufré planted Chile's first grapevines here at the site of an old Incan village called Macul. The property changed hands over the centuries until it was bought by coal magnate Matías Cousiño in 1856. His only son, Luis, along with his wife, Isabel Goyenechea, founded the present winery in 1871. The Cousiños also erected a home in Santiago, the magnificent **Palacio Cousiño** (see "Seeing the Sights," in chapter 11). The winery is still owned by the Cousiño family today, and wine-tasting tours include a visit to a small museum that charts the property's history as well as a viewing of the tremendous collection of red wines.

Tours include a visit to the antique bodegas and a demonstration of wine-bottling, and visitors can purchase wine at discount prices. To get here by car from Santiago, take Avenida Américo Vespucio Sur and at the Quilín turnabout, take Avenida Quilín toward the Andes; the winery is behind the park. This is another winery that is close enough to take a taxi.

Av. Quilín 7100, Peñalolen, Santiago. (© 2/284-1011. www.cousinomacul.cl. Free admission. Wine tasting $1 per glass. Bilingual tours Mon–Sat 11am; reservations required..

Ruta del Vino ★★ This half- or full-day tour takes you to several up-and-coming wineries, many of them good to excellent, including Viña Montes, Viña Bisquertt, Casa Lapostolle, Viu Manent, and more. A full-day tour includes two wineries and the **Museo de Colchagua** (see "The Central Valley," later in this chapter), or visits to three wineries. You may use your own rental vehicle and hire a guide to accompany your group, or you can join their shuttle van, which leaves from the plaza, typically from the Hotel Santa Cruz Plaza. The included lunch for the full-day tour is at the Hotel Santa Cruz.

Plaza de Armas 6, 2nd floor. (© 72/823199. www.rutadelvino.cl. Reservations required 24 hr. in advance. Bilingual tours cost, per person, full-day $65 and 1/2-day $40 for parties of 2 (includes lunch), and full-day $41 and 1/2-day $23 for 6 guests. Maximum 16 guests.

Viña Santa Rita ★★★ *Moments* Located about an hour from downtown Santiago, Santa Rita is a top-notch day trip. Santa Rita isn't just a winery; it's also a first-class bed-and-breakfast hotel with a splendid restaurant. Founded in 1880 by Domingo Fernández Concha near his hacienda Alto Jahuel, which once gave refuge to Bernardo O'Higgins after his failed bid for independence in 1814, Santa Rita is a wonderful place to wander among fragrant, lush gardens, built in the late 1800s by a French landscape architect. Just as fascinating is a wander around the striking estate, a lovingly restored 19th-century property with bubbling fountains and a sizeable chapel. Tours on Saturday, Sunday, and holidays require that visitors have lunch, followed by a free tour (see below for information about the hotel and restaurant). The tour takes visitors through the old bodega and a national monument. Wine tasting is not conducted; for a sample one must buy a glass in their restaurant. To get here by car, head south on the Ruta Panamericana for 42km (26 miles) until Buin, where you'll see signs for Santa Rita.

Hendaya 60, #202, Las Condes, Santiago. ℂ 2/362-2594 or 2/362-2520. Fax 2/228-6335. www.santa rita.com. Bilingual tours, reservations required, Tues–Fri at 10:30, 11:30am, 12:15, 3, and 4pm; Sat and Sun 12:30 and 3:30pm (lunch required). Tours $4 per person.

WHERE TO STAY AND DINE

Hotel Viña Santa Rita ⭐⭐⭐ *(Finds)*   One of the loveliest places to spend the night near Santiago is Santa Rita winery's picturesque 19th-century hotel. Built in 1885 and refurbished in 1996, this wonderful bed-and-breakfast is surrounded by lush gardens and mixes contemporary decor with antique lamps, rugs, and furniture. It's a very exclusive place, and the price certainly reflects that. A stunning, neo-Gothic chapel on the property offers a quiet place for reflection, as does the pretty patio with its bubbling fountain. There is also an old-fashioned game parlor with a pool table imported from England and a piano. Two outstanding restaurants can be found on-site, one at the winery and one within the hotel itself. Rates include breakfast only; lunch and dinner rates run from $10 to $20 per person for a set menu.

Camino Padre Hurtado 0695, Alto Jahuel. ℂ 2/821-9966. www.santarita.cl. 16 units. $220 double. AE, DC, MC, V. **Amenities:** 2 restaurants, game room.

6 The Nearby Ski Resorts

Every year, hundreds of Americans and Europeans head to Chile from mid-June to mid-October to ski or snowboard the Andes at one of Chile's famed ski resorts. The reason? The terrain is awesome, offering everything from easy groomers to frightening steeps; the season runs during the Northern Hemisphere's summer, and some come escaping the heat back home; parents can take their kids with them because they are on summer vacation; and ski and snowboard classes are about one-third the price back home, meaning aficionados can come and improve their technique at "summer camp."

The major resorts in Chile are top-notch operations with modern equipment and facilities. Resorts centered on the Farallones area, such as Valle Nevado, La Parva, and El Colorado, can be reached in a 1- to 2-hour drive from Santiago or the airport. At a little over 2 hours from Santiago, the venerable, world-renowned Portillo is a very viable option, too, and anyone thinking of skiing for several days or a week might consider bunking in its all-inclusive hotel.

GETTING TO THE RESORTS   Two companies offer transfer service to the resorts near Farallones. **Ski Total** (ℂ 2/246-6881) offers minivan transfers for around $10 per person. You must come to their offices at Av. Apoquindo 4900, #40 (in the Omnium shopping mall in Las Condes—the best way to get there is by taxi) for one of their 8 or 8:30am shuttles; if your hotel is reasonably close, they'll pick you up. For downtown pickups, call **Manzur Expediciones** (ℂ 2/777-4284). Manzur requires a reservation and might charge extra for hotel pickup, but in general the cost is around $15 round-trip. Call for more information. These services head to Portillo, which also has its own transfer service (see below).

PORTILLO

For 54 years, the world-renowned Portillo Ski Resort has hosted everyone from the U.S. Ski Team to Fidel Castro, and it continues to entertain a veritable Who's Who in skiing and snowboarding. Portillo is set high in the Andes on the shore of beautiful Lake Inca, a little more than 2 hours from Santiago, near the Argentine border. Although open to the public for day skiing, Portillo really operates as a weeklong, package-driven resort that includes lodging, ski tickets, all meals, and use of their plentiful amenities. There are no other hotels in the area, ensuring no lift lines and lots of untracked powder. The resort encompasses a variety of terrain, from beginner to some of the steepest runs found anywhere in the world. There's heli-skiing too, if you want to get far out in the Andes.

Portillo's greatest asset is the heavy snowfall it receives each year (although there's snow-making equipment just in case), which also means that the road to the resort can close for days and tire chains are frequently required. Also an asset is Portillo's 450-guest limit, which creates a social ambience found at few other resorts in the world. In early July, the resort is popular with families who appreciate the day care, activity programs, and superb ski school; from late July to September there's a more adult crowd. Special weeks include Chilean Wine Week, Friends & Singles Week, and Gastronomic Week.

The grand yet rustic hotel forgoes glitz for a more relaxed atmosphere encouraged by its American owners. Rooms are average-size and bathrooms are somewhat cramped, but hot, powerful showers make up for it. The suites have recently been renovated and come with a living area, and families can rent an "apartment" with connecting rooms. See "Where to Stay," below, for more lodging information.

The resort sells Saturday to Saturday ski packages, which are recommended for the Portillo "experience," but check availability if you only have fewer days, especially during the weekdays.

There are 12 lifts, including five chairs, eight T-bars, and a unique Va et Vient "slingshot" lift that leaves skiers at the top of short but vertiginous chutes. The terrain is 43% beginner and intermediate, 57% advanced/expert. Lift tickets are $25 adults, $20 kids 12 and under; the first and last three weeks of the season, two kids under 12 per family ski free.

WHERE TO STAY   **Hotel Portillo**'s 7-day packages include lodging, lift tickets, four meals per day, and use of all facilities. Per person rates are: double with lake view $970 to $2,045, suites $1,550 to $3,275; family apartments (minimum 4 people) $840 to $1,760. Children under 4 are free, kids 4 to 11 pay half price, and kids 12 to 17 pay about 25% less than adults. The **Octagonal Lodge** features four bunks to a room (you may have to share with strangers), and includes the same amenities as above for $620 to $1,100. The **Inca Lodge,** another bunkhouse, popular with 20-somethings, charges $390 to $450. The first and last three weeks of the season, two kids under 12 per family ski free.

Guests of the hotel and the Octagonal Lodge take their meals in the hotel's dining room, which serves an international menu, from gourmet to hamburgers, including a kid's menu. Guests of the Inca Lodge take their meals in a cafeteria on the first floor. There's also a bar that hosts nightly live music, and a disco.

For more information or to make reservations at any of the lodges mentioned, contact the resort at ℂ **800/829-5325** in the U.S., or 2/263-0606; fax 2/263-0595; www.skiportillo.com. Resort amenities (available to guests at any of the lodges) include a restaurant, cafeteria, outdoor heated pool, fitness center and sauna, full-court gymnasium, disco, cybercafe, and a cinema.

VALLE NEVADO

Valle Nevado is a 9,000-hectare (22,230-acre), full-service ski resort featuring three hotels, seven restaurants, a condominium complex, and a dozen shops squeezed into one compact village that straddles a ridge overlooking a plunging canyon. It is French-designed, somewhat like the St. Moritz of Chile, and it offers plenty of groomed, intermediate runs. The terrain at Valle Nevado is not as challenging as Portillo, but it is larger and has longer runs. The resort hosts the FIS Snowboard World Cup every season, and they have developed a world-class half-pipe and terrain park. Valle Nevado also has a popular heli-skiing operation.

Out of the three resorts at Farallones, Valle Nevado is the only one to offer a tourism infrastructure instead of just condos for Santiago weekenders. Many Santiaguinos, especially families with kids, head to Valle Nevado for the day because of its close proximity to the city; that also means it can get *very* busy on weekends even though the parking lot closes after 200 cars. Valle Nevado offers lodging in three comfortable hotels with singles, doubles, and suites; there are no double beds, however. Verify what's open toward the end of the season as two of the three hotels close and only one restaurant remains open (an Italian pasta restaurant). However, during this time the slopes are less crowded and the spring skiing is great. Valle Nevado recently closed their disco and reopened it as a spa, with facial treatments, sauna, massage, and special wellness programs.

Prices include lodging, ski tickets, breakfast, après-ski, and dinner, which can be taken in any one of the resort's restaurants.

The ski resort has 27 runs serviced by three chair lifts and six T-bars, as well as a helicopter service for those who want to ski steep powder. There's also hang gliding, paragliding, and organized ski safaris. The terrain is 15% expert, 30% advanced, 40% intermediate, and 15% beginner.

WHERE TO STAY   Prices include breakfast and dinner, and lift tickets, and are per person, based on double occupancy. The range reflects low to high season (prices drop as length of stay increases). The most upscale option is the **Hotel Valle Nevado,** which features full amenities and a ski-in, ski-out location for $175 to $320 per night. There's also a piano bar, glass-enclosed gym, sauna, cozy lounge, and more.

The four-star **Hotel Puerta del Sol,** which is the most popular among North Americans and Europeans, consists mostly of suites that go for $145 to $375 a night, which isn't that much more than a double. North-facing rooms with balconies and views of the mountain are $143 to $276 per night; south-facing rooms that overlook the parking lot and do not have balconies are $116 to $296 per night. Amenities at the Puerta del Sol include cable TV, sauna, game room, piano bar, Internet cafe, and gym.

Hotel Tres Puntas has many bunk-bed rooms; each features a minibar, cable TV, and a full bathroom. This hotel is frequented by a younger crowd and has the liveliest bar; room prices range from $100 to $192 per night.

Valle Nevado has many good, even excellent restaurants that serve international, French, Italian, and Chilean cuisine—and there is sushi in the lounge bar. There is a second bar in the Hotel Tres Puntas.

Lift tickets are $30 adults, $20 kids 12 and under. For more information or to make reservations at any of the hotels mentioned, contact the resort at © 2/ **206-0027;** fax 2/208-0695; www.vallenevado.com. In addition to the amenities mentioned for each specific hotel, the following amenities are offered for all hotels: outdoor heated pool, fitness gym, spa, game room, and cinema. For the public, there's a bank, boutiques, and a minimarket.

LA PARVA

La Parva is the smallest and most exclusive of the group, with excellent terrain that doesn't see the crowds that flock to Valle Nevado. For a few bucks more, you can ski the two with an interconnecting ticket. La Parva is somewhat like a private club for well-heeled families from Santiago, many of whom own a condo or chalet here. There are few lodging options for the outside visitor, but if you're coming up for the day only, it's not an issue. La Parva offers extensive off-piste skiing options, and the steepest inbounds terrain of the resorts in the area. For a quick taste of back-country skiing, check out La Chimenea, accessed via a short but steep hike off the Piuquenes Lift. Avalanche gear is essential when exploring out of bounds here in the Andes.

The resort's terrain breaks down into 10% expert, 30% advanced, 45% intermediate, and 15% beginner. There are four chairs and 10 surface lift runs, such as T-bars. There are several on-slope cafes for lunch and an Alpine, fondue-style restaurant at the base called **La Marmita de Pericles** (no phone).

Lift tickets are $25 to $30 adults, $17 to $22 kids 5 to 12 and seniors, $6.50 to $9 kids 4 and under. Interconnect tickets with Valle Nevado are $35 to $40 adults, $22 to $27 kids 12 and under. A 20% discount is offered to women on Wednesday and students on Thursday. For more information, contact the resort (© 2/264-1466 in Santiago, or 2/220-9530 direct; fax 2/264-1575; www.laparva.cl).

EL COLORADO/FARELLONES

El Colorado ✮ is the closest ski resort to Santiago (but not by much), and it is made up of two villages, Villa Farellones and Villa Colorado, that are connected by two ski lifts. Farellones is La Parva's blue-collar brother, an older, more economical option located just slightly downhill from Colorado. The center is popular with beginning skiers, tubing aficionados, snowman builders, and the like. El Colorado's center is really the hub of the resort, and skiers generally come directly here. The resort features a wide variety of terrain, fewer people than its neighbors, and often better snow, but the lift system is not as advanced.

There is plenty of beginner and intermediate terrain, and the best advanced terrain can be found on the east side known as the Cono Este. Be sure not to ski beyond the Cono Este T-bar or you will be in Valle Nevado where your ticket is not honored. For the expert looking for good backcountry skiing, the chutes that drop down to the road *leading* to Valle Nevado offer excellent skiing or snowboarding. You will have to hitchhike or arrange transportation back to the base.

The resort has five chair lifts and 17 surface lifts, such as T-bars. There's a bit of off-piste skiing, and there are 22 runs: four for experts, three advanced, four intermediate, and eleven beginner. Lift tickets low to high season: $25 to $32 adults, $16 to $20 kids 5 to 12, $6 seniors and kids 4 and under. Prices are $18 to $24 on Wednesday for women, Monday for students. For more information, contact the resort at © 2/246-3344; fax 2/206-4078; www.elcolorado.cl.

7 The Central Valley

The minute you drive out of Santiago, the scenery changes dramatically to wide fields of grapevines, a testament to the nation's thriving wine industry. As you head farther south, the smog begins to thin and more fields unfold until you enter what's known as the Central Valley. The region has both rich soil and a Mediterranean climate conducive to agriculture, and the fresh fruits and vegetables grown here can be bought from one of the many food stands that dot the Panamericana Highway. The region is indeed a food-lover's delight, with so many savory country restaurants along the Panamericana just outside Santiago that many call it the gastronomic axis.

The "Wild West" of South America

During the colonial period, the Central Valley was fundamentally agrarian and largely dependent on cattle production. Wealthy families, who owned the bulk of land, developed their property into ranches called *haciendas* or *estancias*. To tend their giant herds of cattle, hacienda owners hired Chilean "cowboys" called *huasos*.

You'll recognize a *huaso* by his wide-brimmed hat, a poncho that is either colorful and short-waisted or long and earth-toned, and metal spurs the size of a pinwheel. Often, especially when attending a special event, the *huaso* wears black leather chaps that cover the leg from ankle to knee and are adorned with tassels.

The *huaso* struts his stuff in one of the occasional **rodeos** that are popular in the Central Valley. The rodeos take place in a half-moon arena called a *medialuna*. Here *huasos* begin the match by demonstrating their agility atop their mounts, followed by the main event in which a *huaso* attempts to pin a young bull against a wall while on horseback.

Rodeos are held from September to May, especially during the Independence holiday on September 18 and September 19. The city of Rancagua hosts the rodeo championships in September. For more information, call the Federación del Rodeo Chileno at ℂ **2/699-0115.**

The Central Valley is both urban and rural: Semis and cars race along the Panamericana from Santiago to flourishing cities such as Rancagua and Talca, but outside those cities, a quick detour off the interstate puts you between poplar-lined, patchwork fields on dirt roads that see more hooves than wheels. Below are a few of this region's highlights, all the way down to Chillán.

SANTA CRUZ

Three hours south of Santiago, Santa Cruz is undeniably the hub of what is quickly becoming the Napa or Sonoma Valley of Chile, with a well-designed Wine Route, high-end wineries, and a new four-star hotel. Frequent buses head to Santa Cruz, leaving from the bus station at the Univ. de Santiago Metro station. **Ace Turismo** specializes in custom-made wine country and culture trips (ℂ **2/335-6309**), or try **Chip Tours,** which offers a variety of day tours to the Maipo and Colchagua Valley (ℂ **2/735-9044;** www.chiptravel.cl). Nearly all the travel agencies listed in chapter 10 offer day trips.

Once here, do not miss the **Museo de Colchagua** (no phone; open Mon–Sun 10am–6pm; admission $4). The diverse collection includes historical artifacts, from pre-Hispanic throughout the Americas, to local Indian artifacts, to Spanish conquest-era helmets and artillery, to immigrant household items and farm machinery, and more. The museum is the private collection of Carlos Cardoen, who also owns the Hotel Santa Cruz.

For the Ruta del Vino (Wine Route), see "The Wineries of the Central Valley," earlier in this chapter.

Hotel Santa Cruz Plaza ★★ *Finds* This hotel has turned the town of Santa Cruz into a destination in its own right, although visitors come to wine taste and visit the town's outstanding museum more than the town itself. The three-year-old hotel sits on the main plaza yet is relatively inconspicuous with its mellow mustard wash and ironwork window terraces, a style reminiscent of colonial Mexico. The guest rooms and bathrooms are not huge, but they offer enough space for comfort, and are decorated in a terra cotta–colored, country style featuring antiques and decorations found throughout the Santa Cruz area.

Service is this hotel's weak spot, but the staff is friendly enough and will assist you with your day plans. Once at the hotel, dining in their restaurant is really the only option in town, and thankfully the cuisine is varied and very good. Their buffet breakfast is terrific. The hotel offers a super deal for 1 night/2 days that includes accommodation, full board, and visits to Colchagua's vineyards and the Colchagua Museum, for $145 per person. They can arrange a transfer for you from Santiago for an additional charge.

Plaza de Armas 286, Santa Cruz. ©/fax 72/821010. www.hotelsantacruzplaza.cl. 41 doubles, 3 suites. Double $105–$115, breakfast included. AE, DC, MC, V. **Amenities:** Restaurant; outdoor pool; sauna; babysitting; laundry service. *In room:* A/C, TV.

A THERMAL SPA

Termas de Cauquenes ★★ This out-of-the-way thermal spa (about 115km/71 miles from Santiago) is worth the journey if you have the time, for its beautiful spa facilities inspired by Vichy in France, its historical appeal, and its lovely, oak-lined park. Termas de Cauquenes was founded by Spaniards in 1646, although Indians in the area had already enjoyed the curative waters for some time. General San Martín soaked here, and so did Bernardo O'Higgins. Charles Darwin even paid a visit in 1834.

In 1876, a millionaire by the name of Apolinario Soto bought the property and renovated the grounds with a hacienda-style hotel centered on a well-manicured garden and bubbling fountain. There is a tiny chapel and a beautiful, Gothic-style thermal pavilion fitted with colorful stained glass, marble floors, and two facing rows of cubicles with marble bathtubs. The marble bathrooms are tiny and antiquated, being more than a century old, but they've added modern whirlpools.

Termas de Cauquenes is now owned by a Swiss chef and his daughter, both experts at whipping up fine cuisine. The changing menu features fresh seafood and meats that embrace regional recipes. The dining area is sunny and spacious, with leather chairs and a long oak bar. A fixed lunch here costs $14 per person.

The hotel's age means some creaky floors and old-fashioned bathrooms. The rooms are very humble and could stand to be updated. Some open onto the garden patio; others face the river and are soaked in afternoon sun. You can visit for the day, and the cost is $6 for use of the baths only; the swimming pool is for hotel guests only. There are also massages, manicures, and pedicures offered.

Road to Cauquenes, near Rancagua. ©/fax 72/899010. 50 units. $77 per person double, full pension and bathrooms; $53 per person double, breakfast only and baths. AE, DC, MC, V. **Amenities:** Restaurant; bar; outdoor pool (guests only); massage; thermal baths. *In room:* TV, minibar.

EN ROUTE TO THE SPA

If you're driving to the hotel, head south toward Rancagua, and take the road left marked EL TENIENTE or COYA. **El Teniente** is the world's largest underground copper mine. The road branches off to El Teniente, but continue ahead until you see the sign for the branch-off to Cauquenes. There is another posted access road from the Panamericana south of Rancagua, but don't take it—it's long and bumpy. To get to the spa by bus, you need to take a bus to the Rancagua terminal, and from there a bus to the hotel. Buses leave from Rancagua twice daily, once in the morning and once in the late afternoon. Call the hotel for a current schedule.

While in the area, you'll want to pay a visit to the **Reserva Nacional Rio Los Cipreses,** a relatively unknown gem of a nature reserve 14km (9 miles) from Cauquenes; it's open daily from 8:30am to 6pm (8pm Dec–Feb); admission is $3. There is a park administration center with information, including trails and a guide to the flora and fauna of the reserve. Here it is possible to watch wild parrots swoop from trees and tiny caves high on cliffs; there are also rabbitlike *vizcachas* and red foxes, and of course a blanket of cypress trees.

This reserve is highly recommended, but you'll need your own car to get here. If you plan to stay in the hotel, inquire as to whether they can take you there.

A LOVELY RANCH, FOR A DAY TRIP OR OVERNIGHT

Hacienda Los Lingues ★★★ *Moments* About 125km (78 miles) south of Santiago and nestled among poplar-lined country fields and rolling hills is the Hacienda Los Lingues. The Hacienda is one of the oldest and best-preserved haciendas in Chile, and is now run as a splendid, full-service hotel as a member of the exclusive Relais & Châteaux group. If you can't stay overnight, consider a day tour ($46 per person) that includes a welcome cocktail, tour of the hacienda, lunch in the cavernous wine bodega, a horse demonstration, and optional use of a swimming pool. There's also horseback riding at an additional cost.

King Phillip III bestowed this beautiful estate to the first mayor of Santiago in 1599, and it has remained in the same family for 400 years. The center of the estate features portions of the structures that were built here in the early 17th century, but most of the buildings were built around 250 years ago and have been superbly maintained.

Every room is accented with crystal chandeliers, Oriental rugs, and antique furniture, and literally brimming with decorative pieces, family photos, collector's items, and fascinating odds and ends. The guest rooms are decorated individually with antique armoires and tables, iron bed frames and crocheted bedspreads, ancestral family photos, fresh flowers, and a bucket of champagne. A bountiful breakfast is served to you in bed.

Hacienda Los Lingues is actually a working ranch that grows fruit, such as pears and lemons, for export. The estate is also home to one of the most prestigious horse breeding farms in Latin America.

The hotel is currently run by the charismatic and very talkative Don Germán, a family descendent who likes to keeps guests entertained at dinner—which, by the way, is excellent, and served family-style at a long table. You'll want to join Germán for an after-dinner drink in the French salon for interesting stories about the estate.

Round-trip transportation from Santiago on the hotel's shuttle is $320 for one to six people. The cheaper alternative is to rent a car or take a bus to San Fernando (in Santiago, ride to the Universidad de Santiago Metro stop for the bus terminal), then a taxi to the hotel. No matter how you get here, try to plan a trip here if you have the time.

Reservations in Santiago: Av. Providencia 1100, #205. ✆ 2/235-5446. Fax 2/235-7604. www.loslingues.com. 19 units, 2 suites. $236 double with breakfast; $452 double with full board. Day tours $46. AE, DC, MC, V. **Amenities:** Outdoor pool; 2 clay tennis courts; game room; room service; horseback riding; fly-fishing.

8 Chillán & Termas de Chillán Resort

407km (252 miles) S of Santiago

Chillán is a midsize city known for three things: It's the birthplace of Chilean liberator Bernardo O'Higgins; the **Termas de Chillán,** one of South America's largest and most complete ski and summer resorts, is here; and it's home to the **Feria de Chillán,** one of the largest crafts and food markets in the country.

A tidy city of 145,000, with five attractive plazas and tree-lined streets, Chillán is a pleasant enough place to spend an afternoon, but it really offers little more of interest to the foreign visitor. If you're driving south to the Lake District, you might consider spending the night here.

Chillán is divided into two sectors: the downtown area and Chillán Viejo, or Old Chillán. The town's history is one of relocations and disasters. Founded as a fort in 1565, Chillán was attacked, abandoned, and rebuilt several times until the government moved the whole settlement to what is now Chillán Viejo.

Probably the worst tragedy to hit the town happened in 1939, when an earthquake destroyed 90% of the city and killed 15,000 of its residents. Fronting the city's central Plaza Bernardo O'Higgins is the **Cathedral,** whose utilitarian design seems aimed more at seismic protection than style. Here you'll notice a monumental cross in remembrance of the many who died during the earthquake.

From the plaza, walk 1 block southeast on Constitución and right on Avenida 5 de Abril for 2 blocks until you reach the **Feria de Chillán** ✿. Here you'll find baskets, *huaso* clothing and saddles, chaps and spurs, pottery, knitwear, and more. There's a colorful fish and vegetable market here, too. The market is safe, but beware of pickpockets. The market is open every day.

If you still have time, head to the **Mexican Murals** at the Escuela Mexico, Av. O'Higgins 250; it's open Tuesday through Friday from 9:30am to 12:30pm and 3 to 6pm; Monday and Saturday from 9:30am to 12:30pm. Admission is free. Two famous muralists from Mexico, David Siqueiros and Xavier Guerrero, painted the interior library and stairwell of this school in remembrance of Chillán's residents who were killed in the 1939 earthquake.

ESSENTIALS
GETTING THERE   By Air   Chillán is served by the Aeropuerto Carriel Sur in Concepción, about an hour away. **LanChile** offers direct flights from Santiago several times daily. If you've made hotel reservations in town or in Termas de Chillán, their transfer service will pick you up. If not, you must take a taxi to the bus terminal where buses for Chillán leave every 20 minutes.

By Bus   Línea Sur and **Tur Bus** offer daily service from most major cities, including Santiago. The trip from Santiago takes about 5 to 6 hours and costs $11 one-way. The bus terminal in Chillán is located at Av. O'Higgins 010, and from there you can grab a bus for the Termas.

By Train   Ferrocarriles del Sur offers a 5-hour train trip from Santiago, leaving from the Estación Central and arriving in Chillán at the station at Calle Brasil. The cost is $9 per person and there are three trips daily.

VISITOR INFORMATION   Sernatur can be found at 18 de Septiembre 455 (© 42/223272); it's open Monday through Friday from 8:30am to 1:30pm and 3 to 6pm, and closed on weekends. It has a large amount of published material.

WHERE TO STAY & DINE
If you're looking for local color and cheap prices, go to the **Municipal Market** across the street from the Feria de Chillán, where simple restaurants prepare seafood and local dishes, some featuring Chillán's famous sausages. Also, across the street from the Café París is the **Fuente Alemán** (© 42/212720), with good sandwiches, quick meals, and food to go.

Tips **Get Your Funds in Order Before You Arrive**

Note that there are no ATMs anywhere in Termas de Chillán or Las Trancas, so do your banking beforehand.

Café París CAFE/CHILEAN   The París has a cafe on its bottom floor and a smaller restaurant upstairs, both offering the same menu, but diners usually order full meals upstairs and sandwiches below. The upstairs is a little tacky, but comfortable, and the staff is friendly. The menu is exhaustive, with sandwiches, soups (and a very good *cazuela,* a chicken soup), quick dishes, meats, seafood, empanadas, even a mini ice-cream parlor.

Arauco 666. ℭ **42/223881**. Main courses $3–$8. AE, DC, MC, V. Daily 24 hr.

Gran Hotel Isabel Riquelme   The Gran Hotel faces the main plaza and is a huge green building with a flat, unadorned facade. This was Chillán's first hotel, but others have since surpassed the hotel in quality. The rooms have good linens, but the design is somewhat old-fashioned and dowdy. Rooms are, however, very spacious, almost twice the size of the rooms at Las Terrazas, and the price is economical. There is a large restaurant just past the lobby, which serves Chilean and international fare, and there's a bar, but both tend to be closed during the winter on weekdays. Call to inquire.

Arauco 600, Chillán. ℭ **42/213663**. Fax 42/211541. 75 units. $41 double. AE, DC, MC, V. **Amenities:** Restaurant. *In room:* TV.

Hotel Las Terrazas ⍟   Las Terrazas is really the best hotel in Chillán, and it is popular with business executives—the reason they jack up prices on weekdays. The hotel is in a commercial building; the lobby is on the fifth floor, guest rooms are on the sixth, and most have lofty views, some of the Chillán volcano in the distance. All rooms are first-rate, with classic design and matching floral curtains and bedspreads. The lounge has cushy couches to sink into, and there are tables and chairs for cafe service and breakfast.

Constitución 664, Chillán. ℭ **42/227000**. Fax 42/227001. www.lasterrazas.cl. 36 units, 2 suites. $64 double weekday; $47 double weekend. AE, DC, MC, V. **Amenities:** Restaurant; bar; room service; laundry service. *In room:* A/C, cable TV, minibar.

Paso Nevado ⍟ *Value*   The Paso Nevado is a good value for its comfortable rooms and amicable service, and it always seems willing to negotiate lower rates. Rooms are average size, accented with wood furniture, and in good shape due to the relative newness of the establishment. There's a small interior patio with tables and a bar. The hotel is several blocks from the main plaza, across the street from a movie theater. They also have transfers to Termas de Chillán.

Av. Libertad 219, Chillán. ℭ **42/221827**. Fax 42/237666. www.chile-travel.com/paso-nevado-chillan-hotel.html. 15 units. $41 double. AE, DC, MC, V. **Amenities:** Cafe; bar; tours and transfers to ski resort. *In room:* TV.

TERMAS DE CHILLAN

About 80km (50 miles) from the city is Termas de Chillán, a full-season resort that is principally known for skiing, but offers great hiking, biking, and horseback riding opportunities in the summer. Most visitors to Chile head to Pucón, Puerto Varas, or even Patagonia for those kinds of summer-season activities because the locations are more uniquely beautiful than Chillán. However, you might find a hot springs spa and the 5-hour distance from Santiago to be more appealing.

The resort is nestled in a forested valley under the shadow of the 3,212m (10,535-ft.) Chillán Volcano. The resort has 28 runs, 3 chair lifts, and 5 T-bars, as well as heli-skiing, dog-sledding, an international ski school, equipment rental, and restaurants.

But what really makes the Termas stand out from the pack are its spa facilities. There are nine thermal pools, steam baths in caves, and three state-of-the-art spa centers that offer hydrotherapy, aromatherapy, mud baths, and massages. Special treatments like anti-inflammatory plant wraps, and a space-age "Sensory Capsule" pretty much put it in a class of its own. It is possible to visit the thermal pools and spa for the day, for an extra charge (depending on which pools and services you opt for). Contact the hotel for updated prices.

There are two hotels here: the newish, luxury five-star **Gran Hotel Termas de Chillán** with 120 rooms, and the three-star **Hotel Shangri-La** with 48 rooms. The Gran Hotel is sumptuous, with a rich, warm lobby accented by contemporary wood art and a roaring fire.

Rooms are everything you'd expect in terms of comfort, but they are somewhat unremarkable for the price. Rates include breakfast and dinner, ski tickets, and spa facilities (low to high season: $815–$1,605 per week, per person). The Shangri-La is the older unit, but it's comfortable and wraps around an outdoor thermal pool (rates include the same amenities as the Gran Hotel; low to high season: $595–$1,095). The complex has several restaurants, as well as a squash court, gym, three outdoor pools, a game room, and a disco.

Lift tickets are about $40 adults, $25 children, but prices fluctuate throughout the season. For more information, contact the resort at ✆ **42/223887** (in Chillán) or 2/233-1313 (in Santiago).

A BRIEF STOP IN LAS TRANCAS

You'll pass through the tiny village of Las Trancas just before you get to Termas de Chillán. There are many lodging options here, including cabins. If interested, check out the website www.vallelastrancas.cl for a listing.

Hotel Parador Jamón, Pan y Vino 🐾   This is a good bet in Las Trancas, although the lobby and game room are cold and battered. Rooms are fairly comfortable and laid out motel-like around a summer-only pool. The A-framed cabins come with kitchenettes and are equally standard. The restaurant is one of the best in the area, however, especially with its cozy ambience of a medieval-style fireplace and beams festooned with hams, gourds, and corncobs; it's open Monday through Sunday from 1 to 4pm and 7pm to midnight.

10km (6 miles) from Termas de Chillán. ✆ **42/242316.** Fax 42/211054. 15 units. $37–$52 double; $110 cabin. AE, MC, DC, V. **Amenities:** Restaurant; game room. *In room:* TV.

Hotel Robledal 🐾🐾   This newer hotel, surrounded by oak and beech trees and serenaded by a babbling creek, is an excellent choice for lodging outside the Termas de Chillán ski resort. The entrance is flanked on one side by an airy, comfortable lobby with a copper fireplace and bar, and on the other by a restaurant. Guest rooms feel like condominiums, starkly decorated, but brightly lit by an abundance of windows; some have terraces. Among the amenities are an outdoor pool, gym, a sauna, a whirlpool, a game room, and child care.

8km (5 miles) from Termas de Chillán. ✆/fax **42/214407.** www.hotelrobledal.cl. 22 units. $113–$64 per person, double occupancy, includes breakfast and dinner. AE, DC, MC, V. **Amenities:** Restaurant; bar; outdoor pool; gym; Jacuzzi; sauna; babysitting. *In room:* Cable TV, minibar.

13

The Desert North & San Pedro de Atacama

Northern Chile is home to the driest desert in the world and the wonderful adobe village San Pedro de Atacama. Just 10 years ago, few besides copper miners came to this region. And often, San Pedro never even made it onto maps of the country. What a difference a decade makes! Once-sleepy San Pedro is now home to several elegant hotels, good restaurants, lively bars, and more outfitters than grocery stores.

EXPLORING THE REGION

The town of **Calama** is not a destination in itself, but a gateway of sorts. It's the nearest airport to San Pedro, and the city is a convenient jumping-off point to the outdoor attractions and colonial villages that lie in the Atacama Desert region. Plan for at least 4 days to visit this region's highlights, or 6 to 7 days to really explore the region thoroughly. The best—and really only—place to base yourself is San Pedro; from here you can take part in a multitude of day trips. You may consider spending a night in Calama, especially if you want to visit the Chuquicamata mine.

Immense distances between sites of interest means the traveler would do best to focus on one area of Chile's northern desert rather than trying to pack in too many stops. We've covered Chile's "hot spot" in the northern desert, the Atacama Desert and the village of San Pedro, but many tour operators offer multiple-day excursions to a variety of locations in this beautiful environment, some of which may not be highlighted in this book. If you've rented a car or have signed on with a tour agency, it is imperative that you consider safety first. **Bring plenty of water**—a gallon per person per day—and extra food, as well as sunscreen, a hat, warm clothing and even a blanket (in the event you have to spend a chilly night on the road) and sunglasses. Ask your rental car agency (or your tour operator) about procedures for road emergencies and breakdowns, and *always* double-check the state of any spare tires. Be certain to give at least one person your planned itinerary, even if it's the car-rental agency. For obvious reasons, solo travel is *not* the ideal way to explore this region.

Another serious consideration is **flash floods.** Though the region receives only a few days of rainfall each year, it can come in a torrential downpour known as the "Bolivian Winter," which drowns the region in flash floods and causes substantial damage to roads and bridges. The Bolivian Winter can strike anywhere during the summer between December and early March.

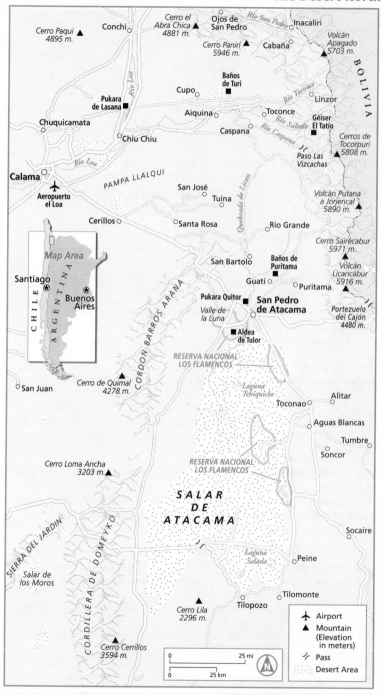

Cerro Paqui ▲
4895 m.

Conchi ○

Cerro el
Abra Chica ▲
4881 m.

Ojos de
San Pedro ○

Río San Pedro

Inacaliri ○

Volcán
Apagado ▲
5703 m.

Cerro Paniri ▲
5946 m.

Cabaña ○

B O L I V I A

Río Loa

Pukara
de Lasana ■

Cupo ○

Baños
de Turi ■

Río Toconce

Linzor ○

Chuquicamata ○

Aiquina ○

Toconce ○

Géiser
El Tatío ○

Chiu Chiu ○

Caspana ○

Río Salado

Río Caspana

Cerros de
Tocorpuri ▲
5808 m.

Río Loa

Paso Las
Vizcachas

Calama ●

PAMPA LLALQUI

Aeropuerto
el Loa ✈

San José ○

Volcán Putana
a Jorjencal ▲
5890 m.

Cerillos ○

Tuina ○

Quebrada de Licán

Santa Rosa ○

Río Grande ○

Cerro Sairécabur
5971 m. ▲

Map Area

Santiago ✪

CHILE

ARGENTINA

Buenos
Aires ✪

San Bartolo ○

Baños de
Puritama ■

Guati ○

Puritama ○

Volcán
Licancábur ▲
5916 m.

Pukara Quitor ■

San Pedro
de Atacama ●

Valle de
la Luna

Portezuelo
del Cajón
4480 m.

Aldea
de Tulor ■

CORDON BARROS ARANA

RESERVA NACIONAL
LOS FLAMENCOS

San Juan ○

Cerro de Quimal ▲
4278 m.

Laguna
Tebiquiche

Toconao ○

Alitar ○

Aguas Blancas ○

Tumbre ○

Soncor ○

Cerro Loma Ancha
3203 m. ▲

RESERVA NACIONAL
LOS FLAMENCOS

SIERRA DEL JARDIN

CORDILLERA DE DOMEYKO

S A L A R
D E
A T A C A M A

Socaire ○

Salar de
los Moros

Laguna
Salada

Peine ○

Tilomonte ○

Cerro Lila ▲
2296 m.

Tilopozo ○

✈ Airport

▲ Mountain
(Elevation
in meters)

✗ Pass

Desert Area

Cerro Cerrillos ▲
3594 m.

0 ——— 25 mi

0 ——— 25 km

1 Calama & the Chuquicamata Copper Mine

1,574km (976 miles) N of Santiago; 98km (61 miles) NW of San Pedro de Atacama

Calama, a city of 120,000, is alive due primarily to the mining interests in the area. Most travelers spend the night here only when they're on their way in or out of the area, or if they're interested in visiting the Chuquicamata Copper Mine. The Indian ruins **Pukará de Lasana** and the colonial village **Chiu Chiu** are also close to Calama, although they can be visited on the way back to Calama from San Pedro via the Tatío Geysers.

GETTING THERE

BY PLANE Calama's **Aeropuerto El Loa** (no phone) is served by LanChile (© 2/526-2000) and has 3 flights daily. A taxi to Calama costs around $2. To get to San Pedro de Atacama, hire one of the transfer services outside for around $10 per person, or take a taxi, which will cost about $30 to $35—be sure to fix a price before leaving the airport.

BY BUS It takes around 22 hours to reach Calama by bus from Santiago. Buses are an economical choice, but even a *cama salón* with reclining seats hardly mitigates a torturously long ride. **TurBus** leaves from Santiago's Terminal Alameda at O'Higgins 3750 (© 2/270-7500), and **Pullman Bus** leaves from the Terminal Norte at the Central Station (© 2/778-7086).

BY CAR Few actually drive to Calama from Santiago (a 20–22 hr. trip), but many find it convenient to rent a car in Calama to explore at their own pace. A word of caution, however, if you choose to rent. This is a vast desert and most areas are fairly isolated; roadside service is not unheard of, but it's not very common either. Travel prepared for the worst, and bring extra water and food and warm clothes in case you must spend the night on the road. Also, consider renting a 4×4 if you plan to really explore along poorly maintained roads. Rental car companies in Calama include: **Avis** at Pedro Lyon Gallo 1883 (© 55/363120, or 55/363325 airport); **Budget** at Granaderos 2875 (© 55/361072); and **Hertz** at LaTorre 1510 (© 55/341380). There are also rental agency kiosks at the airport.

WHAT TO SEE & DO

TOUR OPERATORS The following tour operators offer excursions around the north of Calama and trips to the Tatio Geysers and San Pedro de Atacama: **Tour Aventura Valle de La Luna** at Abaroa 1620 (© 55/310720); **Tungra Expediciones** at Turi 2098 (© 55/363010); and **Atacama Explorer** at Lascar 4182, Villa Ayquina (© 55/335527).

CHUQUICAMATA COPPER MINE

The northern desert is full of ghost towns left over from Chile's nitrate-mining days, but the copper mining industry is alive and well, as is evident by Calama's Chuquicamata mine, the largest open-pit mine in the world. Few wonders generate the visual awe a visitor experiences when gazing into this gigantic hole in the ground. The mine is so big that it can be seen from space. The principal pit measures 4km (2½ miles) across and more than half a kilometer deep—everything at its bottom looks Lilliputian. The Guggenheim brothers initiated construction of the mine in 1911, but did not produce a bar of copper until 1915. Today, the mine yields more than 600,000 tons of copper per year and is owned by the government-controlled company Codelco. There is a planned company town at the edge of the mine, with about 13,000 residents.

Tours run every day, except holidays (call © **55/321861** for information). There's just one tour a day, at 8:30am; there's limited space, so arrive early. To get there, take a taxi from the main plaza in Calama on Calle Abaroa to the company mining town, and sign up for the tour at the Sede de Chuqui Ayuda a la Infancia Desvalida at José Miguel Carrera and Tocopilla streets. There is no admission price; however, they do accept donations. For safety reasons, it is recommended that visitors wear pants and long sleeved shirts and closed shoes.

OTHER ATTRACTIONS

Museo Arqueológico y Etnográfico ★   This museum sits in the El Loa park, about 2km (1 mile) from the city center, so you'll need to grab a taxi to get there. The museum holds an interesting collection of artifacts from the Atacama region and displays interpreting pre-Columbian history and civilization.

Parque El Loa. No phone. Admission $1, free for seniors. Tues–Sun 10am–1pm and 3–7:30pm.

WHERE TO STAY

Hotel El Loa   Budget travelers will find the El Loa a very simple but decent option in Calama. It's a little low on style, but it's very clean, and there's a kitchen that can be used by guests. The hotel has a fair number of singles, so if you're traveling alone and looking for cheap digs, this is your place. It can get crowded in the summer, so reserve in advance.

Abaroa 1617. © **55/341963**. 30 units. $9 per person. No credit cards. *In room:* No phone.

Hotel El Mirador ★   This is one of the more interesting hotels in Calama. The small El Mirador is a spotless, old-fashioned hotel furnished with antiques and featuring hardwood floors, a plant-filled patio, and a pleasant sitting area decorated with old photos of the region. Most of the rooms are ample in size, and the largest room has a bathroom with a claw-foot tub. The hotel offers several tours around the area.

Sotomayor 2064. ©/fax **55/340329**. 15 units. $49 double. AE, MC, V. *In room:* TV.

Park Hotel ★   The Park Hotel is perhaps Calama's best hotel, and it is a good bet for travelers seeking dependable, high-quality accommodations—and free airport pick-up. The hotel is owned by the Park Plaza hotel in Santiago, and stays true to the region's architectural design, with interiors painted in desert pastels, off-white couches, and iron and wood furniture. Rooms feature the same pastel-colored decor, with striped bedspreads and wooden headboards; they are roomy and very comfortable. The large, circular, outdoor pool makes for a refreshing desert respite.

Camino Aeropuerto 1392. © **55/319900**. Fax 55/319901. www.parkplaza.cl. 102 units. $120 double standard; $150 double superior. AE, DC, MC, V. **Amenities:** Restaurant; bar; outdoor pool; tennis court; gym; sauna; car rental; room service; laundry service. *In room:* A/C, TV, minibar, safe.

WHERE TO DINE

If you're looking for hearty Chilean cuisine, try **Bavaria** at Sotomayor and Abaroa (© **55/341496**); it serves barbecued meats, seafood, and sandwiches. Calama locals' favorite for Chinese is **Tong Fong,** Calle Vivar 1951 (no phone). For fine dining and international cuisine, head to the **Park Hotel** at Camino Aeropuerto 1392 (© **55/319990**).

NEARBY EXCURSIONS TO COLONIAL VILLAGES & PUKARAS

A memorable excursion near Calama is a visit to the several colonial-era villages that still function as agricultural centers, and the Atacama Indian ruins built in the 12th century. Most tour companies in Calama offer trips to this region for around $15 per person.

Chiu Chiu is a colonial village founded by the Spanish in the early 17th century, and it boasts the most picturesque church in the north, the **Iglesia San Francisco,** open Tuesday to Sunday 9am to 1pm and 3 to 7pm. The white-washed adobe walls of this weather-beaten beauty are 120cm (47-in.) thick, and its doors are made of cedar and bordered with cactus, displaying a singular, Atacamanian style. Inside are interesting items such as a crucifix used in processions and a painting of the Passion of Christ. Chiu Chiu was first occupied by Indians around 1000 B.C. and was part of an extensive trading route that included Brazil; it continued as such until the railway began service in 1890.

Another fascinating attraction is the **Pukará de Lasana,** a 12th-century Indian fort abandoned after the Spanish occupation and restored in 1951. You'll want to spend some time wandering the labyrinthine streets that wind around the remains of 110 two- to five-story buildings.

North of Chiu Chiu is the engaging village of **Caspana,** surrounded by a fertile valley cultivated in a formation much like steps. The flowers and vegetables grown here are sold to markets in Calama. In the center, visitors will find a tiny museum dedicated to the culture of the area and an artisan shop selling textiles made from alpaca. Don't buy any item made of cactus, as the species is closing in on extinction. Also in Caspana is the charming **Iglesia de San Lucas,** built in 1641 of stone, cactus, and mortar and covered in adobe. The church is not officially open for visitors, but if you find the caretaker, he will unlock the door for you.

Near Caspana is the **Pukará de Turi,** which was the largest fortified city of the Atacama culture, built in the 12th century, and widely believed to be an Incan administrative center. The size of these ruins is impressive, with wide streets, circular towers, and buildings made of volcanic stone and adobe. The Pukará is well worth a visit.

2 San Pedro de Atacama

98km (61 miles) SE of Calama; 1,674km (1,040 miles) N of Santiago

Quaint, unhurried, and built of adobe brick, San Pedro de Atacama sits in the driest desert in the world, a region replete with bizarre land formations, giant sand dunes, jagged canyons, salt pillars, boiling geysers, and one smoking volcano. Better to call it a moonscape than a landscape. For adventure seekers there is a wealth of activities to participate in, including hiking, mountain biking, and horseback riding—or you can just sightsee with a tour van. This region was the principal center of the Atacamanian Indian culture, and relics such as Tulor, an ancient village estimated to have been built in 800 B.C., still survive. There's also a superb archaeology museum that boasts hundreds of artifacts that have been well preserved by the desert's arid climate.

But it is perhaps San Pedro's intangible magic that captivates its visitors in the end. Many will tell you it is as much of a place for one's "inside" as it is for one's "outside." One well-known Chilean architect has been noted to say, "The first day you begin to discover things; the third day you throw away your agenda; and by the seventh day you don't even know who you are, and that is the most fabulous moment, one that many associate with God." This spiritual penchant has fomented somewhat of an artistic, bohemian atmosphere in San Pedro.

Important Info to Know Before Arriving in San Pedro
Although San Pedro boasts several luxury hotels, there are no banks or pharmacies in town, and medical service is limited to a small clinic. San Pedro is at 2,438m (7,997 ft.) above sea level, and a small percentage of visitors may be affected by the high altitude; see "Health" in chapter 10, for remedies.

Unfortunately, as with any uniquely beautiful place, San Pedro has been discovered, and today it is a thriving tourism center that is so popular from October to March that visitors might feel overwhelmed by the presence of so many gringos. Somehow, however, San Pedro maintains its mellow charm. This is one of my favorite places in Chile for its one-of-a-kind, breathtaking beauty.

ESSENTIALS

GETTING THERE   By Car   From Calama, head southeast on the route marked "San Pedro de Atacama" and continue for 98km (61 miles).

By Bus   Several bus companies provide service to San Pedro from Calama: **Buses Frontera,** Antofagasta 2041 (© **55/318543**), offers the most daily trips; **Gemenis,** Antofagasta 2239(© **55/263968**) and **TurBus** LaTorre 3055 (from Antofagasta; © **55/220240**) also offer daily service to San Pedro.

VISITOR INFORMATION   Sernatur operates a small visitor center at the plaza on the corner of Antofagasta and Toconao (© **55/85-1420**). Hours are Saturday through Thursday from 9:30am to 1:30pm and 3 to 7pm.

ORIENTATION   San Pedro de Atacama is divided into several *ayllus,* or neighborhoods; however, the principal area of the town can be walked in about 10 minutes or less. Most businesses do not list street numbers (their addresses contain the abbreviation "s/n" for *sin número,* or without number). Many sights are within walking or biking distance, such as Quitor and Tulor, and it is possible to bike to the Valley of the Moon and through the Devil's Canyon. You'll need a tour to get to the Tatio Geysers.

WHAT TO SEE AND DO

TOUR OPERATORS   The boom in tourism has given birth to dozens of tour operations, offering everything from sightseeing to active travel. The following are a few reliable operators. Two tour companies who arrange custom tours, specifically ones that require equipment or cultural tours, are **Atacama Desert Expeditions,** Tocopilla 411, an upscale operation that works in conjunction with the Lodge Terrantai (© **55/85-1045;** www.adex.cl), and **Nativa Expeditions,** Tocopilla s/n, which can arrange 1-day and multiple-day trips that lean more toward adventure travel (© **55/85-1095;** nativaexp@yahoo.com). All-inclusive trips cost a bit more, anywhere from $60 to $90 a day per person. **Azimut 360,** Caracoles s/n (© **55/851469;** base-spa@netline.cl), offers adventure trips and classic day trips, including horseback riding, trekking and biking, and more advanced expeditions for those with outdoor know-how. For trips to any of the destinations listed below, try **Desert Adventure** at the corner of Tocopilla and Caracoles (©/fax **55/85-1067;** www.desertadventure.cl); or **Cosmo Andino Expediciones** at Caracoles s/n (© **55/85-1069**). **Pangea Expediciones,** Tocopilla s/n (no phone; pangeaexp@yahoo.com), has bike rentals.

The average price for tours to the Valle de la Luna is $7; the Tatio Geysers tour costs about $20, which includes the entrance fee at the thermal baths. A full day tour including the Salt Flats and the Flamingo Reserve averages $35.

A CAN'T-MISS ATTRACTION IN TOWN

Museo Arqueológico Padre le Paige ★★★   This tiny museum near the plaza is one of Chile's best, offering a superb collection of pre-Columbian artifacts gathered by Padre le Paige, a Belgian missionary who had a fondness for archaeology. What makes this museum especially unique is the well-preserved state of the artifacts, due to the arid conditions of the region. You'll find thousands of ceramics, textiles, tablets used for the inhalation of hallucinogens, tools, and more displayed according to time period. However, the unquestionable highlights here are the well-preserved mummies, including "Miss Chile," a female mummy that still has bits of skin and hair intact, and the creepy display of skulls that shows how the elite once used cranial deformation as a show of wealth.

Toconao and Padre le Paige. No phone. Admission $2. Jan–Feb daily 10am–1pm and 3–7pm; rest of the year Mon–Fri 9am–noon and 2–6pm, Sat and Sun 10am–noon and 2–6pm.

VALLE DE LA LUNA

The **Valle de la Luna (Valley of the Moon)** ★★ is a popular destination for its eerie, freeze-dried land formations encrusted with veins of pure salt. The best time to come is when the sun sets, to watch the colors of the desert melt from pink to gold, but you'll often have to share the view with a dozen or more tourists. This valley is also at its best on the eve of a full moon, when ghostly light makes the land formations appear even stranger. The Valley of the Moon sits about 15km (9 miles) from San Pedro and can be reached by bicycle or vehicle. To get here, head west out of town on Caracoles and turn left on the signed, dirt road (the old road to Calama). All tour companies offer this excursion.

SALAR DE ATACAMA & THE FLAMINGO NATIONAL RESERVE

San Pedro sits on the edge of a gigantic mineralized lake that is covered in many parts by a weird, putty-colored crust. This *salar*, or salt flat, is a basin that collects water but has no outlet, leaving behind an accumulation of minerals, including a sizeable percentage of the world's lithium reserves. A highlight is a stop at the Flamingo Reserve near Solcor, which allows a chance to glimpse a few of the birds that come here to nest. There's also an interpretive center (no phone), open daily September through May 8:30am to 8pm, and June through August 8:30am to 7pm. To get here, head south toward Toconao, 33km (20 miles) from San Pedro. Once you've passed through Toconao, keep your eyes open for the entrance to the flamingo reserve signed LAGUNA CHAXA.

GEYSERS DEL TATIO/BAÑOS DE PURITAMA

Without a doubt a highlight in the Atacama Desert, the **Geysers del Tatio (Tatio Geysers)** ★★★ are nonetheless not the easiest excursion—there's not a lot of physical activity required, but tours leave at the crack of dawn (the geysers are most active around 6–8am). At 4,321m (14,173 ft.), these are the highest geysers in the world. Exercise extreme caution when walking near thin crust; careless visitors burn themselves here frequently. Herds of *vicuñas*, the llama's wild cousin, are known to graze in this area, so keep your eyes open for these delicate creatures. The geysers are 95km (59 miles) north of San Pedro. Those driving their own vehicle will want to pay sharp attention to the road and signs, especially because visitors set out in darkness to reach Tatio. Ask for a detailed map and directions at your car-rental agency. Head north out of San Pedro toward the Azufrera Polán. At the 45km mark you'll turn right at a signed intersection until, at the 54km mark you reach the camp Volcán Apagado. Continue straight ahead until the next intersection at 68km and head right to Campamento Apagado. Another intersection at 73km will point you toward the airstrip Tocopuri, where, at 79km you'll head left until 84km, where you'll turn right and continue until passing Campamento Corfo and arriving at the geyser field.

There's a hot spring pool near the geyser field, but the best hot springs are on the road to the geysers at **Baños de Puritama** ★★, an oasis composed of well-built rock pools that descend down a gorge, about 60km (37 miles) from the geysers. They are run by the luxury Hotel Explora (see "Where to Stay," below), and cost $10 to enter; there are changing rooms and bathrooms here. Most tour companies leave around 4 to 5am for the 2½-hour journey to Tatio, and they usually include a stop at Puritama. For travelers with a rental car, it is possible to continue on to Calama from here, so you may want to save this excursion for your last day. Note that some visitors have experienced difficulty driving here due to unfamiliarity with the road and vague turn-off points, so be sure to get good directions before you head out.

PUKARA DE QUITOR

This 12th-century, pre-Inca defensive fort clings to a steep hillside some 3km (2 miles) outside San Pedro. Although formidable, the fort was no match for the Spanish with their horses and arms made of metal, and it was conquered in 1540 by Francisco de Aguirre and 30 men. To get there, walk, bike, or drive west up Tocopilla Street and continue along the river until you see Quitor at your left.

ALDEA DE TULOR

This fascinating attraction is the Atacama's oldest pueblo, estimated to have been built around 800 B.C. Tulor remained intact in part because it had been covered with sand for hundreds of years, and today it is possible to see the walls that once formed the structures of this town. There are a few reconstructed homes on view as well. It's 9km (5½ miles) southwest of San Pedro.

OUTDOOR ACTIVITIES

BIKING   The Atacama region offers superb terrain for mountain bike riding, including the Quebrada del Diablo (Devil's Gorge) and Valle de la Muerte (Death Valley); however, it is also enjoyable to ride across the flat desert to visit sites such as Tulor. For bikes, try **Pangea Expediciones,** Tocopilla s/n (no phone), which rents high-quality mountain bikes for $12 per day and plans excursions such as a descent from the Altiplano (an elevated region created from volcano ash). It also has detailed maps for riders.

HORSEBACK RIDING   Horseback riding is a fun way to experience the Atacama, especially if you're adept at galloping. **Rancho Cactus,** Toconao 568 (© **55/851506;** ranchocactus@sanpedroatacama.com), owned by friendly couple Farolo and Valérie, rents horses by the hour for about $6 an hour. They also plan multiple-day, full-service excursions ranging from a $45 day trip to a $150 2-day camping trip.

VOLCANO ASCENTS   Climbing one of the four volcanoes in the area requires total altitude acclimatization and a good physical state—previous mountaineering experience wouldn't hurt either. The most popular volcanic ascent is up Volcano Láscar to 5,400m (17,712 ft.). Many tour companies offer this excursion; try **Nativa Expediciones,** Tocopilla s/n (𝄪 **55/851095;** nativaexp@yahoo.com), or **Azimut 360** (Caracoles s/n; 𝄪 **55/851469;** base-spa@netline.cl).

WHERE TO STAY
VERY EXPENSIVE

Hotel Explora ★★★   With the boom in tourism in San Pedro, a luxury hotel was inevitable. Although Explora encompasses a considerable chunk of desert, it manages to keep a low profile, tucked away at the end of a dusty street. Like its counterpart in Patagonia, the Explora in Atacama is elegant yet unpretentious. Inside, the lounge and guest rooms are tastefully decorated with local art and painted in quiet, primary tones. Cut-out window displays hold Atacama Indian artifacts found when the hotel broke ground, and in many ways the collection rivals San Pedro's museum. The lounge, with soaring ceilings, is enormous, stretching the length of the building and scattered with plush, multicolored couches and wicker chairs draped in sheepskin. The rooms have ultra-comfort-able beds made with crisp linens and fluffy down comforters; each bathroom comes with a Jacuzzi tub. Each room has a blue-trimmed window that stretches the length of the building—if you can, try to get a room facing the Volcano Licancabúr. Above the main building is an open deck with an outstanding view of the desert. A slatted walkway takes guests to the oasislike, irrigation-style swimming pools, each with its own sauna.

Explora operates as an all-inclusive hotel, offering packages that include trans-fers, an open bar, all excursions, all meals (cuisine is superb), and an afternoon tea. Every evening one of their full-time bilingual guides meets with guests to plan daily excursions.

Domingo Atienza s/n (main office: Américo Vespucio Sur 80, Piso 5, Santiago). 𝄪 **55/851110** (local), 2/206-6060 in Santiago (reservations). Fax 2/228-4655. Toll-free fax 800/858-0855 (U.S.), 800/275-1129 (Canada). www.explora-chile.com. 52 units. All-inclusive rates, double occupancy, per person: 3 nights $1,296; 4 nights $1,706; 7 nights $2,441. Reduced tariffs available for children and teens. AE, DC, MC, V. **Amenities:** Restau-rant; bar; 4 outdoor pools; sauna; massage; babysitting; laundry service; mountain bikes; horseback riding; TV room; library.

EXPENSIVE

Hotel Altiplanico ★★   The newest addition to lodging options in San Pedro sits just outside of town, on the road to the Pukará de Quitor. Like its prede-cessors, the striking architecture stays true to the style of the zone: river rock patios, adobe walls, peaked straw roofs, tree trunks left in their spindly, natural state. It is quite an attractive hotel and about on par as La Aldea (see below) in terms of price; La Aldea has a slight edge in architecture, but the Altiplanico is located on a spacious property with better views. Rooms are simple, with little decoration and cutout windows that let in streams of soft light. All rooms face east toward the Andes and therefore offer outstanding views. The friendly staff arrange excursions at an additional price.

Domingo Atienza 282. 𝄪 **55/851212.** Fax 55/851238. 16 units. $100 double, $200 family apt for 5. AE, DC, MC, V. **Amenities:** Cafeteria; large outdoor pool; bicycles. *In room:* No phone.

Hotel Tulor ★   This hotel is owned by the person who discovered the Tulor ruin site, hence the name. The Tulor is on a quiet street just down from the Hotel Kimal (see below) and behind an adobe wall. The circular buildings are made of adobe and thatched roofs. The rooms are unremarkable, with nondescript beige walls, thin carpet, and a tiny table and chair; some seem crammed with too many beds. For the price, you'd do better at the Kimal; however, the Tulor does come with a patio and kidney-shaped swimming pool, and its stand-alone restaurant is very appealing. The owner will gladly share information about the Tulor site and arrange excursions there and to other attractions in the area.

Domingo Atienza s/n. ℂ/fax **55/851027.** www.tulor.cl. 9 units. $90 double. AE, DC, MC, V. **Amenities:** Restaurant; bar (high season only; cafeteria rest of year); outdoor pool.

La Aldea ★★ This chic adobe hotel is owned by two architects, who have bestowed great taste to its interiors. The principal drawback here is the 10-minute dusty walk to the center of town, which can be a bother. The welcoming lobby, lounge, and restaurant are built of stone, adobe walls, cinnamon-colored wood, ironwork, and thatched roofs. A curving stairwell leads to a game room and lounge. Several rooms branch off from the main unit, and although they are slightly dark, they have a cooling effect on a hot day. They are also spacious enough to give some breathing room. Perhaps the best rooms are in the separate *cabañas* for three, which are cylindrical two-stories with fresh white walls and lots and lots of light; two of them are brand-new. Outside is a turquoise pool, surrounded by a pebbled courtyard.

Solcor s/n. ℂ/fax **55/851247** or 55/851333. www.hotelaldea.cl. 9 units, 3 *cabañas*. $96 double; $138 3-person *cabaña*. AE, MC, V. **Amenities:** Restaurant; outdoor pool; room service; laundry service; TV room; bicycles; horseback riding.

Lodge Terrantai ★★ If the prices at the Explora are a little beyond your budget, but you're looking for something of comparable quality, you might try this exclusive little hotel near the main street. The Terrantai is in a 100-year-old home that was renovated by a well-known Chilean architect, who preserved the building's flat-fronted facade, adobe walls, and thatched roof. The style is pure minimalism, and every inch of the interior hallways and the rooms are made of stacked river rock. The rooms are very comfortable, with down comforters, linen curtains, soft reading lights, and local art. Most rooms have large floor-to-ceiling windows that look out onto a pleasant garden patio. The Terrantai has a small restaurant; dinner is served here only during the summer, which means that prices are slightly cheaper during the off season. There is also outdoor dining. The Terrantai offers all-inclusive packages that include meals, airport transfers, and daily excursions with English-speaking guides.

Tocopilla 411. ℂ **55/85-1045.** Fax 55/85-1037. www.terrantai.com. 14 units. $137 double; all-inclusive, English-guided package doubles, per person: 2-night $542, 3-night $733, 4-night $870, 5-night $1,018. MC, V. **Amenities:** Restaurant; outdoor pool (more like a soak tub); laundry service; daily excursions with bilingual guides.

MODERATE

Hostería San Pedro de Atacama ★ Hostería San Pedro was the first hotel in the area. The motel-like establishment has comfortable rooms spread across a large property that includes San Pedro's only gas pump—the reason you'll see a fair amount of traffic drive in and out throughout the day. Across from the main building are seven *cabañas*—each with two bedrooms and spacious bathrooms, but no living area—that sleep a total of four to five people; these units are the loudest, especially when a tour bus or two starts its engine. For a quieter respite, choose one of the detached, sunny double rooms in back that look out onto a very nice pool/Jacuzzi/patio area. More rooms can be found in the hotel's main building, with stone walls and larger bathrooms, but less light. All are carpeted and clean. The pool area, with its patio filled with tables for relaxing or eating, is a strong point, as is the *hostería's* restaurant, which serves an ample selection of international/Chilean dishes.

Solcor 370. (℃) **55/851011.** Fax 55/851048. hosteria@sanpedroatacama.com. 25 units. $60 double; $100 *cabaña* for 4. AE, DC, MC, V. **Amenities:** Restaurant; bar; outdoor pool; shop; gas station. *In room:* No phone.

Hotel Kimal ★★ This appealing little hotel is tucked behind an adobe wall, with tiled walkways that lead to the 10 rooms, each with its own small outdoor seating area. The hotel feels more intimate than most in San Pedro. The rooms are fringed outside by pimiento trees and are fairly straightforward: adobe walls, thick foam beds, a bathroom, and a freestanding closet, but they're softly lit by skylights and are very soothing. Of all the hotels in this price range, I enjoy the Kimal the most, especially for its good, on-site restaurant Paacha. The hotel is run by an amiable English woman, and is on a quiet side street.

Domingo Atienza 452 (at Caracoles). (℃) **55/851152.** Fax 55/851030. kimal@entelchile.net. 10 units. $60 double. AE, DC, MC, V. **Amenities:** Restaurant. *In room:* No phone.

La Casa de Don Tomás The Don Tomás seems a bit expensive for what it has to offer. The hotel is made of adobe brick centered on a gravel courtyard/parking lot, and there are a few large *cabañas* behind the main unit. The main building has a dining area and a mini-lounge; a dozen rooms branch off from this central area, but the majority have separate entrances, much like a motel. The rooms are average-size, with white ceramic floors and surprisingly so-so beds. The service is perhaps better than the accommodations. On the average it's a decent place, but you might want to check out other hotels before booking here.

Tocopilla s/n. (℃) **55/85-1055.** Fax 55/851175. www.rdc.cl/dontomas. 38 units. $80 double; $200 cabin for 8. AE, DC, MC, V. **Amenities:** Restaurant; outdoor pool. *In room:* No phone.

INEXPENSIVE

Hotel Tambillo ★ The Tambillo is the best option in this price range. The 12 rooms are lined along both sides of a narrow, attractive pathway inlaid with stone. Rooms have arched windows and doors, and no decoration other than two boldly striped bedspreads, but it's not unappealing—on the contrary, the atmosphere is fresh and clean. There's a large restaurant and a tiny sheltered patio. It's a 4-block walk to the main street.

Gustavo Le Paige s/n (℃)/fax **55/851078.** tambillo@sanpedroatacama.com. 12 units. $40 double. No credit cards. **Amenities:** Cafeteria. *In room:* No phone.

Residencial Casa Corvatsch The Casa Corvatsch is a popular place with budget travelers. The main building has attic rooms that are very unremarkable and have shared bathrooms—they're literally a room with a bed, nothing else. A walkway out back leads to the other option, which is four carpeted rooms with private bathrooms, brick walls, and better beds. The Casa Corvatsch is owned by a Swiss-Chilean couple, and they run excursions, offer airport transfers, and have Internet access on site. It's about a 5-block walk to the main street.

Gustavo Le Paige 178. (℃)/fax **55/851101.** corvatsch@sanpedroatacama.com. 28 units. $25 double, private bathroom; $8 double, shared bathroom. MC, V. *In room:* No phone.

WHERE TO DINE

If you're looking for a quick, light lunch, try **Petro Pizza** at Toconao 447 ((℃) **09/2916347;** pizzas $1-$4), which serves a variety of stone oven–baked pizzas with toppings for vegetarians and meat eaters. They also offer tacos and empanadas.

MODERATE

Adobe ★★ CONTEMPORARY CHILEAN   This is one of the best choices in San Pedro. The Adobe is a popular place for eating, drinking, or just hanging out in front of the bonfire that blazes every evening in the semi-enclosed outdoor area. The best seats are at the wooden tables under a thatched roof that wraps around the fire area. The Adobe is known for its set breakfasts, which can include pancakes, eggs, a fruit salad, and espresso, but really any meal is delicious here. The menu offers typical Chilean treats such as empanadas, but there's also pasta, salads, grilled meats, and a set menu for $7 to $9 that includes a soup, main dish, and dessert. There's also live music Thursday through Saturday starting at 10pm, and an Internet cafe.

Caracoles 211. ✆ 55/851132. www.cafeadobe.cl. Main courses $5–$8. AE. Daily 8am–1am.

Restaurant Milagro ★ CHILEAN   The newest addition to San Pedro's restaurant scene, Restaurant Milagro could essentially be a copy of its predecessors (adobe walls, rock floors, open-air ceiling). Nevertheless, the ambience is as enjoyable as at the Adobe, and the food isn't half-bad either. Each evening the restaurant builds a bonfire, which diners and drinkers gather round for conversation and to look up at the stars. The menu includes salads, sandwiches, vegetarian items, and grilled meats, such as kebabs.

Caracoles 241. ✆ 55/851515. Main courses $3.50–$7. AE. Daily 8am–1am.

La Casona ★ CHILEAN   La Casona is a newly renovated restaurant/bar housed in an old colonial building with soaring ceilings and whitewashed walls. Candelit, wooden tables adorned with a few sprigs of flowers and a crackling fireplace set a quieter ambience. There's also a pool table and pub in the rear room that can get fairly lively, as can the outdoor bar, featuring music and a roaring fire. The owner is from Finland, but the menu is typically Chilean, with appetizers such as a *palta reina* (avocado stuffed with tuna) or *palta york* (stuffed with chicken) and main dishes such as grilled tenderloin in a creamy pepper sauce. They also serve pastas, vegetarian dishes, and *picoteos* (appetizer plates).

Caracoles 195. ✆ 55/851004. www.restaurantlacasona.com. Reservations not accepted. Main courses $5–$9; sandwiches $1.50–$4. AE, DC, MC, V. Daily 9am–11pm.

La Estaka ★ INTERNATIONAL/CHILEAN   La Estaka is part hip, part hippie, and one of the most popular restaurants in San Pedro, especially in the evening when the music is turned up and the wine starts to flow. The plentiful yet simple menu offers both meat and vegetarian dishes, including omelets, pasta, salads, and even sushi in a funky ambience that features semi-outdoor seating with a netlike roof, dirt floor, and molded banquettes, and a spacious indoor eating area with lofty ceilings and large wood tables. The lunch hour is quite mellow, but at night the bar gets pretty loud. There's a deejay Fridays and Saturdays.

Caracoles 259. ✆ 55/851201. www.laestaka.cl. Reservations not accepted. Main courses $5–$10; sandwiches $2–$4.50. AE, DC, MC, V. Daily 8:30am–1:30am.

INEXPENSIVE

Café Todo Natural ★ CAFE   This tiny cafe is known for its vegetarian, whole-meal empanadas made from scratch while you wait. Of course, the wait can be long, but it's worth it. Café Todo Natural makes every pizza and bread item the same way. For breakfast there's nothing quite like toast made from freshly baked bread, especially when you pair it with an espresso and fresh fruit juice; they also serve pancakes. Seating is limited, but they'll make a sandwich or empanada to go if you can't get a seat.

Caracoles s/n. No phone. Empanadas and sandwiches $2.50–$4. No credit cards. Daily 9am–10:30pm.

Café Etnico CAFE   This is a good all-in-one spot: coffee, fresh baked pies and cakes, sandwiches, a good book exchange, and four Internet terminals. What Café Etnico has on offer changes daily according to the mood of the bar guys behind the counter. They also give tourist information about excursions around San Pedro, including little-known areas. If the Internet terminals here are occupied, there is another cafe serving light snacks and coffee, **Rincón Pintado** at Caracoles 101-b (© **55/851470;** no credit cards). The Rincón Pintado also has outdoor seating.

Tocopilla 423. © **55/85–1377.** Snacks $1.50–$5. No credit cards. Daily 7am–9:30pm.

14

The Chilean Lake District

The region south of the Biobío River to Puerto Montt is collectively known as the Lake District, a fairy-tale land of emerald forests, white-capped volcanoes, frothing waterfalls, and plump, rolling hills dotted with hundreds of lakes and lagoons that give the region its name. It is one of the most popular destinations in Chile, not only for its beauty, but also for the diverse outdoor and city-themed activities available and a well-organized tourism structure.

The Lake District is home to the Mapuche Indians, who fiercely defended this land against the Spanish for 300 years. German settlers came next, clearing land and felling timber for their characteristic shingled homes. Both ethnic groups have left their mark on the region through architecture, art, and food.

The region is dependent on fishing, tourism, and, unfortunately, the timber industry, which has done much to destroy the Lake District's once nearly impenetrable forests. However, the many national parks and reserves give visitors a chance to surround themselves in virgin forest that is unique for its stands of umbrella-shaped *araucaria* and 1,000-year-old *alerce* trees (see "The *Alerce* & the *Araucaria:* Living National Monuments," later in this chapter).

The weather here during summer is usually balmy, but in winter this region sees a *heavy* amount of rainfall, much like the Pacific Northwest of the United States.

EXPLORING THE REGION

The Lake District is composed of the **Región de la Araucanía,** which includes the city **Temuco** and the resort area **Pucón,** and the **Región de los Lagos,** where you'll find the port cities **Valdivia** and **Puerto Montt;** charming villages such as **Puerto Varas** and **Frutillar;** and the island **Chiloé** (see chapter 15). There's plenty more to see and do outside these principal destinations, including hot springs, boat rides, adventure sports, beaches, and kilometer after kilometer of bumpy dirt roads that make for picturesque drives. Towns such as Puerto Varas and Pucón make for excellent bases to take part in all of these activities. Another great attraction here is Chile's proximity to the **Argentine Lake District** (see chapter 8), where you'll find the equally beautiful cities **Bariloche** and **San Martín de los Andes.** If you're planning on visiting both countries, it makes sense to cross the border in the Lake District, where Chile and Argentina are separated by a 1- to 2-day boat ride or several hours by road. It is entirely feasible to loop through both country's Lake Districts; most visitors find they need just 2 to 4 full days to explore each destination.

1 Temuco

677km (420 miles) S of Santiago; 112km (69 miles) NW from Pucón

Outside magazine called Temuco one of "The World's Great Towns," and although that claim might seem dubious to the average visitor, Temuco offers enough attractions to warrant a half day getting to know Chile's third-largest city. Unless you're flying in or out it does not really warrant an overnight stay.

Historically known as La Frontera (The Frontier), this is where the Mapuche Indians kept Spanish conquistadors at bay for 300 years until Chile's Frontier Army founded a fort on the shore of the River Cautín in 1881. The city grew like a boomtown as Spanish, German, French, Swiss, and English immigrants poured into the region. Temuco is still one the country's fastest-growing cities, as is evident by the thundering buses, bustling downtown crowds, and increasingly poor air quality that threaten to absorb whatever charm remains in this historic town.

Temuco serves as a jumping-off point to a handful of national parks, such as **Conguillío, Villarrica,** and **Huerquehue.** It is also the gateway to the wildly popular **Pucón.** If you plan to use Temuco solely as a transfer point for outlying regions, try to at least stop at the Mercado Municipal (Municipal Market), described in "What to See & Do," below.

ESSENTIALS
GETTING THERE
BY PLANE   **Manquehue Airport,** ZCO (no phone), is about 8km (5 miles) from the city center. To get to Temuco, hire a cab outside or arrange transportation with Transfer & Turismo de la Araucanía, a minivan service at the airport that charges $6 for door-to-door service (© **45/339900**). This transfer service will also take a maximum of six people directly to Pucón for $42. Lan-Chile serves Temuco with an average of four daily flights from Santiago, a daily flight to Valdivia and twice-weekly service to Osorno and Puerto Montt. There's also one weekly flight to Conception.

BY BUS   To get to Temuco from Santiago by bus, try **TurBus** (© **2/270-7500**), which leaves from the Terminal Alameda at Avenida Bernardo O'Higgins 3750; or **Cruz del Sur** (© **2/770-0607**), which leaves from the Terminal Santiago at Avenida Bernardo O'Higgins 3848. The trip takes 7 to 8 hours and a one-way economical ticket costs about $9; a seat in executive class costs about $20. Most buses arrive at Temuco's new **Terminal Rodoviario** (no phone). From here you can take a taxi to your hotel.

BY TRAIN   EFE (© 2/632-2802 in Santiago, or 45/233416 in Temuco; www.efe.cl) offers one of the few train services in Chile, with economy, salon, and sleeper coaches. Opinions about the service are varied; however, most say that quality and comfort are decent, but the clackety-clack of the rails keeps more than a few riders up all night. EFE's "La Frontera" has daily service to Santiago, leaving at 9pm and arriving at 8:45am; from Santiago to Temuco the departure time is 9:30pm with an arrival at 9:15am. The train station in Temuco is at Barros Arana and Lautaro; in Santiago, the station is at Bulnes 582. Tickets are $17 sleeper, $14 economy.

BY CAR   The Panamericana drives right through town. Follow the signs to downtown to the left.

VISITOR INFORMATION
Sernatur operates a well-stocked tourism office at the corner of Claro Solar and Bulnes streets at Plaza Aníbal Pinto (© **45/211969**). Hours from December to March are Monday through Saturday from 8:30am to 7:30pm; the rest of the year, Monday through Friday from 9:30am to 1pm and 3 to 7pm.

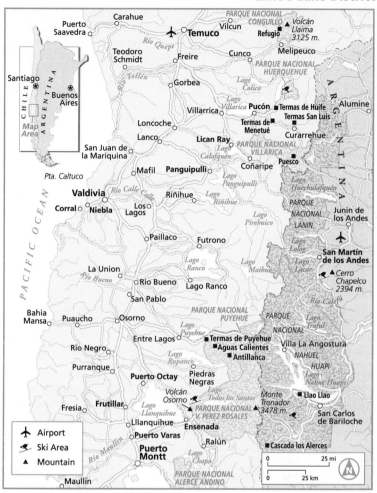

NEARBY GUIDED TOURS

MultiTour, Bulnes 307, #203 (© **45/237913;** fax 45/233536; www.chile-travel.com/multitur.html), offers a wide variety of bilingual excursions, including city tours, day trips to Conguillío National Park, and 3-hour, 8-hour, and overnight cultural trips through Mapuche communities. These cultural trips include visits to a *ruca,* a typical Mapuche Indian home, and the opportunity to visit with Mapuches; the "working" overnight requires participation in tasks such as chopping wood and taking animals out to pasture.

GETTING AROUND

Getting around Temuco is easy by foot. To get to outlying areas such as national parks, it's best to rent a car or go with a tour. To get to Pucón (see "Villarrica & Pucón," later in this chapter), try **Buses JAC,** corner of Balmaceda and Aldunate (© **45/231340**), which operates from its own terminal, leaving every half hour on weekdays and every hour on weekends and holidays.

If you want to rent a car to see the outlying sights, Hertz, Avis, and First all have kiosks at the airport. In downtown Temuco, **Hertz** can be found at Las Heras 999 (✆ **45/235385**); **Avis** at Vicuña Mackenna 448 (✆ **45/238013**); **First** at Antonio Varas 1036 (✆ **45/233890**); and **Dacsa** at A. Bello 770 (✆ **45/ 211515**).

FAST FACTS: TEMUCO

Currency Exchange   There are a few *casas de cambio* and banks with 24-hour cash machines along Calle Bulnes at the main plaza.

Hospital   **Clínica Alemana,** Senador Estenbanez 645 (✆ **45/244244**).

Laundry   **Marva** laundromat has two locations: 415 and 1099 Manuel Montt.

Travel Agency   Try **Agencia de Viajes y Cambios Christopher,** Bulnes 667, #202 (✆ **45/211680**).

WHAT TO SEE & DO

For a sweeping view of Temuco, take a taxi or hike up the heavily forested **Cerro Ñielol,** which also features four trails and a restaurant near the summit. It's open Monday through Sunday from 8am to 10pm; admission is 70¢ adults, 25¢ children. At the site marked LA PATAGUA, you'll find a plaque commemorating the agreement signed here in 1881 between the Mapuche Indians and the Chilean Army for peaceful settlement of Temuco. If you're there between March and May, the Cerro Ñielol is also an ideal spot to catch Chile's national flower in bloom, the crimson, trumpet-shaped *copihue.*

The manicured grounds of **Plaza Aníbal Pinto** ✫ in the city center are a relaxing break from the commercial bustle surrounding it. Within the plaza you'll find the sizeable *La Araucanía* monument depicting the clash between the Mapuche and the Spanish. There's also a gallery with temporary exhibits.

Walk up Calle Bulnes to Portales to enter one of Chile's finest markets, the **Mercado Municipal** ✫, open Monday through Saturday from 8am to 8pm, Sunday and holidays from 8:30am to 3pm; from April to September the market closes at 6pm. Rows of stalls sell high-quality woven ponchos, knitwear, textiles, woodwork, hats, silver Mapuche jewelry, *mate* gourds, and assorted arts and crafts. Around the perimeter, fishermen and food stalls aggressively vie for business while butchers in white aprons hawk their meats from behind dangling sausages and fluorescent-lit display cases. Another market, the **Feria Libre** at Aníbal Pinto, offers a colorful chaos of fruit and vegetable stands as well—the highlight here is the traditional Mapuche Indian vendors who come in from *reducciones* to sell their goods. The market is open Monday through Sunday from 8:30am to 5pm; from March to December, it closes at 4pm.

Temuco also has the **Museo Regional La Araucana** at Alemania 084 (✆ **45/ 211108**), open Tuesday through Friday from 10am to 5:30pm, Saturday from 11am to 5:30pm, Sunday from 11am to 2pm; admission is 70¢. The museum features exhibits charting Indian migration and history, along with displays of Mapuche jewelry and weapons. There's really not a lot to see, so you should consider visiting this museum only if you've run out of things to do.

WHERE TO STAY

Holiday Inn Express *(Kids)*   Predictable the way a Holiday Inn always is, this hotel is best used as an overnighter for those on their way out of Temuco. With clean rooms, comfortable beds, cable TV, and a location a half block from an American-style shopping mall with the usual fast-food joints, you might feel like you never left the States. The principal drawback of this hotel is its distance from downtown; however, it is close to the locally renowned La Estancia barbecue restaurant (see below). Kids under 18 can room with their parents for free.

Ortega 1800, Temuco. © 800/36666 or 45/223300. Fax 45/224100. www.sixcontinentshotels.com. 40 units. $65 double. Rate includes buffet breakfast. AE, DC, MC, V. **Amenities:** Small outdoor pool; exercise room; Jacuzzi; business center. In room: A/C, TV, coffeemaker, safe.

Hotel Aitué   This family-owned and -operated hotel offers good value for the price, including a business center with an Internet connection and free airport pickup. Double rooms are average size; junior suites are substantially larger. Each well-lit room comes with mahogany furniture and fairly comfortable beds. The staff is knowledgeable and friendly and strives to make guests feel at home. The hotel has a popular convention salon downstairs, and it also offers a small bar and lounge, as well as a fireside dining area serving breakfast and snacks.

Antonio Varas 1048, Temuco. © 45/211917. Fax 45/212608. www.hotelaitue.cl. 38 units. $40 double; $52 junior suite. AE, DC, MC, V. **Amenities:** Restaurant; bar; lounge. In room: TV, minibar.

Hotel Continental ★ *Moments*   Inaugurated in 1889, the Continental is the oldest hotel in Chile, with a rich local history and a guest book that has registered names such as Gabriela Mistral and Pablo Neruda. Virtually nothing has changed at the Continental, certainly not the wooden bar where locals still meet for the dice game *cacho,* nor the elegant dining room with period bronze chandeliers and mounted deer antlers. The stark rooms come with high ceilings, antique furniture, and a sink; most have tiny windows; room no. 9 is the only one with a TV. The major drawbacks at the Continental are squeaky floors, thin walls, and the beds (all singles), which seemingly haven't been changed since 1889. On the other hand, this hotel is your best bet for old-world, romantic charm. Where else can you spend the night in the same room as ex-presidents Aguirre and Salvador Allende (room no. 11)? Recommended for a visit even if you choose not to stay. See below for a review of the restaurant.

Antonio Varas 708, Temuco. © 45/238973. Fax 45/233830. www.turismochile.cl/continental. 40 units. $46 double with bathroom; $31 with shared bathroom. Rates include continental breakfast. AE, DC, MC, V. **Amenities:** Restaurant; bar.

Tierra del Sur *Kids* *Value*   This small, modern hotel sits just across a set of railroad tracks where the paved road turns to dirt. Designed and built by a local architect (including simple, handcrafted furniture), the Tierra del Sur has bold blue- and mustard-colored stucco walls and a compact, motel-like layout. Seven new rooms were added in 2002 on the first floor of the main building; each comes with bright yellow wallpaper and a small but very clean bathroom. Apartments are average-size and come with small kitchenettes and a tiny bar-and-stool setup for eating. The 10-minute, unattractive walk to the downtown plaza is really the only negative point of the Tierra del Sur. Service is friendly, and inside the lobby there's a bright cafe serving breakfast and lunch. A nice touch is the *quincho,* a covered barbecue house near the pool for grilling dinner.

Bulnes 1196, Temuco. ©/fax 45/232439. www.tierradelsur.cl. 22 units. $36 double; from $39 apt. AE, DC, MC, V. **Amenities:** Restaurant; 2 small pools (1 indoor, 1 outdoor); sauna; Turkish steam bath. In room: TV, fridge.

WHERE TO DINE

Head to the **Mercado Municipal,** open Monday through Saturday from 8am to 8pm, and Sunday from 8:30am to 3pm, for a quick, inexpensive lunch at one of the market's dozen or so restaurants. To get there, enter at Portales at Bulnes or Adulante streets. Waiters will harangue you until you feel suckered enough to choose their establishment, but the best bet is at **La Caleta.** For sandwiches and other quick meals, try **Dino's** at Bulnes 360 (© **45/213660**), **ñam ñam** at the corner of Portales and Prat (no phone), or **Bierstube** at Vicuña Mackenna 530, if you like your sandwich with sauerkraut (no phone).

The Continental Hotel ★ *(Finds* CHILEAN   Located in an antique hotel of the same name (see above), the Continental is still the traditional favorite in town. The food is prepared simply, with many dishes following the standard fried entree with mashed potatoes format. Several highlights are cheese soufflé, crab stew, and Parmesan scallops. One of the best reasons to dine at the Continental is for the old-world ambience. Inside the century-old, barn-size dining area, giant bronze chandeliers hang from a soaring ceiling; the room is so spacious that conversation echoes when there are only a few diners. The restaurant offers a set menu for lunch Monday through Friday for $6.

Antonio Varas 708. © **45/238973**. Main courses $4–$10. AE, DC, MC, V. Daily noon–3pm and 8–11pm.

La Estancia STEAKHOUSE   This restaurant is regionally known as one of the best Chilean *parrillas* (grills) in the south of Chile, although La Pampa (see below) is nipping at its heels. Sizzling cuts of beef can be ordered individually or as part of a *parrillada* (mixed grill), and there are also chicken, fish, salads, and a range of appetizers, including excellent Serrano ham. The surrounding grounds are quite pleasant and include an expansive garden.

Ortega 2340. © **45/221385**. Main courses $5–$12. AE, DC, MC, V. Mon–Sat noon–3pm and 8pm–midnight; Sun noon–4pm.

La Pampa STEAKHOUSE/ARGENTINE   Excellent grilled meats, fresh salads, seafood, and an extensive wine list that includes export-only varieties make La Pampa a good place to dine. It was opened 5 years ago by two Argentine transplants who came for a visit and never went home. Try the trout with Roquefort sauce, or one of the Argentine specialties such as *matambre,* thin meat rolled with spinach and egg. Don't miss the weekend-only *asado criollo,* thick ribs slowly grilled for 3 hours.

Caupolicán 155. © **45/882116**. Main courses $6–$16. AE, DC, MC, V. Mon–Sat noon–4pm and 7:30pm–midnight; Sun noon–4pm.

Quick Biss *(Value* *(Kids* CAFETERIA   This modern cafeteria, with wooden booths and zebra-striped walls, is very popular with downtown workers for its reasonable prices. Diners fill their trays with items such as salads, hot dishes, sandwiches, soups, and desserts, or a simple empanada. Solo diners often sit at a large bar near the entrance where they watch the news or a soccer game while eating. The *autoservicio,* or self-service, lunch runs from 12:30 to 4pm, dinner from 6 to 9pm, and there is also a simple menu offered all day.

Antonio Varas 755. © **45/211219**. Main courses $3–$5. AE, DC, MC, V. Daily 11am–11pm.

EXCURSIONS FROM TEMUCO
PARQUE NACIONAL TOLGUACA

This compact, 6,400 hectare (15,808-acre) national park offers several enjoyable hiking trails and the **Hotel Termas de Tolguaca** (© **45/881211**; www.termas detolhuaca.co.cl), a hot springs complex and hotel. Tolguaca's highlights are its valley surrounded by glacier-scoured peaks and Volcán Tolguaca. Two of the park's popular trails, **Mesacura** and **Lagunillas,** both 12km (7½ miles) long, are full-day hikes that wind through a virgin forest of laurel, *araucaria,* and evergreen

The *Alerce* & the *Araucaria:* Living National Monuments

The Lake District and its neighboring forests in Argentina are home to two of the oldest trees on the planet: the *alerce* and the *araucaria,* otherwise known as larch and monkeypuzzle trees, respectively. The *alerce* is a sequoia-like giant that grows less than 1mm each year, and can live for more than 3,000 years, making it the world's second-oldest tree after the California bristlecone pine. They are best viewed in the Alerce Andino National Park and Pumalín Park.

The *araucaria,* called *pehuén* by the Mapuche, is unmistakable for its gangly branches and thick, thorny leaves that feel waxy to the touch. Mature trees can grow as high as 50m (164 ft.), and take on the appearance of an umbrella, which is why they're often called Las Paraguas (The Umbrellas). They do not reach reproductive maturity until they are about 200 years old, and they can live as long as 1,250 years. They are best seen in Tolguaca, Villarrica, and Conguillío national parks, but they're virtually everywhere around the Lake District. The *araucaria* seed, an edible nut, was the principal source of food for the Mapuche Indians; later the tree was coveted for its quality wood and, as with the *alerce,* aggressive harvesting destroyed the majority of its forests. Today, both the *alerce* and the *araucaria* have been declared protected national monuments.

beech, some of which tower more than 30m (98 ft.) tall. The Lagunillas trail ends at a panoramic vista point that looks directly out at Volcán Tolguaca. To get to these trails, hikers must first take the **Salto Malleco** trail, which passes the **Río Malleco** and its namesake lagoon (where you can fish) until it comes upon a thundering, 50m (164 ft.) waterfall; this moderate trail is 8km (5 miles) long. From here the trail forks; the left trail is Mesacura and the right Lagunillas. The park is open from November to April only, daily from 8am to 8pm. Admission is $2.50 for adults, 75¢ for children under 12, and there are several campsites and picnic areas (for more information, call © **45/236312**). During the summer, park rangers give daily talks. Another feature of the park is its hot springs, the **Termas de Tolguaca,** with a pleasant hotel, a restaurant, and two large thermal pools with hydromassage lounge seats. Pool day-use costs $10 adults, $5 kids; it's free if you stay at the hotel. You'll need your own vehicle to get here, or you can arrange a trip with a tour company. Bring rain gear regardless of the season.

CONGUILLIO NATIONAL PARK ★★

Ranked as one of Chile's finest national parks, Parque Nacional Conguillío surrounds the spectacular smoking cone of Volcán Llaima and features a dense forest of spindly *araucaria* trees, which the park was created to protect. It's a lovely park and a great attraction year-round due to several splendid hiking trails, a ski resort, and an outstanding park information center. Volcán Llaima is one of the most active volcanoes on earth and has registered 40 eruptions since 1640, most recently in 1994. In the southern section of the park it is possible to witness the tremendous destruction lava has wreaked on the surrounding forest. Conguillío is divided into three separate sectors with as many access points. The western side of the park is commonly known as **Las Paraguas (The Umbrellas);** the eastern side is accessed from the north in sector Laguna Captren, and the south at Sector Truful-Truful. Visitors will find the park's administration center, campgrounds, and most hiking trails here in the eastern sector.

The eastern access point is at the village **Cherquenco;** from here a 21km (13-mile) rutted road ends at the **Centro Esquí Las Araucarias (**© **45/ 562313)** in Las Paraguas. This ski center has two T-bars, a ski school, equipment rental, and a restaurant and bar. Ticket prices are $14 Monday through Friday and $20 on weekends. The center offers dormitory-style lodging with two single-sex rooms and about 10 bunk beds without bedding for $11 per person. There's also a condominium with units for six that go for $90 a night. It's a fun little resort nestled in a forest of *araucaria,* and the views are simply breathtaking.

An unpaved and poorly maintained road connects a Conaf **visitor center,** which is open daily from 9am to 1pm and 3 to 7pm (© **45/212121),** with the towns **Curacautín** in the north and **Melipeuco** in the south. The information center has interpretive displays highlighting the park's flora, fauna, and physical geology, including an interesting section devoted to volcanism. During the summer, park rangers offer informative talks and walks and a host of educational activities, which they post in the visitor center.

There's an easy, hour-long, self-guided trail that leaves from the Conaf center, but if you really want to get out and walk, you'll want to take the **Sierra Nevada trail.** This moderate, 5-hour hike is the best in the park, taking visitors through thick forest and rising to two lookout points that offer sensational volcano and lake views, before dropping back down to the Captrén Lagoon near the Conaf center. The trail head is on the western shore of Lake Conguillío at the Conaf center. A second, 5-hour hike along moderate terrain, **Los Carpinteros,** weaves its way through stands of *araucaria* trees that are several hundred, some more than 1,000, years old. This trail leaves from Laguna Captrén at the Conaf center. Keep your eyes peeled for woodpeckers.

GETTING THERE & BASICS If you plan to rent a vehicle, try to get one with a high clearance—it's not essential, but it helps. Most tour companies in Temuco plan excursions to this park. Bus service from Temuco's main terminal is available only to Curacautín and Melipeuco; from here you'll need to take a taxi or hitch a ride. The road is paved only to the park entrance, so during the winter you'll usually need a 4×4 or tire chains to get to the ski center.

The park is open daily April through November from 8am to 11pm and May through October 8:30am to 5pm. The park entrance fee is $5 for adults and $1 for children. There is a cafeteria and a store at Conaf's park information center in Sector Truful-Truful.

WHERE TO STAY There are seven campsites along the shore of Lago Conguillío; backcountry camping is not permitted. Campsites cost about $21. From October to April the park service has cabins that go for an average of $50 per night; information about rentals can be found inside the store next to the visitor center in Sector Truful-Truful (© **45/213299).** A great option is one of the wooden cabins at **La Baita (**© **45/581075),** for $85 per night, located midway between Conaf and the town Melipeuco. Here, you'll find a restaurant, a store, park information, and guided excursions such as hiking, skiing, and snowshoeing.

A REMOTE LODGE OUTSIDE TEMUCO

El Hotel Trailanqui *Finds* *Kids*   This out-of-the-way resort should appeal to anyone looking to get away from it all. Families especially love this resort for its wealth of activities, including fishing, horseback riding, and swimming—there's even a mini-golf course—that keep everyone busy. The resort is spread out along the shore of a crystal-clear river, and it offers hotel rooms, apartments, cabins, and campsites. Its spacious lounge has a huge fireplace made of volcanic rock and floors made of cypress trunks. Actually, the Trailanqui is made entirely of cypress, offset with large picture windows, sheepskin rugs, and deer antler chandeliers. Double "full" rooms are substantially larger than double standard rooms and are the same price. Apartments have two bedrooms and a wood-burning stove, but no kitchen. *Cabañas* come fully stocked and have decks overlooking the river, where there's a beach and swimming platform.

It can get a little crazy here in January and February, but the off season promises tranquillity. If you're not staying at the hotel and want to use their pool, you may drop in for a $10 fee.

Guests typically take meals in the hotel's restaurant (guests in *cabañas* can cook their own), which is also open year-round to the public. The restaurant serves a fixed-price menu of home-style Chilean dishes during the high season in a dining area down by the river; they serve from a regular menu (chicken, meat, and seafood dishes) during the low season in the restaurant within the hotel.

Los Laureles a Colico Km 5. © 45/578218, or for reservations in Temuco 45/234119. Fax 45/214915. www.trailanqui.cl. 22 units, 9 *cabañas*. $81 double; $139 suite; $120–$144 *cabaña*. AE, DC, MC, V. **Amenities:** Restaurant; bar; lounge; heated outdoor pool; 9-hole golf course; tennis courts; spa; bike rental; game room; room service; laundry service.

2 Villarrica & Pucón *★ ★*

Villarrica is 25km (16 miles) W of Pucón and 764km (474 miles) S of Santiago; Pucón is 112km (69 miles) E of Temuco and 789km (489 miles) S of Santiago

Villarrica is a quiet town that never really took off as a vacation resort. Cheaper accommodations can be found here, and the town is decidedly less touristy, but it sits a half-hour ride away from the more popular Pucón and attractions such as Villarrica and Huerquehue national parks and the ski resort.

Nationally and internationally known as the **"Adventure Capital of Chile,"** Pucón offers a multitude of outdoor activities, including fly-fishing, rafting, hiking, and skiing. Yet what makes Pucón a great destination is its flexibility. There's also an abundance of low-key activities, such as hot spring spas and scenic drives through spectacular landscapes. Or you can just hang out on the beach and sun yourself, as hundreds do during the summer.

VILLARRICA

Decidedly less popular than neighboring Pucón, Villarrica does have a charm of its own. It's a more authentic Lake District *pueblo;* the compact downtown area hums with activity as regular townsfolk go about their daily business. The town is also closer to Temuco and attractions such as Lican Ray on Lake Calafquén, Panguipulli, and the Coñaripe hot springs.

GETTING THERE   Buses JAC (© 45/442069) leave Villarrica every half hour for Pucón from its location at Bilbao 610, near Pedro de Valdivia. In Pucón, JAC's location is O'Higgins 492. The fare is under a dollar. A taxi to or from Pucón costs about $10. For more information on getting to the region, see "Getting There" for Pucón, below.

VISITOR INFORMATION   A good **tourism office** can be found at Av. Pedro de Valdivia 1070 (℃ **45/411162**). It's open daily from 8:30am to 11pm from December 15 to March 15 and daily from 8:30am to 6:30pm the rest of the year; it often closes on winter afternoons when the weather is rotten. You can also visit www.villarrica.com for more information.

WHAT TO SEE & DO
You might consider a 2-hour trip to Villarrica to stroll the streets, have lunch, and drop in to visit the **Museo Histórico y Arqueológico** (Pedro de Valdivia 1050; no phone), with displays of Mapuche items and trademark silver pieces and jewelry. Outside you'll find an authentically thatched *ruca,* a traditional Mapuche home. The museum is open Monday through Friday from 9am to 1pm and 3 to 7:30pm. The festival **Muestra Cultural Mapuche** takes place here in Villarrica from January to late February, with music, handcrafts, dancing, and other activities (for more information, call the visitor center at ℃ **45/411162**).

WHERE TO STAY
Hostería de la Colina ✿, Casilla 382 (℃/fax **45/411503;** aldrich@entel chile.net), is owned and managed by an American couple, Glen and Beverly Aldrich, who have lived in Chile for 14 years. The inn is located on a hill with a panoramic view of the lake and volcanoes and offers 7 comfortable rooms in the main house and two cottages located in the peaceful gardens, as well as a Jacuzzi. The owners will help you plan your stay, and they serve hearty Chilean meals in the pleasant dining room. Doubles run from $65 to $85; cottages start at $98. Rates include full breakfast.

   Hostería Kiel, General Korner 153 (℃ **45/411631;** fax 45/410925), has comfortable rooms ($55–$65 double) and a direct view of Volcán and Lake Villarrica that you can enjoy from your very own porch. Or try **Cabañas Monte Negro** at Pratt and Montt streets (℃ **45/411371**); it charges $110 for two to six people (no credit cards), and has eight newer cabins near the lake with a direct view of the volcano. Private parking or ample street parking is available and free.

A NEW LUXURY HOTEL
Villarrica Park Lake ✿✿ *Finds*   Inaugurated by the President of Chile in November 2002, this is the region's top new hotel. Luxurious and expansive, this property is striving to be the best in Southern Chile. It only has 69 rooms, but it feels like a big corporate hotel with its large lobby and aloof but polite staff. Extra-wide doors made of local wood lead into comfortable and spacious modern rooms, all with sliding French doors that open up onto a balcony with a view of the lake. The marble bathrooms come with shower/tub combinations and heated towel racks. The spa has an exquisite selection of facials and bodywork offerings. This is an excellent base for travelers who prefer large, full-service hotels, although you'd be well advised to book way in advance as it occasionally fills up with corporate retreat groups for days at a time. Always request promotional rates when making your reservations.

Camino Pucón–Villarrica Km 13. ℃ **45/450000.** Fax 45/450202. www.villarricaparklakehotel.cl. 69 units. $180–$255 double; from $220 suite. AE, DC, MC, V. **Amenities:** Restaurant; bar; lounge; heated indoor pool; health club and spa; limited watersports equipment; concierge; business center; salon; room service; massage; dry cleaning; laundry service. *In room:* TV, minibar, hair dryer, safe.

WHERE TO DINE

For excellent seafood dishes, try **El Rey de Marisco,** on the coast at Valentín Letelier 1030 (© **45/412093**), or **Hostería Kiel,** General Korner 153 (© **45/ 411631**), for simple Chilean fare and a superb view of Volcán Villarrica. **The Travellers,** Valentín Letelier 753 (© **45/412830**), has that international traveler's hostel vibe, and a menu to match with Chinese, Indian, Mexican, Thai, and Chilean dishes, plus the ever-popular happy hour from 6 to 9:30pm.

PUCÓN ☆☆

Pucón is a picturesque little town almost entirely dependent on tourism, but thankfully it has not embellished its streets with gaudy tourist traps. Instead, a creative use of timber creates the architectural tone. During the early 1900s, Pucón's economy centered on the timber industry, but the town's fate as a travel destination was sealed when the first hotel went up in 1923, attracting hordes of fishermen. Ten years later, the government built the stately Hotel Pucón, drawing hundreds more visitors each year, who at that time had to travel here by boat from Villarrica. Today, there are many lodging options, and even more adventure outfitters ready to fill your days.

It is important to note that the summer season, particularly from December 15 to the end of February, as well as Easter week, is jam-packed with tourists. Hotel and business owners gleefully take advantage of this and jack up their prices, sometimes doubling their rates.

GETTING THERE   By Plane   Visitors normally fly into Temuco's **Manquehue Airport** and then arrange transportation for the 1- to 1½-hour ride into Villarrica or Pucón. Most hotels will arrange transportation for you, although it's usually at an additional cost. Transfer & Turismo de la Araucanía (© **45/ 339900**), a minivan service at the airport, will take a maximum of six guests to Pucón for $45. Pucón's new airport is now operational and equipped to handle jets, but for the time being only two flights a week (on Fri and Sun) touch down here from Santiago and only during the highest season, from mid-December to late February. Additional service is expected to be added as demand continues to increase; for fares and up-to-the-minute schedule information contact **LanChile** at (© **600/600-4000;** www.lanchile.com.)

By Car   From the Panamericana Highway south of Temuco, follow the signs for Villarrica onto Ruta 199. The road is well marked and easy to follow. If coming from Valdivia, take 205 to the Panamericana Norte (Hwy. 5). Just past Loncoche, continue east, following signs for Villarrica and Pucón.

By Bus   TurBus (© **2/270-7500;** www.TurBus.cl) offers service to Pucón from destinations such as Santiago, stopping first in Temuco and Villarrica. The trip is about 9 to 11 hours and generally a night journey; the cost is about $19 for an economy seat and $31 for an executive seat. **Buses JAC** has service from Temuco every half hour from its terminal at Bustamante and Aldunate.

VISITOR INFORMATION   Sernatur (© **45/443338**) operates a helpful tourism office at the corner of Brasil and Caupolicán streets; it's open daily from 8:30am to 10pm December through March and from 8:30am to 8pm the rest of the year. The city of Pucón has an excellent website at **www.pucon.com**.

GETTING AROUND   There are dozens of tour companies providing transportation and tours to all points of interest around Pucón; they generally advertise everything in their front windows. However, this is another place where renting a car is a great option if you want to get out and leisurely see the sights.

In Temuco, **Hertz** has an office at Las Heras 999 (© **45/441664**) and they operate a branch in Pucón at Ansorena 181 © **45/441664.** In Pucón, try **Christopher** in front of the supermarket (© **45/449013**), **Pucón Rent A Car** on the
Camino Internacional 1395-1510 (© **45/441992**), or **SP Comercial Rent A
Car** at 191 Ansorena (© **45/444485**). Rates start at $34 for a small car, per day.

OUTDOOR ACTIVITES

With so many outdoor adventures available here, it's no wonder there's a surplus
of outfitters eager to meet the demand. When choosing an outfitter in Pucón,
remember that you get what you pay for. Be wary of seemingly fly-by-night
operations or those that treat you like just another nameless tourist. You want a
memorable experience for the fun you've had, not for the mishaps and accidents.
Most outfitters include insurance in the cost of a trip, but first verify what their
policy covers.

For more things to see and do in this area, see "Hot Springs Outside Pucón"
and "Natural Attractions Outside Pucón," later in this chapter.

TOUR OPERATORS **Politour,** O'Higgins 635 (© **45/441373;** www.politur.
com), is a well-respected tour company that offers fishing expeditions, Mapuche-
themed tours, and sightseeing trips around the Seven Lakes area, in addition to
volcano ascents. They're slightly more expensive than other agencies, but are
worth it. **Aguaventura,** Palguín 336 (© **45/444246;** www.aguaventura.com),
is run by a competent, dynamic French trio and specializes in snowboarding in
the winter with a shop that sells and rents boards, boots, and clothing. In the
summer the focus is rafting and kayaking, and they offer a great half-day
canyoneering and rappelling excursion; they also plan horseback rides. **Trancura,**
O'Higgins 211-c (© **45/441189;** www.trancura.com), operates a variety of
excursions, but it's known for rafting and volcano climbs. Trancura seems to offer
just about everything, including ski rental at several locations along the main
strip. It's a large company with the lowest prices around, but there have been
complaints about lackluster service. Still, they're the only tour agency that offers
wild-boar hunting. **Sol y Nieve,** O'Higgins and Lincoyán (© **45/441070;**
www.chile-travel.com/solnieve.htm), has been on the scene for quite a while,
offering rafting and volcano ascents, as well as fishing, airport transfers, and
excursions in other destinations around Chile. **[ue]école!,** General Urrutia 592
(© **45/441675;** trek@ecole.mic.cl), offers a unique trip to a private *araucaria* forest, **Cañi.** If you can't get to Conguillío, you'll want to see the *araucaria* trees here.
It's a good excursion, especially if it's raining and you're unsure what to do.

BIKING Several outfitters on the main street, O'Higgins, rent bicycles by the
hour and provide trail information and guided tours. Bicycle rentals run an average of $8 for a half day. You can also just pedal around town, or take a pleasant,
easy ride around the wooded peninsula.

CLIMBING THE VOLCANO ★★ An ascent of Volcán Villarrica is perhaps
the most thrilling excursion available here—but you've got to be in decent shape
to tackle it. The excursion begins early in the morning, and the long climb
requires crampons and ice axes. There's nothing like peering into this percolat-
ing, fuming crater. The descent is a combination of walking and sliding on your
behind in the snow. Volcán Villarrica is perpetually on the verge of exploding,
and last year trips were called off for some time until the rumbling quieted
down. Tour companies that offer this climb are **Trancura, Politour, Aguaventura,** and **Sol y Nieve** (see "Tour Operators," above). The average cost is $35,
and does not include lunch.

FISHING You can pick up your fishing license at the visitor center at Caupolicán and Brasil. Guided fishing expeditions typically go to the Trancura River or the Liucura River. See a list of outfitters above for information, or try **Off Limits,** Fresia 273 (© **45/441210**).

GOLFING Pucón's private, 18-hole Península de Pucón golf course is open to the playing public. For information, call © **45/441021,** ext. 409. The cost is $42 for 18 holes.

HIKING ☆ The two national parks, Villarrica and Huerquehue, offer outstanding hiking trails that run from easy to difficult. An average excursion with an outfitter to Huerquehue, including transportation and a guided hike, costs about $22 per person.

HORSEBACK RIDING Half- and full-day horseback rides are offered throughout the area, including in the Villarrica National Park and the Liucura Valley. The **Centro de Turismo Huepil** (© **9/643-2673**) offers day and multiple-day horseback rides, including camping or a stay at the Termas de Huife, from a small ranch about a half hour from Pucón (head east out of Pucón and then north toward Caburgua; take the eastern road toward Huife and keep your eyes open for the signs to Centro de Turismo Huepil). You'll need to make a reservation beforehand. All-inclusive multiple-day trips cost about $100 per person, per day. A wonderful couple, Rodolfo and Carolina, run this outfit. Rodolfo is a superb equestrian professor who used to train the Spanish Olympic team. Beginning riders are given an introductory course in the corral before setting out. Contact a tour agency for day rides in Villarrica Park, which go for about $60 for a full day. Tour agencies will also organize rides that leave from the **Rancho de Caballos** (© **45/441575**) near the Palguín thermal baths. If you're driving, the Rancho is at 30km on the Ruta International toward Argentina.

RAFTING ☆ Rafting season runs from September to April, although some areas might be safe to descend only from December to March. The two classic descents in the area are the 14km (8½-mile) Trancura Alto, rated at Class III to IV, and the somewhat gentler Trancura Bajo, rated at Class II to III. Both trips are very popular and can get crowded in the summer. The rafting outfitter **Trancura** (see "Tour Operators," above) also offers an excursion rafting the more technical Maichin River, which includes a barbecue lunch. The 3-hour rafting trip on the Trancura Alto costs an average of $20; the 3-hour Trancura Bajo costs an average of $8.

SKIING The **Centro Esquí Villarrica** gives skiers the opportunity to schuss down a smoking volcano—not something you can do every day. There's a sizeable amount of terrain here, and it's all open-field skiing, but regrettably the owners **(The Grand Hotel Pucón)** rarely open more than two of the five chairs. You'll need to take a chair lift to the main lodge, which means that non-skiers too can enjoy the lovely views from the lodge's outdoor deck. There's a restaurant, child-care center, and store. The Centro has a ski school and ski equipment rental; there are slightly cheaper rentals from Aguaventura, Sol y Nieve, and Trancura, among other businesses along O'Higgins. Lift ticket prices vary but average about $23. Most tour companies offer transport to and from the resort. For more information contact one of the tour operators above.

WHERE TO STAY

Pucón is chock-full of lodging options, nearly all of them good to excellent. If you're planning to spend more than several days in the region, you might consider renting one of the abundant *cabañas*. Keep in mind that Pucón is very busy during the summer, and accommodations need to be reserved well in advance for visits between December 15 and the end of February. Prices listed below show the range from low to high season; high season is from November to February, but verify each hotel's specific dates. You might consider visiting during the off season, when lodging prices drop almost 50%; November and March are especially good months to visit.

Expensive

Gran Hotel Pucón *(Kids)*   The Gran Hotel is a landmark built by the government in 1936 when fishing tourism began to take off in Pucón. It is a good choice for families, but otherwise we have mixed opinions about it. The owners renovated the premises somewhat recently, but one has the feeling they still have a ways to go. The hotel's palatial hallways, stately dining areas, and lovely checkerboard patio seem to belie the ugly teal they saw fit to paint the hotel recently. Indeed, the old-world beauty of these common areas, with their marble and parquet floors, lofty ceilings, and flowing curtains, still look a tad scruffy. The paint is peeling in the lobby and the carpets in the hallways are stained and fading fast. The rooms are not exactly noteworthy, but they are not bad either: spacious, with comfortable beds and views of the volcano or the lake. The superior room has an alcove with one or two additional beds for kids; bathrooms are spacious and clean. The hotel is run somewhat like a cruise ship, with nightly dinner dances, stage shows, music and comedy, as well as a team of activity directors who run a kids' "miniclub" and host classes for adults, such as cooking or tango. The hotel sits on the most popular beach in Pucón.

Clemente Holzapfel 190, Pucón. (©)/fax **45/441001**, or for reservations (in Santiago) 2/353-0000. Fax 2/233-3174. www.granhotelpucon.cl. 145 units. $95–$160 double. Kids under 10 stay free in parent's room. AE, DC, MC, V. **Amenities:** Restaurant; outdoor cafe; bar; lounge; large outdoor pool; small indoor pool; health club; children's programs; concierge; tour desk; limited room service; dry cleaning; laundry service. *In room:* TV, minibar, safe.

Hotel Antumalal *★★★* *(Moments)*   The minute you arrive here you know you've come upon something special. Perhaps it is the Antumalal's unique Bauhaus design and its lush, beautiful gardens, or perhaps it's the sumptuous view of sunset on Lake Villarrica seen nightly through the hotel's picture windows or from its wisteria-roofed deck. Either way, this is simply one of the most unique hotels in Chile. Low-slung and literally built into a rocky slope, the Antumalal was designed to blend with its natural environment. The lounge is a standout, with walls made of glass and slabs of *araucaria* wood, goatskin rugs, tree-trunk lamps, and couches built of iron and white rope. It's retro-chic and exceptionally cozy, and the friendly, personal attention provided by the staff heightens a sense of intimacy with one's surroundings. The rooms are all the same size, and they are very comfortable with large panoramic windows that look out onto the same gorgeous view, as well as honeyed-wood walls, a fireplace, and a big, comfortable bed. Guests don't just walk into a room; they *sink* into it. The aging bathrooms are slowly being renovated and should all be complete by early 2004. There's also a "Royal Cottage" for rent that comes with two bedrooms, a living room and fireplace—perfect for families; a rustic lakeside cabin with a private terrace close to the water is also available.

The owners are very involved in the day-to-day management of the hotel, and will sit down with guests to help them plan their stay and arrange for any special requests. The bar is especially interesting, with high-backed leather chairs and a stone fireplace, and the dining room not only serves up a spectacular view, it also serves some of the best food in Pucón. Lovely, terraced gardens zigzag down the lakeshore, where guests have use of a private beach. A kidney-shaped pool is half-hidden under a lawn-covered roof, and the tennis courts are a short walk away. It's all fit for a queen—indeed, Queen Elizabeth graced the hotel with her presence several decades ago, as have Jimmy Stewart and Barry Goldwater.

Camino Pucón–Villarrica, Km 2. © 45/441011. Fax 45/441013. www.antumalal.com. 16 units. $153–$212 double; from $380 Royal Cottage. Rates include full breakfast. AE, DC, MC, V. **Amenities:** Restaurant; bar; lounge; small outdoor pool; tennis court; room service; massage; laundry service.

Hotel del Lago ⋆ *(Kids)*   Pucón's sole five-star luxury hotel boasts a casino, the only cinema in town, and so many amenities that you might not feel like leaving the hotel. Attractively designed and recently built, the Hotel del Lago is airy and bright, with a lobby covered by a lofty glass ceiling. All the hotel's furnishings were imported from the United States, and the elegant, comfortable rooms are tastefully decorated with furniture and wood trim made of faux-weathered pine, accented with iron headboards, crisp linen, and heavy curtains colored a variety of creamy pastels, all very light and bright.

The bathrooms are made of Italian marble and are decently sized, as are double-size rooms—note that a double standard comes with two twins. The suites feature a separate living area. The Suite Volcán has the volcano view, but rooms facing west enjoy the late afternoon sun. A concierge can plan a variety of excursions for guests, as well as transport to the ski center. The hotel offers many promotions and package deals from March to December, often dropping the double price to $110, so be sure to check their website for seasonal promotions.

Miguel Ansorena 23, Pucón. © 45/291000. Fax 45/291200. www.hoteldellago.cl. 82 units. $120–$240 double; $200–$300 suite. Rates include buffet breakfast. AE, DC, MC, V. **Amenities:** 2 restaurants; bar; lounge; small indoor pool; large outdoor pool; state-of-the-art health club; spa; sauna; children's programs; game room; concierge; business center; room service; massage; babysitting; dry cleaning service; laundry service. *In room:* TV, minibar, safe.

Hotel Huincahue ⋆ *(Finds)*   If you like to be in the center of town, steps from all the shops and restaurants, in a quiet and sophisticated setting, then this is your best bet. Pucón's newest hotel sits right on the main plaza and has an elegant homey feel to it. From the cozy lobby lounge with a fireplace and adjoining library to the peaceful pool in the lovely garden, this place feels more like a private mansion than a hotel. Rooms have pleasant beige carpets, and nice wrought iron and wood furniture, and a few have spectacular views of the volcano (room no. 202 is best). Second-floor rooms have small balconies. The marble bathrooms are large and many have windows, as well. The staff tries hard to accommodate, but their English is minimal, so be patient.

Pedro de Valdivia 375. ©/fax 45/443540 or 442728. www.hotelhuincahue.cl. 20 units. $85–$120 double. Rates include continental breakfast. AE, MC, V. **Amenities:** Restaurant; bar; lovely outdoor pool; room service; massage; babysitting; laundry service. *In room:* TV.

Moderate

Hotel & Spa Araucarias   The rooms could use a lick of paint, but otherwise the Hotel & Spa Araucarias is a good bet for its well-manicured grounds, attractive indoor pool, outdoor deck, and extras such as an on-site gift shop. The size of the rooms is a little tight—not too much space to walk around in, but enough to open your suitcase. If you're looking for something a little more independent and spacious, try one of the four connected cabins in the back. The hotel has a "spa" room with a sauna and a great, heated indoor pool fitted with hydromassage lounges. The name comes from the *araucaria* trees that flank the entrance; there's also an *araucaria* sprouting from a grassy courtyard in the back. An attractive restaurant serves lunch and dinner.

Caupolicán 243, Pucón. ✆/fax **45/441963**. www.araucarias.cl. 25 units. $60–$75 double. Rates include continental breakfast. AE, DC, MC, V. **Amenities:** Restaurant; lounge; heated indoor pool; Jacuzzi; sauna; massage. *In room:* TV.

Hotel Munich   The Hotel Munich is a nice, moderately priced hotel with a touch of charm here and there. The rooms have enough elbowroom, and each comes with its own terrace; they are also clean and well lit. The lobby is filled with oil paintings that the owner displays as part of a makeshift gallery; the lounge feels like a living room. There is a small dining area for buffet breakfast or afternoon tea and snacks; you can also order breakfast in your room. The service is friendly, but a little lax.

Gerónimo de Alderete 275, Pucón. ✆/fax **45/442056**. munich@pucon.com. 10 units. $54–$76 double. Rates include buffet breakfast. AE, DC, MC, V. **Amenities:** Bar; lounge; room service. *In room:* TV.

La Posada Plaza   This traditional hotel is housed in a 78-year-old home built by German immigrants, located on the main square 2 blocks from the beach. Everything about this old-fashioned hotel, from its exterior to its dining area to its backyard swimming pool, is very attractive—except the rooms, that is, which are plain and inexplicably do not keep up the charm of the hotel's common areas. These old buildings always seem to come with fun-house floors that creak and slant in every direction. All in all, it's a comfortable enough place to hang your hat for the evening.

Av. Pedro de Valdivia 191, Pucón. ✆ **45/441088**. Fax 45/441762. laposada@unete.com. 17 units. $42–$66 double. Rates include buffet breakfast. AE, DC, MC, V. **Amenities:** Restaurant; pool snack bar; lounge; large outdoor pool; laundry service. *In room:* TV.

Malahue Hotel   This attractive, newer hotel is about a 15-minute walk from town, but offers excellent value in handsome accommodations. It was designed to feel like a modern mountain lodge, made of volcanic rock and native wood, and is set on an open space in a residential area. The interiors are impeccably clean, and rooms are decorated with country furnishings. There's a restaurant and a cozy lounge with a fireplace and couches. *Cabañas* have two bedrooms, a trundle bed in the living area, and a fully stocked kitchen. The location isn't ideal, but the accommodations are fine.

Camino Internacional 1615, Pucón. ✆ **45/443130**. Fax 45/443132. www.pucon.com/malalhue. 24 units, 3 *cabañas*. $46–$70 double; $70–$98 *cabaña*. Rates include buffet breakfast. AE, DC, MC, V. **Amenities:** Restaurant; bar; lounge; room service. *In room:* TV.

Inexpensive

¡école! ☆ *Value*   Nearly 40 partners own this pleasant hostel, which offers small but clean and comfortable rooms with beds that come with goosedown comforters. ¡école! sees a predominantly international crowd, from backpackers to families traveling on a budget. It has a very good vibe throughout, and a nice outdoor patio with picnic tables. The hostel provides great reading material in the small lounge, from travel guides to environment-oriented literature to logging protest rosters. The hostel is part restaurant/part lodging/part ecology center, offering day trips to various areas, but especially to the private park Cañi, an *araucaria* reserve. It's very popular in the summer, when it's wise to book at least 1 or 2 weeks in advance.

General Urrutia 592, Pucón. ℂ/fax **45/441675**. www.ecole.cl. 16 units. $24–$27 double. Rates include continental breakfast. DC, MC, V. **Amenities:** Restaurant.

La Tetera   Rooms at La Tetera are simple but meticulously clean, and shared bathrooms are not much of an issue as they are just outside your door. It's all squeezed in pretty tight, but guests have use of a private, sunny common area with chairs and a picnic table, and a short walkway connects to an elevated wooden deck. A Swiss-Chilean couple own La Tetera; they offer a book exchange and good tourism information, and will arrange excursions and help with trip planning. La Tetera (the teakettle) lives up to its name with two menu pages of teas, along with sandwiches, daily specials, and pastries. A common area next to the cafe has the only TV in the place. The staff can arrange for Spanish lessons, even if you're here for a short time.

General Urrutia 580, Pucón. ℂ/fax **45/441462**. www.tetera.cl. 6 units. $20–33 double. Rates include continental breakfast. No credit cards. **Amenities:** Restaurant; bar.

Cabañas

Almoni del Lago Resort ★★ *Finds*   Location is everything at the Almoni, with its lush, gorgeous grounds leading down to the lapping shores of Lake Villarrica just a few meters from the deck of your cabin. Cabins for two, four, and eight guests are available; ask for specials for multiple-day stays. Cabins are fully equipped, very comfortable, and elegant; guests are given their own remote gate opener to help control access. A kiosk sells basic food items and other sundries. Most *cabañas* have their own deck right on the water, others have a deck farther up the hill. Either way, the cabins are fairly close together, so you might end up getting to know your neighbor. Prices drop 50% in the off season.

Camino Villarrica a Pucón, Km 19. ℂ **45/210676**. Fax 45/442304. www.almoni.cl. 8 *cabañas*. $47–$90 *cabaña* for 2. MC, V. **Amenities:** Large outdoor pool; tennis courts. *In room:* TV, kitchen.

Cabañas Ruca Malal   These custom-made, cozy wooden cabins are tucked away in a tiny forested lot at the bend where busy O'Higgins becomes the road to Caburga. The grounds, however, are peaceful, and they burst with bamboo, beech, magnolias, and rhododendron. The design of each cabin features log stairwells, carved headboards, and walls made of slabs of evergreen beech trunks cut lengthwise. They are well lit and have full-size kitchens and daily maid service. A wood-burning stove keeps the rooms toasty warm on cold days. In the center of the property is a kidney-shaped swimming pool; there's also a Jacuzzi and sauna, but unfortunately you'll have to pay extra to use them. As with most cabins, those designed for four people means one bedroom with a double bed and a trundle bed in the living area; book a cabin for six if you prefer two bedrooms. Those with a sweet tooth will delight in Ruca Malal's on-site chocolate shop.

O'Higgins 770, Pucón. ℂ/fax **45/442297**. avalle@cepri.cl. 9 units. $36–$98 cabin for 4; $66–$110 cabin for 6. MC, V. **Amenities:** Lounge; small outdoor pool; Jacuzzi; sauna; laundry service. *In room:* TV, kitchen.

Las Cabañas Metreñehue   These pastoral *cabañas* are surrounded by dense forest and bordered by the thundering Trancura River, about a 10-minute drive from downtown Pucón, and are for those seeking a country ambience away from town. There are cabins built for seven guests; a few two-storied cabins can fit eight. All are spacious and very comfortable, with wood-burning stoves, decks, and ample kitchens. Some come with bathtubs, and a few have giant picture windows; all have daily maid service. The two *cabañas* in the back have a great view of the volcano. Around the 3-hectare (7-acre) property are walking trails, a swimming pool, a volleyball court, a soccer field, and a river where guests can fish for trout. The cabins are popular with families in the summer, and sometimes large groups take advantage of the *quincho,* the poolside barbecue site. There's also mountain bike rental. The German owners are gracious and multilingual, and live in the main house (and reception area), near the cabins. Parties of two to five will have to pay a $110, six-guest rate during the summer.

Camino Pucón a Caburga, Km 10. ⓒ/fax 45/441322. www.pucon.com/metrenehue. 7 units. $50–$110 for 2; $90–$110 for 6. AE, DC, MC, V. **Amenities:** Restaurant; large outdoor pool; bike rental; laundry service. *In room:* TV, kitchen.

Puerta Pucón Cabañas *(Kids)*   These newer wooden cabins are spread out over a large grassy lot overlooking Lake Villarrica (a road separates the cabins from the beach). They are comfortable and relatively inexpensive, and a good bet for families with kids, especially for the pool, play area, "kids' clubhouse," and babysitting service; daily maid service is also included. All cabins have tiny kitchens, living areas, wood-burning stoves, small decks with table and chairs, and sweeping views of the lake. However, five of the cabins *(cabañas chicas)* are large cabins split into two units, and are somewhat cramped. Solitary cabins for four are larger, but the view shrinks. One cabin built for seven guests could really be called a house. The spacious property features walking trails, and there's also a private beach and docking area a 5-minute walk down the hill and across the road. Puerta Pucón is a 3-minute drive from downtown.

Camino Pucón–Villarrica, Km 4.5. ⓒ 45/442496. Fax. 45/442498. www.puertapucon.com. 14 units. $36–$64 for 2; $44–$95 for 4. No credit cards. **Amenities:** Lounge; bar; large outdoor pool. *In room:* TV, kitchen.

WHERE TO DINE

Pucón has a good selection of cafes that serve *onces,* the popular late-afternoon, coffee-and-cakes snack, in addition to a lunch menu. **Holzapfel** at Holzapfel 524 (ⓒ **45/443546**) offers promotional lunches that usually include a free beer, but it's really known for its desserts and out-of-this-world chocolates. **Café de la "P,"** Licoyán 395 (ⓒ **45/442018**), has a menu with sandwiches, cakes, coffee drinks, and cocktails. It's a nice place to unwind with a drink in the evening, and is open until 4am in the summer.

Alta Mar SEAFOOD   Seafood is the specialty here, as you can tell by the marine decor. It's the best spot for seafood in Pucón, offering a wide range of fish usually served grilled, fried, or sautéed in butter and bathed in a sauce. Their ceviche is tasty, and so are the razor clams broiled with Parmesan cheese. Outdoor seating is available on the front deck during warm months.

Fresia 301. ⓒ **45/442294**. Main courses $4–$8. No credit cards. Daily noon–4pm and 7:30pm–midnight.

Antumalal *(★★)* *(Moments)* INTERNATIONAL   The Hotel Antumalal's restaurant serves some of the most flavorful cuisine in Pucón, with creative dishes that are well prepared and seasoned with herbs from an extensive garden. In fact most of the vegetables used here are local and organic; the milk comes from the family's own dairy farm. Try a thinly sliced beef carpaccio followed by chicken stuffed with smoked salmon, grilled local trout, or any one of the pastas. There's a good selection of wine and an ultra-cool cocktail lounge for an after-dinner drink. It's worth a visit for the view of Lake Villarrica alone, and it's our favorite dining experience in Pucón.

Camino Pucón–Villarrica, Km 2. ⓒ **45/441011**. Fax 45/441013. Reservations recommended. Main courses $5–$9. AE, DC, MC, V. Daily noon–4pm and 8–10pm.

Buonatesta Pizzería PIZZERIA   Buonatesta has great pizzas, but they're not the saucy versions most are typically used to. The tiny restaurant, located behind the Puerto Pucón, has a cozy dining area with framed photos of Mapuches. The menu features more than a dozen combinations of pizzas, from sausage and onions to vegetarian, as well as fresh pastas and salads.

Fresia 243. © 45/441434. Pizzas $4–$11. AE, DC, MC, V. Daily 11am–4pm and 6:30–11:30pm.

¡école! VEGETARIAN *Value*   This vegetarian restaurant includes one salmon dish among heaps of creative dishes like calzones, quiche, pizza, burritos, chop suey, and more. Sandwiches come on homemade bread, and breakfast is good, featuring American breakfast as well as Mexican and Chilean. ¡école! uses locally and organically grown products and buys whole wheat flour and honey from a local farm. There are also fresh salads. There's a lovely outdoor patio where you can dine under the grapevine in good weather. The service is slightly disorganized; they usually offer a shorter menu during the winter.

General Urrutia 592. ©/fax 45/441675. Main courses $3–$5. MC, V. Daily 8am–11pm.

La Maga ⋆ URUGUAYAN STEAKHOUSE   Pucón's newest *parrilla* opened in the fall of 2002 and is proving very popular with locals. It originated in the beach town of Punta del Este, Uruguay. The food is excellent, especially the meat, chicken, and fish grilled on the giant barbecue on the patio. Order a bottle of wine and a large fresh salad and watch the people go by the large picture windows overlooking the street. Try the grilled salmon with capers, if you're in the mood for fish. But, really, the best cuts here are the beef filets, known as *lomos,* served with mushrooms, Roquefort, or pepper sauce. The *bife de chorizo* (sirloin) is thick and tender. For dessert, the flan here is excellent.

Fresia 125. © 45/444277. Main courses $4–$8. No credit cards. Daily noon–4pm and 7pm–midnight.

La Marmita de Pericles ⋆ FONDUE   Cozy and candlelit, La Marmita specializes in warm crocks of fondue, as well as the other Swiss favorite, *raclette.* Both involve a diner's participation, which usually makes for an amusing dinner. Fondue can be ordered a variety of ways, with standard bread cubes, squares of breaded meat, or vegetables. A *raclette* runs along the same lines; diners heat cheese to eat with cured meats and potatoes; it's not as fun as fondue, but enjoyable nevertheless. Unfortunately, this restaurant closes during the winter, which is the perfect season for this kind of food.

Fresia 300. © 45/441114. Fondue for 2 about $22. AE, DC, MC, V. Daily 7:30–11pm. Closed Apr–Nov.

Marmonhi ⋆ *Finds* CHILEAN   If you'd like to have lunch with the locals, then this place, a good 20-minute walk from the center of town, is worth the hike. The food is typically Chilean, prepared by the amiable Elena, who runs a tight ship. Many of Pucón's residents stop by here to pick up lunch or dinner for their families, although the simple dining room is pleasant for a leisurely meal and there's a small patio for outdoor dining in good weather. Specials change daily, according to what Elena finds at the market. Vegetable or beef empanadas are a great start to the meal. Then order a big Chilean salad (fresh tomatoes and lots of sweet onion) and one of the special chicken or fish dishes. They're simply yet deliciously prepared: marinated and grilled and served with vegetables and rice. There's excellent baked lasagna, as well. For dessert, have one of the decadent tarts that locals rave about but skip the coffee, which is instant and tasteless.

Ecuador 175. © 45/441972. Main courses $3–$7. No credit cards. Daily noon–4pm and 7–10:30pm.

Puerto Pucón *Finds* SPANISH   Puerto Pucón pays homage to its owner's Spanish heritage through its design and well-made classics such as paella. Seafood is the focus here, and it is served in a multitude of ways: Have your razor clams, shrimp, and calamari sautéed in garlic or wrapped in a crepe and smothered in crab sauce. The atmosphere is typical Spanish, with white stucco walls, bullfight posters, flamenco-dancer fans, and racks of wine bottles; the fireplace is especially nice, and there's a small bar. The sangria is excellent and during warmer months there's seating on the front deck, which can get packed.

Fresia 246. ⓒ 45/441592. Main courses $6–$8. AE, MC, V. Daily 11am–3:30pm and 7–11:30pm (until 2am during summer).

PUCON AFTER DARK

Pucón's **casino** can be found inside the five-star Hotel del Lago (see "Where to Stay," above), with three gaming rooms and a bingo hall. There's a good bar here that appeals to all ages, and the place is open very late. The Hotel del Lago also has the town's only **cinema;** contact them for playlists (ⓒ 45/291000), or check the newspaper. For bars, **Bar Bazul,** Lincoyán 361 (no phone), has food and outdoor seating, and **El Living,** at the corner of Colo Colo and O'Higgins (no phone), has sushi by day and techno music by night; it's open very late.

HOT SPRINGS OUTSIDE PUCON ★★

All the volcanic activity in the region means there's plenty of *baños termales,* or hot springs, that range from rustic rock pools to full-service spas with massage and saunas. Nothing beats a soothing soak after a long day packed with adventure. Also, like the Cañi Reserve, the hot springs make for a good rainy-day excursion.

Termas de Huife ★   Termas de Huife, a relaxing escape for the body and mind, is popular with tourists and locals alike for its idyllic thermal baths and setting. Nestled in a narrow valley on the shore of the transparent River Liucura, Huife operates as a full-service health spa for day visitors and guests who opt to spend the night in one of their *cabañas* or suites. This is one of my favorite *termas,* both for its cozy accommodations and gorgeous landscaping, complete with narrow canals that wind through the property and river-rock hot springs flanked by bamboo and palm fronds. The complex features two large outdoor thermal pools kept at 96°F to 98°F (36°C–37°C) and a cold-water pool, as well as private thermal bathtubs, individual whirlpools, and massage salons arranged around an airy atrium. The four-person *cabañas* and double suites are housed in shingled, rust-colored buildings along the river, about a 2-minute walk from the main building. All come with wood-burning stoves, and the *cabañas* have a living area. The bathrooms deserve special mention for their Japanese-style, sunken showers and bathtubs that run thermal water.

Nearby, a swinging bridge takes guests to a nature trail that winds through a forest of beech and laurel. The service is good, and the gracious owner strives to see that every visitor leaves rested and feeling physically in top shape. The resort has a transfer from the airport and Pucón for an additional cost, and can plan excursions throughout the area. To get here, take the road east out of Pucón toward Lago Caburgua until you see a sign for Huife, which turns off at the right onto an unnamed dirt road. Follow the road until you see the well-marked entrance for Termas de Huife.

Road to Huife, 33km east of Pucón. ⓒ/fax 45/441222. www.termashuife.cl. 10 units. $118–$135 double. Day-use fee $9 adults, $4.30 children 10 and under. AE, DC, MC, V. Thermal baths open daily 9am–8pm, year-round. **Amenities:** Restaurant; cafeteria; 3 outdoor pools; exercise room; Jacuzzi; sauna; game room; massage. *In room:* TV, minibar.

Termas de Menetúe   These thermal baths are better for a day visit than an overnighter because the cabins sit so far away from the complex. There are two pools here. The reception area and restaurant look out onto a giant, grass-encircled swimming pool, and a short path takes visitors around to a woodsier setting, with one average-size pool serenaded by a gurgling waterfall. It's a relaxing, bucolic place with giant ferns and a gently flowing stream. The spa house has individual baths, but they're rather creepy and dark; better to join the floating masses in one of the outdoor pools. The pine cabins are for two to six people. They come with a fully stocked kitchen and wood-burning stove, and are a 5-minute walk from the baths. Menetúe rents out bicycles and can point out a few trails for walking. A restaurant serves decent Chilean cuisine, and there's a snack bar near the second pool.

Camino Internacional, Km 30. ©/fax **45/441877.** www.menetue.com. 6 *cabañas.* $50–$64 *cabaña* for 2. Day-use fee $6.50 Apr–Nov, $8 Dec–Mar. No credit cards. Thermal baths open Dec–Mar 9am–9pm; Apr–Nov 9am–6pm. **Amenities:** Restaurant; bar; 2 large outdoor pools; spa. *In room:* TV, kitchen.

Termas Los Pozones *(Finds*   Los Pozones is Huife's rustic neighbor, well known in the region for its cheaper prices, natural setting, and late hours—they stay open 24 hours a day, year-round, for the (mostly) young adults (many of them local) who want to keep the party going after leaving the discos in Pucón. The hot springs are reached by walking down a long, steep path, which means a long, steep climb after your soak (there are plans for a cable-operated people mover). One other drawback is the unsightly iron pipe that cuts through the property, bringing thermal water to its neighbor Huife. Los Pozones expanded in 2000 from two to six rock pools, and has built three *cabañas* high above the springs across from the road. The simple but pleasant *cabañas* come with kitchens and have lovely views, although it's a walk to get to the springs.

Road to Huife, 34km from Pucón, just past Termas de Huife. No phone. $42–$58 *cabañas* for 4. Day-use fee $6. No credit cards. Thermal baths open 24 hr. *In room:* Kitchen.

Termas San Luis *(* *(Kids*   Located high in the saddle of the Curarrehue Valley, the attractive Termas San Luis is popular for its well-built thermal pools and view of Volcán Villarrica, but mostly for the rare paved access road that gets you there. The compact resort is centered on two swimming pools built with stone tiles, one outdoor and the other covered by a fiberglass shell much like a greenhouse; both are surrounded by plastic lounge chairs for reclining after a long soak. If you'd like to spend the night, San Luis has six wooden cabins perched on a slope overlooking, unfortunately, the parking lot, although a few are hidden behind trees. The cabins sleep four to six guests, meaning one double bed, three singles, and a living-room trundle bed. They are bright and very pleasant, but can get very cold in the winter unless the wood-burning stove is continually stoked. The spa house features a tiny sauna and a massage salon at an additional cost. The restaurant serves Chilean specialties and uses some organic produce such as spinach and lettuce, grown in a greenhouse on the hillside.

Ruta Internacional Pucón, Km 27. © **45/412880.** www.termasdesanluis.cl. $100 double. Day-use fee $9 adults, $5 children, and $7 for a private bathtub. No credit cards. Thermal baths open 9am–11pm summer; 10am–7pm winter. **Amenities:** Restaurant; large outdoor pool; large indoor pool; spa; sauna; limited room service; massage. *In room:* TV, kitchen.

NATURAL ATTRACTIONS OUTSIDE PUCON
PARQUE NACIONAL HUERQUEHUE

Smaller than its rivals Conguillío and Villarrica, though no less attractive, Parque Nacional Huerquehue boasts the best short-haul hike in the area, the **Sendero Los Lagos.** This 12,500-hectare (30,875-acre) park opens as a steeply walled amphitheater draped in matted greenery and crowned by a forest of lanky *araucaria* trees. There are a handful of lakes here; the first you come upon is Lago Tinquilco, which is hemmed in by steep forested slopes. At the shore you'll find a tiny, ramshackle village with homes built by German colonists in the early 1900s. A few residents offer cheap accommodations, but the best place to spend the night is in a campground near the entrance or at the Refugio Tinquilco (see "Where to Stay," below).

There's a self-guided trail called **Ñirrico** that is a quick 400m (436-yd.) walk, but if you're up for a vigorous hike, don't miss the spectacular **Tres Lagos** trail that begins at the northern tip of Lake Tinquilco. The path first passes the **Salto Nido de Aguila** waterfall, then winds through a forest of towering beech, climbing to a lookout point with a beautiful view of Lago Tinquilco and the Villarrica volcano. From here the trail begins zigzagging up and up through groves of billowy ferns and more tall trees until finally (2–3 hr. later) arriving at the beautiful, *araucaria*-ringed **Lago Chico,** where you can take a cool dip. A relatively flat trail from here continues on to the nearby **Verde** and **Toro** lakes. Bring plenty of food and water, and come prepared with rain gear if the weather looks dubious.

On your way to or from the park you can make a detour to the **Ojos de Caburga,** where two aqua-colored waterfalls crash into the tiny Laguna Azul. There are a few picnic tables here, and you can take a dip if the weather's nice. The turn-off point is about 15km (9 miles) from Pucón.

GETTING THERE & BASICS The park is 35km (22 miles) from Pucón. There is no direct bus service to the park, but most tour companies offer minivan transportation and will arrange to pick you up later should you decide to spend the night. If you're driving your own car, head out of Pucón on O'Higgins toward Lago Caburga, until you see the sign for Huerquehue that branches off to the right. From here it's a rutted, dirt road that can be difficult to manage when muddy. Conaf charges $5.75 for adults and $1.50 for kids to enter, and is open daily from 8:30am to 6pm.

WHERE TO STAY Conaf has a campground near Lago Tinquilco and charges $18 per site, maximum six people. The best option for a roof over your head is the attractive **Refugio Tinquilco** (© 2/777-7673; fax 2/735-1187), a spacious lodge with bunks for $8 per person (you'll need your own sleeping bag), and regular rooms with complete bedding for $55 double. They also have a good restaurant and offer full pension for an additional $9.

PARQUE NACIONAL VILLARRICA

This gem of a park is home to three volcanoes: the show-stealer Villarrica, Quetrupillán, and Lanín. It's quite a large park, stretching 61,000 hectares (150,670 acres) to the Argentine border and that country's Parque Nacional Lanín, and is blanketed with a thick, virgin forest of *araucaria* and evergreen and deciduous beech. A bounty of activities are available year-round, including skiing and climbing to the crater of the volcano (see "Outdoor Activities" under "Pucón," earlier in this chapter), hiking, horseback riding, bird-watching, and more.

The park has three sectors. Most visitors to the park head to **Sector Rucapillán** (the Mapuche's name for Volcán Villarrica, meaning House of the Devil). Volcán Villarrica is one of the most active volcanoes in the world, having erupted 59 times from the 16th century until now. Every day, Villarrica belches out several dozen minor explosions; last year the explosions were so earth-rattling that all activity in the area had to be shut down. There are two trails here, the 15km (9-mile) **Sendero Challupén** that winds through lava fields and *araucaria,* and the 5km (3-mile) **Sendero El Glaciar Pichilancahue,** which takes visitors through native forest to a glacier. The park ranger booth at the entrance can point out how to get to the trail heads. You'll also find the interesting **Cuevas Volcánicas** in this sector. Ancient, viscous lava that flowed from the volcano created underground tunnels, 400m (1,312 ft.) of which have been strung with lights and fitted with walkways that allow you to tour their dark, dripping interiors.

Visitors are provided with a hard hat; the cave's humid, cold air requires that you bring warm clothing regardless of the season. There are also exhibits describing volcanism and bilingual tours. It's open daily from 10am to 8:30pm during the summer and from 10am to 6:30pm during the winter; admission is a steep $10 for adults and $4.50 for children (© **45/442002**).

The second sector, **Quetrupillán,** is home to wilder, thicker vegetation and a multiple-day backpacking trail that wanders through virgin forest and past the **Termas de Palguín** (which is also accessible by road), a rustic hot springs. Here you'll also find several waterfalls, including the crashing **Salto el León.** There's a horse stable here (see "Horseback Riding" under "Pucón," earlier in this chapter) that offers trips around the area. The dirt road to Palguín that branches off from the road to Curarrehue is rough but passable; however, the road from Palguín to Coñaripe is nearly impossible to pass, even with four-wheel-drive.

Finally, the third sector, **Puesco,** is accessed by Ruta 119 south of Curarrehue. There's a Conaf post and several hikes through the park's wildest terrain, including pine forests, lakes, and rugged mountains.

3 Siete Lagos: Panguipulli & Lican Ray

Panguipulli is 54km (33 miles) south of Villarrica; Lican Ray is 31km (19 miles) S of Villarrica

Few daylong sightseeing drives surpass the beauty of the Siete Lagos (Seven Lakes) region south of Pucón, where you can follow a half-paved, half-dirt loop around Lago Calafquén, with stops in the picturesque resort towns Panguipulli and Lican Ray. As its name implies, the region is home to seven lakes, one of which is across the border in Argentina, and all are set among rugged, verdant mountains that offer photo opportunities at every turn. (For more on the Argentina side of the Lake District, see chapter 8.)

DRIVING THE SIETE LAGOS ROUTE

Renting a car is the best option here, but several tour companies offer this excursion. Going south from Villarrica, you drive first to Lican Ray and then through Coñaripe, circling the lake until reaching Panguipulli. From here you take the paved road toward Lanco (although signs might say LICAN RAY as well), until you see the sign for Lican Ray and Villarrica. This rough dirt road continues to Villarrica (there's a good lookout point along the way), or forks to the right to Lican Ray, where you can again catch the paved road to Villarrica. Take a good look at the map before making any decisions; note that none of these roads are

---

A Note on Camping

The road between Lican Ray and Coñaripe is full of campsites, some of which are quite nice, with showers and barbecue pits. Try **Cabañas and Camping Foresta** (✆ **45/211954**) at 2km (1¼ miles) from Lican Ray, which has well-built sites and comfortable cabins for four guests (about $75–$105 during the summer, $38–$65 during winter).

---

numbered or have names. Of course, the trip can be done in the reverse direction, which might be more desirable for an afternoon soak at the hot springs just south of Coñaripe (see "Hot Springs Outside Pucón" above).

Termas de Coñaripe *(Finds* These *termas* boast a magnificent location in a narrow valley hemmed in by lush, sheer mountains and Lago Pellaifa. Location aside, Coñaripe is handsomely built with touches of Japanese design. There are four outdoor pools, one with a slide, and one indoor pool with whirlpool lounges and a waterfall. A babbling creek meanders through the property. The thermal spa's on-site trout fishery means there's fresh fish for dinner every evening, and kids love to feed the teeming schools of trout. Inside the lobby and the hallways, the floors are made of a mosaic of cypress trunks. Rooms are carpeted and spacious, and suites come with a queen bed. If you require quiet, you might not want a room near the busy pool. The *cabañas* come with two rooms with double beds and one with two twins.

Along with all this beauty and the deluxe amenities comes the inevitable crush during the summer months, and it's not unusual for these hot springs to see almost 1,000 visitors per day at peak high season from January 1 to February 15. There are so many people that guests who have booked for a week often leave, shell-shocked, after only a few days. During this time the hotel opens a special fast-service cafeteria to alleviate the packed dining room at lunch; a restaurant serves Chilean food year-round. Off-season crowds drop dramatically, and during the winter you might have the place to yourself.

Camino Coñaripe to Liquiñe at Km 15. ✆ 45/431407. Fax 45/411111. www.termasconaripe.com. 14 units, 3 *cabañas*, 1 apt. $85–$110 double standard; $108–$142 double standard with full board. Day-use fee $9 adults, $4 children for use of outdoor pools, and an additional $3 for indoor pool. DC, MC, V. Thermal baths open daily 9am–11pm, year-round. **Amenities:** Restaurant; lounge; 4 outdoor pools; indoor pool; tennis courts; exercise room; sauna; bike rental; game room; room service; massage; laundry service. *In room:* TV.

LICAN RAY

This tiny resort town hugs the shore of Lago Calafquén, offering toasty beaches made of black volcanic sand and a forested peninsula for a leisurely drive or stroll. The lake is warmer than others in the region, and is therefore better suited for swimming; you can also rent a boat here. The name comes from Lican Rayén, a young Mapuche woman from the area who is said to have fallen in love with a Spanish soldier. The town was founded as a trading post, and today there are about 2,000 permanent residents, except for the period from December 15 to February 28 when the population doubles with the arrival of summer vacationers.

The first weekend in January is the busiest time of year—the town hosts its **Monumental Barbecue of Lican Ray,** when residents line up 100 barbecues along the main street, General Urrutia, to roast lamb and throw an enormous outdoor party. There's also the **Noche Lacustre** the second week in February, when the bay fills with boats for a variety of contests and activities, followed by an evening fireworks display. Lican Ray is less crowded and less expensive than Pucón, and during the off season you'll practically have the place to yourself.

There are a few places to stay here: **Hotel Becker,** Manquel 105 (© **45/ 431021**), has modest but comfortable rooms, a restaurant, and a deck from which you can enjoy the lakefront view, and charges $34 double in off season, $58 double in high season. **Hostería Inaltulafquén,** Cacique Punulef 510 (©/fax **45/431115**), has good rooms and an even better dining area and deck, and it is ideally located across from the Playa Grande beach; it charges $28 to $48 double. The *hostería* is run by two helpful Canadians, who also offer excursions. For dining, try the restaurant at the *hostería* or **Noñas,** General Urrutia 105 (© **45/431021**), with an extensive menu that offers everything from barbecue meats to clay oven–baked pizzas. It also has outdoor seating during the summer.

PANGUIPULLI

This little town with the impossible-to-pronounce name (try "pan-gee-*poo*-yee") occupies a cove on the shore of Lago Calafquén. During the summer, Panguipulli's streets bloom a riot of colorful roses, which the town celebrates in January during the **Semana de las Rosas (Rose Week)** festival. Panguipulli was founded as a timber-shipping port and today has nearly 8,300 residents. The town's primary attraction is its charming **Iglesia Parroquial,** Diego Portales and Bernardo O'Higgins (in front of the gas station). Mass is held from November to February Thursday and Saturday at 8pm; Sunday and holidays 8:30am and 11am; the church is open all day (no phone). The Swiss priest who initiated the building of this church in 1947 modeled its architecture after churches he had seen in Switzerland, with two latticed towers painted in creamy beige and red and topped off with black shingled steeples.

If you decide you'd like to stay in this region, you might want to check out the **Hotel Riñimapu,** Casilla 512, Lake Riñihue, Panguipulli (© **63/311388,** or ©/fax in Santiago 2/696-1786), south of Panguipulli and on the shore of Lago Riñihue. The Riñimapu is a wonderful remote lodge that draws guests from around the world for its fly-fishing, horseback riding, and hiking—but it is the tranquillity here that encourages guests to really lose themselves in the beauty of the surroundings. The woodsy lodge has 16 attractive rooms, a restaurant, a bar, and a tennis court, and it charges $64 to $72 double, about $50 more for meals. To get here, head south out of Panguipulli on the paved then dirt road toward Lago Riñihue, and continue for 20km (13 miles) until reaching the hotel.

4 Valdivia ⟨★⟩

839km (520 miles) S of Santiago; 145km (90 miles) SW of Pucón

Valdivia is a large University town that always gets mixed reviews from visitors. Chileans tend to enjoy visiting here more than foreigners. It's a funky city with some charm evident through its colonial homes and vibrant waterfront, but it is as though every building from every decade from every architectural style were thrown in a bag, shaken up, and randomly scattered about the city.

The city is vibrant, bustling, and very tenacious. Valdivia has suffered attacks, floods, fires, and the disastrous earthquake of 1960 that nearly drowned the city under 3m (10 ft.) of water. During World War II, Valdivia's German colonists were blacklisted, ruining the economy. So if Valdivia looks a little weary—well, it's understandable. If you're in Pucón or Temuco, Valdivia makes for an interesting 1- or 2-day diversion, especially to visit the tiny towns and ancient forts at the mouth of the bay that protected the city from seafaring intruders. There's a pleasant fish market and several good restaurants. Some of the best museums and galleries in Chile can be found here, too.

Valdivia, with about 125,000 residents, is divided by a series of narrow rivers, notably the Río Valdivia and the Río Calle Calle that wrap around the city's downtown area. Along the Río Valdivia is the city's bustling waterfront, where fishmongers peddle their fresh catches of the day and pleasure boats disembark for a variety of journeys around the region's twisting waterways. These rivers have produced some of the world's top rowing athletes, and many mornings you can see spidery figures plying the glassy water. Across the Río Valdivia is the Isla Teja, a residential area that's home to the Universidad Austral de Chile, the reason you see so many students riding bikes around town.

ESSENTIALS
GETTING THERE
BY AIR   Valdivia's **Aeropuerto Pichoy,** ZAL (© **63/272294**), is about 30km (19 miles) northeast of the city; LanChile has one daily flight from Santiago, and once-weekly flights to Concepción, Temuco, and Puerto Montt. A taxi to town costs about $10, or you can catch a ride on one of Transfer Valdivia's minibuses for $2.50.

BY BUS   The bus terminal can be found at Anwandter and Muñoz, and nearly every bus company passes through here; there are multiple daily trips from Pucón and Santiago (the average cost for a ticket from Santiago to Valdivia is $10; from Pucón to Valdivia it is $3.50).

BY CAR   From the Panamericana Highway, take Ruta 205 and follow the signs for Valdivia. A car is not really necessary in Valdivia, as most attractions can be reached by boat, foot, or taxi. It's about a 2-hour drive from Pucón, 1½ hours from Temuco, or 3 hours from Puerto Montt.

VISITOR INFORMATION
Sernatur's helpful **Oficina de Turismo,** near Muelle Schuster at Arturo Prat 555 (© **63/215739**), has a well-stocked supply of brochures. The office hours from March to November are Monday through Friday from 8:30am to 1pm and 2:30 to 6:30pm; from December to February, hours are Monday through Saturday from 9am to 7pm and Sunday from 10am to 7pm. There's also an information kiosk at the bus terminal open daily from 8am to 9pm and a website with lots of information at www.valdiviachile.cl.

If you require more personal assistance, contact Elisabeth Lajtonyi at **Outdoors Chile** (© **63/253377;** www.outdoorschile.com). She can arrange for your entire trip, from reserving hotels to airport transfers and personalized sightseeing tours.

SPECIAL EVENTS
The city hosts a grand yearly event, the **Semana Valdiviana,** with a week of festivities that culminates with the **Noche Valdiviana** on the third Saturday in February. On this evening, hundreds of floating candles and festively decorated boats fill the Río Valdivia; in the evening the city puts on a fireworks display. Note that Valdivia is crowded during this time, so hotel reservations are essential.

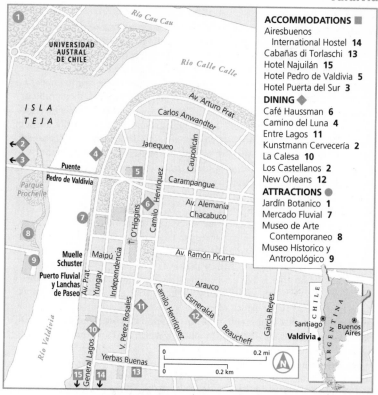

ACCOMMODATIONS ■
Airesbuenos
  International Hostel **14**
Cabañas di Torlaschi **13**
Hotel Najuilán **15**
Hotel Pedro de Valdivia **5**
Hotel Puerta del Sur **3**
DINING ◆
Café Haussman **6**
Camino del Luna **4**
Entre Lagos **11**
Kunstmann Cervecería **2**
La Calesa **10**
Los Castellanos **2**
New Orleans **12**
ATTRACTIONS ●
Jardín Botanico **1**
Mercado Fluvial **7**
Museo de Arte
  Contemporaneo **8**
Museo Hístorico y
  Antropológico **9**

FAST FACTS: VALDIVIA

Car Rental   **Assef y Mendez Rent A Car** can be found at General Lagos 1335 (© **63/213205**), and **Hertz** at Ramón Picarte 640 (© **63/218316**); both have airport kiosks.

Currency Exchange   *Casas de cambio* can be found at **La Reconquista** at Carampangue 325 (© **63/213305**), and **Turismo Cochrane,** Arauco 435 (© **63/212214**), but banks **Banco Santander** at Pérez Rosales 585 and **Banco Corpbanca** at Ramón Picarte 370 have ATM machines in addition to money exchange. **Red Bank** ATMs are scattered throughout the city.

Hospital   The hospital can be found at Simpson 850 (© **63/214066**).

Laundry   Self-service laundromats are **Lavamatic** at Walter Schmidt 305, #6 (© **63/211015**), or **Lavazul** at Chacabuco 270, #12 (© **63/211122**).

WHAT TO SEE & DO

Several tour companies offer trips to Niebla (see "Niebla, Corral & Isla Mancera," below) and other surrounding areas, including city tours. Try **Turismo Kohler,** José Martí 83 (© **63/255335**), **Agencia Cochrane,** Arauco 4351 (© **63/212213**), and **Turismo Cristopher,** calles Independencia and Arauco (© **63/225144**). All offer travel agency services and can book plane tickets.

BOAT TRIPS

An enjoyable way to explore the Valdivia region is with one of the many boat tours that depart from the pier Muelle Schuster at the waterfront, including yachts, catamarans, and an antique steamer. Tours are in full swing during the summer, and although there's limited service during the off season, it's possible for a group to hire a launch for a private trip. The most interesting journeys sail through the **Carlos Anwandter Nature Sanctuary** to the **San Luis de Alba de Cruces Fort** and to **Isla Mancera** and **Corral** to visit other 17th-century historic forts; both tours run about 5 to 6 hours round-trip and usually include meals. The Nature Sanctuary was created after the 1960 earthquake sank the banks of the Río Cruces, thereby spawning aquatic flora that, with the surrounding evergreen forest, is now home to more than 80 species of birds, including black-neck swans, red gartered coots, and buff-necked ibis.

Tour Fluvial Bahía (no phone) operates throughout the year with quick trips around Isla Teja ($4.50 per person), and tours to Isla Mancera and Corral (see "Niebla, Corral & Isla Mancera," below) can be arranged during the off season with a negotiated price or when there are enough passengers; children under 10 ride free. Other trips to Isla Mancera and Corral are offered by **Orión III** (© **63/210533**; hetours@telsur.cl), which also includes a stop at the Isla Huapi Natural Park; the price is $25 per person, including lunch and snacks, and there are discounts for children under 10. By far the most luxurious is the **Catamarán Extasis** (© **63/295674**), which offers Isla Mancera and Corral tours with lunch and snacks included, and evening dinner cruises; both cost about $28 per person. The cheapest is the *Tatiana* (no phone), which leaves at 1pm and returns at 6pm; cost is $2 per person.

An interesting journey is aboard the *Collico* (© **09/319-3284**), a completely restored 1907 German steamer, with tours to the Nature Sanctuary and historical sightseeing journeys along the Río Calle Calle and the Collico area. There's a required minimum of 10 guests (or a negotiated fee), and reservations must be made at least 48 hours in advance ($20 per person, includes lunch). **Isla del Río** (© **63/225244**) also offers full-day tours of the Nature Sanctuary from 1:30 to 7:30pm for $30 per person, including lunch.

OTHER ATTRACTIONS

The bustling **Mercado Fluvial** at Muelle Schuster (Av. Prat at Maipú) is the principal attraction in Valdivia, and is worth a visit for the dozens of fishermen who hawk fresh conger eel, hake, and spindly king crabs in front of colorful fruit and vegetable stands. Take a peek behind the fish stands to view the lanky pelicans and enormous sea lions barking for handouts. Across the street, the **Mercado Municipal** holds few attractions apart from a couple of souvenir shops and decent, inexpensive restaurants. Hours for the various shops here are erratic, but generally Monday through Sunday from 9am to 6pm, with some restaurants open later.

A block up from the waterfront, turn right on Yungay and head south until the street changes into **General Lagos** at San Carlos. A pleasant stroll for several blocks along General Lagos offers picturesque evidence of German immigration to the area through the stately, historic homes that dot the street. The houses, built between 1840 and 1930, belonged to affluent families and many have been restored and maintained, despite the various earthquakes and other natural disasters that have beset them since construction.

An interesting stop along the way is the **Centro Cultural El Austral,** General Lagos 733 (no phone), commonly known as the Casa Hoffman for the Thater-Hoffman family, who occupied the home from 1870 until 1980. It's open Tuesday through Sunday from 10am to 1pm and 4 to 7pm; admission is free. The first floor of this handsome building has been furnished to re-create the interior as it would have looked during the 19th century, complete with period antiques, paintings, and a few very garish chandeliers. Upstairs, the center holds temporary art exhibitions and painting classes. At the junction of General Lagos and Yerbas Buenas, you'll find the **Torreón Los Canelos,** a 1781 defensive tower built to protect the southern end of the city.

ISLA TEJA

Isla Teja is a tranquil residential area that is also home to the Universidad Austral de Chile and a splendid history museum, the **Museo Histórico y Antropológico Mauricio van de Maele** (© 63/212872). It's open Monday through Sunday from 10am to 1pm and 2 to 8pm from December 15 to March 15, and Tuesday through Sunday from 10am to 1pm and 2 to 6pm the rest of the year; admission is $2 adults, 50¢ children 12 and under. To get there, cross the Pedro de Valdivia bridge, walk up a block, turn left, and continue for half a block. The museum is housed in the grand family home of Karl Anwandter, brewery owner and vociferous supporter and leader of German immigrants. Outside, two 19th-century carriages flank the entrance. Inside on the first floor is a varied collection of antiques culled from local well-to-do families and notable figures such as Lord Cochrane, including furniture (even a double piano), photos, letters, medals, and everyday objects. There are also a few conquest-era artifacts, such as a Spanish helmet, as well as an excellent display of Mapuche Indian silverwork, textiles, and tools. An interesting collection of sepia-toned photos depicts settlers' images of Mapuches.

Leaving the museum, turn right and continue north on Los Laureles until you reach the **Universidad Austral de Chile.** Once inside the campus, the road veers right; follow it and the signs to the **Jardín Botánico,** a lovely botanical garden created in 1957 that features a labeled collection of native trees and vegetation from every region in Chile and around the world. It's open from December to March daily from 8am to 8pm; from April to November daily from 8am to 7pm. Cut west through the campus to Calle Los Lingues and turn right until you reach the gated entrance to **Parque Saval,** a sizeable park with rodeo stands, a children's playground, a picnic area, and the pretty Laguna Los Lotos. Admission is 25¢, and it's open daily from 8am to 8pm.

NIEBLA, CORRAL & ISLA MANCERA

These three villages offer a chance to view Valdivia's historic defense system through its weathered 17th-century forts strategically situated near the estuary's door to the Pacific, their rusty cannons still pointed at enemies long past. **Niebla** lies 18km (11 miles) from Valdivia and is home to the **Castillo de la Pura y Limpia Concepción de Monfort de Lemus** (no phone), an interesting defensive fort founded in 1671 and renovated in 1767. It's open December through February daily from 10am to 7pm, and March through November from 10am to 5:30pm, closed Monday; admission is 70¢, free for kids under 8. The fort is carved partially out of rock and features details such as cannons and a powder room, as well as a small museum. The town itself is mostly a hodgepodge of seafood restaurants and *cabañas* popular with students for the cheap rent, but it's not unattractive, and there are a few beaches for walking.

To get there, take a private taxi for about $5, or grab a *colectivo* taxi for 30¢ at the waterfront. In the summer it is possible to take a tour boat to Niebla; in the off season, you'll need to take the road. It's a pleasant 15- to 20-minute drive from Valdivia to Niebla.

Across the bay sits **Corral** (take a taxi to get here from Niebla) and the area's first and most powerful fort, the **Castillo San Sebastian de la Cruz,** built in 1645 and reinforced in 1764. From December 15 until the end of February, mock soldiers in 1777 uniforms perform a reenactment that includes firing cannons and muskets twice daily, at 3 and 5pm. The city itself is a picturesque jumble of brightly painted wooden homes and fishing boats, an old German colony that never really recovered from the tidal wave that wiped out a significant chunk of the town after the 1960 earthquake. Before-and-after pictures can be seen inside the tiny **Museo de Corral** (no phone) at the dock, which is open from December 15 to March 15 daily from 9am to 1pm and 2 to 6:30pm, and the rest of the year daily except Wednesday from 2 to 6pm. To get to Corral, take a tour boat from Valdivia during high season, or take a ferry from the fishing dock just before entering Niebla.

Either on the way to Corral or on the way back, ask to be dropped off at idyllic **Isla Mancera** (and ask to be picked up!) for a pleasant stroll and a visit to the fort **Castillo de San Pedro de Alcántara** (no phone). Admission is 70¢, and it's open from November 15 to March 15 daily from 10am to 1pm and 4 to 8pm, and Tuesday through Sunday from 10am to 1pm and 2 to 6pm the rest of the year. It was built in 1645 and restored in 1680 and again in 1762 to house the Military Government of Valdivia. Inside the grounds are the crumbling ruins of the San Francisco Convent and an underground supply room. It is possible to walk the circumference of the island in 20 to 30 minutes, and there is a site for picnics with great views.

WHERE TO STAY
EXPENSIVE

Hotel Naguilán ★ *Moments*   Although it sits about a 20-minute walk from the edge of downtown, the Hotel Naguilán, now part of Best Western, boasts a pretty riverfront location and solid, attractive accommodations. The hotel is housed in an interesting structure (ca. 1890) that once held a shipbuilding business. All rooms face the Río Valdivia and the evening sunset; from here it's possible to watch waterfowl and colorful tugs and fishing skiffs motor by. The rooms are divided into 15 newer units in a detached building and 17 in an older wing. The newer "Terrace" units sit directly on the riverbank and feature contemporary floral design in rich colors, classic furniture, ample bathrooms, and a terrace patio. The older wing is more economical and features a few dated items, such as 1960s lime-green carpet, but the entire hotel, is impeccably clean.

The staff offers professional and attentive service, and the hotel has a private dock from which guests board excursion boats. More than anything, though, the handsome design and great view make this hotel a winner. The Naguilán's restaurant, serving international cuisine, is one of the most attractive features of the property, with the river passing just outside the window.

General Lagos 1927, Valdivia. © **63/212851.** Fax 63/219130. www.valdivianet.com/naguilan. 32 units. $78 standard double (older units); $89 double (newer units); from $120 suite. AE, DC, MC, V. **Amenities:** Restaurant; bar; outdoor pool; game room; concierge; room service; laundry service. *In room:* TV, minibar.

Hotel Pedro de Valdivia ★ *Moments*   The Pedro de Valdivia is located in the heart of the city in front of a plaza, and it is popular for its proximity to the waterfront, Isla Teja, and shops and restaurants. The oldest hotel in Valdivia, it has just embarked on an ambitious renovation project that will refresh the entire property. All double rooms with queen-size beds have terraces and face north toward the river, and are better than doubles with two twins that face the busier plaza. The bright suites are not significantly bigger than the doubles; all rooms have spacious bathrooms. There are also four two-bedroom guest rooms with one bathroom. Perhaps the nicest part of the hotel is its airy, well-lit lobby with a giant mural painted by two well-known artist brothers depicting the arrival of Pedro de Valdivia to this area, as well as its cozy bar and the lovely outdoor patio and pool. The Don Pedro restaurant is renowned in the city for serving consistently good Chilean and international specialties. In the winter, the restaurant is upstairs near a giant fireplace; in the summer it can be found downstairs.

Carampangue 190, Valdivia. ℂ 63/212931. Fax 63/203888. www.valdivianet.com/pedrodevaldivia. 77 units. $114 double; from $135 suite. AE, DC, MC, V. **Amenities:** Restaurant; bar; large outdoor pool; room service; business center with Internet access; laundry service. *In room:* TV.

Puerta del Sur *Overrated* *Kids* This quiet resort just across the bridge on Isla Teja offers all the amenities a guest would expect from a five-star hotel but its drab decor and mediocre service don't quite live up to expectations. However, it does boast a gem of a location on the shore of the Nature Sanctuary. It's about a 7-minute walk to downtown, but you'll feel miles away. All rooms come with views of the river and are fairly comfortable; double superiors are roomy, as are the sparkling bathrooms. This is one of the few hotels in Chile to offer doubles with either a queen or two full-size beds instead of singles. The suites come with giant, triangular picture windows, but are not much larger than a double superior.

Outside, a path winds past the pool and whirlpool to a private dock where guests can be picked up for boat tours or launch one of the hotel's canoes. There are also bikes available for guests at no extra charge. The airy lobby is set off by a second-story U-shaped balcony and brocade couches next to two fireplaces. The hotel has a semiformal restaurant serving international cuisine. When making reservations, request promotional rates and ask about the discounted stays of 3 to 7 days that include some meals. Most room rates do not include breakfast.

Los Lingues 950, Isla Teja, Valdivia. ℂ **63/224500,** or for reservations (in Santiago) 2/633-5101. Fax 63/211046. www.hotelpuertadelsur.com. 40 units. $90–$114 double; from $162 suite. AE, DC, MC, V. **Amenities:** Restaurant; bar; large outdoor pool; tennis court; Jacuzzi; sauna; game room; room service; babysitting; laundry service. *In room:* TV.

MODERATE

Cabañas Di Torlaschi *Value* *Kids* These fully equipped *cabañas* feature charming exteriors, pleasant, well-lit kitchens, and a decent location on a residential street near downtown; they're also quiet due to the grammar schools at the front and side that empty at the end of the day. The friendly owners and staff strive to make guests feel at home, and offer a wealth of tourism information. The 16 wood *cabañas* are situated around a courtyard walkway planted with climbing ivy. Guests park just outside their door, and there is a security gate that shuts during the evening. Each *cabaña* is identical, with two bedrooms upstairs (1 comes with a double bed and the other, 2 twins) and a sofa that unfolds into a bed downstairs, with a maximum of six guests allowed. Kitchens come with full-size fridge and microwave. These *cabañas* are popular with European visitors.

Yerbas Buenas 283, Valdivia. ℂ **63/224103.** Fax 63/224003. www.aparthotelitaliano.cl. 16 *cabañas.* $43–$50 double. No credit cards. **Amenities:** Tour desk; laundry service. *In room:* TV, kitchen.

INEXPENSIVE

Airesbuenos International Hostel ⭐ *Value*   This beautiful house is a historical monument in Valdivia and dates back to 1890. The young and friendly owner, Lionel Brossi, has meticulously restored the entire house and oversees the day-to-day operation of the hostel. There's a special touch everywhere, which is rare when it comes to budget accommodations. A vintage staircase leads to eleven rooms of varying sizes, all with beautiful (and original) hardwood floors. Some of the rooms have bunk beds and are the top choice for traveling European and American backpackers; the bathroom in the hallway is clean and spacious. The five rooms with private bathrooms are pleasant and bright; the front room even has a balcony with river views. All beds come with cute blue and gold cotton sheets. There's Internet access for guests in the foyer, and the owner will arrange free transportation from the bus station if you give him advance notice. The hotel is located about a 15-minute walk from the market and most restaurants.

General Lagos 1036, Valdivia. ©/fax **63/206304**. www.airesbuenos.cl. 11 units. $8.50 per person in a shared room; $40 double with private bathroom. Rates include breakfast. No credit cards. **Amenities:** Lounge; Internet access.

WHERE TO DINE

For an inexpensive meal, try the **Municipal Market** near the waterfront at Yungay and Libertad, where you'll find several basic restaurants with fresh seafood and Chilean specialties.

Café Haussman CAFE *Moments*   The Haussman is known for its *crudos* (steak tartare and raw onion spread on thin bread), which it has served since opening its doors in 1959. The tiny, old-fashioned cafe has just four booths and a counter, and is frequently packed with downtown workers. There are no frills, but good sandwiches, local color, and Kunstmann beer on tap.

O'Higgins 394. © **63/202219**. Sandwiches $1.50–$4. No credit cards. Mon–Sat 8am–9pm.

Camino de Luna SEAFOOD   The Camino de Luna serves excellent seafood and other dishes aboard a floating restaurant moored at the waterfront. The menu includes delicious fare such as seafood crepes, abalone stew, and *congrio* steamed in wine, bacon, asparagus, and herbs, as well as Greek and chef salads and a long list of terrific appetizers. Inside, the well-appointed, candlelit tables are much nicer than the pea-green facade and red Coca-Cola neon outside would indicate. The restaurant does sway when vessels speed by, but not much.

Costanera at Arturo Prat. © **63/213788**. Main courses $6–$10. AE, DC, MC, V. Daily 12:30–11:30pm; bar open until 2am.

Entre Lagos CAFE *Value*   Entre Lagos is one of the best-known shops in the region for its mouth-watering chocolates and colorful marzipan, and its neighboring cafe is equally good. Nothing on the menu is short of delicious, from the juicy sandwiches and french fries down to the heavenly cakes and frothy cappuccinos. The restaurant serves a dozen varieties of crepes, such as ham and cheese, and abalone and shrimp in a creamy crab sauce. Entre Lagos is a great spot for lunch or to relax for an afternoon *once* or coffee. It also offers a set menu for $6 that includes a main dish, soup, and coffee.

Pérez Rosales 622. © **63/212047**. Main courses $4–$8. AE, DC, MC, V. Daily 9am–8pm.

Kunstmann Cervecería GERMAN PUB   This is a nice place to stop on the way back from Niebla (see "Niebla, Corral & Isla Mancera," above); it's a 10-minute drive from town. The popular Kunstmann brewery serves four varieties of beer on tap (they'll let you sample before ordering), in a newer, microbrew-styled restaurant with wooden tables and soft, yellow light. The hearty fare includes appetizer platters of grilled meats and sausages, German-influenced dishes such as smoked pork loin with cabbage, and sandwiches, salads, and spaetzle. Kunstmann also has an on-site brewery museum.

950 Ruta T-350. ✆/fax **63/292969**. Main courses $5–$10. DC, MC, V. Mon–Sat noon–midnight; Sun noon–7:30pm.

La Calesa ★ *(Finds* PERUVIAN   Owned and operated by a Peruvian family, the cozy La Calesa features spicy cuisine served in the old Casa Kaheni, a gorgeous, 19th-century home with high ceilings, wood floors, and antique furnishings. The menu features Peruvian fare along with several international dishes. Standouts include grilled beef tenderloin and sea bass in a cilantro sauce; *ají de gallina,* a spicy chicken and garlic stew with rice; or any of the nightly specials. The *pisco* sours are very good, as is the wine selection. There's a great wooden bar lit by giant windows looking out onto a garden and the river.

Yungay 735. ✆ **63/225467**. Dinner reservations recommended. Main courses $9–$12. Daily 1–3:30pm and 8–12pm.

Los Castellanos ★ *(Moments* SEAFOOD   If you're hankering for seafood while enjoying an ocean view, then drive or take a taxi to Niebla (a 20-min. trip). Los Castellanos sits on a hill overlooking the bay and is elegantly decorated with handsome wood floors and large picture windows overlooking the water. Always be sure to ask what fish arrived that morning and order accordingly. Usually, there's an excellent salmon carpaccio and a sampler seafood plate that may include scallops, mussels, shrimp, and other delicacies. For the main course, you can't go wrong with any of the fresh grilled fish such as congrio eel, salmon, or tuna. There are over 110 wines to choose from, and the bartender whips up a mean pisco sour here. The waiters are rather slow and they speak no English so be patient; the views and the food are worth the effort.

Antonio Ducce 875 in Niebla. ✆ **63/282082**. Reservations recommended in high season. Main courses $7–$10. MC, V. Daily noon–4pm and 7–11pm.

New Orleans INTERNATIONAL   This is Valdivia's most popular restaurant, tucked away on a side street a few streets in from the river, and it seems to always be busy. There's a pleasant outdoor patio with tables very close together and a charming dining room with more spacious seating. The food here is consistently good and fresh and the menu changes often. Main courses often include pastas, grilled salmon or tuna, chicken, and steak. This is a loud, boisterous place, often filled with families with children early in the evening. Later, the atmosphere is more pub-like.

Esmeralda 682. ✆ **63/218771**. Dinner reservations recommended. Main courses $9–$10. AE, DC, MC, V. Mon–Fri noon–4pm and 7pm–midnight; Sat–Sun 5pm–midnight.

5 Puyehue ★

Termas de Puyehue is 73km (45 miles) E of Osorno; 95km (59 miles) W of Antillanca; 93km (58 miles) W of the Argentine border

This region is chiefly known for the **Termas de Puyehue** hot springs and the **Antillanca** ski and summer resort at the base of the Casablanca Volcano in Puyehue National Park. The region, including its namesake lake and national park, is remarkably beautiful, with thick groves of junglelike forest, emerald lakes, picture-perfect volcano backdrops, waterfalls, and roads narrowed by over-grown, enormous ferns. You won't find a tourist-oriented town here, such as Pucón or Puerto Varas, but there are several good lodging options in the area. You'll also find a fair amount of outdoor activities, scenic drives, and one of the best lookout points in Chile, which can reached by car during the summer.

Puyehue is a worthwhile diversion from Osorno or Puerto Montt, and a great stopover point on the road to or from Argentina. Some travelers opt to loop through the Lake Districts of Argentina and Chile by booking a one-way ticket to Bariloche via the popular "lake crossing" (see "Parque Nacional Vicente Pérez Rosales & the Lake Crossing to Argentina," later in this chapter) and later taking a bus to Puyehue, passing first through Villa Angostura at the Argentina-Chile border and crossing at the international pass Cardenal Antonio Samore.

The road from Osorno to Puyehue is rather flat and banal, but the scenery viewed when crossing from Villa Angostura to Puyehue is stunning. Note that during the winter, chains might be required when crossing the border. The city of Osorno holds few attractions, and is used as a transportation hub only.

GETTING THERE

BY PLANE   LanChile serves **Osorno airport,** ZOS (no phone), with two daily flights from Santiago; both flights stop in Temuco. Osorno is a 1-hour drive from Puyehue. LanChile has much more frequent flights from Santiago to Puerto Montt (PMC), which is about a 2-hour drive from Puyehue.

BY BUS   Bus service from Osorno is provided by **Bus Norte,** with daily serv-ice to and from Puyehue: From Bariloche, Argentina, **Andes Mar** and **Río de la Plata** buses head to Osorno and stop along the highway near Puyehue or directly at the Hotel Termas de Puyehue. If you're trying to get to Puyehue from Puerto Montt, you'll need to transfer at Osorno.

BY CAR   Termas de Puyehue is about 75km (47 miles) east from Osorno via Route 215. The border with Argentina, Control Fronterizo Cardenal Antonio Samore, is open daily November through March from 8am to 9pm, and April through October from 8am to 7pm. The road is a bit curvy and there are some potholes on the Chilean side, so plan on driving slowly.

EXPLORING PUYEHUE NATIONAL PARK

Puyehue National Park is one of Chile's best-organized national parks, offering a variety of trails to suit all levels, well-placed park information centers, lodging, camping, restaurants, and hot springs. The 107,000-hectare (264,290-acre) park sits between the Caulle mountain range and the Puyehue Volcano, and is divided into three sectors: **Anticura, Aguas Calientes,** and **Antillanca.** Visitors head east toward Argentina to access Anticura, where they'll encounter a park ranger information station just before the border, as well as trail heads for day hikes and the 16km (10-mile) backpacker's trail up and around the Puyehue Volcano. There's a self-guided, short hike to the Salto del Indio waterfall where you'll see 800-year-old evergreen beech trees, known locally as *coigue.*

To get to Antillanca, visitors pass first through the Agua Calientes sector, where there are hot springs, cabins, and campgrounds, as well as a park infor-mation center. The most popular excursion in this region is the absolutely spec-tacular ascent to a lookout point atop the Raihuén crater, reached by foot or vehicle about 4km (2½ miles) past the Antillanca hotel and ski resort. This *mirador* can be reached only during temperate months, and is not worthwhile on a heavily overcast day. The park ranger information stations are open daily from 9am to noon and 2:30 to 6pm, or contact Conaf (© **64/374572**). They sell an information packet about the region's flora and fauna and issue fishing licenses. For information about day visits to the hot springs at Termas de Puyehue or Aguas Calientes, see "Where to Stay & Dine," below. To get here, you need to catch a bus in Osorno, or book a tour with an operator out of Temuco or Pucón.

OTHER ATTRACTIONS

Along the road to Puyehue, at about Km 25 on Ruta 215, just before the ramshackle town of Entre Lagos, is Chile's first car museum, the well-designed **Auto Museum Moncopulli** (© **64/204200**; www.moncopulli.cl). Admission is $2 adults, $1.50 students, and 70¢ kids; it's open from April to October, Tuesday through Sunday from 10am to 6:30pm, and from November to March, Tuesday through Sunday from 10am to 8pm. Owner Bernardo Eggers has assembled a collection of 40 Studebakers from the years 1930 to 1961, plus other vehicles, such as a 1929 Model A fire engine.

WHERE TO STAY & DINE

Aguas Calientes Turismo y Cabañas   These A-frame cabins are a cheaper alternative to Termas de Puyehue, and are owned by the same company. There's a hot spring/spa facility here included in the price of the *cabañas,* and it can be used for the day for a fee. The *cabañas* sleep four to eight guests, and are simple affairs with fully stocked, plain, but decent kitchenettes. The drawback here is that the beds are really crammed into small spaces. A cabin for five, for example, has one bedroom with a double bed, and three twins in the living room that leave little room for the dining table. Ask for a cabin with two floors; those come with separate living/eating areas. All cabins come with decks and a barbecue. There are also two nicely developed campgrounds called Chanleufu and Los Derrumbes, with barbecue pits, free firewood, and hot showers ($10–$14 for 1–4 campers, $18–$26 for 5–8 campers).

The hot springs facility features indoor and outdoor pools (the outdoor pool is far nicer); there are also a sauna and picnic area. Day-use fees are $6 adults, $2.50 kids for the indoor pool; $1.50 adults, 70¢ kids for the outdoor pool. A private herbal bath costs $11. There is also massage for $21 an hour.

Camino a Antillanca, Km 4. ©/fax **64/236988**. www.puyehue.cl. 23 *cabañas.* $45–$90 cabin, 2 guests; $60–$95 cabin, 4 guests. AE, DC, MC, V. **Amenities:** Large outdoor pool; indoor pool; Jacuzzi; massage. *In room:* TV, kitchen.

Antillanca Hotel and Tourism Center   Antillanca is really nothing to write home about, but the lovely surroundings and the ski/summer resort is really one of Chile's gems—if you can hit it on a good weather day. The resort is open year-round, offering trekking, fishing, mountain biking, canoeing, and ascents of Volcán Antillanca in addition to skiing. The ski resort is a local favorite, tiny but steep, with three T-bar lifts and one chair lift. Heavy, powdery snowfall makes for great skiing, but often a storm or *huelche* (a freezing western wind) blows in, essentially ruining the day; also note that car chains are often required during the winter, but they can be rented from a guard's post before driving up the winding road. A lookout point boasts one of the most magnificent views in Chile.

The hotel could really stand to renovate its rooms, especially considering the price. Couples would do well to view the options, as the only room that comes with a double bed also comes with two twins and is considered a quadruple. The rooms are fairly spacious, but many are nothing more than dormitory style, with four bunks to a room and early '80s furniture to boot.

If you're looking for something cheaper, you might consider the *refugio*, the slightly shabby, older wing of the hotel popular with students and young adults for its rooms costing about a third less. The split-level lobby/restaurant/bar/lounge area is a delight, however, cozy and with character derived from pillars made of tree trunks that still have branches and a giant fireplace. There's also a deck for sunbathing and complimentary use of mountain bikes for registered guests.

Ski Resort: Lift tickets Monday through Friday cost $26 adults, $14 students; Saturday and Sunday and holidays cost $28 adults, $22 students. Ski and snowboard equipment rental is available and sold in packages that include a lift ticket for $38 adults and $26 students. If you're not skiing but want to ride a chair lift to the top, the cost is $6.

Road to Antillanca, at about 10km past Ñilque, or (in Osorno) O'Higgins 1073. ⓒ/fax **64/235114.** antillanca@ telsur.cl. 73 units. $80–$110 double superior; $55–$70 double standard. MC, V. **Amenities:** Restaurant; bar; lounge; exercise room; sauna; game room; room service; laundry service.

Termas de Puyehue *Overrated*   The first thing you'll notice about this classic, grand hotel is its size; the entrance's stone facade alone nearly dwarfs guests as they enter. Termas de Puyehue is more aptly called a lodge, for its lofty ceilings, giant stone fireplaces, wood walls and floors, and country setting. The compound features a view of Lake Puyehue and two attractively designed, enormous thermal pools, as well as massage rooms, mud baths, herbal baths, saunas, game rooms, and more. Termas de Puyehue was built between 1939 and 1942, and has undergone recent, substantial renovations as well as the addition of 52 brand-new, elegant and roomy suites. Standard double rooms have all been nicely appointed with thick cotton bedding and drapes in soft colors, but are not extraordinary, which is surprising for such an esteemed hotel. Rooms are fairly small but with very comfortable beds. Standard rooms on the first floor are cheaper because they are supposedly of lower quality, but the difference is negligible.

The rooms and public areas are now more attractive than ever, but the staff has no concept of customer service and the complaints of bad service, problems with plumbing, and problems with the staff continue to drive people away. But the activities and excursions offered, including horseback riding, trekking, mountain biking, windsurfing, fishing, tennis, and farm tours through organic gardens (all for an extra cost), might make a stay worthwhile. The spa facilities (which you can use even if you don't stay here) are more upscale than those at Aguas Calientes, including an attractive, "tropical" indoor pool under a glass roof. The costs charged to day visitors are indoor pool, $10 adults, $7 kids; outdoor pool, $6.50 adults, $3 kids. Hours are Monday through Thursday from 9am to 8pm, and Friday through Sunday and holidays from 9am to 9pm. Herbal, mud, sulfur, and marine salt baths run $9 to $12. Guests take their meals either at the cafeteria, the casual eatery, or the semi-formal restaurant. There's also a cozy bar and a lounge with a giant stone fireplace.

Ruta 215, Km 76. ⓒ **2/293-6000.** Fax 2/283-1010. www.puyehue.cl. 132 units. $90–$165 double. AE, DC, MC, V. **Amenities:** 3 restaurants; bar; lounge; large outdoor pool; large indoor pool; spa; Jacuzzi; sauna; limited watersports equipment rental; bike rental; game room; shopping arcade; room service; massage; dry cleaning service; laundry service. *In room:* TV, minibar.

6 Lago Llanquihue, Frutillar & Puerto Varas ★ ★

Lago Llanquihue is the second largest lake in Chile, a body of clear, shimmering water whose beauty is superseded only by the 2,015m (6,609-ft.), perfectly conical, snowcapped Volcán Osorno that rises from its shore. The peaks of Calbuco, Tronador, and Puntiagudo add rugged beauty to the panorama, as do the rolling, lush hills that peek out from forested thickets along the perimeter of the lake. But the jewel of this area is without a doubt the 253,780-hectare (626,837-acre) Vicente Pérez Rosales National Park, the oldest park in Chile and home to Volcán Osorno and the strangely hued emerald waters of Lago Todos los Santos.

> **A Health Warning**
>
> Every January, this region is beset by horrid biting flies called *tábanos.* Avoid wearing dark clothing and any shiny object, which seem to attract them; they are also usually more prevalent on sunny days.

This splendid countryside and the picturesque, German-influenced architecture of the homes and villages that ring Lago Llanquihue draw thousands of foreign visitors each year. Many adventure-seekers come to take part in the vast array of outdoor sports and excursions to be had here, including fly-fishing, rafting, volcano ascents, trekking, or just sightseeing. Puerto Varas is similar to Pucón in that it offers a solid tourism infrastructure, with quality lodging and restaurants, nightlife, and several reliable outfitters and tour operators. Consider lodging in Frutillar, Puerto Varas, or Ensenada instead of Puerto Montt, as these three towns are nicer and closer to natural attractions than Puerto Montt.

FRUTILLAR & PUERTO OCTAY ★
58km (36 miles) S of Osorno, 46km (29 miles) N of Puerto Montt

Frutillar and Puerto Octay offer a rich example of the lovely architecture popular with German immigrants to the Lago Llanquihue area, and both boast dynamite views of the Osorno and Calbuco volcanoes. The towns are smaller than Puerto Varas, but just as charming. They make a great day trip, and the coastal dirt road that connects the two is especially beautiful, with clapboard homes dotting an idyllic countryside—bring your camera. Apart from all this scenic beauty, there are a few museums documenting German immigration in the area.

Frutillar was founded in 1856 as an embarkation point with four piers. Later, the introduction of the railway created a spin-off town that sits high and back from the coast, effectively splitting the town in two: Frutillar "Alto" and "Bajo," meaning high and low, respectively. You won't find much worth seeing in the Alto section, a semi-ratty collection of wood homes and shops.

Puerto Octay was founded in the second half of the 19th century by German immigrants; folks in the region know it for a well-stocked general goods store— the only one in the region—run by Cristino Ochs. In fact, the name *Octay* comes from "donde Ochs hay," roughly translated as "you'll find it where Ochs is." Today there are about 2,000 residents in this sleepy town, which can be reached by renting a car or with a tour.

ESSENTIALS
VISITOR INFORMATION   The **Oficina de Información Turística** is located along the coast at Constanera Philippi (℃ **65/421080**); it's open

January through March daily from 8:30am to 1pm and 2 to 9pm; April through December Monday through Friday from 8:30am to 1pm and 2 to 5:45pm.

GETTING THERE   See the information under the "Puerto Varas" section, below.

WHAT TO SEE & DO

Excursions to **Parque Nacional Vicente Pérez Rosales** from Frutillar can be arranged by your hotel with a company such as AlSur or Aguamotion out of Puerto Varas (see "Outdoor Activities" under "Puerto Varas," below). In Frutillar, spend an afternoon strolling the streets and enjoying the town's striking architecture. The town really gets hopping during the last week of January when it hosts, for 9 days, the **Semanas Musicales,** when hundreds of Chilean and foreign musicians come to participate in various classical music concerts. Call the visitor center at (© **65/421080;** tickets are never hard to come by.

The two most-visited attractions in town are **the Museo de la Colonización Alemana de Frutillar** and the **Reserva Forestal Edmundo Winkler.** The museum (© **65/421142**) is located where Arturo Prat dead-ends at Avenida Vicente Pérez Rosales. Admission is $2 adults, 70¢ kids 12 and under; it's open from April to November, daily from 10am to 1:30pm and 3 to 6pm, and from December to March, daily from 9:30am to 1:30pm and 3 to 7pm. It features a collection of 19th-century antiques, clothing, and artifacts gathered from various immigrant German families around the area.

The Reserva is run by the University of Chile, and features a trail winding through native forest, giving visitors an idea of what the region looked like before immigrants went timber crazy and started chopping down trees. It's open year-round, daily from 10am to 7pm; admission costs 70¢ for adults and 25¢ for kids. To get there, you'll have to walk a kilometer up to the park from the entrance at Calle Caupolicán at the northern end of Avenida Philippi. You might also consider paying a visit to the town **cemetery,** which affords a panoramic view of the lake. To get there, continue farther north up Avenida Phillipi.

WHERE TO STAY

If you're on a tight budget, stay at **La Suizandina Guesthouse,** Camino Internacional Km 28 (© **09/884-9541;** www.suizandina.com), which has *cabañas* that sleep two to four people for $10 per person in dormitory-style lodging, or $40 for a double room with private bathroom, in a charming hostel.

Hotel & Cabañas Centinela *★★ (Moments*   At the tip of a peninsula, at the end of a lush tree-lined dirt road, 10 minutes from town and right on the lake, you'll find this hidden gem with its own private beach. Originally built in 1913 as a bordello, it has long since been turned into a homey lodge with 12 rooms and 18 *cabañas.* Rooms in the main building are quaint, with thick beige Berber carpets, down comforters, and antique furnishings. The new bathrooms are of varying sizes, simple and very clean. The downstairs living room has a beautiful fireplace; there's a satellite TV and free Internet access as well. The restaurant serves excellent Chilean cuisine; there's a daily fixed price three-course meal for $12 for lunch and dinner. This place exudes charm, not luxury; there's no spa but there's a rustic wood-fired hot tub. Six of the *cabañas* sit right on the water's edge; request numbers 21 to 26 when making your reservations and you'll have the best views. The 12 A-frame *cabañas* that sit back from the water are pleasant for families and come with kitchenettes; all the *cabañas* have rather small bathrooms. The hotel's friendly staff can arrange for fishing trips, including fly-fishing expeditions; they can also arrange for transfers from the airport.

Península de Centinela, Puerto Octay. ©/fax **64/391326.** www.hotelcentinela.cl. 30 units. $63–$86 double; from $84 cabana for 2 people. Rates include full breakfast. AE, DC, MC, V. **Amenities:** Restaurant; lounge; Jacuzzi; limited watersports equipment rental. *In room:* Fridge (in *cabañas* only).

Hotel Ayacara ★ *Finds* The Ayacara is a top choice in Frutillar, housed in a superbly renovated, 1910 antique home on the coast of Lago Llanquihue. The interior of the hotel is made of light wood and this, coupled with large, plentiful windows, translates into bright accommodations. The rooms come with comfy beds, crisp linens, wood headboards, country furnishings, and antiques brought from Santiago and Chiloé. The Capitán room is the largest and has the best view. An attractive dining area serves dinner during the summer, and there's a small, ground-level outdoor deck and a TV/video lounge. The staff can arrange excursions around the area; fly-fishing excursions are their specialty.

Av. Philippi 1215, Frutillar. ©/fax **65/421550.** www.hotelayacara.com. 8 units. $42–$60 double; $85–$110 Capitán double. Rates include full breakfast. AE, DC, MC, V. **Amenities:** Restaurant (summer only); bar; tour desk.

Hotel Elun ★ This four-star, azure-colored hotel is a good bet for anyone seeking modern accommodations, a room with a view, and a quiet, forested location. The hotel, opened in 1999, is made almost entirely of light, polished wood, and was designed to take full advantage of the views. The lounge, bar, and lobby sit under a slanted roof that ends with picture windows; there's also a deck should you decide to lounge outside. Double standard rooms are decent size and feature Berber carpet and spic-and-span white bathrooms. The superiors are very large and come with a comfy easy chair and a table and chairs. Room no. 24 looks out over Frutillar. The hotel is attended by its owners, who will arrange excursions. A restaurant serves dinner during the summer, and breakfast can be ordered in your room.

200m (218 yd.) from start of Camino Punta Larga, at the southern end of Costanera Phillipi, Frutillar. © **65/420055.** www.hotelelun.cl. 14 units. $54–$80 double. Rates include continental breakfast. DC, MC, V. **Amenities:** Restaurant (summer only); lounge; mountain bike rental; tour desk; room service; laundry service. *In room:* TV.

Hotel Klein Salzburg The Hotel Klein Salzburg is housed in a large wooden home built in 1911 and painted blue and white. It sits on the lakefront, but only one room has a view—the "VIP" room, which is larger than the rest and has a small balcony. The hotel has a lot of antique charm, complete with creaky wooden floors, but the decoration is as sugary sweet as the delicious cakes and tortes it serves in its tearoom: flowered wallpaper, duck motifs, and pink trim, all a tad cutesy, but not too overbearing. One unit has a separate kids' room with two twins in a claustrophobic attic alcove, but kids like it.

Av. Philippi 663, Frutillar. © **65/421201.** Fax 65/421750. 8 units. Rates include continental breakfast. $30–$53 double. AE, DC, MC, V. **Amenities:** Restaurant. *In room:* TV.

Hotel Residenz Am See This pleasant wooden hotel is a steal in the low season when you factor in the lakefront view and its clean, comfortable accommodations. Run by an elderly German couple, the Residenz has rooms that range in size, and a few of the doubles are large enough to fit an extra twin. The rooms that look out onto the lake are slightly more expensive than those facing the back, but the rooms in the back receive glorious afternoon sun. The owners have a shop selling arts and crafts and have decorated the place with woven wall hangings that are for sale. Downstairs there's a tea salon where guests are served German breakfast; in the afternoon, folks drop by for tea.

Av. Philippi 539, Frutillar. ℂ 65/421539. Fax 65/421858. 6 units. $36–$57 double; from $71 suite. Rates include German breakfast. AE, DC, MC, V. **Amenities:** Restaurant. *In room:* TV.

Hotel Villa San Francisco *(Moments* The Villa San Francisco sits high on a cliff and features a layout similar to the Elun Lihue (see above), with rooms that all face the lake, some with a view of the volcano. All of the rooms are identical, decorated with simple but attractive furnishings that include comfortable beds and wicker headboards. Some guests might find the rooms a little on the small side, but most come with a terrace and four have corner windows. The new owners of this hotel have invested a great deal in idyllic gardens that surround the property. There's also a great barbecue area that sits on a grassy perch looking straight out toward the volcano, as does a pleasant glass-enclosed dining area. The staff will arrange excursions around the area for guests.

Av. Philippi 1503, Frutillar. ℂ/fax **65/421531.** iberchile@telsur.cl. 15 units. $57–$64 double. AE, MC, V. **Amenities:** Restaurant; bar. *In room:* TV.

WHERE TO DINE

Club Alemán GERMAN/CHILEAN   Nearly every city in the Lake District has a Club Alemán, and Frutillar is no exception. You'll find a few German dishes here, such as pork chops with sauerkraut, but the menu leans heavily toward traditional Chilean fare. Periodically, game specials such as duck and goose are on the menu, and there are set lunch menus for $6 on weekdays and $10 on Sundays that include a choice of fish or meat. The atmosphere is congenial, and the service is very good.

San Martín 22. ℂ **65/421249.** Main courses $4–$10. AE, DC, MC, V. Daily noon–4pm and 7:30pm–midnight.

El Ciervo CHILEAN   This newer restaurant specializes in smoked meats and game, and lives up to its name (which means "deer" in Spanish) by offering a tasty grilled venison in pepper sauce. There are other delights, such as smoked pork chops "Kassler" with mashed potatoes and sauerkraut, filet mignon in a mushroom sauce, and pork leg pressure-cooked to tenderness and served with applesauce. Mounted deer antlers don't do much to add to the cold atmosphere. It's a good spot for lunch, as it serves lighter fare such as sandwiches.

San Martín 64. ℂ **65/420185.** Main courses $5.50–$10. AE, DC, MC, V. Daily noon–3:30pm and 7–10pm.

Selva Negra INTERNATIONAL/GERMAN   Expect delicious food and creative dishes at this semi-casual restaurant housed in a hutlike replica of a German dry-goods bodega. German-influenced dishes abound, such as white sausage and sauerkraut, and smoked pork chops with red cabbage. There is also a host of other interesting options, such as half a pineapple filled with sautéed shellfish, chicken with orange sauce, pork steeped in port, and cuts of meat from a barbecue grill. Top it all off with hot bananas bathed in caramel sauce. The owners speak English, German, and French, and service is friendly.

Antonio Varas 24. ℂ **65/421164.** Main courses $5.50–$8.50. AE, DC, MC, V. Daily noon–4pm and 7:30pm–midnight.

PUERTO VARAS ★★

20km (12 miles) N of Puerto Montt; 996km (618 miles) S of Santiago

Puerto Varas is on the shore of Lago Llanquihue, and is also an adventure travel hub and gateway to the **Parque Nacional Vicente Pérez Rosales** (see "Parque

Nacional Vicente Pérez Rosales & the Lake Crossing to Argentina," below). It is a tidy little town, with lovely architecture and a bustling center. Puerto Varas extends more services to its visitors than Frutillar, including a spanking-new casino, tour operators, and more, but it's busier too, and can get crowded during the summer months (but not as much as Pucón). The city was founded by German immigrants and later became a port for goods being shipped from the Lago Llanquihue area to Puerto Montt. Today, Puerto Varas relies heavily on tourism, but it's also a residential community for Puerto Montt's workers.

ESSENTIALS

VISITOR INFORMATION   The **Oficina de Turismo Municipal** at San Francisco 441 is open from December 15 to March 15 Monday through Sunday from 8am to 9pm, and the rest of the year Monday through Friday from 8am to 4:45pm (© **65/232437**).

GETTING THERE   By Plane   El Tepaul (PMC) airport (© **65/252019**) lies an almost equal distance from Puerto Montt and Puerto Varas; it's about 25km (16 miles) from the airport to Puerto Varas. A taxi from the airport costs $14 to $24, or you can arrange a transfer with **Andina del Sud** (© **65/257797;** adsmontt@chilesat.net) for about $6 per person. LanChile serves the El Tepaul airport with five to six daily flights from Santiago. Ask your hotel about transfers.

By Bus   The following buses offer service to and from major cities in southern Chile, including Santiago: **Buses Cruz del Sur,** San Pedro 210 (© **65/233008**); **Buses Tas Choapa,** Walker Martínez 230 (© **65/233831**), and **Buses Lit,** Walker Martínez 227-B (© **65/233838**). Buses **Tas Choapa** and **Andesmar** (© **65/252926**) both offer daily service to Bariloche, Argentina.

By Car   Puerto Varas is just 20km (12 miles) north of Puerto Montt and 88km (55 miles) south of Osorno via the Panamericana. There are two exits leading to Puerto Varas, and both deposit you downtown. To get to Frutillar, you need to get back on the Panamericana, go north, and take the exit for that town.

GETTING AROUND   By Bus   Buses Cruz del Sur offers transportation to Chiloé and nearly 15 daily trips to Puerto Montt, leaving from an office in Puerto Varas, at San Pedro 210 (© **65/233008**). There are also cheap minibuses that leave frequently from the corner of San Bernardo and Walker Martínez, across from the pet shop, leaving you at the bus terminal in Puerto Montt. You'll also find minibuses at San Bernardo and Martínez that go to Ensenada, Petrohué, and Lago Todos los Santos every day at 9:15am, 11am, 2pm, and 4pm, and **Andina del Sud,** Antonio Varas 437 (© **65/257797**), has daily trips to this area as well.

By Car   Renting a car is perhaps the most enjoyable way (but also the most expensive) to see the surrounding area. Try **Llancahue Rent a Car,** San José 301 (© **65/233745**); **Turismo Nieve,** San Bernardo 406 (© **65/232299**); **Adriazola Turismo,** Santa Rosa 340 (© **65/233477**); or **Travi Viajes,** Camino Ensenada, Km 1 (© **65/233491**).

WHERE TO STAY
Expensive

Colonos del Sur ⭐   Boasting a waterfront location next door to the new casino and charming German colonial architecture, the Colonos del Sur is a standard favorite among travelers to Puerto Varas and one of the nicer hotels in town. The common areas are large and plentiful, including a tea salon and lounge, and feature a quaint yet handsome decor sprinkled with various antique furnishings. The tea salon is one of the best in Puerto Varas. The rooms are not especially noteworthy but do offer solid quality. Doubles with a lake view are slightly larger, for the same price; others face the casino. The large suites, however, stand out, with wraparound windows, sparkling bathrooms, and attractive decorations like crocheted bedspreads.

Del Salvador 24, Puerto Varas. ℭ **65/233369**, or for reservations 65/233039. Fax 65/233394. www.colonos delsur.cl. 54 units. $75–$110 double; from $132 suite. AE, DC, MC, V. **Amenities:** Restaurant; lounge; bar; small indoor pool; sauna; room service; dry cleaning service; laundry service. *In room:* TV, minibar, safe.

Hotel Cabañas del Lago ⭐ *Kids* Recent renovations and sweeping views of Puerto Varas and Volcán Osorno make Hotel Cabañas del Lago the highest quality lodging available in town. The lakeview and park suites are luxuriously appointed and colossal in size; one could get lost in the bathroom alone. A junior suite is a slightly larger double, and might be worth booking for the larger windows and better decoration. Doubles are not overly spacious, and have cramped bathrooms, but curtains and bedding have been updated. Doubles with a lake view are the same price as rooms that overlook the *cabañas*.

The hotel takes advantage of its location with lots of glass in its attractive lounge and restaurant, which, like all the rooms, sports a country decor. The common areas have the feel of a mountain lodge, complete with deer antler chandeliers. There's also a large sun deck. The small, two- to five-person *cabañas* are not as pleasant as the hotel rooms but are a bargain for a family of four, if you're willing to be a bit cramped. The excellent **El Ciervo** restaurant serves wild game and other daily specials from an extensive menu.

Klenner 195, Puerto Varas. ℭ **65/232291**. Fax 65/232707. www.cabanasdellago.cl. 65 units, 21 *cabañas*. $100–$114 double; $124–$136 junior suite; $95–$130 *cabañas* for up to 4 people. Rates include buffet breakfast. AE, DC, MC, V. **Amenities:** Restaurant; bar; lounge; indoor heated pool; sauna; game room; room service; babysitting; laundry service. *In room:* TV.

Moderate

Cabañas Altué ⭐ *Finds* Located at the quiet end of the beach in Puerto Chico, about a 10-minute drive from downtown Puerto Varas, these *cabañas* have lovely views (but not of the volcanoes) and are situated among one of the most impressive arboreal gardens in the region. Guests arrive to a circular driveway ringed with roses and fronted by a huge magnolia tree; the *cabañas* themselves are surrounded by *araucaria*, pine, *alerce*, and more. The nine cabins are perched above the beach behind a row of eucalyptus trees, with a vista of Puerto Varas and the beach. The cabins were freshly painted recently and are decent and comfortable, with a separate kitchen/dining room and a deck. Nearly every plant or tree in the surrounding garden is unique, often from other regions in Chile. This is a place for those who want direct beach access, fragrant surroundings, and an address outside town.

Av. Vicente Pérez Rosales 1679, Puerto Varas. ℭ/fax **65/232294**. www.altue-chile.cl. 9 units. $30–$84 *cabañas* for 2–3; $55–$110 *cabañas* for 4–6. No credit cards. *In room:* TV.

Hotel & Cabañas Los Alerces This hotel/*cabaña* complex is for travelers who want beach access and/or an independent *cabaña* with cooking facilities (it's about a 2-min. drive out of Puerto Varas). Los Alerces has undergone substantial renovations as a result of new ownership and the results are wonderful. Each of the rooms is decorated differently, but with a common country decor accentuated with framed antique photos and other period pieces. The rooms are arranged around a bright atrium, and all are designed so that they take advantage of the view of the lake—but the hotel's neighboring lots are not particularly eye-catching. Each identical *cabaña* comes with three bedrooms and a large living area with real couches that are not considered an extra bed. They come with a fully stocked, open kitchen, giant corner windows, leafy surroundings, and a cozy wood-burning stove. Internet access is available for guests in the lobby.

Av. Vicente Pérez Rosales 1281, Puerto Varas. © **65/235984.** Fax 65/23621. www.cabanaslosalerces.cl. 44 units, 10 *cabañas*. $65–$85 double; $42–$135 *cabaña* for 2–3. AE, DC, MC, V. **Amenities:** Restaurant; bar; small indoor heated pool; laundry service. *In room:* TV.

Hotel Bellavista *(Moments (Kids*   Another waterfront hotel with gorgeous views, the Bellavista also has four larger guest rooms that face a forested cliff for those seeking quieter accommodations, and duplex units with three to four upstairs beds that are great for families with kids. It also has one of the best suites in town, a two-story apartment with giant windows and a thoroughly contemporary, country design. A lounge and bar also face the back, and are lit by wall and ceiling windows; the separate restaurant/coffee shop looks out over the lake. It's not highly noticeable, but the walls of the rooms could use a lick of paint. Doubles are just slightly worn, with unremarkable furnishings. This hotel is considered the closest competition to the Licarayén (see below); the Bellavista is larger but the Licarayén has the slight edge with its renovations and friendlier service. The Bellavista's restaurant has a good range of international dishes.

Av. Vicente Pérez Rosales 60, Puerto Varas. © **65/232011.** Fax 65/232013. www.hotelbellavista.cl. 38 units. $70–$84 double; from $120 suite. Rates include buffet breakfast. AE, DC, MC, V. **Amenities:** Restaurant; bar; lounge; laundry service. *In room:* TV.

Hotel El Greco *(Value*   This is an excellent value in Puerto Varas, both for its low price and delightful interiors. A block's walk from downtown, the hotel is an antique, shingled home painted lemon and lilac. A comfortable living area is packed with antiques, magazines, and photo books, and there's a small dining area and a separate common area lit by skylights, with tables, a classic jukebox, and a computer with Internet access. The rooms are small, but they're as comfortable as your own bedroom. The amiable owner is a painter himself; he has a gallery here containing hundreds of paintings and drawings that was set up to give local artists a much-needed space to hang their pieces.

Mirador 134, Puerto Varas. © **65/233388.** Fax 65/233380. www.hotelelgreco.cl. 12 units. $34–$50 double. Rates include continental breakfast. AE, DC, MC, V. **Amenities:** Restaurant; laundry. *In room:* TV.

Hotel Licarayén *(Value*   This is one of Puerto Varas's best values, for its comfortable accommodations, waterfront views, and central location. The lobby and rooms are cheery and well lit, and the double standard rooms are average-size. Double superior rooms come with lake views, balconies, and whirlpool tubs. Superiors are also substantially larger than standards and come with big, bright bathrooms. Only a few standards have lake views, so ask for one; suites are ample, and come with a couch. The hotel may not have the antique character of Colonos del Sur (see above), but the rooms are just as good, if not better. There's a pleasant dining area for breakfast, again with lake views. The hotel sits on the main plaza and is close to everything. The service is cordial and professional.

San José 114, Puerto Varas. © **65/232305.** Fax 65/232955. 23 units. $70 double standard. Rate includes continental breakfast. AE, DC, MC, V. **Amenities:** Sauna; room service. *In room:* TV.

Inexpensive

Casa Azul   You can't beat Casa Azul for price, access to a fully stocked kitchen, and stylish, comfortable accommodations. This tiny home was recently converted into a hostel, and offers small rooms furnished with beds, tables, and chairs made entirely of tree trunks and branches. There's a back bedroom for three with a garden/lake view, three bedrooms for two, and the "cave," a tiny attic room with a double bed on the floor and not much headroom. The German-Chilean couple who runs Casa Azul is very friendly, and will help you arrange excursions and car rentals. Bathrooms are shared here. An enormous dog, Butch, guards the front door. The kitchen is really a bonus for those tired of eating out, and it's set up so you have your own storage area. Breakfast is not included.

Manzanal 66 (at Rosario), Puerto Varas. ℂ 65/232904. www.casaazul.net. 8 units. $26 double with private bath; $20 double with shared bath; $11 per person dorm-style room. No credit cards. **Amenities:** Lounge.

Colores del Sur   The Colores del Sur offers the same character as Casa Azul, with inexpensive lodging and a central living area with large tables and couches. It's a comfortable place where you can use the kitchen, but it is not organized as well as Casa Azul. There are a couple of bright bedrooms that face the street. This hostel is frequented by a younger backpacker and budget traveler crowd, and is often confused with the more upscale hotel Colonos del Sur. Bathrooms are shared, and breakfast is not included.

Santa Rosa 318, Puerto Varas. ℂ 65/338588. Fax 65/311311. 5 units. $9–$14 per person. No credit cards. **Amenities:** Lounge.

WHERE TO DINE

Puerto Varas has a handful of excellent restaurants, but the best restaurant in the region is in Ensenada, at the Yan Kee Way lodge (see below).

Café Mamusia *Value* CHILEAN CAFE/BAKERY   The Mamusia is locally renowned for its delicious desserts and pastries, especially the homemade empanadas, cake, and *kuchen* it sells from its bakery. The atmosphere is somewhat like a tearoom or ice-cream parlor, but there are delicious sandwiches and full meals throughout the day as well. Café Mamusia is also a great place for breakfast, and serves a continental version for $4.75. Typical Chilean favorites such as *pastel de choclo* and *escalopas* are served here, as well as lasagna, pizza, and grilled meats and fish; sandwiches come on homemade bread.

San José 316. ℂ 65/233343. Main courses $5–$8; sandwiches $5.50. MC, V. Summer daily 8:30am–2am; winter Mon–Fri 9am–10:30pm, Sat–Sun 10am–11pm.

Club Alemán GERMAN/CHILEAN   This Club Alemán seems to offer more German specialties than its fellow clubs, with goose, duck, and bratwurst served with onions, potatoes, and applesauce; pork chops with caramelized onions and sauerkraut; goulash with spaetzle; steak tartare; and other dishes, in addition to Chilean favorites. Sandwiches are much cheaper than main dishes ($2–$5) and are substantial. There are also appetizing desserts, such as crepes *diplomático*, with bananas, ice cream, and chocolate sauce.

San José 415. ℂ 65/232246. Main courses $8–$13. DC, MC, V. Daily 11am–midnight.

Color Café INTERNATIONAL   The Color Café has a stylish decor, good wine list, and diverse menu. Clean, crisp interiors offset by contemporary oil paintings, a long bar, and a blazing, wood-burning stove set the ambience. The periodically changing menu features delicious bistro-style cuisine, including Caesar salads, soups, quiches, pastas, sandwiches, and main courses such as Roquefort filet and chicken stuffed with ham and cheese in a mustard-chive sauce. It's a good place for a cocktail and an appetizer of regional smoked salmon. The Color Café is about a 5-minute drive from downtown Puerto Varas.

Los Colonos 1005. ✆ 65/234311. Main courses $6–$11. AE, DC, MC, V. Dec–Mar daily noon–1am; Apr–Nov daily 8pm–midnight.

Dane's _Value_ CHILEAN CAFE   It's often hard to get a table during the lunch hour in this extremely popular restaurant. Dane's serves inexpensive, hearty food in good-size portions, plus mouth-watering desserts. The interior is simple and unassuming, and much of the food is standard Chilean fare, all of it good or very good. The fried empanadas, especially shellfish, deserve special mention. Dane's serves a daily set menu for $5 Monday through Saturday, and $8 on Sunday, as well as a special dish, or _plato del día,_ for $3.50. It's less busy before 1pm or after 3pm. You can also buy food to go from the front counter.

Del Salvador 441. ✆ 65/232371. Main courses $3.50–$8; sandwiches $2–$5.50. MC, V. Daily 8am–11pm.

Ibis ✿ INTERNATIONAL/CHILEAN   This popular restaurant is one of the best in Puerto Varas, namely for its creative cuisine and vast menu featuring everything from meat to pasta to sushi. Menu highlights include the flambéed Ecuadorian shrimp in cognac, pistachio salmon, beef filet in a sauce of tomato, garlic, and chipotle pepper, and lamb chops with mint sauce. To begin, you might try a salad such as endive and Roquefort, and end the meal with crêpes suzette. The eating area is small but warm, and is decorated with crafts-oriented art; there's also a bar. The wine list also merits mention for its variety.

Av. Vicente Pérez Rosales 1117. ✆ 65/232017. Main courses $7–$12. AE, DC, MC, V. Mon–Sat 12:30–3pm and 8pm–midnight.

Kika's ✿✿ _Finds_ CHILEAN/INTERNATIONAL   This is one of the newest and most charming eateries in town and it's tucked away in a lovely old house, a few blocks in from the lake. The bright dining room has hard wood floors, a beautiful fireplace, and lots of plants. There's a very young and casual atmosphere, but the food is quite sophisticated. The fresh seafood is outstanding and Kika's is known for its combination plates, such as the salmon and congrio eel with crab sauce or the jumbo shrimp served with a tender filet mignon. There are also several duck and wild game choices, depending on the season. To drink with your dinner, choose from over 60 award-winning Chilean wines. Desserts are heavenly—try the delicate raspberries baked with orange liquor.

Walker Martínez 584. ✆ 65/234703. Main courses $7–$12. AE, DC, MC, V. Daily 9am–11pm.

Mediterráneo ✿ _Moments_ INTERNATIONAL   Boasting an excellent location right on the Costanera, this new restaurant has a glass-enclosed terrace with water views. The cheerful orange tablecloths add to its brightness as does the pleasant waitstaff. Mediterráneo is known for its imaginative dishes (think Chilean-Mediterranean fusion) that change weekly. The owners use mostly local produce, including spices bought from the Mapuche natives. Here, you'll find big fresh salads mixing such ingredients as endives, Swiss cheese, anchovies, olives, and local mushrooms. For the main course, the venison here is excellent, served with a yummy zucchini gratin. Other standouts are the fresh seabass with a caper white-wine sauce and a delicious lamb cooked in a rosemary wine reduction and served with roasted potatoes. For dessert, try one of the yummy fruit sorbets.

Santa Rosa 068, corner of Portales. ✆ 65/237268. AE, DC, MC, V. Main courses $11–$14. Daily noon–3:30pm and 7:30–11pm.

Merlin ✿✿ _Finds_ CHILEAN   Merlin is arguably the finest restaurant in the center of town, located on a hillside just a block up from the lake. It is also one of the only restaurants in Chile that has managed to take Chilean cooking to a new level by exchanging the same tired recipes for creative dishes while still using only local (and mostly organic) ingredients. The setting is elegant, with hardwood floors, and a lovely view overlooking a small park (from the back dining area). The front dining room overlooks the street. The German chef who has been running this restaurant for 10 years changes the menu seasonally. A few examples include sea bass *ceviche,* crawfish bisque, smoked salmon–and–chive ravioli, rabbit with asparagus and olive risotto, and curried scallops, shrimp, and vegetables served with almond rice. The wine list also deserves mention for its selection of fine varietals not usually seen in this region.

Imperial 0605. ℂ **65/233105.** Reservations recommended. Main courses $11–$13. AE, DC, MC, V. Daily noon–3pm and 7pm–midnight.

WHAT TO SEE & DO: A WALK AROUND TOWN

Puerto Varas is compact enough to explore by foot, which is the best way to view the wooden colonial homes built by German immigrants from 1910 until the 1940s. Eight of these homes have been declared national monuments, yet there are at least a dozen more constructed during the period of expansion that began with the installation of the railroad connecting Puerto Varas with Puerto Montt.

Walk up San Francisco from Del Salvador until reaching María Brunn, where you turn right to view the stately **Iglesia del Sagrado Corazón de Jesús,** built between 1915 and 1918. The neo-Romantic design of the church, made entirely of oak, was modeled after the Marienkirche in the Black Forest. Continue along María Brunn and turn right on Purísima, where you'll encounter the first group of colonial homes. The first is **Casa Gasthof Haus** (1930), now run as a hotel, then **Casa Yunge** (1932), just past San Luis on the left, and on the right, **Casa Horn** (1925), and finally **Casa Kaschel** at Del Salvador, where you turn left. If you'd like to see more, walk to Calle Dr. Giesseler and turn right, following the train tracks for several blocks, passing the **Casa Opitz** on the right (1913, and now a hotel) until you see **Casa Maldonado** (1915) on the left.

Turn left on Nuestra Señora del Carmen to view the five homes left and right, including the **Casa Juptner** (1910). Double back and continue along Dr. Giesseler, turn left on Estación and then right on Decher, passing the **Casa Emhart** (1920) and several other homes on the left. Continue until reaching **Parque Philippi,** where you'll find a lookout point. Double back, turn left on Bellavista, right on Klenner, and left on Turismo, at whose corner sits the eclectic **Casa Kuschel** (1910), with its Bavarian baroque tower. At the end of Turismo is the Avenida Costanera; turn right and take a stroll down the boardwalk.

OUTDOOR ACTIVITIES

TOUR OPERATORS & OUTFITTERS   Puerto Varas has a few reliable, competent outfitters and tour operators offering excursions around the region, and even as far away as the Aisén region along the Carretera Austral. Perhaps the most difficult excursion in this region is an ascent up Volcán Osorno, which requires adequate physical fitness and a guided tour company that can provide necessary gear such as ropes and crampons. **Tranco Expediciones,** Santa Rosa 580 (ℂ **65/311311**), and **Aquamotion Expediciones,** San Pedro 422 (ℂ **65/ 232747;** fax 65/235938; www.aquamotion.cl), offer ascents to the top of Volcán Osorno, as well as trekking, rafting, sea kayaking, horseback riding, canyoneering, rock climbing, horseback riding, photo safaris, and more. They also custom-plan excursions and offer packages that include accommodations. Both are competent, solid bets with excellent guides.

For city tours and sightseeing tours around the Lake District, including trips to Frutillar, Puyehue, Chiloé, and Parque Nacional Alerce Andino, try **Andina del Sud,** at Del Salvador 72 (© **65/232811;** www.andinadelsud.com). Andina del Sud is the company that provides boat excursions on Lago Todos los Santos and the Chilean leg of the lake crossing to Argentina (for information, see "Parque Nacional Vicente Pérez Rosales & the Lake Crossing to Argentina," below).

BOATING   During the summer it is possible to rent kayaks and canoes at the pier, located near the main plaza. For a sailing cruise around Lago Llanquihue, try **Motovelero Capitán Haase** (© **65/235120;** fax 65/235166; captain@chilesat.net). Mr. Haase, the amicable owner and captain, offers four daily cruises aboard his yacht, built in 1998 in an attractive, antique design. The "Sunrise" cruise from 7:30 to 10:30am, including breakfast, is geared primarily toward fishermen. An early afternoon cruise from 11:30am to 1:30pm, with snacks, is for families with kids. "Sunset with the Captain" from 6 to 9:30pm is a quiet, romantic trip using sails and no motor. A "Party Cruise" goes from 10pm to 2am, and ships out only when there's a minimum of 20 passengers.

FISHING   This region is noted for its excellent fly-fishing opportunities, namely along the shores of Río Puelo, Río Maullín, and Río Petrohué. The premiere and most exclusive fishing is offered at the Yan Kee Way Lodge (see "Where to Stay," below). Many hotels will set up tours with guides, but the central hub for information, gear, and fishing licenses is at **Gray's Fly-Fishing Supplies,** which has two shops at San José 192 and San Francisco 447 (© **65/310734;** www.grayfly.com). Gray's has a roster of fly-fishing guides who will arrange outings to all outlying areas, for river and lake fishing.

The exclusive, full-service **Río Puelo Lodge** (© **2/960-1001** in Santiago) caters to fly-fishermen but also offers horseback riding, boat rides, water-skiing, and more. The stately wood-and-stone lodge is tucked well into the backcountry on the shore of Lago Tagua Tagua. Packages average around $300 per person, per day, including meals, open bar, guide, boats, horseback riding, trekking, and heated pool. Ask about discounts for non-anglers.

HORSEBACK RIDING   **Campo Aventura,** San Bernardo 318, Puerto Varas (© **65/232910;** www.campo-aventura.com), offers horseback riding from October 15 to April 15, leaving from a camp in Valle Cochamó, south of the national park, with day and multiple-day trips. Gear and bilingual guides are provided, and guests can lodge in their mountain bunkhouses. Other tour companies, such as **Aquamotion** (see "Tour Operators & Outfitters," above), offer day horseback-riding trips in Vicente Pérez Rosales National Park.

RAFTING   Few rivers in the world provide rafters with such stunning scenery as the Río Petrohué, whose frothy green waters begin at Lago Todos los Santos and end at the Reloncaví Estuary. Rafters are treated to towering views of the volcanoes Osorno and Puntiagudo. The river is Class III and suitable for nearly everyone, but it is not a slow float, so timid travelers might consult with their tour agency before signing up. The tour operators listed above offer rafting.

A SIDE TRIP FROM PUERTO VARAS TO ENSENADA

Ensenada is a tiny settlement at the base of Volcán Osorno. Its proximity to Petrohué and Lago Todos los Santos makes it a convenient point for lodging if you plan to spend a lot of time around the Vicente Pérez Rosales National Park. About 4km (2½ miles) outside Puerto Varas on the way to Ensenada is a Chilean rodeo *medialuna* ("half moon"), where events are held during February and on Independence days September 18 to September 19.

GETTING THERE If you have your own vehicle, take the coastal road east out of Puerto Varas and continue for 46km (29 miles) until you reach Ensenada. In Puerto Varas, you'll find minibuses at the intersection of San Bernardo and Martínez that go to Ensenada, Petrohué, and Lago Todos los Santos every day at 9:15am, 11am, 2pm, and 4pm. **Andina del Sud,** Del Salvador 72 (© **65/ 232811**), has daily trips to this area as well.

Where to Stay

Hotel Ensenada *Value* The Hotel Ensenada is a veritable museum, with a lobby jam-packed with colonial German antiques. The hotel itself is a living antique, built more than 100 years ago. Although it offers an acceptable level of comfort, the rooms do reflect the hotel's age. It's such a fun place, though, that most visitors, 90% of them foreigners, don't seem to mind. All rooms on the second floor have private bathrooms, and for the most part the rest share with just one other room. Rooms are sparsely decorated. If they're not too full, ask to see several rooms as each one is differently sized. The hotel is situated on a 500-hectare (1,235-acre) private forest that's perfect for taking a stroll or riding a bike—which comes free with the room—and there's a tennis court, canoes, and motorboats. The old-fashioned kitchen serves simple, Chilean cuisine with vegetables straight from the garden. The hotel closes from May to September.

Ruta Internacional 225, Km 45. © 65/212017. Fax 65/212028. 25 units. $60 double; $90 double with volcano view. AE, DC, MC, V. Open Oct–Apr. **Amenities:** Restaurant; lounge.

Yan Kee Way ★★★ *Finds* The name "Yan Kee Way" is a play on words, a gringo's pronunciation of Llanquihue, and coincidentally it's owned and managed by Americans. The lodge is luxury at its finest, and it is patronized by wealthy entrepreneurs, Chilean military generals, actors, sports stars, and more. The setting is ideal: nestled in a thick forest of cinnamon-colored *arrayán* trees on the shore of Lago Llanquihue, and offering up an astounding view of the volcano directly in front of the lodge.

The complex is made entirely of wood painted terra cotta and forest green. Lodging options come in a variety of shapes and sizes: There are two chalets, eight bungalows, five two-bedroom suites, and four standard hotel rooms. The chalets are the most elegant, but also come with full kitchens. The bungalows are cozier, but also modern and extremely well designed. Prices can often be negotiated; contact the hotel or its Web page to inquire about full-service packages. The first-class decor features dark green walls, ebony leather couches, and furniture and art imported from Mexico and Argentina.

The hotel's outstanding main bar and dining area, Latitude 42 (see below) has to be seen to be believed, but even if you don't stay here, do try to make a stop for lunch or dinner to view this gorgeous lodge with your own eyes.

The hotel began as a fishing lodge—there are five on-staff guides—but now offers a wide variety of activities, including the region's only sailcraft for floating on the lake. There's a lovely lounge with large-screen satellite TV, and free Internet access for guests. Two wood-fired hot tubs face the lake and the volcano.

Road to Ensenada east of Puerto Varas, Km 42. © 65/212030. Fax 65/212031. www.southernchilexp.com. 18 units. $100–$150 double; from $250 1-bedroom chalet; $318 per person all-inclusive package, per day. Package includes all meals and house wines with dinner. MC, V. **Amenities:** Restaurant; bar; lounge; spa; Jacuzzi; sauna; exercise room; watersports equipment; room service; massage; laundry service; wine-tasting cellar; cigar bar. *In room:* Fridge, hair dryer, safe.

Where to Dine

Latitude 42 ★★★ *(Moments)* INTERNATIONAL   This is the finest restaurant in Southern Chile, located right on the lake overlooking the volcano. The decor is perfect: Marble and brass chandeliers, fireplaces made of volcanic rock, orangey leather chairs, picture windows overlooking the water, a basement "cave" for wine tasting, and a cigar bar that sells Havanas. Service is superb. The very talented chef, Rocío, uses only the highest quality produce, mostly local and organic, to create the most tantalizing dishes. The smoked salmon is smoked in-house using the finest cognac, and the meat is aged on the premises. Fish is brought daily from Puerto Varas, usually sea bass and conger eel. Specials change daily and the entire menu changes weekly. The cellar houses outstanding wines, an impressive collection from over 50 vineyards. Pastries and desserts are also terrific; even the heavenly chestnut ice cream is homemade.

In the Yan Kee Way Lodge, Road to Ensenada, east of Puerto Varas, Km 42. *(C)* **65/212030.** Main courses $9–$16. AE, DC, MC, V. Closed May–Oct.

PARQUE NACIONAL VICENTE PEREZ ROSALES & THE LAKE CROSSING TO ARGENTINA

About 65km (40 miles) from Puerto Varas sits Chile's oldest national park, Vicente Pérez Rosales, founded in 1926. It covers an area of 250,000 hectares (617,500 acres), incorporating the park's centerpiece, Lago Todos los Santos, and the Saltos de Petrohué, and three volcanoes: Osorno, Tronador, and Puntiagudo. The park is open daily, from 9am to 8pm during the summer from and from 9am to 6pm during the winter; admission to the Saltos de Petrohué is $1.75. Conaf's **information center** (no phone) can be found towards the end of the dirt road; the center is open daily and adheres loosely to these hours: December through February from 8:30am to 8pm, March through November from 8:30am to 6:30pm.

By far the most popular excursions here are boat rides across the unbelievably emerald waters of **Lago Todos los Santos,** and there are several options. **Andina del Sud** offers a 2-hour sail around Isla Margarita and a 3-hour sail to Peulla, where visitors are given the option to lodge in the Peulla Hotel, then return or continue on to Bariloche with the Argentine company Cruce de Lagos. Andina del Sud has a ticket office at the pier and an office in Puerto Varas, at Del Salvador 72 (*(C)* **65/232811**). The boat ride to Bariloche is spectacular, offering rugged, panoramic views; however, some travelers have complained that 1-day trips to Bariloche are not worth the money on stormy days, and that the companies shuttle passengers in and out too quickly. The ferry portions of this journey are broken up by short bus rides from one body of water to the other.

There are relatively few hiking trails here. The shortest and most popular trail leads to the **Saltos de Petrohué,** located just before the lake (admission $3). Here you'll find a wooden walkway that has been built above the start of the Río Petrohué; from here it is possible to watch the inky-green waters crash through lava channels formed after the 1850 eruption of Volcán Osorno. If you're serious about backpacking, pick up a copy of the JLM map *Ruta de los Jesuitas* for a description of longer trails in the park, one of which takes you as far as Lago Rupanco and Puerto Rico (the town, not the Caribbean island!), where you can catch a bus to Osorno. Day hikes take visitors around the back of Volcán Osorno. A trail to a rustic hot springs called **Termas de Callao** can be completed in a day, but it is accessed solely by boat, which you'll need to hire at the Petrohué dock (6-person maximum, $50). The round-trip hiking time is 5 to 6 hours, and you must arrange with the boat's captain to pick you up later.

Hotel Peulla *Finds*   Passengers on the 2-day journey to Bariloche stop for the night at this giant lodge, which sits on the shore of Lago Todos los Santos. It's possible to spend several days here if you'd like, to take part in trekking, fishing, and kayaking in the area. The lodge's remoteness is perhaps its biggest draw, surrounded as it is by thick forest and not much else. The Peulla is a mountain lodge, with enormous dining rooms, roaring fireplaces, and lots of wood. It's an agreeable place, with a large patio and sprawling lawn, although the price is a bit high. Try reserving rooms at a lower rate through a travel agency.

Lago Todos los Santos. ℰ/fax **2/889-1031** in Santiago. 78 units. $131 double. AE, MC, V. **Amenities:** Restaurant; bar; watersports equipment; game room. *In room:* Satellite TV.

7 Puerto Montt

20km (12 miles) N of Puerto Varas; 1,016km (630 miles) S of Santiago

This port town of roughly 110,000 residents is the central hub for travelers headed to Lagos Llanquihue and Todos los Santos, Chiloé, and the national parks Alerce Andino and Pumalín. It is also a major docking zone for dozens of large cruise companies circumnavigating the southern cone of South America and several ferry companies with southern destinations to Laguna San Rafael National Park and Puerto Natales in Patagonia.

The town presents a convenient stopover point for travelers, but is not a particularly attractive destination in itself. However, Puerto Montt's small downtown can be a pleasant place to take a stroll on a sunny day, and the city offers great restaurants and an extensive outdoor market that sells Chilean handicrafts.

Puerto Montt was founded in 1853 by German immigrants and their stalwart promoter Vicente Pérez Rosales, who named the town after another promoter of immigration, President Manual Montt. The waterfront here was rebuilt after the devastating earthquake of 1960, which had destroyed the city's port, church, and neighborhood of Angelmó. Today, it is the capital of Chile's Región X, a thriving city that invests heavily in salmon farming, shipping, and tourism.

ESSENTIALS
GETTING THERE
BY PLANE   Puerto Montt's **El Tepaul** (PMC) airport (ℰ **65/252019**) is currently served only by one major airline, and that's **LanChile/LanChile Express,** San Martín 200 (ℰ **65/253141**), with six to eight daily flights to Santiago; two to four daily flights to Punta Arenas; three daily flights to Balmaceda; and once-weekly flights to Valdivia and Temuco. Since it has no competition, LanChile charges high rates and has very low levels of customer service. The wait at ticket counters can be enormous while dealing with inefficient and poorly trained staff. **Sky Airlines,** a new privately owned company, began services in early 2003 using a small fleet of Boeing 737 jets. As of this writing, it operated two flights a day between Santiago and Puerto Montt; it doesn't yet have a website, but you can make reservations by calling ℰ **600/6002828** toll-free from within Chile, or 2/353-3169. **Aero Met,** Urmeneta 149 (ℰ **65/252523**), has two or three daily flights from Chaitén and the cost is $100 round-trip. A bus from the airport to the city's downtown bus terminal costs $1; a taxi costs $8.50. Agree on the fare before getting into the cab. There are several car-rental agencies at the airport, including Hertz and Avis.

BY BUS   Puerto Montt's main terminal is at the waterfront, about a 10-minute walk from downtown, and there are taxis. Regular bus service to and from most major cities, including Santiago, is provided by **Cruz del Sur** (ℰ **65/254731**),

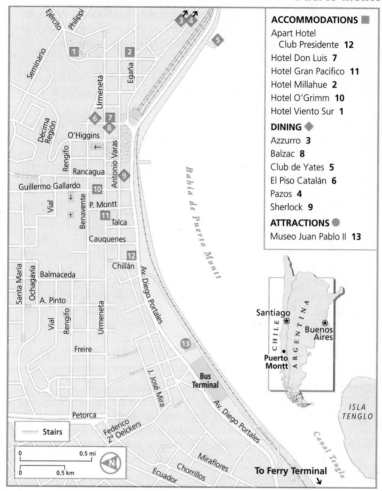

ACCOMMODATIONS ■
Apart Hotel
  Club Presidente **12**
Hotel Don Luis **7**
Hotel Gran Pacifico **11**
Hotel Millahue **2**
Hotel O'Grimm **10**
Hotel Viento Sur **1**
DINING ◆
Azzurro **3**
Balzac **8**
Club de Yates **5**
El Piso Catalán **6**
Pazos **4**
Sherlock **9**
ATTRACTIONS ●
Museo Juan Pablo II **13**

TurBus (☎ 65/253329), **Tas Choapa** (☎ 65/254828), and **Bus Norte** (☎ 65/252783).

BY CAR The Panamericana Highway ends at Puerto Montt.

VISITOR INFORMATION

The municipality has a small **tourist office** in the plaza at the corner of Antonio Varas and O'Higgins (☎ 65/261700); it's open December through March daily from 9am to 9pm, and April through November Monday through Friday from 9am to 1pm and 2:30 to 6:30pm, Saturday and Sunday from 9am to 1pm. There is also an office in the bus terminal on the second floor, and two new kiosks on the pedestrian street Calle Talca near Calle Urmeneta.

ORIENTATION

Puerto Montt is divided into *poblaciones,* or neighborhoods, scattered around the city's hilltops. From the city center to the east is the **Pelluco** district, where many of the city's good restaurants can be found, and to the west is the district

Angelmó, with the city's fish market, port departures, and Feria Artesanal with great shopping; the two districts are connected by the coastal road Diego Portales. The city center is laid out on a grid system that abuts a steep cliff.

GETTING AROUND

BY FOOT   The city center is small enough to be seen on foot. The crafts market and fish market in Angelmó are a 20-minute walk from the center, but you can take a cab. You'll need a taxi to reach the Pelluco district.

BY BUS   **Buses Cruz del Sur** (© 65/252783) leaves for Puerto Varas 15 times daily from the bus terminal, and so do the independent white shuttle buses to the left of the coaches; look for the sign in the window that says PUERTO VARAS. Cruz del Sur also serves Chiloé, including Castro and Ancud, with seven trips per day. **TransChiloé** (© 65/254934) goes to Chiloé 11 times per day from the terminal.

BY CAR   This is one of those places where renting a car can come in handy, given the ample sightseeing opportunities and pleasant drives. Local car-rental agencies in Puerto Montt include **Hertz** at Antonio Varas 126 (© **65/259585;** www.hertz.com), **Avis** at Urmeneta 1037 (© **65/253307;** www.avis.com), **First** at Av. G. Gallardo 211 (© **65/252036**), **Econo Rent** at Av. G. Gallardo 450 (© **65/254888**), **Hunter Rent A Car** at Antonio Varas 449 (© **65/251524**), and **Ace Turismo** at Antonio Varas 445 (© **65/254988;** www.geocities.com/ lagosandinos). Hertz, Avis, and Ace Turismo rent cars for the Carretera Austral, leaving the vehicle in Coyhaique or Punta Arenas. Some companies insist that you rent a 4×4 (the importance of this during the summer is debatable; during the winter it could help if the road turns muddy). Calling the local office of each company is usually the best way to get bargain rates.

SPECIAL EVENTS

The second week in January Puerto Montt hosts a **Día del Curanto,** preparing this popular Chilote dish the traditional way—in earthen holes—in public places around the city. In the first half of February the city holds its annual **Semana Puertomontina,** with weeklong festivities that culminate with a fireworks display over the bay. The festival celebrates Puerto Montt's anniversary.

FAST FACTS: PUERTO MONTT

Currency Exchange   **Turismo Los Lagos,** Talca 84; **Trans Afex,** Av. Diego Portales 516; **Inter/Cam,** O'Higgins 167, 1st floor; **La Moneda de Oro,** in the bus terminal, Office #37; and **Eureka Tour,** Antonio Varas 445. Exchange houses are generally open Monday through Friday from 9am to 1pm and 2 to 6pm, Saturday from 9am to 1pm. For ATMs, try Banco de A. Edwards at Pedro Montt 55 (© **65/264520**) or Banco Santander at Antonio Varas 501 (© **65/ 252412**). Banks are open Monday through Friday from 9am to 2pm.

Hospital   **Hospital Base Seminario** s/n (© **65/261100**) and the **Hospital de la Seguridad** at Panamericana 400 (© **65/257333**).

Internet Cafe   **Mundo Sur Cibercafe,** San Martín 232; **Tetris Entel,** Antonio Varas 529; and **Travellers Center,** Av. Angelmó 2456 (© **65/262099**). Internet service cost averages $3 per hour but many hotels are slowly adding free access for guests; inquire when you arrive at your hotel.

Laundry   **Narly** at San Martín 167 (no phone), or **Lavandería Center** at Antonio Varas 700 (© **65/252338**).

WHAT TO SEE & DO

TOUR OPERATORS & TRAVEL AGENCIES   **Ace Turismo** at Antonio Varas 445 (© **65/254988**) offers just about everything, including tours to Vicente Pérez National Park, the Termas de Puyehué, Chiloé, sightseeing tours around the circumference of Lago Llanquihue, 2-night treks around Volcán Osorno with an overnight in a family home, and more.

   Petrel Tours at Benavente 327 (© **65/251780**) is a full-service travel agency and offers city tours and sightseeing excursions around the area and to the Vicente Pérez Rosales National Park. **Andina del Sud** at Antonio Varas 447 (© **65/257797**) is another agency offering classic trips such as city tours and sightseeing journeys, and has a transportation service to attractions, as well as the monopoly on Lago Todos los Santos for the lake crossing to Bariloche. **Travellers** at Av. Angelmó 2456 (© **65/262099;** travlers@chilesat.net) is somewhat like a one-stop travel shop, with information and booking arrangements with nearly every outfitter, hotel, and program around Chile.

Museo Juan Pablo II   This museum contains a medley of artifacts culled from this region. There's an interesting interpretive exhibit of the Monte Verde archaeological dig that found bones estimated to be 12,000 years old. There's also an open-air railway exhibit next to the museum. Truthfully, the museum really holds little of interest, but if you're in the area it's worth a quick stop.

Av. Diego Portales 991. No phone. Admission 70¢. Mar–Dec daily 9am–noon and 2–6pm; Jan–Feb daily 9am–7pm.

SHOPPING   Puerto Montt is a great place to pick up souvenirs. On Avenida Angelmó, from the bus terminal to the fish market, is the **Feria Artesanal de Angelmó** ๙ (open daily 9am–7pm), with dozens of stalls and specialty shops that peddle knitwear, ponchos, handicrafts, jewelry, regional foods, and more from areas around the Lake District, including Chiloé. It's about a 15-minute walk from the plaza, or you can take a taxi.

WHERE TO STAY
EXPENSIVE

Apart Hotel Club Presidente   This well-tailored hotel's classic, nautical-themed design appeals equally to executives and tourists, and handy kitchenettes give guests a little extra freedom. Located on the waterfront in a central location close to shops, the Presidente is on busy Portales Avenue, but double-paned windows keep noise to a minimum. All rooms have either queen- or king-size beds. The doubles are spacious, but the superiors are much larger and worth the extra $5; they also have ocean views. Most come with a small loveseat and a table and chairs. The rooms are decorated with creams and navy blue, striped curtains, and nubby bedspreads. A breakfast buffet is served daily in the comfortable restaurant/bar next to the lobby.

Av. Diego Portales 664, Puerto Montt. © **65/251666.** Fax 65/251669. www.presidente.cl. 50 units. $60–$95 double. Rates include buffet breakfast. AE, DC, MC. **Amenities:** Restaurant; bar; small heated pool; sauna; small business center; laundry service. *In room:* TV.

Gran Pacífico ๙   Opened in late 2001, the Gran Pacífico is the city's only luxurious boutique hotel, and its imposing seven-story structure towers over the waterfront. The Art Deco lobby is sleek and modern with lots of wood and marble. The rooms follow the same motif and are spacious, modern, and very bright. They have wood headboards, off-yellow wallpaper, and large-screen TVs.

Those overlooking the water have breathtaking views (request an upper level oceanview floor when you check in). The marble bathrooms are a tad small but the size of the room makes up for it. For such a high caliber hotel, the staff is not too efficient nor do they speak much English, so be patient.

Urmeneta 719, Puerto Montt. ⓒ 65/482100. Fax 65/482110. Reservas@hotelpacifico.cl. 48 units. $95–$160 double. AE, DC, MC, V. **Amenities:** Restaurant; bar; lounge; exercise room; sauna; room service; laundry service. *In room:* TV, minibar, safe, dataport.

Hotel Don Luis   The Don Luis is part of the Best Western chain, and offers pleasant, comfortable accommodations with traditional decor. For the price, you'd do better staying at the Club Presidente (see above), but occasional discounts might make this hotel more attractive. The lobby has glass walls, shiny white floors, and English-style furniture. The hotel renovated its rooms and sparkling white bathrooms in 2000, but not the carpet, which could stand to be replaced. Corner rooms and those on the seventh and eighth floors have the best views. Junior suites have a terrace, and superiors come with a queen-size bed. Double-paned windows ensure tranquil evenings. The hotel often caters to executives and conventioneers.

Calle Urmeneta and Quillota, Puerto Montt. ⓒ 65/259001. Fax 65/259005. www.hoteldonluis.cl. 60 units. $98–$110 double; from $112 suite. Rates include buffet breakfast. AE, DC, MC, V. **Amenities:** Restaurant; bar; lounge; exercise room; sauna; small business center; room service; laundry service. *In room:* TV.

Hotel Viento Sur   The main body of this appealing bed-and-breakfast style hotel is within an 80-year-old home clinging to a cliff, with a decade-old, added-on wing below that keeps with the architectural uniformity of the establishment. The hotel has luminous, blonde-wood floors and is brightly lit by a generous supply of windows that look out over Puerto Montt's bay. The rooms are unique, each with a folk-art and nautical theme, but simple and not luxurious at all. The upstairs rooms in the old house have tall ceilings, the rooms in the lower wing have the cozy feel of a ship's cabin, and rooms on the fourth floor have terraces or balconies. Doubles come in standard and superior, and nearly all have a view of the bay. A large patio juts out from the front of the hotel.

One of the perks at the Viento Sur is the delicious breakfast buffet served in the restaurant, which is locally considered one of the best in Puerto Montt (see "Where to Dine," below).

Ejército 200, Puerto Montt. ⓒ 65/258701. Fax 65/258700. www.hotelvientosur.cl. 27 units. $75–$90 double standard; $85–$98 double superior. Rates include buffet breakfast. AE, DC, MC, V. **Amenities:** Restaurant; sauna; laundry service. *In room:* TV.

O'Grimm   One of the city's most established hotels, the O'Grimm is run by a friendly English-speaking staff and is adjacent to the popular O'Grimm Pub. Rooms are of varying sizes and all come with sleek black and gray furniture and dark satin-like bedspreads. There's no view to mention, really, and the rooms are not as inviting as the price may suggest. Bathrooms are small and aging, but clean. The restaurant, pub, and bustling atmosphere downstairs is pleasant and there's live music several nights of the week.

Guillermo Gallardo 211, Puerto Montt. ⓒ 65/252845. Fax 65/258600. www.Ogrimm.com. 26 units. $80–$100 double; from $110 suite. AE, DC, MC, V. **Amenities:** Restaurant; bar; business center with Internet access. *In room:* TV, safe, minibar.

MODERATE

Hotel Millahue   This older hotel is not particularly fancy, but it does offer clean, large double rooms and friendly service. All double rooms are sized differently but priced the same, and rooms on the fourth and fifth floors are the nicest, especially those whose numbers end in 06 and 07. There's a dining area for breakfast and hearty, set-menu Chilean meals should you decide to eat in. Beds are average but offer standard comfort. The hotel is run by its owner, a friendly woman who strives to make guests feel at home.

Copiapó 64, Puerto Montt. ℂ 65/253829. Fax 65/256317. jacortes@entelchile.net. 25 units. $30–$45 double. Rates include buffet breakfast. No credit cards. **Amenities:** Restaurant; laundry service.

WHERE TO DINE

Puerto Montt is Chile's seafood capital. If you're feeling adventurous, try a Chilean favorite, such as abalone, sea urchin, or the regional barnacle. And where better to see, smell, and taste these fruits of the sea than the **Fish Market of Angelmó,** located at the end of Avenida Angelmó where the artisan market terminates; it's open Monday through Sunday from 10am to 8pm. Like most fish markets, it's a little grungy, but it's a colorful stop nevertheless and there are several restaurant stalls offering the freshest local specialties around. A word of caution: There have been reports that a few food stalls like to overcharge tourists, so double-check your bill with the menu.

Apart from the restaurants below, there are a handful of inexpensive cafes in Puerto Montt, including **Central** at Rancagua 117 (ℂ 65/254721), **Dino's** at Antonio Varas 550 (ℂ 65/252785), and **Super Yoco** at Quillota 259 (ℂ 65/252123), which has lunches, empanadas, and appetizer platters. If you're in the mood for pizza, try **Di Napoli** at Av. General Gallardo 119 (ℂ 65254174).

Azzurro ITALIAN   Fresh pasta served in rich sauces is this Italian eatery's mainstay, but that's not all they serve—the stuffed Roquefort chicken and pizzas are also very good. The folk-artsy blue dining area has hand-painted stenciling and is decorated with craftwork; it's a fun, pleasant atmosphere. The pastas are to die for, such as lasagna, fettuccine, or cannelloni stuffed with crab and spinach, or with ricotta, walnuts, eggplant, and fresh basil and bathed in a choice of 11 sauces. The specialty is smoked trout ravioli, for which the restaurant won a regional culinary award. There are also salads and an extensive wine list.

Av. General Gallardo at Av. España, Pelluco. ℂ 65/318989. Reservations recommended on weekends. Main courses $4–$8. No credit cards. Mon–Sat 1–3:30pm and 8pm–midnight.

Balzac ⋆ CHILEAN/FRENCH   Balzac is one of the best restaurants in Puerto Montt, and is accordingly popular with local residents and tourists alike. The idea behind Balzac is to create innovative dishes with a French flavor, using only fresh, regional products and ingredients. Plenty of Chilean specialties abound, such as garlic shrimp *pil pil* or conger eel with a caper or chardonnay sauce. You'll see a few French classics here, such as *boeuf bourguignon,* but the emphasis is seafood, of which there's a large variety, including albacore tuna or a *curanto* stew for two. The brightly painted interior is an attractive surrounding for enjoying your meal. The wine list features fine Chilean varieties.

Calle Urmeneta 305. ℂ 65/313251. Main courses $7–$9. No credit cards. Mon–Fri noon–3:30pm and 8–11:30pm; Sat–Sun 8–11:30pm.

Club de Yates SEAFOOD   The light-blue Club de Yates looks like a traditional seafood restaurant that sits out over the water like a pier. Inside, though, the atmosphere is white tablecloths, candlesticks, and sharp waiters in bow ties; it's one of the more elegant dining areas in town. This is a good place to come if you're looking for typical Chilean seafood dishes, such as razor clams broiled with Parmesan, sea bass *Margarita,* a creamy shellfish sauce, avocado halves filled with shrimp salad, and the like. It has a great waterfront view, and is located about 1km (½ mile) from the plaza toward Pelluco.

Av. Juan Soler Manfredini 1. ℂ 65/263606. Main courses $6–$13. AE, DC, MC, V. Daily noon–3pm and 8–11pm.

El Piso Catalán *Value* SPANISH   The Piso Catalán is a great choice for a good, inexpensive lunch, which is why this tiny second-story restaurant is usually packed with downtown workers. The atmosphere is as enjoyable as the menu; the dining areas are in two rooms of an old wooden home, artistically decorated and well lit. The regular menu offers a bounty of tapas, those little Spanish appetizers that range from garlic shrimp to an egg tortilla—all cost between $2.50 and $7 each. There are just seven main dishes here, so you might consider ordering several tapas instead and sharing with your dining partner.

Quillota 185, 2nd floor. ℂ 65/313900. Main courses $5–$13. No credit cards. Daily 12:30–4:30pm and 8pm–2am.

Hotel Viento Sur CONTEMPORARY CHILEAN   Like Balzac (see above), the Viento Sur takes regional ingredients and puts them to work in flavorful, well-prepared dishes. Another reason to come here is for the intimate dining area with its expansive view of the bay—if you get a table near the window, that is. The restaurant is built of polished blond wood, with linen tablecloths and a nautical theme. Mouth-watering dishes include beef tenderloin in a cilantro sauce, saffron conger eel, and chicken marinated in port with almonds. A most unusual dish is the exquisite smoked salmon soup with spinach. Although there are set hours for dining, the restaurant serves cocktails, tea, and cakes all day, should you be looking for a good place to take a break. There's also a tiny bar.

Ejército 200. ℂ 65/258701. Main courses $7–$10. AE, DC, MC, V. Daily 12:30–3:30pm and 7:30–10:30pm.

Pazos CHILEAN   This is the place to come if you're interested in sampling *curanto* but don't have time to make it to Chiloé. *Curanto* is that island's specialty, a mixture of mussels, clams, sausage, chicken, pork, beef, and a gooey pancake steamed in a large pot and served with a cup of broth. Pazos also serves a variety of other seafood items, such as sea urchin omelets and the shellfish cornucopia, *sopa marinera*. The restaurant is on the waterfront in Pelluco, in a 90-year-old home. It's very popular with summer visitors to Puerto Montt.

Liboro Guerrero 1, Pelluco. ℂ 65/252552. Main courses $4–$9. No credit cards. Mon–Sat 12:15–3pm and 8:15–10pm; Sun 12:15–3pm.

Sherlock ⭐ *Finds* CHILEAN/PUB   The newest and most happening place in Puerto Varas is this centrally located pub, cafe, and restaurant all rolled into one. There's lots of charm, a nice bar, and wood furniture, and it fills with locals at all hours of the day. This is a good place to get some local color, and they serve excellent home-made Chilean cuisine and delicious sandwiches. Try the albacore steak with a Chilean tomato and onion salad or the Sherlock sandwich with beef strips, tomato, corn, cheese, bacon and grilled onion ($5).

Antonio Varas & Rancagua 117. ℂ 65/288888. Main courses $6–$10. Sandwiches $3–$5. No credit cards. Daily 9am–2am.

8 Ferry Crossings to the Carretera Austral & Sailing to Patagonia Through the Fjords

Few fjordlands in the world surpass the elegant beauty of Chile's southern region. The entire coast of Chile is composed of thousands of little-explored islands, canals, and sounds. **Navimag** offers a popular sailing trip through the southern fjords to Puerto Natales in Patagonia. The company also offers journeys to the Laguna San Rafael Glacier, as does the freight ferry **Transmarchilay** and the luxury liners *Skorpios* and *Patagonian Express* (which leaves from Puerto Chacabuco). Both cruises are unforgettable.

For information about the journey to the Laguna San Rafael Glacier, see chapter 16.

Navimag ★ *Moments*   Navimag offers a sensational 4-day/3-night journey through the southern fjords to **Puerto Natales,** near Torres del Paine National Park (the trip can also be done in the reverse direction—see the section on Puerto Natales in chapter 17 for departure dates and times). Navimag's ship, M/N *Puerto Edén,* is a passenger and freight ferry with a variety of cabins, all of which are pretty basic. The cruise is not only unforgettable for the spectacular views it offers, but also for the camaraderie that occurs among the passengers. The journey goes through fjords and channels, and past coves, and across the Golfo de Penas, or "Gulf of Grief," where, depending on climatic conditions, passengers may experience seasickness.

The *Puerto Edén* leaves Puerto Montt every Monday and arrives at Puerto Natales on Thursday. The return trip is shorter, leaving Puerto Natales on Thursday evening and arriving back here on Sunday.

Cabin prices include all meals. Check to see if your cabin has a private bathroom and interior or exterior windows. You may have to share with strangers unless you fork over the entire price of a Cabina Armador (about $1,584 for 2). The most deluxe accommodations go for about $792 per person, double occupancy, then $398 per person, quadruple occupancy. Prices drop from here all the way down to $250 per person, but be forewarned that the very cheapest bunks are booked by young backpackers and are separated by curtains, and many are close to the engine room and get stuffy and incredibly noisy. Prices drop for off-season travel; check Navimag's website for specials from April to October.

Offices in Puerto Montt at Av. Angelmó 2187 in the Terminal de Transbordadores ((*C*) **65/432300**) and Santiago at El Bosque Norte 0440 ((*C*) **2/442-3120**); in Chaitén, call (*C*) **65/731570.** www.navimag.com. AE, DC, MC, V.

FERRY SERVICES   Puerto Montt is the hub for all ferry companies. If you are planning a trip down the Carretera Austral, you'll need to travel to or from Puerto Montt by ferry (unless you enter through Argentina). During the summer, passengers and autos can cross into Pumalín Park and Caleta Gonzalo by ferry. This route is preferred, but available only from December to March. For information about ferry crossings to Caleta Gonzalo, see the section on Pumalín Park in chapter 16.

Throughout the year, Transmarchilay and Navimag offer service to Chaitén from Puerto Montt, and Transmarchilay also goes to Chaitén from Quellón, Chiloé.

Catamaranes Del Sur, Diego Portales 510, Puerto Montt ((*C*) **65/482308;** www.catamaranesdelsur.cl), has introduced speedy service from Puerto Montt to Chaitén aboard their luxury catamarans. The trip takes 4 hours 15 minutes and is very pleasant. The service operates Monday, Wednesday, and Friday from September 16 to March 30. Catamarans depart Puerto Montt at 9am; the return trip leaves the same days and departs Chaitén at 2pm. The price is $40 one-way or $72 round-trip and includes a snack.

Navimag's (see above) ferries to **Chaitén** leave once a week (usually Fri) from March 15 to November, and three times per week during the summer; call for days because they tend to vary. The trip takes 10 hours, and costs $16 per person for the right to stay in the salon with tables and chairs, or $22 per person for a semi-reclining seat.

Transmarchilay, in Puerto Montt at Av. Angelmó 2187, Terminal de Transbordadores (© **65/270416;** www.transmarchilay.cl), offers ferry crossings to **Chaitén** aboard the ship *Pincoya* leaving Monday at noon and Tuesday, Thursday, and Friday at 8pm for $26 per passenger and an additional $100 for autos (prices slightly lower in the low season); bikes are charged $10. The trip takes 10 hours and passengers sleep in reclining seats. From Chaitén, the return trips depart on Monday, Wednesday, and Sunday at 11pm and 9am on Friday.

15

Chiloé

The "Grand Island of Chiloé" is a land of myths and magic—of emerald, rolling hills shrouded in mist and picturesque bays lined with brightly painted fishing boats. Residents here live in *palafitos,* rickety and charming shingled houses with corrugated roofs that rise above the water on stilts. Throughout the region, lovely wooden churches modeled after a Bavarian, neoclassic style appear like a beacon in every cove.

Visually appealing as it is, Chiloé is truly defined by its people, the hardy, colorful Chilotes who can still be seen plowing their fields with oxen or pulling in their catch of the day the same way they have for centuries. Spanish conquistadors occupied Chiloé as early as 1567, followed by Jesuit missionaries and Spanish refugees pushed off the mainland by Mapuche Indian attacks. For 3 centuries Chiloé was the only Spanish stronghold south of the Río Biobío, and its isolation produced a singular culture among its residents who, after so much time, are now a *mestizo* blend of Indian and Spanish blood. The Chilotes' rapid and closed speech, local slang, mythical folklore, and style of food, tools, and architecture was and still is uniquely different from their counterparts on the mainland. The downside of Chiloé's extremely limited contact with the outside world is a dire poverty that has affected (and continues to affect) many of the island's residents. Most residents live in pastoral settings, and each family typically has its own small farm and basic livestock, most of the animals of which can usually be seen pecking and grazing along the side of the road. Here it is as common to see residents traveling on horseback or by fishing skiff as it is by vehicle.

The rectangular body of Chiloé and the tiny islands on the eastern shore that complete the archipelago render it South America's second-largest island, bordered by the Pacific Ocean on the west and the Gulf of Ancud on the east. Chiloé's principal cities are **Ancud** in the north, **Castro** on the island's eastern shore, and **Quellón** at the southern tip, and visitors can take a recommended short ferry ride to **Isla Quinchao.** Chiloé also boasts the **Parque Nacional de Chiloé** on the western shore. The island's tourism infrastructure is improving, but as of yet visitors should expect to find modest accommodations, usually within old homes or in simple hotels.

EXPLORING THE ISLAND

Most visitors use Castro as a central base for exploring the island, since the busy town of Ancud (the island's largest city) does not really warrant an overnight stay. Quellón is considered primarily a ferry departure point for Chaitén on the Carretera Austral (see chapter 16). On a clear day—not very often—one can see Volcán Osorno and the towering, snowcapped Andes in the distance.

You'll need a day to explore Castro, Dalcahue, and Achao, a day to see the national park (more if you want to do a lot of hiking or camping), and a half-day to tour Ancud, with a stop in Chacao.

1 Chiloé Essentials

GETTING TO THE ISLAND

BY BOAT   There's been talk of building a bridge between the mainland and Chiloé, but until then, two ferry companies operate continuously between Pargua (on the mainland) and Chacao (on the island), shuttling passengers and vehicles. If you are taking a bus to Chiloé, you won't need to worry about paying the fare because it's included in the price of the bus ticket, but if you've rented a car the cost is $9 one-way. The ride lasts 30 to 40 minutes. (And, yes, there are toilets on board the ferry!)

> **Tips** **Driving to Chiloé**
>
> If you're driving your own rental car onto the ferry don't line up behind the trucks and buses but go to the front of the line and park to the left—that will make you visible to the ferry attendants and they'll squeeze you onto the next available ferry.

BY BUS   Several companies provide service to Ancud, Castro, and Quellón from Puerto Montt and even Santiago and Punta Arenas. In Puerto Montt, daily departures for Ancud and Castro leave from the bus terminal: **Cruz del Sur** (© 65/254731) has 16 trips per day; **TransChiloé** (© 65/254934) has 11 trips per day, as does **Queilén Bus** (© 65/621140). From Puerto Varas, try **Cruz del Sur** at San Pedro 210, with 5 trips per day. **Cruz del Sur** (© 2/779-0607) offers service from Santiago to Chiloé; the trip takes about 17 hours. Buses ride over on the ferry; you can remain in your seat or step out and walk around.

GETTING AROUND THE ISLAND

Chiloé's beauty is best revealed by sightseeing with a car in order to stop along the way at historic churches and the many well-built lookout points throughout the archipelago. The best plan is to rent a car in Puerto Montt or in Chiloé. In Ancud, car rental can be found at **Eben Ezer,** Copec Pudeto Bajo s/n (© 65/623793). In Castro, car rental is at **ADS Rent A Car** at Esmeralda 260 (© 65/637373). Local bus service from town to town is frequent and inexpensive. More information about bus service can be found in the sections for each specific town below.

2 Ancud

95km (59 miles) SE of Puerto Montt; 146km (91 miles) N of Castro

Ancud is Chiloé's largest city, founded in 1767 as a defensive fort to monitor passing sea traffic to and from Cape Horn. It was for many years the capital of Chiloé until the provincial government pulled up stakes and moved to Castro in 1982. Ancud is a bustling, rambling port town with about 40,000 residents and is convenient for its proximity to Puerto Montt (but keep in mind that Castro is a more convenient base if you want to reach the island's outlying areas). This was the last Spanish outpost in Chile, and visitors can view the fort ruins here; there's also a good museum depicting Chilote history and culture.

GETTING THERE & DEPARTING   **By Bus**   For regular bus service from Puerto Montt to Ancud, see "Chiloé Essentials," above. Ancud has a central bus station, the **Terminal Municipal,** at the intersection of Avenida Aníbal Pinto and Marcos Vera; from here, you'll need to take a taxi to the center of town, or

Chiloé

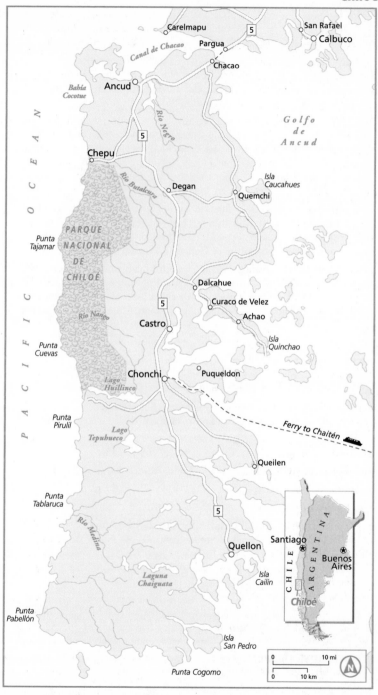

Carelmapu

San Rafael

Calbuco

5

Pargua

Canal de Chacao

Chacao

Bahía
Cocotue

Ancud

Golfo
de
Ancud

Río Negro

5

Chepu

Río Butalcura

Isla
Caucahues

Degan

Quemchi

Punta
Tajamar

PARQUE
NACIONAL
DE
CHILOÉ

Río Nanigo

Dalcahue

Curaco de Velez

Achao

Castro

Isla
Quinchao

Punta
Cuevas

Lago
Huillinco

Chonchi

Puqueldon

Punta
Pirulil

Lago
Tepuhueco

Ferry to Chaitén

Punta
Tablaruca

Río Medina

Queilen

5

Quellon

Santiago

Buenos
Aires

ARGENTINA

CHILE

Isla
Cailín

Chiloé

Laguna
Chaiguata

Punta
Pabellón

Isla
San Pedro

0   10 mi

0   10 km

Punta Cogomo

a local bus headed toward the plaza. Frequent buses leave from this station for destinations such as Castro, Dalcahue, and Quellón; try **Cruz del Sur** (© 65/622265), **Transchiloé** (© 65/622876), or **Queilen Bus** (© 65/621140).

By Car Ruta 5 (the PanAmerican Hwy.) is a well-paved road that links Ancud with nearly every city on the island. Beware of road works to widen the highway south of Ancud; expect delays (and muddy conditions on rainy days) until early 2004. The paved highway ends just south of Quellon.

ORIENTATION Ancud is spread across a tiny peninsula, with the Canal de Chacao to the east and the Golfo de Quetalmahue to the west, and it is 27km (17 miles) from the Chacao ferry dock. The city is not laid out on a regular grid pattern, and its crooked streets might easily confuse anyone driving into the city. **Avenida Aníbal Pinto** is the main entrance road that funnels drivers into the center of town. Most attractions are located within several blocks of the plaza.

VISITOR INFORMATION Sernatur's office is on the plaza, at Libertad 655 (© 65/622800). It's open daily from 8:30am to 8pm during January and February; the rest of the year it's open Monday through Thursday from 8:30am to 5:30pm and Friday from 8:30am to 4:30pm, and closed on weekends.

SPECIAL EVENTS From the second week in January to the last week of February, the city hosts the **"Different and Magical Summer of Ancud."** The event kicks off with classical music concerts and a 3-day food and folklore festival at the Arena Gruesa (3rd week in Jan) and a shore-fishing contest the second week of February, and culminates with a fireworks display, again in Arena Gruesa, the third week of February. For more information, call © **65/622800.**

FAST FACTS: ANCUD

Currency Exchange There are no places to exchange money here, but there are a couple of ATMs on Ramírez near the plaza.

Ferry Offices for the ferry company, Transmarchilay, for the Quellón-Chaitén connection, are next to the Sernatur office on the plaza at Libertad 669 (© 65/622317).

Hospital The hospital is at A. Latorre 301 (© **65/622356**).

Internet Access On the Costanera, Salvador Allende 740 (no phone).

Laundry **Clean Center,** Pudeto 45, half a block from the plaza.

WHAT TO SEE & DO

For boating excursions around Chiloé, try **Austral Adventures** (© 65/625977 or 09/642-8936; www.austral-adventures.com). These North American and British outfitters offer excursions by boat around Chiloé, as well as Pumalín Park. They also have excursions on land around the island and can arrange for transfer from Puerto Montt.

Fuerte San Antonio Built in 1770 and fortified with cannons aimed at the port entrance, Fort San Antonio was Spain's last stronghold in Chile after the War of Independence. The Spanish flag last flew here on January 19, 1826, and just 6 days later Peru's El Callao surrendered, ending Spanish rule in South America forever. The site affords a sweeping ocean view.

San Antonio and Cochrane (below Hostería Ancud). No phone. Free admission.

Museo Regional de Ancud Audelio Bórquez Canobra This handsome, well-designed museum features a wide variety of exhibits related to the history and culture of Chiloé. The museum includes a large courtyard with sculptures depicting the mythological characters that form part of Chilote folklore, as well as a replica of the ship *Ancud* that claimed possession of the Strait of Magellan in 1843, and a replica of a thatched Chilote house. Inside, two salons offer interactive displays and a variety of archaeological items, such as Indian arrowheads and nautical pieces, as well as displays explaining the farming and wool production techniques used by Chilotes. Temporary exhibits feature such themes as "Centuries of Textile Art in Chiloé."

Libertad 370. *Ⓒ* 65/622413. Admission 85¢ adults, 45¢ children. Jan–Feb Mon–Fri 11am–7:30pm, Sat–Sun 10am–7pm; Mar–Dec Mon–Fri 10am–6pm, Sat–Sun 10am–2pm.

SHOPPING

For a selection of regional handicrafts, including knitwear, baskets, and carved wooden utensils and crafts, try the **Centro Artesanal** in the Municipal Market (irregular hours, open late during the summer and to around 4pm during the winter). For superb smoked salmon and other local foodstuffs, stop on your way in or out of Chiloé at **Die Raucherkate,** a German-owned smokery located about 2km (1 mile) before the Chacao ferry dock (*Ⓒ* 65/622990). There is a huge "Smoked Salmon" sign that you won't miss, just off the main road.

WHERE TO STAY

Cabañas Las Golondrinas   This is a good choice for travelers seeking a little independence as well as crashing views of the ocean. Las Golondrinas offers pleasant accommodations complete with kitchens. They include cabins with two bedrooms that sleep up to six (2 sleep in the living area on *very* basic foam settees); bungalows with three bedrooms for up to six guests; and apartments that sleep four. All guest rooms sit precariously high on a cliff, about 10m (30 ft.) up from the beach, and the complex is just 4 blocks from Ancud's plaza. The interiors are made of wood, with giant windows and decks.

Baquedano s/n, Balneario Arena Gruesa, Ancud. *Ⓒ*/fax 65/622823. fmallagaray@LatinMail.com. 5 *cabañas*, 2 bungalows, 7 apts. $30 *cabaña* for 2, low season; $68 bungalow for 2, high season. AE, MC, V. **Amenities:** Restaurant; laundry service. *In room:* TV, fridge.

Hospedaje Alto Bellavista   The green-and-red Bellavista sits on a winding street a block from downtown, in an old home with one of the kitschiest living rooms around, crammed with photos, woodcarvings, and other fun knickknacks. The friendly owner offers clean but very modest accommodations. A steep stairwell leads to most of the rooms on the second floor, with a variety of double- and triple-bed arrangements, but the two rooms on the first floor are perhaps the best of the lot, with crisper furnishings. There's a small breakfast area.

Calle Bellavista 449, Ancud. *Ⓒ* 65/622384. 10 units. $17–$27 double. No credit cards. **Amenities:** Breakfast room. *In room:* No phone.

Hostal Lluhay   This hostal is on a dirt road 1 block from the pier, and it caters to a predominately international crowd. Rooms are slightly dark and very humble, but many bathrooms have been newly tiled. The open lounge has a fireplace and a picture window that looks out onto the sea, which should make you overlook an occasional hole in the burgundy carpet. The couple who own the Lluhay couldn't be nicer, and they're eager to show off their 200-year-old piano and antique Victrola.

Lord Cochrane 458, Ancud. *Ⓒ*/fax 65/622656. lluhay@entelchile.net. 10 units. $15–$25 double. No credit cards. **Amenities:** Lounge. *In room:* No phone.

"Sea-food" Everywhere: What to Eat on Chiloé

Part of Chiloé's appeal is the wide variety of seafood available around the island's shores and the typical dishes found only here on the island. Below are a few regional specialties to keep an eye out for:

Cancato   Salmon stuffed with sausage, tomatoes, and cheese and steamed in tinfoil.

Carapacho   A rich crab "casserole" with a breaded crust.

Curanto   Perhaps the most famous dish here in Chiloé, traditionally prepared in a hole in the ground (similar to a New England clambake). First, hot rocks are placed in the hole and then layered with mussels, clams, beef, pork, chicken, sausage, and potatoes and topped off with chewy pancakes called *milcaos*. Of course, most restaurants cook this dish in a pot, and often call it *pulmay*; it is then served with a cup of broth.

Hostería Ahui   The weatherbeaten, shingled facade of the Ahui would be appealing in a rustic sort of way if it weren't for the FOR SALE sign posted out front—which indicates a somewhat uncertain future for this barn of a hotel. The older couple who own this humble place don't seem to be having much luck selling (it's been on the market for over 3 years) so it's worth a shot to score one of the five sunny rooms that face the ocean. The simple rooms are what you'd expect for this price range, with very average furnishings and beds. The hotel's size gives guests some breathing room, unlike many hostals in town. The staff is open to negotiating a lower price, especially in low season, so it's worth bargaining once you get here.

Costanera 906, Ancud. (C) **65/622415.** 22 units. $24 double. Kids stay free in parent's room. No credit cards. **Amenities:** Lounge. *In room:* No phone.

Hostería Ancud ★   Part of the Panamerican Hotel chain, the Hostería Ancud is the best option in this price range, especially for its location fronting the Gulf of Quetalmahue and next to the ruins of the old Fort San Antonio. All rooms come with a partial view of the ocean, as does the airy, split-level lounge and restaurant and the large outdoor deck. Rooms are somewhat tight, but offer all the necessary comforts. The interior bedroom walls are made of polished alerce logs, and the lobby is adorned with woodcarvings from the region. The *hostería* also has one of the better restaurants in town (see "Where to Dine," below) as well as a cozy bar with a giant fireplace.

San Antonio 30, Ancud. (C) **65/622340.** Fax 65/622350. www.hosteriancud.com. 24 units. $60–$74 double. AE, DC, MC, V. **Amenities:** Restaurant; bar; lounge. *In room:* TV.

Hotel Galeón Azul   Like the Hostería Ancud, this hotel's strength is its location—perched high on a cliff above the sea—and although the rooms are not nearly as nice, some travelers prefer the character of this bed-and-breakfast to the Ancud. With porthole windows, a nautical motif, and curved walls, the big, sunflower-yellow hotel feels somewhat like a ship—an aging ship, that is. Upstairs an intriguing, narrow hallway has a high ceiling that peaks into skylights. The hotel is next to the regional museum; large windows look out onto the museum's sculpture garden. The rooms are very so-so, with dated furnishings, stained carpets, and walls that look suspiciously as though made of plywood; the small bathrooms could also use a face-lift. The most attractive part of the hotel is its sunny restaurant, with glass walls that look out onto the ocean.

Av. Libertad 751, Ancud. ℂ 65/625234. Fax 65/625235. 16 units. $42–$60 double. No credit cards. **Amenities:** Restaurant. *In room:* TV, no phone in some rooms.

Hotel Caulín *Finds* *Kids*   This is the spot for anyone looking for a waterfront location outside town. The Hotel Caulín has a dining area and four comfortable rooms in a pretty, antique home, but what's really nice are the cabins, eight of which sit 33m (100 ft.) from the shore and seven that sit high on a bluff. This lodging option is really better for those with a private vehicle because the hamlet of Caulín is about 25km (16 miles) from Ancud, although taxi service is available for a moderate cost. All cabins look out over a splendid estuary, and they are backed by forest. Each cabin has two bedrooms, one with a full-size bed and the other with a twin and bunk bed. The spacious living area has wood floors and is warmed by a *cancahua,* a ceramic fireplace typical of the region. The interiors are rustic with tweedy bedspreads and curtains, and there's a fully stocked kitchen. The Hotel Caulín also has a restaurant but most guests opt to dine a few minutes walk down the beach at the popular Ostras Caulín (see "Where to Dine," below).

Road to Caulín, 9km (5½ miles) from port of Chacao. ℂ 65/267150. Fax in Santiago 2/225-8697. 4 units, 15 cabins. $35–$58 cabin. No credit cards. **Amenities:** Restaurant; outdoor pool; tennis court; sauna. *In room:* No phone.

WHERE TO DINE

For good, inexpensive seafood meals, including Chilote dishes such as *curanto, carapacho,* and *cancato,* try **La Pincoya** at Av. Prat 61 (ℂ **65/622613**), which also offers great views of fishermen at the pier engaging in hectic business from their colorful fishing skiffs. One restaurant popular with tourists and locals alike is **Sacho** (no phone), which can be found inside the market. Across from the market is **El Cangrejo** (no phone), which specializes in crab *carapacho* and features walls covered in graffiti and business cards. Another good bet is **Kurantón** at Prat 94 (ℂ **65/622216**), which, as the name implies, specializes in *curanto.* None of the restaurants here get busy enough to warrant making reservations.

Galeón Azul CHILEAN   The Galeón's yellow-painted dining area offers great views, so be sure to get a table that sits up against the front windows. The menu here features several Chilote specials such as *curanto,* as well as the standard Chilean fish and meat grilled and served with a choice of sauces. Try the salmon stuffed with ham and mushrooms or the garlicky *locos* (abalone).

Av. Libertad 751. ℂ 65/625234. Main courses $4–$7. No credit cards. Daily 11am–3pm and 7–11pm.

Hostería Ancud INTERNATIONAL/CHILEAN   The expansive dining area here commands a superb view of the ocean, and there's a good offering from the menu that mixes Chilean specialties with international dishes. Seafood such as oysters on the half shell and king crab are offered as appetizers, as well as king crab casserole and conger eel with sea urchin sauce. Meat dishes include pork loin with mustard sauce and risotto. There's also a bar for a quiet evening drink. If weather permits, you can watch the sunset from the deck.

San Antonio 30. ℂ 65/622340. Main courses $5–$8. AE, DC, MC, V. Daily noon–11pm.

Ostras Caulín ★ *(Finds)* CHILEAN/OYSTERS   Oyster lovers should not miss this tiny restaurant on the shore of Caulín, about 9km (5½ miles) from Chacao and 25km (16 miles) from Ancud (from the ferry, follow the signs and turn right onto a gravel road). The restaurant, with its hardwood floors and red tablecloths, sits on an estuary, where they farm their own oysters, and they offer three sizes: *especial, extra,* and *exportación,* all on the half shell and all exceptionally fresh. The menu is limited, offering just oysters, cream of oyster soup, and beef stew. Afternoon tea is served with cakes and sandwiches daily from 3 to 7pm. The service here is attentive, and the dining area has a nice view. The restaurant caters almost exclusively to visiting foreigners, so don't expect to mingle with locals here.

On the shore in Caulín. ⓒ/fax **09/643-7005.** Main courses $5–$7. AE, DC, MC, V. Daily 8am–10pm (until midnight Jan–Feb).

3 Castro

146km (91 miles) S of Ancud; 99km (61 miles) N of Quellón

Castro is spread across a promontory on the western shore of Chiloé, midway from Ancud and Quellón. It is the capital of Chiloé and Chile's third-oldest city, boasting a population of about 21,000 inhabitants. Visitors to the island often choose Castro as a base for its central proximity to a host of attractions. But the town has a charm all its own, with its city church brightly painted like an Easter egg, and the city's colorful homes on stilts, known as *palafitos.*

ESSENTIALS

GETTING AROUND   By Bus   You'll find the bus terminal at the corner of Esmerelda and Sotomayor. For buses to Dalcahue and Isla Quinchao, take **Buses Arriagada** at San Martín 681; for Dalcahue and Chonchi, take **Colectivos** from the Terminal Municipal; for Isla Lemuy, take **Buses Gallardo** from its office at San Martín 681; and for transportation to the national park, take **Buses Arroyo** or **Buses Ojeda** from the Terminal Municipal. The majority of these bus companies are independently owned and operated, so it's difficult to obtain reliable information about schedules and fares in advance. We recommend showing up at the terminal or checking at the tourist information kiosk (see "Visitor Information," below) to ask questions or book a tour.

By Car   To get to Castro from Ancud, head south on the island's only highway for 146km (88 miles), and from Quellon, north on the highway for 99km (59 miles). Please note that until early 2004 there will be extensive road-works on the highway South from Ancud to Castro. Be prepared for delays—figure in an extra 20 to 30 minutes to your trip.

VISITOR INFORMATION   A tiny, privately run **tourism kiosk** on the main plaza offers a fairly poor selection of information. During the summer, the kiosk is open all day, but during the winter it can close unexpectedly.

SPECIAL EVENTS   Every February, for 1 week, Castro hosts one of the more interesting events in Chile, the **Festival Costumbrista Chilote,** a celebration of the unique Chilote culture, history, and mythical folklore that make up Chiloé. The festival highlights the island's gastronomy, played out through expositions and booth after booth selling mouth-watering samples. There are also demonstrations of the giant wooden press used to make *chicha,* an alcohol usually made from fermented apples. For more information, call ⓒ **65/632289.**

FAST FACTS: CASTRO

Currency Exchange   Julio Barrientos, Chacabuco 286 (© **65/635079**), is open Monday through Friday from 9am to 12pm and 3 to 7pm; Saturday from 9am to 12pm; from December to March they do not close for lunch.

Hospital   Hospital Augusta Rifat, Freie 852 (© **65/632444**).

Internet Access   Hostería Castro (see below) offers Internet access for its guests, free of charge. If you're not staying there, try **Café de la Brújula,** O'Higgins 308 (© **65/633229**); open daily from 10am to midnight.

Laundry   Clean Center, Serrano 490 (© **65/633132**).

Travel Agency   LanChile's representative is **Pehuén Expediciones,** Blanco 229 (© **65/635254**); open Monday through Friday from 9am to 1:30pm and 3 to 7pm, Saturday from 10am to 1pm, closed Sunday.

WHAT TO SEE & DO IN CASTRO

You might begin a tour of Castro at the plaza and the neo-Gothic **Iglesia de San Francisco** ★★ church, painted brightly in peach, lilac, and white. It's impossible to miss, and that's really the point; this 1912 national monument always stands out, especially on dreary, gray Chiloé days (which is pretty much ¾ of the year).

From there, head down Esmerelda toward the waterfront and drop by the town's small **Museo Regional de Castro,** half a block from the plaza (© **65/635967**). It's open from January to February Monday through Saturday from 9:30am to 8pm and Sunday from 10:30am to 1pm; from March to December, Monday through Friday from 9:30am to 1pm and 3 to 6:30pm, Saturday from 9:30am to 1pm, and closed on Sunday; admission is free although a small donation is suggested. The museum features displays of Chilote farming and household wooden implements, such as plows and weaving looms; religious icons; Indian artifacts such as arrowheads, bones, and *boleadores;* as well as an interesting photographic exhibit of the damage done to Castro after the 1960 earthquake and flood.

Castro's main attraction would have to be its *palafitos,* colorful houses built near the shore but atop stilts over water. There are four main spots to view these architectural oddities. The first two sites are at the town entrance, the third site is on the coast at the end of San Martín, and the fourth is at the cove of the Castro Fjord, on the way out of town on Ruta 5. Residents are often baffled as to why tourists find these dwellings so fascinating because locally they are considered Castro's "ghetto," occupied by poor folk with questionable sanitary conditions.

A short taxi ride will take you to the **Parque Municipal,** home to the Costumbrista Festival in February and the surprisingly well-designed **Museo de Arte Moderno (MAM;** © **65/635454**). Admission is free, and it's open daily January and February from 10am to 6pm; November, December, and March from 11am to 2pm. It's closed April through October; you might be able to arrange a private viewing if you call ahead. If the weather is clear, visitors to the park are treated to superb views of Castro and the Andes. The MAM, housed in several renovated shingled buildings, is one of the only contemporary art museums in the country, and it often hosts exhibitions by some of Chile's most prominent artists.

SHOPPING

The **Feria Artesanal,** on Lillo at the port, brings together dozens of artisans who offer a superb selection of handknitted woolen goods and handicrafts. Here you'll find the island's typical tightly woven ponchos; the raw wool used makes them water resistant. Vendors open their booths independently, and hours are roughly from 10am to 5pm April through November, and from 10am to 9pm December through March.

WHERE TO STAY

Hostal Kolping *(Value)* This hostal is a great value for the price, and really the best place to stay if you're looking for inexpensive lodging. The rooms are sunny and immaculately clean, and they come with beds with thick foam mattresses that are adequately comfortable. The rooms are all rather nondescript, but they are reasonably spacious and so are the bathrooms. The exteriors are attractive, with a newly replaced shingled facade; the deck has also been covered, thereby creating a bright dining area and wide foyer. A German company owns this and other Kolping hostals around the Lake District, including the Termas de San Luis, and they can be relied on for economical, quality lodging.

Chacabuco 217, Castro. Ⓒ/fax **65/633273**. 11 units. $22–$34 double. No credit cards. **Amenities:** Lounge. *In room:* TV.

Hostería Castro *⭐* This *hostería* is about as upscale as hotels get in Castro. Built in 1970, the hotel has done a decent job of maintaining the place, but a slight renovation wouldn't hurt, as evidenced by the dated leather sofas and end tables with faded glass rings. The bar and its giant cast-iron fireplace contribute to the warm atmosphere. The hotel overlooks the ocean, and all rooms on the eastern side (rooms ending in odd numbers) have views of the water; rooms on the western side have a leafy view of a stand of trees. Rooms are very cramped, so much so that it is hard to walk around the bed. A few are slightly more spacious for the same price, so be sure to ask for one. The white-tiled bathrooms are ample. The A-frame, shingled roof has a skylight in the form of a glass band that runs through the roof's middle, letting in a cascade of light that brightens the interior hallways. Service is exceptionally friendly and the bar is popular with traveling Europeans, as is Las Araucarias restaurant (see "Where to Dine," below). There's also a computer with free Internet access for guests.

Chacabuco 202, Castro. Ⓒ **65/632301**. Fax 65/635688. Hoboston@telsur.cl. 29 units. $53–$64 double. AE, DC, MC, V. **Amenities:** 2 restaurants; bar; room service; laundry service. *In room:* TV.

Hotel Casita Española All 13 rooms are exactly the same here, set up motel-like with two stories. The lobby faces the street, but the rooms are reached via a pretty walkway sandwiched between a tall residential building and the hotel. You won't be wowed when you walk into your room, but the quality is about par for the price: thick foam mattresses, drab but decent decor, a tiny desk used primarily as a TV stand, and okay bathrooms with tubs. There's an eating area next to the reception area for breakfast.

Los Carrera 359, Castro. Ⓒ/fax **65/635186**. 13 units. $25–$40 double. AE, MC, V. **Amenities:** Lounge. *In room:* TV.

Hotel Esmeralda This newer hotel is just steps from the main plaza and is a good alternative to the Hostería Castro, but not nearly as charming. Rooms are small but modern and have flowery bedspreads and decent mattresses. The bathrooms, though clean, are tiny. The best unit is the large suite with its enormous whirlpool tub next to the king-size bed, and a separate shower in the spacious bathroom. There's a good restaurant on the top (3rd) floor offering the usual Chilean specialties at reasonable prices. But if you stay here you'll probably want to dine at the nearby Anoz Luz (see "Where to Dine," below). There's also a room with two billiard tables. If you're traveling alone, be sure to request one of the discounted "single rooms" that come with one small bed.

Esmeralda 266, Castro. ⓒ **65/637900.** Fax 65/637910. Hesmeralda@telsur.cl. 32 units. $42–$58 double; from $69 suite. MC, V. **Amenities:** Restaurant; bar; room service. *In room:* TV.

Unicornio Azul *Overrated*   Many people say this is the best place to stay in Castro—but we'll let you be the judge. It's a fun place to stay, but don't expect regal comfort. Certainly the hotel has character; it's housed in a pretty Victorian on the waterfront, with funky interiors decorated with framed prints of unicorns. But the quality the Unicornio Azul seems to promise from the lobby falls short once you step into the rooms. The best rooms sit high above the main building facing out toward the water, and they come with tiny balconies and wooden floors. But they're unremarkable, and you have to hike up a long flight of stairs to get to them. Downstairs rooms are darker but carpeted, and a few come with bathtubs. The hotel was built in 1910 and renovated in 1986—both "Years of the Comet," as the staff likes to say. The exterior is painted as pink as a Mary Kay Cadillac, and much of the wooden beams and floor-runner carpets are sugary shades of pink, too. The owners of this hotel also own Ancud's Galeón Azul.

Pedro Montt 228, Castro. ⓒ **65/632359.** Fax 65/632808. 17 units. $61–$81 double. No credit cards. **Amenities:** Restaurant; bar. *In room:* TV.

WHERE TO DINE

Anoz Luz ✫ *Value* INTERNATIONAL/PUB   Right on the main plaza, this is the newest and most happening place in Castro. The attractive main dining area with its hardwood floors has windows looking out onto bustling San Martín street where locals sip coffee, pisco sours, and beer. A simple but delicious selection of salads, sandwiches, and a few meat dishes are served. The smoked salmon salad is yummy, with lots of fresh green lettuce and locally smoked salmon, and the steak and fries is the top choice for a main course. The back area has more of a pub feel, with tables closer together and local Castro "yuppies" drinking pint-size beers. The unusual bar area is carved out from a real wooden boat.

San Martín 309. ⓒ **65/532-700.** Main courses $4–$6. MC, V. Daily 9am–midnight.

Café La Brújula del Cuerpo CAFE   This sizeable cafe on the plaza (the name translates as "the Body's Compass") is the social center for residents of Castro. It's perennially active thanks to its friendly service and extensive menu offering sandwiches, salads, main dishes, ice cream, desserts, espresso, and delicious fresh juices. The cafe/restaurant is open all day, and you'll often find travelers writing out postcards here. There's one computer for Internet use.

O'Higgins 308. ⓒ **65/633229.** Main courses $4–$7; sandwiches $2–$4. MC, V. Daily 10am–midnight.

Las Araucarias ✫ INTERNATIONAL/CHILEAN   Las Araucarias is Hostería Castro's restaurant, and is one of the top places to dine in town. The atmosphere is better during lunchtime, with the view and the airy interiors brought on by the two-story-high ceilings and a wall of windows; at night the dining room's size seems to encourage echoes, but it is comfortable nevertheless. The menu is steak and seafood, featuring Chilean classics and Chiloé specialties such as *carapacho* and *curanto*. Other delicious seafood dishes offered are crab casserole, sea-urchin omelets, and garlicky squid. There's also a wide selection of meat dishes, such as filet mignon wrapped in bacon and served with sautéed vegetables. You might want to call ahead; the hotel often has a buffet special that is usually themed (German food, for example), and although it is quite good, it might not be what you're in the mood for.

Chacabuco 202. ✆ **65/632301**. Fax 65/635688. Main courses $5–$9. AE, DC, MC, V. Mon–Sat noon–midnight; Sun (Dec 15–Mar 15 only) noon–11pm.

Octavio _Finds_ CHILEAN   Octavio has the best atmosphere in Castro, with an idyllic, airy dining area that sits directly over the water, and a panorama of windows showcasing the view. It also has a woodsy, shingled exterior and interior. Octavio is a great place to come for Chilote specials—it's known around town for its _curanto_. It also serves seafood specials such as _mariscal_, a shellfish stew made with onion and cilantro, and other typical Chilean dishes, such as breaded cutlets and filet mignon. Fish is delivered daily so be sure to ask what's freshest. Simple menu and simple food, but all very good, and a few sandwiches and soups. Octavio is typically more popular with visitors to Castro, while Sacho (see below) is more popular with locals.

Pedro Montt 261. ✆ **65/632855**. Main courses $5–$9. No credit cards. Daily 10am–midnight.

Sacho ✦ _Value_ SEAFOOD/CHILEAN   Sacho serves the best cuisine in Castro, a fact clearly evident by the throngs of locals who patronize the restaurant daily. There are two seating areas, neither of which is particularly eye-catching, but the upstairs dining room at least has large windows and a view of the water. The specialty here is seafood, and they serve the most inexpensive abalone _locos_ we've seen anywhere in Chile. Try starting off with a plate of clams Sacho raw, steamed, or broiled and served with onion, lemon, whisky, and Parmesan, then follow it up with a _cancato_. Typically the only fish served here is _congrio_ (conger eel) and salmon, but they do have hake and sea bass from December to March.

Thompson 213. ✆ **65/632079**. Main courses $4–$7. No credit cards. Daily noon–4pm and 8pm–midnight.

4 Excursions Outside Castro ✦

Few Chilean towns supersede the charming beauty of **Dalcahue, Achao,** and **Curaco de Vélez,** the latter two located on the **Isla Quinchao.** The towns and the countryside separating them are Chiloé highlights, offering gorgeous scenery and a glimpse into the Chilote's culture and day-to-day life.

DALCAHUE & ISLA QUINCHAO

Just off of Route 5, the island's only major highway, **Dalcahue** is a little town whose prosperity is best illustrated by the hustle and bustle of salmon industry workers at the pier, unloading and loading crates of fish byproducts to be processed. Dalcahue's other thriving industry (although to a smaller scale) is its **Feria Artesanal,** located at the waterfront about 2 blocks southwest of the plaza. Every Thursday and Sunday, artisans come to Dalcahue from the surrounding area to hawk their knitwear, baskets, hand-carved wood items, clothing, and more. At the plaza you'll have a chance to view another of the island's famous parochial churches. This particular attractive church features a scalloped portico and is one of the largest in Chiloé. Across the plaza, on the corner, you'll find the **Museo Histórico Arqueológico Etnográfico** (no phone); it's open daily from 10am to 6pm, with a cluttered array of stuffed birds and Indian and colonial-era artifacts.

For directions to Dalcahue, see "Essentials" under Castro, above. All transportation stops in Dalcahue first, before crossing over to Quinchao.

Several blocks away at Dalcahue's pier, you'll find the ferry to **Isla Quinchao.** The ferry makes the 5-minute ride almost continuously from 7am to 10:30pm every day ($1.50 for cars, $2.50 for pickup trucks). This is one of Chiloé's most-populated islands, a magical landscape of plump, rolling hills where smoke slowly wafts from picturesque, wooden homes, and Chilote farmers can be seen tilling their land with oxen and a plow. The island also affords the visitor with spectacular views of the Gulf of Ancud and the scattered, pint-size islands that sit between the Isla Quinchao and the mainland.

The first town you'll encounter upon exiting the ferry is **Curaco de Vélez,** a historic village whose former prosperity brought about by wool production and whaling can be witnessed through the grand, weatherbeaten homes that line the streets. The homes are characterized by a great variety of shingle styles, from concave to convex, circular to triangular. The town's antique church unfortunately burned to the ground in 1971.

Continue southeast along the island's single, unnamed main road to **Achao,** a former Jesuit colony founded in 1743 that features the oldest church in Chiloé. Made entirely of cypress, alerce, and mañío, this church appears as plain as a brown paper bag from the outside, but one step inside and all impressions change due to its multicolored interiors and whimsical decorations. Throughout the Island of Quinchao, you'll find wooden gazebos atop well-designed lookout points. Here's hoping the weather allows you to take full advantage of them.

PARQUE NACIONAL CHILOE

Chiloé National Park, on the western coast of Chiloé, covers 43,000 hectares (106,210 acres) and is divided into three sectors: **Chepu, Islote Metalqui,** and **Anay,** the latter of which is connected by a dirt road that branches off Ruta 5, about 25km (15 miles) south of Castro. For transportation to the national park, take **Buses Arroyo** or **Buses Ojeda** (no phone) from the Terminal Municipal. The park is wild and wet—very, very wet. Many backpackers come in the summer to hike through the park's primordial forest and along vast stretches of sandy beach that often peak into sand dunes

Visitors first arrive at the tiny village of **Cucao,** the gateway to the national park, which was devastated by a 1960 tidal wave; today it is a collection of rickety homes. **Posada Darwin** (© 65/633040), closed June and July, is a restaurant that serves pizzas and seafood and offers inexpensive *cabañas*. Across the suspension bridge visitors will find the park interpretation center run by Conaf (Chile's national park service), which has environmental displays and information about hiking trails. From here hikers have an option of three trails. The short, 770m (839-yd.) **Sendero el Tepual** winds through thick, humid tepú forest. The **Sendero Dunas de Cucao** is about 1km (a little over ½ mile), and it passes alternately through dense vegetation and open stretches of sand dunes. The most beautiful hike is a 20km (12-mile) backpacking route via a long trail on the coast, which weaves in and out of evergreen forest and sandy beach until arriving at Conaf's backcountry refuge, **Cole.** From here it's another 2 hours to Conaf's other refuge, **Anay.** Parque Nacional Chiloé has a variety of campsites, and it is open every day from 9am to 7pm; admission is 70¢ adults, free for children. While here, keep your eyes open for the miniature deer (*pudú*).

GUIDED TOURS AND OTHER ACTIVITIES

Pehuén Turismo at 299 Blanco in Castro (© 65/635254; pehuentr@entelchile. net) offers a huge variety of tours in the area, including hiking in the national park, guided visits to Dalcahue and Achao, horseback riding, boat tours, and overflight tours that give passengers an aerial view of the island. It's really the most complete tour agency; however, **Queilén Travels** at Gamboa 502 (© 65/ 632594) also offers guided tours around the area.

16

The Carretera Austral

South of Puerto Montt the population thins and the vegetation thickens. This is La Carretera Austral, or the Southern Highway, a region that has only recently opened itself up to the traveling public. The Carretera Austral is a 1,000km (620-mile) dirt and gravel road that bends and twists through thick, virgin rainforest; glacial-fed rivers and aquamarine lakes; jagged, white-capped peaks that rise above open valleys; and precipitous cliffs with cascading ribbons of waterfalls at every turn. If you like your scenery remote and rugged, this is your place.

The Carretera Austral runs from **Puerto Montt** in the north to **Puerto Yungay** in the south, and passes through two regions: the southern portion of the **Región Los Lagos** and

the **Región Aisén,** whose capital city **Coyhaique** is home to more than half the population in the area. Apart from Coyhaique, the region was previously accessible from other locations only by ferry or plane, and vehicles servicing the tiny villages and fishing hamlets that make up the area's civilization had to enter from Argentina. It's no wonder they call it the "last frontier."

The road exists thanks to ex-dictator Augusto Pinochet, whose paranoia of Argentine encroachment convinced him that a road would fortify Chile's presence in this isolated region. Construction of the Carretera Austral began in 1976, but wasn't fully completed until 1996, at a staggering cost: more than $300 million (and counting) and the lives of more than two dozen men.

1 Driving the Carretera Austral ★ ★

Although it is possible to reach most destinations in this region by ferry, bus, or plane, road improvements and an expansion of services mean an increasing number of travelers are choosing to drive the Carretera Austral. It's not as enormous an undertaking as it sounds, but it can be costly, especially when you factor in the cost of ferry rides, drop-off fees, and gas.

Several agencies in Puerto Montt and Coyhaique offer one-way car rentals, and some allow you to cross into Argentina or leave the car as far away as Punta Arenas, Chile. (See "Essentials" under "Puerto Montt," in chapter 14.) Alternatively, you could rent a car in Coyhaique and drive north, stopping in Puyuhuapi and on to Futaleufú. Although you'd have to backtrack to Coyhaique to return the car, this is a less expensive option. (See "Coyhaique," later in this chapter, for information.)

The most troublesome considerations are flat tires, gas shortages, and foul weather, any of which can strike at any time. With advance preparation, however, these obstacles can be overcome.

FERRY CROSSINGS The trip from Puerto Montt to Caleta Gonzalo or Chaitén requires a ferry crossing (in operation Dec–Mar only). For crossings to Caleta Gonzalo, see "Ferry Crossings to Caleta Gonzalo" below under "Parque

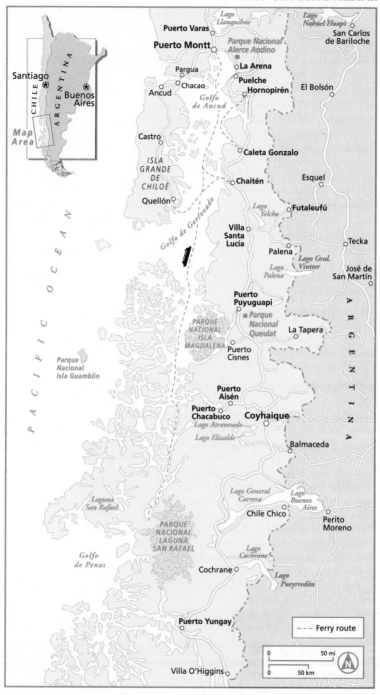

Lago Llanquihue
Lago Nahuel Huapi
San Carlos de Bariloche
Puerto Varas
Puerto Montt
Parque Nacional Alerce Andino
Pargua
La Arena
Puelche
Chacao
Hornopirén
El Bolsón
Ancud
Golfo de Ancud
Castro
Caleta Gonzalo
ISLA GRANDE DE CHILOÉ
Chaitén
Esquel
Quellón
Lago Yelcho
Futaleufú
Golfo de Corcovado
Villa Santa Lucía
Tecka
Palena
Lago Gral. Vintter
José de San Martín
Lago Palena
Puerto Puyuguapi
Parque Nacional Queulat
La Tapera
PARQUE NACIONAL ISLA MAGDALENA
Puerto Cisnes
Parque Nacional Isla Guamblin
Puerto Aisén
Puerto Chacabuco
Coyhaique
Lago Atravesado
Lago Elizalde
Balmaceda
Laguna San Rafael
Lago General Carrera
Lago Buenos Aires
Chile Chico
Perito Moreno
PARQUE NACIONAL LAGUNA SAN RAFAEL
Lago Cochrane
Golfo de Penas
Cochrane
Lago Pueyrredón
Puerto Yungay

- - - Ferry route

| 0 | | 50 mi |
| 0 | | 50 km |

Villa O'Higgins

CHILE
ARGENTINA
Santiago
Buenos Aires
Map Area

PACIFIC OCEAN

361

Nacional Alerce Andino." See "Ferry Crossings to the Carretera Austral & Sailing to Patagonia Through the Fjords" in chapter 14 for information on ferries to Chaitén.

GAS Service stations can be found at reasonable intervals, and some smaller towns such as Futaleufú sell gas in jugs from stores or private residences, but most travelers take precautions by carrying a backup canister of fuel. Canisters can be purchased from any service station.

CROSSING INTO ARGENTINA Drivers who head into Argentina must prove that they are the owner of their car, or have their rental agency set up the proper paperwork to show they are driving a rental car. Make sure to ask your rental agency about this. There's also an extra insurance that usually has to be purchased, averaging around $130 per car. Drivers must fill out a detailed form and are then given a copy to carry with them until crossing back into Chile.

ROAD CONDITIONS The Carretera Austral is made entirely of dirt and gravel, which can get slippery during a storm. A 4×4 vehicle isn't necessary, but can help, especially if snow is in the forecast. Giant potholes are the exception, not the norm, but they can cause a car to spin out or even flip if driving too fast. For this reason, drivers are cautioned to keep speed between 40kmph (25 mph) and 60kmph (37 mph). When it's wet or the road curves, you need to slow down even more.

HITCHHIKERS Road courtesy dictates that you might have to pick up a hitchhiker or two along the way. Most hitchhikers are humble, local folk who simply do not have the means to get from place to place (during the summer many foreign backpackers try to get a lift, too). Use your own judgment. You should always lend a hand to anyone whose car has broken down.

GETTING AROUND BY BUS

There's inexpensive, frequent summer service and intermittent winter service to and from destinations along the Carretera Austral for those who choose not to drive. It takes longer, and you won't have the opportunity to stop at points of interest along the way; however, every town has a tour operator that can usually get you to outlying sites for day trips. Also, the breathtaking scenery never fails to dazzle, even if you can't get off the bus.

For the 5-hour journey from Puerto Montt to Hornopirén (for the summer-only ferry to Caleta Gonzalo), take **Buses Fierro** (© **65/253600**), which leaves from the main bus terminal three times daily. The bus makes one 30-minute ferry crossing before landing in Hornopirén (cost is $6). From there you take another ferry to Caleta Gonzalo, where buses meet ferry arrivals for the journey to Chaitén. Buses from Chaitén leave for Futaleufú an average of five to six times per week during the summer, and about three times per week during the winter.

Buses from Chaitén to Coyhaique, stopping first in Puyuhuapi, leave up to four times per week during the summer and twice per week during the winter. For information about buses from Chaitén, see "Getting There" under "Chaitén," below. Note that bus schedules are subject to change without notice.

2 Parque Nacional Alerce Andino ★★

32km (20 miles) SE of Puerto Montt

The Carretera Austral begins as Ruta 7, just outside the city limits of Puerto Montt, and follows the coast of Reloncaví Sound until it reaches **Parque**

Nacional Alerce Andino, one of Chile's little-known national parks. This 39,255-hectare (96,960-acre) park is home to the *alerce,* which is often compared to the sequoia for its thick diameter and height. These venerable giants can live more than 3,000 years, making them the second-oldest tree, after the American bristlecone pine. The *alerce* was designated a national monument in 1976, and heavy fines are levied against anyone caught harming or cutting one down. Other species in the park include evergreen beech, *mañío, canelo, ulmo,* and thick crops of ferns. It can get pretty wet here year-round, so bring rain gear just in case.

The park itself is serviced by a rough dirt road that leads to a **Conaf guard station** in what's known as the **Chaica sector,** where there is a campground and the trail head for the half-hour round-trip walk to a waterfall and a fenced-off 3,000-year-old *alerce* tree. The walk to Lago Triángulo is about 10km (6 miles) from the campground. Roads, trails, and campgrounds are often washed out or impeded by falling trees. Be sure to check the park's condition before heading out. For more information, contact the Conaf office in Puerto Montt at Ochagavía 464 (© 65/290712; www.conaf.cl).

The park's second sector at **Lago Chapo** also has campgrounds and two muddy trails for day hikes through the park's rainforest, a section of which has a thick stand of alerce trees. Though this sector sees fewer visitors, it is more difficult to get to if you do not have your own vehicle because buses go as far as the pueblo Correntoso, a 2-hour walk from the park entrance (although it is possible to arrange a tour; see "Getting There," below). At the park ranger station here it is possible to rent canoes for a paddle across Lago Chapo.

GETTING THERE   If you're driving, head south on Ruta 7, winding past tiny villages on a gravel road until you reach Chaica, about 35km (22 miles) from Puerto Montt, where a sign indicates the road to the park entrance at the left. The park ranger station is open from 9am to 5pm, so leave your car outside the gate if you plan to return later than 5pm. Travelers without a vehicle can take **Buses Fierro** (© 65/253600) headed in the direction of Hornopirén from the main terminal in Puerto Montt (ask to be dropped off at Chaica); however, the bus, which costs $1.15, leaves visitors at an entrance road 4km (2½ miles) from the park ranger station. You might consider hiring a tour operator to take a day trip or possibly to organize an advance pickup date if you plan to camp. To get to the Lago Chapo sector, head south on Ruta 7 for about 9km (5½ miles) to Chamiza; just before the bridge, take a left toward the town Correntoso and drive 19km (12 miles) to the park entrance. Buses Fierro (© 65/253600) has several daily trips, costing $1.30, to Correntoso that leave from the main terminal in Puerto Montt; from here, it's a 2-hour walk to the park entrance. For tours to either of the park's sectors, try **Andina del Sud,** in Puerto Varas at Antonio Varas 437 (© 65/257797; crucedelagos@chilesat.net); the company also has an office in Puerto Montt, at del Salvador 72 (© 65/232811).

WHERE TO STAY

Alerce Mountain Lodge ★ *(Finds)*   This quiet, remote lodge sits on the shore of a small lake—which must be crossed by a hand-drawn ferry—at the edge of the national park, and is surrounded by dense stands of stately, 1,000-year-old *alerce* trees.

The lodge is about a 1-hour drive from Puerto Montt (they provide transportation from there), and is built almost entirely of handcrafted *alerce* logs, with giant trunks acting as pillars in the spacious, two-story lobby. The woodsy effect continues in the cozy rooms, which are decorated with local crafts and feature forest views. The cabins have a view of the lake and come with a living room and two bedrooms, and accommodate a maximum of five guests. One of the highlights at this lodge is that the surrounding trails are not open to the general public, so you practically have them to yourself. Bilingual guides lead horseback rides and day hikes that can last as long as 7 hours or as little as a half hour.

Carretera Austral, Km 36. ©/fax **65/286969**. www.mountainlodge.cl. 11 units, 3 *cabañas*. All-inclusive packages run per person, double occupancy: 1 night/2 days $230; 3 nights/4 days $680. Inquire about other packages and off-season discounts. AE, DC, MC, V. **Amenities:** Restaurant; bar; Jacuzzi; sauna; game room; laundry service.

FERRY CROSSINGS TO CALETA GONZALO

The portion of the Carretera Austral from Puerto Montt to Caleta Gonzalo crosses two bodies of water—meaning you'll have to make two ferry crossings, or get to Caleta Gonzalo by driving up from the south. The first ferry crossing from La Arena to Puelche runs year-round; unfortunately the second, from Hornopirén to Caleta Gonzalo, is available January and February only. This means that the rest of the year the only ways to get from Puerto Montt to Caleta Gonzalo are: to travel through Argentina, reenter Chile at Futaleufú and then drive north; or to take the year-round ferry from Puerto Montt to Chaitén (see chapter 14)—or the ferry from Quellón, in Chiloé (see chapter 15), to Chaitén—and then drive from Chaitén to Caleta Gonzalo.

Leaving from Chaica, south of Puerto Montt, the road continues for 13km (8 miles) to Caleta La Arena, departure and arrival point for the 30-minute ferry ride that connects with Caleta Puelche. **Transmarchilay** ferries, Av. Angelmó 2187, Puerto Montt (© **65/270416;** www.transmarchilay.cl), make about nine runs a day, from 8am to 9pm or so, depending on the season and any unforeseen changes. From Puelche it's a 54km (34-mile) drive to Hornopirén, a pretty village that is the summer ferry terminal for trips to Caleta Gonzalo, in Pumalín Park (a 5-hr. crossing). Transmarchilay offers service between Hornopirén and Caleta Gonzalo every day except Monday and Friday, leaving Hornopirén at 4pm and Caleta Gonzalo at 9am; the fare is $20 per person, $100 per car.

3 Pumalín Park ★★

The Pumalín Park Project, the world's largest private nature reserve, spans roughly 303,500 hectares (750,000 acres) and incorporates a breathtaking landscape that includes temperate rainforest, glaciers, fjords, thundering waterfalls and rivers, and stands of ancient *alerce* trees. It's a marvelous place that exists thanks to American millionaire and philanthropist Douglas Thompkins, who bought his first chunk of land here in 1991.

It was a controversial move. Although any nature-lover would think Thompkins did Chileans and the world a favor by spending his money on this ecological cause, the move did not sit well with the Chilean government. Understandably, the government was uneasy with the foreign ownership of so much land, especially because it stretched from the Pacific Ocean to the Argentine border.

Years have passed, the public and the government have slowly grown to accept the project, and today Pumalín boasts a growing number of visitors. Thompkins plans to eventually donate this park to the Fundación Pumalín, who will run it as a national park under a private initiative. The facilities are superb, with exceptionally attractive cabins, well-groomed campgrounds, and a cafe selling tasty meals.

A soggy walk through this jungle, with its tall moss-draped trees and enormous, billowy ferns, is worth the journey, and makes for an excellent introduction to the Carretera Austral. But remember this is a rainforest, and torrential downpours can go on for days, even in the middle of summer.

WHAT TO SEE & DO

The park's **main information center** is at **Caleta Gonzalo,** reached by ferry from Hornopirén in the summer and by Chaitén in the winter (visitors must first take a ferry to Chaitén from Puerto Montt, or from Quellón in Chiloé). The northern section of the park is accessible by road from Hornopirén, which has an information center (© **65/217256**), but the park is cut in two, and visitors will need to take a ferry to Caleta Gonzalo regardless to reach the southern section. In the Caleta Gonzalo center, visitors will find photos, brochures, and locally produced crafts. There's also a new information center in Chaitén, at O'Higgins 62 (© **65/731341**), and in Puerto Montt (© **65/250079**). For advance information, request brochures in the United States (© **415/229-9339; pumalin@earthlink.org**).

HIKING At Caleta Gonzalo, trails include the 3-hour round-trip **Sendero Cascada,** which meanders along a footpath and elevated walkways through dense vegetation before terminating at a crashing waterfall. The **Sendero Tronador,** 12km (7½ miles) south of Caleta Gonzalo, takes visitors across a suspension bridge and up, up, up a steep path and wooden stepladder to a lookout point, with views of Volcán Michinmáhuida, then down to a lake with a campground, round-trip about 3½ hours. The **Sendero los Alerces** is an easy, 40-minute walk through old stands of *alerce*. There is also a tough-going, 3-day backpacking trip, the **Sendero Inexplorado,** for experienced hikers only.

OTHER ACTIVITIES Pumalín offers **horse pack trips** and trips to the remote **Cahuelmo Hot Springs,** all with advance reservation only. You can also tour an **organic farm** or sign up for **boat trips** around the fjord and to the sea lion rookery. For more information and reservations, contact the official outdoor operator for the park, **Alsur Expeditions,** in Puerto Varas at Del Salvador 100 (©/fax **65/232300;** www.alsurexpeditions.com).

ORGANIZED TOURS **Altué Sea Kayaking,** based out of Santiago at Encomenderos 83, Las Condes (© **2/232-1103;** www.seakayakchile.com), offers kayak trips in Pumalín that it often combines with kayaking in Chiloé.

WHERE TO STAY & DINE

Cabañas and Camping Pumalín These rustic and charming cabins are built for two to six guests and feature details like nubby bedspreads, gingham curtains, and carved wood cabinets. Only one comes with a kitchen, the "family" cabin at Reñihué, a more remote cabin with fishing access that goes for $90 for four. The cabins are small but cozy, with a double bed and twin on the bottom floor and two twins above in a loft; all offer lots of light.

The sites at **Camping Pumalín,** on the beautiful Fiordo Reñihué, are well-kept rooms offering a firepit (firewood costs extra), a sheltered area for cooking, bathrooms with cold-water showers, and an area for washing clothing; the cost is $2 per person. About 14km (8½ miles) south of Caleta Gonzalo is the **Cascadas Escondidas Campground,** with sheltered tent platforms, picnic tables, cold-water showers, bathrooms, and the trail head to three waterfalls. The cost to camp here is $10 per group. There are more than 20 campsites throughout the park, many of them accessible by boat or by backpacking trail; consult the park for more information.

Caleta Gonzalo s/n. (✆ **65/250079,** or 415/229-9339 in the U.S. Fax 65/255145, or 415/229-9340 in the U.S. 7 units. $65 double; $10 each additional guest. AE, DC, MC, V. **Amenities:** Restaurant.

4 Chaitén

420km (260 miles) N of Coyhaique

Chaitén is a sleepy hamlet that serves as a jumping-off point for exploring Pumalín, Futaleufú, and the Carretera Austral. There's not much to see or do here, but visitors often find that it makes a convenient stopover point, especially during the winter when ferry service is limited. The town's main attraction is the view of **Volcán Michinmáhuida** in the distance, although perennial wet weather often impedes visibility of anything except the puddled, potholed streets.

GETTING THERE

BY BOAT   For information about ferries to Chaitén, see chapter 14 under "Ferry Crossings to the Carretera Austral & Sailing to Patagonia Through the Fjords." The Catamaranes del Sur office in Chaitén is located at Av. Juan Todesco 180 ((✆ **65/482308;** www.catamaranesdelsur.cl).

BY AIR   There are two to three daily flights from Puerto Montt offered by **Aeromet** at Todesco 55 ((✆ **65/731275;** www.aeromet.cl), and air-taxi **Aerosur** at Carrera Pinto and Almirante Riveros ((✆ **65/731228;** aerosur@telsur.cl). It is not recommended that travelers fly in stormy weather.

BY BUS   Bus schedules in this region are always subject to change, and both **Chaitur,** Diego Portales 350 ((✆ **65/731429)** and **B&V Tours,** Libertad 432 ((✆ **65/731390),** have information about service to destinations such as Caleta Gonzalo, Futaleufú, Puyuhuapi, and Coyhaique. Buses to all destinations leave daily from December to March; from April to November, buses to Futaleufú leave three times weekly, as do buses to Caleta Gonzalo, and two times weekly to Coyhaique, with a stop at Puyuhuapi.

VISITOR INFORMATION & TOUR OPERATORS

Sernatur has an office at Av. Bernardo O'Higgins 254 ((✆ **65/731280;** www. sernatur.cl) and several tour operators offer set trips and custom-built trips to outlying areas. Try **Chaitur,** Diego Portales 350 ((✆ **65/731429;** nchaitur@ hotmail.com), or **Ñuke Mapu** in the Galería Genisis ((✆ **65/731578)**—both agencies often work together, offering trips to the Yelcho Glacier and Pumalín Park, horseback riding, rock climbing, kayaking, and even mountain biking to destinations as far away as Coyhaique. Pumalín Park has an office in Chaitén at O'Higgins 52 ((✆ **65/731341),** and it is actually the best place to pick up information about the area.

WHERE TO STAY

Hostal El Verde Puma (*Value*)   Owned and operated by the Pumalín Park Project, this newer hostal offers the most attractive and modern accommodations in Chaitén. The cream and forest green hostal is in an old but newly renovated shingled building, and sits above the park's information center and gift shop. The rooms are quite small, but the interiors are very pleasant, with contemporary decorations and linens. There's one bedroom for two with a full-size bed, and another with three beds that singles must share with other travelers. The wooden gourmet kitchen has a large, copper-hooded stove and a cozy eating area where guests can take meals. Out back is a wonderful apartment consisting of one large room with a double bed and a long counter and kitchenette.

O'Higgins 52, Chaitén. ✆ **65/731184.** 2 units, 1 apt. $28–$50 per person. Rates include breakfast. No credit cards. **Amenities:** Lounge.

Hostería Los Coihues *(Value)*

This is one of the nicer hotels in Chaitén, and it's downright cheap. The unassuming, log-cabin building sits several blocks back from the waterfront, and has a comfortable dining area/lounge with windows facing Volcán Michinmáhuida. The rooms have wood floors and are somewhat plain, but are warm, and the bathrooms sparkle. Doubles have a full-size bed or two twins, and triples have a twin and bunk bed. The friendly Argentine family who own and run the hotel came to Chaitén and were so smitten they never left; one family member is a mountaineer enthusiast who organizes outdoor adventures. Daily excursions are available for an additional cost. Packages include transportation from/to Chaitén airport, so ask for other arrangements if you plan to arrive by ferry or catamaran.

Pedro A. Cerda 398, Chaitén. ✆/fax **65/731461.** coihues@telsur.cl. 8 units. $38 double. AE, DC, MC, V. **Amenities:** Lounge; tour desk.

Hotel Mi Casa

The Hotel Mi Casa is located on a hill just above town, offering a direct view of Volcán Michinmáhuida and the colorful rooftops below, all taken in from a winding deck. The unadorned rooms are nothing to go wild about, but the warm, friendly service, decent restaurant, and extra amenities give it a slight edge above several of its competitors. Two rooms have a double bed and an extra twin for parents traveling with a child. Although many have thin carpet, the rooms are large enough and kept toasty warm. A winding path out back leads to a gym with weights and a Ping-Pong table and continues to a sauna and massage cabin. Several sitting areas in the hotel include a TV room with a VCR. A fun extra is the hotel's *quincho*, where they often host lamb, beef, and pork barbecues grilled the Chilean way on a spit over a roaring fire. Internet access is available for guests for a small fee.

Av. Norte 206, Chaitén. ✆/fax **65/731285.** www.gochile.cl/hotel/micasa. 21 units. $50–$75 double. No credit cards. Rates include full breakfast. **Amenities:** Restaurant; bar; exercise room; sauna; massage; game room.

Hotel Schilling

The Hotel Schilling has a bright, cheery lobby and a waterfront location, but the rooms are dowdy and not a great value. Nevertheless, it's still one of the better hotels in Chaitén, and it's possible to negotiate the price, especially in the off season or for multiple-day stays. Some rooms come with private bathrooms, although rooms with shared bathrooms are slightly cheaper. The decor consists of colorful velveteen bedspreads and frilly lamps, and rooms are heated only by a wood-burning stove in the hall; a few come with a TV. There's a nice dining area and bar on the bottom level.

Av. Corcovado 230, Chaitén. ✆ **65/731295.** Fax 65/731298. $16–$28 per person. No credit cards. **Amenities:** Lounge; bar.

Residencial Astoria

If you can get past the dark, musty bottom floor, this *residencial* is a good bet for inexpensive accommodations. There are two bedrooms on the first level, but better accommodations are on the sunny second floor, which has a giant living room with windows that face out over the ocean (and a Copec gas station). Low ceilings, especially in the shower, are inconvenient for anyone over 1.8m (6 ft.), and it can get fairly cold in the rooms. The walls are thin, but the *residencial* is very clean and the beds are comfortable.

Av. Corcovado 442, Chaitén. © **65/731263**. 8 units. $12–$18 private bathroom; $8–$12 shared bathroom. No credit cards. **Amenities:** Lounge.

WHERE TO DINE

Hotel Mi Casa ★ CHILEAN This restaurant has a sweeping view of Chaitén and the waterfront and its dining room is nicer in the day than the evening, when fluorescent lights go on. The menu features simply prepared, average dishes, such as filet mignon with mashed potatoes. All the food is organic, however, and the staff will arrange a special lamb barbecue for couples and groups, if you call ahead.

Av. Norte 206. ©/fax **65/731285**. Main dishes $2–$6. No credit cards. Daily 6am–11pm.

Restaurant Brisas del Mar CHILEAN This is one of Chaitén's better restaurants, but it's open only during the summer. Brisas del Mar sits on the waterfront and has a sunny, semi-casual dining area. The menu offers a typically Chilean selection of seafood and meats.

Av. Corcovado 278. © **65/731266**. Main courses $3–$9. MC, V. Dec–Mar daily 8:30pm–midnight.

Restaurant Flamengo CHILEAN The best thing that can be said about the Flamengo is that it is open all day, year-round. However, it's somewhat expensive given the simple dishes it serves and its casual atmosphere. Flamengo offers grilled meats, fish, and chicken with a choice of a dozen sauces and often has shellfish specials during the summer.

Av. Corcovado 218. No phone. Main courses $5–$9. No credit cards. Daily 8:30am–1am high season; daily 10am–11pm low season.

5 South from Chaitén: Futaleufú ★

155km (96 miles) SE of Chaitén

The road south between Chaitén and Villa Santa Lucía, where drivers turn for Futaleufú, passes through mountain scenery that affords spectacular views of Volcán Michinmáhuida, the Yelcho Glacier, and Lago Yelcho. At 25km (16 miles), you'll arrive at Amarillo, a tiny village and the turn-off point for the 5km (3-mile) drive to Termas de Amarillo.

Termas de Amarillo This seemingly half-built hot springs site is a good place for a soak. There's a large temperate pool along with several outdoor and private indoor pools (private meaning a cement pool inside a shack). There are several sites for camping here, or you can lodge at the modest, family-run **Cabañas y Hospedaje Los Mañíos** about 100m (109 yd.) from the hot springs, for $9 per person, or $36 for a cabin for six (© **65/731210**).

No phone. $3.50 adults, $1.50 children 12 and under; $3.50 for camping. Nov–Apr daily 9am–8pm; Mar–Oct daily 9am–6pm.

CONTINUING ON TO FUTALEUFU

Farther south the road curves past the northern shore of Lago Yelcho and the Yelcho en la Patagonia Lodge (see below), and at 60km (37 miles) crosses the Puente Ventisquero, which bridges a milky green river; this is where you'll find the trail head to the **Yelcho Glacier.** To get there, take the short road before the bridge and then walk right at the almost imperceptible sign indicating the trail. A muddy 1½-hour hike takes you through dense forest to the Yelcho Glacier.

At Villa Santa Lucía, the Carretera Austral continues south to Puyuhuapi, but visitors should consider a trip to Futaleufú, an idyllic mountain town with adventure activities and one of the most challenging rivers to raft in the world. The road to Futaleufú is worth the trip itself for its majestic views at every turn, first winding around the southern end of Lago Yelcho before passing the Futaleufú River and Lakes Lonconao and Espolón and on to the emerald valley surrounding the town of Futaleufú.

AN ADVENTURE LODGE

Yelcho en la Patagonia Lodge ⭐ *(Finds)*   The Yelcho Lodge enjoys a privileged location on the shore of Lago Yelcho, and is this general region's only complete resort, with elegant, attractive accommodations and a full range of excursions, especially fly-fishing. Yelcho offers three options: suites, *cabañas* for two to six guests, and 15 well-equipped campsites complete with barbecues. The white, shingled *cabañas* come with spacious kitchens, but there's also a restaurant that serves gourmet cuisine, as well as barbecue roasts. The cabins have a deck and barbecue and a view of the lake seen through a stand of *arrayán* trees; note that cabins for six mean two sleep in the living area. The lodge and the indoor accommodations have handsome two-tone floors made of *mañío* and *alerce*. The lodge offers excursions with bilingual guides for fly-fishing the Yelcho River and Lago Yelcho, locally renowned for its plentiful salmon and trout, and treks to the Yelcho Glacier, mountain biking, horseback riding, and visits to the Amarillo hot springs and Futaleufú. The lodge will pick you up from nearly any nearby location.

Lago Yelcho, Km 54, Carretera Austral, Región X. ℭ **65/731337**, or for reservations, 2/334-1309 in Santiago. www.yelcho.cl. 8 suites; 6 *cabañas;* 15 camp sites. $54–74 double; $90 *cabaña* for four. Rates include full breakfast. MC, V. **Amenities:** Restaurant; tour desk.

FUTALEUFU ⭐
155km (96 miles) SE of Chaitén; 196km (122 miles) NE of Puyuhuapi

Futaleufú is one of the prettiest villages in Chile, a town of 1,200 residents who live in colorful clapboard homes nestled in an awe-inspiring amphitheater of rugged, snowcapped mountains. Futaleufú sits at the junction of two rivers, the turquoise Río Espolón and its world-renowned cousin the Río Futaleufú, whose whitewater rapids are considered some of the most challenging on the globe. Every November to April, this quaint little town becomes the base for hundreds of rafters and kayakers who come to test their mettle on the "Fu," as it's colloquially known, although just as many come to fish, hike, mountain bike, paddle a canoe, or raft the gentler Río Espolón. Futaleufú is just kilometers from the Argentine border; it's possible to get here by road from Puerto Montt by crossing into Argentina, a route sometimes preferred for its paved roads.

Note that there are no banks or gas stations here in Futaleufú. Residents do, however, sell gas out of wine jugs and other unwieldy containers; just look for signs advertising BENCINA.

GETTING THERE & AWAY

BY PLANE   Aerosur offers air-taxi charter flights from Puerto Montt and even Chaitén, weather permitting (ℭ **65/252523** in Puerto Montt, or 65/731268 in Futaleufú; aerosur@telsur.cl). It's entirely feasible to fly into Esquel in Argentina from Buenos Aires and then travel by road 65km (40 miles) to Futaleufú, just be sure to factor in the possible delay at the border crossing and give yourself plenty of time to make the journey (3–4 hr.). Most travelers, however, either fly into Chaitén or take the Catamaran there from Puerto Montt (see "Getting There" in "Chaitén," above) and then transfer to Futaleufú. From

Chaitén, there's a daily van service that departs from the Chaitur at Diego Portales 350 (© **65/731429;** nchaitur@hotmail.com) office every afternoon at 3:30pm for the 3-hour journey.

BY BUS   There isn't a bus terminal here, so ask at your hotel or call each company for schedules, locations, and prices. Winter service is sketchy; try calling **B&V Tours** in Chaitén to see if they have an upcoming trip (© **65/731390**). **Skorpios Turismo,** which operates out of the Hospedaje Emita at Miraflores 1281 (© **65/250725**), offers service to Puerto Montt via Argentina, leaving Futaleufú on Tuesday and Puerto Montt on Thursday. The bus leaves at 8am and arrives 12 hours later.

BY CAR   From Chaitén, take Ruta 7 south and go left to Ruta 235 at Villa Santa Lucía. The road winds around the shore of Lago Yelcho until Puerto Ramírez, where you head northeast on Ruta 231 until you reach Futaleufú.

WHAT TO SEE & DO

Futaleufú was put on the map by travelers with one goal in mind: to raft or kayak the internationally famous, Class V waters of the village's namesake river. This is one of the most challenging rivers in the world. You've got to be good—or at least be experienced—to tackle frothing whitewater so wild that certain sections have been dubbed "Hell" and "The Finisher." But rafting and kayaking companies will accommodate more prudent guests with shorter sections of the river. If you just can't handle the Futaleufú, the Río Espolón offers a gentler ride.

American Olympic kayaker Chris Spelius now runs the Futaleufú-based **Expediciones Chile,** a rafting and kayaking excursion center. It's headquartered at the Hostería Río Grande, O'Higgins 397 (© **65/721320,** or 888/488-9082 in the U.S.; www.raftingchile.com). He also offers a kayak skills course from a remote tent camp with lodge support. Day trips can be organized on the spot, but it's best to reserve ahead of time.

For **fishing licenses,** go to the municipal building at O'Higgins 596 (© **65/ 721241**); it's open Monday through Friday from 8am to 1:30pm and 2:30 to 5pm. For more information on fishing, see "Fly-Fishing Lodges in the Futaleufú Area," below.

WHERE TO STAY IN THE AREA

It's slim pickings here, and you'll be charged a lot for what you get. Outside Futaleufú there are several options for lodging, including campsites that dot the road between here and Villa Santa Lucía. If you'd like to do a little fishing, check out the **Hostal Alexis** (© **65/731505**), located just before Puerto Ramírez and situated on the grassy bank of Lago Yelcho. There's a hotel in an old, converted farmhouse, and a dozen campsites with wooden half-walls that protect sites from the wind. You can fish directly from the shore here, but the owners also offer fishing excursions. Open from November to April only, $32 double.

Hospedaje Familiar Ely   The friendly woman who owns and runs Hospedaje Familiar Ely offers decent but no-frills accommodations in an old, shingled building. The rooms are somewhat cramped and the floors squeak, but that's pretty common for lodging in this price range for this town. Two of the rooms share a bathroom. Guests take breakfast in a downstairs living room that also acts as a lobby. There's also a backyard cement patio.

Balmaceda 409, Futaleufú. © 65/721205. 5 units. $28 double. Rate includes continental breakfast. No credit cards. **Amenities:** Lounge. *In room:* No phone.

Rafting on the Río Futaleufú

The Futaleufú river is known as one of the best whitewater rivers in the world. An excellent, U.S.-based company that offers rafting on the Río Futaleufú is **Bío Bío Expeditions** ★★ (© **800/246-7238;**or 530/582-6865 in the U.S.; www.bbxrafting.com). Their programs are unique in that they are very sensitive to local culture; the company manages a beautiful Lodge and Adventure Spa with a high regard to the surrounding environment. The 8-day trips include daily guided rafting trips, horseback riding adventures, and gourmet meals. All-inclusive packages are $2,500 per person.

Hostería Río Grande   This wooden, two-story *hostería* is popular with foreign tourists for its outdoorsy design and especially its restaurant and pub. It's one of the better hotels in town, with walls painted boldly in tangerine and blue, although the rooms seem slightly expensive for their dull, standard furnishings and office-building carpet. However, the atmosphere is relaxed and guests can expect a standard level of comfort. There's also an apartment (but no kitchen) for six guests. The Río Grande's restaurant is the unofficial hangout spot in town, and it has a nice atmosphere for relaxing with a beer. One of the owners is an American who has tailored the menu to satisfy the tastes of gringo clientele, so there's a lot on offer. There's seafood throughout the week, but try to make it on Wednesday and Saturday when the restaurant receives its fresh fish delivery by air.

O'Higgins 397, Futaleufú. © 888/488-9082 in the U.S., or 65/721320. www.raftingchile.com. 10 units, 1 apt for 6. $100 double. MC, V. Hotel and restaurant closed June–Sept. **Amenities:** Restaurant; bar; extensive watersports equipment rental. *In room:* No phone.

Posada La Gringa *Finds*   This attractive white-and-green clapboard hotel sits on a large, grassy property with excellent views of the countryside stretched out before it. With well-maintained, clean, pleasant rooms, the hotel is open from November to April only.

Sargento Aldea s/n, corner of Aldea, Futaleufú. © 65/258633. 8 units. $64 double. Rates include full breakfast. No credit cards. Hotel closed May–Oct. **Amenities:** Lounge. *In room:* No phone.

WHERE TO DINE

Apart from the Hostería Río Grande's restaurant (see above), there's **Restaurant Skorpios,** Gabriela Mistral 255 (© **65/731228**), which offers about four choices per day of simple meat and seafood dishes (no credit cards accepted). **Café Restaurant Futaleufú,** Pedro Aguirre Cerda 407 (© **65/721295**), has a short menu with 10 or so simple dishes that all cost the same ($5; no credit cards accepted). Sample items include homemade spaghetti and chicken stewed with peas; there's also a range of sandwiches.

FLY-FISHING LODGES IN THE FUTALEUFU AREA

Futaleufú Lodge ★ *Finds*   The Futaleufú is an intimate little lodge nestled in the Las Escalas Valley in the mountains 8km (5 miles) from town, on the shore of the Futaleufú River. Like the Isla Monita Lodge, the Futaleufú is rustic yet very comfortable, but unlike the Isla Monita, which has a more masculine aesthetic, this lodge is aimed at couples (the capacity here is 6 people). The owners, American Jim Repine and his wife Sonia, are very amiable, and the setting is ideal, on their very own 81 hectares (200 acres). They offer trekking and horseback riding, and can arrange a kayak or rafting trip down the Futaleufú River (at an additional cost).

8km from Futaleufú, Route 231, Futaleufú, Región X. ℂ/fax **32/812659.** jimrepine@worldangler.com. All-inclusive, 7-day packages $4,200 per person. **Amenities:** Restaurant; bar; lounge. *In room:* No phone.

Isla Monita Lodge This exclusive, newly renovated lodge can be found on a 101-hectare (250-acre) private island in Lago Yelcho, and its location affords anglers the most diverse fly-fishing conditions found in Chile. Fly-fishers have their choice of the Palena, Futaleufú, or Yelcho rivers, all within a short drive from the lodge, and there are wading and floating excursions. The lodge has room for just eight guests. You can't beat the location, encircled by a ring of rugged peaks. Guests typically reach the lodge by plane from Chaitén. The season runs from November to April.

Lago Yelcho, Futaleufú, Región X. Tours are arranged through Frontier Tours in the U.S.; call ℂ **800/245-1950.** Information also available in Santiago at ℂ 2/273-2198. Fax 412/935-5388 in the U.S. Average, all-inclusive packages run $3,600 per person, not including transportation. **Amenities:** Restaurant; bar; lounge. *In room:* No phone.

Río Palena Lodge Situated on the shore of the Río Palena and offering front-door fishing, this handsome lodge, owned by Spencer Moore, an American, is made entirely of native wood. It backs up against a leafy slope, and there's a long deck for kicking back and telling fish tales. The lodge has space for just eight guests, who normally spend their days pulling in brown and rainbow trout. There's also hiking, horseback riding, and bird watching for non-anglers. The season here is from November to May.

Km 14 outside Palena, Route 235. ℂ **888/891-3474** in the U.S. Fax 860/434-8605 in the U.S. www.flyfishing chile.com. 7-night/8-day packages average $3,800 per person, including lodging, meals, guides, and transportation from Puerto Montt or Palena. **Amenities:** Restaurant; bar; lounge with fireplace. *In room:* No phone.

6 Puyuhuapi ⊹

198km (123 miles) S of Chaitén; 222km (138 miles) N of Coyhaique

Just south of Villa Santa Lucía is the end of Chile's Región X Lake District (also called Región Los Lagos) and the beginning of Región XI, better known as Región Aisén. South of here you enter a flat valley and the utilitarian town La Junta. The only thing of any interest there is a gas pump and well-stocked store. The view begins to pick up farther along, until the scenery goes wild as the valley narrows and thick green rainforest rises steeply from the sides of the road, just outside the entrance of Parque Nacional Queulat. When the valley opens, the Seno Ventisquero (Glacier Sound) unfolds dramatically, revealing the charming town of Puerto Puyuhuapi on its shore.

Puerto Puyuhuapi was founded by four young immigrant German brothers and their families who set up camp here in 1935. They ran a surprisingly successful **carpet factory,** whose humble, shingled building you can still visit Monday through Friday at 10:30, 11, 11:30am, 4, 4:30, and 5pm; Saturday, Sunday, and holidays the tour is offered just once at 11:30am. Admission is $1.70 adults and 70¢ kids.

The most popular attractions in this region are **Parque Nacional Queulat** and the five-star **Termas de Puyuhuapi Spa & Hotel** (see "Outside Puerto Puyuhuapi," below) just south and on the other side of the sound a 5-minute boat ride away. If the Termas de Puyuhuapi's prices are beyond your limit, you might opt to stay at a more economical hotel in Puerto Puyuhuapi or, during the off season, at El Pangue *cabañas,* and take a soak in the hot springs for the day. You can then spend the following day exploring Parque Nacional Queulat.

EXPLORING PARQUE NACIONAL QUEULAT

Parque Nacional Queulat's scenery will make your jaw drop. Every national park has a unique characteristic and Queulat's is its emerald, virgin rainforest, some of it so thick and impenetrable that it has yet to be explored. What makes this park special is that you can drive through the heart of it, and there are several spectacular lookout points reached by car or a brief walk. Be sure to keep your eyes open for the *pudú,* a miniature Chilean deer that is timid but can often be seen poking its head out of the forest near the road.

The 154,093-hectare (380,610-acre) park has several access points but few trails and no backpacking trails. If entering from the north, you first pass a turnoff that heads to the shore of **Lago Risopatrón** and a very attractive camping spot that charges $12 per site. There's a 14km (8½-mile) round-trip trail here that leads trekkers through rainforest and past Lago los Pumos (a 5–6 hr. hike). Continuing south of Puerto Puyuhuapi, visitors arrive at the park's star attraction, the **Ventisquero Colgante,** a tremendous, U-shaped river of ice suspended hundreds of feet above a sheer granite wall. From the glacier, two powerful cascades fall into Lago los Témpanos below. To enter this part of the park, Conaf charges $2.50 per adult and 35¢ per child 12 and under; visitors can drive straight to a short trail that takes them to the glacier's lookout point. To get closer, cross the hanging bridge that's before the campground and take the **Sendero Mirador Ventisquero Colgante,** a moderate, 3- to 4-hour hike that takes you to the lake below the glacier. As of this writing, a concession has made plans to offer a 45-minute boat ride around this lake for $3 per person; check at the Conaf station, which is open daily December through March from 8:30am to 9:30pm and April through November from 8:30am to 9:30pm. To camp in this area, the park charges $12 per site. For more information, contact Conaf's offices in Coyhaique at © **67/212125;** www.conaf.cl.

Traveling farther south, the scenery becomes more rugged as the road takes visitors up the Cuesta de Queulat and to views of glacier-capped peaks, and then down again where the road passes the trail head to the **Sendero Río Cascada.** Even if you don't feel like walking the entire 1.7km (1-mile) trail, at least stop for a quick stroll through the enchanting forest. The trail leads to a granite amphitheater draped with braided waterfalls that fall into an ice-capped lake. Note that Conaf is slow-moving when it comes to clearing trails of fallen trees, especially on the Río Cascada trail. If you're able, you can scramble over the trees, but it takes some maneuvering that will tack extra time onto your journey. Check with Conaf at the Ventisquero Colgante entrance for the status of a trail, or factor obstacles into your trip time. The station is open daily December through March from 8:30am to 9:30pm and April through November from 8:30am to 9:30pm; © **67/212125.**

WHERE TO STAY & DINE
IN PUERTO PUYUHUAPI

Try **Café Rossbach,** Aysé s/n (© **67/325202**), if you're looking for something to eat—cakes are the specialty. The Rossbach is next to the carpet factory. **El Pangue** has a restaurant, but it's 18km (11 miles) away. Call beforehand to see if you can get a table (see "Outside Puerto Puyuhuapi," below).

Hostería Alemana *Finds* The German woman who runs this hotel emigrated to Puerto Puyuhuapi more than 30 years ago, and her roots are reflected in the style of the establishment, including delicious breakfasts with sliced meats and *kuchen.* The hotel is in a well-maintained, flower-bordered antique home that just got a fresh coat of paint this year. Only one room comes with a private bathroom, and one triple comes with a wood-burning stove. All are spacious and scrubbed.

Av. Otto Uevel 450, Puerto Puyuhaupi. ℂ **67/325118.** Hosteria_alemana@entelchile.net. 6 units. $33–$39 double. Rates include full breakfast. No credit cards. **Amenities:** Lounge. *In room:* No phone.

Residencial Marily Just across the street from the Hostería Alemana is this inexpensive *residencial.* The place doesn't have much style, but it is clean and the beds are surprisingly comfortable. The floors are wood, the walls mauve and light blue, and some rooms share a bathroom; there is a TV in the lounge. The best thing about this place has to be the stuffed puma in the living room.

Av. Otto Uevel s/n, Puerto Puyuhaupi. ℂ **67/325201.** Fax 67/325102. 7 units. Per person, $21 private bathroom; $17 shared bathroom. No credit cards. **Amenities:** Lounge. *In room:* No phone.

OUTSIDE PUERTO PUYUHUAPI

El Pangue ★ *Finds* El Pangue is located at a breathtakingly beautiful site just kilometers from the edge of Parque Nacional Queulat, 30m (100 ft.) from Lago Risopatrón, and 18km (11 miles) from Puerto Puyuhuapi. Dense rainforest encircles the complex; a winding stream provides a fairy-tale spot for a quiet walk or a quick dip. The staff and facilities are commendable, and although the lodge focuses heavily on fly-fishing from November to May, other excursions include mountain biking, hiking, canoeing, and boat rides. Guided fly-fishing is offered here and around the region.

Lodging consists of cozy, attractive wood cabins that fit two to three guests. There are also two "houses" with kitchens for seven guests each; only four of the cabins have kitchens. The open-room, split-level cabins have a small table and chairs and an extra bed/couch; bathrooms have sunken tubs. The main building houses an excellent restaurant, game room, and lounge; outside is a *quincho* where there are frequent lamb barbecues. There is an interesting aviary of sorts with ducks, geese, pheasants, and chickens. Off-season rates drop dramatically.

Carretera Austral Norte, Km 240, Región XI. ℂ/fax **67/325128.** www.elpangue.cl. 13 *cabañas.* $66–$109 double. Rates include buffet breakfast. No credit cards. **Amenities:** Restaurant; bar; lounge; outdoor heated pool; Jacuzzi; sauna; limited watersports equipment; mountain bike rental; business center; room service; business center; laundry service. *In room:* No phone.

Termas de Puyuhuapi Spa & Hotel ★★ *Moments* This region's top attraction is an extraordinary place to spend the night or visit for the day. Termas de Puyuhuapi Spa & Hotel is perhaps the best hotel/thermal spa complex in Chile, and it draws visitors from all over the world for its remote, magnificent location, elegant design, thermal pools, and full-service spa. The hotel is nestled in thick rainforest on the shore of the Seno Ventisquero; to get here, guests must cross the sound via a 5-minute motorboat ride. There, visitors find an indoor complex with a giant pool, whirlpools, steam baths, spa, and three open-air pools, one a rock pool framed by ferns.

The Termas was just a handful of ramshackle cabins until German Eberhard Kossmann bought the property and built his handsome complex of shingles and glass; the only remaining original building is one of the *cabañas,* which is probably the least appealing lodging option. Nine large suites are on the shore, and they come with a deck that hangs out over the water during high tide. There are six newer, and smaller, nonsmoking suites that come with a more stylish decor (especially the "Captain's Suite"). Other options include a duplex with a fireman's ladder that leads to a loft with three twins for kids, and two cabins that sleep four to six people, but they do not come with a kitchen stove or a view. Of special note is the superb cuisine served in the hotel's charming dining room. Outside, a winding path takes guests to two short hikes through the rainforest, and there's a pier where you can drop a kayak in the sound. But the big outdoor attractions here are Puyuhuapi's fly-fishing expeditions and the connection with *Patagonia Express,* a boat that takes visitors to the Laguna San Rafael Glacier (see "Puerto Aisén, Puerto Chacabuco & Laguna San Rafael National Park," later in this chapter). Both are sold as packages. Guests typically fly into Coyhaique and transfer to the Termas by vehicle. On the return trip they board the *Express* for a visit to the glacier, and get dropped off in Puerto Chacabuco for the night, then back to the airport. If you're not staying at the hotel but want to use the facilities, there's a $24 day-use fee; more for sauna use or a massage.

Puerto Puyuhuapi, Región XI. ℂ/fax in Santiago **2/225-6489,** or in Puyuhuapi 67/325103. www.patagonia-connection.com. 25 units. $150–$175 double, meals not included. 3-night packages including the cruise to Laguna San Rafael cost about $1,000 per person; ½-price for kids. AE, DC, MC, V. **Amenities:** Restaurant; bar; lounge; large indoor pool; 3 outdoor pools; spa; Jacuzzi; thermal pools; sauna; massage; room service.

7 Coyhaique

222km (138 miles) S of Puyuhuapi; 774km (480 miles) N of Cochrane

The province Aisén includes the capital city Coyhaique and a handful of natural reserves whose rivers and lakes draw thousands every year for superb fly-fishing opportunities. Visitors who are not traveling the Carretera Austral can fly into Coyhaique from Santiago or Puerto Montt; travel to southern Patagonia from here requires that you fly again to Punta Arenas, unless you have your own car and plan to take the long and gravelly road through flat Argentine pampa.

Driving south out of Parque Nacional Queulat, the scenery provokes oohs and ahhs at every turn. The pinnacle of Cerro Picacho comes into view before you enter Villa Amengual, a service village for farmers. The scenery is marred at times, unfortunately, by the terrible destruction caused by settlers who burned much of the area for pastureland. Tall, slender, evergreen beech tree trunks bleached silver from fire can still be seen poking out from regrowth forest or littered across grassy pastures in a messy testament to these fires.

The road passes through rinky-dink towns such as Villa Mañihuales before arriving at a paved road that appears like a heaven-sent miracle after hundreds of kilometers of jarring washboard. At a junction south of Mañihuales, drivers can head to Puerto Aisén and Puerto Chacabuco, the departure point for boat trips to Laguna San Rafael and Puerto Montt, and then southeast toward Coyhaique, passing first through the Reserva Nacional Río Simpson.

Coyhaique is a compact, urban city that is home to more than half the population of the entire Aisén region—about 36,000 residents. It's really the only city in the region with a full range of services—most important, banks. The city boasts a beautiful location at the base of a basalt cliff called Cerro MacKay and is surrounded by green rolling hills and pastures. The city also sits at the confluence of the Simpson and Coyhaique rivers, both renowned for trout and salmon fishing and the reason so many flock to this region. The other prime attraction here is the Laguna San Rafael Glacier, an enormous glacier that can be visited on a modest ship or a luxury liner from Puerto Chacabuco. Beyond fishing, visitors can choose from a wealth of activities within a short drive of the city.

ESSENTIALS
GETTING THERE & AROUND

BY PLANE   Coyhaique's new **Aeropuerto de Balmaceda, BBA** (no phone), is a 50-minute drive from downtown. This is where the large jets arrive. **Lan-Chile** is the only scheduled airline flying here; it has three to four flights daily from Santiago with a stop in Puerto Montt (there are no nonstops from Santiago); there's also one weekly flight from Punta Arenas. The LanChile office is at General Parra 211 (© **67/231188;** www.lanchile.com). A variety of minibus shuttles await each arriving flight, offering transportation to Coyhaique for about $5 to $7. Charter flights (all small propeller planes) to closer destinations such as Villa O'Higgins, Chile Chico, or Cochrane leave from the **Teniente Vidal airport** (no phone) just outside town. **Aerohein,** Baquedano 500 (© **67/ 232772;** www.aerohein.cl), offers charter flights; **Transporte Don Carlos,** Subteniente Cruz 63 (© **67/231981;** www.doncarlos.cl), offers regional flights.

BY BOAT   It is possible to arrive by boat at Puerto Chacabuco near Puerto Aisén (from Puerto Montt), then travel by road for the 67km (42 miles) to Coyhaique. For schedule information, see "Puerto Aisén, Puerto Chacabuco & Laguna San Rafael National Park," later in this chapter. Ferry company offices in Coyhaique are at **Transmarchilay,** Av. 21 de Mayo 417 (© **67/ 231971;** www.transmarchilay.cl), and **Navimag,** Ibáñez 347 (© **67/233306;** www.navimag.cl).

BY BUS   Coyhaique has a bus terminal at Lautaro and Magallanes streets, but many companies use their own office for departures and arrivals. For buses with a final destination in **Chaitén,** try Buses Norte at General Parra 337 (© **67/ 232167**), which leaves on Tuesday and Saturday. For **Puerto Aisén** and **Chacabuco,** try Buses Don Carlos at Subteniente Cruz 63 (© **67/232981;** www.doncarlos.cl) with five trips per day, or Buses Suray at Eusebio Ibar 630 (© **67/ 238287**). For **Puerto Ibáñez,** try Minibus Don Tito at Pasaje Curico 619 (© **67/250280**).

BY CAR   Heading south on Ruta 7, the highway comes to a fork—one paved road and one dirt. The choice here is clear, especially if you've been driving on gravel all day. The well-signed, paved route heads first toward Puerto Aisén, and then switches, heading southeast for a beautiful drive through the Río Simpson National Reserve before hitting town. At the city entrance, a sign points left for the center of town.

Car Rental for Local Trips & the Carretera Austral

Among the companies to try: **AGS Rent a Car,** Av. Ogana 1298, and at the airport (© **67/235354;** fax 67/231511); **Rent a Car Aisén,** Francisco Bilbao 926 (© **67/231532;** fax 67/233555); **Turismo Prado,** Av. 21 de Mayo 417 (©/fax **67/231271**); **Ricer Rent a Car,** Horn 48 (©/fax **67/232920**); and **Automundo AVR,** Francisco Bilbao 510 (© **67/231621;** fax 231794). If you can't find what you want with these companies, request a list from the visitor center, as there are many independent offices that rent cars here in Coyhaique.

ACCOMMODATIONS ■
Cabañas Los Pinos **12**
El Reloj **2**
Hostal Araucaria **11**
Hostal Belisario Jara **5**
Hostería Coyhaique **10**
Hotel Los Nires **3**
Hotelera San Sebastián **1**
Patagonia Hotel **4**

ⓘ Information

DINING ◆
Restaurante Café Ricer **7**
La Olla **8**
Casino de Bomberos **9**
La Fiorentina **6**

VISITOR INFORMATION

A helpful **Sernatur** office can be found at Bulnes 35 (© **67/231752**; www.serna tur.cl); it's open December through February daily from 8:30am to 8:30pm, and March through November Monday through Friday from 8:30am to 5:30pm. Sernatur produces a glossy magazine packed with information about the region and full listings of services. For information about the surrounding natural parks and reserves, you can try **Conaf**'s office at Av. 12 de Octubre 382 (© **67/ 212125**; www.conaf.cl).

ORIENTATION

Coyhaique claims possibly the most unusual city layout in Chile due to its pentagon-shaped plaza and one-way streets that can be totally confusing to the visitor, especially when driving. Most services and hotels are near the plaza, and you'll find it convenient to stick to walking when in the city. The rest of the city is on a regular grid pattern.

FAST FACTS: COYHAIQUE

Currency Exchange Options include **Turismo Prado** at Avenida 21 de Mayo (© **67/231271**), **Emperador** at Francisco Bilbao 222 (© **67/233727**), and **Lucía Saldivia** at Condell 140 (© **67/231125**). Exchange houses are open Monday through Friday from 9:30am to 7:30pm and Saturday from 8:30am to 1pm.

Hospital The city's Regional Hospital is at Calle Hospital 68, near Carrera. For emergencies, dial **131.**

Internet Access **Entel** has Internet access and a calling center at Prat 340 (© **67/231223**).

Laundry There's a **Lavandería Q.L.** at Francisco Bilbao (tel **67/232266**) and a **Lavaseco Universal** at General Parra 55, #2 (© **67/231769**). Both are open Monday through Saturday from 9am to 1pm and 3 to 7pm.

Outdoor & Fishing Gear **Patagonia Outdoors,** Horn 47 (no phone), has a wide selection.

Post Office **Correos de Chile** is at Cochrane 202 (no phone).

WHAT TO SEE & DO IN COYHAIQUE

Museo Regional de la Patagonia Central This museum has two compact rooms, one a natural history exhibit packed with stuffed birds, armadillos, and turtles as well as rock and petrified wood samples, the other an ethnographic exhibit featuring photographs, colonial machinery, and other antique items. There is also one interesting photo exhibit of workmen building the Carretera Austral.

Av. Baquedano 310. © **67/213176.** Admission 75¢ adults, free for students. Open Dec–Feb daily 8:30am–8pm; Mar–Nov Mon–Fri 8:30am–1:30pm and 2:15–5:30pm.

Reserva Nacional Coyhaique You don't need to go far in Coyhaique to surround yourself in wilderness. This little reserve is just under 3km (2 miles) from town on the road to Puerto Aisén, and is a great place to go for a walk through native forest, have a picnic, pitch a tent, or hike to the spectacular lookout point that affords views of the entire region. A ranger station at the entrance has complete trail information. From here, a short trail leads to a campground and then continues to Laguna Verde, with picnic areas. The longest (and most rewarding) trail is the Sendero Las Piedras, which rewards hikers with wide-open views of the surrounding area and city below. The reserve's proximity to the city means it's entirely feasible to walk there. **Aventura Turismo** and **Tour Australis** (see "Outdoor Activities in the Area," below) can both arrange a trip there.

4km (2½ miles) from Coyhaique on the road to Puerto Aisén. © **67/212125.** Admission 75¢, camping $6. Open daily 8:30am–6pm.

Reserva Nacional Río Simpson The only way to see this reserve, really, is by car—which you'll do anyway if you take the road from Coyhaique to Puerto Aisén. The road winds along the shore of the Río Simpson, passing through impressive scenery and offering two crashing waterfalls, the Bridal Veil and the Virgin, which are signposted. There's also a museum here without anything of much interest and an information center. Unfortunately, trails in this reserve are not regularly maintained and therefore tough to hike; inquire at the information center as to their status.

Road to Puerto Aisén. © **67/212125.** Free admission. Museum open daily 8:30am–1:30pm and 2:15–6:30pm.

OUTDOOR ACTIVITIES IN THE AREA

TOUR OPERATORS In addition to horseback riding, **Aventura Turismo** at General Parra 222 (© **67/234748;** aventuraturismo@entelchile.net) also offers rafting on the Río Simpson (depending on river conditions) or trips south to Lago Elizalde and the Marble Cathedrals of Lago Carrera. **Expediciones**

Coyhaique at Portales 195 (© **67/232300;** www.expecoy.es.vg) is the best bet for fly-fishing, and their guide, Julio Meier, is the man who knows where to find the choice spots. For sightseeing trips along the Carretera Austral and to Puerto Aisén, and trips to view Telhuelche Indian rock, call **Tour Australis,** Moraleda 589 (© **67/239696;** taustralis@patagoniachile.cl). They typically offer trips from November to May only, but can put together a trip for a small group any time of the year. This company also acts as a full-service travel agency.

FISHING   Since their introduction in the late 1800s, trout and salmon have thrived in the crystalline waters in southern Chile, but nowhere in the country has fly-fishing taken off as it has here in the Aisén region. The burgeoning amount of fly-fishing guides alone bears testament to the truth of this region's claim as one of the premier fishing destinations on the globe, drawing thousands of anglers from around the world to reel in 3-, 5-, and even 10-pounders. Even if you've never fished before, this might be your opportunity to give it a go. **Sernatur** (see "Visitor Information," above) issues a complete listing of all fly-fishing guides in the Aisén region, some of whom work independently, some with a tour operator. If you're coming here mainly to fly-fish, there are several full-service luxury lodges in the region. All have on-site guides, both Chilean and foreign, especially American. Most offer activities for non-angling spouses and friends (see "Fly-Fishing Lodges Around Coyhaique," below).

Tour operators organize day, multiple-day, and weeklong excursions to fly-fishing spots such as Simpson, Baker, and Nirehuao rivers and Bertrand and General Carrera lakes. Some combine excursions with other activities such as horseback riding or hiking.

HORSEBACK RIDING   Trips often head to the Coyhaique Reserve and Lago Margaritas, but tour companies offer a variety of destinations. Some arrange all-inclusive, multiple-day trips. Aventura Turismo (see "Tour Operators," above) offers a full-day horseback riding trip for $50 per person to Coyhaique Alto, including a hike and a barbecue.

SKIING   The **Centro Esquí El Fraile** (© **67/250023**) is located 25km (16 miles) from Coyhaique, offering five ski runs serviced by two T-bars. It's a tiny resort, but can make for a fun day in the snow, and it's one of the few resorts in Chile that has tree skiing. There are also cross-country skiing opportunities here. Tickets cost $21 per day, and it's possible to rent equipment for an average of $17. Again, Aventura Turismo is the one to call for transfer service here.

WHERE TO STAY

For decent, but very, very basic accommodations that usually come with a shared bathroom, try the following hostels. **Hospedaje María Esther,** Lautaro 544 (© **67/233023**), has six rooms and kitchen facilities for $9 to $14 per person. **Hospedaje Lautaro,** Lautaro 269 (© **67/238116**), charges about the same rate, and although it's a little nicer than María Esther, it's usually closed during the winter.

EXPENSIVE

Cabañas La Pasarela *Moments*   These attached rooms and cabins nestled on the shore of Río Simpson are good for those who'd like a more rural surrounding not too far from town. The complex is on the other side of the river, away from the main road, and to get there guests must first cross a wooden suspension bridge. Cabañas La Pasarela is geared toward fly-fishermen, with private guides from Chile and the United States. But guests also like this lodge because you can fish right at the bank of the Río Simpson outside your door. The cozy restaurant is one of the best in town, and the fireside bar is a great place to unwind with a drink. All of the structures are made of cypress logs and have black, shingled roofs. In 2002, the main lobby, bar and restaurant areas were refurbished and are now a bit more elegant than before but the rooms are a bit on the dark side. The two new "VIP" suites are worth a splurge for their pleasant decor and come with queen bed and minibar. A pebbled walkway goes up to four A-frame *cabañas*. Note that you've got to be family or really good friends to rent one of the cabins, because three twins are in the bottom living area next to the kitchen.

Km 1.5, road to Puerto Aisén, Coyhaique. © 67/234520. www.lapasarela.cl. 11 units, 4 *cabañas*, 2 apts. $36–$57 double; $135 cabin for 5; $50–$71 suite. Rates include buffet breakfast. AE, DC, MC, V. **Amenities:** Restaurant; bar; lounge. *In room:* TV.

Hostal Belisario Jara ★ *(Value)*   This boutique hotel is Coyhaique's best lodging in this price range. The charming architectural design features honey-colored wood frames nailed together in varying angles, giving every room and sitting area a unique size and shape. A twisting hallway winds around the rooms, and the roof is a cupola topped off with a steeple and weathervane. The hotel is made of army-green stucco and windows aplenty, so it's bright and airy, and the crisp, white walls are accented here and there with local arts and crafts. Rooms are average size, some brighter than others, and all have ceramic floors. The softly lit, cozy dining area/bar is the highlight of the hotel, with a wooden table and chairs for relaxing fireside. French doors open out onto the front garden; the hotel sits on a busy street but is set back far enough so that you do not notice. The hotel has an apartment on the second floor of an old home on the main road, separate from the main building, that comes with a kitchen and can fit up to six.

Francisco Bilbao 662, Coyhaique. © 67/234150. www.belisariojara.itgo.com. 9 units, 1 apt. $55–$65 double. Rates include buffet breakfast. No credit cards. **Amenities:** Bar; lounge; laundry service. *In room:* TV.

Hostería Coyhaique ★   This *hostería* is Coyhaique's largest, and it sits in a quiet part of town surrounded by a well-trimmed lawn and garden. It is a more traditional hotel with loads of services, including its own boat service to the Laguna San Rafael Glacier. A leafy hallway leads guests to their rooms, which come with gleaming bathrooms and a classic decoration colored in rich green and maroon. The doubles come in two sizes; the matrimonial double with a full bed is larger than the double with two twins, but they're the same price. A dark-wood lobby leads into the bar, and around the corner is a semiformal restaurant; there's a more casual restaurant downstairs with great views of the countryside. Outside, there's a kidney-shaped pool and lots of grass for kids to romp around. The hotel offers packages that include lodging, most meals, and various excursions; contact the hotel for details.

Magallanes 131, Coyhaique. © 67/231137. Fax 67/233274. www.hotelsa.cl. 40 units. $65–$85 double. Rates include buffet breakfast. MC, V. **Amenities:** Restaurant; bar; lounge; outdoor pool; tour desk; room service; laundry service; nonsmoking rooms. *In room:* TV, minibar.

Patagonia Hotel   The Patagonia Hotel is another good option in this price range. This unassuming hotel sits on a quiet residential street and offers average-size rooms with mahogany furniture and comfortable beds. The hotel's main interior is dominated by an airy restaurant and bar, which has a towering, slanted ceiling with prominent wood beams, blond wood, and peach walls offset by stone. Although the Patagonia offers high quality, the style is a little sterile.

General Parra 551, Coyhaique. ©/fax **67/236505**. www.patagoniahotel.cl. 12 units. $64 double. Rate includes buffet breakfast. AE, DC, MC, V. **Amenities:** Restaurant; bar; tour desk; laundry service. *In room:* TV, minibar.

MODERATE

Cabañas Los Pinos *Finds*   These neat, handcrafted log cabins are nestled in a pine forest on the shore of Río Simpson, about a 5-minute drive from downtown. There are cabins for three, four, or six people with a wood-burning stove; the cabin for six has one bedroom with a full-size bed and one with two bunks. The cabin for four is a little tight, but the charm of the place makes up for it. The cabin for six comes with a kitchen; the other two cabins share a separate eating area, which guests usually don't mind considering the eating area is an idyllic little cabin with a beautiful view, great cooking facilities, and two tables for four. Two additional cabins are being built in 2003; inquire as to the size and rate when making your reservations. The couple who own and run the property are very friendly, and they have a vehicle for excursions.

Camino Teniente Vidal, Parcela 5, Coyhaique. © **67/234898**. 5 *cabañas.* $80 double. Rates include continental breakfast. No credit cards. *In room:* No phone.

El Reloj   This bed-and-breakfast–style hotel is housed in a forest-green-and-lemon old home flanked by two *araucaria* trees. The hotel is surrounded by an abundance of greenery, which is pleasant, but it shades the windows, so the rooms are fairly dark. The rooms are a little on the small side, but are appealing; some have stone walls, and all have old wood floors. It's a cozy enough place and very clean. There's a common living area, and a small restaurant serving local fare, such as wild hare, sheep cheese, and fresh salmon. The restaurant is open to the public, but limited seating keeps the numbers low. The hotel also has a tiny shop that sells various souvenirs.

Av. Baquedano 828. ©/fax **67/231108**. Htlelreloj@patagoniachile.cl. 9 units. $51 double. Rate includes buffet breakfast. No credit cards. **Amenities:** Restaurant. *In room:* TV.

Hotelera San Sebastián   This hotel's mustard exterior is so nondescript you might miss it the first time you pass by. But don't let the outside fool you: Inside, each room offers high-quality interiors and all but one has lovely views of the Coyhaique River meandering through grassy countryside. Huge bedrooms are tastefully painted in rose and cream, with matching linens and curtains, and are impeccably clean (most rooms were renovated in 2002) as are the bathrooms. The eating area is a bit cold, with linoleum floors and metal chairs, but a full renovation is promised for 2003. The hotel is on a busy street, but it sits back, tucked away between two buildings and therefore is very quiet.

Av. Baquedano 496, Coyhaique. © **67/233427**. 11 units. $50–$55 double. Rates include buffet breakfast. No credit cards. **Amenities:** Restaurant. *In room:* TV.

Hotel Los Nires   The Hotel Los Nires is a good mid-range choice, offering clean, bright rooms with decent, average furnishings. All the bathrooms were renovated in 2002 and are sparkling clean. The rooms are average size, but if you want extra space the staff can put a full-size bed in a room built for a triple (triple rate is $49–$57). The hotel has a large restaurant on the bottom floor that is open to the public, but guests take their breakfast in a sunny dining area off the lobby. The hotel's wood facade repeats itself indoors, with wood slat paneling.

Av. Baquedano 315, Coyhaique. © 67/232261. Fax 67/233372. Info@doncarlos.cl. 21 units. $39 double. Rate includes continental breakfast. AE, DC, MC, V. **Amenities:** Restaurant. *In room:* TV.

INEXPENSIVE

Hostal Araucaria   The Hostal Araucaria sits on a quiet street across from the Hostería Coyhaique's large garden park. This slightly weathered hostel is slowly getting a makeover. In 2002 the bathrooms were renovated and some of the beds were changed, but it still could use a touch of paint here and there and a new roll of carpet. There's an upstairs sitting area and a downstairs dining area that feels a bit like someone's own living room. The woman who owns and runs this hostel is very welcoming.

César Gerardo Vielmo 71, Coyhaique. © 67/232707. 6 units. $36 double. Rate includes buffet breakfast. No credit cards. *In room:* TV.

WHERE TO DINE

There are several cafes downtown that are good for a quick bite, such as **Café Oriente** (© 67/231622), Condell 201, with pizzas and sandwiches. The **Café Alemana** (© 67/231731) is a very nice cafe almost next door at Condell 119—despite its name, it does not serve German food. You'll find quick meals and sandwiches here, including a towering club sandwich.

Casino de Bomberos *Finds* CHILEAN   Chile's unpaid firemen need some way to make a buck, and here's their solution: Open a cafe in the fire station. The atmosphere is plain but fun, and the menu features classic dishes like roasted chicken and calamari with tomato sauce. The food is tasty and the fixed-price lunch is a steal at $4.25, with an appetizer, main dish, and dessert. On Sunday, there are baked and fried fresh empanadas.

General Parra 365. © 67/231437. Main courses $4–$7.50. No credit cards. Daily noon–4pm and 7pm–midnight.

Hostería Coyhaique ⭐ INTERNATIONAL/CHILEAN   Decent cuisine and ambience put this *hostería* above most restaurants in Coyhaique. The spacious, semiformal restaurant features an extensive menu serving international and Chilean fare, including pastas, salads, grilled meats, and pan-fried seafood, with a choice of sauces such as garlic or peppercorn. There's another restaurant downstairs, which is really more enjoyable for its cozier ambience and valley view. If you're waiting for a table, the Hostería Coyhaique has a bar and small lounge; if you just feel like a cocktail and an appetizer platter of cheeses and meat or shellfish, this is your spot.

Magallanes 131. © 67/231137. Main courses $5–$10. MC, V. Daily noon–11pm.

La Fiorentina *Value* PIZZA/CHILEAN   La Fiorentina serves a long list of pizzas and hearty, home-style dishes that can even be ordered to go—and stays open all day. The fixed-price lunch offers two selections and costs $3.50; it's very popular with the locals, who usually sit alone at lunchtime with their eyes glued to the TV blaring in one eating area. The atmosphere is very, very casual, but the service friendly and attentive.

Francisco Bilbao 574. © 67/238899. Individual pizzas $2.50–$5. MC, V. Daily 11am–midnight.

La Olla CHILEAN   This tiny restaurant offers a brightly lit, semi-casual dining area with floral tablecloths and attentive service. The Olla looks as though it promises more, but the menu is surprisingly brief. The fare is typical Chilean, with classics such as beef tenderloin and fried conger eel paired with the usual french fries or mashed potatoes. The food is hearty and good, but too simple. There is, however, a decent paella on Sunday. The owner is usually on hand and likes to chat with customers.

Prat 176. ℂ 67/234700. Main courses $5–10. MC, V. Daily noon–3:30pm and 8pm–midnight.

La Pasarela ⚲ CHILEAN   La Pasarela is about the best thing going in town. To get here, you need to take a taxi ride just outside town and across a wooden suspension bridge. The atmosphere is great: stone walls, wood beams, a roaring fireplace, and a comfortable bar for relaxing with a pisco sour. Through the windows, diners watch the Río Simpson rush by. The Pasarela is part of a *cabaña*/hotel complex, and usually whips up specials according to the guests' whims. Standbys include grilled meats and pastas. There is usually a fixed-price meal for lunch and dinner, including appetizer, main dish, dessert, and coffee for about $7 for lunch and $11 for dinner. Diners who are not lodging at La Pasarela must always call ahead for a reservation for dinner.

Road to Puerto Aisén, Km 1.5. ℂ 67/234520. Reservations required. Main courses $6–$10. AE, DC, MC, V. Daily 8am–midnight.

Restaurante Café Ricer *Finds* CHILEAN/INTERNATIONAL   This restaurant is a favorite with traveling gringos, and just about everyone else in town, too. The large, pub-style restaurant is fashioned of logs, and a handcrafted wood staircase leads to a mellower, slightly more formal dining area upstairs. The food is fairly good, although slightly overpriced; a salmon with sausage and onions means one bite of sausage and a few slivers of onion only. The fixed-price menu is a good deal at $7 and includes an appetizer, main course, and dessert. The waitresses' frumpy diner uniforms and distracted service don't seem to reflect the style of the restaurant. The atmosphere is lively, though, and it's a good place for a casual meal and a beer—and it stays open very late.

Horn 48. ℂ 67/232920. Main courses $8–$13. AE, DC, MC, V. Daily 8:30am–2am (to 3am in summer).

SOUTH FROM COYHAIQUE
A SIGHTSEEING EXCURSION AROUND LAGO ELIZALDE

The Seis Lagunas (Six Lagoons) and Lago Elizalde region just south of Coyhaique offers a sightseeing loop that passes through fertile, rolling farmland and forest and past several picturesque lakes, all of which are known for outstanding fly-fishing. This area is little visited and is a great place to escape the crowds. If you're tempted to stay and fish for a few days here, there are lodges that cater to this sport, described in "Fly-Fishing Lodges Around Coyhaique," below. If you rent your own car, pick up a good map because many of these roads have no signs. Aventura Turismo (see "Tour Operators," above) offers an excursion here.

Leaving Coyhaique via the bridge near the Piedra del Indio (a rock outcrop that resembles the profile of an Indian), head first to Lago Atravesado, about 20km (12 miles) outside town. The road continues around the shore and across a bridge and enters the Valley Lagunas. From here, you'll want to turn back and drive the way you came until you spy a road to the right that heads through country fields, eventually passing the "six lagoons." Take the next right turn toward Lago Elizalde. This pretty, narrow lake set amid a thick forest of deciduous and evergreen beech is a great spot for picnicking and fishing. There is often a boat-rental concession here in the summer. There's a lodge here, but it's open only occasionally, usually when it books a large group. From here you'll need to turn back to return to Coyhaique; follow the sign for Villa Frei, which will lead you onto the paved road to Coyhaique instead of backtracking the entire route. Keep an eye open for El Salto, a crashing waterfall that freezes solid in the winter.

LAGO GENERAL CARRERA & THE MARBLE CATHEDRALS

The Lago General Carrera straddles the border of Argentina (where it is known as Lago Buenos Aires) and is Chile's largest lake. There are two reasons to pay a visit here: the robin's-egg blue hue of the water and the "Marble Cathedral," a series of limestone caves polished and sculpted by centuries of wind and water whose black and white swirls are a magnificent contrast to the blue water below. It's entirely feasible to make an entire circuit around Lago Carrera, crossing by ferry between Chile Chico and Puerto Ibáñez (reservations are a good idea for travelers with a vehicle; © 67/237932), but it's not recommended for anyone with a short amount of time in Chile as you will need to spend the night somewhere along the way, most likely in Chile Chico. Try the charming **Hostería de la Patagonia,** just outside town on the Camino Internacional (© 67/411337), with an in-house restaurant. It charges $28 double; no credit cards accepted.

If you're looking for a day trip, however, a boating excursion to the Marble Cathedrals is a very interesting option—but at 223km (138 miles) from Coyhaique along a paved, then dirt road, it's a long round-trip drive to get to the dock in Puerto Tranquilo. A charter boat service takes visitors around and inside the marble caves for a half-day journey. You could plan a picnic and kick back along the shore. The lake is also great for fishing.

FLY-FISHING LODGES AROUND COYHAIQUE

El Saltamontes Lodge ⭐ This rustic, charming lodge can be found on the shore of the Nireguao River, about 100km (62 miles) from Coyhaique. This river is one of the highest rated in South America for the big, fat trout who gorge on the area's abundance of grasshoppers. Two anglers are paired with a guide, who leads them to various spots accessible by foot, horse, or vehicle. Beginners usually have a lot of luck here. The lodge has four bedrooms, each with a view.

Casilla 565, Coyhaique. ©/fax **67/232779.** Reservations arranged by The Fly Shop in the U.S. (© 800/669-3474; www.theflyshop.com). 2 *cabañas*, 1 suite. All-inclusive packages average $3,450 per angler, $2,500 for non-anglers per week. AE, DC, MC, V. **Amenities:** Restaurant; bar. *In room:* No phone.

Heart of Patagonia Lodge This lodge is closest to Coyhaique, if convenience is a big issue for you. The well-appointed lodge on the shore of Río Simpson is owned by an American and his Chilean wife, who offer good-natured service. Lunches are prepared streamside so as not to interrupt your fishing. They'll take you to other rivers and lagoons for shore and drift fishing. The owners charge less for non-angling guests, who can hike and horseback ride. They also charge a 1- to 2-night fee if you're not interested in a package.

Casilla 324, Coyhaique. ©/fax **67/233701.** mjenkins@netline.cl. 5 units. Average 7-day, full-service packages cost $4,025 per person; $450 per person, per day, non-angler. No credit cards. **Amenities:** Restaurant; lounge. *In room:* No phone.

Paloma Lodge The Paloma is about 35km (22 miles) from Coyhaique, and is good for its proximity to the city, a wide variety of excursions, and a remote location near Lago Elizalde. Beyond fly-fishing, in which two to three guests are paired with a guide, there are hiking and boat excursions. Fishing here is along the Paloma and Simpson rivers and Lakes Azul and Desierto. The lodge offers comfortable accommodations and a fly-tying room.

Freire 436, Coyhaique. ©/fax **67/215848.** 4 units. All-inclusive 7-night packages average $3,000 per person, double occupancy. MC, V. **Amenities:** Restaurant. *In room:* No phone.

The Terra Luna Lodge *Value*   This is a good lodge for anglers with non-fishing spouses. The Terra Luna Lodge is owned by the French-Chilean outfitter company Azimut, which offers excursions all over Chile. The location, on the shore of Lago Carrera, is ideal. There are quite a few things on offer here: Laguna San Rafael, hiking, horseback riding, and, of course, fishing. The lodge is close to the Río Baker. All-inclusive packages include transportation from Coyhaique. Several rooms here are a bit less expensive than those of the lodge's competitors.

Km 1.5, Camino Chile Chico, Puerto Guadal. In Santiago, Arzobispo Casanova 3, Providencia. © 2/737-3048. www.terra-luna.cl. 8 units. $60–$240 double; $38 more per person, per day, for meals. All-inclusive packages run an average of 4 days/3 nights at $850 per person. AE, MC, V accepted only at the main office in Santiago. **Amenities:** Restaurant; Jacuzzi; kayak and bike rental; laundry service. *In room:* No phone.

8 Puerto Aisén, Puerto Chacabuco & Laguna San Rafael National Park ★ ★

Puerto Aisén is 68km (42 miles) W of Coyhaique

Puerto Aisén was a vigorous port town until the 1960s, when silt filled the harbor and ships were forced to move 16km (10 miles) away to Puerto Chacabuco. Puerto Aisén still bustles, but it really offers few attractions to the visitor. The same could be said for Puerto Chacabuco; however, the majority of visitors to this region pass through here at some point to catch a ship or ferry to the spectacular Laguna San Rafael Glacier or to Puerto Montt. Most travelers arriving by ferry from Puerto Montt head straight to Coyhaique, and vice versa, but the full-day ferry ride to Laguna San Rafael leaves early and returns late, so many travelers find it convenient to spend a night here in Puerto Chacabuco.

It's recommended that you at least take a day trip to Puerto Aisén and Puerto Chacabuco, more than anything for the beautiful drive through the Reserva Nacional Río Simpson and the equally beautiful view of Aisén Sound at the journey's end. Both towns have pleasant squares for a quick stroll, and you can have lunch perched above the pier at the Hotel Loberías de Aysen (see "Where to Stay & Dine," below). If you don't have your own transportation, you can try **Buses Suray** at Eusebio Ibar 630 (© **67/238287**). The best bet is to call **Tour Australis** at Moraleda 589 (© **67/239696**; taustralis@patagoniachile.cl), which offers day trips around this area. The tours operate from November 15 to March 15 only, but the agency will arrange trips any time of the year for small groups.

Another excursion that is growing in popularity is a 2-hour boat trip to **Termas del Chilconal** in the middle of the dramatic Aisén Sound. The fare is about $30 per person and is arranged through the travel agency **Turismo Rucarary** in Puerto Aisén at Teniente Merino 668 (© **67/332862;** turismorucaray@entel chile.net). This travel agency offers other excursions around the area and sells ferry tickets.

For more information, there's a good website crammed with information on Aisen at www.puntoaisen.cl.

PARQUE NACIONAL LAGUNA SAN RAFAEL ★★★

If you're not planning a trip to Patagonia, the Laguna San Rafael National Park is a must-see. It's the foremost attraction in the Aisén region, drawing thousands of visitors each year to be dazzled by the tremendous vertical walls of blue ice that flow 45km (28 miles) from the Northern Ice Field and stretch 4km (2½ miles) across the Laguna San Rafael. Around these walls, thousands of aquamarine icebergs float in soupy water, forming jagged sculptures. If you're lucky enough, you'll see a few crash off the iceberg in a mammoth kerplunk.

The glacier is actually receding, and quite quickly. The first explorers here in 1800 described the glacier as having filled three-quarters of the Laguna; when you're here you can appreciate how much has disappeared.

The Laguna San Rafael National Park is a staggering 1.7 million hectares (4 million acres). Most of the park is inaccessible except by ship, on which visitors slowly cruise through narrow canals choked with thick vegetation. Like Torres del Paine, Laguna San Rafael is a UNESCO World Biosphere Reserve. Visitors set sail in Puerto Chacabuco or Puerto Montt aboard an all-inclusive luxury liner or modest ferry for day and multiple-day trips. The ship anchors near the glacier and passengers board zodiacs (inflatable motorized boats) for a closer look at the icebergs and the glacier, which in some places rises as high as 70m (230 ft.). A smaller fraction of visitors book an overflight excursion for a bird's-eye view of the glacier's entirety, which includes a touchdown at the park's center near the glacier for an hour-long visit.

It rains endlessly in this national park, but that's not a reason to cancel a trip to the glacier. Although this region sees heavy rainfall throughout the year, your best bet for clear skies is from November to March. Even on foul-weather days, the glacier is usually visible as the clouds tend to hover just above it. Bring protective rain gear just in case, or inquire when booking a ticket, as many companies provide guests with impermeable jackets and pants.

FERRY JOURNEYS THROUGH THE FJORDS TO LAGUNA SAN RAFAEL ★★

This extraordinary journey is about a 200km (124-mile) sail from Puerto Chacabuco, but many visitors leave from Puerto Montt for a round-trip journey or to disembark in Puerto Chacabuco. Some visitors plan a multiple-day journey to Laguna San Rafael as the focal point of a trip to Chile. When booking a trip, consider the journey's length and whether you will be traveling at night and therefore missing any portions of scenery. If you're doing a loop, you should be able to see everything.

Navimag ★ *Value* Both Navimag and Transmarchilay offer modest passenger and cargo ferry service to Laguna San Rafael, but Navimag has the slight edge in quality and sleeping arrangements. There are several embarkation options here. Navimag's ship M/N *Evangelistas* leaves from Puerto Montt, arrives in Puerto Chacabuco the next day, the Laguna San Rafael the following day, and then returns to Chacabuco and back to Puerto Montt. You can get on or off at Puerto Chacabuco for a cheaper, shorter trip. Like the rest of the companies, guests are taken close to the icebergs aboard a dinghy. There are cabins for four with a private or shared bathroom, and with an exterior or interior view. If you're a couple or alone, you might have to share with strangers, unless you're willing to fork out the entire price for a four-person cabin. Like Navimag's ship to Puerto Natales, the cheapest bunks are for the adventurous or very young only. Prices include meals, your bunk, and excursions. Vehicles cost $80 to $130 one-way from Puerto Montt to Chacabuco.

Offices in Puerto Montt at Av. Angelmó 2187 in the Terminal de Transbordadores (✆ **65/432300**) and Santiago at El Bosque Norte 0440 (✆ 2/442-3120). In Chaitén, call ✆ 65/731570. In Coyhaique, Ibáñez 347 (✆ 67/233306). www.navimag.cl. Prices vary, but average $160–$460 per person for the 4-night, round-trip journey from Puerto Montt. The 2-night, round-trip journey from Puerto Chacabuco costs about $245–$370 per person. AE, DC, MC, V.

Patagonia Expedition Not to be confused with Patagonia Express, the Expedition is another high-quality boat service offering day trips from Puerto

Chacabuco and package tours that include a stay in the Hostería Coyhaique, which owns this company. The Flash San Rafael 3-day tours include lodging, a 1-day trip to the glacier, and a day excursion south of Coyhaique to the beautiful Lago Elizalde region, where guests are treated to a lamb barbecue. The Flash Plus 5-day package offers the same activities, but guests spend the fourth night at the hotel in Lago Elizalde (minimum of 6 guests required). The Expedition is of the same general quality as the Patagonia Express. Kids here are given less of a discount than the Express, but the Expedition operates from December to March and the Express from January to February only.

In Santiago, Av. Providencia 2331, #602. © **2/335-5951.** Fax 2/335-0581. In Coyhaique, Magallanes 131 (in the Hotel Coyhaique). © 67/231137. Fax 67/233274. www.hotelsa.cl. The day excursion from Puerto Chacabuco is $325 per person. The Flash San Rafael 3-day program costs $543 per person; the 4-night/5-day program costs $528 per person, double occupancy. Kids under 12 receive a 30% discount. Includes lodging, meals, and excursions. AE, DC, MC, V.

Patagonia Express   Patagonia Express works in conjunction with the Termas de Puyuhuapi (see "Where to Stay & Dine" under "Puyuhuapi," above), leaving from Puerto Montt and including a 2-night stay at the hotel and 1 night in Puerto Chacabuco. This is another premium excursion with sharp service and wonderful accommodations, but unlike Skorpios, you do not spend the night on board the ship. If the package price is beyond your reach, Patagonia Express operates a day trip leaving from Puerto Chacabuco on Friday, from January to February.

In Santiago, Fidel Oteíza 1921, #1006. © **2/225-6489.** Fax 2/274-8111. www.patagonia-connection.com. Prices average $1,000 per person for the 3-night package, including 1 night in Puerto Chacabuco and 2 nights at Termas de Puyuhuapi; ½-price for kids under 16. The day excursion from Puerto Chacabuco (Jan–Feb only) is $290 per person, ½-price for kids under 16. Includes all meals and excursions. AE, DC, MC, V.

Skorpios   Skorpios is the upscale cruise service to Laguna San Rafael, offering deluxe on-board accommodations, great food, and all-around high quality. The wood-hewn cabins come with berths or full-size beds (or both, for families), in standard rooms or suites. There are three ships: the *Skorpios I, II,* and *III,* for 70, 160, and 110 people, respectively, although the trips are not usually heavily booked. Skorpios offers 6-day cruises leaving from Puerto Montt and 4-day cruises from Puerto Chacabuco. The 6-day takes visitors first along the coast of Chiloé near Ancud, then down to the glacier. On the return trip, the ship detours up the Fjord Quitralco to visit the remote hot springs there. Heading back to Puerto Montt, the ship cruises along the southern coast of Chiloé, stopping in Castro for an afternoon excursion. The 4-day journey also includes a stop at the hot springs. Skorpios offers service from September to May.

In Santiago, Augusto Leguía Norte 118, Las Condes. © **2/231-1030.** Fax 2/232-2269. In Puerto Montt, Av. Angelmó 1660. © 65/256619. Fax 65/258315. www.skorpios.cl. Cost for the 6-day/6-night journey is $800–$3,800 per person; the 4-day/4-night journey is $430–$1,600 per person. Prices include all meals, drinks, and excursions, and vary from high season to low season. ½-price for kids when they room with their parents. AE, DC, MC, V.

OVERFLIGHT TRIPS TO THE LAGUNA SAN RAFAEL

Two companies arrange overflight trips to the Laguna San Rafael, which include a few hours near the glacier. It is a spectacular experience to view the glacier in its entirety (which means you won't want to do this trip on a cloudy day). These are charter flights, so you'll have to get a group together or fork over the entire price. Prices range from $575 for a five-seater plane to $1,000 for an eight-person twin engine. Try **Transportes Don Carlos** at Subteniente Cruz 63

(© 67/231981; www.doncarlos.cl) or **Aerohein** at Av. Baquedano 500 (© 67/ 232772; www.aerohein.cl).

WHERE TO STAY & DINE

Hotel Loberías de Aysen   Puerto Chacabuco's slight shabbiness belies its lovely location on the shore of Aisén Sound, and thankfully this hotel does it justice with wraparound windows in a large dining area and lounge. The Loberías de Aysen is the obvious choice for its location right above the pier, and because it is the only decent hotel in Puerto Chacabuco. This is where most travelers with ferry connections spend the night when they don't want to make the early-morning journey from Coyhaique. It's a large complex with a garden, a kid's play area, 60 bedrooms, and 12 cabins with two and three bedrooms for four to six guests. Only the cabins for four come with kitchens, and unfortunately none come with views. The rooms have been recently renovated with new wallpaper, paint, and linens. Even if you're not planning on staying here, stop by for a coffee or pisco sour before heading back to Coyhaique.

Carrera 50, Puerto Chacabuco, Región XI. © 67/351112. Fax 67/351188. 60 units. $65–$10 double. Rates include buffet breakfast. DC, MC, V. **Amenities:** Restaurant; bar; lounge; sauna; laundry service. *In room:* TV.

Patagonia & Tierra del Fuego

Few places in the world have captivated the imagination of explorers and travelers like Patagonia and Tierra del Fuego. It has been 4 centuries since the first Europeans sailed through on a boat captained by Ferdinand Magellan. And yet this vast, remote region is still for the most part unexplored. Sailors from around the world continue to test their luck and courage in these harrowing straits and fjords. Mountaineers stage elaborate excursions through rugged territories only to be beaten back, like their predecessors, by unrelenting storms. A traveler can drive for days without seeing another soul on the vast Patagonian pampa, his perception of time and distance so warped that he believes he is the only human left on the planet. What seduces so many people to Patagonia is the idea of the "remote"—

indeed, the very notion of traveling to The End of the World. It is a seduction, but also an illusion. After all, people do live here—very few people, but those who do are hardy survivors.

A harsh, wind-whipped climate and Patagonia's geological curiosities have produced some of the most beautiful natural attractions in the world: the granite towers of Torres del Paine and Los Glaciares national parks, the Southern and Northern Ice Fields with their colossal glaciers, the flat pampa broken by multicolored sedimentary bluffs, the emerald fjords and lakes that glow an impossible sea-foam blue. In the end, this is what compels most travelers to plan a trip down here. Beyond landscapes, the region's "cowboys" (called *gauchos* in Argentina or *baquedanos* in Chile) lend a certain air of romanticism.

EXPLORING THE REGION

Patagonia and Tierra del Fuego are surprisingly easy to travel. It's entirely feasible to plan a circuit that loops through, for example, Ushuaia, Punta Arenas, Torres del Paine, and then El Calafate and El Chaltén. There's so much to see and do here, you'll really want to include a visit to this region in your trip to Argentina or Chile, if possible. How much time you plan on spending in Patagonia is entirely up to you. If you're planning a backpacking trip in Torres del Paine, for example, you'll want to spend between 5 and 10 days there—however, those with plans for a few light walks and sightseeing drives in that national park might find that 4 days are enough. A quick trip to Patagonia might include 2 days in El Calafate, 3 in Torres del Paine, and 2 days in Punta Arenas. A longer journey could begin with several days in El Chaltén, 2 in El Calafate, 5 in Torres del Paine, 2 in Punta Arenas, and a flight or cruise to Ushuaia for 3 to 4 days.

Prices jump and crowds swell from early November to late March, and some businesses open during this time frame only. The busiest months are January and February, but these summer months are not necessarily the best months to visit Patagonia, as calmer weather prevails from mid-October to late November, and from mid-March to late April.

Calling Between Chile & Argentina

One would think that two neighboring countries would offer low telephone rates for calls made from one to the other, but not so with Chile and Argentina. Visitors can expect to pay the same or higher rates as a call to the U.S., often around $1 per minute. When calling from Argentina to Chile, first dial **00-56,** then the area code and number. The prefix for Chilean cellphones is **09,** but callers from Argentina will drop the "0;" so to call a Chilean cellphone from Argentina, dial **00-56-9,** then the number.

When calling from Chile to Argentina, you must first call whichever carrier you're using (ask your host, your hotel, or at a calling center for the carrier prefix, usually either **123, 181,** or **120**), followed by **0-54,** then the area code and number. Argentine area codes always begin with a "0" prefix, which you'll drop when dialing from Chile. For example, if dialing from Punta Arenas, Chile, to Ushuaia, Argentina, you'll dial 123 (or whichever carrier you're using), then 0-54-2901 and the number. When dialing Argentine cellphone numbers (which begin in 15), drop the 15 and replace it with the region's area code.

1 Punta Arenas, Chile

254km (158 miles) SE of Puerto Natales; 3,090km (1,916 miles) S of Santiago

Punta Arenas, with a population of 110,000, is the capital of the Magellanic and Antarctic Region XII, and it is Patagonia's most important city; its streets hum with activity and its airport and seaports bustle with traffic. The town has made a living from carbon mines, wool production, petroleum, fishing, and as a service center for cargo ships.

Punta Arenas's earliest wealth is reflected in the grand stone mansions that encircle the main plaza, which were built with earnings from the sheep *estancias,* or ranches, of the late 1800s. Gold fever followed, and then flight from the First World War, when hundreds poured into the region from Yugoslavia, Russia, Spain, and Italy. Today, Punta Arenas's streets are lined with residential homes with colorful, corrugated rooftops, business offices and hotels downtown, and an industrial port. The city considers itself somewhat of an independent republic due to its isolation from the rest of Chile, and this in turn has affected the personality of its people, an indefatigable bunch who brace themselves every summer against the gales that blow through this town like a hurricane. The wind, in fact, is so fierce at times that ropes are strung up in and near the plaza for people to hold onto. If that weren't enough, residents here now have to contend with the ozone layer, which opened completely for the first time a few years ago.

All of this history and the extremity of Punta Arenas's climate, as well as its position overlooking the renowned Magellan Strait, make for a fascinating place to explore. There's enough to do here to fill 1 or 2 days, and you'll want to at least spend the night here, even if you plan to head directly to Torres del Paine.

GETTING THERE

BY PLANE Punta Arenas's **Aeropuerto Presidente Ibáñez** is 20km (12 miles) north of town, and, depending on the season, it's serviced with three to five daily flights from Santiago (all stop in Puerto Montt) by **LanChile/ LanChile Express,** Lautaro Navarro 999 (© **600/661-3000** or 61/241100).

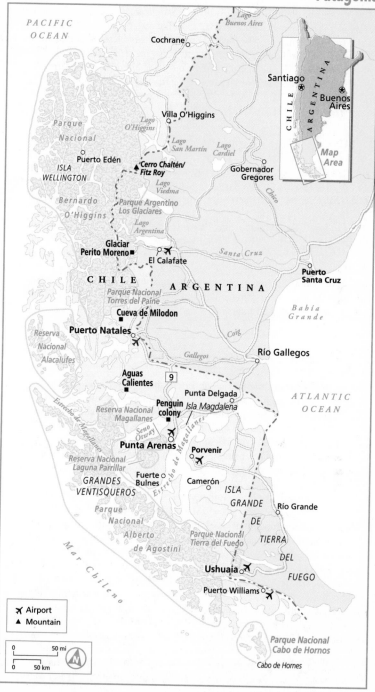

Patagonia

PACIFIC
OCEAN

Lago Buenos Aires

Cochrane

CHILE
ARGENTINA
Santiago
Buenos Aires

Map Area

Villa O'Higgins

Lago O'Higgins

Parque Nacional

Puerto Edén

Lago San Martín

Lago Cardiel

▲ Cerro Chaltén/
Fitz Roy

Gobernador
Gregores

Chico

ISLA WELLINGTON

Bernardo O'Higgins

Lago Viedma

Parque Argentino Los Glaciares

Lago Argentina

Glaciar
Perito Moreno

El Calafate

Santa Cruz

Puerto
Santa Cruz

C H I L E

A R G E N T I N A

Parque Nacional Torres del Paine

Bahía Grande

Cueva de Milodon

Coig

Puerto Natales

Reserva Nacional Alacalufes

Gallegos

Río Gallegos

Aguas
Calientes

9

Punta Delgada

ATLANTIC OCEAN

Penguin
colony

Isla Magdalena

Reserva Nacional Magallanes

Seno Otway

Punta Arenas

Porvenir

Reserva Nacional Laguna Parrillar

Estrecho de Magallanes

Fuerte
Bulnes

Camerón

ISLA GRANDE

Río Grande

GRANDES VENTISQUEROS

Parque Nacional

DE

Alberto de Agostini

Parque Nacional Tierra del Fuego

TIERRA

Mar Chileno

DEL

Ushuaia

FUEGO

Puerto Williams

✈ Airport
▲ Mountain

0   50 mi
0   50 km

Parque Nacional Cabo de Hornos

Cabo de Hornes

391

There's also one flight a week (usually on Sat) from Balmaceda. The airline **Aerovías DAP,** O'Higgins 891 (© **61/223340;** www.aeroviasdap.cl), has flights to and from Ushuaia every Wednesday and Friday from October to March, and Wednesday only from April to September; it also has daily service to Porvenir and the only air service to Puerto Williams and Cape Horn. To get to Punta Arenas, hire a taxi for about $8 or take one of the transfer services there (which can also arrange to take you back to the airport): **Ecotour** (© **61/223670**) and **Buses Transfer** (© **61/229613**) have door-to-door service for $5 per person; Buses Transfer has bus service to and from its office for $3 per person.

BY BUS From Puerto Natales: **Bus Sur** at José Menéndez 565 (© **61/ 244464**) has four daily trips; **Buses Fernández** at Armando Sanhueza 745 (© **61/242313**) has seven daily trips; **Buses Transfer** at Pedro Montt 414 (© **61/229613**) has two daily trips; and **Buses Pacheco** at Av. Colón 414 (© **61/242174**) has three daily trips. The cost is about $5 and the trip takes 3 hours.

To and from Ushuaia, Argentina: **Buses Tecni Austral** and **Buses Ghisoni** at Lautaro Navarro 975 (© **61/222078**) leave Punta Arenas Tuesday, Thursday, Saturday, and Sunday and return from Ushuaia on Monday, Wednesday, and Saturday. **Buses Pacheco** at Av. Colón 900 (© **61/242174**) has service to Ushuaia on Monday, Wednesday, and Friday and returns on Tuesday, Thursday, and Saturday. Buses cross through Porvenir or Punta Delgada. Bus fare is about $19, and the trip takes 12 hours.

 ## Cruising from Punta Arenas to Ushuaia

Cruceros Australis operates an unforgettable journey between Punta Arenas and Ushuaia aboard its ship, the M/V *Mare Australis.* This cruise takes passengers through remote coves and spectacular channels and fjords in Tierra del Fuego and then heads into the Beagle Channel, stopping in Puerto Williams on Isla Navarino and later Ushuaia, Argentina. The trip can be done as a 7-night, 8-day round-trip journey, a 4-night one-way from Punta Arenas, or a 3-night, one-way journey from Ushuaia.

The beauty of this cruise is that you are taken to places in Tierra del Fuego that few have a chance to see. Passengers are shuttled to shore via zodiacs (motorized inflatable boats) for two daily excursions that can include visits to glaciers or a sea elephant rookery, walks to view elaborate beaver dams, or horseback rides. There are several excellent bilingual guides who give daily talks about the region's flora, fauna, history, and geology. Service aboard the *Mare Australis* is excellent, and the food is quite good. The accommodations are comfortable, ranging from suites to simple cabins. All-inclusive, per person prices (excluding cocktails) range from $785 to $1,903 one-way from Punta Arenas and $1,152 to $2,537 round-trip. This cruise operates from late September to mid-April. For reservations or information, contact the offices in Santiago, at Av. El Bosque Norte 0440 (© **2/442-3110;** fax 2/203-5025), or in Punta Arenas, at Av. Independencia 840 (© **61/ 224256**); or visit www.australis.com.

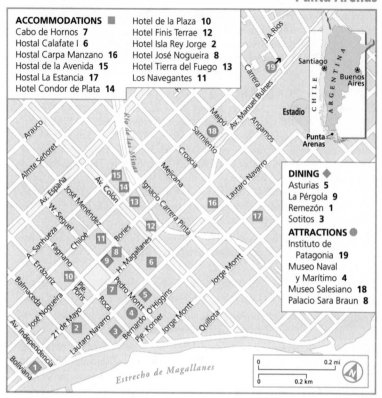

ACCOMMODATIONS ■
Cabo de Hornos 7
Hostal Calafate I 6
Hostal Carpa Manzano 16
Hostal de la Avenida 15
Hostal La Estancia 17
Hotel Condor de Plata 14

Hotel de la Plaza 10
Hotel Finis Terrae 12
Hotel Isla Rey Jorge 2
Hotel José Nogueira 8
Hotel Tierra del Fuego 13
Los Navegantes 11

DINING ◆
Asturias 5
La Pérgola 9
Remezón 1
Sotitos 3

ATTRACTIONS ●
Instituto de
  Patagonia 19
Museo Naval
  y Marítimo 4
Museo Salesiano 18
Palacio Sara Braun 8

BY CAR Ruta 9 is a paved road between Punta Arenas and Puerto Natales. Strong winds often require that you exercise extreme caution when driving this route. To get to Tierra del Fuego, there are two options: Cross by ferry from Punta Arenas to Porvenir, or drive east on Ruta 255 to Ruta 277 and Punta Delgada for the ferry crossing there (for more information, see "The Far South: Puerto Williams, Chile," later in this chapter).

CAR RENTAL **Hertz** at O'Higgins 987 (℃ 61/248742), **Lubac** at Magallanes 970 (℃ 61/242023), **Budget** at O'Higgins 964 (℃ 61/241696), **Emsa** at Roca 1044 (℃ 61/241182), **First** at O'Higgins 949 (℃ 61/220780), and **Rus** at Av. Colón 614 (℃ 61/221529).

GETTING AROUND

Punta Arenas is compact enough to explore on foot; however, taxis are plentiful and you can hail one off the street. Travel anywhere within the city limits will not cost more than $3; always confirm the fare with your driver before getting in the car. Buses are also abundant and run either north-south on calles Bulnes and Noguiera or east-west along Independencia. Bus fare is about 70¢.

VISITOR INFORMATION

There's an excellent **Oficina de Turismo** (℃ **61/200610**) inside a glass gazebo in the Plaza de Armas. The staff is helpful and they sell a wide range of historical and anthropological literature and postcards. The office is open from October to March, Monday through Friday from 8am to 8pm, Saturday from 9am to 6pm, and Sunday from 9am to 2pm. From April to September, it's open Monday through Friday from 8am to 7pm only. **Sernatur**'s office at Waldo Seguel 689 (© **61/225385;** www.sernatur.cl), on the other hand, is harried and inattentive; it's open Monday through Friday from 8:15am to 8pm.

FAST FACTS: PUNTA ARENAS

Currency Exchange   Exchange money at **La Hermandad,** Lautaro Navarro 1099 (© **61/248090**); **Cambios Gasic,** Roca 915, #8 (© **61/242396**); **Cambio de Moneda Stop,** José Nogueira 1168 (© **61/223334**); or **Scott Cambios,** corner of Avenida Colón and Magallanes (© **61/245811**). Casas de cambio are open Monday through Friday from 9am to 1pm and 3 to 7pm and Saturday from 9am to 1pm. For banks with 24-hour ATMs, go to Banco Santander at Magallanes 997 (© **61/247145**), Banco de Chile at Roca 864 (© **61/206033**), or Banco de A. Edwards at Plaza Muñoz Gamero 1055 (© **61/241175**). Banks are open Monday through Friday from 9am to 2pm.

Hospital   The local hospitals are **Hospital de las FF. AA. Cirujano Guzmán,** Avenida Manuel Bulnes and Guillermos (© **61/207500**), or the **Clínica Magallanes,** Av. Manuel Bulnes 1448 (© **61/211527**).

Internet Access   Try **Telefónica,** Bories 798 (© **61/248230**) or **Calafate,** Magallanes 22 (© **61/241281**). Internet service costs an average of $3 per hour.

Laundry   Try **Lavandería Antártida,** Jorge Montt 664; **Autoservicio Lavasol,** O'Higgins 969; or **Lavandería Lavasuper,** José Nogueira 1595.

Pharmacy   Go to **Farmacias Cruz del Sur,** Bories 658 (© **61/227018**) and José Nogueira 1120 (© **61/244871**); **Farmacia Marisol,** Fagnano 681 (© **61/224650**); or **Farmacias Salco** at Bories 683 (© **61/229241**) and Bories 970 (© **61/229227**).

Post Office   The central post office is at José Menéndez and Bories (© **61/222210**); hours are Monday through Friday from 9am to 6pm and Saturday from 9am to 1pm.

WHAT TO SEE & DO IN PUNTA ARENAS

Begin your tour of Punta Arenas in the Plaza Muñoz Gamero, where you'll find a bronze sculpture of Ferdinand Magellan. The leafy plaza is a beautiful place to take a seat, and several vendors here have set up stands selling crafts and souvenirs. From the plaza on Avenida 21 de Mayo, head north toward Avenida Colón for a look at the Teatro Municipal, designed by the French architect Numa Mayer and modeled after the Teatro Colón in Buenos Aires. Head down to the waterfront and turn south toward the pier, where you'll find a 1913 clock imported from Germany that has a complete meteorological instrumentation and hands showing the moon's phases and a zodiac calendar.

City Cemetery   They say you can't really understand a culture until you see where they bury their dead, and in the case of the cemetery of Punta Arenas, this edict certainly rings true. The City Cemetery was opened by the Governor Señoret in 1894 and features a giant stone portico donated by Sara Braun in 1919. Inside this necropolis lies a veritable miniature city, with avenues that connect the magnificent tombs of the region's founding families, settlers, and civic workers and a rather solemn tomb where lie the remains of the last Selk'nam Indians of Tierra del Fuego. You can walk here, but it's a good 20 minutes or more from the plaza. Av. Manuel Bulnes and Angamos. No phone. Free admission. Daily 7:30am–8pm.

Instituto de Patagonia/Museo del Recuerdo   The Instituto de Patagonia is run by the University of Magallanes and directed by the region's chief historian Dr. Mateo Martinic. Here you'll find an engaging exhibit of colonial artifacts called the Museum of Remembrances. Antique machinery and horse-drawn carts are displayed around the lawn and encircled by several colonial buildings that have been lifted and transported here from ranches around the area. One cabin shows visitors what home life was like for a ranch hand, another has been set up to resemble a typical dry goods store, another is a garage with a 1908 Peugeot, and another, a carpenter's workshop. There's a library on the premises with a collection of books and maps on display and for sale. To get into the colonial buildings, you'll need to ask someone in the museum's office to unlock them for you. The museum is about 4km (2½ miles) out of town, so you'll need to take a taxi. The Zona Franca (a duty-free shopping center) is just down the street, so you could tie in a visit to the two.

Av. Manuel Bulnes 01890. © 61/217173. Admission 70¢. Mon–Fri 8:30–11am and 2:15–6pm; Sat 8:30–12:30pm.

Museo Salesiano Maggiorino Borgatello ⭐   This fascinating museum is well worth a visit, offering insight into the Magellanic region's history, anthropology, ecology, and industrial history. The first room you enter is a dusty collection of stuffed and mounted birds and mammals that at turns feels almost macabre. It's an old collection, and some specimens such as the pygmy owl are in such desperate shape that it nearly provokes a laugh; nevertheless, it allows you to fully appreciate the tremendous size of the condor and the puma. In the adjoining room is a reproduction of the Milodon cave near Puerto Natales, where remains of a prehistoric giant sloth were found. Several rooms in the museum hold displays of Indian hunting tools, ritual garments, jewelry, an Alacalufe bark canoe, and colonial and ranching implements. The beautiful black-and-white photos of the early missionary Alberto d'Agostini are well displayed, and there's a sizable exhibit charting the region's petroleum production.

Av. Manuel Bulnes and Maipú. © 61/221001. Admission $2. Tues–Sun 10am–12:30pm and 3–6pm.

Museo Naval y Marítimo   Punta Arenas's tribute to its seafaring history is this Naval and Maritime Museum. Here you'll find photos depicting the various ships and the port activity over the past century, as well as small ship replicas and other artifacts. This museum is really recommended only for those with a strong interest in nautical-related items.

Pedro Montt 981. No phone. Admission $1. Tues–Sat 9:30am–12:30pm and 3–6pm.

Palacio Sara Braun and Museo Regional Braun Menéndez ⭐ *Moments*   These two attractions are testament to the staggering wealth produced by the region's large-scale, colonial-era sheep and cattle *estancias*. The museums are the former residences of several members of the families Braun, Nogueira, and Menéndez, who believed that any far-flung, isolated locale could be tolerated if one were to "live splendidly and remain in constant contact with the outside world." Splendid is an understatement when one gets a glimpse of these veritable palaces. The Palacio Sara Braun is now partially occupied by the Hotel José Nogueira and the Club de la Unión, a meeting area for the city's commercial and political leaders. Sara Braun, who emigrated from Russia with her brother Mauricio Braun, was the widow of the shipping, wool, and cattle magnet José Nogueira. The Museo Regional Braun Menéndez is the former residence of Mauricio Braun and Josefina Menéndez, a marriage that united the two largest fortunes in the Magellanic region. With the falling price of wool and the nationalization of *estancias* during the 1960s, the families lost a large percentage of their holdings, and their descendants have since moved out, settling in places such as Buenos Aires.

The homes are national monuments and both have been preserved in their original state. French architects planned the neoclassical exteriors, and European craftsmen were imported to craft marble fireplaces and hand-paint walls to resemble marble and leather. The interior fixtures and furniture were also imported from Europe, including gold and crystal chandeliers, tapestries from Belgium, Arabian tables inset with abalone, stained-glass cupolas, English and French furniture, hand-carved desks, and more. For some visitors, the knowledge that these families single-handedly exterminated the Native Indians in the region on their quest for wealth may temper the awe inspired by the grandeur of these palaces. The Museo Menéndez also has a salon devoted to the ranching and maritime history of the region. Tours are conducted in Spanish; however, the museums offer literature in English.

Palacio Sara Braun: Plaza Muñoz Gamero 716. (*C*) 61/248840. Admission $1.50 adults; free for under 16. Tues–Sat 11am–1pm and 6–8pm.

Museo Regional Braun Menéndez: Magallanes 949. (*C*) 61/244216. Admission $1.15 adults, 60¢ children under 16. Sun and holidays free. Mon–Fri 10:30am–5pm; Sat–Sun 10:30am–2pm.

SHOPPING

Punta Arenas is home to a duty-free shopping center called the **Zona Franca,** with several blocks of shops hawking supposedly cheaper electronics, home appliances, imported foodstuffs, sporting goods, perfumes, clothing, toys, booze, and cigarettes. The savings here are negligible, except for alcohol, and the selection isn't what you'd hope for, although there certainly is a lot on offer, including a few supermarkets. Really, this is a good place to stock up on supplies if you're planning a backpack trip to Torres del Paine—otherwise, forget it. The Zona Franca is located on Avenida Manuel Bulnes, just outside town. Because of its proximity to the Museo del Recuerdo (see "What to See & Do in Punta Arenas," above), you might want to tie a visit in here with that attraction; take a taxi to get there. It's open Monday through Saturday from 10am to 12:30pm and 3 to 8pm, and closed Sunday and holidays.

For regional crafts, try the great selection available at **Chile Típico,** Carrera Pinto 1015 ((*C*) **61/225827**), or **Artesanía Yoyi,** Av. 21 de Mayo 1393 ((*C*) **61/229156**). Both have knitwear, carved wood items, lapis lazuli, and more.

EXCURSIONS OUTSIDE PUNTA ARENAS
TOUR OPERATORS

Many tour operators run conventional city tours and trips to the Seno Otway colony and Fuerte Bulnes, as well as short visits and multiday, all-inclusive trekking excursions to Torres del Paine National Park. However, more and more adventure-travel outfitters are popping up around town, offering day and weeklong trips to Tierra del Fuego, including all-inclusive kayaking, mountaineering, hiking, fly-fishing, and horseback combination trips.

Turismo Yamana, Av. Colón 568 ((*C*) **61/240056;** www.turismoyamana.cl), offers kayak trips on the Strait of Magellan for a half day ($30 per person) or full day ($65), minimum two persons. The company also offers multiple-day trips to Lago Blanco in Tierra del Fuego for trekking, horseback riding, and fishing as well as all-inclusive trips to Torres del Paine, and even El Calafate, Argentina.

The tour company **VientoSur,** Fagano 585 (© **61/226930;** www.vientosur. com), offers all conventional tours, as well as tours to Torres del Paine (some overnight). They also arrange tours to Porvenir.

FUERTE BULNES

In 1843, Captain Juan Williams, the naturalist Bernardo Philippi, 16 sailors and soldiers, and two women set sail from Ancud in Chiloé to the Strait of Magellan to plant the Chilean flag in this region before European colonists could beat them to it. They chose a rocky promontory that dominated the strait and named it **Fuerte Bulnes.** Although this promontory was strategically appropriate for monitoring seafaring traffic, the location proved undesirable, and they pulled up stakes and moved 25km (16 miles) north, founding what is today Punta Arenas. In recognition of the historical value of Fuerte Bulnes, the Chilean government reconstructed the site in 1943, its centenary anniversary, and made it a national monument. Here you'll find reproductions of the log cabins that housed the settlers, a chapel, and several cannons. There are no set hours, and admission is free.

Just before Fuerte Bulnes is a short road leading to **Puerto Hambre.** The site was founded as Rey Felipe by Pedro Sarmiento de Gamboa in 1584, and settled by 103 colonists who were tragically stranded after tremendous storms prevented their ships from returning to shore. The name Puerto Hambre (Port Hunger) was given by the British captain Thomas Cavendish who found only one survivor when he docked here in 1587 (the rest had died of starvation and exposure). In 1993, the Chilean ambassador José Miguel Barros found the plan for Rey Felipe in the library of the Institute of France in Paris, and it is the oldest known document of urban history in Chile. The only thing you'll find here is a plaque and the remains of a chapel, but imagining yourself in the place of these settlers on this forsaken plot is worth the visit. Admission for both Fuerte Bulnes and Puerto Hambre is free, with unspecified hours. To get here, drive south from Punta Arenas to the road's end, or take a tour with **Buses Transfer,** Pedro Montt 966 (© **61/229613**), or **Eco Tour Patagonia,** Lautaro Navarro 1091 (© **61/223670;** www.ecotourpatagonia.com). Buses Transfer leaves at 9am, Eco Tour at 9:30am; the cost is $12 per person.

PENGUIN COLONIES AT SENO OTWAY & ISLA MAGDALENA

One of the highlights of a visit to Punta Arenas is a trip to the penguin colonies at Seno Otway or Isla Magdalena. At both colonies visitors are allowed to watch the amusing Magellanic penguins (also called Jackass penguins for their characteristic bray) at their nesting sites, whisking out sprays of sand or poking their heads out of their burrows. These penguins form lifelong partnerships and divide their chores equally: Every morning around 10am and in the afternoon around 5pm, the penguin couples change shifts—one heads out to fish, the other returns from fishing to take care of their young. When this changing of the guard begins, the penguins politely line up and waddle to and from the sea. Viewing takes place from September to late March, but they're best viewed from November to February.

Seno Otway is a smaller colony, with an estimated 3,000 penguins, and it's accessible by road about 65km (40 miles) from Punta Arenas. A volunteer study group has developed the sight with roped walkways and lookout posts, including a peek-a-boo wall where you can watch the penguins diving into the ocean.

Tours are offered in four languages, and there is a tiny cafe here, too. Admission is $3.50; it's open daily September through April from 8am to 8:30pm. Both **Buses Transfer,** Pedro Montt 966 (© **61/229613**) and O'Higgins 1055 (© **61/ 243984**), and **Eco Tour Patagonia,** Lautaro Navarro 1091 (© **61/223670; www.ecotourpatagonia.com**), offer transportation to Seno Otway, leaving at 4pm daily (most tour companies also have similar trips). The cost, not including the entrance fee, is $12. Your hotel can probably arrange a tour here as well. If you drive here in your own vehicle, come for the morning shift-change, when the crowds are thinner. Take Ruta 9 toward Puerto Natales, then turn left on the dirt road that branches out near the police checkpoint.

Isla Magdalena is much larger than Seno Otway, with an estimated 150,000 penguins sharing nesting space with cormorants. These penguins are more timid than those at Seno Otway, but the sight of so many of these birds bustling to and fro is decidedly more impressive. To get here, you need to take a ferry, which makes for a pleasant half-day afternoon excursion. **Turismo Comapa,** Av. Independencia 830, 2nd floor (© **61/225804**), puts this tour together. Its boat, the *Barcaza Melinka,* leaves from the pier at 3:30pm and returns at 8:30pm on Tuesday, Thursday, and Saturday from December to February ($28 for adults, $13 children under 12).

SKIING IN THE AREA

Punta Arenas has a ski resort that operates from mid-June to mid-September: the **Centro de Esquí Cerro Mirador,** situated at the border of the Reserva Nacional Magallanes. If you're here during the season, this little resort is a fun place to spend the afternoon, notable more than anything for its view of the Strait of Magellan, Tierra del Fuego, and—on a clear day—Dawson Island. During the summer they often run their only chair lift to carry you to the top of the peak, or you can hike the hill yourself. The resort has 10 runs, ski rental, and a cafeteria. Ski lift tickets cost about $18. The resort (© **61/241479**) is very close to town; to get here, take a taxi.

WHERE TO STAY

In general, lodging in Punta Arenas is somewhat expensive for the caliber of accommodations available. Note that price ranges reflect the low to high season—high season being from October 15 to April 15—and that each hotel is willing to negotiate a price, especially if you book the more expensive hotels with a travel agent. Always ask for "promotional rates" when calling a hotel, and check the hotel's website (when available) for Internet-only discounted rates.

EXPENSIVE

Cabo de Hornos   In 1962, the Cabo de Hornos was built as the first grand hotel in Punta Arenas. The style of the lobby, especially the Hornos's retro-chic bar, is reminiscent of this era, and not in an unattractive way. But then there are the rooms, which seem carelessly mismatched with clashing fabrics and outmoded furniture. The bathrooms here are circa 1962, with clunky toilets and bidets, but they've been well maintained. The best things this hotel has to offer are its direct view of the Strait of Magellan (try to get a corner room), the location directly overlooking the main plaza, and a tremendous breakfast buffet. Even so, the price is much higher than you'd expect for what's offered. The Cabo de Hornos is part of the Panamericana Hotel chain.

Plaza Muñoz Gamero 1025, Punta Arenas. © **61/242134.** Fax 61/229473. www.hch.co.cl. 90 units. $166 double. Rate includes buffet breakfast. AE, DC, MC, V. **Amenities:** Restaurant; bar; room service; laundry service. *In room:* TV, safe.

Hotel Finis Terrae   This hotel is very popular with foreigners, especially Americans, and it's part of the Best Western chain. The well-lit accommodations here are exceptionally comfortable, with king beds in double rooms and a softly hued decor in peach and beige, with wood trim and wooden headboards. And although Richard Gere stayed here in November 2002 (he chose the spacious 5th floor suite with a whirlpool tub and minibar) on his way to Antarctica to film a documentary, the rooms are by no means luxurious. The singles here are tiny, so be sure to ask for a larger double for the single price, which they will likely agree to, especially during slower months. The simple yet panoramic penthouse restaurant has an enormous A-frame ceiling fronted with windows on both ends that look out over the city and the Strait of Magellan. There's an adjoining lounge where visitors can relax and order a drink. The view from these two salons is undoubtedly the best in Punta Arenas.

Av. Colón 766, Punta Arenas. ℂ 61/228200. Fax 61/248124. www.hotelfinisterrae.com. 64 units, 2 suites. $149–$179 double; $189–$290 superior suite. Rates include buffet breakfast. AE, DC, MC, V. **Amenities:** Restaurant; lounge; room service; laundry service. *In room:* TV.

Hotel Isla Rey Jorge ⭐ *Finds*   This hotel is housed in an antique English-style mansion, 2 blocks from the plaza. There's a compact lounge lit by a pergola-like glass ceiling, decorated with a blue country-style theme. Altogether it's a lovable little hotel, especially since the wallpaper and bedspreads were changed in 2002. The snug rooms with angled eaves are just slightly dark, but kept toasty warm. Rooms have a classic, executive-style decor, in navy blue and burgundy offset with brass details. The junior suites are the most spacious, with king-size beds and whirlpool tubs. The friendly staff let it be known that they rarely charge the advertised price, so ask for a discount. Downstairs, in what was the brick-walled cellar, is an intimate restaurant and a popular pub (with a separate entrance), where they serve, among more standard fare, regional dishes such as Calafate (a wild berry) mousse and grilled beaver.

Av. 21 de Mayo 1243, Punta Arenas. ℂ/fax **61/248220**. www.Islareyjorge.com. 25 units. $146 double; from $189 junior suite. Rates include buffet breakfast. AE, DC, MC, V. **Amenities:** Restaurant; pub; room service; laundry service. *In room:* TV.

Hotel José Nogueira ⭐⭐ *Moments*   The best hotel in town is in this partially converted neoclassical mansion once owned by the widow of one of Punta Arenas's wealthiest entrepreneurs; half of the building is still run as a museum. The mansion was built between 1894 and 1905 on a prominent corner across from the plaza, with materials imported entirely from Europe. The José Nogueira is appealing for its historical value, but also offers classic luxury. The rooms here are not as large as you would expect, but high ceilings accented by floor-to-ceiling curtains compensate for that. All are tastefully decorated, either in rich burgundy and navy blue–striped wallpaper or rose and cream combinations, Oriental rugs, and lithographs of local fauna; the marble bathrooms are sparkling white. The Nogueira's singles are unusually spacious. The suites have ample bathrooms with Jacuzzi tubs and a living area in the open bedroom. The maids here dress in old-fashioned long smocks. The brief lobby with two leather couches leads into the popular restaurant La Pérgola, which is housed under the Nogueira's glass-enclosed terrace that once served as a "winter garden." The parlor and conference center that are connected to the lobby can be used for special meetings, but they are typically toured as part of the museum. Downstairs is a popular pub in what once was the wine cellar.

Bories 959, Punta Arenas. (②) **61/248840.** Fax 61/248832. www.hotelnogueira.com. 25 units, 3 suites. $119–149 double; suite from $199. Rates include buffet breakfast. AE, DC, MC, V. **Amenities:** Restaurant; bar; room service; laundry service. *In room:* TV, minibar.

Los Navegantes   Los Navegantes is another recommended hotel, and it's a bit cheaper than the Hotel Finis Terrae (see above). A few years ago the hotel renovated all of its rooms with fresh curtains, paint, and bright yellow wallpaper, but they are still rather nondescript. Even the restaurant was revitalized, in a Tuscan motif with mustard-colored walls and spiraling iron chandeliers. The bathrooms are a bit cramped, but they've been kept sparkling clean. The hotel is located downtown, and rooms come with a view of the city or a bland interior view, but they are the same price. The Los Navegantes isn't as cozy as the Finis Terrae, due to its stark hallways and fluorescent-lit lobby, but the rooms are fine, and the old-fashioned, low-lit bar with leather banquettes provides a comfortable place to sink into with an evening drink. Professional service and airport transfers round out this hotel.

José Menéndez 647, Punta Arenas. (②) **61/244677.** Fax 61/247545. www.hotel-losnavegantes.com. 50 units. $79–$108 double. AE, DC, MC, V. **Amenities:** Restaurant; bar; lounge; room service; laundry service. *In room:* TV, minibar.

Tierra del Fuego ★ *Value*   If you're looking for good value in this price category, then look no further. The Tierra del Fuego offers some of the most spacious accommodations in Punta Arenas, especially if you request the second floor rooms that come with kitchenette at no extra charge. Rooms are comfortable but don't expect much elegance: brown carpet, flowery bedspreads, and dark wood furniture. The marble bathrooms are clean but small. The focus of the hotel is the ground floor pub that pulls in many of the city's young professionals and visiting businessmen. It gives the hotel a vibrant, youthful atmosphere. There's also a computer with Internet access available to guests for a small fee.

Colon 716, Punta Arenas. (②)/fax **61/226200.** www.puntaarenas.com. 26 units. $98 double; suite from $130. Rates include buffet breakfast. AE, MC, V. **Amenities:** Restaurant; pub; room service; laundry service. *In room:* TV, minibar, hair dryer, dataport.

MODERATE

Hostal Carpa Manzano   If you're looking for a moderate lodging option, this is the best deal going. This comfortable little hostel is located in a residential area about a 7-block walk from the main plaza, so it's not exactly centrally located, but it is quiet. There's a front common area that looks like the dining area of a home and tidy, sunny rooms that face a plot of flowers. The beds are comfortable, and each room has a private bathroom.

Lautaro Navarro 336, Punta Arenas. (②)/fax **61/248864.** 10 units. $38–$52 double. Rates include continental breakfast. No credit cards. **Amenities:** Lounge. *In room:* TV.

Hostal de la Avenida   This olive-colored, homey hostel looks as though it were run by a little old lady, judging by the sugary dining area decorated in floral prints and porcelain figurines. A plant-filled walkway is half-covered with a fiberglass ceiling, and the three rooms that face the covered portion are dungeon-like dark; ask for one of the four rooms upstairs that receive more light. Rooms are simple, with brick walls.

Av. Colón 534, Punta Arenas. (②)/fax **61/247532.** 7 units. $36–$43 double. Rates include continental breakfast. AE, DC, MC, V. **Amenities:** Lounge. *In room:* TV.

Hotel de la Plaza   The Hotel de la Plaza was built almost a hundred years ago as a home for men who worked for the sheep rancher José Menéndez. Its lobby feels like a hangout in a college dorm, but the antique rooms with high ceilings, crisp linens, and antique furnishings make up for it. The rooms are bright, with white walls and tall windows that look out onto the plaza or neighboring buildings; each room still has its original wood molding. The bathrooms are dark and tiny. The halls are adorned with historic black-and-white photos from the region, and the lobby displays posters celebrating climbing achievements by mountaineers who have stayed here in the past. The receptionists don't speak much English and aren't too helpful, either.

José Nogueira 1116, Punta Arenas. (C) **61/241300.** Fax 61/248613. hplaza@chileaustral.com. 17 units. $55– $80 double. AE, DC, MC, V. **Amenities:** Lounge. *In room:* TV.

INEXPENSIVE

Hostal Calafate I and II   The Hostal Calafate I and II are joint-owned hostels. Calafate I is in an old white–and–mint green wooden home and is perhaps the best inexpensive lodging option in town—the reason it tends to book up days in advance. It's nothing special, but the owners are gracious and each room is clean and comes with cable TV. It is ideal for anyone looking for three or four individual twin beds, as there is just one room with a double bed. The best deal here is the sole apartment out back, which has a fully stocked kitchen, three twin beds, and a separate entrance. The Calafate II is more like a standard hotel, and it's located around the corner from the plaza with an adjoining Internet cafe very popular with locals. Rooms and the bathrooms (some shared) in both hotels are pretty tight but clean.

Hostal Calafate I: Lautaro Navarro 850, Punta Arenas. (C) **61/248415.** 5 units. $28 double with shared bathroom. No credit cards. **Amenities:** Lounge. *In room:* TV.

Hostal Calafate II: Magallanes 22, Punta Arenas. (C) **61/241281.** 18 units. $38 double with private bathroom; $32 double with shared bathroom. No credit cards. **Amenities:** Internet cafe. *In room:* TV.

Hostal La Estancia   If you're trying to keep expenses down, the Hostal La Estancia offers low-cost rooms and a kitchen that guests may use to cook meals. The hostel, located in a residential area that is a 10-minute walk from downtown, is an old home with creaky wooden floors, humble rooms, and a sunny, pleasant dining area with a TV.

O'Higgins 765, Punta Arenas. (C) **61/249130.** 8 units, all with shared bathroom. $26 double. AE, DC, MC, V. **Amenities:** Lounge.

WHERE TO DINE

There are plenty of good restaurants in Punta Arenas, most of which serve local fare such as lamb, king crab, and shellfish. All major hotels have decent restaurants if you feel like dining in. For a quick bite, try the casual cafes **El Quijote,** Lautaro Navarro 1087 (C **61/241225**), open daily from 10am to 11pm, or **Patiperros,** Av. Colón 782 (C **61/245298**), open daily from 11am to 1am. Another local favorite, although slightly overpriced, is the diner-style **El Mercado,** Mejicana 617 (C **61/247415**). If you're not planning a trip to Chiloé, you might want to try El Mercado's version of that island's specialty: *curanto,* a heaping surf-and-turf platter with tomato broth.

Asturias SPANISH/CHILEAN   Locals rave about Asturias, but we find that other restaurants have slowly usurped it, especially in terms of ambience. The dining room features Spanish pink stucco and ironwork, but is too plain and over-lit to encourage intimacy. Asturias specializes in Spanish cuisine, such as paella, and seafood. You'll find standard salmon, sea bass, and shellfish dishes here, and great abalone loco appetizers when in season. Asturias is best known for its mouth-watering salmon dish prepared with cheese and sausage and steamed in a tinfoil pouch with garlic and wine.

Lautaro Navarro 967. ℂ **61/243763**. Main courses $6–$12. AE, DC, MC, V. Mon–Sat noon–3pm and 8–11pm.

La Pérgola *★ Moments* REGIONAL   La Pérgola is located inside the glass-enclosed, vine-draped "winter garden" that once was part of the stately mansion owned by Sara Braun, now part of the Hotel José Nogueira. The ambience is as lovely as the cuisine. The menu provides photos of each dish, including king crab quiche, curried lamb with glazed carrots, filet mignon in three sauces, and pork loin in a cherry sauce. There's even salmon sashimi. An ample wine list and desserts such as tiramisu round out the menu. Small tables make this restaurant unsuitable for large groups.

Bories 959. ℂ **61/248840**. Main courses $9–$13. AE, DC, MC, V. Daily noon–3:30pm and 7:30pm–midnight.

Remezón *★★ Finds* CONTEMPORARY REGIONAL   One of the best restaurants in the region, Remezón breaks from the traditional mold with a warm, intimate dining area decorated with a jumble of art and slightly kitsch items that are as personal as the chef's daily changing menu. The food is, in a word, divine: not too pretentious but always prepared with fresh, regional vegetables, seafood, and meats seasoned to delicious perfection. The menu features five appetizers and as many main dishes handwritten on a chalkboard; usually the chef approaches your table and explains each item to diners before ordering. Sample dishes include delicious garlic soup; broiled Parmesan scallops; calamari, zucchini and avocado salad; goose marinated in pisco and lemon; and crepes stuffed with king crab and cream. There's always a vegetarian dish on offer, such as vegetable *pastel de choclo,* a casserole topped with a corn crust. The gracious owners love good cooking, and it shows. Remezón is located on the edge of town in a somewhat grungy neighborhood so taking a taxi here would be best.

Av. 21 de Mayo 1469. ℂ **61/241029**. Main courses $8–$13. AE, DC, MC, V. Daily noon–3pm and 7:15pm–midnight. Closed Mon Apr–Sept.

Restaurant Hotel Finis Terrae CHILEAN/INTERNATIONAL   This restaurant is located on the top floor of the Hotel Finis Terrae. The food is not as good as what you'll find at the other restaurants mentioned in this section, but it's decent; what makes this restaurant unique are the incredible views seen through enormous arched windows that wrap around the dining area. This is a great place for breakfast, and it opens early, at 6:30am. The ambience leans toward the casual, and the menu has enough options to satisfy anyone, from beef stuffed with king crab in an herb sauce to sea bass with mussels and spinach; there are also soups and sandwiches for a light lunch and a variety of pasta dishes. For dinner, there's usually a $15 fixed-price meal—your choice of an appetizer, main course, and dessert. There's a decent wine list, as well.

Av. Colón 766. ℂ **61/228200**. Main courses $6–$13; fixed-price 3-course meal $15. AE, DC, MC, V. Daily 6:30am–11pm.

Sotitos CHILEAN   Don't be fooled by the plain green front with the weathered sign: Sotitos has handsomely renovated its semiformal interiors with brick walls and white linen tablecloths. If you're looking for traditional Chilean cuisine, this is your restaurant. Sotitos offers everything and more than most Chilean restaurants, including steak and seafood, local baked lamb, Valencia shellfish rice (which must be ordered ahead of time), pastas, and fresh salads.

The key is that everything is of high quality, regardless of how simple the dish. The service here is superb, attentive but not overbearing. On Friday, Saturday, and Sunday they fire up their *parrilla* (grill) for barbecued meats. There's a non-smoking section up front, but it's usually empty.

O'Higgins 1138. © **61/221061.** Main courses $6–$13. AE, DC, MC, V. Mon–Sat 11:30am–3pm and 7–11:45pm.

PUNTA ARENAS AFTER DARK

The city has a fair amount of bars and pubs, plus a few discos, which we recommend only if you like to hang out with teenagers and listen to bad techno music. One of the most popular pubs for all ages is in the **La Taberna** (© **61/248840**) cellar bar, below the Hotel José Nogueira at the corner of Bories and Sequel across from the plaza; appetizers are available. Another popular spot is the **Pub 1900** (© **61/242759**), at the corner of Avenida Colón and Bories; yet another pub is the **El Galeón** at Av. 21 de Mayo 1243, below the Hotel Isla Rey Jorge (© **61/248220**). If you just can't get enough karaoke, head to **El Coral,** Bories 817 (© **61/243851**), which also serves food. The **Cabo de Hornos Hotel** (© **61/242134**), on the plaza, has a 1960s-chic bar with abstract paintings and pinhole lights. The cinema **Commercial Cine Magallanes,** at Plaza Muñoz Gamero 765 across from the tourism kiosk at the plaza (© **61/223225**), has one screen; call or check newspaper listings for what's playing.

2 Puerto Natales, Chile

254km (158 miles) NW of Punta Arenas; 115km (71 miles) S of Torres del Paine

Puerto Natales is a rambling town of 15,000, spread along the sloping coast of the Señoret Canal between the Ultima Esperanza Sound and the Almirante Montt Gulf. This is the jump-off point for trips to Torres del Paine, and nearly all visitors to the park will find themselves spending at least one night here. The town itself is nothing more than a small center and rows and rows of weather-beaten tin and wooden houses, but it has a certain appeal, and it boasts a stunning location with grand views out onto a grassy peninsula and glacier-capped peaks in the distance. From May to September, the town virtually goes into hibernation, but come October, the town's streets begin to fill with travelers decked out in parkas and hiking boots on their way to the park.

Puerto Natales is the capital of the Ultima Esperanza Sound, founded in 1911 as a residential center and export port for local sheep ranches. Tourism has now replaced wool as a dominant economic force, evident by the plethora of hostels, restaurants, and tour companies found here.

ESSENTIALS
GETTING THERE & GETTING AROUND

BY PLANE   The tiny Puerto Natales airport (no phone) has only one scheduled flight per day and that is a nine-passenger propeller plane from El Calafate. Contact **Aerovías DAP,** in Punta Arenas, at O'Higgins 891 (© **61/223340;** www.aeroviasdap.cl), for information and reservations. At this writing, the one-way fare is $50 for the short hop to Argentina. A taxi from Puerto Natales to the airport costs $1.50 and is only a 5-minute drive.

BY BUS   Puerto Natales is the hub for bus service to Torres del Paine National Park and El Calafate, Argentina. For information about bus service to and from Torres del Paine, see "Parque Nacional Torres del Paine," later in this chapter.

There are frequent daily trips between Punta Arenas and Puerto Natales. In Puerto Natales each bus company leaves from its own office.

To & from Punta Arenas **Buses Fernández,** Eberhard 555 (© **61/411111**), has seven daily trips; **Bus Sur,** Baquedano 558 (© **61/411325**), has six daily trips; **Buses Pacheco,** Baquedano 244 (© **61/414513**), has six daily trips (and the most comfortable buses); and **Transfer Austral,** Baquedano 414 (© **61/412616**), has three daily trips. The trip takes about 3 hours and the cost is $5 one-way.

To El Calafate, Argentina **Buses Zaahj,** Arturo Prat 236 (© **61/412260**), leaves at 9am; **Bus Sur,** Baquedano 534 (© **61/411325**), leaves at 9am; and **Cootra,** Baquedano 244 (© **61/412785**), leaves at 6:30am. The cost is $22 one-way. The trip takes 5 to 6 hours, depending on the traffic at the border crossing. Note that most of this voyage is on unpaved dirt roads.

BY CAR Ruta 9 is a paved road that heads north from Punta Arenas. The drive is 254km (158 miles) and takes about 2½ to 3 hours. If you're heading in from El Calafate, Argentina, you have your choice of two international borders: Cerro Castillo (otherwise known as Control Fronterizo Río Don Guillermo) and Río Turbio (otherwise known as Controles Fronterizos Dorotea y Laurita Casas Viejas). Cerro Castillo is the preferred entry point for its easier access. Both are open 24 hours from September to May, and daily from 8am to 11pm the rest of the year.

Car rentals in Puerto Natales are offered by **Motorcars** at Baquedano 380, #3 (© **61/413593**), **EMSA** (an Avis representative) at Av. Manuel Bulnes 632 (© **61/410775**), and **Bien al Sur** at Av. Manuel Bulnes 433 (© **61/414025**).

BY BOAT **Navimag** runs a popular 3-night ferry trip between Puerto Natales and Puerto Montt, passing through the southern fjords of Chile. This journey passes through breathtaking scenery, and it makes for an interesting way to leave from or head to Chile's Lake District. The trip is described in chapter 14, under "Ferry Crossings to the Carretera Austral & Sailing to Patagonia Through the Fjords." Navimag leaves every Thursday evening; its offices are next to the Hotel CostAustralis at Pedro Montt 262 (© **61/414300;** www.navimag.com).

ORIENTATION

Puerto Natales is built on a grid pattern, and you'll find you spend most of your time within a 5-block radius. There is the main plaza, Plaza de Armas, along which runs Calle Eberhard, the street where you'll find the post office and the town's yellow cathedral. Calle Eberhard dead-ends a block away at Blanco Encalada; this street, Avenida Manuel Bulnes (1 block to the right), and Baquedano (1 block up from Blanco Encalada) are the principal streets, with most of the supermarkets, banks, and tourism-oriented businesses. Along the shore of Puerto Natales runs Pedro Montt, also called the Costanera. The Costanera is an excellent place for a stroll.

VISITOR INFORMATION

Sernatur operates a well-stocked and informed office on the Costanera at Pedro Montt and Philippi (© **61/412125;** www.sernatur.cl); it's open October through March, Monday through Friday from 8:30am to 8pm, Saturday and Sunday from 9:30am to 1pm and 2:30 to 6:30pm; April through September, it's open Monday through Friday from 8:30am to 1pm and 2:30 to 6:30pm, closed Sunday and holidays. **Conaf** has its park headquarters at O'Higgins 584

(© **61/411438;** www.conaf.cl), but you'll get better park information from a tour operator for information (see "Tour Operators & Adventure Travel Outfitters," below).

FAST FACTS: PUERTO NATALES

Currency Exchange   There are several exchange houses on Blanco Encalada; try **Mily,** Blanco Encalada 183, and their other office on the same street, at 266 (© **61/411262;** open Mon–Sat 10am–8pm). The only ATM in town is at the **Banco de Santiago,** located at the corner of Blanco Encalada and Manuel Bulnes (the ATM is open 24 hr.).

Hospital   Frankly, the town's public hospital is horrible. It's on the corner of Pinto and O'Higgins (© **61/411583**). For major medical emergencies, it's best to get yourself to Punta Arenas.

Internet Access   Turismo Mily, Blanco Encalada 183 (© **61/413834**), and **Turismo María José,** Av. Manuel Bulnes 386 (© **61/414312**), have Internet services. Connections in Puerto Natales are excruciatingly slow.

Laundry   Try **ServiLaundry,** Av. Manuel Bulnes 513 (no phone). Hours vary, but it's open more or less Monday through Saturday from 9am to 1pm and 2 to 8pm.

Pharmacy   Farmacias Marisol is at Baquedano 331 (© **61/411591**).

Post Office   The post office is on the Plaza de Armas next to the cathedral (no phone; open Mon–Fri 9am–6pm, Sat 9am–1pm).

EXCURSIONS OUTSIDE PUERTO NATALES
CUEVA DE MILODON

In 1896, Capitan Eberhard found a scrap of hairy skin and a few bones in a large cave near his property that were later determined to be from a *Milodon,* a prehistoric ground sloth. The story of the *Milodon* was popularized by Bruce Chatwin's travelogue *In Patagonia.* Although the *Milodon* is depicted in a full-size replica at the cave's entrance, most of the *Milodon's* remains were shipped off to London, which means the real attraction is the 30m (98-ft.) high, 200m (656-ft.) deep cave itself, which has a weird shaggy roof and is surrounded by interesting conglomerate rock formations. There's an interpretative center with a few *Milodon* bones and a display showing the geological formation of the cave, as well as a historical display of the Indians who inhabited this and nearby caves as far back as 12,000 years ago. This attraction is really recommended only if you happen to be passing by, or if you've run out of things to do in Puerto Natales. The cave is located 24km (15 miles) north of Puerto Natales, so you'll

---

Tips **Renting Camping Equipment**

If you don't feel like lugging your own gear down here, there are several agencies that rent equipment. Typical daily rental prices are two-man tents $5 to $6, sleeping bags $2, stoves $1.50, sleeping mats $1.50, and backpacks $3. During the high season, it's best to reserve these items. The following companies rent equipment: **Casa Cecilia,** Tomás Roger 60 (© **61/ 411797;** redcecilia@entelchile.net); **Onas,** Eberhard and Blanco Encalada (© **61/412707;** onas@chileaustral.com); and **Fortaleza Aventura,** Arturo Prat 234 (© **61/410595;** monofortaleza@hotmail.com).

need your own car or a tour to get here. To get here, take the road to Torres del Paine; at 20km (13 miles) turn left, and then drive for 4km (2½ miles) to the cave's turn-off. The site is managed by Conaf and open daily from 8:30am to 7pm; admission is $4 adults, $2 children (© **61/411438** in Puerto Natales).

SAILING TO PARQUE NACIONAL BERNARDO O'HIGGINS

This national park encompasses a tremendous amount of terrain, but it's unreachable except for boat tours to the glaciers Balmaceda and Serrano. There are several boat excursions that leave from Puerto Natales, sailing first through the Ultima Esperanza Sound past the Península Antonio Varas, stopping for a walk up to the narrow Serrano Glacier that plunges into a small bay choked with icebergs. The boat then sails past the Balmaceda Glacier. This journey is highly recommended, although it's a full-day excursion and might bore some travelers because it doubles back along the same route. The best way to do it is to leave Torres del Paine via one of the zodiac services that drops riders off at the Serrano Glacier, then take the boat back to Puerto Natales, or vice versa (see "Getting There & Away" under "Parque Nacional Torres del Paine," later in this chapter).

There are two companies that offer the excursion. The cutter *21 de Mayo* with offices at Eberhard 554 (© **61/411978;** www.turismo21demayo.cl), leaves at 8:30am and arrives at the Serrano Glacier at 11:30am, where it stays for 1½ hours, returning at 5pm. The cost is $30 per person, not including lunch (box lunches are provided for $9 more). A new service offered by **Aventour** at Av. Manuel Bulnes 689 (© **61/243354;** www.aventouraventuras.com) takes visitors along a similar route aboard its wooden yacht *Nueva Galicia,* leaving at 7:30am and arriving at the Serrano Glacier at 11am for a half hour, then across the adjoining river to its lodge, the Hostería Monte Balmaceda (see "Where to Stay," below). There, visitors can take a walk around the self-guided nature trail, have lunch in the restaurant, and reboard, arriving at Puerto Natales at 5:30pm. The cost for this trip is $55 per person.

TOUR OPERATORS & ADVENTURE TRAVEL OUTFITTERS

The glut of tour operators in Puerto Natales can be divided into two groups: conventional sightseeing day tours to Torres del Paine, the Perito Moreno Glacier in Argentina's Los Glaciares National Park, the Nordenskjold Trail, and the icebergs at Lago Grey; and adventure travel outfitters that arrange multiday, all-inclusive excursions, including trekking the "W" or the Circuit (see "Trails in Torres del Paine," later in this chapter) and climbing in Torres del Paine; kayaking the Río Serrano in Parque Nacional Bernardo O'Higgins; and horseback trips. Keep in mind that it's very easy to arrange your own trekking journey in Torres del Paine; the bonus with these outfitters is that they carry the tents (which they'll set up) and food (which they'll cook). They also will pick you up from the airport and provide guided information about the flora and fauna of the park.

CONVENTIONAL DAY TOURS   These tours are for people with a limited amount of time in the area. Tours typically leave at 7:30am and return around 7:30pm, and cost about $26 per person, not including lunch or park entrance fees. Try **Turismo Mily,** Blanco Encalada 183 (© **61/413834**), **Turismo María José,** Av. Manuel Bulnes 386 (© **61/414312**), and **Turismo Zaahj,** Arturo Prat 236 (© **61/412260**); Zaahj includes a stop at the Cueva de Milodon.

ADVENTURE TRAVEL   Apart from the local guiding outfitters here in Puerto Natales, several American and Chilean companies offer well-planned trekking excursions in Torres del Paine, specifically Mountain-Travel Sobek and Cascada Expediciones (both have bases here and in Punta Arenas; see "The Active Vacation Planner," in chapter 10, for more information). **Bigfoot Expeditions,** Blanco Encalada 226 (© **61/414611;** www.bigfootpatagonia.com), is the leader of the pack here in Puerto Natales; in Santiago, its office is at Helvecia 210 (© **2/335-1796;** fax 2/335-1798). Bigfoot offers a variety of multiday trekking journeys through the park that can include kayaking, horseback riding, and sailing. Bigfoot also owns the concession for the ice walk across Glacier Grey (described in "Parque Nacional Torres del Paine," later in this chapter), and they are the ones to call for climbing and mountaineering in the park. Bigfoot can arrange custom tours, and all-inclusive tours include all lodging, transfers, meals, and equipment. **Onas,** Blanco Encalada and Eberhard (©/fax **61/412707;** www.onaspatagonia.com), is another adventure travel company that offers trekking excursions in Torres del Paine. Onas also has a half-day zodiac trip down the Río Serrano; see "Getting There & Away" under "Parque Nacional Torres del Paine," later in this chapter. **Aventour,** Av. Manuel Bulnes 689 (© **61/410253;** www.aventouraventuras.com), works mainly out of Parque Nacional Bernardo O'Higgins, and has a variety of excursions, transfers, and boat journeys that can get you to the park through the back route up the Río Serrano. **Turismo Yamana,** out of Punta Arenas, is a very reliable company that offers all-inclusive trekking trips to Torres del Paine; for more information, see "Tour Operators" under "Excursions Outside Punta Arenas," earlier in this chapter.

WHERE TO STAY

It seems that anyone and everyone who owns a home large enough to rent out a few rooms has decided to hang an HOSPEDAJE sign above their door. These simple, inexpensive accommodations can be found everywhere, but higher-end (and more expensive) options are to be had as well. The high season in Puerto Natales is longer than in any other city in Chile, generally considered to run from October to April, and the price range shown reflects this.

EXPENSIVE

Hostería Monte Balmaceda *(Moments* This *hostería* sits along the Río Serrano and across from the glacier of the same name—a remote, stunning location that can be visited only by boat. Although the site provides a direct view of the glacier as it tumbles down the mountain, it unfortunately cannot be viewed from any of the rooms. Why the owner decided to design the rooms in three rows like army barracks that face each other can only be explained by the fact that he is an ex-military man. Nevertheless, the circular, separate restaurant is lovely (and comes with views), and the self-guided trail they've built around the property is really a delight, giving visitors lots of space to quietly walk and enjoy nature; there are fishing opportunities here as well. The rooms are not noteworthy, but brand-new and spacious enough. If you plan to stay here and visit Torres del Paine, it's possible to take the spectacular ride up the Río Serrano to a drop-off point near Conaf's administration and visitor center (see "Sailing to Parque Nacional Bernardo O'Higgins," above).

Aventour's office in Puerto Natales, Av. Manuel Bulnes 689. © 61/410253. Fax 61/410825. www.aventour aventuras.com. 16 units. $45 May–Sept; $100 Oct and Apr; $145 Nov–Mar. AE, DC, MC, V. **Amenities:** Restaurant.

Hotel CostAustralis ✪ This hard-to-miss, sunflower-yellow hotel on the coast offers the highest caliber lodging in Puerto Natales. Floor-to-ceiling windows face out onto the sound, which means that whether you're in the bar, the restaurant, or the lounge, you always have sweeping views and a splendid evening sunset. The CostAustralis is the town's largest hotel, but it retains a certain coziness with its grasscloth wallpaper offset by wooden trim and ceilings, stiff potted palms, and soft light. Unfortunately, the coziness translates to also being able to hear your neighbor's plumbing upstairs, so try to request a top-floor room. The Dickson Bar is a great place to unwind with one of its well-prepared pisco sours. Spacious doubles come with a sea view or a truly depressing view of the buildings in the back; all feature glossy wood paneling and attractive furnishings. The price is fairly high, even by U.S. standards, and therefore might not be appealing to anyone who plans to arrive late and leave early. The hotel has two restaurants, one for breakfast, and a semiformal dining area for dinner (see "Where to Dine," below) and is popular with European tour groups.

Pedro Montt 262, Puerto Natales. ⓒ 61/412000. Fax 61/411881. www.australis.com. 50 units. $75–$181 double. Rates include buffet breakfast. AE, DC, MC, V. **Amenities:** 2 restaurants; bar; room service; laundry service. *In room:* TV.

Hotel Martín Guisinde   This hotel sits on a residential street near the casino, and its boxy, brown exterior is an odd match for its classically designed rooms. Every room is a little tight but comfortable, with crisp linens, rich floral-and-stripe wallpaper with matching bedspreads, and wood furniture. The hallways are a little cold, but the restaurant in front is a comfortable place for a meal or a drink, and they serve a hearty breakfast. The Martín Guisinde is owned by the same people who run the Hostería Lago Grey (see "Where to Stay & Dine in Torres del Paine," later in this chapter), and they will arrange excursions around the region.

Bories 278, Puerto Natales. ⓒ 61/412770. Fax 61/412820. hgrey@ctcreuna.cl. 20 units. $55–$135 double. Rates include buffet breakfast. AE, DC, MC, V. **Amenities:** Restaurant; lounge; room service; laundry service. *In room:* TV.

MODERATE

Hostal Francis Drake   The Hostal Francis Drake is nearly identical to the Los Pinos (see below)—the only difference is about $30, but you might want to give negotiating a try (if you pay cash you get a discount). Both are located on the same block, and like the Los Pinos, this small inn has just 12 rooms, all very clean. The exterior is appealing, with latticed wood trim; inside there's a plant-filled eating area for breakfast. There's also a salon with a TV. The friendly owner who runs the hotel can help with transfers and travel information and provide box lunches for excursions.

Philippi 383, Puerto Natales. ⓒ/fax 61/411553. 12 units. $34–$69 double. Rates include continental breakfast. DC, MC, V. **Amenities:** Lounge. *In room:* TV.

Hostal Los Pinos *(Value)*   The Hostal Los Pinos is a great value for the price. It's tucked behind two cypress trees, across from the local high school and 3 blocks from the plaza. The friendly owners make you feel at home, especially while relaxing in the ample living area. Oriental rug runners lead to squeaky clean rooms with enough details here and there that bring them a step above most moderate accommodations found in town. The bathrooms aren't huge, but they'll do. The new mattresses and TVs, added in 2002, round out this excellent value.

Philippi 449, Puerto Natales. ⓒ 61/411735. Fax 61/411326. 12 units. $32 double. Rate includes continental breakfast. No credit cards. **Amenities:** Lounge. *In room:* TV.

Hotel Capitán Eberhard   The Capitán Eberhard was the first hotel in Puerto Natales, built 30 years ago on the Costanera and featuring a commanding view of the sound and the peaks behind it. The rooms could use an update, with low-to-the-floor beds and drab furnishings, but the bar and restaurant are still as handsome as ever. Try to get a room with a view of the sound (no extra charge); otherwise, look for lodging elsewhere, because the price is too high for what you get. The hotel is offset with various ornaments, such as a stuffed eagle, fox pelts, antique photos, and the like. The black and wood bar is the best in Puerto Natales, but the lounge upstairs is a pinch tacky and reeks of smoke.

Pedro Montt (the Costanera) 58, Puerto Natales. © **61/411208.** Fax 61/411209. Heberhard@terra.cl. 24 units. $34–$109 double. Rates include buffet breakfast. AE, DC, MC, V. **Amenities:** Restaurant; bar; room service. *In room:* TV.

Hotel Cisne Cuello Negro *Kids*   This hotel sits a 3km (2-mile) taxi ride outside town, and it's ideal for those who want to be surrounded by a bit of greenery and history. The Hotel Cisne is in the old mutton-canning and wool plant that once operated as a collection and export site for various sheep ranches. The old wooden buildings provide great places to walk and explore, especially if you have kids. The hotel itself is a three-story white building with red tin awnings, and it fronts a grassy slope that leads into the sound. After a fire burned part of the building, they rebuilt an airy restaurant lit by a plant-filled atrium. Rooms are spacious and comfortable, with good beds and sunny views. There are two large suites surrounded by floor-to-ceiling windows. Much of the time the hotel sells packages to guests that include transportation from Punta Arenas, 3 nights' accommodation, a 1-day tour through Torres del Paine, and a catamaran journey to Parque Nacional Bernardo O'Higgins and the Serrano Glacier.

Road to Torres del Paine, NE of Puerto Natales, Km 3. In Punta Arenas, José Menéndez 918. © **61/411498,** or reservations 61/244506. Fax 61/248052. www.pehoe.com. 39 units. $71 double. Rate includes buffet breakfast. AE, DC, MC, V. **Amenities:** Restaurant; bar; laundry service. *In room:* TV.

Hotel Glaciares   The Hotel Glaciares's best deal going is the fleet of transfer vehicles they use to shuttle guests in and out of the park for day trips or to locations as far away as Ushuaia. Guests here are usually satisfied with their accommodations; we think it's a little overpriced. The rooms are modest, but comfortable. The four newest rooms, added in 2002, are done in loud pink and red colors and have in-room safes. Upstairs there's a bright lounge area, but the grenadine-colored carpet will make your teeth hurt. Service is adequate.

Eberhard 104, Puerto Natales. © **61/412189.** Fax 61/411452. 22 units. $41–$86 double. Rates include buffet breakfast. AE, DC, MC, V. **Amenities:** Restaurant; lounge. *In room:* TV, minibar.

Hotel Lady Florence Dixie ★ *Value*   This hotel is about as downtown as downtown gets in Puerto Natales, located on bustling Avenida Manuel Bulnes. The owners have recently gone through a substantial renovation, tearing down the old home that fronted the establishment (the rooms are set far back from the street), and rebuilding a new unit that includes four brand-new superior rooms. Guests enter the wooden gate and find a courtyard and a motel-like setup that's nicely designed, with wooden banisters and trim. The rooms are comfortable, and it's one of the few hotels in this price range that has cable TV, if that's important to you. You might consider one of the front rooms because they are spanking new, with gleaming bathrooms, and they have soundproof windows. The two women who run the place are very accommodating.

Av. Manuel Bulnes 655, Puerto Natales. © **61/411158.** Fax 61/411943. Florence@chileanpatagonia.com. 19 units. $75 double Oct–Apr; $42 double May–Sept. AE, DC, MC, V. **Amenities:** Lounge. *In room:* TV.

Kotenk Aike Cabañas These cabins are about 2km (1¼ miles) outside of town on an exposed grassy slope, and they're a good bet if you're looking for your own room with a kitchen. The German-style, A-frame *cabañas* sit apart from each other, and each has two upstairs bedrooms, one with a full-size bed and one with three twins; all are brightly lit. There's a tidy kitchen with a burner, a microwave, and a table. The distance from town means you'll have to walk or taxi (costing about $1), but the all-embracing views are worth it.

Costanera (Pedro Montt), NE of Puerto Natales, Km 2. © 61/412581. Fax 61/225935 (in Punta Arenas). 5 *cabañas*. $64 *cabaña* for 5. MC, V. *In room:* TV, kitchen.

INEXPENSIVE

Casa Cecilia *Value* Casa Cecilia is a budget favorite in Puerto Natales, consistently garnering rave reviews from guests for its full range of services, pleasant rooms, and delicious breakfasts. The front lobby acts as a travel agency of sorts, providing information, arranging excursions, and renting camping equipment; beyond that is a common area and a kitchen that guests can use—and they do. Rooms are stacked on two floors and encircle an atrium; some come with private bathrooms, some shared, and they are a good value for the price. Two new rooms were added in 2002 and boast bright burgundy carpet and new mattresses. However, rooms are lit by the interior atrium, not from the outside. The Swiss-Chilean couple (she's Cecilia) speak several languages and are very friendly. This hostel is popular with a wide range of ages and types.

Tomás Roger 60, Puerto Natales. ©/fax 61/411797. redcecilia@entelchile.net. 15 units. Nov 15–Feb $32 double, $21 double with shared bathroom; Mar–Nov 14 $20 double, $14 double with shared bathroom. Rates include full breakfast. AE, DC, MC, V.

Concepto Indigo *Finds* The Concepto Indigo is a hip, outdoorsy hostel/restaurant located along the Costanera. It's a purple barn of a building with a rock-climbing wall, so you won't have any trouble spotting it. The rooms are inexpensive, but remarkable only for the tremendous view of the sound seen through giant windows—especially the corner room, which has a full-size bed and a twin. Only one room comes with a private bathroom, but there are several bathrooms, so you most likely won't find that sharing is a problem. The best thing about Concepto Indigo is its restaurant downstairs, with wraparound views, stacks of magazines, and a few couches to kick back in. When the wind picks up (which it usually does), the place really whistles and shakes.

Ladrilleros 105, Puerto Natales. © 61/413609. Fax 61/410169. www.conceptoindigo.com. 8 units. $40 double; $28 double with shared bathroom. MC, V. Closed May–Aug. **Amenities:** Restaurant; bar.

WHERE TO DINE

Along with the following restaurants, there are several that serve inexpensive fare, such as **RePizza,** Blanco Encalada 294 (© 61/410361), a popular place for pizzas, and **El Cristal,** Av. Manuel Bulnes 439 (© 61/411850), which has a very basic menu of sandwiches, grilled or breaded meats, french fries, and the like, as well as a daily set lunch for about $5.

Concepto Indigo *Finds* VEGETARIAN This cozy and happening eatery is one of the few in town with a water view. The menu here is on the vegetarian side; the only meat item is a ham sandwich. The menu is simple, with grilled or sautéed salmon, scallops, king crab, pastas, and spongy pizzas. The sandwiches are served on wagon-wheel bread, and are hefty enough for a dinner. There's also a good wine selection. Concepto Indigo has a great atmosphere, with hip decor and candlelit tables, good music, and an evening slide-show presentation of

Torres del Paine. The bar is a good place for a late evening drink, and there's a computer with Internet access in the adjoining lounge.

Ladrilleros 105. ⓒ **61/413609**. Main courses $3.50–$7. AE, DC, MC, V. Daily 11am–11pm; bar closes at 1am. Closed May–Aug.

El Living ✦✦ *Finds* CAFE/VEGETARIAN   If you're looking for a friendly, comfortable place to kick back and spend the evening, then look no further. At El Living, recently opened by a British expatriate couple, you can lounge on a comfortable sofa with a pisco sour or have an excellent vegetarian dinner at one of their hand-made wooden dining tables. The menu is simple and inexpensive but fresh and delicious. The Sweet and Sour Red Salad is a perfect mix of beet-root, red cabbage, kidney beans, and onion; the veggie burger is delicious and served on a whole-wheat baguette. This is the only place in Chile that serves a peanut-butter-and-jelly sandwich. There's also French toast with fried bananas, a divine toasted banana sandwich, and a variety of cakes baked daily. A full bar and wine list round out this excellent place.

Arturo Prat 156. ⓒ **61/411140**. Main courses $2.50–$3.75. No credit cards. Daily 11am—11pm.

El Rincón de la Tata PIZZA/CHILEAN   This little cafe doesn't have the best cuisine in town, but it undoubtedly has a good atmosphere, candlelit and warm. It's kind of like a pub, casual and friendly, with walls adorned with old Chilean kitsch. Better to stick with one of the huge sandwiches or a pizza and a beer than any of the main courses.

Arturo Prat 238. No phone. Main courses $5.50–$8. MC, V. Daily 11am–midnight.

Hotel Capitán Eberhard ✦ *Kids Finds* CHILEAN   Like the CostAustralis (see below), this restaurant features a lovely view of the sound, but the difference is the Eberhard is cozier and full of old-fashioned Puerto Natales charm. Nothing has changed in this dining room since the hotel's inception 30 years ago, includ-ing the unique notched wooden ceiling. The menu features typical Chilean fare and very good salmon dishes, such as salmon with a creamy seafood sauce. Try the abalone in salsa verde appetizer. There's also a kid's menu. The bar is hand-somely designed, with a black bar and tables offset by cinnamon-colored wood. The fixed price menu is a steal at $9 and includes a soup or salad, a main course and dessert.

Pedro Montt 58. ⓒ **61/411208**. Main courses $7–$11; 3-course fixed-price menu $9. AE, DC, MC, V. Daily 7am–10am, 12:30–2:30pm, and 8–11pm.

Hotel CostAustralis ✦✦ *Moments* INTERNATIONAL   This is as close as you'll get to fine dining in Puerto Natales. If you're looking for tasty cuisine and a wonderful ambience, look no further. The sunset views from the picture win-dows in combination with your candlelit table make for a sumptuous environ-ment. The new chef is very talented and tries hard to maintain the regional angle in the menu. A good example is the lamb and potato stew typical of this region but not easy to find in restaurants. Salmon and conger eel are usually the fresh catches of the day. Other specialties include wild hare marinated in red wine and herbs, and pork loin with mustard and whiskey. Top off your dinner with the apricots and peaches stewed in syrup and served with cream of wheat, or minty pears poached in wine with chocolate ice cream.

Pedro Montt 262. ⓒ **61/412000**. Main courses $8–$13. AE, DC, MC, V. Daily noon–3pm and 7:30–11pm.

La Caleta *Value* CHILEAN   La Caleta is a simple restaurant that belies the quality of its food. Neither the dining room nor the presentation is worth writing home about, but the food is consistently good, and the portions are hearty. Try the abalone in a creamy salsa verde or "Congrio Caleta," conger eel with seafood sauce; it's very rich, but satisfying, as is the steak with pepper sauce. La Caleta has begun serving lamb roasted on a revolving spit in the typical Patagonian style. They also have a parsley *ceviche* and mussels in garlic. The cantina-style homemade borgoña won't win any wine awards, but it goes with the atmosphere.

Eberhard 169. ℂ 61/413969. Main courses $3.50–$7. No credit cards. Daily 11am–1am.

Restaurant Marítimo SEAFOOD Locals and tourists flock to this restaurant that lacks any sort of ambience inside but has windows overlooking the water. The seafood is fresh, and the location is ideal on the Costanera, but the food is bland, the service is absent-minded, and the nighttime fluorescent lights are blinding. The appetizers are good here—abalone salad and lemony king crab among them—but the fish dishes are fried to a crisp and served three ways: with butter, with butter and garlic, and without. The prices are reasonable, however.

Pedro Montt 214-A. ℂ 61/414467. Main courses $3–$5. No credit cards. Daily 11am–11pm.

3 Parque Nacional Torres del Paine, Chile ⓐⓐⓐ

113km (70 miles) N of Puerto Natales, 360km (223 miles) NW of Punta Arenas

This is Chile's prized jewel, a national park so magnificent that few in the world can claim a rank in its class. Granite peaks and towers soar from sea level to upward of 2,800m (9,184 ft.). Golden pampas and the rolling steppes are home to grazing guanacos and more than 100 species of colorful birds, such as parakeets and flamingos, that come to nest each spring. Antarctic beech emits a strong cinnamon aroma. Chilean firebush blooms a riotous red; delicate porcelain orchids and ladyslippers seem unfit for such inhospitable terrain. Electric-blue icebergs cleave from Glacier Grey. Resident gauchos ride by atop sheepskin saddles. Condors float effortlessly even on the windiest day. The park is not something you visit; it is something you experience.

Although it sits next to the Andes, **Parque Nacional Torres del Paine** is a separate geologic formation created roughly 3 million years ago when bubbling magma began growing and pushing its way up, taking a thick sedimentary layer with it. Glaciation and severe climate weathered away the softer rock, leaving the spectacular Paine Massif whose prominent features are the *Cuernos* (which means "horns") and the one-of-a-kind *Torres*—three salmon-colored, spherical granite towers. The black sedimentary rock can still be seen atop the elegant Cuernos, named for the two spires that rise from the outer sides of its amphitheater. *Paine* is the Tehuelche Indian word for "blue," and it brings to mind the varying shades found in the lakes that surround this massif—among them the milky, turquoise waters of Lagos Nordenskjold and Pehoé. Backing the Paine Massif are several glaciers that descend from the Southern Ice Field.

Torres del Paine was once a collection of *estancias* and small-time ranches; many were forced out with the creation of the park in 1959. The park has since grown to its present size of 242,242 hectares (598,338 acres), and in 1978 was declared a World Biosphere Reserve by UNESCO for its singular beauty and ecology. This park is a backpacker's dream, but just as many visitors find pleasure staying in lodges here and taking day hikes and horseback rides—even those with a short amount of time here are blown away by a 1-day visit. There are options for everyone, part of the reason the number of visitors to this park is growing by nearly 10,000 per year.

ESSENTIALS
WHEN TO COME & WHAT TO BRING
This is not the easiest of national parks to visit. The climate in the park can be abominable, with wind speeds that can peak at 161kmph (100 mph) and rain and snow even in the middle of summer. The periods in which your chances are highest of avoiding wind and rain are from early October to early November and from mid-March to late April, but even then the weather is unpredictable. Spring is a beautiful time for budding flowers and birds; during the fall the beech forests turn striking shades of crimson, orange, and yellow. The winter is surprisingly temperate, with relatively few snowstorms and no wind—but short days. You'll need to stay in a hotel during the winter, but you'll practically have the park to yourself. Summer is ironically the worst time to come, especially from late December to mid-February, when the wind blows at full fury and crowds descend upon the park. When the wind blows it can make even a short walk a rather scary experience or just drive you nuts—just try to go with it, not fight it, and revel in the excitement of the extreme environment that makes Patagonia what it is.

Equip yourself with decent gear, especially hiking boots (if you plan to do any trekking), weatherproof outerwear, and warm layers, even in the summer. The ozone problem is acute here, so you'll need sunscreen, sunglasses, and probably a hat. Don't ever go outside without slathering on sunscreen.

VISITOR INFORMATION
The park's administration and visitor center can be reached at © **61/691931;** open daily from 8:30am to 8pm. The entrance fee to the park is $9.25; 70¢ for kids.

GETTING THERE & AWAY
Many travelers are unaware of the enormous amount of time it takes to get to Torres del Paine. There are no direct transportation services from the airport in Punta Arenas to the park, except with package tours and hotels that have their own vehicles. The earliest flight from Santiago to Punta Arenas arrives at around noon; from there it's a 3-hour drive to Puerto Natales. The last bus to the park leaves at 2:30pm for the 2-hour journey to the park. If you're relying on bus transportation (as most do), it's only logical that you will need to spend the night in Punta Arenas or Puerto Natales. If you've arranged a package tour or hotel stay that picks you up at the airport, remember that the trip can be very tiring if you factor in a 4-hour flight from Santiago and 5 hours in a vehicle.

BY BUS   Several companies offer daily service from October to April. During the low season, only two companies, Bus Sur and JB, offer service to the park. Buses to Torres del Paine enter through the Laguna Amarga ranger station, stop at the Pudeto catamaran dock, and terminate at the park administration center. If you're going directly to the Torres trail head at Hostería Las Torres, there are minivan transfers waiting at the Laguna Amarga station that charge $3 one-way. The return times given below are when the bus leaves from the park administration center; the bus will pass through the Laguna Amarga station about 45 minutes later.

JB at Arturo Prat 258 (© **61/412824**) leaves at 7, 8am, and 2:30pm and returns at 1, 2:30, and 6:30pm; **Fortaleza Aventura** at Arturo Prat 234 (© **61/410595**) leaves at 7am and 2pm, returning at 2 and 6pm; **Buses Paori** at Eberhard 577 (© **61/411229**) leaves at 7:30am, returning at 2pm; **Turismo María**

José at Av. Manuel Bulnes 386 (℃ **61/414312**) leaves at 7:30am, returning at 2pm; and **Andescape** at Eberhard 599 (℃ **61/412592**) leaves at 7am, returning at 12:15pm. The cost is around $7 one-way.

BY TOUR VAN   If you have just a little time to spend in the park, or would like to get there at your own pace, check into the minivan tour services that plan stops at the Salto Grande waterfall and carry on to Lago Grey for a walk along the beach to view giant icebergs (see "Tour Operators," under Puerto Natales above).

BY CAR   Heading north on Pedro Montt out of town, follow the dirt road for 51km (32 miles) until you reach Cerro Castillo. From here the road turns left and heads 47km (29 miles) toward the park (keep your eyes open for another left turn that is signed TORRES DEL PAINE). You'll come to a fork in the road; one road leads to the Lago Sarmiento Conaf station, another to the Laguna Amarga station. If you are planning to head to the Torres trail head and Hostería Las Torres hotel complex on your way out, then take the Lago Sarmiento entrance; it's faster, and you'll get to view the blue, blue waters of Lago Sarmiento. You can park your car at the Hostería Las Torres, the park administration center, the Pudeto catamaran dock, or the Lago Grey ranger station.

CROSSING LAGO PEHOE BY CATAMARAN   At some point you'll likely cross Lago Pehoé. The catamaran *Our Lady of the Snows* has several crossings per day and is timed to meet all buses; the cost is a steep $14 one-way. Times vary according to demand and season; they are posted outside the refugio Pehoé, and every *refugio* (cabin) in the park has a time schedule.

GETTING TO THE PARK BY BOAT   Relatively few people are aware that they can arrive by a zodiac-catamaran combination that takes visitors from Puerto Natales through the Ultima Esperanza Sound and up the Río Serrano, or vice versa. This is a highly recommended way to do one leg of the trip rather than ride both ways in a vehicle, but it's an all-day affair. Along the winding turquoise river, visitors are taken through territory that rivals Alaska, past the glaciers Tyndall and Geike, and eventually to the Serrano Glacier. Here they disembark for a walk up to the ice, then board another boat for a 3½-hour ride to Puerto Natales. It's not cheap—the cost runs about $60 to $90 per person, depending on the season. You can also do a round-trip journey leaving from and returning to the park for about $60. See "Tour Operators & Adventure Travel Outfitters" under "Puerto Natales," earlier in this chapter for more information. **Onas** is the oldest-running company with zodiac service, leaving daily at 8:30am from the administration office (they'll pick you up from longer distances for an extra charge). Two companies, **Aventour** and **21 de Mayo,** also take guests down the Río Serrano. **Aventour** includes an additional stop at its lodge and offers round-trips up and down the river that start from its lodge near the Serrano Glacier. Be aware that the zodiacs are not roofed.

WHERE TO STAY & DINE IN TORRES DEL PAINE
HOTELS AND HOSTERIAS
Hostería Lago Grey   This spruce little white *hostería* is tucked within a beech forest, looking onto the beach at Lago Grey and the astounding blue icebergs that drift to its shore. It's well on the other side of the park, but they have a transfer van and guides for excursions to all reaches of the park. The 20 rooms are spread out from the main common area, with a restaurant and lounge area. The rooms are comfortable, but the walls are a tad thin. Also, when the wind

whips up, this side of the park is colder, but the location is more tranquil than that of Las Torres, and there are plenty of trails that branch out from here, including the stroll along the beach out to the Pingo Valley and the strenuous hike up to Mirador Ferrier. The transfer van will pick you up from anywhere in the park.

Office in Punta Arenas, Lautaro Navarro 1061. © 61/410172. 20 units. Oct–Apr $200 double; May–Sept $85 double. Rates include buffet breakfast. AE, DC, MC, V. **Amenities:** Restaurant; lounge.

Hostería Las Torres   This *hostería* sits at the trail head to the Torres on an *estancia* that still operates as a working cattle ranch. The complex includes a ranch-style hotel, a large campground, and a hostel, meaning there's a fair amount of traffic coming in and out daily. The main building has a restaurant, a bar, and half the guest rooms; the other half of the rooms are located in a brand-new separate unit, but the newer rooms are identical to the old. The superior rooms are slightly larger than the standard, and they come with central heating; other than this, the difference is slight. The rooms are not especially noteworthy, but they are comfortable, and there's a relaxing lounge with couches and game tables for guests only. The entire building is made of terra-cotta–colored logs, situated on an idyllic grassy expanse that is backed by the Paine Massif. The *hostería* offers guided excursions and horseback rides. The *hostería's* restaurant deserves special note for its delicious evening buffet dinner for $24.

Office in Punta Arenas, Magallanes 960. ©/fax 61/226054. 20 units. $195 double superior; $135 standard. Rates include buffet breakfast. AE, DC, MC, V. **Amenities:** Restaurant; lounge; tour desk; room service; laundry service.

Hostería Mirador del Payne ⭐   This *hostería* is an old *estancia* outside the park, and it boasts a commanding view of the Cuernos rising behind a grassy field and Lake Verde. If you really want to get away from crowds, this is your hotel, although it doesn't put you directly near the Paine Massif. The rooms are in a unit separate from the main lodge, which has a restaurant, bar, and fireside lounge. The *hostería* offers great horseback-riding opportunities for an additional cost of $20 for 3 hours. Access to the *hostería* is via one of two ways: by a road that branches off before arriving at the park or by a moderate 2-hour trail that leads to the park administration center. Guests arrive by road, but more than a few opt to end their stay here with a horseback ride to the park administration center to continue on to another hotel within the park's boundaries.

Office in Punta Arenas, Fagnano 585. © 61/228712. www.mundosur.com/mirpayne. 20 units. Oct–Mar $138 double; Apr–Sept $90 double. AE, DC, MC, V. **Amenities:** Restaurant; bar; lounge; laundry service.

(*Tips*   **Advance Planning**

It's not easy to arrange for your own accommodations before arriving here; phones sometimes are inoperable, there's no e-mail, and the wind wreaks havoc with the postman. If you need help setting up your trip in advance, e-mail or call Alfonso Lopez Rosas, manager of the largest tour operator in the park. Through his office in Puerto Natales, he'll secure whatever you need, contact the hotels, and even arrange for your transportation. Path@gone Travel is at Ebarhard 595, Puerto Natales (© 61/413291; pathgone@entelchile.net). Alfonso can sometimes negotiate lower hotel rates at the park's *hosterías* as well as arrange for everything from camping equipment to horseback riding trips.

Hotel Explora Salto Chico ★★★ (Moments)   Few hotels in Chile have garnered as much fame as the Hotel Explora, and deservedly so. The Explora's location is simply stunning, looking out over the blue waters of Lago Pehoé and directly at the dramatic Cuernos formation. A band of picture windows wrap around the full front of the building and there are large windows in each room—even the bathrooms come with cut-outs in the wall so that while you're brushing your teeth, you'll still have your eyes on the gorgeous panorama. Explora's style is comfortable elegance. The softly curving, blonde-wood interiors were built entirely from native deciduous beech, as was the handcrafted furniture. The rooms are superb, with checkered linens imported from Barcelona, wicker furniture, handsome slate-tiled bathrooms, powerful showers, and warming racks for drying gear.

Explora operates as a full-service lodge with packages that include direct airport transfers, meals, open bar, and excursions. Every evening, 3 of the 10 full-time guides meet with guests to discuss the following day's excursions, which range from easy half-day walks to strenuous full-day hikes. There are about seven excursions to choose from, including horseback rides and photo safaris. In the morning, a fleet of vans whisks guests off to their destination and back again for lunch; guides carry picnic lunches for full-day hikes. The set menu is limited to two choices, generally a meat and vegetarian dish, and it must be said that the food quality has at times been uneven—never bad, but not as outstanding as one would expect from a hotel of this caliber. Americans make up a full 50% of the guests, who typically leave thrilled with their visit. Note that the first-day arrival to the hotel is around 6pm, time for a short hike to a lookout point only, and the last day isn't really a day at all, as guests leave after breakfast for the drive back to the airport. The hotel's downstairs lounge has a satellite TV, videos of the park, and a small library.

In Santiago, Américo Vespucio Sur 80, 5th floor. ⓒ **22/066060.** Fax 2/228-4655. www.explora-chile.com. 31 units. Packages per person, double occupancy: 3 nights/2 days $1,234; 4 nights/3 days $1,624; 7 nights/ 6 days $2,323. Rates include all meals. AE, DC, MC, V. **Amenities:** Restaurant; bar; lounge; large indoor pool; outdoor Jacuzzi; sauna; massage.

REFUGIOS & ALBERGUES

These cabin-like lodging units can be found at the base of trails or in the backcountry. They are moderately priced options for those who are not interested in pitching a tent, and although most have bedding or sleeping bags for rent, your best bet is to bring your own. All come with hot showers, a cafe, and a common area for hiding out from bad weather. Simple meals and sandwiches are sold, or you can bring your own food and cook in their kitchens. Each *refugio* has rooms with two to six bunks, which you'll have to share with strangers when they're full. Per-person rates average $16. Some of these *refugios* are very attractive, and all are situated in gorgeous locations. During the high season you'll need to book a bed at least 2 days in advance, but busier *refugios* can book up to 4 to 5 days ahead. All agencies in Puerto Natales take reservations, or you can call or e-mail (shown below). There is a *refugio* near the park administration center, but it has a lousy sleeping arrangement, with an upper floor and two rows of sleeping berths, much like a camp-out. This *refugio* is on a first-come, first-serve basis.

The following *refugios* can be reserved by calling or faxing ⓒ **61/226054.**

- **Refugio Chileno.** This is probably the least-frequented *refugio,* due to its position halfway up to the Towers (most do the trail as a day hike). Still, it's nicer to stay in this pretty valley than down below.

- **Albergue Las Torres.** This *albergue* (lodge) sits near the Hostería Las Torres, with a full-service restaurant. Horseback rides can be taken from here.
- **Refugio Los Cuernos.** This may be the park's loveliest *refugio*, at the base of the Cuernos and with two walls of windows that look out onto Lago Nordenskjold.

The following *refugios* can be reserved at ©/fax **61/412592.** These three *refugios* are exactly the same in terms of their cabinlike design.

- **Refugio Grey.** Tucked in a forest on the shore of Lago Grey, this *refugio* is a 10-minute walk to the lookout point for the glacier. It's an ideal setting, and it has a cozy fireside seating area.
- **Refugio Dickson.** This is another less-frequented *refugio* for its location well on the other side of the park. It has a fantastic location on a grassy glacial moraine, and looks directly at the Dickson Glacier.
- **Refugio Pehoé.** This *refugio* is the hub for several of the trail heads to the park administration center, Glacier Grey, and the French Valley, as well as the docking site for the catamaran. It is, therefore, constantly busy and service is notoriously bad here.

CAMPING IN TORRES DEL PAINE

Torres del Paine has a well-designed campground system with free and concession-run sites. All *refugios* have a campground, and all concession sites charge $4 per person, which includes showers (hot water is available at Los Cuernos, Chileno, and the site at Hostería Las Torres only), water, and bathrooms. The site at Las Torres provides barbecues and firewood. Free campgrounds are run by Conaf, and they can get a little dingy, with deplorable outhouses. Beginning in March, mice become a problem for campers, so always leave food well stored or hanging from a tree branch. The JLM hiking map (available at every bookstore, kiosk, and travel agency and at the park entrance) denotes which campgrounds are free and which charge a fee.

TRAILS IN TORRES DEL PAINE

There is a multitude of ways to hike or backpack in Torres del Paine. Which you choose depends on how much time you have and what kind of walking you're up for. The best way to plan a multiple-day hike is to begin at the Hostería Las Torres, reached from the Laguna Amarga ranger station, although some prefer to begin by crossing Lago Pehoé by catamaran and start the trip up to the glacier or the French Valley. Pick up one of JLM's Torres del Paine maps (sold everywhere) to plan your itinerary. Walking times shown below are average. The minimum amount of days shown assumes walking 4 to 8 hours a day; plan for extra days if you want to take it easy, and maybe a 1 or 2 days for bad weather.

LONG-HAUL OVERNIGHT HIKES

The "W" ★★   This segment of the Paine Massif is so called because hikers are taken along a trail that forms a W. This trail takes hikers to the park's major geological features—the Torres, the Cuernos, and Glacier Grey—and it's the preferred multiple-day hike for its relative short hauls and timeframe that requires 4 to 5 days. As well, those who prefer not to camp or carry more gear than a sleeping bag, food, and their personal goods can stay in the various *refugios* along the way. Most hikers begin at Hostería Las Torres and start with a day-walk up to the Torres. From here, hikers head to the Los Cuernos *refugio* and spend the night, or continue on to the Italiano campsite near the base of the valley; then they walk up to the French Valley. The next stop is Pehoé *refugio,* where most spend the night before hiking up to Glacier Grey. It's best to spend a night at Refugio Grey and return to the Pehoé *refugio* the next day. From here, take the catamaran across Lago Pehoé to an awaiting bus back to Puerto Natales.

Approximately 56km (35 miles) total. Beginning at Hostería Las Torres or Refugio Pehoé. Terrain ranges from easy to difficult.

The Circuit ★ The Circuit is a spectacular, long-haul backpacking trip that takes hikers around the entire Paine Massif. It can be done in two ways: with the "W" included or without. Including the "W," you'll need 8 to 11 days; without it, from 4 to 7 days. The Circuit is less-traveled than the "W" because it's longer and requires that you camp out at least twice. I don't recommend doing this trail if you have only 4 or 5 days. This trail is for serious backpackers only because it involves several difficult hikes up and down steep, rough terrain and over fallen tree trunks. You'll be rewarded for your effort, however, with dazzling views of terrain that varies from grassy meadows and winding rivers to thick, virgin beech forest, snowcapped peaks and, best of all, the awe-inspiring view of Glacier Grey seen from atop the John Garner Pass. If you're a recreational hiker with a 4- to 6-hour hike tolerance level, you'll want to sleep in all the major campgrounds or *refugios.* Always do this trail counter-clockwise for easier ascents and with the scenery before you. If you're here during the high season and want to get away from crowds, you might contemplate walking the first portion of this trail beginning at Laguna Azul. This is the old trail, and it more or less parallels the Circuit but on the other side of the river, passing the gaucho post La Victorina, the only remaining building of an old *estancia.* At Refugio Dickson you'll have to cross the river in the *refugio's* dinghy for $4. To get to Laguna Azul, you'll need to hitchhike or arrange private transportation.

Approximately 60km (37 miles) total. Beginning at Laguna Amarga or Hostería Las Torres. Terrain ranges from easy to difficult.

DAY HIKES

These hikes run from easy to difficult, either within the "W" or from various trail heads throughout the park. Again, the times given are estimates for the average walker.

Glacier Grey ★★★ This walk is certainly worth the effort for an up-close look at the face of Glacier Grey. The walk is not as steep as the Las Torres hike, but it's longer. The walk takes hikers through thick forest and open views of the Southern Ice Field and the icebergs slowly making their way down Lago Grey. A turn-off just before the lookout point takes you to Refugio Grey.

3½ hr. one-way. Moderate.

Lago Grey *(Moments* Not only is this the easiest walk in the park, it is one of the most dramatic for the gigantic blue icebergs that rest along the shore of Lago Grey. There's a peninsula with a fairly easy trail that takes walkers to a lookout point where you can see the glacier in the distance. This walk begins near the Hostería Lago Grey; they offer an hour-long zodiac trip around the icebergs and are currently attempting to bring back boat service to the glacier. Ask for more information at the *hostería* (see "Hotels and Hosterías," above).

Departing from the parking lot past the entrance to Hostería Lago Grey. 1–2 hr. Easy.

Lago Pingo *(Finds* Lago Pingo consistently sees fewer hikers, and is a great spot for bird-watching. The trail begins as an easy walk through a beautiful valley, past an old gaucho post. From here the trail heads through forest and undulating terrain and past the Pingo Cascade until it eventually reaches another old gaucho post, the run-down but picturesque Zapata *refugio*. You can make this trail as long or as short as you'd like. The trail leaves from the same parking lot as the Lago Grey trail.

Departing from the Lago Grey parking lot past the entrance to Hostería Lago Grey. 1–4 hr. one-way. Easy/moderate.

Las Torres (The Towers) The trail to view the soaring granite Towers is a classic hike in the park, but certainly not the easiest. It leaves from the Hostería Las Torres. The beginning is a steep, 45-minute ascent, followed by up-and-down terrain for 1½ hours to another 45-minute steep ascent up a granite moraine. Don't give up—the Torres do not come into full view until the very end.

3 hr. one-way. Difficult.

Mirador Nordenskjold The trail head begins near the Pudeto catamaran dock. This trail begins with an up-close visit to the crashing Salto Grande waterfall. Then it winds through Antarctic beech and thorny bush to a lookout point with dramatic views into the French Valley and the Cuernos, looking over Lago Nordenskjold. This trail is a good place to see wildflowers.

1 hr. one-way. Easy.

Valle Francés (French Valley) There are several ways to hike this trail. From Refugio Pehoé, you'll pass by the blue waters of Lake Skottsberg and through groves of Chilean firebush and open views of the granite spires behind Los Cuernos. From Refugio Los Cuernos, you won't see the French Valley until you're in it. You can walk a bit into the valley for direct views of the hanging glacier that descends from Paine Grande, or continue the steep climb up into the valley itself for a view of an enormous granite amphitheater.

Departing from Refugio Pehoé or Refugio Los Cuernos. 2½–4½ hr. one-way. Moderate/difficult.

OTHER OUTDOOR ACTIVITIES IN THE PARK
HORSEBACK RIDING
A horseback ride in Torres del Paine can be one of the most enjoyable ways to see the park, especially from the Serrano pampa for big, bold views of the Paine Massif. Contact **Path@gone Travel** in Puerto Natales, Eberhard 595 (C **61/413291;** pathgone@entelchile.net). They can arrange a wide variety of trips across the Serrano pampa to Lago Grey and excursions around the Laguna Amarga and Laguna Azul sectors. They also offer multiple-day trips that include camping and stays in *refugios*. The cost depends on the number of riders (10 maximum), but averages $28 to $50 per person for 1- to 3-hour rides. Most trips require prior experience. **Hostería Las Torres** has horseback riding to Refugios Chileno and Los Cuernos; its Punta Arenas office is at Magallanes 960 (C/fax **61/226054**). The full-day trips cost $75 per person, and they leave from the hotel.

ICE CLIMBING
There is nothing as thrilling as a walk across Glacier Grey. Trips begin from the Refugio Grey at 9am and return at 5pm, with an hour walk to the entrance site and then back to the *refugio*. Guests are provided with full equipment, including crampons, ice axes, ropes, and harnesses, and are given basic ice-climbing instructions. Visitors who have taken this hike have consistently given rave

reviews for the chance to peer into deep blue crevasses and explore the glacier's otherworldly contours up close. Bigfoot Expeditions runs this concession, and reservations are recommended, although there is often space for walk-ins. You need to spend the previous night at the Refugio Grey or in its campsite; the office in Puerto Natales is at Blanco Encalada 226 (© **61/414611;** www. bigfootpatagonia.com). The cost is $60 per person, which includes a box lunch; credit cards are accepted at their concession site at Refugio Grey.

4 El Calafate, Argentina ★★

222km (138 miles) S of El Chaltén; 2,727km (1,691 miles) SW of Buenos Aires

El Calafate is a tourist-oriented village that hugs the shore of turquoise Lago Argentino, a location that, combined with the town's leafy streets, gives it the feel of an oasis in the desert pampa of this region. The town depends almost entirely on its neighboring natural wonder, the Perito Moreno Glacier, for tourism. Thousands of visitors come for the chance to stand face-to-face with this tremendous wall of ice, one of the few glaciers in the ice field that isn't retreating.

The town was named for the calafate bush found throughout Patagonia that produces a sweet berry commonly used in syrups and jams. As the economy in Buenos Aires deteriorated, many Argentines fled to the countryside and some came here, to El Calafate, which had suffered from a tourist trap mentality for years. Thankfully this tendency is waning as more migrants head south to set up businesses that are meant to really serve visitors. The town itself is quite a pleasant little place, but you won't find many attractions here—they are all within the confines of Los Glaciares National Park. What you will find are several good restaurants and a charming main street lined with boutiques boasting fine leather goods and shops selling locally manufactured chocolates, jams, and delicious caramel cookies called *alfajores.*

ESSENTIALS
GETTING THERE
BY PLANE   El Calafate's brand-new **Aeropuerto Lago Argentino** (no phone) has dramatically changed transportation options here; before you would have to fly into Río Gallegos and then take a long bus ride across the flat pampa. Service is from Argentine destinations only: **Aerolíneas Argentinas/Austral** (© **11/ 4340-3777** in Buenos Aires; www.aerolineas.com.ar) has a daily flight from Buenos Aires. During high season (Dec–Mar), there may be up to three daily flights; there's also a daily flight from Ushuaia and three flights a week from Bariloche. New in 2003 are flights arriving directly from Ezeiza International Airport in Buenos Aires (before, all flights left from Aeroparque, downtown). Be sure to specify which airport you'd like to fly from.

Aerovías Dap (no phone; www.aeroviasdap.cl) has a daily morning flight to Puerto Natales aboard a nine-seater propeller; but that service is frequently canceled due to high winds. Neither company has an office in El Calafate, but any travel agency can book tickets for you. From the airport, **Aerobús** (© **02901/ 492492**) operates a bus to all the hotels in town for $2.25; they can also pick you up for your return trip if you call 24 hours ahead. A taxi into town should cost no more than $6.50 for up to four people. There's a brand new Hertz Rental Car desk (no phone; www.Hertz.com) at the airport, as well.

BY BUS   El Calafate has a bus terminal located on Julio A. Roca, reached by taking the stairs up from the main street Avenida del Libertador. To and from

> **Tips   Departure Taxes**
>
> If you're departing from El Calafate airport, remember to pay the departure tax of $4.85 before going through security. They'll take your money and stamp your boarding pass. Otherwise, you won't be allowed to board the flight. There are no signs posted saying you must do this, nor do the airline agents remind you of this when checking in.

Puerto Natales, Chile: **Buses Sur** (© 02901/491631) and **Turismo Zaahj** (© 02902/411325) have five weekly trips leaving at 8am, as does **Cootra** (© 02902/491444). The trip takes 5 to 6 hours, depending on how long you get held up at the border. To get to El Chaltén, take **Chaltén Travel,** which leaves daily at 8am and returns from Chaltén at 6pm (© 02902/492212); **Caltur** (© 02902/491842); or **Interlagos Turismo** (© 02902/491179); the latter two leave daily at 7:30am and return from El Chaltén at 5pm.

BY CAR   Ruta 5, followed by Ruta 11, is paved entirely from Río Gallegos to El Calafate. From Puerto Natales, cross through the border at Cerro Castillo, which will lead you to the famous Ruta Nacional 40 and up to the paved portion of Ruta 11. The drive from Puerto Natales is roughly 5 hours, not including time spent at the border checkpoint.

GETTING AROUND

For information about transportation to and from the Perito Moreno Glacier, see "Parque Nacional Los Glaciares & the Perito Moreno Glacier," later in this chapter. If you'd like to rent a car, you can do so at the new **Europcar** office at Av. del Libertador 1741 (© 02902/493606; www.europcar.com.ar). Rates begin at $21 per day, including insurance and taxes.

VISITOR INFORMATION

The city's **visitor information kiosk** can be found inside the bus terminal. They offer an ample amount of printed material and can assist in planning a trip to the Perito Moreno Glacier; open October through April from 8am to 11pm daily and May through September from 8am to 8pm daily (© 02902/491090).

A good website to check is www.elcalafate.com.ar.

If you require help arranging any aspect of your trip, a very helpful agency to contact is **SurTurismo,** 25 de Mayo 23 (© 02902/491266; suring@cotecal. com.ar). They can secure everything from airport transfers to hotel reservations at discounted rates. They also provide private and licensed guides for treks and tours of the region.

WHAT TO SEE & DO IN EL CALAFATE

El Calafate serves mostly as a service town for visitors on their way to visit the glaciers (see "Parque Nacional Los Glaciares & the Perito Moreno Glacier," below), but it does present a pleasant main avenue for a stroll, and as expected, there are lots of souvenirs, bookstores, and crafts shops to keep you occupied. Heading out of town on Avenida del Libertador, you'll pass the **Museo Municipal** (no phone; free admission), open Monday through Friday from 8am to 1pm and 3 to 9pm, with a collection of farming and ranching implements, Indian artifacts, and historical and ethnographical displays. It's worth a stop if you have the time. And that's about it here in El Calafate, although if you are interested in bird-watching, you could take a short walk to the Bahía

Redonda at the shore of Lago Argentino to view upland geese, black-necked swans, and flamingos.

ATTRACTIONS & EXCURSIONS AROUND EL CALAFATE

For information about visiting the glaciers and the national park, see "Parque Nacional Los Glaciares & the Perito Moreno Glacier," below.

HORSEBACK RIDING **Cabalgata en Patagonia,** Julio A. Roca 2063 (© 02902/493203; cabalgataenpatagonia@cotecal.com.ar), offers two horseback riding options: a 2-hour ride to Bahía Redonda for a panoramic view of El Calafate ($10) and a full-day trip bordering Lago Argentino, with an optional stop at the Walicho Caves where one can supposedly view Indian "paintings," which are billed as real but are really reproductions. This tour costs $15 per person and includes lunch. Book directly or with a travel agency.

VISITING AN _ESTANCIA_ An interesting option worth looking into is one of the several _estancias,_ or ranches, that have opened their doors to the public, offering day activities, restaurant services, and even lodging should you opt to spend the night. Perhaps the most exclusive and well known is the **Estancia Helsingfors,** open from October to March and located on the shore of Lago Viedma about 150km (93 miles) from El Calafate. Helsingfors offers lodging, horseback riding, overflights, bird-watching, boat trips, and fine dining. For more information, contact their offices in Río Gallegos at Av. del Libertador 516 (©/fax **02966/420719**).

All of the following _estancias_ offer lodging, a restaurant, horseback riding, trekking, vehicle excursions, and transportation from El Calafate. The closest to El Calafate is the **Estancia Huyliche,** about 3km (2 miles) from downtown, open from October to April; they also offer boating excursions (© **02902/ 491025;** teresanegro@cotecal.com.ar). **Estancia Alice El Galpón,** open October through April, is 20km (12 miles) from El Calafate on Ruta 11, and offers activities that lean more toward ranching, including sheep-shearing and wool-packing demonstrations, sheep round-ups, and maintenance of the animals, as well as bird watching (© **02902/492290;** info@elgalpon.com.ar). **Estancia Alta Vista,** at 33km (20 miles) from El Calafate on the dirt road Ruta 15 near the beautiful area of Lago Roca, is open October through March and offers ranch activities and fishing (© **02902/491247;** altavista@cotecal.com.ar). **Estancia Nibepo Aike** is picturesquely nestled on the southeast edge of the national park about 6km (37 miles) from El Calafate, and it's also near Lago Roca, offering fishing and ranch activities October through April (© **02966/ 422626;** nibepo@internet.siscotel.com.ar).

WHERE TO STAY
EXPENSIVE

Hotel El Mirador del Lago At a 15-minute walk from downtown, the Mirador del Lago isn't as conveniently located as its competitors, but the exceptionally friendly, personal service and amenities more than make up for it. The brick hotel with its peaked green awnings faces Lago Argentino, an otherwise interesting landscape if it weren't for a yellow building that somewhat mars the view. Rooms aren't huge, but they're not cramped either. Unfortunately, they have not been too well maintained; the carpets are fading, a little paint is peeling here and there, and the checkered bedspreads are starting to look a bit aged. That said, the hotel's strong suit is its friendly staff and pleasant manager who really work to make certain your stay is above average. Beyond the TV room with regional videos, there is a library chock-full of multilingual information about the area and a souvenir and crafts shop. The hotel frequently offers promotional discounts so be sure to ask. The bright, plant-filled restaurant serves breakfast as well as a wide variety of regional and Argentine dishes.

Av. del Libertador 2047, El Calafate. © **02902/493176.** Fax 02902/493213. www.miradordellago.com.ar. 20 units. $45–$120 double. Rates include buffet breakfast. MC, V. **Amenities:** Restaurant; bar; lounge; sauna; room service; laundry service. *In room:* TV, hair dryer, safe.

Hotel Kosten Aike ★★ (Value)   This charming newer hotel offers modern and attractive accommodations paired with high-quality service. The Kosten Aike is priced lower than its competitor, the Posada los Alamos (see below); but the only difference here is that the Posada's design is buttoned-up conservative and the Kosten Aike is fresh and stylish. Both the architect's and the designer's good taste saved the Kosten Aike from the cookie-cutter style usually seen in new hotels. Furnishings and artwork imported from Buenos Aires include matching drapes and bedspreads in rust and beige accented with black geometric squiggles, papier-mâché lamps, iron and rosewood tables and chairs, and petal-soft carpets, and all rooms feature sumptuous bathrooms. Some rooms have bay windows and are very large; they aren't any more expensive, so ask for one when booking. The airy lobby is inlaid completely with gray stone. The Kosten Aike has a chic restaurant off the lobby that serves contemporary regional and Argentine fare.

Gobernador Moyano 1243, El Calafate. © **02902/492424,** or 11/4811-1314 (reservations). Fax 02902/491538. www.kostenaike.com.ar. 60 units. $63–$97 double. AE, DC, MC, V. **Amenities:** Restaurant; wine bar; fireside lounge; exercise room; spa; game room; concierge; room service; laundry service. *In room:* TV, dataport, minibar, hair dryer, safe.

Hotel Posada Los Alamos ★★ (Finds)   The Posada Los Alamos is as conservative as a Brooks Brothers suit. Because of the low-key design of the "complex" and the slightly aloof service, you can't help shake the feeling that you're in a private country club. The style is classic: a red-brick exterior fringed with the hotel's namesake alamo trees, plaid carpet, old English furniture, and windows with wooden, triangular eaves. Downstairs is a comfortable lounge, and the lobby's large windows look out onto an expansive lawn. Rooms have ample space and each has a slightly different color and style. Ask for one that looks out onto the quiet, grassy backyard instead of the dusty dirt road. The hotel's excellent restaurant, La Posta, is reviewed under "Where to Dine," below.

Gobernador Moyano and Bustillo, El Calafate. © **02902/491144.** Fax 02902/491186. www.posada losalamos.com. 144 units. $92–$163 double; from $240 suite. AE, MC, V. **Amenities:** Restaurant; bar; lounge; golf course; tennis court; tour desk; room service; massage; laundry service; dry cleaning. *In room:* TV, minibar, safe.

MODERATE
Hostería Sierra Nevada ★ (Finds)   This charming *hostería* is a 15-minute walk from all the shops and restaurants. It's the only recommended property right on the lake (not across the street like the Mirador del Lago, above), and every room comes with a water view. Built in 2000, the two-story building has a pleasant expansiveness to it and the rooms are fresh and modern with wrought iron furniture, firm mattresses, and beautiful granite tiled bathrooms and showers. Large French doors in each room slide open to reveal the garden and the lake just beyond. Most of the guests here are South American, so the staff members don't speak much English, but they're friendly and pleasant and will try their best.

Libertador 1888, El Calafate. © **02902/493129.** Sierranevada@cotecal.com.ar. 18 units. $52–$70 double. Rates include buffet breakfast. MC, V. **Amenities:** Restaurant; bar. *In room:* TV, safe.

Hotel Kapenke *Value* This hotel is a good option for moderately priced lodging in El Calafate. The Kapenke underwent a minor renovation in 2000, installing new wallpaper and, in the hallway, lemon-yellow paint. The bathrooms are cramped, but the rooms are decently sized and come with a large chest of drawers and comfortable beds—ask for a room on the second floor as they are brighter. Apart from a few corner sitting areas spread about each floor, there is a large lounge with lots of padded wooden chairs. The staff isn't as energetic or as helpful as one would hope.

Av. 9 de Julio 112, El Calafate. ©/fax **02902/491093.** www.kapenke.com.ar. 32 units. $43 double. MC, V. **Amenities:** Restaurant; bar; lounge; room service. *In room:* TV, hair dryer, safe, dataport.

Michelangelo Hotel The Michelangelo is very popular with traveling foreigners, especially Europeans. The well-maintained hotel sits about a 2-block walk from the main street and catty-corner from the phone center, a convenient yet quiet location, and is recognizable by its A-frame porticos. Probably the best thing about the Michelangelo is its excellent restaurant (reviewed under "Where to Dine," below) and its comfortable rooms, although they're not especially noteworthy. Rooms are average size with white walls, dark beams, and little decoration; new mattresses were added in 2002. The softly lit lounge has a handful of chairs, a banquette, and potted plants. The staff is exceptionally friendly and helpful here, and speak passable English.

Gobernador Moyano 1020, El Calafate. © **02902/491045.** Fax 02902/491058. michelangelohotel@cotecal. com.ar. 20 units. $55–$61 double. AE, MC, V. **Amenities:** Restaurant; bar; lounge; room service. *In room:* TV, minibar.

INEXPENSIVE

Hostal Lago Argentino Like Los Dos Pinos (see below), the Hostal Lago Argentino offers different options for budget travelers. There are $6 beds in two-bunk, shared rooms in one wing and, across the street in a pink and blue building, modest yet tidy doubles with private bathrooms that for $18 make for a great value in El Calafate. The rooms aren't huge, but there's a small seating area should you need a little space. The *hostal* is about a block from the bus terminal.

Campaña de Desierto 1070, El Calafate. © **02902/491423.** 8 units. $18 double. No credit cards. Closed July to mid-Aug. **Amenities:** Lounge.

Hotel Amado The Hotel Amado sits on the main street next to all the shops and restaurants. The hotel is an okay choice, far from exceptional but not particularly bad either. The hallway and the rooms are on the dark side, and doubles always come with an extra single that cramps the room—ask if they can move the single for extra breathing space. The red cotton bedspreads are somewhat tired, but beds have regular mattresses and box springs instead of a foam mattress. All in all, very clean if a bit worn.

Av. del Libertador 1072, El Calafate. © **02902/491023.** Fax 02902/491134. familiagomez@cotecal.com.ar. 20 units. $20–$24 double. AE, MC, V. **Amenities:** Lounge. *In room:* TV.

Los Dos Pinos The Los Dos Pinos has just about every and any combination for budget travelers. At the bottom of the rung is the grassy campground, which comes with barbecue pits and costs $2 per person; next up is the $6 option for a bed in a six-bunk room that you might or might not have to share with strangers during the high season. There are several cabins and a few rooms that come with a kitchen. One floor has three rooms and a hall that leads to a shared kitchen and bathroom. The *cabañas* have kelly-green cement interiors and two bedrooms with one single and one bunk bed and a shared eating area and kitchen. The "deluxe" rooms are simple doubles with a private bathroom but no kitchen, and are a good deal for the price. The hostal sits at the end of a gravely dirt road about a 4-block walk to the main street, not exactly a choice location, but peaceful. Also, the surrounding grounds are unattractive because the lot seems to be in a perpetual state of half-completed construction.

Av. 9 de Julio 358, El Calafate. ℂ/fax 02902/491271. losdospinos@cotecal.com.ar. 25 units. $17 double; $8 per person *cabaña*. MC, V. **Amenities:** Lounge.

WHERE TO DINE

If you're just looking for a pleasant place away from the main street crowds in which to unwind with a cup of tea, then try **Kau Kaleshen** (Gobernador Gregores 1256; ℂ **02902/491188**). Opened in the fall of 2002 in a charming house on a side street, this tea house is open daily from 5pm to midnight and offers a "Te Completo" for $5 which includes your choice of either tea or specialty coffee along with homemade breads and jam, a selection of pastries, and toasted sandwiches. Credit cards are not accepted.

MODERATE

La Posta ★★★ ARGENTINE.   Although it's in a building separate from the Posada Los Alamos, the La Posta is considered to be part of that hotel. This is El Calafate's most upscale restaurant, serving great cuisine and choice wines in a cozy, candlelit environment. The menu, printed in four languages, offers well-prepared dishes that effectively blend Argentine and international-flavored fare, like filet mignon in a puff pastry with rosemary-roasted potatoes, king crab ravioli, almond trout, or curried crayfish. Desserts are superb. If you're staying at the hotel, a lovely breakfast buffet is served here every morning, and the service both morning and night is exquisite.

Gobernador Moyano and Bustillo. ℂ 02902/491144. Reservations recommended in high season. Main courses $5–$8. AE, DC, MC, V. Daily 7pm–midnight.

INEXPENSIVE

Casablanca CAFE/BAR   The Casablanca is the local hangout for a beer and a quick meal, and one of the few places you can grab a meal at odd hours. There's a wooden bar and a dining area with tile floors and metal chairs and tables, and an elevated TV that's usually on. The menu is mostly pizzas, sandwiches, and empanadas, with one special and a popular steak and fries plate for $3.50, but sandwiches are your best bet here. This is a good spot for writing out postcards and sipping a cold beer on a warm afternoon.

Av. 21 de Mayo and Av. del Libertador. ℂ 02902/491402. Main courses $3.50–$5; sandwiches $1.50–$3. No credit cards. Daily 10am–3am.

Casimiro ★ *Moments* REGIONAL   This new wine bar and restaurant opened in the fall of 2002 and has quickly become the number one hot spot in El Calafate. The sleek and modern black and white decor; thick tablecloths and flickering candles on every table; and young and energetic waitstaff make this place a winner. You can sample one of the many wines while enjoying an appetizer platter of regional Patagonian specialties such as smoked trout, smoked wild boar, and a variety of cheeses. Main courses change frequently but usually range from a simple steak to an elaborate pasta with salmon, cream, and capers in white-wine sauce; there's always a chicken and seafood offering, as well. If you're celebrating a special occasion, this would be an excellent place to try a glass of dry Argentine sparkling wine.

Av. del Libertador 963. ℂ 02902/492590. Main courses $4–7. MC, V. Daily 10am—1am.

El Rancho PIZZA   El Rancho's brick interior, with its white lace curtains and old photos, is cozy and inviting, but the restaurant's tiny size means you might have to wait for a table on busy evenings. There are 32 varieties of pizza on offer here and 5 varieties of hefty empanadas. Also on the menu are fresh salads and a couple of steaks. They also deliver, free of charge.

Gobernador Moyano and Av. 9 de Julio. 🕐 **02902/491644.** Pizzas $2–$5. DC, MC, V. Tues–Sun 6:30pm–midnight.

La Cocina *(Value)* BISTRO   This little restaurant serves bistro-style food, including fresh pastas such as raviolis and fettuccine, fresh trout, and meats that are prepared simply but are quite good. Try the crepes stuffed with vegetables or combinations such as ham and cheese, or meat items such as steak with a pepper and mustard sauce. Of all the restaurants on the main street with a similar appearance, such as the Paso Verlika, La Cocina is without a doubt the best.

Av. del Libertador 1245. 🕐 **02902/491758.** Main courses $2–$4.25. MC, V. Tues–Sun noon–3pm and 7:30–11pm.

La Tablita ★★ *(Value)* STEAKHOUSE   Carnivores need not look any further. La Tablita is all about meat, and it's one of the local favorites in town for its heaping platters and giant *parrilladas* (mixed grills) that come sizzling to your table on their own mini-barbecues. The *parrilladas* for two cost $9, but they really serve three diners given the size and assortment of chicken, sausage, beef, lamb, and a few innards you may or may not recognize. The filet mignon is incredibly tender here, and at $4 is one of the least expensive filets that we've ever had. The sunny, airy restaurant can be found on the other side of the bridge that spans the Arroyo Calafate, about a 2-minute walk from downtown.

Coronel Rosales 24. 🕐 **02902/491065.** Main courses $2–$4.25. AE, MC, V. Daily 11am–3pm and 7pm–midnight (Wed closed for lunch).

Michelangelo *(Finds)* ARGENTINE   The Michelangelo Hotel's restaurant is as popular with the public as it is with its guests. The semi-elegant dining area is very pleasing, with low ceilings, stone-and-mortar walls, and candlelit tables. The Michelangelo has added more exotic fare to its menu than La Posta, such as wild hare and smoked venison. The lamb in red-wine sauce with roasted potatoes is quite good as are other meat dishes, such as filet mignon, or chicken with a balsamic and tarragon vinaigrette. The fresh pastas and fish dishes are light and simple, as are the salads.

Gobernador Moyano 1020. 🕐 **02902/492104.** Main courses $3.50–$6. MC, V. Daily noon–3pm and 8pm–midnight.

Parrilla Mi Viejo STEAKHOUSE   Mi Viejo is another local barbecue favorite, with enough variety on the menu to satisfy everyone. Mi Viejo ("My Old Man") seems to refer to the crusty character manning the lamb barbecue spit at the restaurant's front entrance, serving up weighty, delicious cuts of meat. Three to five diners could eat from a $10 *parrillada* meat assortment, depending on their hunger. The menu also offers trout and salmon dishes and a few interesting plates such as pickled hare. The restaurant is located on the main drag, and its dining room is warm and pleasant.

Av. del Libertador 1111. 🕐 **02902/491691.** Main courses $3–$5. MC, V. Daily 11am–3pm and 7pm–midnight.

Pura Vida ★ *(Finds)* VEGETARIAN/REGIONAL   The friendliest place in town is a short walk from downtown but is worth finding. Set in a woodsy location overlooking the lake, this is the best place in El Calafate for homestyle cuisine that favors vegetarians. Try the delicious pumpkin soup or the gnocchi in saffron sauce. If you're wanting to try a regional specialty then go for the *cazuela de cordero* (hearty lamb stew with mushrooms). For dessert, both the rice pudding and the pumpkin ice cream are delicious. Fresh fruit shakes, sandwiches, and afternoon tea with homemade rolls and jams are also offered. The service is laid back, the crowd young and relaxed, and the view of the lake is divine.

Av. del Libertador 1876. $©$ 02902/493356. Main courses $3.50–$5. No credit cards. Thurs–Tues 4pm–12:30am (to 1:30am Fri–Sat).

Tango Sur DINNER/SHOW   The Porteño owner of this restaurant/ nightclub has brought tango to the south of Argentina. The Tango Sur, in a lovely raspberry-colored building made of old brick, serves light meals and a nightly tango show of crooning and dancing. The interiors are crammed with memorabilia and antiques such as a megaphone, records, microphones, and anything related to tango that the owner could find. The menu is brief, serving grilled steak, beef *milanesas* (breaded filets), and sandwiches—better to order a drink and an appetizer platter.

Av. 9 de Julio 265. $©$ 02902/491550. Main courses $3–$6. No credit cards. Tues–Sun 7pm–5am.

PARQUE NACIONAL LOS GLACIARES & THE PERITO MORENO GLACIER ★★★

The Los Glaciares National Park covers 600,000 hectares (1.5 million acres) of rugged land that stretches vertically along the crest of the Andes and spills east into flat pampa. Most of Los Glaciares is inaccessible to visitors except for the park's two dramatic highlights: the granite needles, such as Fitz Roy near El Chaltén (covered in "El Chaltén & the Fitz Roy Area, Argentina," below), and this region's magnificent Perito Moreno Glacier. The park is also home to thundering rivers, blue lakes, and thick beech forest. Los Glaciares National Park was formed in 1937 and declared a World Heritage region by UNESCO in 1981.

If you don't get a chance to visit Glacier Grey in Torres del Paine, the Perito Moreno is a must-see. Few natural wonders in South America are as spectacular or as easily accessed as this glacier, and unlike the hundreds of glaciers that drain from the Southern Ice Field, the Perito Moreno is one of the few that are not receding. Around 1900, the Perito Moreno was measured at 750m (2,460 ft.) from the Península Magallanes; by 1920 it had advanced so far that it finally made contact with the peninsula. Each time the glacier reached the peninsula, which would occur every 3 to 4 years, it created a dam in the channel and the built-up pressure would set off a calving explosion for 48 to 72 hours, breaking the face of the glacier in a crashing fury. The phenomenon has not occurred in many years, but the Perito Moreno is usually reliable for a sending a few huge chunks hurling into the channel throughout the day.

What impresses visitors most is the sheer size of the Perito Moreno Glacier, a wall of jagged blue ice measuring 4,500m (14,760 ft.) across and soaring 60m (197 ft.) above the channel. To give you some perspective of its length: You could fit the entire city of Buenos Aires on this glacier. From the parking lot on the Península Magallanes, a series of vista-point walkways descend, which take visitors directly to the glacier's face. It's truly an unforgettable, spellbinding experience. There are opportunities to join an organized group for a walk on the glacier as well as boat journeys that leave from Puerto Banderas for visits to the neighboring glaciers Upsala and Spegazzini.

GETTING THERE & ESSENTIALS

At Km 49 (30 miles) from El Calafate, you'll pass through the park's entrance, where there's an information booth with erratic hours (no phone; www. calafate.com). Entrance fee is $5.75 per person. If you're looking for information about the park and the glacier, pick up an interpretive guide or book from one of the bookstores or tourist shops along Avenida del Libertador in El Calafate. There is a restaurant near the principal lookout platform near the glacier, and a good, though expensive, restaurant inside the Los Notros hotel (see "Lodging Near the Glacier," below).

To get to the park:

BY CAR   Following Avenida del Libertador west out of town, the route turns into a well-maintained dirt road. From here it's 80km (50 miles) to the glacier.

BY TAXI OR *REMISE*   If you want to see the glacier at your own pace, hire a taxi or *remise* (a private taxi). The cost averages $40 for two, $65 for three, and $90 for four, although many taxi companies will negotiate a price. Be sure to agree on an estimated amount of time spent at the glacier.

BY ORGANIZED TOUR   Several companies offer transportation to and from the glacier, such as **Interlagos,** Av. del Libertador 1175 (② **02902/ 491175;** interlagos@cotecal.com.ar); **City Tour,** Av. del Libertador 1341 (② **02902/492276;** morresi@cotecal.com.ar); **Caltur** at Av. del Libertador 1177 (② **02902/491368;** caltur@cotecal.com.ar); and **TAQSA** in the bus terminal (② **02902/491843**). These minivan and bus services provide bilingual guides and leave around 9am, spending an average of 4 hours at the peninsula; the cost is $25 to $30 per person, not including lunch. For a more personalized tour (a private car with driver and a bilingual, licensed guide), contact **SurTurismo** at 25 de Mayo 23 (② **02902/491266;** suring@cotecal.com.ar); they can arrange for a half-day trip costing $60 to $75 for two people; prices vary with the seasons.

OUTDOOR ACTIVITIES

There are several exciting activities in this region, including a "mini-trek" that takes guests for a walk upon the glacier. The trip begins with a 20-minute boat ride across the Brazo Rico, followed by a 30-minute walk to the glacier. From here guests are outfitted with crampons and other safety gear, then spend approximately 1½ hours atop the ice, complete with a stop for a whisky on the thousand-year-old "rocks." This great trip gives visitors the chance to peer into the electric-blue crevasses of the glacier and truly appreciate its size. You can book this trip through any travel agency.

   Companies that can arrange this trip for you include **Solo Patagonia,** Av. del Libertador 963 (② **02902/491298;** www.solopatagonia.com.ar), which offers visitors navigation through the Brazo Rico to the face of the Perito Moreno, including trekking to the base of the Cerro Negro with a view of the Glacier Negro. Both Solo Patagonia and **Upsala Explorer** ⊛, Av. 9 de Julio 69 (② **02902/491034;** www.upsalaexplorer.com.ar), offer a variety of combinations from Puerto Banderas to Los Glaciares National Park's largest and tallest glaciers, respectively the Upsala and Spegazzini. Upsala Explorer makes a stop at the Estancia Cristina for lunch and optional trekking and 4×4 trips to the Upsala Lookout. Solo Patagonia offers similar journeys, including a stop at the Onelli area for trekking, as well as navigation-only journeys. Both companies charge $87 to $99 for this all-day excursion.

LODGING NEAR THE GLACIER

Los Notros ★★★ *Moments*   Few hotels in Argentina boast as spectacular and breathtaking a view as Los Notros—but it doesn't come cheap. This luxury lodge sits high on a slope looking out at the Perito Moreno Glacier, and all common areas and rooms have been fitted with picture windows to really soak up the marvelous sight. Although the wood-hewn exteriors give the hotel the feel of a mountain lodge, the interior decor is contemporary. Each room is slightly different, with personal touches like antique lamps and regional photos; crocheted or gingham bedspreads; lilac, peach, or lemon-yellow walls; padded floral headboards or iron bed frames; and tweedy brown or raspberry corduroy chairs. Bathrooms are gleaming white, and premium rooms in the newer wing have whirlpool baths. The older "Cascada bungalow" rooms have very thin walls; if you're a light sleeper, be sure to request a top floor room or a room in the newer "Premium" (and more expensive) wing.

Inside the main building is a large, chic, expensive restaurant renowned for serving creative regional cuisine; guests can expect to pay $38 for a fixed-price dinner, $20 at lunch. Upstairs is an airy lounge area with chaise longues positioned in front of panoramic windows; here you'll find a TV room with a selection of nature videos. Guests at the Los Notros frequently opt for one of the multiple-day packages that includes airport transfers, meals, box lunches for expeditions, nightly discussions, guided trekking, boat excursions, and ice walks. Although Los Notros offers 4-night packages, you might find that length of time too long unless you're looking to get away from it all for a while. Note that prices jump substantially during Christmas, New Year's, and Easter week.

Main office in Buenos Aires: Arenales 1457, 7th floor. © **11/4814-3934.** Fax 11/4815-7645. www.losnotros. com. 32 units. $330 double Cascada bungalow; $390 double superior; $480 double premium. Rates include buffet breakfast. All-inclusive, 2-night packages average $843 in a premium room, per person. AE, DC, MC, V. **Amenities:** Restaurant; bar; lounge; tour desk; room service; laundry service. *In room:* Minibar.

5 El Chaltén & the Fitz Roy Area, Argentina ★★

222km (138 miles) N of El Calafate

El Chaltén is a tiny village of about 200 residents whose lifeblood, like El Calafate's, depends entirely on the throng of visitors who come each summer. This is the second most-visited region of Argentina's Los Glaciares National Park and quite possibly its most exquisite for the singular nature of the granite spires that shoot up, torpedo-like, above massive tongues of ice that descend from the Southern Ice Field. In the world of mountaineering, these sheer and ice-encrusted peaks are considered some of the most formidable challenges in the world, and they draw hundreds of climbers here every year.

Little more than 5 years ago, El Chaltén counted just a dozen houses and a hostal or two, but the Fitz Roy's rugged beauty and great hiking opportunities have created somewhat of a boomtown. The town sits nestled in a circular rock outcrop at the base of the Fitz Roy and is fronted by the vast, dry pampa. Visitors use El Chaltén either as a base from which to take day hikes or as an overnight stop before setting off for a multiple-day backpacking trip.

ESSENTIALS

GETTING THERE

BY PLANE   All transportation to El Chaltén originates from El Calafate, which has daily plane service from Ushuaia and Buenos Aires. From El Calafate you need to take a bus or rent a car; the trip takes from 3 to 3½ hours.

BY CAR Take the Ruta Nacional 11 west for 30km (19 miles) and turn left on Ruta Nacional 40 north. Turn again, heading northwest, on Ruta Provincial 23 to El Chaltén. The road is unpaved.

BY BUS Buses from El Calafate leave from the terminal, and all cost about $30 round-trip. **Chaltén Travel,** with offices in El Chaltén in the Albergue Rancho Grande on Avenida del Libertador (© 02962/493005; chaltentravel@ cotecal.com.ar), leaves El Calafate daily at 8am and El Chaltén at 6pm. Chaltén Travel can arrange private tours and day trips to outlying destinations such as Patagonian ranches, as well as summer-only transportation up Ruta Nacional 40 for those crossing into Chile. **Caltur,** which leaves from El Chaltén's Hostería Fitz Roy at Av. San Martín 520 (© 02962/493062; caltur@cotecal.com.ar), leaves El Calafate daily at 7:30am and leaves El Chaltén at 6pm. **Los Glaciares,** San Martín 100 (© 02962/493063; www.losglaciaresturismo.com), leaves El Calafate daily at 8am and returns at 5:30pm.

VISITOR INFORMATION

There is a $5.75 fee to enter the park. The Park Service has an **information center** located at the entrance to town; here you'll find maps, pamphlets, and brief interpretive displays about the region's flora and fauna. It's open daily from 8am to 8pm. El Chaltén also has a well-organized visitor center at the town's entrance—the **Comisión de Fomento,** Perito Moreno and Avenida Güemes (© 02962/493011), open daily from 8am to 8pm. In El Calafate, the **APN Intendencia** (park service) has its offices at Av. del Libertador 1302, with a visitor center that is open daily from 9am to 3pm (© 02902/491005).

OUTDOOR ACTIVITIES

TOUR OPERATORS **Fitz Roy Expediciones** ⭐, Lionel Terray 212 (©/fax 02962/493017; fitzroyexpediciones@videodata.com.ar), offers a full-day excursion trekking through the Valle de Río Fitz Roy combined with ice climbing at the Glacier Torre. No experience is necessary, but they do ask that you be in fit condition. They can also arrange for you to make the descent back to the base on horseback. Fitz Roy Expediciones offers a variety of trekking excursions, including a complete 10-day circuit around the backside of the Fitz Roy and Cerro Torre peaks, for $1,083 per person, all equipment and meals included, as well as 2 nights' lodging in an *albergue*. **Alta Montaña** at Lionel Terray 501 (© 02962/493018; altamont@infovia.com.ar) also offers summer-only, day-trekking excursions. There are several resident mountaineering and trekking guides who speak English and can be hired on a freelance basis including Alberto del Castillo (© 02962/493017), Jorge Tarditti (© 02962/4993013), and Oscar Pandolfi (© 02962/493016).

HIKING & CAMPING If you're planning on doing any hiking in the park, you'll want to pick up a copy of Zagier & Urruty's trekking map, "Monte Fitz Roy & Cerro Torre," available at most bookstores and tourist shops in El Calafate and El Chaltén. You'll also need to register at the park service office at the entrance to El Chaltén. You won't find a well-defined circuit here as you do in Torres del Paine, but there is a loop of sorts, and all stretches of this 3- to 4-day loop can be done one leg at a time on day hikes. Trails here run from easy to difficult and take anywhere from 4 to 10 hours to complete.

One of the most spectacular day hikes, which can also be done as an overnight, 2-day hike, is the 19km (12-mile) trail to the **Mirador D'Agostini,** also known as Maestri, that affords exhilarating views of the spire Cerro Torre.

The hike takes 5½ to 6 hours to complete and is classified as easy, except for the last steep climb to the lookout point. It's possible to camp nearby at the D'Agostini campground (formerly Bridwell). Leaving from the Madsen campground, a more demanding, though beautiful, trail heads to several campsites and eventually the Laguna de los Tres, where there is a lookout point for views of Mount Fitz Roy. This walk is best done as an overnight trip; it's too much to undertake in 1 day. Campgrounds inside the park's boundaries are free, but do not have services; paid campgrounds (outside the park) have water and some have showers.

HORSEBACK RIDING   There's nothing like horseback riding in Patagonia, and two outfitters offer several day excursions: **Rodolfo Guerra** at Las Loicas 773 (© **02962/493020**) has horseback rides and a horsepack service for carrying gear to campsites. Also try the **El Relincho** at Av. del Libertador s/n (© **02962/493007**).

WHERE TO STAY IN EL CHALTEN

El Puma ⭐   El Puma offers the most stylish and comfortable accommodations in El Chaltén. The owners of this hotel work with the outfitter Fitz Roy Expediciones, who have an office next door. The hotel sits back from the main road, and faces out toward snowy peaks, although without a view of Fitz Roy. Inside, warm beige walls and wooden beams interplay with brick, and are offset with soft cotton curtains and ironwork. Although the common areas have terra-cotta ceramic floors, all rooms are carpeted. The rooms are well designed and bright; the lounge has a few chairs that face a roaring fire. There's also an eating area with wooden tables and a small bar. Very friendly service.

Lionel Terray 512, El Chaltén. © 02962/493095. Fax 02962/493017. Elpuma@videodata.com.ar. 8 units. $83 double. Rate includes buffet breakfast. No credit cards. Open Nov–Mar. **Amenities:** Restaurant; bar.

Hostería El Pilar *(Finds)*   The Hostería El Pilar is undoubtedly the choice lodging option in the area. True, the hotel's location 15km (9 miles) from El Chaltén toward Lago del Desierto does put guests far from restaurants and shops, but then lovely, peaceful surroundings are what many guests look for when they come to visit the national park. The yellow-walled and red-roofed El Pilar was once an *estancia;* now it's tastefully and artistically decorated with just enough detail to not distract you from the outdoors. The lounge offers a few couches and a fireplace and is a comfy spot to lounge and read a book. Rooms are simple but attractive, with peach walls, comfortable beds, and sunlight that streams through half-curtained windows. Guests normally take their meals at the hotel's restaurant, which serves great cuisine. The hotel offers guided excursions and is located next to several trail heads. If you're driving here, really keep an eye open for the sign to this hotel because it's easy to miss.

Ruta Provincial 23, 9 miles (15km) from El Chaltén. ©/fax 02962/493002. 16 units. $80 double. MC, V. Open Oct–Apr; rest of the year with a reservation. **Amenities:** Restaurant; bar; lounge.

Hostería Fitz Roy   This mint-green hotel is spread out somewhat ranch-style, with a popular restaurant and regular bus service to El Calafate. The hallways are very dark, but the rooms receive decent light, and none have a view of much of anything. The rooms at the Fitz Roy are simple but clean. If by chance you're traveling with five people and you all want to sleep in the same room, they've got one to fit you. This hotel is a decent value, but the service could use a smile.

Av. San Martín 520, El Chaltén. © 02962/493062, or 02902/491368 (reservations). Fax 02902/492217. www.elchalten.com/fitzroyinn. 24 units. $48–$62 double. MC, V. Open Sept–May. **Amenities:** Restaurant.

Hostería Los Ñires This *hostería* offers unremarkable but clean and comfortable accommodations. In one wing are rooms with a private bathroom; the other is a hostal setup with shared bunks and bathrooms and a common area with a kitchen. The rooms have white walls and no decoration other than a view of the Fitz Roy peak, and a wide variety of combinations, including several quadruples. If it's fairly slow in the hostal, they'll make sure you don't have to share your three-bed room with a stranger. The main building has a roomy restaurant and lounge. Breakfast is not included for guests in the hostal.

Lago del Desierto s/n, El Chaltén. ℂ 02962/493009. Losnires@sanjulian.com.ar 12 units. $30 double with private bathroom; $8 bunk with shared bathroom. MC, V. **Amenities:** Restaurant; laundry service.

Posada Poicenoit & Albergue Rancho Grande These two jointly owned lodging options sit next to each other. The Posada Poicenoit is a tiny, attractive hotel built of wood with just three rooms: two doubles and a quadruple, all with private bathrooms. There's a small foyer with high ceilings, filled with several wooden tables for breakfast or snacks. The rooms are simple but comfortable and sunny. Next door, an equally attractive hostal caters to a predominantly backpacker crowd. Each room has two bunk beds, and rooms are shared if you don't have three friends to help you fill it. The restaurant and eating area is a great place to unwind, with long wooden tables, a lofty ceiling, and broad windows. The best deal here is the *albergue*'s kitchen, which guests may use, including guests from the Posada Poicenoit.

Av. del Libertador s/n, El Chaltén. ℂ 09262/493005. chaltentravel@cotecal.com.ar. 3 units, 8 dormitory-style rooms. $20 double; $6 per person dormitory. AE, MC, V. Open Oct–Apr. **Amenities:** Restaurant; lounge.

WHERE TO DINE

During the winter only one restaurant valiantly stays open: **La Casita,** Avenida del Libertador at Lionel Terray, in the pink building (ℂ **02966493042**). La Casita offers average, home-style fare, including sandwiches, meats, pastas, stuffed crepes, and absent-minded service; it accepts American Express, MasterCard, and Visa. At other times of the year, the best restaurant in town for food and ambience is **Patagonicus,** Güemes at Andreas Madsen (ℂ **02966/493025**). Patagonicus serves mostly pizza and enormous salads in a woodsy dining area; no credit cards accepted. Another good restaurant can be found inside the **Hostería Fitz Roy,** Av. San Martín 520 (ℂ **02966/493062**), which serves Argentine and international fare such as grilled meats and seafood, pastas, and more in a pleasant dining area with white linen-draped tables; it accepts MasterCard and Visa. For sandwiches, snacks, coffee, and cakes, try the **Albergue Rancho Grande,** Av. del Libertador s/n (ℂ **02966/493005**); no credit cards accepted.

6 The Far South: Puerto Williams, Chile

Puerto Williams has a population of 2,500 and is a small naval base and town located on Isla Navarino on the southern shore of the Beagle Channel. As a destination, it's superseded by its Argentine neighbor Ushuaia, chiefly due to the town's isolation and the difficulty getting there—which for some is part of its draw. Apart from a few hiking trails and a museum, there's not a lot to do, but adventurers setting out for or returning from sailing and kayaking trips around Cape Horn use the town as a base. Several boat companies leaving from Ushuaia or Punta Arenas stop off here. It's worth a walk through town past the colorful jumble of tin houses picturesquely nestled below verdant peaks. Alternatively, visitors can fly here for a multiple-day sailing adventure.

GETTING THERE

BY AIR   **Aerovías DAP** (© **61/223340** in Punta Arenas, 61/621051 in Puerto Williams; www.aeroviasdap.cl) flies to Puerto Williams from Punta Arenas three times a week (see "Getting There," under "Punta Arenas, Chile," earlier in this chapter).

BY BOAT   Several companies in Ushuaia, Argentina offer sailing excursions to Puerto Williams: **All Patagonia Viajes y Turismo,** in Ushuaia, Juana Fadul 26 (© **02901/433622;** allpat@tierradelfuego.org.ar), offers 2-day/1-night trips for $220 per person, including lodging aboard its sailboat and meals. From Puerto Williams, **Karanka Expeditions,** Casilla 09, Puerto Williams, offers sailing cruises as far as the Cape Horn for $90 per person, per day, with gourmet meals included (© **61/621127;** vademasi@ctc.internet.cl), and **Canales Australis,** on the plaza (© **61/621050;** vcaselli@munitel.cl), has 10-hour trips on a motorized boat around remote locations in the Beagle Channel for $50 per person, including lunch. **Tekenika Sea Ice Mountains** has sailboat adventures that can leave guests in Ushuaia; its office is on the tiny plaza (© **61/627750**). The cruise ship *Mare Australis* makes a stop here; for information, see "Cruising from Punta Arenas to Ushuaia" under "Punta Arenas, Chile," earlier in this chapter.

WHAT TO SEE & DO

The **Museo Maurice van de Maele,** at Aragay 01 (© **61/621043**), is open from 10am to 1pm and 3 to 6pm, featuring a good collection of Yaghan and Yamana Indian artifacts, ethnographic exhibits, and stuffed birds and animals. The museum's docent is an excellent anthropologist and naturalist who can provide tours in the area. Just outside town, next to the waterfall that cascades down to the road, is a **hiking trail** that eventually splits into two trails. For a 2-hour round-trip climb up to Cerro La Bandera, take the trail leading left; for an 8-hour round-trip hike to the peak Dientes de Navarino, head right when the trail splits. There is a longer backpacking trail called Los Dientes, but it's recommended only for those with ample backpacking experience and good map and compass skills. The best map is JLM's "Tierra del Fuego" map, sold in most shops and bookstores. **Inhóspita Patagonia** in Punta Arenas, Lautaro Navarro 1013 (© **61/224510;** inhospita@chileanpatagonia.com), arranges guided treks through this region.

WHERE TO STAY & DINE

The pickings are slim ever since the Wala Hotel closed in 2001, but basic, clean accommodation can be found at the **Hostal Camblor,** Calle Patricio Cap Deville (© **61/621033**), which has six brand-new rooms for $18 per person. The Camblor also has a restaurant that serves as the local disco on Friday and Saturday nights, so noise could be a problem. Another comfortable place is the **Hostal Pusaki,** Piloto Pardo 222 (© **61/621116**), which has three rooms and charges $14 per person. The amiable owners of the Pusaki are also owners of Puerto Williams's pub and restaurant, **The Micalvi** (© **61/621020**), housed in an old supply ship that is docked at the pier, and the meeting spot for an international crowd of adventurers sailing around the Cape Horn. Another dining option is **Los Dientes de Navarino** (no phone), on the plaza.

7 Tierra del Fuego: Ushuaia, Argentina ⟨★⟨★

461km (286 miles) SW of Punta Arenas; 594km (368 miles) S of Río Gallegos

The name *Ushuaia* comes from the Yamana Indian language meaning "bay penetrating westward," a fairly simple appellation for a city situated in such a

---

Moments Flying To Antarctica

In early 2003, the Argentine Air Force began flying a revamped cargo jet, a Hercules C-130, twice weekly between Ushuaia and Seymour Island (known as Marambio to the locals) 1,006km (625 miles) to the south. After landing, the 70 passengers are given a 3-hour tour of Antarctica before returning to Ushuaia. The 1-day excursion is organized by Aerored in Buenos Aires (in cooperation with LADE, the Argentine Air Force's commercial airline). Departure from Ushuaia is at 5am, returning at 2pm; the days vary weekly. For rates and detailed information, contact **Aerored** in Buenos Aires at Esmeralda 740 (© **11/4328-1923;** fax 11/4328-4187 www. aeroredes.com.ar).

---

spectacular location. It's the southernmost city in the world (although the naval base and town Puerto Williams is farther south across the channel). Ushuaia is encircled by a range of rugged peaks and fronted by the Beagle Channel. It was first inhabited by the Yamana Indians until the late 1800s, then it became a penal colony until 1947. The region grew as a result of immigration from Croatia, Italy, and Spain and migration from the Argentine mainland, with government incentives such as tax-free duty on many goods being part of the draw. Today, the city has about 40,000 residents. Ushuaia is a great destination with plenty of activities, and many use the city as a jumping-off point for trips to Antarctica or sailing trips around Cape Horn.

ESSENTIALS
GETTING THERE
BY PLANE   There is no bus service to town from the Ushuaia Airport, but cab fares are only about $1.50; always ask for a quote before accepting a ride. **Aerolíneas Argentinas/Austral,** Roca 116 (© 02901/421218; www.aerolineas. com.ar), has one to three daily flights to Buenos Aires; air service frequency increases from November to March when there's also a daily flight from El Calafate. **LAPA,** Av. 25 de Mayo 64 (© 02901/432112; www.lapa.com.ar), has a daily flight to Buenos Aires, with a stopover in Río Gallegos. **Aerovías DAP** now has air service to and from Punta Arenas for $120 one-way (plus $5 airport tax), leaving Wednesday only at 9am from Punta Arenas and 10:30am from Ushuaia; its offices are at Av. 25 de Mayo 62 (© **02901/431110;** www.aeroviasdap.cl). During high season, DAP increases flights from Punta Arenas to five weekly in addition to a daily flight from Cape Horn.

BY BUS   Service from Punta Arenas, Chile, costs $19 and takes about 12 hours. **Tecni Austral** (© **02901/431407** in Ushuaia, or 61/222078 in Punta Arenas) leaves Monday, Wednesday, and Friday at 7am; tickets are sold in Ushuaia from the Tolkar office at Roca 157, and in Punta Arenas at Lautaro Navarro 975. **Tolkeyen,** Maipú 237 (© **02901/437073;** tolkeyenventas@ arnet.com.ar), works in combination with the Chilean company Pacheco for trips to Punta Arenas, leaving Tuesday, Thursday, and Saturday at 8am; it also goes to Río Grande, with three daily trips. Both companies take the route to Punta Arenas via Bahía Azul. Techni Austral offers service to Punta Arenas via Porvenir for the same price, leaving Saturday at 6am. **Lidded LTD,** Gobernador Paz 921 (© **02901/436421**), Techni Austral, and Tolkeyen all have multiple day trips to Río Grande.

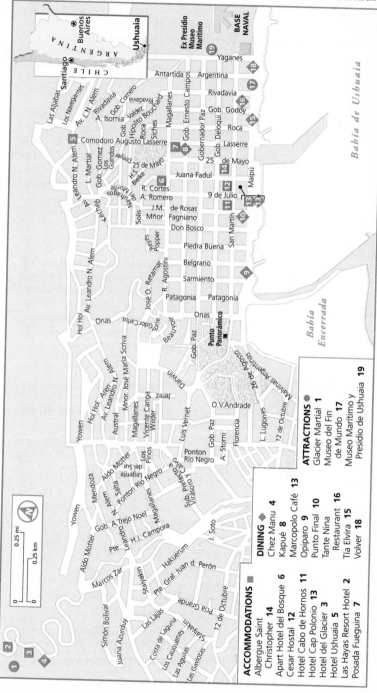

Ushuaia

ACCOMMODATIONS ■
Albergue Saint
  Christopher **14**
Apart Hotel del Bosque **6**
Cesar Hostal **12**
Hotel Cabo de Hornos **11**
Hotel Cap Polonio **13**
Hotel del Glacier **3**
Hotel Ushuaia **5**
Las Hayas Resort Hotel **2**
Posada Fueguina **7**

DINING ◆
Chez Manu **4**
Kapué **8**
Marcopolo Café **13**
Opiparo **9**
Punto Final **10**
Tante Nina
  Restaurant **16**
Tía Elvira **15**
Volver **18**

ATTRACTIONS ●
Glacier Martial **1**
Museo del Fin
  de Mundo **17**
Museo Marítimo y
  Presidio de Ushuaia **19**

Bahía de Ushuaia

Bahía Encerrada

BASE NAVAL

Ex Presidio
Museo Marítimo

435

BY BOAT   The company **Crucero Australis** operates a cruise to Ushuaia from Punta Arenas and vice versa aboard its ship the M/V *Mare Australis;* departures are Saturday from Punta Arenas and Wednesday from Ushuaia, from late September to April. If you have the time, this is a recommended journey for any age, and it's covered in the box "Cruising from Punta Arenas to Ushuaia," under "Punta Arenas, Chile," earlier in this chapter.

GETTING AROUND

BY CAR   Everything in and around Ushuaia is easily accessible via bus or taxi or by using an inexpensive shuttle or tour service, so renting a car is really not necessary. Rentals, however, are very reasonable, from $20 to $45 per day. **Avis** at Avenida del Libertador and Belgrano drops its prices for multiple-day rentals (© 02901/422744; www.avis.com); **Cardos Rent A Car** is at Av. del Libertador 845 (© 02901/436388); **Dollar Rent A Car** is at Maipú and Sarmiento (© 02901/432134; www.dollar.com); **Localiza Rent A Car** is at Av. del Libertador 1222 (© 02901/430739); and **Seven Rent A Car** rents 4×4 Jeeps with unlimited mileage at Av. del Libertador 802 (© 02901/437604).

VISITOR INFORMATION

The **Subsecretaría de Turismo** has a helpful, well-stocked office at Maipu 505 (© **02901/423340;** fax 02901/430694; info@tierradelfuego.org.ar). They also have a counter at the airport that is open to assist passengers on all arriving flights. From November to March, the office is open daily from 8am to 10pm; the rest of the year it's open Monday through Friday from 8am to 9pm, weekends and holidays from 9am to 8pm. The national park administration office can be found at Av. del Libertador 1395 (© **02901/421395;** open Mon–Fri 9am–3pm).

FAST FACTS: USHUAIA

Currency Exchange   Banco Sud at Avenida del Libertador and Godoy (© **02901/432080**) and **Banco Nación** at Av. del Libertador 190 (© **02901/ 422086**) both exchange currency and have 24-hour ATM machines.

Laundry   Los Tres Angeles, Rosas 139, is open Monday through Saturday from 9am to 8pm.

Pharmacy   Andina at Av. del Libertador 638 (© **02901/423431**) is open 24 hours a day.

Post Office   Correo Argentino is at Avenida del Libertador and Godoy (© **02901/421347**), open Monday through Friday from 9am to 7pm, Saturday from 9am to 1pm; the private postal company **OCA** is at Maipú and Avenida 9 de Julio (© **02901/424729**), open Monday through Saturday from 9am to 6pm.

Travel Agency/Credit Cards   American Express travel and credit card services are provided by All Patagonia, Juana Fadul 26 (© **02901/433622**).

WHAT TO SEE & DO IN & AROUND TOWN

An in-town walk can be taken to the city park and **Punto Panorámico,** which takes visitors up to a lookout point with good views of the city and the channel. It can be reached at the southwest terminus of Avenida del Libertador, and is free.

Museo del Fin de Mundo ⭐   The main room has an assortment of Indian hunting tools and colonial maritime instruments. There's also a natural history display of stuffed birds and a "grandfather's room" set up to resemble an old general store, packed with antique products. But the strength of this museum is its 60 history and nature videos available for viewing and its reference library with more than 3,650 volumes, including a fascinating birth record. Its store has an excellent range of books about Patagonia for sale.

Maipú 175. © **02901/421863**. Admission $1.50 adults, 60¢ students, free for children under 14. Daily 10am–1pm and 3–7:30pm.

Museo Marítimo y Presidio de Ushuaia ★ *Moments*   Ushuaia was founded primarily thanks to the penal colony set up here in the late 1800s for hundreds of Argentina's most dangerous criminals. The rehabilitation system consisted of forced labor to build piers and buildings, and creative workshops for teaching carpentry, music, tailoring, and other trades—all of which coincidentally fueled the local economy. The museum offers a fascinating look into prisoners' and prison workers' lives through interpretive displays and artifacts. There's a restaurant here, with "prison" meals and other theme items.

Yaganes and Gobernador Paz. © **02901/437481**. Admission $2 adults, $1.50 seniors, 70¢ children ages 5–12, free for children under 5. Daily 10am–1pm and 3–8pm.

Glacier Martial/Aerosilla *Finds*   The Glacier Martial is a pleasant excursion that sits literally in the backyard of Ushuaia. Avenida Luis Fernando Martial winds 7km (4 miles) up from town to the base of a beautiful mountain amphitheater, where you'll find a chair lift that takes visitors to the small Glacier Martial. It's a long walk up the road, and there are no buses to take you there. Visitors usually hire a taxi for $2 and walk all the way back down, or arrange for the driver to pick them up later. At the base of the chair lift, don't miss a stop at **La Cabaña** ★ (© **02901/424257**), an excellent teahouse with a wraparound outdoor deck and mouth-watering cakes and pastries.

Av. Luis Fernando Martial, 7km (4 miles) from town. No phone. Admission $2 adults, $1 children under 9. Daily 10:30am–5:30pm.

OUTDOOR ACTIVITIES

BOATING   Navigation excursions are very popular here, with several companies offering a variety of trips. The most popular excursion is a half-day trip cruising the Beagle Channel to view sea lions, penguins, and more. You'll find a cluster of kiosks near the pier offering a variety of excursions. **Motonave Barracuda** leaves twice daily for its 3-hour trip around the channel for $18 per person, visiting Isla de Lobos, Isla de Pájaros, and a lighthouse (© **02901/436453**). **Motovelero Tres Marías** also leaves twice daily and sails to the same location; however, they have a maximum of nine guests and add an hour's walk, crab fishing, cognac, and an underwater camera to the package (© **02901/421897**). **Tierra del Sur** combines a bus/boat trip, visiting Estancia Harberton (see below) first, then embarking for a 1½-hour sail to a penguin colony during penguin season from November to April (© **02901/421897**). **Motovelero Patagonia Adventure** has an 18-passenger maximum and leaves daily; it visits the sea lion colony and includes a walk on the Isla Bridges for $20. This company also works with the Aventuras Isla Verde in the park for a full-day sail; inquire at their kiosk.

FISHING   For a fishing license and information, go to the Club de Pesca y Caza at Av. del Libertador 818 (no phone). The cost is about $12 for foreigners per day.

SKIING Ushuaia's new ski resort, **Cerro Castor** (© 02901/422244; www. cerrocastor.com), is surprisingly good, with more than 400 skiable hectares, 15 runs, three quad chairs and one double, a lodge/restaurant, and a slopeside bar. Day tickets cost $17 to $24, depending on low or high season, and the resort is open from June 15 to October 15. To get there, take the shuttle buses **Pasarela** (© 02901/433712) or **Bella Vista** (© 02901/443161); the fare is $4.

TOUR OPERATORS

All Patagonia Viajes y Turismo, Juana Fadul 26 (© 02901/433622; allpat@ tierradelfuego.org.ar), is the local American Express travel representative, and acts as a clearinghouse for everything—if they don't offer it themselves, they'll arrange an excursion with other outfitters, and they can reserve excursions in other destinations in Argentina and Chile. All Patagonia offers three glacier walks for those in physically good shape, scenic flights over Tierra del Fuego ($35 per person for 30 min.), and treks and drives in its Land Rover with nature guides. If you're not sure what you want, start here. **Canal Fun & Nature,** Rivadavía 82 (© 02901/437395; www.canalfun.com), is a great company with excellent guides who provide 4×4 trips and walks culminating with a barbecue, as well as kayaking and nighttime beaver watching, and they'll custom-build a trip for you. **Rumbo Sur,** Av. del Libertador 350 (© 02901/430699; www. rumbosur.com.ar), and **Tolkeyen/PreTour,** Maipú 237 (© 02901/437073; tolekeyenventas@arnet.com.ar), are two operators that deal with larger groups and arrange more classic excursions, such as a city tour and guided visits to the national park and Lagos Escondido and Fagnano.

EXCURSIONS AROUND USHUAIA

One of the most intriguing destinations around Ushuaia is the **Estancia Harberton,** the first ranch founded in Tierra del Fuego. It is now run as a museum. The ranch is located on the shore of the Beagle Channel, and can be reached by road or boat. The entrance fee is $2 April through October and $4 November through March. Transportation to the *estancia,* 90km (56 miles) from Ushuaia, is provided by most travel agencies in town, for an average cost of $45 per person plus the entrance fee, provided you are a group of 4 or more. Roughly from October to April, several tour companies offer a catamaran ride to the *estancia,* a 6-hour excursion for $65 per person; try **All Patagonia,** Juana Fadul 26 (© 02901/433622). Tour groups will also arrange a boat excursion to a **penguin colony** from the *estancia,* an add-on excursion that costs about $24 per person.

After the turnoff for Estancia Harberton, Ruta 3 begins to descend down to **Lago Escondido,** a beautiful lake about 60km (37 miles) north of Ushuaia that

---

A Ride in the Park

If you don't feel like walking but would like to take in the sights at Parque Nacional Tierra Del Fuego, you can take a ride on **El Tren del Fin del Mundo,** a vapor locomotive that is a replica of the train used to shuttle prisoners to the forest to chop wood (© 02901/431600; www.trendelfin delmundo.com.ar). The train departs from its station (which houses a souvenir shop and cafe) near the park entrance four times daily; the journey is 1 hour and 10 minutes one-way. The cost is $16 adults, $5 kids, plus the $3.50 park entrance fee.

provides a quiet spot for relaxation or fishing the mammoth trout that call the lake home. The lake is home to a stately, gorgeous lodge, the **Hostería Petrel** (© 02901/433569). The wood and stone lodge has nine rooms, and seven splendid wooden cabins have just been constructed on the shore. Each cabin has one bedroom and a trundle bed for two more in the living room, with folksy furniture made of thin tree trunks, and an ultra-peaceful front deck for kicking back and casting a line. The cabins cost $60 April through October and $80 November through March; double rooms in the lodge are $40 to $65 for the same dates. The cabins do not come with a kitchen, but the lodge has a restaurant; they also have a gift shop and Jacuzzi, and they hire a summer season fishing guide.

PARQUE NACIONAL TIERRA DEL FUEGO

Parque Nacional Tierra del Fuego was created in 1960 to protect a 63,000 hectare (155,610-acre) chunk of Patagonian wilderness that includes mighty peaks, crystalline rivers, black-water swamps, and forests of *lenga,* or deciduous beech. Only 2,000 hectares (4,940 acres) are designated as recreation areas, part of which offer a chance to view the prolific dam building carried out by beavers introduced to Tierra del Fuego in the 1950s.

The park's main claim to fame is that it's the only Argentine national park with a maritime coast. If you've been traveling around southern Argentina or Chile, chances are you won't be blown away by this park. Much of the landscape is identical to the thousands of kilometers of mountainous terrain in Patagonia, but the park offers easy and medium day hikes to get out and stretch your legs, breathe some fresh air, take a boat ride, or bird-watch. Also, there are areas where the road runs through thick beech forest and then abruptly opens into wide views of mountains whose dramatic height can be viewed from sea level to more than 2,000m (6,560 ft.). Anglers can fish for trout here in the park, but must first pick up a license at the National Park Administration office at Av. del Libertador 1395 (© **02901/421395;** open Mon–Fri 9am–3pm), in Ushuaia. The park service issues maps at the park entrance showing the walking trails here, ranging from 300m (980 ft.) to 8km (5 miles); admission into the park is $3.50. Parque Nacional Tierra del Fuego is 11km (7 miles) west of Ushuaia on Ruta Nacional 3. Camping in the park is free; there are no services, but potable water is available. At the end of the road to Lago Roca, there is a snack bar/restaurant. At Bahía Ensenada you'll find boats that take visitors to the Isla Redonda, where there are several walking trails. The cost is about $7 or $14 with a guide. All tour companies offer guided trips to the park, but if you just need transportation there, call these shuttle bus companies: **Pasarela** (© **02901/ 433712**) or **Bella Vista** (© **02901/443161**).

WHERE TO STAY

Accommodations are not cheap in Ushuaia, and quality is often not on par with price. Below are some of the best values that can be found here.

VERY EXPENSIVE

Hotel del Glaciar *Overrated* *Kids*   This large hotel is approximately the same size as the Las Hayas (see below), and it sits just above it, offering the same stunning views. The difference between the two is that this hotel is bland and slightly fading and Las Hayas is meticulously maintained. The Hotel del Glaciar caters mostly to large tour groups and does not have much personalized service. It's a good choice, away from the hubbub of downtown, but don't expect luxury here.

The simple exterior and the tremendous lobby are built entirely of wood, and there's a partially sunken lounge centered on a freestanding fireplace, and yet another high-ceilinged lounge with massive windows that look out onto the Beagle Channel. The bright rooms are decent size, with a fresh, country decor; half come with a view of the glacier-topped mountain or, for $20 more, a view of the Beagle Channel. There's a winter activity center housed in a "barn" out back, where you can sign up for dog-sledding trips or rent snowshoes and snow boots. The hotel is an hour's walk (or a $1.50 taxi ride) up a winding road from town, but they operate a transfer shuttle. The hotel's restaurant, Temaukel, serves local specialties and international cuisine; there's also a coffee shop and bar, and a computer with Internet access. Don't expect much from the poorly trained staff.

Av. Luis Fernando Martial 2355, Ushuaia. ⓒ **02901/430640**, or 11/4393-4444 (reservations in Buenos Aires). Fax 11/4893-1435. Glaciar@infovia.com.ar. 123 units. $90–$159 double. Rates include buffet breakfast. AE, MC, V. **Amenities:** Restaurant; bar; lounge; sauna; game room; room service; massage; laundry service. *In room:* TV, minibar.

Las Hayas Resort Hotel ★★ *Finds* Ushuaia's sole five-star, luxury hotel has prices as sky-high as its location on the road to Glacier Martial, but if you're looking for elegant accommodations, this is for you. This member of the Leading Hotels of the World sits nestled in a forest of beech just below the Hotel del Glaciar (see above), a location that gives sweeping views of the town and the Beagle Channel. It's at least 3km (2 miles) from downtown, however, so you'll need to take a cab, hike, or use one of the hotel's summer-only transfer shuttles. The sumptuous lounge stretches the length of the building; here you'll find a clubby bar, formal restaurant, and fireside sitting area. The rooms are lavishly decorated with rich tapestries, upholstered walls, and bathrooms that are big and bright. The ultra-comfortable beds with thick linens are dreamy. There are three suites: junior suites (which are hardly bigger than doubles); junior suite superiors with a couch and separate entryway; and gala suites with a separate living area and four-poster beds. A glass-enclosed walkway leads to one of Ushuaia's few swimming pools and an indoor squash court; the hotel also offers automatic membership at the region's golf club. The owner of Las Hayas promotes an air of genteel exclusivity, making the hotel not entirely suitable for children. The hotel's gourmet restaurant changes its menu weekly, but specializes in black hake and king crab dishes. Downstairs, there's a more casual restaurant and an indoor garden dining area.

Av. Luis Fernando Martial 1650, Ushuaia. ⓒ **02901/430710**. Fax 02901/430719. www.lashayas.com.ar. 93 units. $170–195 double; $220–252 junior suite superior; $238–$285 deluxe junior suite; $355 gala suite. Rates include buffet breakfast. AE, DC, MC, V. **Amenities:** 2 restaurants; bar; lounge; indoor swimming pool; Jacuzzi; sauna; exercise room; concierge; room service; massage; laundry service; dry cleaning. *In room:* TV, hair dryer, safe.

EXPENSIVE

Hotel Cap Polonio This hotel is a good choice for its central location and bustling, adjoining restaurant that essentially forms part of the hotel's entrance lobby. The hotel has a bright yellow and red exterior and sits on busy Avenida del Libertador; for this reason you'll want to request a room in the rear of the hotel to avoid the noise. The rooms here at the Cap Polonio are some of the better rooms in town, but the shag carpet and frilly bedspreads are a little dowdy. Also, as with most hotels in town, a single bed is laughably narrower than a twin and might be uncomfortable for anyone over the age of 10; ask for a double instead.

Av. del Libertador 746, Ushuaia. © **02901/422140.** www.hotelcappolonio.com.ar. 30 units. $68–$89 double. AE, MC, V. **Amenities:** Restaurant; bar; room service. *In room:* TV.

Hotel Ushuaia   This hotel is another that offers sweeping views; however, it is only an 8-block walk to downtown—convenient for anyone who wants to be closer to restaurants and services. In this price range, the Hotel Ushuaia is one of the city's better values, offering very bright interiors and comfortable, spacious rooms, although everything is aging fast. From the vine-draped reception area, long hallways stretch out on both sides; centered in the middle is a second-story restaurant with a lofty, V-shaped ceiling from which hang about 100 glass bubble lamps, a style that is somewhat 1970s, but attractive nevertheless. All doubles cost the same but range in three sizes; when making a reservation, ask for the largest double they have, which, incidentally, they'll also give to singles when they're not full.

Lasserre 933, Ushuaia. © **02901/423051.** Fax 02901/424217. 58 units. $63 double. Rate includes buffet breakfast. AE, MC, V **Amenities:** Restaurant; bar; lounge; room service; laundry service. *In room:* TV.

Posada Fueguina ★★ *Finds*   This is one of our favorite hotels in Ushuaia, full of flavor and cozier than anything in town. The Fueguina has hotel rooms and a row of inviting, wooden *cabañas* (no kitchen) on a well-manicured lot, and their freshly painted cream and mauve exteriors stand out among the clapboard homes that surround them. Inside, Oriental floor-runners, dark glossy wood, and tartan curtains set the tone. Everything is meticulously maintained. Most rooms are spacious; the second and third floors have good views, and the three rooms on the bottom floor are brand-new. Bathrooms are sparkling clean; many received new fixtures in 2002. The cabins do not have interesting views, but they're so comfy you probably won't mind. The hotel is a short 3-block walk to downtown.

Lasserre 438, Ushuaia. © **02901/423467.** Fax 02901/424758. www.posadafueguina.com.ar. 23 units, 5 *cabañas*. $112 double Apr–Dec; $80 double Jan–Mar. Rates include buffet breakfast. AE, MC, V. **Amenities:** Bar; lounge. *In room:* TV, minibar, hair dryer.

MODERATE

Apart Hotel del Bosque *Value*   The Apart Hotel del Bosque gives guests a huge amount of space, including a separate living/dining area and a kitchenette. However, the kitchenette is intended more than anything for heating water, not cooking—for that reason they include breakfast, which is not common with apart-hotels. The 40 guest rooms are spread out much like a condominium complex, each with a separate entrance and maid service. The exteriors and the decor are pretty bland, but very clean. Inside the main building there's a cozy restaurant with wooden tables where they serve fixed-price meals. The hotel is located in a residential area about a 3-minute walk from downtown.

Magallanes 709, Ushuaia. ©/fax 02901/430777. www.hostaldelbosque.com.ar. 40 units. $35 double Apr–Sept; $60 double Oct–Mar. Rates include continental breakfast. AE, DC, MC, V. **Amenities:** Restaurant; room service; laundry service. *In room:* TV, minibar, hair dryer, kitchen.

Cesar Hostal   This basic hotel is located on Avenida del Libertador, just steps away from most services—it's a busy street, so ask for a room in the back if you need peace and quiet. The Cesar is a little lacking in style (read: 1970s furniture and shag carpet), but the rooms are comfortable and generally acceptable for this price range. The windows are small and the bedspreads a bit faded, but they're clean, and if you plan to spend the majority of your time outdoors, you probably won't mind. Some of the beds are mini-twins that don't particularly allow you to stretch out, so ask for a *cama matrimonial* (double bed).

Av. del Libertador 753, Ushuaia. ℂ 02901/421460. cesarhostal@infovia.com.ar. 29 units. $32 double. Rate includes buffet breakfast. AE, MC, V. **Amenities:** Restaurant. *In room:* TV.

INEXPENSIVE

Albergue Saint Christopher This fun, inviting *hostal* is for those who are looking to spend a lot less, but you'll have to share a room with strangers if you don't have your own group. Rooms have two to three bunk beds, and are not always separated by gender, but they'll try to find you a same-sex room if you ask. The *hostal* attracts a vivacious crowd that ranges in age from 20 to 40 years of age. The staff are entertaining, and the common area is a great place to hang out and chat. Guests have use of the kitchen facilities, and the *hostal* is packed with information about excursions around the area.

Gobernador Deloqui 636, Ushuaia. ℂ 02901/430062. hostel_christopher@yahoo.com. 5 shared units. $9 per person. No credit cards. **Amenities:** Lounge.

WHERE TO DINE

A dozen cafes can be found on Avenida del Libertador between Godoy and Rosas, all of which offer inexpensive sandwiches and quick meals. The most popular among them is **Tante Sara,** San Martín 137 (ℂ **02901/435005**), where a two-course meal of salad and ravioli or gnocchi costs $5. A block away, the Tante Sara Café is the place to sip coffee with locals in the afternoons. In addition to the restaurants listed below, you might consider the Hotel Las Hayas's **Luis Martial** (ℂ **02901/430710**). It offers great views and gourmet dining, as well as fixed meals and weekly changing menus.

Chez Manu ★ *Finds* SEAFOOD/FRENCH The Chez Manu offers great food and even better views seen through a generous supply of windows. The two transplants from France who run this restaurant, one of whom was once the chef at the five-star resort Las Hayas, stay true to their roots with a menu that offers French-style cooking using fresh local ingredients. Dishes include black hake cooked with anise and herbs, or Fueguian lamb. Before taking your order, the owner/chef will describe the catch of the day, usually a cold water fish from the bay such as Abejado or a Merlooza from Chile. The side dishes include a delicious eggplant ratatouille, made with extra-virgin olive oil and herbes de provence. The wine list includes several excellent regional dry whites.

Av. Fernando Luis Martial 2135. ℂ 02970/432253. Main courses $4–$8. AE, MC, V. Mon–Sun noon–3pm and 8pm–midnight.

Kapué Restaurant ★★★ ARGENTINE FINE DINING This is undoubtedly the best restaurant in Ushuaia, for its superb cuisine, lovely view, and warm, attentive service. Kapué, which means "at home" in Selk'nam, is owned and operated by the friendly, gracious Vivian family—the husband, Ernesto, is chef and his wife runs the dining area and waits tables, and often one of their kids can be found behind the bar. The menu is brief, but the offerings are delicious. Don't start your meal without ordering a sumptuous appetizer of king crab wrapped in a crepe and bathed in saffron sauce. Main courses include seafood, beef, and chicken; sample items include tenderloin beef in a plum sauce or a subtly flavored sea bass steamed in parchment paper. Kapué offers a special "sampler" with appetizers, a main dish, wine, dessert, and coffee for $26 per person. The extensive gourmet wine list ranges in price from $4 to $35; there's also wine by the glass. Finish it all off with a sorbet in a frothy champagne sauce. Kapué's dining area is cozy, and candlelit tables exude evening romance.

Roca 470. ℂ **02901/422704.** Reservations recommended on weekends. Main courses $7–$9. AE, MC, V. Nov 15–Apr 15, daily noon–2pm and 6–11pm; rest of the year, dinner only 7–11pm.

Marcopolo Café Restaurant INTERNATIONAL   This newer, stylish restaurant is a good place for lunch, both for its varied menu and its atmosphere. The softly lit dining area has warm yellow walls and beige linen tablecloths, both of which are offset with artsy ironwork knickknacks, colorful candles, and watercolor paintings. The menu will satisfy most tastes, as it includes creative renditions and simple, familiar items such as chef salads and shrimp cocktails. Try a local specialty, such as trout stuffed with king crab or Fueguian lamb in a flaky potato pastry. There's also fresh, homemade pasta with a choice of six sauces. The Marcopolo is open early for breakfast and also has a cafe menu that offers sandwiches, soups, and pastries, which can be ordered all day.

Av. del Libertador 746. ℂ **02901/430001.** Main courses $2–$7. AE, MC, V. Daily 7:30–10:30am, noon–3pm, and 8pm–midnight.

Opiparo *Value* PIZZA/PASTA   This diner-style restaurant can be found on the waterfront, and it serves pizza, pasta, and quick meals like chicken and beef *milanesas* with fries. There's two long pages of different kinds of pizza, which can be ordered individually or shared. The pastas are fresh, but very simple. This is where to go if you're looking for something casual.

Maipú 1255. ℂ **02901/434022.** Main courses $1.50–$5. MC, V. Daily noon–midnight.

Punto Final ★★ *Moments* CLUB/INTERNATIONAL   Opened in the fall of 2002, Punto Final has quickly become the most hip and happening place in Ushuaia. The location couldn't be better: right on the waterfront with fabulous bay and mountain views from the large windows that wrap around the entire building. The atmosphere is much like a big city club, with leopard-print fabric upholstery on the booths and bar stools. Techno music plays in the background during the early evening when full meals are served. You'll find dishes such as sliced melon with ham, grilled steaks, chicken breast with white wine and cream sauce, and a simple trout with butter sauce. Most of the trendy people who come here come for drinks, and after midnight, to dance. This place is a zoo from midnight to 3am, and even later on the weekends. If you're looking to live it up with young Argentines, then this is your place for the night.

Maipú 822. ℂ **02901/422423.** Main courses $4–$6. AE, MC, V. Daily 11am–4am. (to 5am Fri–Sat).

Tante Nina ★ *Finds* SEAFOOD/ARGENTINE   For the best atmosphere and water views in the center of town, Tante Nina is your best bet. The elegant dining room has huge picture windows overlooking the bay, handsome wooden chairs, and white tablecloths. This place is becoming very popular since it opened a year ago, and many of the local elite choose to dine here. Specialties are the seafood casseroles (known as *cazuelas*) most of which come with fresh king crab (all for $9). There's a delicious Hungarian style cazuela with king crab, tomatoes, cream, and mushrooms; a long list of fish prepared many different ways; and of course grilled chicken, tenderloin, and the very interesting pickled Patagonian rabbit for the terribly adventurous. For dessert, try the homemade almond ice cream or the luscious lemon sorbet. Service here is refined, if slightly aloof, and the diners tend to be on the older side.

Gobernador Godoy 15. ℂ **02901/432444.** Reservations recommended for dinner in high season. Main courses $7–$9. AE, MC, V. Daily 11am–3pm and 7pm–midnight.

Tía Elvira Restaurante ARGENTINE BISTRO   Tía Elvira is part restaurant, part mini-museum, with walls adorned with antique photos of the region and various artifacts its owners have collected during its 30 years in business. The menu features fairly straightforward Argentine dishes such as grilled meats, but the restaurant serves mostly simply prepared seafood, including king crab, trout, sea bass, and cod in a variety of sauces, such as Roquefort or Parmesan. There's also a list of homemade pastas, including lasagna and stuffed cannelloni. The restaurant is on the waterfront, with up-close views of the canal and the pier, and caters mostly to foreign tourists.

Maipú 349. ⓒ **02901/424725.** Main courses $3.50–$8. MC, V. Daily noon–3pm and 7–11:30pm.

Volver ARGENTINE   Even if you don't eat here, don't fail to stop by just to see this crazy, kitschy restaurant on the waterfront. Volver is inside a century-old, yellow, tin-pan house. Old newspapers and signs wallpaper the interiors, which are also packed with oddball memorabilia, photos, gadgets, trinkets, and antiques. The food is pretty good, too, serving regional dishes such as trout, crab, lamb, plus homemade pastas. King crab is served in a dozen different ways, including soups, casseroles, or naturally with a side sauce. The desserts are primarily crepes with local fruits like calafate. One complaint: Service can often be absent-minded or hurried.

Maipú 37. ⓒ **02901/423977.** Main courses $5–$8. MC, V. Daily noon–3pm and 7:30pm–midnight. Closed for lunch Mon.

Appendix:
Argentina & Chile in Depth

To understand how Argentina's European heritage impacts its South American identity, you must identify its distinct culture. Tango is the quintessential example—a sensual dance originated in the suspect corners of Buenos Aires's San Telmo neighborhood, was legitimized in the ballrooms of France, and was then re-exported to Argentina to become this nation's great art form. (For more on the tango, see "Tango: Lessons in the Dance of Seduction & Despair," in chapter 3.) Each journey you take, whether into a tango salon, an Argentine cafe, or a meat-only *parrilla,* will bring you closer to the country's true character.

But beyond the borders of Argentina's capital and largest city, you will find a land of vibrant extremes—from the Northwest's desert plateau to the flat grasslands of the Pampas, from the rainforest jungle of Iguazú to the towering blue-white glaciers of Patagonia. The land's geographic diversity is similarly reflected in its people: Witness the contrast between the capital's largely immigrant population and the indigenous people of the Northwest.

On the other side of the Andes, Chile capitalizes on a stunning array of landscape and geology: the desert volcanoes of Atacama, the Mediterranean climes of the Central Valley, the snowcapped peaks of the Lake District, and the vast plains and granite cathedral peaks of Patagonia. But for all its natural wonder, Chile remains deliciously undiscovered. Chile is considered a "hot spot" for outdoor adventure, but much of the country still has regions that are little-visited or unexplored—both by foreigners *and* by Chileans.

Spectacular, untrammeled landscapes are just the beginning: Chileans themselves are a warm, inviting, and proud people. A staggeringly long coastline provides the country with what is arguably the richest variety of seafood in the world. A thriving capital city, a strong economy, and a modern infrastructure promise high-quality amenities and services. And, of course, activities abound—from skiing to hiking to rafting to biking to some of the world's best fly-fishing. What follows is a historical and cultural introduction to a country where adventure, beauty, and hospitality await the willing traveler.

1 Argentine History 101

by Shane Christensen

EARLY SETTLEMENT & COLONIZATION

Several distinct indigenous groups populated the area now called Argentina well before the arrival of the Europeans. The Incas had made inroads into the highlands of the Northwest. Most other groups were nomadic hunters and fishers, such as those in the Chaco, the Tehuelche of Patagonia, and the Querandí and Puelche (Guennakin) of the pampas. Others (the Diaguitas of the Northwest) developed stationary agriculture.

Many present-day Argentines feel they're really Europeans settled in South America, a perception fed by the heritage of the country's Spanish, Italian,

German, and French immigrants. In 1502, Italian Amerigo Vespucci was the first European to arrive. Ferdinand Magellan arrived at the Río de la Plata in 1520, and Sebastian Cabot in 1526. Cabot established a fort at Sancti Spíritus. He also sent word back home of the presence of silver.

In 1535, Spain—having conquered Peru and aware of Portugal's presence in Brazil—sent an expedition headed by Pedro de Mendoza to settle the country. Mendoza was initially successful in founding Santa María del Buen Aire, or Buenos Aires (1536), but the lack of food proved fatal. Mendoza, discouraged by Indian attacks and mortally ill, sailed for Spain in 1537; he died on the way.

Northern Argentina (including Buenos Aires) was settled mainly by people traveling from the neighboring Spanish colonies of Chile, Peru, and the settlement of Asunción in Paraguay. Little migration occurred directly from Spain, but early communities forged a society dependent on cattle and horses imported from Spain, as well as such native crops as corn and potatoes. Pervasive Roman Catholic missions played a strong role in the colonizing process. The Spanish presence grew over the following centuries as Buenos Aires became a critical South American port.

INDEPENDENCE

The years 1806 and 1807 saw the first stirrings of independence. Buenos Aires fought off two British attacks in battles known as the *Reconquista* and the *Defensa*. Around this time, a civil war had distracted Spain from its colonial holdings, and many Argentine-born Europeans began to debate the idea of self-government in Buenos Aires. On July 9, 1816 (Nueve de Julio), Buenos Aires officially declared its independence from Spain, under the name United Provinces of the Río de la Plata. Several years of hard fighting followed before the Spanish were defeated in northern Argentina. But they remained a threat until Peru was liberated by Gen. José de San Martín (to this day a national hero) and Simón Bolívar from 1820 to 1824. Despite the drawing up of a national constitution, the territory that now constitutes modern Argentina was frequently disunited until 1860. The root cause of the trouble, the power struggle between Buenos Aires and the rest of the country, was not settled until 1880, and even after that, it continued to cause dissatisfaction.

Conservative forces ruled for much of the late 19th and early 20th centuries, at one point deposing an elected opposition party president from power through military force. By the turn of the 20th century, Argentina had become one of the world's 10 richest nations, thanks to agricultural expansion and foreign investment. Despite the Conservatives' efforts to suppress new social and political groups—including a growing urban working class—their power began to erode.

THE PERON YEARS

In 1943, the military overthrew Argentina's constitutional government in a coup led by then–army colonel Juan Domingo Perón. Perón became president in a 1946 election and was re-elected 6 years later. He is famous (though by no means universally applauded) for his populist governing style, which empowered and economically aided the working class. His wife, Eva Duarte de Perón (Evita), herself a controversial historical figure, worked alongside her husband to strengthen the voice of Argentina's women. (For more on Evita, see "Evita Perón: Woman, Wife, Icon," in chapter 3.) In 1955, the military deposed Perón, and the following years were marked by economic troubles (partly the result of Perón's expansive government spending) and social unrest, with a surge in terrorist activity by both the left and the right. While Perón was exiled in Spain, his power base in Argentina strengthened, allowing his return to the presidency in 1973. When he died in 1974, his third wife (and vice president), Isabel, replaced him.

THE DIRTY WAR & ITS AFTERMATH

The second Peronist era abruptly ended with a March 1976 coup that installed a military junta. The regime of Jorge Rafael Videla carried out a campaign to weed out anybody suspected of having Communist sympathies. Congress was closed, censorship imposed, and unions banned. Over the next 7 years, during this "Process of National Reorganization"—a period known as the *Guerra Sucia* (Dirty War) or *El Proceso*—between 10,000 and 30,000 (some believe more) intellectuals, artists, activists, and others were tortured or executed by the Argentine government. The mothers of these *desaparecidos* (the disappeared ones) began holding Thursday afternoon vigils in front of the presidential palace in Buenos Aires's Plaza de Mayo as a way to call international attention to the plight of the missing. Although the junta was overturned in 1983, the weekly protests continue to this day.

The dictatorship's control of the country was undermined by public outrage over the military's human-rights abuses combined with Argentina's crushing defeat by the British in the 1982 war over the Falkland Islands (called Las Islas Malvinas by South Americans). An election in 1983 restored constitutional rule and brought Raúl Alfonsín of the Radical Civic Union to power. In 1989, political power shifted from the Radical Party to the Peronist Party (established by Juan Perón), the first democratic transition in 60 years. Carlos Saúl Ménem, a former governor from a province of little political significance, won the presidency by a surprising margin.

A strong leader, Ménem pursued an ambitious but controversial agenda with the privatization of state-run institutions as its centerpiece. With the peso pegged to the dollar, Argentina enjoyed unprecedented price stability, allowing Ménem to deregulate and liberalize the economy. However, world financial crises in the late 1990s, including those in Mexico, East Asia, Russia, and Brazil, increased the cost of external borrowing and made Argentine exports and commodity industries uncompetitive. This added to charges of government corruption eroded investor confidence, and the national deficit began to soar.

After 10 years as president—and a constitutional amendment that allowed him to seek a second term—Ménem left office. By that time, an alternative to the traditional Peronist and Radical parties, the center-left FREPASO political alliance, had emerged on the scene. The Radicals and FREPASO formed an alliance for the October 1999 election, and the alliance's candidate, running on an anti-corruption campaign, defeated his Peronist competitor.

President Fernando de la Rúa, not as charismatic as his predecessor, was forced to reckon with the recession the economy had suffered since 1998. In an effort to eliminate Argentina's ballooning deficit, de la Rúa followed a strict regimen of government spending cuts and tax increases recommended by the International Monetary Fund. However, the tax increase crippled economic growth, and political infighting prevented de la Rúa from implementing other needed reforms designed to stimulate the economy. With a heavy drop in production and steep rise in unemployment, an economic crisis was looming.

The economic meltdown arrived with a run on the peso in December 2001, when investors moved en masse to withdraw their money from Argentine banks. Government efforts to restrict the run by limiting depositor withdrawals fueled anger through society, and Argentines took to the streets in sometimes violent demonstrations. De la Rúa resigned on December 20, as Argentina faced the worst economic crisis of its history. A series of interim governments did little to improve the situation, as Buenos Aires began to default on its international debts. Peronist President Eduardo Duhalde unlocked the Argentine peso from the dollar on January 1, 2002, and the currency's value quickly tumbled.

Argentina's economic crisis has severely eroded the population's trust in the government. Increased poverty, unemployment surpassing 20%, and inflation hitting 30% has resulted in massive emigration to Italy, Spain, and other destinations in Europe and North America. But despite these profound economic troubles, Argentina retains a large middle class with a healthy standard of living, and the country is rich in natural resources, human capital, and productive and tourist infrastructure.

2 Chile's History 101

by Kristina Schreck

EARLY HISTORY

Little is known of Chile's history before the arrival of the Spaniards. Archaeologists have had to reconstruct Chile's indigenous history from artifacts found at burial sites, in ancient villages, and in forts. Because of this, much more is known about the northern cultures of Chile than their southern counterparts: The north's extraordinarily arid climate has preserved, and preserved well, objects as fragile as 2,000-year-old mummies. Northern tribes such as the Atacama developed a culture that included the production of ceramic pottery, textiles, and objects made of gold and silver, but for the most part, early indigenous cultures in Chile were small, scattered bands that fished and cultivated simple crops. The primitive, nomadic tribes of Patagonia and Tierra del Fuego never developed beyond a society of hunters and gatherers because severe weather and terrain prevented them from ever developing an agricultural system.

In the middle of the 15th century, the great Inca civilization pushed south in a tremendous period of expansion. Although the Incas were able to subjugate tribes in the north, they never made it past the fierce Mapuche Indians in southern Chile.

THE SPANISH INVADE

In 1535, and several years after Spaniards Diego de Almagro and Francisco Pizarro had successfully conquered the Inca Empire in Peru, the conquistadors turned their attention south after hearing tales of riches that lay in what is today Chile. Already flushed with wealth garnered from Incan gold and silver, an inspired Diego de Almagro and more than 400 men set off on what would become a disastrous journey that left many dead from exposure and famine. De Almagro found nothing of the fabled riches, and he retreated to Peru.

Three years later, a distinguished officer of Pizarro's army, Spanish-born Pedro de Valdivia, secured permission to settle the land south of Peru in the name of the Spanish crown. Valdivia left with just 10 soldiers and little ammunition, but his band grew to 150 by the time he reached the Aconcagua Valley, where he founded Santiago de la Nueva Extremadura on February 12, 1541. Fire, Indian attacks, and famine beset the colonists, but the town nonetheless held firm. Valdivia succeeded in founding several other outposts including Concepción, La Serena, and Valdivia, but like the Incas before him, he was unable to overcome the Mapuche Indians south of the Río Biobío. In a violent Mapuche rebellion, Valdivia was captured and suffered a gruesome death, sending frightened colonists north. The Mapuche tribe effectively defended its territory for the next 300 years.

Early Chile was a colonial backwater of no substantive interest to Spain, although Spain did see to the development of a feudal land-owning system called an *encomienda*. Prominent Spaniards were issued a large tract of land and an *encomienda*, or a group of Indian slaves, that the landowner was charged with caring for and converting to Christianity. Thus rose Chile's traditional and nearly self-supporting *hacienda* known as a *latifundio*, as well as a rigid class system that defined the population. At the top were the *peninsulares* (those born in Spain), followed by the *criollos* (Creoles, or Spaniards born in the New World). Next down on the ladder were *mestizos* (a mix of Spanish and Indian blood), followed by Indians themselves. As the indigenous population succumbed to disease, the *latifundio* system replaced slaves with rootless *mestizos* willing, or forced, to work for a miserable wage. This form of land ownership would define Chile for centuries to come.

CHILE GAINS INDEPENDENCE

Chile was given its first taste of independence after Napoléon's invasion of Spain in 1808 and the subsequent sacking of King Ferdinand VII, who Napoléon replaced with his own brother. On September 18, 1810, leaders in Santiago agreed that the country would be self-governed until the king was reinstated as the rightful ruler of Spain. Although the self-rule was intended as a temporary measure, this date is now celebrated as Chile's independence day.

Semi-independence was not enough for many *criollos*, and soon thereafter, Jose Miguel Carrera, the power-hungry son of a wealthy *criollo* family, appointed himself leader and stated that the government would not answer to Spain or the viceroy of Peru. But Carrera was an ineffective and controversial leader, and it was soon determined that one of his generals, Bernardo O'Higgins, would prove to be a more adept leader. Loyalist troops from Peru took advantage of the struggle between the two and crushed the fragile independence movement, sending Carrera, O'Higgins, and their troops fleeing to Argentina. This became known as the Spanish "reconquest." Across the border, in Mendoza, O'Higgins met José de San Martín, an Argentine general who had already been plotting the liberation of South America. San Martín sought to liberate Chile first and then launch a sea attack on the viceroyalty seat in Peru from Chile's shore. In 1817, O'Higgins and San Martín crossed the Andes with their well-prepared troops and quickly defeated Spanish forces in Chacabuco, securing the capital. In April 1818, San Martín's army triumphed in the bloody battle of Maipú, and full independence from Spain was won. An assembly of prominent leaders elected O'Higgins as Supreme Director of Chile, but discontent within his ranks and with landowners led him to quit office and spend his remaining years in exile in Peru.

THE WAR OF THE PACIFIC

The robust growth of the nation during the mid- to late 1800s saw the development of railways and roads that connected previously remote regions with Santiago. The government began promoting European immigration to populate these regions, and it was primarily Germans who accepted, settling and clearing farms around the Lake District.

Increased international trading boosted the economy, but it was northern Chile's mines, specifically nitrate mines, that held the greatest promise. Border disputes with Bolivia in this profitable region ensued until a treaty was signed giving Antofagasta to Bolivia in exchange for not raising taxes on Chilean mines. Bolivia did an about-face and hiked taxes, sparking the War of the Pacific that pitted allies Peru and Bolivia against Chile, all fighting for their share of the nitrate fields. The odds were against Chile, but the country's well-trained troops were a force to reckon with. The war's turning point came with the surrender of Peru's major warship, the *Huáscar*. Chilean troops then invaded Peru and didn't stop until they had captured Lima. With Chile as the final victor, both countries signed treaties that conceded Peru's Tarapacá region and Antofagasta to Chile, increasing Chile's size by one-third with nitrate- and silver-rich land, and cutting Bolivia off from the coast.

THE MILITARY DICTATORSHIP

No political event defines current-day Chile better than the country's former military dictatorship. In 1970, Dr. Salvador Allende, Chile's first socialist president, was narrowly voted into office. Allende vowed to improve the lives of Chile's poorer citizens by instituting a series of radical changes that might redistribute the nation's lopsided wealth. Although the first year showed promising signs, Allende's reforms ultimately sent the country spiraling into economic ruin. Large estates were seized by the government and by independent, organized groups of peasants to be divided among rural workers, many of them uneducated and unprepared. Major industries were nationalized, but productivity lagged, and this, along with the falling price of copper, reduced the government's fiscal intake. Spending began outpacing income, and soon, the country's deficit soared. Worst of all, uncontrollable inflation and price controls led to shortages, and Chileans were forced to wait in long lines to buy basic goods.

Meanwhile, the United States (led by Richard Nixon and Henry Kissinger) had been closely monitoring the situation in Chile. With anti-Communist sentiment running high in the U.S. government, the CIA allocated $8 million to undermine the Allende government by funding right-wing opposition and supporting a governmental takeover.

On September 11, 1973, military forces led by Gen. Augusto Pinochet toppled Allende's government with a dramatic coup d'état. Military tanks rolled through the streets and jets dropped bombs on the presidential palace. Inside, Allende refused to surrender and accept an offer to be exiled. After delivering an emotional radio speech, Allende took his own life.

Many Chileans, especially wealthier citizens who had lost much under Allende, celebrated the coup as an economic and political salvation. But nobody was prepared for the brutal repression that would haunt Chile for the next 17 years. Congress was shut down, political parties and the news media were banned or censored, a strict curfew was imposed, and military officers took over previously nationalized industries and universities. Pinochet snuffed out his adversaries by rounding up and killing or torturing nearly 7,000 political activists, journalists, professors, and any other "subversives." Thousands more fled the country.

Pinochet set out to rebuild the economy using free-market policies that included selling off nationalized industries, curtailing government spending, reducing import tariffs, and eliminating price controls. From 1976 to 1981, the economy grew at such a pace that it was hailed as the "Chilean Miracle," but the miracle did nothing to address the country's high unemployment rate, worsening social conditions, and falling wages. More importantly, Chileans were unable to speak out against the government and those who did often "disappeared," taken from their homes by Pinochet's secret police never to be heard from again. Culture was filtered, and artists, writers, and musicians were censored.

The worldwide recession of 1982 put an end to Chile's economic run, but the economy bounced back again in the late 1980s. The Catholic Church began voicing opposition to Pinochet's brutal human-rights abuses, and a strong desire for a return to democracy saw the beginning of nationwide protests and international pressure, especially from the United States. In a pivotal 1988 "yes or no" plebiscite, 55% of the voting public said no to military rule, and Patricio Alywin was democratically elected president of Chile. Pinochet agreed to hand over power, but not before he redesigned the constitution so that it would protect him and the military from future prosecution.

CHILE TODAY

Chile is on its third democratically elected president since the dictatorship, the left-leaning Ricardo Lagos. Even today, the country remains divided over the legacy of Pinochet. There are his fervent supporters who claim that deaths and torture were an inevitable evil required to put Chile back on track, and there are his adversaries, those who were exiled and many of whom lost relatives during the dictatorship. Pinochet appeared impossible to prosecute until 1998, when a visit to London to undergo surgery prompted a Spanish judge to level murder and torture charges against the former dictator and issue a request for his extradition. Lengthy legal wrangling ended with Pinochet's release and return to Chile; however, he is now under fire from Chilean prosecution and has been stripped of his immunity. At press time, the 85-year-old is undergoing medical examinations to determine if he is fit enough for trial, but Pinochet is already pointing the finger at officers within his ranks.

The early 1970s were a time of desperate economic hardship for Chileans. After the military coup, the Pinochet government hired a group of economic advisors who instituted radical economic liberalization policies, such as privatization and reduced trade tariffs, and sought to wean the country from its dependence on copper exports. It was a bumpy road, with many companies going bust when faced with international competition and a deep recession in the early 1980s. Workers' rights went ignored during the first decade, as the military government outlawed labor unions. Today, however, despite a somewhat sluggish past few years, the Chilean economy is the strongest in Latin America. The country is rich in natural resources; accordingly, its top industries are mining, forestry, fishing, agriculture, wine, and tourism. Chile's political stability and strong economy have boosted its credit rating, and many companies now look abroad for investment. Unfortunately, more than half the country's citizens still do not earn a decent living wage. Literacy is at an all-time high, but analysts claim that Chile could do much to increase education, especially with the onset of the electronic age.

Index